Staying on Track Guide, Revision Guide, and a list of Common Errors boxes appear at the back of this book.

How to find what you need in *The Penguin Handbook*:

If you want a quick overview of what's in this book, then you can look at the **Brief Contents** to the left.

If you see a chapter that interests you in this Brief Contents, then you can go to the page number listed or turn to the appropriate **Part opening page** for that general topic. On the back of this page is a detailed list of the contents of that part of the book.

If you want to know more about what's in a particular chapter or part, then you can also find a **detailed table of contents** beginning on page v.

If you want to know where to find help for a very specific issue or if you need to look up a particular term, then you can refer to the **Index** on page 857.

You will also find **more help** at the back of this book:

- A list of **Common Errors** of grammar, punctuation, and mechanics that many writers make

- A list of all the new **Staying on Track** boxes that help you to avoid pitfalls during writing

- A **Revision Guide** of editing and proofreading symbols

- A **Glossary** with basic grammatical and usage terms, on page 823

You can also find additional help and resources for writing and research in the E-book version of *The Penguin Handbook* available at www.mycomplab.com.

Why Do You Need This New Edition?

If you're wondering why you should buy this new edition of *The Penguin Handbook*, here are six great reasons!

1 Save time while writing your research project, using the **new expanded coverage of research**. If, like most students, your research starts with Google, new chapters (17 and 18) on database and Web sources will help you research more efficiently and teach you to distinguish worthwhile from unreliable information. There's also a new chapter (20) to aid you with field research, from interviewing to observing to conducting surveys.

The new Five-Step Documentation Guide (at the beginning of Part 6) eliminates documentation headaches by teaching you the essentials of the process, so you can properly cite any source. New citation examples cover an even wider range of sources, from YouTube videos to podcasts and wikis. **2**

3 **New coverage of writing in different disciplines**, because writing isn't just for English majors. A whole new Part 3 helps you understand general expectations for writing in all of your courses, providing mini-guides for writing an essay exam, a case study, a lab report, a résumé, and more.

More student writing samples make it easier to understand what's expected of you. This edition adds a new sample informative paper, sample argument paper, and sample APA research paper to provide models for your own work.

5 New **Staying on Track boxes** throughout the book highlight common writing and research problems and offer concrete "on track" and "off track" examples.

6 *The Penguin Handbook* gets even better when used with **Pearson's unique MyCompLab site**— the gateway to a world of online resources developed specifically for you!

THE
Penguin
Handbook

Third Edition

LESTER FAIGLEY
University of Texas at Austin

PEARSON
Longman

New York   San Francisco   Boston
London   Toronto   Sydney   Tokyo   Singapore   Madrid
Mexico City   Munich   Paris   Cape Town   Hong Kong   Montreal

Executive Editor: Lynn M. Huddon
Director of Development: Mary Ellen Curley
Senior Marketing Manager: Windley Morley
Senior Supplements Editor: Donna Campion
Senior Media Producer: Stefanie Liebman
Production Manager: Donna DeBenedictis
Project Coordination, Text Design, and Electronic Page Makeup: Pre-Press PMG
Senior Cover Design Manager: Nancy Danahy
Cover Designer: Base Art Co.
Cover Images (Clockwise from top right): © Iconica/Getty Images; © Stanislav
    Popov/iStockphoto; © Stockbyte/Getty Images; © photosindia/Getty Images; © Alix
    Minde/PhotoAlto Agency/Getty Images; © Marcelo Wain/iStockphoto; © PNC/Digital
    Vision/Getty Images; © Noel Henderson/Photographer's Choice/Getty Images
Photo Researcher: Jody Potter
Senior Manufacturing Buyer: Dennis J. Para
Printer and Binder: R.R. Donnelley & Sons/Crawfordsville
Cover Printer: Phoenix Color Corporation

For permission to use copyrighted material, grateful acknowledgment is made to the copyright holders
on pp. 895–896, which are hereby made part of this copyright page.

Library of Congress Cataloging-in-Publication Data
Faigley, Lester, 1947–
    The Penguin handbook / Lester Faigley. -- 3rd ed.
        p. cm.
    Includes index.
        ISBN-13: 978-0-205-50581-4
        ISBN-10: 0-205-50581-3
        ISBN-13: 978-0-205-55994-7 (pbk.)
        ISBN-10: 0-205-55994-8 (pbk.)
    1. English language--Rhetoric--Handbooks, manuals, etc. 2. English language--Grammar--
Handbooks, manuals, etc. 3. Report writing--Handbooks, manuals, etc. I. Title.
    PE1408.F25 2008
    808'.042--dc22

                                                                        2007046224

Please visit us at www.pearsonhighered.com

ISBN-13: 978-0-205-55994-7
ISBN-10: 0-205-55994-8

1 2 3 4 5 6 7 8 9 10—DOC—11 10 09 08

Contents

PART 2
Writing for Different Purposes   77

PART 3
Writing in the Disciplines   153

PART 4
Designing and Presenting   189

PART 5
Researching   233

PART 7
Effective Style and Language 499

PART 8
Understanding Grammar   557

PART 9
Understanding Punctuation and Mechanics   669

PART 10
If English Is Not Your First Language 783

Preface

The third edition of *The Penguin Handbook* grows out of my experiences as a writing teacher at a time when the tools for writing, the uses of writing, and the nature of writing itself are undergoing astounding and rapid transformation. Yet with millions of words, images, and graphics now dashing around the planet at speeds measured in nanoseconds, the traditional qualities of good writing—clarity, brevity, readability, consistency, effective design, accurate documentation, freedom from errors, and a human voice—are prized more than ever.

Each edition of *The Penguin Handbook* has started with the question: How do students learn best? Stated simply, the answer is that students learn best when they can find the right information when they need it without being overwhelmed with detail. To accomplish this goal, the design of *The Penguin Handbook* makes key points stand out visually and verbally, allowing students to browse to find content and keeping them oriented. Complicated subjects are broken down into processes, giving students strategies for dealing with problems in their writing. Many thousands of students have become better writers with the help of *The Penguin Handbook*.

What's new in this edition?

The Penguin Handbook has been revised extensively in order to give students the best, most up-to-date writing instruction available.

Expanded coverage of research

- New chapters on database sources and Web sources guide students on where to find worthwhile information and how to recognize what is not reliable.

- A new chapter on field research gives strategies for interviewing, observing, and conducting surveys.

New and expanded documentation coverage

- A new guide at the beginning of Part 6 provides an overview of the five key steps needed to cite any source to help students better understand the documentation process before moving on to the specifics of MLA, APA, CMS and CSE styles.
- New citation examples cover an even wider range of sources, from YouTube videos to podcasts and wikis.

New coverage of writing in the disciplines

- In an all-new Part 3, Chapter 10 introduces students to the general expectations and conventions for writing in all of their courses.
- A new Chapter 11 features mini-guides, pointers, and examples of an essay examination, an observation, a case study, a lab report in the sciences, a letter of application, and a résumé.

Expanded coverage of argument

- Part 2 gives added instruction and student examples for writing position and proposal arguments.

New guides give students an overview of the writing process

- New writing guides in Part 2 offer specific advice on critical issues such as taking into account the knowledge and beliefs of the audience, providing the necessary background, and addressing other points of view.

Innovative new features keep students on track

- New Staying on Track boxes offer concrete advice with examples.

Expanded coverage of images and graphics in writing

- New coverage of using visuals effectively throughout the writing process shows how to explain with visuals, how to use visuals as evidence, and how to create effective visuals for presentations.

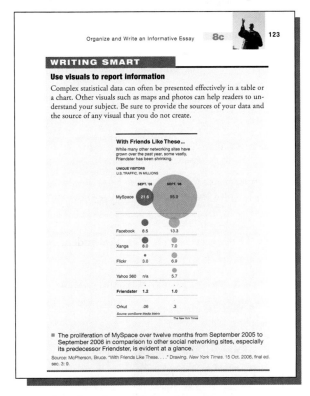

More samples of student writing throughout

- *The Penguin Handbook* now includes a new sample informative essay (Chapter 8), a new sample position argument (Chapter 9), new model documents for writing in the disciplines (Part 3), and a new sample student APA research paper (Chapter 24).

Students learn best when complicated processes are explained step by step.

Wherever possible, this handbook breaks down complicated information into uncomplicated steps and elements. For example, a new "Five Steps for Documenting Sources" guide in Part 6 gives students everything they need to understand the basics of this process. Also, the innovative illustrated source samples and citation models have been updated and augmented with additional online and media examples such as blogs, wikis, and podcasts.

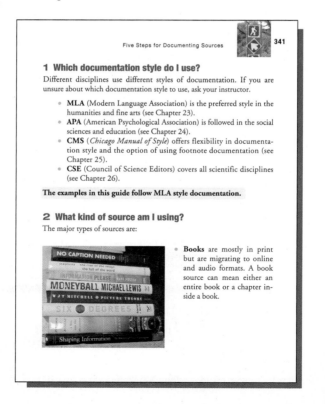

Five Steps for Documenting Sources   **341**

1 Which documentation style do I use?
Different disciplines use different styles of documentation. If you are unsure about which documentation style to use, ask your instructor.

- **MLA** (Modern Language Association) is the preferred style in the humanities and fine arts (see Chapter 23).
- **APA** (American Psychological Association) is followed in the social sciences and education (see Chapter 24).
- **CMS** (*Chicago Manual of Style*) offers flexibility in documentation style and the option of using footnote documentation (see Chapter 25).
- **CSE** (Council of Science Editors) covers all scientific disciplines (see Chapter 26).

The examples in this guide follow MLA style documentation.

2 What kind of source am I using?
The major types of sources are:

- **Books** are mostly in print but are migrating to online and audio formats. A book source can mean either an entire book or a chapter inside a book.

Students learn best when they can see examples of what does and doesn't work in writing.

By showing both effective and ineffective examples, this handbook helps students see and learn the key patterns for successful writing in college. For example, new Staying on Track boxes focus on various common writing and research problems that students encounter, offering "on track" and "off track" examples to help students deal with such problems.

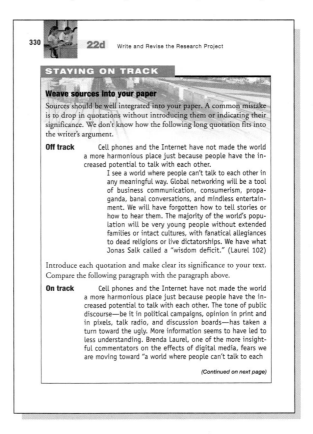

330   **22d**   Write and Revise the Research Project

STAYING ON TRACK

Weave sources into your paper

Sources should be well integrated into your paper. A common mistake is to drop in quotations without introducing them or indicating their significance. We don't know how the following long quotation fits into the writer's argument.

Off track   Cell phones and the Internet have not made the world a more harmonious place just because people have the increased potential to talk with each other.
I see a world where people can't talk to each other in any meaningful way. Global networking will be a tool of business communication, consumerism, propaganda, banal conversations, and mindless entertainment. We will have forgotten how to tell stories or how to hear them. The majority of the world's population will be very young people without extended families or intact cultures, with fanatical allegiances to dead religions or live dictatorships. We have what Jonas Salk called a "wisdom deficit." (Laurel 102)

Introduce each quotation and make clear its significance to your text. Compare the following paragraph with the paragraph above.

On track   Cell phones and the Internet have not made the world a more harmonious place just because people have the increased potential to talk with each other. The tone of public discourse—be it in political campaigns, opinion in print and in pixels, talk radio, and discussion boards—has taken a turn toward the ugly. More information seems to have led to less understanding. Brenda Laurel, one of the more insightful commentators on the effects of digital media, fears we are moving toward "a world where people can't talk to each

(Continued on next page)

Students learn best from looking at models and examples of real writers at work in college.

This handbook is written with the understanding that students learn best by seeing *examples* of what writers do, not by just reading long descriptions of what they do. For example, a new Chapter 11 features documents from across the disciplines, such as essay exams, observations, case studies, lab reports, letters of application, and résumés, with mini-guides to writing each of these genres and examples of each.

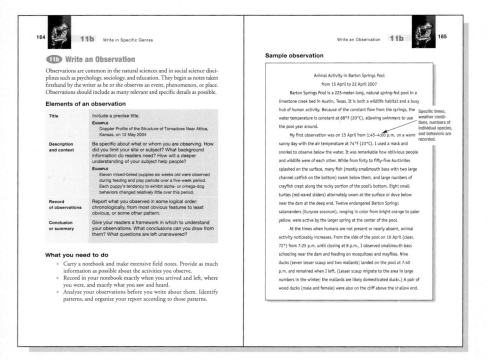

Students learn best when they can quickly find answers to common writing questions.

The Penguin Handbook is designed to be browsed in addition to being accessed through the table of contents and the Index. Common Errors boxes make it easy for students to find guidance on grammar, punctuation, and mechanics issues. Writing Smart boxes give practical tips, including advice on using computers.

---

630   **36a**   Pronouns

COMMON ERRORS

Who or whom

In writing, the distinction between *who* and *whom* is still often observed. *Who* and *whom* follow the same rules as other pronouns: *Who* is the subject pronoun; *whom* is the object pronoun. If you are dealing with an object, *whom* is the correct choice.

Incorrect	Who did you send the letter to?
	Who did you give the present to?
Correct	To whom did you send the letter?
	Whom did you give the present to?

Who is always the right choice for a subject pronoun.

Correct	Who gave you the present?
	Who brought the cookies?

If you are uncertain of which one to use, try substituting *she* and *her* or *he* and *him.*

Incorrect	You sent the letter to she [who]?
Correct	You sent the letter to her [whom]?

Incorrect	Him [Whom] gave you the present?
Correct	He [Who] gave you the present?

Remember: *Who* = subject
                  Whom = object

For step-by-step discussion, examples, and practice exercises, visit this page of the E-book at www.mycomplab.com.

Students learn best when they have an overview of the writing process with specific strategies for invention, drafting, and revising.

All-new guides for organizing and writing a rhetorical analysis, a reflective essay, an informative essay, and position and proposal arguments are included in Part 2. For example, the guide for writing a rhetorical analysis in Chapter 6 gives strategies for analyzing the text, the immediate context, and the larger cultural context. Each guide is accompanied by a model example of student writing.

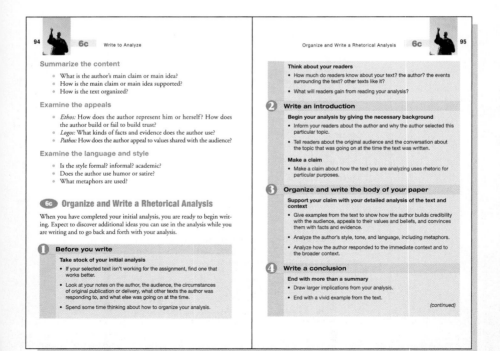

Summarize the content

- What is the author's main claim or main idea?
- How is the main claim or main idea supported?
- How is the text organized?

Examine the appeals

- *Ethos:* How does the author represent him or herself? How does the author build or fail to build trust?
- *Logos:* What kinds of facts and evidence does the author use?
- *Pathos:* How does the author appeal to values shared with the audience?

Examine the language and style

- Is the style formal? informal? academic?
- Does the author use humor or satire?
- What metaphors are used?

6c **Organize and Write a Rhetorical Analysis**

When you have completed your initial analysis, you are ready to begin writing. Expect to discover additional ideas you can use in the analysis while you are writing and to go back and forth with your analysis.

1 **Before you write**

Take stock of your initial analysis

- If your selected text isn't working for the assignment, find one that works better.
- Look at your notes on the author, the audience, the circumstances of original publication or delivery, what other texts the author was responding to, and what else was going on at the time.
- Spend some time thinking about how to organize your analysis.

Think about your readers

- How much do readers know about your text? the author? the events surrounding the text? other texts like it?
- What will readers gain from reading your analysis?

2 **Write an introduction**

Begin your analysis by giving the necessary background

- Inform your readers about the author and why the author selected this particular topic.
- Tell readers about the original audience and the conversation about the topic that was going on at the time the text was written.

Make a claim

- Make a claim about how the text you are analyzing uses rhetoric for particular purposes.

3 **Organize and write the body of your paper**

Support your claim with your detailed analysis of the text and context

- Give examples from the text to show how the author builds credibility with the audience, appeals to their values and beliefs, and convinces them with facts and evidence.
- Analyze the author's style, tone, and language, including metaphors.
- Analyze how the author responded to the immediate context and to the broader context.

4 **Write a conclusion**

End with more than a summary

- Draw larger implications from your analysis.
- End with a vivid example from the text.

(continued)

Students learn best when concepts are explained using clear, accessible language.

Since the first edition, *The Penguin Handbook* has been praised by teachers and students alike for the way that it "talks" to students. Whenever possible, writing, research, and grammar terms are defined simply and key concepts are presented with concise, to-the-point explanations.

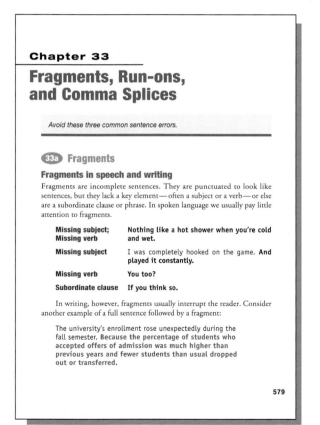

Chapter 33

Fragments, Run-ons, and Comma Splices

Avoid these three common sentence errors.

33a Fragments

Fragments in speech and writing

Fragments are incomplete sentences. They are punctuated to look like sentences, but they lack a key element—often a subject or a verb—or else are a subordinate clause or phrase. In spoken language we usually pay little attention to fragments.

Missing subject; Missing verb	Nothing like a hot shower when you're cold and wet.
Missing subject	I was completely hooked on the game. **And played it constantly.**
Missing verb	You too?
Subordinate clause	If you think so.

In writing, however, fragments usually interrupt the reader. Consider another example of a full sentence followed by a fragment:

The university's enrollment rose unexpectedly during the fall semester. Because the percentage of students who accepted offers of admission was much higher than previous years and fewer students than usual dropped out or transferred.

579

Supplements

Accompanying *The Penguin Handbook* is an array of supplements for both instructors and students, including book-specific resources.

MyCompLab E-book

An E-book of *The Penguin Handbook*, available within Longman's premier composition Web site, *MyCompLab*, provides a complete, engaging multimedia experience for students:

- MyCompLab is a Web application that offers comprehensive and integrated resources for every writer. With MyCompLab, students can access a dynamic e-book version of *The Penguin Handbook*; learn from interactive tutorials and instruction; practice and develop their skills with grammar, writing, and research exercises; share and collaborate on their writing with peers; and receive comments on their writing from instructors and tutors. Go to www.mycomplab.com to register for these premier resources and much more!

- The E-book of *The Penguin Handbook* includes hyperlinks to relevant MyCompLab tutorials, quizzes, and other instruction.

- In the E-book students will also find unique, interactive, book-specific resources that support and supplement the chapters of *The Penguin Handbook,* such as:

    - **Student Writing Samples with Audio Commentary**, offering complete papers in a number of disciplines with additional audio commentaries by the author.

    - **Writing in the World Projects**, providing complete scenarios and situations for a variety of writing and research assignments.

    - **Writing and Researching Worksheets,** which help students focus on particular stages of the writing, design, and research process and can be used independently or in conjunction with a specific project.

- **Common Errors Workbook**, providing additional exercises and activities directly related to the most frequent problem areas encountered by student writers.
- **Common ESL Errors Workbook**, providing additional practice and exercises to help nonnative speakers and writers recognize common grammar and style problems.
- **Punctuation Personality Quiz**, offering students a fun way to discover how punctuation adds personality to their writing.

References to this E-book can be seen throughout the handbook, where this icon is displayed ——————. Please visit the E-book at **www.mycomplab.com**.

VangoNotes

vango Students can study on the go with VangoNotes. They just download chapter reviews from the text and listen to them on any mp3 player. Now wherever they are—whatever they're doing—they can study by listening to the lessons following the grammar and punctuation chapters in this handbook:

- **Big Ideas:** The "need to know" for each chapter
- **Practice Test:** A gut check for the Big Ideas—tells students if they need to keep studying
- **Key Terms:** Audio flash cards to help to review key concepts and terms
- **Rapid Review:** A quick drill session—students can use it right before the test

VangoNotes are **flexible**; students can download all the material or only the chapters they need. And they're **efficient**. Use them in a car, at the gym, walking to class, wherever. Find out more at VangoNotes.com.

Instructor's Resource Manual

An *Instructor's Resource Manual*, by Susan Schorn of the University of Texas at Austin, offers guidance to new and experienced teachers for using the handbook and its ancillary package to the best advantage.

To see a complete listing of the student supplements and instructor support materials available upon adoption of *The Penguin Handbook*, please visit the book's online catalog page, which can be accessed at www.pearsonhighered.com.

Answer Key

A separate *Answer Key* is also available to instructors for the exercises contained in *The Penguin Handbook*.

Acknowledgments

The scope and complexity of a handbook require a talented, experienced team, and I have been extremely fortunate to have three of the best editors in the country on my team. Executive Editor Lynn Huddon and I have worked together on ten previous books and editions—none of which would have achieved success without Lynn's creative mind and hard work. Joseph Opiela, editor-in-chief, has contributed a great deal to the previous two editions, indeed to all of my books with Longman, and I have greatly benefited from working with him directly on the third edition. My immediate collaborator has been Mary Ellen Curley, director of development, who has brought a wealth of knowledge, thoroughness, and the attention to detail that a handbook demands. She has been a superb editor throughout the long process. I could not be blessed with better colleagues.

Others at Longman who have contributed their wisdom and experience are Windley Morley, senior marketing manager; Donna Campion, senior supplements editor; Nancy Danahy, senior cover design manager; and Donna DeBenedictis, production manager. Melissa Mattson at

Pre-Press PMG has skillfully guided the production. My copy editor, Elsa van Bergen, has worked in some capacity on all three editions, and she has taught me a great deal along the way in addition to being a joy to work with. Christopher Stolle was a meticulous proofreader.

I thank Susan "George" Schorn, who made major contributions to the chapters on writing in the disciplines and elsewhere in the book, and also helped update and improve the online resources available for this edition in the E-book. Victoria Davis created new exercises for the third edition, and John Jones helped with the new APA example paper along with offering many good ideas. I am grateful for the students I have been fortunate to teach at the University of Texas at Austin and who produced the splendid work that is included in this edition. I also appreciate the help and support of numerous colleagues in the Departments of English and Rhetoric and Writing and in the Undergraduate Writing Center at Texas.

I would like to thank the many students who provided feedback and who gave us suggestions for this new edition of *The Penguin Handbook*, particularly the students from the University of South Florida, the University of Texas at El Paso, Lower Columbia College, and San Jose State University.

Over the years I've learned and continue to learn from colleagues around the country. I am fortunate to have an expert group of reviewers, who were not only perceptive in their suggestions but could imagine a handbook that breaks new ground. They are Sue Beebe, Texas State University, San Marcos; Jennifer Bottinelli, Kutztown University; Mickey Hall, Volunteer State Community College; Gary Sligh, Lake-Sumter Community College; Nancy Hull, Calvin College; Dominic Delli Carpini, York College of Pennsylvania; Linda C. Mitchell, San Jose State University; Conni Kendall, University of Kentucky; and Jane Leach, Minneapolis Community and Technical College. A. Suresh Canagarajah, then of Baruch College of the City of New York, now at The Pennsylvania State University, offered invaluable feedback on the advice to students writing in English as a second language; Louise Klusek, Head of Reference at the William and Anita Newman Library of Baruch College of the City of New York, provided essential, up-to-the-minute information on the resources students can use during the research process today. I'd also like to acknowledge the work of Gerald Graff and Cathy Birkenstein on strategies for developing arguments.

As always, my greatest debt of gratitude is to my wife, Linda, who makes it all possible.

LESTER FAIGLEY

PART

1

Planning, Drafting, and Revising

Chapter 1

Think as a Writer

Learning to write well is the most valuable part of your college education.

1a Think About the Process of Communication

Whether you are writing a research paper for a political science course, designing a Web site for a small business, or preparing slides for a sales presentation, you are participating in a complex process. That process — communication — involves the interaction of three essential elements: the writer or speaker, the audience, and the subject. These three elements are often represented by a triangle (Figure 1.1).

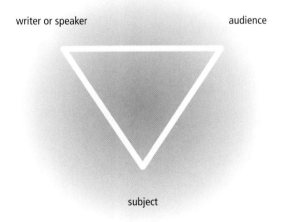

writer or speaker   audience

subject

Figure 1.1   The rhetorical triangle

Speaker, subject, and audience are each necessary for an act of communication to occur. These three elements interact with one another. Speakers make adjustments to their presentations of a subject depending on the audience (think of how you talk to small children). Just as speakers adjust to audiences, audiences continually adjust to speakers (think of how your attitude toward speakers changes when they are able to laugh at themselves).

1b Think About How to Persuade Others

The ancient Greeks recognized that the dynamic nature of the **rhetorical triangle** is the key to understanding how an audience is persuaded. The most important teacher of rhetoric in ancient Greece, Aristotle (384–323 BCE), defined rhetoric as the art of finding the best available means of persuasion in any situation. He set out three primary tactics of persuasion: appeals based on the trustworthiness of the speaker (*ethos*); appeals to the

Ethos	*Pathos*
appeals to the character and expertise of the writer or speaker	appeals to the beliefs and values of the audience

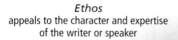

Logos
appeals based on logic, reasoning, and
evidence concerning the subject

Figure 1.2   Persuasive appeals

emotions and deepest-held values of the audience (*pathos*); and appeals to logic, reasoning, and evidence (*logos*). These appeals likewise can be represented using the rhetorical triangle (Figure 1.2).

Aristotle's insight into how people can be persuaded remains relevant today. To give an example, imagine that you drive every day on Lakeside

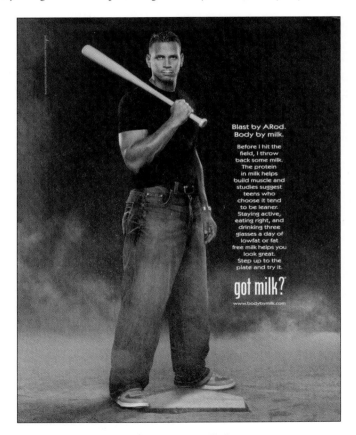

Figure 1.3   *Ethos*. "Blast by ARod. Body by milk."

Figure 1.4 *Pathos.* "Start talking before they start drinking."

Figure 1.5 *Logos.* "You may get to retire in the sun and fun, but your old cell phones don't. Rather than retire them to the trash bin or an old sock drawer, recycle. You'll help our environment and help your neighbors in the process."

Boulevard, a divided highway with a grass median. You've read about numerous accidents on Lakeside Boulevard and witnessed two horrible accidents when cars skidded across the median and collided head-on with traffic in the opposite lanes. You want your city council to vote to erect a concrete barrier that will prevent these frequent head-on collisions. One approach would be to use logic and evidence, documenting that Lakeside Boulevard has far more fatal accidents per mile than other streets in your city (logos). Another would be to invite an expert on traffic safety to speak to the city council (ethos). A third way would be to appeal to the council about the unnecessary loss of life caused by the unsafe street (pathos). Often you will use all of these appeals to gain support from an audience.

Exercise 1.1   Read the following passages and decide which appeal (to logic, to credibility and trustworthiness, to emotions and values) is being addressed.

1. Today I am an inquisitor. And hyperbole would not be fictional and would not overstate the solemnness that I feel right now. My faith in the Constitution is whole; it is complete; it is total. And I am not going to sit here and be an idle spectator to the diminution, the subversion, the destruction, of the Constitution.
   —Barbara Jordan, Speech before the U.S. House Judiciary Committee Impeachment Hearings, 1974

2. When in the course of human events, it becomes necessary for one people to dissolve the political bands which have connected them with one another, and to assume among the powers of the earth, the separate and equal station which the Laws of Nature and of Nature's God entitle them, a decent respect to the opinions of mankind requires that they should declare the causes which impel them to the separation.
   —Thomas Jefferson, *Declaration of Independence,* 1776

3. The pundits like to slice-and-dice our country into Red States and Blue States; Red States for Republicans, Blue States for Democrats. But I've got news for them too. We worship an awesome God in the Blue States, and we don't like federal agents poking around in our libraries in the Red States. We coach Little League

in the Blue States and yes, we got some gay friends in the Red States. There are patriots who opposed the war in Iraq and patriots who supported the war in Iraq. We are one people, all of us pledging allegiance to the stars and stripes, all of us defending the United States of America."

—Barack Obama, Keynote Address at 2004 Democratic National Convention

4. I got to tell you . . . there are a lot of people here who are very upset, and very angry, and very frustrated. And when they hear politicians . . . thanking one another, it just, you know, it kind of cuts them the wrong way right now. Because literally there was a body on the streets of this town yesterday being eaten by rats, because this woman had been laying in the street for 48 hours. And there's not enough facilities to take her up. Do you get the anger that is out here?

—Anderson Cooper, Interview with Louisiana Senator Mary Landrieu about Hurricane Katrina, *Anderson Cooper 360°*, September 1, 2005

5. I supported the decision to go to war in Iraq. Many Americans did not. I stand that ground not to chase dreams of empire; not for a noxious sense of racial superiority over a subject people; not for cheap oil; not for the allure of chauvinism; not for a foolishly romantic conception of war. I stand that ground because I believed, rightly or wrongly, my country's interests and values required it.

—Senator John McCain, Keynote Address at Columbia University, May 16, 2006

1c Think About Your Audience

When you talk with someone face-to-face, you receive constant feedback from that person, even when you're doing all the talking. Your listener may nod in agreement, frown, act bored, and give you a variety of other signals. Unless your listener is deliberately acting, you have a sense of how he or she is responding to what you are saying.

When you write, you rarely receive immediate response from readers. Most of the time you don't know exactly how readers will react to what you write. You have to think consciously about your readers and anticipate how they might respond.

Readers of college writing expect more than what they can find out from a Google search or an online encyclopedia. Facts are easy to obtain from databases and print sources. Readers want to know how these facts are connected. Good college writing also involves an element of surprise. If readers can predict exactly where a writer is going, even if they fully agree, they will either skim to the end or stop reading. Readers expect you to tell them something that they don't know already.

WRITING SMART

Understand your audience

- Who is most likely to read what you write?
- How much does your audience know about your subject? Are there any key terms or concepts that you will need to explain?
- How interested is your audience likely to be? If they lack interest in your subject, how can you engage them?
- What is their attitude likely to be toward your subject? If they hold attitudes different from yours, how can you get them to consider your views?
- What would motivate your audience to want to read what you write?

1d Think About Your Credibility

Some writers begin with a strong ethos because of who they are; they have immediate credibility. Most writers, however, have to convince their readers to keep reading by demonstrating knowledge of their subject and concern with their readers' needs. Furthermore, no matter how much you know about a subject or how good your ideas are, your credibility is destroyed if readers in college, in the workplace, or in public life find your writing poor in quality, especially if it is full of errors and sloppy sentences.

Exercise 1.2   Suppose you are a freelance writer who has lined up several assignments for a variety of publications. Your topics and the publications are listed below. Analyze your intended audience. How much information will they most likely have about your subject (much, none, some); what is their attitude likely to be (positive, negative, neutral); what is their interest level most likely to be (low, moderate, high)? In a few cases, you might need to do some research into the readership for the publication.

1. A chapter about the Vietnam War in a high school textbook
2. An article about ending a relationship in *Men's Health*
3. An opinion piece about gun control for *The Economist*
4. A feature on women's rights in the Middle East for Oprah Winfrey's magazine, *O*
5. An article about the importance of emissions-control features for engines in *Car and Driver*

WRITING SMART

Build your credibility

- How can you convince your audience that you are knowledgeable about your subject? Do you need to do research?
- How can you convince your audience that you have their interests in mind?
- What strategies can you use that will enhance your credibility? Should you cite experts on your subject? Can you acknowledge opposing positions, indicating that you've taken a balanced view on your subject?
- Does the appearance, accuracy, and clarity of your writing give you credibility?

Exercise 1.3   Evaluate the following passages, as well as the example(s) of appeals to ethos you found in Exercise 1.1, for their appeals to credibility. What sort of ethos does the author represent? How might this affect his or her presentation of the topic?

1. Topic: Gay Marriage

   As for the notion that I have argued for same-sex marriage only for the sake of homosexuals, I suggest you take another look at what I've written. Here are a few of the advantages of same-sex marriage for the society as a whole that I have laboriously spelled out: lower rates of promiscuity among gay men, more stable homes for the children of gay parents, less trauma in families with gay offspring, lower rates of disease transmission, more independent and self-reliant members of society, etc., etc. These aren't appeals to sympathy; they're arguments that same-sex marriage would be good for all of us—and for conservative reasons to boot.

   —Andrew Sullivan, "Gay Marriage," *Slate*, April 4, 1997

2. Topic: Proposed Treaty

   Yonder sky that has wept tears of compassion upon my people for centuries untold, and which to us appears changeless and eternal, may change. Today is fair. Tomorrow it may be overcast with clouds. My words are like the stars that never change. Whatever Seattle says, the great chief at Washington can rely upon with as much certainty as he can upon the return of the sun or the seasons. The white chief says that Big Chief at Washington sends us greetings of friendship and goodwill. This is kind of him for we know he has little need of our friendship in return. His people are many. They are like the grass that covers vast prairies. My people are few. They resemble the scattering trees of a storm-swept plain. The great, and I presume—good, White Chief sends us word that he wishes to buy our land but is willing to allow us enough to live comfortably. This indeed appears just, even generous, for the Red Man no longer has rights that he need respect, and the offer may be wise, also, as we are no longer in need of an extensive country.

   —Seattle, Chief of the Suquamish, Treaty Oration, 1854: originally published in the *Seattle Sunday Star*, 29 October 1887

3. Topic: Global Warming

Yet, in spite of all of the clear evidence available all around us, there are many who still do not believe that global warming is a problem at all. And it's no wonder: because they are the targets of a massive and well-organized campaign of disinformation lavishly funded by polluters who are determined to prevent any action to reduce the greenhouse gas emissions that cause global warming out of a fear that their profits might be affected if they had to stop dumping so much pollution into the atmosphere.

—Al Gore, January 16, 2004

1e Think About Your Purpose

The starting point for effective writing is determining in advance what you want to accomplish. Knowing your purpose shapes everything else you do as a writer—your choice of the kind of writing, your subject matter, your organization, and your style.

WRITING SMART

Identify your purposes for writing

- Are you analyzing a verbal or visual text to understand how it persuades readers or how it makes us think and feel in certain ways? (See Chapter 6.)
- Are you describing and reflecting on people, places, experiences, and ideas? Are you writing a personal essay, blog, or travel narrative? (See Chapter 7.)
- Are you writing to report information, to explain a process, to explore questions and problems, or to analyze patterns, connections, and causes? (See Chapter 8.)
- Are you arguing for a position on a controversial issue or arguing to convince people to take a particular course of action? (See Chapter 9.)

1f Think About the Complex Demands of Writing Today

The nature of work and life in general is changing rapidly because of changing technologies and globalization. So too are the demands placed on writers.

- **Writers today use a variety of writing technologies.** People do not throw away their pencils and ballpoint pens when they buy a laptop computer. Each writing tool is well suited to particular uses; it's hard to top a pencil for jotting down a grocery list, although some people may be equally comfortable using PDAs for such daily writing tasks.
- **Writers today do many different kinds of writing:** letters, reports, memos, newsletters, evaluations, articles, charts, Web sites, computer-assisted presentations, press releases, brochures, proposals, résumés, agendas, users' manuals, analyses, summaries, and email. Each kind of writing has its own special set of demands.
- **Writers today have multiple purposes.** An email may convey both business strategies and personal news. A proposal may have as its unacknowledged purpose the request for a new job or wider responsibilities. Even a simple memo often conveys many unstated messages, such as the attitude of the writer toward her coworkers.
- **Writers today have multiple audiences.** Often documents are read by readers who have different interests. The speed of digital media allows many points of view to be expressed simultaneously. Skilled writers in the digital era know they must negotiate among these many points of view.
- **Writers today know how to find and present information relevant to their purposes.** They are efficient researchers who can locate, evaluate, and present information clearly and ethically to their readers. Most readers prefer well-selected information to a barrage of unfiltered data.

- **Writers today often work in teams.** They communicate with colleagues to achieve a common goal, so the ability to collaborate effectively may be an unanticipated need in writing effectively.
- **Writers today know that it is critical to emphasize what is important.** They understand that readers face an overdose of information, have little patience, and want to know quickly what is at stake.
- **Writers today recognize that an active and personal style free from errors is often most effective.** Readers in general prefer a personal and accessible style.
- **Writers today communicate visually as well as verbally.** Computers and digital media give writers the ability to use pictures and graphics in addition to text. Knowing how to communicate visually is important to your success in the digital era.

WRITING IN THE WORLD

Choosing writing tools

Because we are exposed to so much writing in our daily lives—emails, class assignments, instant messages (IM)—it is easy to think that all writing is the same. However, the technologies that we use to write affect that writing. Consider a difference as simple as writing with a pen versus writing with a pencil. What you write with the pen is permanent. Although it can be scratched out or covered with white-out, it will always be on the page. Pencil marks, however, can be erased and written over. Perhaps you prefer to use a pencil because you like to erase mistakes until you are satisfied. Or perhaps you use a pen because you like the solidity and permanence of writing in ink. In either case, the physical tools we use for writing have an effect on that writing and how we think about writing as well.

(Continued on next page)

Similar differences exist with digital writing technologies. Word processing programs provide their users with a number of tools like spell checkers and they provide control over formatting options like typefaces and margins, all of which encourage users to spend time polishing their work. In contrast, the rapid-fire conversations that are characteristic of IM encourage a different kind of writing, one with its own language, standards, and formats.

When you are preparing for a writing assignment, think ahead about the kind of tools you will use and how they will affect your writing. If, say, your project is a reflective journal, you might use a laptop or you might choose a pen and paper. Each has its advantages. But if your project requires collaboration, you might want to choose a Web application that allows multiple authors to add and edit content. As you think about these issues, you will begin to have a wider appreciation of the effect of writing technologies on your work.

Does it matter if you sit down to write a paper in your room or in a coffee shop? If you write an email to a family member sitting in a quiet corner of your school's library or standing at an Internet kiosk in a busy airport?

Exercise 1.4 Write a paragraph describing all of the different types of writing you do in a week. What kinds of tools do you use? How does the audience for the different kinds of writing affect your choice of style? What kind of research do you have to do for this writing? Is there a visual element to any of this writing? If so, what?

Chapter 2

Plan and Draft

Planning begins with thinking about your goals and your readers.

2a ▶ Think About the Expectations of College Readers

Writing in college changes from course to course depending on the requirements of the course's discipline. What is expected in a lab report in biology looks very different from a paper in your English class.

Nevertheless, there are some common expectations about writing in college that extend across disciplines.

Writing in college	Writers are expected to
States explicit claims	Make a claim that isn't obvious. The claim is often called a thesis statement.
Develops an argument	Support their claims with facts, evidence, reasons, and testimony from experts.
Analyzes with insight	Examine in depth what they read and view.
Investigates complexity	Explore the complexity of a subject, challenging their readers by asking "Have you thought about this?" or "What if you discard the usual way of thinking about a subject and take the opposite point of view?"
Organizes with a hierarchical structure	Make the major parts of a presentation evident to readers and indicate which parts are subordinate to others.
Signals with transitions	Indicate logical relationships clearly so readers can follow a pathway without getting lost.
Documents sources carefully	Provide the sources of information so readers can consult the same sources the writer used.

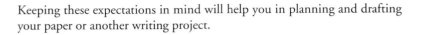

Keeping these expectations in mind will help you in planning and drafting your paper or another writing project.

2b Establish Your Goals

Your instructor will give you specific suggestions about how to think about your audience and topic. Two ways to make your task simpler are

- Be sure you are responding to the assignment appropriately.
- Select a topic that both fits the assignment and appeals to you strongly enough to make you want to write about it.

Look carefully at your assignment

When your instructor gives you a writing assignment, look closely at what you are asked to do. Often the assignment will contain key words such as *analyze, compare and contrast, define, describe, evaluate,* or *propose* that will assist you in determining what direction to take.

- **Analyze:** Find connections among a set of facts, events, or readings, and make them meaningful.
- **Compare and contrast:** Examine how two or more things are alike and how they differ.
- **Define:** Make a claim about how something should be defined, according to features that you set out.
- **Describe:** Observe carefully and select details that create a dominant impression.
- **Evaluate:** Argue that something is good, bad, best, or worst in its class, according to criteria that you set out.
- **Propose:** Identify a particular problem and explain why your solution is the best one.

If you are unclear about what the assignment calls for, talk with your instructor.

Find a topic you care about

If you do not have an assigned topic, a good way to find one is to look first at the materials for your course. You may find something that interests you in the readings for the course or in a topic that came up in class discussion. It's hard to write about something that doesn't engage you, so start by writing down things that do. If your assignment gives you a wide range of options, you might write more than one list, starting with your personal interests. Think also about campus topics, community topics, and national topics that intrigue you. Your lists might resemble these:

Personal
1. Benefits of weight training
2. Wordplay in Marx brothers movies
3. History of hairstyles

Campus
1. Pros and cons of charging computer fees
2. Should my university have a foreign language requirement?
3. Affirmative action admissions policies

Community
1. Helmet laws for people who ride bicycles and motorcycles
2. Bilingual education programs
3. More bike lanes to encourage more people to ride bicycles
4. Better public transportation

Nation/World
1. Advertising aimed at preschool children
2. Censorship of the Internet
3. Effects of climate change
4. Setting aside the laws that govern police searches in an effort to stop terrorism

Often you will find that, before you can begin writing, you need to analyze exactly what you mean by a phrase like "censorship of the Internet." For example, do you mean censorship of Web sites or of everything that goes over the Internet, including private email?

After you make a list or lists, you should review it:

- Put a checkmark beside the topics that look most interesting or the ones that mean the most to you.
- Put a question mark beside the topics that you don't know very much about. If you choose one of these issues, you will have to do research.
- Select the two or three topics that look the most promising.

Exercise 2.1 A student generated the following list for his research paper on the history of the horror movie. Choose a topic for the paper from the list. Then organize the list into categories that the student could address effectively in a paper. Eliminate any dead-end topics or redundancies.

Nosferatu (1922)
Bela Lugosi *Dracula* (1931)
Boris Karloff *Frankenstein* (1931)
Christopher Lee as Dracula in the 1960s
monster movies
Creature from the Black Lagoon (1956)
werewolves
"slasher" films
women
Wes Craven *Scream* (1996)
Hammer Films and Christopher Lee
blood vs. suspense
Japanese horror
The Blair Witch Project (1999)
Stephen King
mutants, aliens, and robots in the 1950s
irony and independent film
demons/possession
what was scary then/now? (1920s to 2000 and beyond)
special effects
cult movies
Friday the 13th (1980)

zombies return in *Dawn of the Dead* (2004) and *Land of the Dead* (2005)
The Exorcist (1973), restored version in 2000
extreme violence returns in 2000s, e.g., *Texas Chainsaw Massacre* (1974), remake (2003)
The Descent (2005)—all female cast
Vincent Price

2c Explore Your Topic

Once you have identified a potential topic, the next step is to determine what you already know about that topic and what you need to find out. Experienced writers use many strategies for exploring their knowledge of a topic and how interesting it really is to them. Here are a few.

Ask questions

These classic reporter's questions will assist you in thinking through a topic:

1. *Who* is doing it?
2. *What* is happening or at issue?
3. *When* is it happening?
4. *Where* is it happening?
5. *How* is it happening?
6. *Why* is it happening?

Freewrite

Another way to find out how much you know about a topic is to **freewrite**: write as quickly as you can without stopping for a set time, usually five or ten minutes. The goal of freewriting is to get as much down as possible. Don't stop to correct mistakes. Let your ideas flow wherever they take you, even if they take you well outside the boundaries of your topic. The constant flow of words should generate ideas—some useful, some not.

If you get stuck, write the same sentence over again, or write about how hungry you are or how difficult freewriting is, until thoughts on your selected topic reappear. After you've finished, read what you have written and single out any key ideas. The following freewrite was composed by Mariela Martinez on a student free speech case that wound up before the United States Supreme Court in March 2007. In 2002 in Juneau, Alaska, high school senior Joseph Frederick was suspended for ten days by principal Deborah Morse after he displayed a banner off of school property during the Winter Olympics Torch Relay. You can read Martinez's essay on pages 142–148.

Freewrite on Morse v. Frederick

I did dumb stuff when I was a senior in high school. I can imagine Joe Frederick sitting around with his friends after they found out that the Winter Olympics Torch Relay would pass by his school. I can imagine what happened. Someone said it would be really cool if we held up a banner that said Bong Hits 4 Jesus in front of the cameras. Everyone else said awesome! The principal will totally freak! But what happens next? That's what Joe and his friends didn't think through. And when it happened, the principal didn't think it through either, but give her credit, she had to react on the spot. She did what she thought was right at the time, but she fell right into the trap. The bottom line is when do stupid statements become illegal? A lot of adults and high school students make stupid statements, but unless they are racist, profane, or libelous, they don't get punished. Joe did get punished. In a school he would have been disruptive, but he wasn't in school. He didn't go to class that day. He was outside on a public sidewalk. And school was called off that afternoon because of the parade.

So he was just a high school student doing something dumb, not something illegal. Joe made the principal look bad, but he embarrassed his school and his parents, and my guess is that if he had it to do over again, he wouldn't have done it. Still, he shouldn't have been punished. He didn't make a serious argument in favor of doing drugs. Or ridicule Christians. The real argument is about the limits of free speech.

Ideas to Use

1. *Joe's banner was in poor taste, but poor taste doesn't meet legal requirement for censorship.*
2. *The principal was embarrassed and made a knee-jerk reaction without thinking.*
3. *The real issue is what free speech rights do young people have.*

You may want to use a key word or idea as a starting point for a second freewrite. After two or three rounds, you will discover how much you already know about your topic and possible directions for developing it.

Brainstorm

An alternative method of discovery is to **brainstorm**. The end result of brainstorming is usually a list—sometimes of questions, sometimes of statements. You might come up with a list of observations and questions, such as these for the free speech case.

- *The student wasn't in the school at the time of the incident.*
- *The principal overreacted.*

- *Drugs are an excuse to give authorities more control.*
- *What is the recent history of free speech cases involving high school students?*
- *Student's citing of Jefferson resulted in more punishment—WHY???*
- *Isn't there protection for satire?*

Make an idea map

Still another strategy for exploring how much you know about a potential topic is to make an **idea map**. Idea maps are useful because they let you see everything at once, and you can begin to make connections among the different aspects of an issue—definitions, causes, effects, proposed solutions, and your personal experience. A good way to get started is to write down ideas on sticky notes. Then you can move the sticky notes around until you figure out which ideas fit together. Figure 2.1 shows what an idea map on the freedom of speech case involving Joseph Frederick might look like.

Respond to something you've read

Most of the writing you do in college will be linked to texts you are reading. Find time to read about your topic before writing about it. Select a book or an article that you find to be a powerful statement about your topic. You don't have to agree with the author completely; in fact, it's more productive if you can "talk back" to the author.

Imagine you are sitting down face-to-face with the author. Find places where you can write things like the following.

- "I agree with your general point, but did you think of this other example? What would you do with it?"
- "Here you seem to be arguing for one side, but later you seem to contradict yourself and give credit to the other side."

- "Your point about one group might be applied to a different group."
- "I don't agree with this claim because your evidence doesn't support your assertion."

Talking back to a text can help you find your own position: "While X sees it this way, I look at it a different way."

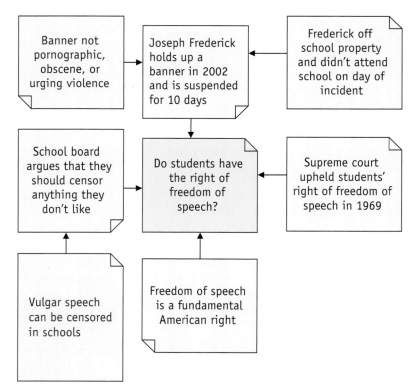

Figure 2.1 Idea map on the Juneau, Alaska, freedom of speech case

Talk and listen

Writing requires concentration, which for many people depends on quiet and solitude. Nevertheless, many ideas come from conversation, and all ideas are born from other ideas. When we talk and listen, we discover. Productive writers are engaged in a community where ideas are discussed. Your writing class is a writing community. To make the community as useful as possible, it is important to ask your peers for specific and genuine feedback on your drafts and to pay close attention to your classmates' writing as well.

If any of your class communication is done through email or online discussion, you will already have a head start on your assigned writing. Emails and online discussions can be used the way journals and freewrites are—as material for essays. When you are planning your essay, you may find that you already have a wealth of written material to draw from.

■ You can get one-on-one help in developing your ideas, focusing your topic, and revising your paper at your writing center.

WRITING SMART

Explore your topic using a blog

One way of keeping track of your exploratory notes is to keep a blog. **Blogs** are a good way to organize multimedia information, including text, images, links, and audio files. For example, after completing a freewriting or brainstorming session, you could quickly edit your notes and post them to your blog. You could also post your idea maps (export your files in PDF format for posting), links and short descriptions of online articles you want to keep track of, or summaries of texts you have read as part of your research.

In addition, most blogs have a commenting feature, which allows others to leave responses to your posts. Invite your classmates or friends to read your exploratory blog and give you feedback. By turning your blog into a conversation about your topic, you will be able to take advantage of their questions and responses about your work as you craft your paper.

Exercise 2.2　　Read the following passage and freewrite for ten minutes. When you are done, look over what you wrote and pick out two or three topics that would be worth pursuing in a paper.

In the years since Darwin published *The Origin of Species,* the crisp conceptual line that divided artificial from natural selection has blurred. Whereas once humankind exerted its will in the relatively small arena of artificial selection (the arena I think of, metaphorically, as a garden) and nature held sway everywhere else, today the force of our presence is felt everywhere. It has become much harder, in the past century, to tell where the garden leaves off and pure nature begins. We are shaping the evolutionary weather in ways Darwin could never have foreseen; indeed, even the weather itself is in some sense an artifact now, its temperatures and storms the reflection of our actions. For a great many species today, "fitness" means the ability to get along in a world in which humankind has become the most powerful evolutionary force. Artificial selection has become a much more important chapter in natural history as it has moved into the space once ruled exclusively by natural selection.

—Michael Pollan, from *The Botany of Desire,* 2001

2d Write a Working Thesis

The initial stage of the planning process involves finding ideas, expanding and broadening your thoughts, and recording ideas from written sources and conversations. The next stage of thinking, after you have decided on a general topic, is *narrowing* your focus to a specific topic. Having a specific focus is the key to writing a strong essay.

Use questions to focus a broad topic

Childhood obesity is certainly a current and interesting research topic, but it is too broad. Ask questions that will break the big topic into smaller ones.

- Why are children becoming obese?
- Why are children today more obese than children of past generations?
- How has the American food industry contributed to childhood obesity?
- What changes in American culture have contributed to childhood obesity?
- What are the adverse health effects of childhood obesity?
- What strategies are effective for preventing childhood obesity?

Consider other angles to expand a narrow topic

Too-narrow topics are rarer than topics that are too broad. Although candy consumption is certainly one factor contributing to obesity in children, this

narrow focus overlooks many other factors that together lead to childhood obesity. For instance:

- Why do some children eat large amounts of candy yet maintain a healthy weight?
- Children have always eaten candy. Why are children today more obese than children of past generations?
- Even when parents keep kids away from candy, some still gain weight. Why?

If you cannot seem to find enough information on your topic to construct an argument, your topic might be too narrow.

Turn your topic into a thesis statement

Your **thesis** states your main idea. Much of the writing that you will do in college and later in your career will have an explicit thesis, usually stated near the beginning. The thesis announces your topic and indicates what points you want to make about that topic.

Your thesis should be closely tied to your purpose—to reflect on your own experience, to explain some aspect of your topic, or to argue for a position or course of action.

Reflective thesis	My experience in a government seminar where other students frequently and sometimes vehemently expressed conflicting views taught me that creating an atmosphere of tolerance can be just as important as passing laws to protect free speech.
Informative thesis	Courts in the United States have consistently upheld the right of free speech on public property if it is not obscene, threatening violence, or inciting violence.
Persuasive thesis	1. A public college or university should have the right to limit free speech in cases of overtly racist or anti-gay language because failing to address

such abuses condones intolerance and threatens students' ability to learn.

2. A public college or university should not have the right to limit free speech, even when it is hateful, because speech that is not obscene or threatening violence is protected on public property.

STAYING ON TRACK

Evaluate your working thesis

Ask yourself these questions about your working thesis.

1. Is it specific?
2. Is it manageable in the length and time I have?
3. Is it interesting to my intended readers?

Consider the following examples.

Example 1

Eating disorders remain a serious problem on college campuses.

Specific? The thesis is too broad. Exactly who suffers from eating disorders? Is the problem the same for men and women?

Manageable? Because the thesis is not limited to a particular aspect of eating disorders, it cannot be researched adequately.

Interesting? The topic is potentially interesting, but most people know that many college students suffer from eating disorders. If you chose this topic, what could you tell your readers that they don't know already?

(Continued on next page)

STAYING ON TRACK *(continued)*

REVISED THESIS

Glamorous images of ultrathin people in the fashion industry, the movie industry, and other media are a contributing cause of eating disorders on college campuses because they influence young people to believe they are fat when in fact their weight is normal.

Example 2

The United States entered World War II when the Japanese bombed Pearl Harbor on December 7, 1941.

Specific? The thesis is too narrow. It states a commonly acknowledged fact.

Manageable? A known fact is stated in the thesis, so there is nothing to research. The general topic of the attack on Pearl Harbor is too large for essay-length treatment.

Interesting? The attack on Pearl Harbor remains interesting to Americans (witness a recent Hollywood film that deals with the subject), but there is no topic to work from.

REVISED THESIS

Although combat between the United States and Japan began at Pearl Harbor, the unofficial war began when President Roosevelt froze Japanese assets in the United States in July 1940 and later declared a commercial embargo.

These examples suggest that the key to writing an effective thesis is finding a topic that is neither too vast nor too narrow—and not obvious. You may have to adjust your working thesis more than once as you plan and begin drafting.

Exercise 2.3   Look at the following theses. What kind (reflective, informative, persuasive) is each?

1. Reading Sylvia Plath's poem "Daddy" awakened me to the violence present in some parent-child relationships.
2. Critics should recognize that the field of trauma studies could not exist without the works of Sylvia Plath.
3. Sylvia Plath's relationship with the poet Ted Hughes affected her later work deeply.
4. No-kill animal shelters are finding creative ways to persuade people to adopt older pets.
5. My experience with Sylvester has given me a great fondness for elderly pets.
6. The city should fine anyone who willfully abandons a pet.
7. Lawmakers need to see that school vouchers will be the death of public schools.
8. My parents, going against their friends' advice, sent me to a public school in the inner city. Their decision made a huge impact on how I, as an adult, feel about education.
9. The voucher issue has set off a heated debate in both major political parties.
10. The school voucher program has worked wonders for many at-risk kids.

Exercise 2.4   Write two summaries of the following passage. In the first summary, provide just the key points, as they appear. When you are done with this summary, rank the ideas in the order of their importance. For your second summary, focus on the top two ideas from your ranking and give more detail from the passage about these ideas. At the end of the second summary, explain why you decided this idea or these ideas were the most important. Finally, rewrite this explanation as one sentence. This is a thesis.

When two people talk, they don't just fall into physical and aural harmony. They also engage in what is called motor mimicry. If you show people pictures of a smiling face or a frowning face, they'll smile or frown back, although perhaps only in muscular changes so fleeting that they can only be captured with electronic sensors. If I hit my thumb with a hammer, most people watching will grimace: they'll mimic my emotional state. This is what is meant, in the technical sense, by empathy. We imitate each other's emotions as a way of expressing support and caring and, even more basically, as a way of communicating with each other.

—Malcolm Gladwell, *The Tipping point: How Little Things Can Make a Big Difference,* 2000

Exercise 2.5   Here are several assignments and the thesis statement that a student has decided to use for that assignment. Evaluate these thesis statements according to their levels of specificity, manageability, and interest. Then, rewrite each one to make it meet all three of the requirements.

1. Design a three-panel brochure intended to educate teenage boys about the responsibilities of fatherhood.
   Thesis: Think before having a baby. They are really expensive.
2. Write a three- to five-page paper for a child development class. The papers from this class will be published on a child advocacy Web site.
   Thesis: Many formerly accepted methods of discipline are now considered child abuse.
3. Write a 10- to 15-page research paper on a revolutionary breakthrough in urban transportation to enter in a contest. Your paper will be evaluated by a panel of graduate students majoring in city planning.
   Thesis: Washington DC has a great subway system called the Metro.
4. Write a 200- to 300-word article for a magazine geared toward 8- to 12-year-olds.
   Thesis: It's never too early to start thinking about a career.
5. Write a one-page paper for your ethics class. You will use this paper to start class discussion.
   Thesis: Reading an employee's email is a violation of privacy.

2e Plan a Strategy

People who write frequently on the job or who make their living by writing have many different ways of producing a successful piece of writing. Some

may plan extensively in advance, either individually or as a team, specifying exactly what will go in each section. Other writers find that putting ideas into words often changes the ideas and generates new ones. These writers know that writing drafts is a way of discovering their subject, and they count on one or two or more rewrites to get their document into shape.

Consider making an outline

At some point in school, you may have been required to produce a formal outline to submit along with a paper. A **formal outline** typically begins with the thesis statement, which anchors the entire outline. Each numbered or lettered item clearly supports the thesis, and the relationship among the items is clear from the outline hierarchy.

> Thesis statement: The United States needs to take concrete steps to reduce obesity in children.
>
> I. A disturbing aspect of the trend of fatter Americans is that children are increasingly obese.
>   A. The percentage of obese children nearly quadrupled between 1974 and 2000.
>   B. Obese children suffer many serious health problems today.
>   C. America has had some success in addressing other teenage health problems including smoking, drug use, and teen pregnancy.
> II. Many causes have been proposed for overweight America.
>   A. One proposed cause is the move to the suburbs, but the population shift to the suburbs occurred before the rapid rise in weight gain.
>   B. The couch potato argument is countered by increases in exercise and participation in athletics.
>   C. The simple answer is that Americans consume about twice as many calories per day as they need.

Consider using a working outline

A working outline is more like an initial sketch of how you will arrange the major sections. Jotting down main points and a few subpoints before you begin can be a great help while you are writing. You can read the complete essay that developed from these outlines in Section 23l.

Addressing Childhood Obesity

Section 1: Begin with a description of the problem including statistics on the rising number of obese children.

Section 2: Discuss the causes that have been proposed for childhood obesity.

Section 3: Discuss how the eating patterns of Americans have changed during the last thirty years and how portions served have increased.

Section 4: Examine how food is being marketed to children.

Section 5: Look at the role of parents and why parents often don't control much of the environment where children eat.

Section 6: Describe solutions: (1) restrict marketing of food to children, (2) educate parents and children, (3) promote healthier lifestyles.

Section 7: Discuss how these solutions can be implemented.

Exercise 2.6   Look again at the list of topics in Exercise 2.1, the freewrite you did for Exercise 2.2, and the summaries and thesis you extracted from the passage in Exercise 2.4. Choose one of these to pursue, and write a short outline for a paper that includes three to five main topics.

2f Compose a Draft

Skilled writers aim at producing a good draft—not a perfect draft. They know that they can go back and revise later.

Essays typically contain an introduction, body, and conclusion. You do not have to write these parts in that order, though. In your **introduction**, you can offer a short example that illustrates the problem being discussed.

You can state a surprising fact. You can begin with a fascinating quotation. Your aim is to interest the reader and to let the reader know the topic of the paper, if not necessarily the thesis.

The **body** of the essay consists of the primary discussion. Remember to guide readers through the discussion by letting them know where you are going. Your readers need road signs to tell them where the discussion is taking them. Road signs are transition words and phrases such as *consequently, the third reason is . . .* , and *on the other hand.*

The last section, the **conclusion**, often repeats what has already been said. If the essay has been long and complex, sometimes this repetition is necessary, but usually the repetition is just that—annoying redundancy. The final paragraph does not have to repeat the main point. It can give a compelling last example or propose a course of action. It can ponder the larger significance of the subject under discussion. It can pose an important question for the reader to think about.

WRITING SMART

Overcome writer's block

1. **If you have an outline, put it on the computer screen or place it beside you.** The outline will give you prompts to help get you started.
2. **Begin writing what you know best.** If you don't know exactly where you are headed, the introduction can be the hardest section to write. The introduction can wait until last.
3. **Resist the urge to revise too soon.** It's more important to keep moving forward. If you stop to polish a section, you will lose momentum, and in the end, you may discard that section anyway.
4. **If you get stuck, try working on another section.** Look again at your notes or outline.
5. **If you are still stuck, talk to someone about what you are trying to write.** If your campus has a writing center, talk to a consultant. Reading more about your subject can also help you to get moving again.

2g Write as a Member of a Team

Almost without exception people in occupations that require a college education write frequently on the job, and much of that writing is done in collaboration rather than alone. The better you understand how to write effectively with other people, the more enjoyable and more productive the process will be for you.

Determine the goals and identify tasks and roles

- Write down the goals as specifically as you can and discuss them as a team.
- Determine what tasks are required to meet those goals. Be as specific as you can. Write down the tasks and arrange them in the order they need to be completed.
- Decide whether the team has the skills and resources to perform those tasks. If you do not possess the necessary skills and resources, adjust the goals to what you can realistically expect to accomplish.

Make a work plan

- Make a time line that lists the dates when specific tasks need to be completed and distribute it to all team members. Charts are useful tools for keeping track of progress.
- Assign tasks to team members. Find out if anyone possesses additional skills that could be helpful to the team.
- Revisit the team's goals often. To succeed, each team member must keep in mind what the team aims to accomplish.
- Decide on a process for monitoring progress. Set up specific dates for review and assign team members to be responsible for reviewing work that has been done.

Understand the dynamics of a successful team

- Teamwork requires some flexibility. Different people have different styles and contribute in different ways. Keep talking to each other along the way.
- It may be desirable to rotate roles during the project.

Deal with problems when they come up

- If a team member is not participating, find out why.
- If team members have different ideas about what needs to be done, find time to meet so that the team can reach an agreement.
- Get the team together if you are not meeting the deadlines you established in the work plan and devise a new plan, if necessary.

WRITING IN THE WORLD

Compose wikis

Wikis are communal Web sites where, in the purest form, each contributor has an equal ability to create and revise a wiki page. Wiki software records each change as it is made, prompting others to make more changes. The most successful wikis have specific goals and methods of communication to discuss problems as they arise. The best-known wiki is *Wikipedia*, the online encyclopedia founded in 2001 with entries that have been collaboratively written by thousands of users.

On your next collaborative project, try using a wiki to organize your group's work. Create a wiki for the text so everyone will be able to see changes to the document in real time. You can even use the wiki to list your group's goals, time line, and the tasks and roles of individual members. Be careful to state explicitly the goals of your wiki and the conditions under which group members can alter important organizational documents.

Compose Paragraphs

Your paragraphs should set out a line of thought for your readers.

3a Focus Your Paragraphs

Readers expect sentences in a paragraph to be closely related to one another. Often writers will begin a paragraph with one idea, but other ideas will occur to them while they are writing. Paragraphs confuse readers when they go in different directions. When you revise your paragraphs, check for focus.

In the following example, notice how much stronger the paragraph becomes when we remove the sentences in green. They distract us from the subject, Royal Chitwan National Park in Nepal and how it is different from Western national parks.

Like everything else in Nepal, Royal Chitwan National Park is different from Western notions of a park. It is a jungle between two rivers, with grass twenty to twenty-five feet tall growing in the swampy land along the rivers. Several rare or endangered species live in the park, including leopards, crocodiles, royal Bengal tigers, and the greater one-horned Asian rhinoceros. In fact, we saw several rhinos during our weeklong visit to the park. To my relief we saw all but one from the safety of an elephant's back. But the boundaries of the park restrict neither the Nepalis nor the animals. The Nepalis cross the river into the park to gather firewood and the tall grass, which they use to make their houses. Some even live within the park. The rhinos and deer raid the Nepalis' fields at night, and the leopards prey on their dogs and livestock. To keep the truce between these competitors, the army patrols the park, mostly to prevent

Deal with problems when they come up

- If a team member is not participating, find out why.
- If team members have different ideas about what needs to be done, find time to meet so that the team can reach an agreement.
- Get the team together if you are not meeting the deadlines you established in the work plan and devise a new plan, if necessary.

WRITING IN THE WORLD

Compose wikis

Wikis are communal Web sites where, in the purest form, each contributor has an equal ability to create and revise a wiki page. Wiki software records each change as it is made, prompting others to make more changes. The most successful wikis have specific goals and methods of communication to discuss problems as they arise. The best-known wiki is *Wikipedia*, the online encyclopedia founded in 2001 with entries that have been collaboratively written by thousands of users.

On your next collaborative project, try using a wiki to organize your group's work. Create a wiki for the text so everyone will be able to see changes to the document in real time. You can even use the wiki to list your group's goals, time line, and the tasks and roles of individual members. Be careful to state explicitly the goals of your wiki and the conditions under which group members can alter important organizational documents.

Compose Paragraphs

Your paragraphs should set out a line of thought for your readers.

3a Focus Your Paragraphs

Readers expect sentences in a paragraph to be closely related to one another. Often writers will begin a paragraph with one idea, but other ideas will occur to them while they are writing. Paragraphs confuse readers when they go in different directions. When you revise your paragraphs, check for focus.

In the following example, notice how much stronger the paragraph becomes when we remove the sentences in green. They distract us from the subject, Royal Chitwan National Park in Nepal and how it is different from Western national parks.

Like everything else in Nepal, Royal Chitwan National Park is different from Western notions of a park. It is a jungle between two rivers, with grass twenty to twenty-five feet tall growing in the swampy land along the rivers. Several rare or endangered species live in the park, including leopards, crocodiles, royal Bengal tigers, and the greater one-horned Asian rhinoceros. In fact, we saw several rhinos during our weeklong visit to the park. To my relief we saw all but one from the safety of an elephant's back. But the boundaries of the park restrict neither the Nepalis nor the animals. The Nepalis cross the river into the park to gather firewood and the tall grass, which they use to make their houses. Some even live within the park. The rhinos and deer raid the Nepalis' fields at night, and the leopards prey on their dogs and livestock. To keep the truce between these competitors, the army patrols the park, mostly to prevent

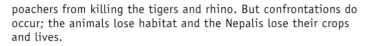

poachers from killing the tigers and rhino. But confrontations do occur; the animals lose habitat and the Nepalis lose their crops and lives.

When to use explicit topic sentences

You were probably taught to begin a paragraph with a topic sentence. Topic sentences alert readers to the focus of a paragraph and help writers stay on topic. Topic sentences should explain the focus of the paragraph and situate it in the larger argument. However, topic sentences do not have to begin paragraphs, and they need not be just one sentence. You will decide what placement and length will best suit your subject.

Topic sentences at the beginning of a paragraph will quickly orient readers, preparing them for the sentences to come. Each sentence that follows elucidates the topic sentence.

Topic sentence at the beginning

We live in a world of risks so much beyond our control that it is difficult to think of anything that is risk free. Even the most basic human acts involve risk—having sex in an era of AIDS, eating in an era of genetically altered food, walking outdoors in an ozone-depleted atmosphere, drinking water and breathing air laden with chemicals whose effects we do not understand. Should we eat more fish in our daily diet? Nutritionists tell us that eating fish reduces the risk of heart disease. Other scientists, however, tell us that fish are contaminated with a new generation of synthetic chemicals.

When a paragraph builds to make a particular point, the topic sentence is more effective at the end of the paragraph.

Topic sentence at the end

We are continually being summoned to change ourselves for the better—through fitness programs, through various kinds of instruction, through advice columns, through self-help books and videos—and somehow we never quite measure up. The blame always comes back on us. If we had eaten better, or exercised more, or paid more attention to our investments, or learned a new skill, or changed our oil every 3,000 miles, then things would have turned out better. Very rarely do we ask how a different social organization might have made things better. Our society incorporates critical thinking without being much affected by the consequences of that thinking.

When to use implicit topic sentences

In some cases, particularly in narrative prose, writers omit explicit topic sentences because they would clash with the tone or style of the paragraph. Instead, these paragraphs use tightly connected, focused sentences to make the topic implicitly clear.

Implicit topic sentence

By the mid-1970s in the United States, the temporary advantage of being the only major power with its industries undamaged following World War II had evaporated, and rust-belt industries failed one after the other against competition from a revived Europe and an emergent Asia. The United States seemed to be going the way of other historical world powers, where efficient trading nations beat out bloated military regimes. Japan appeared to be the model for a fast and light capitalism that the rest of the world would imitate. Just a few years later, however, the American decline reversed. The United States again became the economic leader of the world in the 1990s.

The implicit topic sentence is something like "The United States' economy appeared to be in rapid decline in the 1970s, only to bounce back to world leadership in the 1990s."

Exercise 3.1 Find the topic sentence in each of the following paragraphs. If it implied, write what you think it is.

1. I first got interested in the Civil War as a boy. Any Deep South boy, and probably all Southern boys, have been familiar with the Civil War as a sort of thing in their conscience going back. I honestly believe that it's in all our subconsciouses. This country was into its adolescence at the time of the Civil War. It really was; it hadn't formulated itself really as an adult nation, and the Civil War did that. Like all traumatic experiences that you might have had in your adolescence, it stays with you the rest of your life, constantly in your subconscious, most likely in your conscience, too.

   —Shelby Foote, *Booknotes,* 1997

2. Zach Braff has said that his hit movie *Garden State* (2004) was "a big, life-affirming, state-of-the-union address for twentysomethings." I'm a twentysomething. His new feature, *The Last Kiss,* documents the mental anguish of a 29-year-old commitmentphobe. I'm at the age when commitment looms. If Braff maintains this pace, he'll be making facile observations about our voyage through life's milestones until he films an indie-rock-infused *On Golden Pond*. My only comfort is that one day, we'll both be dead. If Zach Braff is the voice of my generation, can't someone please crush his larynx?

   —Josh Levin, "Why Is This Guy the Voice of My Generation?"
   Slate, September 22, 2006

3. I'm on the subway after a long, hard day in the kitchen, my feet swelling up like twin Hindenburgs; my back killing me; fourteen hours of hot, sweaty, uncomfortable toil and two hundred eighty dinners under my belt; and I want to sit down. There are three seats in front of me in the crowded subway car. Unfortunately, one miserable, fat bastard is taking up all three of them. As he sits glumly but defiantly in the center seat, his gigantic butt cheeks and thighs spill out of the molded plastic bucket onto the seats on both sides, and his beady eyes dare me to try

and squeeze my bony ass into one of the narrow spaces next to him.

—Anthony Bourdain, "The Evildoers," *The Nasty Bits,* 2006

4. But I have said enough. I hope you will treasure up the instructions which I have given you, and make them a guide to your feet and a light to your understanding. Build your character thoughtfully and painstakingly upon these precepts; and by and by, when you have got it built, you will be surprised and gratified to see how nicely and sharply it resembles everybody else's.

—Mark Twain, "Advice to Youth," 1882

3b Organize Your Paragraphs

Well-organized paragraphs in essays usually follow a pattern similar to that of a well-organized paper, but in miniature. Seven strategies for effectively organizing sentences within a paragraph are presented on the following pages. Remember, the form of the paragraph should follow its function in the paper. Chances are you'll use a combination of these strategies in order to get your point across.

Description

Description is a common strategy for informative and narrative writing. Providing concrete details—sights, sounds, smells, textures, and tastes—gives the reader a sensory memory of your subject.

Topic sentence

Details convey a dominant impression.

The airport at Kathmandu resembles one-gate airports in the United States, with a small waiting room and baggage area, except that it is deluged with international tourists. Busloads of young people lug bright nylon rucksacks and duffle bags emblazoned with names like "Australian Wilderness Adventures" and "South Korean Dhaulagiri Winter Expedition." Mingled with them are traders from India and Nepal—some dressed in suits, some in peasant clothes—carrying bulky goods like folding chairs, drums of cooking oil, and boxes of medicine.

This descriptive paragraph relies on a comparison to a place U.S. readers will probably recognize.

As in descriptive writing, in photographs close attention to detail is essential.

The example paragraphs about Nepal are adapted from Lester Faigley, "Nepal Diary: Where the Global Village Ends," *North Dakota Quarterly* 57.3 (1989): 106–29.

Narration or Process

Narrative paragraphs tell a story for a reason. Organized by time, narratives relate a series of events in the order they occur. This approach is useful when the temporal order of ideas or events is essential to their logic, such as in how-to writing.

Verbs establish the sequence of events to orient the reader in time.

The ascent goes easier than they expected. In two hours they reach the yak pastures where they will make the high camp. The view from the high camp is spectacular, with Dhaulagiri in clouds above them and the three sunlit summits of Nilgiri across the valley, with snow plumes blowing from their tops. Jim and Lester drop their packs at the campsite and continue walking to scout the route above the camp that they will follow in the darkness of early morning the next day. They find a steep path that parallels a fern-lined gorge, now rich in fall color. It is the lushest forest they have seen in Nepal. They congratulate each other on their decision to attempt the climb to the Dhaulagiri icefall, unaware that they will soon experience the mountain's furious weather, even on its lower slopes.

Narrative paragraphs often include description to orient the reader in space.

Comparison and Contrast

Paragraphs of comparison assess one subject in terms of its relation to others, usually highlighting what they have in common. Contrasting paragraphs analyze differences between things.

You can organize a comparison or a contrast in two ways: by describing one thing and then describing another, or by moving back and forth between the two items point by point. Often the latter strategy highlights contrasts, as the following paragraph illustrates.

> Nepal was closed to Europeans from 1843 to 1949 and missed the colonial influences of the British. Consequently, Kathmandu remains a medieval city at heart, with a thin overlay of the last two decades of trendy Western culture: Tibetan women dressed in traditional clothes weave rugs on antique looms while humming Sting tunes; a traffic jam on Kathmandu's only wide street is caused by bulls fighting in an intersection; restaurants play U2 and serve tough buffalo steak under the name *chateau briande*; coffee houses serve cappuccino across the street from women drying rice by lifting it into the air with hoes; nearly naked children wearing burlap sacks grab cake slices out of the hands of gawking tourists emerging from a Viennese pastry shop.

Establishes the terms of the comparison.

Each phrase shows the medieval "heart" and the "thin overlay" of Western culture.

This comparison and contrast also uses a cause-and-effect pattern to help organize it. The word *consequently* in the third line is the transition from the cause to the effect.

Definition

Much writing in college depends on establishing the definitions of key terms. Consequently, writers often use entire paragraphs for definitions. Paragraphs organized by definition usually begin with the term and then go on to list its distinguishing features, sometimes using examples. Writers may begin with a standard definition and then qualify or add to that definition in unexpected ways.

Definitions are critical to persuasive writing. If your audience accepts your definitions of key terms, usually you will be convincing.

Usual definition

Tranquility in Western countries is usually equated with getting away from it all. Its synonyms are *calmness, serenity,* and *peace of mind,* and no wonder: We live in a world where it is increasingly difficult to get completely away from human-produced noise. In the Hindu and Buddhist traditions, however, tranquility is thought of as an internal quality that is gained when a person no longer is controlled by worldly desires. While this definition of tranquility may seem foreign to us, the internal state of tranquility is evident when you are in the presence of someone who possesses it.

Extended definition adds a new dimension.

Examples and Illustrations

If you want to prove a point or bring an issue to life, an organization based on examples and illustrations may work well. This structure usually begins with the main idea or point, then moves to a vivid explanation of one or two examples that illustrate the main idea. Examples and illustrations can also work well in opening and concluding paragraphs.

> When religious principles clash with practical realities, ingenuity often comes to the rescue. Upon entering Braga, a Buddhist village built into a cliffside high in the Himalayas, Jim and Lester noticed that the men of the village surrounded two yaks, wrestled them to the ground, and tied their feet together. By a stone wall on the side of the field, an old bearded man read from a holy book while the yaks were stabbed in the heart. They lay panting, bleeding little, taking a long time to die. Three young men poured water down the throats of the yaks, while the other men chanted in their Tibetan dialect. As Buddhists, the people of Braga are forbidden to kill animals, yet the environment demands that they eat meat to survive. They resolve the dilemma by helping the animal to assume a higher form when it is reincarnated.

Point

Illustration

Cause and Effect

Cause-and-effect paragraphs are structured in two basic ways. The paragraph can begin with a cause or causes, then state its effects, or it can begin with an effect, then state its causes. Insightful analysis often requires you to look beyond the obvious to the underlying causes.

Effects

Obvious cause

Underlying cause 1

Underlying cause 2

Underlying cause 3

The loss of the world's forests affects every country through global warming, decreased biodiversity, and soil erosion, but few suffer its impact more than Nepal. Deforestation in Nepal has led to economic stagnation and further depletion of forest resources. The immediate cause of deforestation is the need for more fuel and more farmland by an increasing population. The loss of trees in Nepal, however, has been accelerated by government policies. During the eighteenth and nineteenth centuries, Nepal taxed both land and labor. Farmers could avoid these high taxes for three years if they converted forests to farmland. Others could pay their taxes in firewood or charcoal. While these taxes were reduced in the twentieth century, the government required farmers to register their land, which encouraged clearing of trees to establish boundaries. Furthermore, the stagnant economy led to families' wanting more children to help in the fields at home and to send abroad to find jobs as another source of income.

Classification and Division

Classification and division are valuable strategies for analyzing and explaining a topic. Classifying places items into categories according to their similarities. Dividing takes a single item or concept and breaks it down into its component parts.

Classifying

Nepal is classified as one of the poorest and least developed countries in the world. The average annual income of $220 a year places Nepal alongside the poorest nations in Africa. Only 27% of the population is literate, and over 40% of the population lives below the poverty line. The infant death rate of 76 per 1,000 births is one of the highest in the world.

Category

Characteristics of specific category

Dividing

Nepal is divided into three distinct regions. In the south is the Terai, the flat river plain of the Ganges, occupying 17% of the country. The central hill region is the largest, containing 64% of the land, including the Kathmandu Valley, the country's urban center. The rugged Himalaya mountain region in the north is above 4,000 meters (13,120 feet) and features eight of the ten highest mountains in the world, including the tallest, Mt. Everest (29,028 feet).

Item

Parts of item

Exercise 3.2   A student is writing a paper on New Orleans Mardi Gras celebrations in the United States. The student has the following ideas for paragraphs. Which of the seven common organizational strategies would work best for each?

1. crowd behavior during Mardi Gras
2. history of Mardi Gras in New Orleans
3. the ways different ethnic groups and social classes celebrate Mardi Gras
4. what Mardi Gras really is
5. the difference between celebrations in other parts of the United States and Mardi Gras in New Orleans
6. key parades of Mardi Gras
7. how Hurricane Katrina changed Mardi Gras

Exercise 3.3   Find a paper you wrote either for this class of for another class. Choose one paragraph and rewrite it, organizing it according to one of the strategies from this section. Make sure you choose a strategy that is different from the one you used when you first wrote the paragraph!

3c Make Your Paragraphs Coherent

Your teachers may have told you that your paragraphs should flow. Paragraphs that don't flow make readers struggle to understand how sentences relate to one another, often forcing readers to backtrack. Sentences clash rather than mesh together.

But what exactly does *flow* mean? Writing that flows is coherent. To achieve coherence you must make all the separate parts fit together as a whole. At the level of the paragraph, your first task as a writer is to determine how your sentences fit together. Sometimes you know how your sentences relate to each other as you write them; at other times these relationships become clearer when you are revising. In either case, reiterating key phrases and using transitional terms help writers achieve that elusive quality called flow.

Reiterate key terms and phrases

When you repeat key terms and phrases within paragraphs, your reader will be able to trace major ideas and stay situated in your argument. In the following paragraph, notice that the writer refers back to two central terms, *grass roots activism* and *battleground*. Notice too that the paragraph isn't repeating itself. Repetition without forward momentum is self-defeating.

> The Web has become the primary medium for grass roots activism. Among thousands of Web sites created by individuals are many pages devoted to media criticism and parodies of advertising. This activism has come at a time when the Internet has become the battleground for the deregulated corporate giants. On this battleground, control of the coaxial cable and fiber-optic conduits represents only a small part of the potential fortunes to be made from an array of services carried through the pipe.

Signal relationships with transitional terms

Transitional terms act like warning signs for readers, preparing them for whatever is around the bend. Notice how transitions in the following paragraph make it easier to read by preparing you for what is coming.

> In spite of all the talk about the Internet as cyberspace and a virtual world, the materiality of the Internet as a medium is unavoidable. You sit in front of a machine that has to be turned on and connected to the net. And if you want to access the resources of the World Wide Web, you need an Internet service provider, a modem, and a computer with enough memory to support the current versions of FireFox or Internet Explorer. In the United States the lines do not go to every neighborhood, and in the rest of the world almost the entire continent of Africa outside South Africa is not online. At present the Internet continues the one-way flow of information from the First to the Third World. Can the Internet be a factor in promoting a two-way flow between the margins and the center?

STAYING ON TRACK

Use transitional terms

Be sure to use transitional terms accurately in order to signal the relationships between your sentences.

- **To enumerate:** again, also, and, as well, finally, furthermore, first, second, third, in addition, last, moreover, next, too
- **To generalize:** commonly, in general, for the most part, on the whole, usually, typically
- **To offer an example:** for example, for instance, indeed, in fact, of course, specifically, such as, the following
- **To situate in time:** after a month, afterward, as long as, as soon as, at the moment, at present, at that time, before, earlier, followed by, in the meantime, in the past, lately, later, meanwhile, now, preceded by, presently, since then, so far, soon, subsequently, suddenly, then, this year, today, until, when, while
- **To situate in space:** above, below, beyond, close to, elsewhere, far from, following, here, near, next to, there
- **To conclude:** as a result, hence, in conclusion, in short, on the whole, therefore, thus
- **To contrast:** although, but, even though, however, in contrast, conversely, in spite of, instead, nevertheless, nonetheless, on the one hand, on the contrary, on the other hand, still, though, yet
- **To compare:** again, also, in the same way, likewise, similarly
- **To signal cause or effect:** as a result, because, consequently, for this reason, hence, if, so, then, therefore, thus
- **To sum up:** as I said, as we have seen, as mentioned earlier, in conclusion, in other words, in short, in sum, therefore, thus
- **To concede a point:** certainly, even though, granted, in fairness, in truth, naturally, of course, to be fair, while it's true

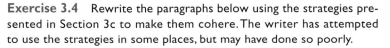

Exercise 3.4   Rewrite the paragraphs below using the strategies presented in Section 3c to make them cohere. The writer has attempted to use the strategies in some places, but may have done so poorly.

1. What do a nineteenth-century rural family, President Andrew Jackson, and two popular movies have in common? The legend of the Bell Witch revolves around a series of strange events experienced by the Bell family of Adams, Tennessee between 1817 and 1821. Events were witnessed by hundreds of people, among them future President of the United States Andrew Jackson. It represents one of the most famous and documented instances of paranormal events in history. It was used as the basis for the 2006 film *An American Haunting* and influenced production of the 1999 film, *The Blair Witch Project*.

2. This may not be true, but the first haunting occurred in 1817, when John Bell saw a strange animal in his cornfield. It had the body of a dog and the head of a rabbit and vanished when it was shot at. Next, a series of strange beating and gnawing noises were heard around, and eventually inside, the Bell residence. The Bell children's bedclothes were regularly pulled off and tossed onto the floor by an invisible force. A choking, grunting voice was heard. Betsy Bell, the family's younger daughter, was violently assaulted.

3. These events became well known in their community. There were reports of a voice conversing loudly and clearly, singing, quoting from the Bible and accurately describing events taking place miles away. Future U.S. President Andrew Jackson heard about them and decided to observe them in person in 1819. Jackson's wagon was stopped in its tracks. He acknowledged that the witch was responsible and the wagon was freed. A man in Jackson's party said he would kill the witch, and he started choking and wriggling. Jackson and his entourage left the Bell property the next day.

4. John Bell was the main target, suffering facial seizures that left him speechless. John Bell died on December 20, 1820. A small bottle containing an unidentified liquid he had apparently ingested was found near the body. The remaining contents were fed to the family cat. It died. The

family heard a voice say "I gave Ol' John a big dose of that last night, and that fixed him." Bell's funeral guests heard a voice laughing and singing.

5. Bell died and it stopped, but Lucy Bell later said a voice told her that it would return in 1828. John Bell Jr. visited later for three weeks and said that a voice communicated with him. It predicted the Civil War, the Great Depression and both World Wars. Many people believe that the spirit returned in 1935, took up residence on the former Bell property, and remains there to the present day. People on the property today still hear the faint sounds of people talking and children playing. No good pictures have ever been taken of the place.

Exercise 3.5   Choose a paragraph from a paper you have written for either this class or another class. Underline any transitional words or phrases you used, and mark spaces where you think you need a transitional word or phrase. Write out the relationships expressed by the transitions you underlined. Then, write out the relationship that needs to be expressed in each place that you marked. What transitional word or phrase could you add to make that relationship clear?

3d Consider Paragraph Length

Paragraph breaks can signal various kinds of shifts:

- A new concept
- The next step in an argument
- The end of the introduction
- The beginning of the conclusion
- A new speaker in dialogue
- A shift in time or place
- A logical pause that gives the reader a breather

What is the ideal length for a paragraph? It depends on what sort of paragraphs you are writing. Business letter writers strive for short paragraphs so their readers can see the essential information at a glance. Fiction writers construct paragraphs of various lengths to produce dramatic effects. For instance, Jack Kerouac's description of staying up all night in a skid row movie theater goes on for thirty-two sentences in *On the Road*. But Harper Lee includes a five-word paragraph—"Jem was a born hero."—in *To Kill a Mockingbird*. Paragraphs in academic essays tend to be about 150 to 200 words long. Academic writers need space to make and support arguments in depth. As a general rule, readers' eyes glaze over when they see paragraphs in an essay that stretch beyond one page. Nevertheless, too many short paragraphs are a sign that the piece lacks either weighty ideas or sufficient development.

3e   Link Across Paragraphs

Transitions at the beginnings and ends of paragraphs guide readers. They explain why a paragraph follows from the previous one. They offer writers the opportunity to highlight the turns in their thinking.

Be aware of transitions in your writing. Ask yourself why one main idea leads into the next. What step or shift takes place between paragraphs? How does this step or shift fit into the overall development of the piece? The answers to these questions can become your transition.

> **Exercise 3.6**   Choose a paper you have written for either this class or another class. Make sure the paper has more than five paragraphs, if possible. Underline any transitional words or phrases you used to link the paragraphs, and mark places where you think you need a transitional word or phrase. Write out the relationships expressed by the transitions you underlined. Then, write out the relationship that needs to be expressed in each place that you marked and specify the transitional word or phrase could you add to make that relationship clear.

3f Write Effective Beginning and Ending Paragraphs

Beginning and ending paragraphs of essays should behave like a smart suitor meeting "the parents" for the first time: dress well; start with a firm handshake; show you are thoughtful and personable; close on a strong note. Because readers are more likely to remember beginning and ending paragraphs, they are your best opportunity to make a good impression.

Understand what beginning paragraphs do

Effective beginning paragraphs convince the reader to read on. They capture the reader's interest and set the tone for the piece. In essays they often state the thesis and briefly map out the way the writing will progress from paragraph to paragraph. Sometimes the work of the beginning paragraph might be carried through three or four paragraphs. A writer might start with a memorable example, then use the example to launch the rest of the essay.

Start beginning paragraphs with a bang

Getting the first few sentences of an essay down on paper can be daunting. Begin with one of the following strategies to get your reader's attention.

A question

How valuable are snow leopards? The director of a zoo in Darjeeling, India, was fired when its snow leopard caught a cold and died.

A hard-hitting fact

Poaching is big business—to be exact, a six-billion-dollar business. The only illegal trade that's larger is drugs.

A pithy quotation

"That the snow leopard is," writes Peter Matthiessen, "that it is here, that its frosty eyes watch us from the mountains—that is enough."

And it has to be enough because, while snow leopards are here now, they may not be here much longer.

Images

Tons of animal pelts and bones sit in storage at Royal Chitwan National Park in Nepal. The mounds of poached animal parts confiscated by forest rangers reach almost to the ceiling. The air is stifling, the stench stomach-churning.

An anecdote

The snow leopard stood so still in the frosty bushes, it wasn't until the goat squealed that we saw it. Its mottled white fur was now spattered with the goat's blood. Steam rose from the animal's wounds. We fumbled for our cameras, hoping to capture this terrible beauty.

A problem

Ecologists worry that the construction of a natural gas pipeline in Russia's Ukok Plateau will destroy the habitat of endangered snow leopards, argali mountain sheep, and steppe eagles.

A concisely stated thesis

If the governments of China and Russia don't soon act decisively, snow leopards will be extinct in a few years.

A contradiction or paradox

Snow leopards are tremendously versatile animals, strong enough to kill a horse and fast enough to chase down a hare. What they can't do is hide from poachers in Nepal and India. And this may be their downfall.

An odd, ridiculous, or unbelievable fact

Caterpillar fungus is a hot commodity. Traditional healers and their clients are willing to pay handsomely for illegally harvested ingredients for their treatments. As a result, demand for the fungus, along with other poached items like rhinoceros horns and snow leopard bones, drives a lucrative and destructive black market in endangered species.

Essays that begin with obvious, overly general, or exaggerated sentences dampen the readers' interest immediately. Use the first sentence to tell readers something they don't know. Begin with a fresh idea, fact, or image.

Understand what ending paragraphs do

Ending paragraphs remind readers where they've been and invite them to carry your ideas forward. Use the ending paragraph to touch on your key points, but do not merely summarize. Leave your readers with something that will inspire them to continue to think about what you have written.

Conclude with strength

The challenge in ending paragraphs is to leave the reader with something provocative, something beyond pure summary of the previous paragraphs. The following are strategies for ending an essay:

Issue a call to action

Although ecological problems in Russia seem distant, students like you and me can help protect the snow leopard by joining the World Wildlife Fund campaign.

Discuss the implications of your argument

Even though the extinction of snow leopards would be a sad event, their end is not the fundamental problem. Instead, their precarious position is a symptom of a larger dilemma: Environmental damage throughout developing nations in Asia threatens their biodiversity.

Explain the applications of your argument

This study of snow leopard breeding behavior can inform captive breeding programs in zoos.

Make recommendations

Russia's creditors would be wise to sign on to the World Wildlife Fund's proposal to relieve some of the country's debt in order to protect snow leopard habitat. After all, if Russia is going to be economically viable, it needs to be ecologically healthy.

Speculate about the future

Unless Nepali and Chinese officials devote more resources to snow leopard preservation, these beautiful animals will be gone in a few years.

Tell an anecdote that illustrates a key point

Poachers are so uncowed by authorities that they even tried to sell a snow leopard skin to a reporter researching a story on endangered species.

Describe a key image

As they watched the pile of confiscated furs and bones burn, Nepali forest rangers flashed proud smiles that seemed to say, "This time we mean business."

Offer a quotation that expresses the essence of your argument

Too often, developed nations impose their high-flown priorities, like protecting snow leopards and tigers, on developing nations.

A Russian farmer summed up the disjunction succinctly. Tigers ate two cows in his herd of fifty. When he was compensated for the two he asked, "What's this? Can't the tiger come back and eat the remaining forty-eight?"

Ask a rhetorical question

Generally the larger and more majestic (or better yet, cute) an endangered animal is, the better its chances of being saved. Bumper stickers don't implore us to save blind cave insects; they ask us to save the whales, elephants, and tigers. But snow leopards aren't cave bugs; they are beautiful, impressive animals that should be the easiest of all to protect. If we can't save them, do any endangered species stand a chance?

Resist the urge to end on a bright note if what comes before doesn't warrant it; you don't want your ending to ring hollow.

Exercise 3.7   Write an introductory and a concluding paragraph for each of the essays described here. Label what each paragraph does, using the types shown in Section 3f, such as asking a question or making a recommendation.

1. An essay explaining the process for applying to colleges
2. A description of a moment when you completely changed your mind about a person
3. A proposal to make talking on a cell phone while driving a felony
4. An analysis of your favorite novel or film
5. A letter to the editor of a newspaper or magazine, responding to an article, editorial, letter, or advertisement you felt was misinformed or inappropriate, or that presented a viewpoint that opposes your opinion on a subject

Chapter 4

Rewrite, Edit, and Proofread

The secret to writing well is rewriting.

4a Switch from Writer to Reader

Even the best writers often have to revise several times to get the result they want. To be able to revise effectively, you have to plan your time. You cannot revise a paper or a Web site effectively if you wait until the last minute to begin working. Allow at least a day to let what you write cool off. With a little time you will gain enough distance to "re-see" it, which, after all, is what *revision* means.

You must also have effective strategies for revising if you're going to be successful. The biggest trap you can fall into is starting off with the little stuff first. *Don't sweat the small stuff at the beginning.* When you see a word that's wrong or a misplaced comma, the great temptation is to fix it. But if you start searching for errors, it's hard to get back to the larger concerns.

Begin your revision by pretending you are someone who is either uninformed about your subject or holds an opposing view. If possible, think of an actual person and pretend to be that person. Read your draft aloud, all the way through. When you read aloud, you will probably hear clunky phrases and outright errors, but do no more at this stage than put checks in the margins so you can find these things later. Once again, you don't want to get bogged down with the little stuff. What you are after in this stage is an overall sense of how well you have accomplished what you set out to do.

Use these questions to evaluate your draft. Note any places where you might make improvements.

Does your paper or project meet the assignment?

- Look again at your assignment, especially at the key words, such as *analyze, define, evaluate,* and *propose.* Does your paper or project do what the assignment asks?
- Look again at the assignment for specific guidelines, including length, format, and amount of research. Does your work meet these guidelines?

Does your writing have a clear focus?

- Does your project have an explicitly stated thesis? If not, is your thesis clearly implied?
- Is each paragraph related to your thesis?
- Do you get off the track at any point by introducing other topics?

Are your main points adequately developed?

- Do you support your main points with reasons and evidence?
- Can you add more examples and details that would help to explain your main points?
- Would additional research fill in gaps or make your case stronger?

Is your organization effective?

- Is the order of your main points clear to your reader? (You may want to make a quick outline of your draft if you have not done so already.)
- Are there any places where you find abrupt shifts or gaps?
- Are there sections or paragraphs that could be rearranged to make your draft more effective?

Do you consider your potential readers' knowledge and points of view?

- Do you give enough background if your readers are unfamiliar with your subject?
- Do you acknowledge opposing views that readers might have?
- Do you appeal to common values that you share with your readers?

Do you represent yourself effectively?

- To the extent you can, forget for a moment that you wrote what you are reading. What impression do you have of you, the writer?
- Does "the writer" create an appropriate tone?
- Has "the writer" done his or her homework?
- Is the writing project visually effective? Has "the writer" selected an attractive and readable font? Does "the writer" use headings and illustrations where they are helpful?

Do you conclude emphatically?

- Conclusions that only summarize tend to bore readers. Does your conclusion offer more than a review of ideas you have already fully discussed?
- Could you use your conclusion to discuss further implications?
- Could you conclude by making recommendations for change or improvement, or by urging readers to take action?
- Have you left your audience with a final provocative idea that might invite further discussion?

When you finish, make a list of your goals for the revision. You may have to write another draft before you move to the next stage.

4b Learn Strategies for Rewriting

Now it's time to go through your draft in detail. You should work on the goals you identified in your review.

1. Keep your audience in mind. Step back and assess your paper from a reader's perspective. Paragraphs with strong, engaging openers keep an audience's attention, establish a writer's credibility, and above all intrigue readers so that they want to read on. Reread each of your paragraphs' opening sentences and ask yourself whether the language is strong and

engaging enough to keep your reader interested in your argument from paragraph to paragraph.

2. Sharpen your focus wherever possible. You may have started out with a large topic but find now that most of what you wrote concerns only one aspect of it. For example, you may have started with the large topic of privacy, but your focus now is on the current practice of some states' selling their driver's license databases to companies that build junk mail lists. Revise your thesis and supporting paragraphs as needed.

3. Check that key terms are adequately defined. What are your key terms? Are they defined precisely enough to be meaningful? If your argument relies on an abstract term such as *justice*, you are obligated to define it specifically.

4. Develop where necessary. Key points and claims may need more explanation and supporting evidence. Look for opportunities to replace generalizations with specific details.

General statement	Grizzly bears and black bears look different.
Specific details	Rely on body shape rather than size and color to distinguish grizzly bears from black bears. Grizzlies have a hump above their front shoulders; black bears lack this hump. In profile, grizzlies have a depression between their eyes and nose, while black bears have a "Roman" profile with a straight line between the forehead and nose.

5. Check links between paragraphs. Carefully crafted transitions between paragraphs accomplish two things: They explain to your reader why a paragraph logically follows the previous one, and they express the twists and turns of your thinking.

If you are struggling with your transitions, try this quick diagnostic: Underline the first and last sentences of each paragraph in your paper and then read these underlined sentences aloud to a friend. Do these sentences together make a logical and coherent argument? If not, spend more time figuring out the relationships between your ideas. Often you can express these relationships more clearly by choosing accurate transitional phrases such as *although, for example, on the other hand, in contrast, similarly,* and so on (see Sections 3c and 3e).

6. Consider your title.   An effective title makes the reader want to read what you have written. Be as specific as you can in your title, and if possible, suggest your stance. "Use of Anabolic Steroids" as a title is vague and bland, and it suggests a topic far too large to be handled well in a few pages. A stronger title would be "Is Andro a Food Supplement or a Steroid?"

7. Consider your introduction.   In the introduction you want to get off to a fast start and convince your reader to keep reading. If your subject is the use of steroids among high school students, don't start with an empty sentence like "Drugs are a big problem in today's high schools." Cut to the chase with a sentence such as "The National Institute of Drug Abuse reports that the number of high school students who abuse anabolic steroids rose steadily during the 1990s, while the perception of the risks involved declined." Then you might follow with a sentence that indicates how you will approach your topic: "My experiences as a high school athlete gave me insights into why students would risk future liver failure, cancer, strokes, heart attacks, and other serious health problems in order to gain a competitive advantage." In two sentences you have established your topic and your own authority to write about it.

8. Consider your conclusion.   Restating your claim usually isn't the best way to finish; conclusions that offer only summary tend to bore readers. The worst endings say something like "in my paper I've said this." In contrast, effective conclusions remind readers where your argument has taken them and then invite further discussion. Try to leave your reader with something interesting and provocative. Think about whether there is an implication you can draw or another example you can include that sums up your position. You might briefly discuss the implications of your argument, or you could argue why your readers' ideas or beliefs should change because of your findings. If you are writing a proposal, your ending might be a call for action.

9. Improve the visual aspects of your text.   Does the font you selected look attractive? (See Section 14c.) Do you use the same font throughout? Are you consistent if you use more than one font? Do you include headings and subheadings to identify key sections of your argument? If you include statistical data, would presenting it in charts be effective? (See Section 14f.) Would illustrations help to establish key points? For example, a map could be very useful if you are arguing about the location of a proposed new highway.

4c Respond to Other Writers' Drafts

Your instructor may ask you to review your classmates' drafts. Writing a response to the work of a fellow student may make you feel uncomfortable. You may think you don't know enough to say anything useful. Remember that you are only charged with letting the writer know how you—one of many potential readers—react.

But you do have to put forth your best effort. Responding to other people's writing requires the same careful attention you give to your own draft. To write a helpful response, you should go through the draft more than once. Before you begin, number the paragraphs if the writer has not already done so.

First reading

Read at your normal rate the first time through without stopping. When you finish you should have a clear sense of what the writer was trying to accomplish.

- **Main idea:** Write a sentence that summarizes what you think is the writer's main idea in the draft.
- **Purpose:** Write a sentence that summarizes what you think the writer was trying to accomplish in the draft.

Second reading

In your second reading, you should be most concerned with the content, organization, and completeness of the draft. Make notes as you read.

- **Introduction:** Does the writer's first paragraph effectively introduce the topic and engage your interest?
- **Thesis:** Where exactly is the writer's thesis? Note in the margin where you think the thesis is located.
- **Focus:** Does the writer maintain a focus on the thesis? Note any places where the writer seems to wander off to another topic.
- **Organization:** Are the sections and paragraphs ordered effectively? Do any paragraphs seem to be out of place? Do you note any abrupt shifts? Can you suggest a better order for the paragraphs?
- **Completeness:** Do any sections and paragraphs lack key information or adequate development? Where do you want to know more?
- **Sources:** If the draft uses outside sources, are they cited accurately? If there are quotations, are they used correctly and worked into the fabric of the draft?

Third reading

In your third reading, turn your attention to matters of audience, style, and tone.

- **Audience:** Who is the writer's intended audience? What does the writer assume the audience knows and believes?
- **Style:** Is the writer's style engaging? How would you describe the writer's voice?
- **Tone:** Is the tone appropriate for the writer's purpose and audience? Is the tone consistent throughout the draft? Are there places where another word or phrase might work better?

When you have finished the third reading, write a short paragraph on each bulleted item, referring to specific paragraphs in the draft by number. Then end by answering these two questions:

1. What does the writer do especially well in the draft?
2. What one or two things would most improve the draft in a revision?

Exercise 4.1   Read the following draft and respond in a paragraph or two answering the following questions:

1. What is the writer's main idea and what is his or her purpose for writing this draft? Are these things clear? How could the writer make them more clear?
2. Does all the information serve the thesis? In other words, is the introduction clear and engaging? Do all of the paragraphs maintain a focus on the thesis? Do the paragraphs need to be reorganized? Is there any information missing? Are sources cited correctly?
3. Who is the writer's intended audience? Are the style and tone appropriate for the subject matter and for the audience? How could the writer make this stronger?
4. What are the writer's strengths? What one or two things would most improve this draft?

Remember to resist the urge to edit sentences and correct mechanical errors—the focus here is on clear and effective presentation of ideas.

We've Come Along Way, Baby

Humans has existed on the Earth for approximately 3.4 million years. That's from when the oldest human ancestor, "Lucy," an Australopithecus, discovered by Donald Johnson and M. Taieb had been found. Lucy was not only the oldest Australopithecus find, they also found over 40% of her skeleton intact, making her one of the most complete, too. Australopithecus africanus, means "southern ape from Africa" (Lewin).

Australopithecine's looked more like primates than modern-day Homo Sapiens. Although they walked upright, they had low, sloping foreheads, protruding jaws, and thick body hair. They were also only about three feet tall. For some reason, they also didn't seem to show any facial expressions (McKie 50).

Humans have evolved a lot over the past three and a half million years. We are almost 6 feet, have lost most of our body hair, have adapted to walking upright all the time, and we've grown brains that are over three times as large as the first Australopithecine's (Larson 123). Besides, humans (Homo Sapiens) have also developed an advanced material culture. We live in cities now and we don't have to live in trees. We also don't have to dig in the ground for our food; we can just buy it at the store. We also can grasp abstract concepts like time and we have art and literature.

But we haven't changed all that much, really. We still are related to primates in many ways. This can be seen in the way our hands, feet, and over all body is structured. Our faces are even very similar (IHO).

There have been four distinct species of human throughout time: Homo Habilis, Homo Erectus, Homo sapiens Neanderthalesis, and Homo sapiens Sapiens. The first major step in evolution was becoming bipedal, or walking upright (Larson 20). As I said before, Australopithecine's were the first to do this. They were really clumsy, though; because their skeleton weren't really able to support the weight, they probably spent most of their time on all fours. They were, however, probably really good at climbing trees. This is not the only way they were more similar to primates than homo sapiens, though (McKie 35). They were tiny, with a tiny (orange size) brain, prominent cheekbones, and thick molars. Like chimps, they had small, underdeveloped thumbs. But their toes were shorter than other primates (IHO).

Australiopithicene also probably lived socailly like chimps. Judging- from the way fossils were at their sites, they probably lived in one place in small groups. We think they lived in groups because usually about 5 individuals are found in the same place. One site even had had 13 in the same place! (Lewin) Scientists think that these groups usually had one male in charge and this was because of their sexual dimorphism. Sexual dimorphism, or the difference in size between the genders, usually means that males are larger (Lewin). So probably the one guy that was big was in charge.

They also weren't very smart. The only tools they had were sticks and rocks. They were also vegetarians. They may not have known animals could be eaten. If they did know, though, they probably couldn't figure out how to kill one anyway. Homo Habilis, though, figured this out (Larson 145). Homo Habilis is the earliest known member of the Homo genus, and has been found only in Africa. Homo Habilis's brain was about 50% larger than Australopithecine's, he was taller, had flatter nostrils, and their faces were nearly hairless (IHO).

Most importantly, though, Homo Habilis figured out, through scavenging, scientists think, that meat was edibLe. Their teeth show that they started to add meat to their vegetarian diets. Homo Habilis lived in Africa until about 1.6 million years ago, when Homo Erectus emerged, causing their eventual extinction. Homo Erectus was the next step. He had a much larger brain (1060 cc) than Homo Habilis (Mc Kie 80). "Homo Erectus" means "Man who Walks Upright" (Lewin).

The larger brain is the main physical change from H. Hablis to Homo Erectus. But they did have smaller jaws and teeth. They also had a larger brow. The brow-ridge was also slightly larger than Homo Habilis. "The term *Homo habilis* means *handy man*, a name selected for the deposits of primitive tools found near *H. habilis* fossils (Lewin).

Homo Erectus lived until about 100,000 years ago, when Homo sapiens Neanderthalesis took over. Homo sapiens Neanderthalesis, or the Neanderthals, lived during the most recent Ice Age (Larson 160).

Evolution happens so slowly that it almost can't be seen. The changes occur in tiny mutations; if you possess a mutation that makes you survive better than others, you are more likely to reproduce and spread that mutation into the next generation. If you have a bad mutation, you die and you don't pass that mutation on. There are lots of examples that prove this, from the problems in royal families to skin color differences that are related to climate (Larson 30).

    We have to remember, though, that all of these things are just physical. Deep down, all humans are really the same so we should love and respect one another.

Works Cited

Institute of Human Origins (IHO). Becoming Human. 2001. 23
    February 2002 <http://www.becominghuman.org/>.
Larsen, Clark Spencer, and Robert M. Matter. Human
    Origins: The Fossil Record. Waveland Press, 1998.
Lewin, Roger. "Australopithecines," Microsoft® Encarta®
    Encyclopedia 99. 1998.
—. "Homo habilis," Microsoft® Encarta® Encyclopedia 99.
McKie, Robin. The Dawn of Man: The Story of Human Evolution.
    London: DK, 2002.

Exercise 4.2   Exchange drafts of a paper you wrote for this class or another class with another student. Read the draft and respond in a paragraph or two by answering the questions listed in Exercise 4.1. Again, resist the urge to edit sentences and correct mechanical errors.

4d Edit for Particular Goals

In your final pass through the text of your paper, you should concentrate on style and eliminate as many errors as you can.

1. Check the connections between sentences.   Notice how your sentences are connected. If you need to signal the relationship from one sentence to the next, use a transitional word or phrase.

2. Check your sentences.   If you noticed that a sentence was hard to read or didn't sound right when you read your paper aloud, think about how you might rephrase it. Often you can pick up problems with verbs (see Chapters 34 and 35), pronouns (see Chapter 36), and modifiers (see Chapter 37) by reading aloud. If a sentence seems too long, you might break it into two or more sentences. If you notice a string of short sentences that sound choppy, you might combine them. If you notice run-on sentences or sentence fragments, fix them (see Chapter 33).

3. Eliminate wordiness.   Writers tend to introduce wordiness in drafts. Look for long expressions that can easily be shortened (*at this point in time* to *now*) and unnecessary repetition. Remove unnecessary qualifiers (*rather, very, somewhat, little*). See how many words you can take out without losing the meaning (see Chapter 28).

4. Use active verbs.   Any time you can use a verb other than a form of *be* (*is, are, was, were*) or a verb ending in *-ing,* take advantage of the opportunity to make your style more lively. Sentences that begin with *There is (are)* and *It is* often have better alternatives:

> **Draft**   It is true that exercising a high degree of quality control in the manufacture of our products will be an incentive for increasing our market share.

> **Revised**   If we pay attention to quality when we make our products, more people will buy them.

Notice too that the use of active verbs often cuts down on wordiness (see Chapter 27).

5. Use specific and inclusive language.   As you read, stay alert for any vague words or phrases (see Chapter 30). Check to make sure that you have used inclusive language throughout (see Chapter 31).

Example of sentence-level editing

It is a widely believed opinion that computers have greatly influenced the lives of the latest generation. I agree with this

~~opinion. I remember back w~~ When I was in the fourth grade, we had a computer *literacy* class every Friday. ~~The classroom held about~~ *in a room equipped with* 20 Apple IIe computers. Besides learning how to type correctly, we were also given simple graphic programming assignments. ~~Thus, I along with m~~ My fellow classmates *and I* were assigned to input VLIN (Vertical Line) and HLIN (Horizontal Line) commands followed by a color and coordinates. ~~When we finished we would have~~ *that created* a picture on the monitor. ~~This was not a photographic quality image by any means.~~ Because the pixels were only slightly smaller than sugar cubes~~,~~ and ~~we were~~ limited to 16 colors, these images made ~~the~~ *our* Nintendo Entertainment System's graphic~~s~~ ~~al output~~ look like the ~~graphic output~~ *quality* of a Hollywood studio production *by comparison*.

4e Proofread Carefully

To proofread effectively, you have to learn to slow down. Some writers find that moving from word to word with a pencil slows them down enough to allow them to find errors. Others read backward to force themselves to concentrate on each word.

1. Know what your spelling checker can and cannot do. Spelling checkers are the greatest invention since peanut butter. They turn up many typos and misspellings that are hard to catch. But spelling checkers do not catch wrong words (e.g., *to much* should be *too much*), missing endings (*three dog*), and other, similar errors. You still have to proofread carefully to eliminate misspellings.

2. Check for grammar and mechanics. Nothing hurts your credibility with readers more than a text with numerous errors. Many job application letters get tossed in the reject pile because an applicant made a single, glaring error. Issues of grammar are treated in Chapters 32 through 37. The conventions for using punctuation, capitalization, italics, abbreviations,

acronyms, and numbers can be found in Chapters 38 through 47. Get into the habit of referring to these chapters.

4f ▸ Learn to Edit the Writing of Others

Editing someone else's writing is easier than editing your own. In your own writing, you know most of the time what you meant to say and often you don't notice where a reader might be stopped or jarred. But editing someone else's writing is also harder because you want to give the writer useful feedback without taking over the writer's task.

1. Make comments in the margins.   If you find a sentence hard to read, let the writer know. If you think a sentence is repetitive, let the writer know. If you think a word was left out, say so in the margin. Also let the writer know when a sentence is especially successful.

> *Word missing here?*
> *Same point as sentence 1?*
> *Can you join this sentence with the previous sentence?*
> *Vivid description!*

2. Use symbols to indicate possible problems.   Draw a wavy line under any phrase or sentence where you think there may be a problem. Even if you are not sure what the problem is, you can ask the writer to look carefully at a particular sentence. If you think a word is misspelled, draw a circle around it. If you think words can be deleted, put parentheses around them.

> A Web cam is a Web page that hosts images or even live video streams served by a (digitel) camera attached to a computer. Web cams serve as surveillance, entertainment, control, and many other services. Web cam technology has become quite popular (with people) since the first Web cams hit the world wide web.

WRITING IN THE WORLD

Standard proofreading symbols

Advanced editing requires learning standard proofreading symbols. Authors, editors, and printers use proofreader's marks to indicate changes. These marks are used in pairs: one mark goes in the text where the change is to be made and the other goes in the margin, close to the change.

Mark in the margin	Mark in the text
ℯ	Delete: take it out
⌒	Close up: foot ball
⋀	Caret: insert here
#	Insert a space: aword
⟨tr⟩	Transpose: the in beginning
⋀	Add a comma: moreover we
⋁	Add an apostrophe: Ellens books
⋁/⋁	Add double quotation marks: James Joyce's Clay
:	Add a colon: 3 45 p.m.
;	Add a semicolon: concluded however, we
⊙	Add a period: last call Next we
¶	Begin a new paragraph
No ¶	No new paragraph
sp	Spell out: 7 dwarfs => seven dwarfs
stet	Ignore correction: in the beginning

Writing for Different Purposes

Chapter 5

Read and View with a Critical Eye

Learn to think critically.

5a   Become a Critical Reader

Critical thinking begins with critical reading. For most of what you read, one time through is enough. When you start asking questions about what you are reading, you are engaging in **critical reading**.

Critical reading is a four-part process. First, begin by asking where a piece of writing came from and why it was written. Second, read the text carefully to find the author's central claim or thesis and the major points. Third, decide if you can trust the author. Fourth, read the text again to understand how it works.

Where did it come from?

- Who wrote this material?
- Where did it first appear? In a book, newspaper, magazine, or online?
- What else has been written about the topic or issue?
- What do you expect after reading the title?

What does it say?

- What is the topic or issue?
- What is the writer's thesis or overall point?
- What reasons or evidence does the writer offer?
- Who are the intended readers? What does the writer assume the readers know and believe?

Can you trust the writer?

- Does the writer have the necessary knowledge and experience to write on this subject?
- Do you detect a bias in the writer's position?
- Are the facts relevant to the writer's claims?
- Can you trust the writer's facts? Where did the facts come from?
- Does the writer refer to expert opinion or research about this subject? Are these sources reliable?
- Does the writer acknowledge opposing views and unfavorable evidence? Does the writer deal fairly with opposing views?

How does it work?

- How is the piece of writing organized? How are the major points arranged?
- How does the writer conclude? Does the conclusion follow from the evidence the writer offers? What impression does the reader take away?
- How would you characterize the style? Describe the language that the writer uses.
- How does the writer represent him or herself?
- Is the page design attractive and correctly formatted? Are photos, tables, and graphics well integrated into the text and clearly labeled?

5b Read Actively

If you own what you are reading, read with a pencil in hand. Pens and highlighters don't erase, and often you won't remember why you highlighted a particular sentence.

Annotate what you read

Using annotating strategies will make your effort more rewarding.

- **Mark major points and key concepts.** Sometimes major points are indicated by headings, but often you will need to locate them.

- **Connect with your experience.** Think about your own experiences and how they match up or don't match up with what you are reading.
- **Connect passages.** Notice how ideas connect to each other. Draw lines and arrows. If an idea connects to something a few pages before, write a note in the margin with the page number.
- **Ask questions.** Note anything that puzzles you, including words to look up.

Critical response

Let's start by imagining a fine Persian carpet and a hunting knife. The carpet is twelve feet by eighteen, say. That gives us 216 feet of continuous woven material. Is the knife razor sharp? If not, we hone it. We set about cutting the carpet into thirty-six equal pieces, each one a rectangle, two feet by three. Never mind the hardwood floor. The severing fibers release small tweaky noises, like the muted yelps of outraged Persian weavers. Never mind the weavers. When we're finished cutting, we measure the individual pieces, total them up—and find that, lo, there's still nearly 216 square feet of recognizably carpetlike stuff. But what does it amount to? Have we got thirty-six nice Persian throw rugs? No. All we're left with is three dozen ragged fragments, each one worthless and commencing to come apart.

Now take the same logic outdoors and it begins to explain why the tiger, *Panthera tigris*, has disappeared from the island of Bali. It casts light on the fact that the red fox, *Vulpes vulpes*, is missing from Bryce Canyon National Park. It suggests why the jaguar, the puma, and forty-five species of birds have been extirpated from a place called Barro Colorado Island—and why myriad other creatures are mysteriously absent from myriad other sites. An ecosystem is a tapestry of species and relationships. Chop away a section, isolate that section, and there arises the problem of unraveling.

—David Quammen, *The Song of the Dodo: Island Biogeography in an Age of Extinctions*, 1996

Quammen begins with the analogy of a Persian carpet.

He develops the analogy with sensory details and humor.

The point of the analogy is that many scraps do not add up to a whole.

Quammen turns to extinct species.

Why does he give Latin names?

The direct connection of the analogy is made with a metaphor; an ecosystem is a tapestry.

5c Recognize Verbal Fallacies

Reasoning depends less on proving a claim than it does on finding evidence for that claim that readers will accept as valid. The kinds of faulty reasoning called *logical fallacies* reflect a failure to provide sufficient evidence for a claim that is being made.

Fallacies of logic

- **Begging the question.** *People who take 8:00 AM classes are crazy because no sane person would choose to get up that early.* The fallacy of begging the question occurs when the claim is restated and passed off as evidence.

- **Either-or.** *Either fraternities must be forced to cancel all parties, or the university will never be able to control its underage drinking problem.* The either-or fallacy suggests that there are only two choices in a complex situation. Rarely, if ever, is this the case. (In this example, the writer ignores the fact that some students under 21 drink when they are not at a fraternity party.)

- **False analogies.** *Permitting children to play computer games in school is like giving them ice cream for watching television.* Analogies always depend on the degree of resemblance of one situation to another. In this case, the analogy fails to consider the content of the computer games and what children might be learning.

- **Hasty generalization.** *We have been in a drought for three years; that's a sure sign of climate change.* A hasty generalization is a broad claim made on the basis of a few occurrences. Climate cycles occur regularly over spans of a few years; climate trends must be observed over centuries.

- **Non sequitur.** *Janet Jackson's "wardrobe malfunction" during the 2004 Super Bowl shows how far contemporary morals have sunk.* A non sequitur (which is a Latin term meaning "it does not follow") ties together two unrelated ideas. In this case, one person's behavior is not indicative of society's morals.

- **Oversimplification.** *If the federal income tax was doubled for all wage brackets, then we could easily provide comprehensive health care for all citizens.* This claim may be true, but the argument would be unacceptable to most citizens. More complex, if less definitive, solutions are called for.
- **Post hoc fallacy.** *The stock market goes down when the AFC wins the Super Bowl in even years.* The *post hoc* fallacy (from the Latin *post hoc ergo propter hoc,* which means "after this, therefore because of this") assumes that things that follow in time have a causal relationship.
- **Rationalization.** *I could have finished my paper on time if my printer was working.* People frequently come up with excuses and weak explanations for their own and others' behavior that avoid actual causes.
- **Slippery slope.** *If the government were to legalize a gateway drug like marijuana, there would be a huge increase in the use of hard drugs like cocaine and heroin.* The slippery slope fallacy maintains that one thing inevitably will cause something else to happen.

Fallacies of emotion and language

- **Bandwagon appeals.** *Since all the power hitters in baseball use steroids, I'll have to use them too if I want to be able to compete.* This argument suggests that everyone is doing it, so why shouldn't you? But on close examination, it may be that everyone really isn't doing it—and in any case, it may not be the right thing to do.
- **Name calling.** Name calling is frequent in politics and among competing groups (*radical, tax-and-spend liberal, racist, fascist, right-wing ideologue*). Unless these terms are carefully defined, they are meaningless.
- **Polarization.** *Feminists are all man haters.* Polarization, like name calling, exaggerates positions and groups by representing them as extreme and divisive.

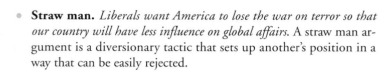

- **Straw man.** *Liberals want America to lose the war on terror so that our country will have less influence on global affairs.* A straw man argument is a diversionary tactic that sets up another's position in a way that can be easily rejected.

Exercise 5.1   Build a collection of fallacies. See if you can find examples of all thirteen fallacies named in Section 5c. If you can't find them all, make up examples for the ones you are missing. You might start with sources you know to be biased, such as political blogs and the Web sites of political media figures. You should also look in editorials, letters to the editor, and opinion pieces in the newspaper or in news magazines. Finally, you might even look at humor publications, such as *The Onion*, and comedy shows that have a news format, such as *The Colbert Report* and *The Daily Show with Jon Stewart*. Make sure you cite the sources for your fallacies.

5d   Become a Critical Viewer

Critical viewing is similar to critical reading. An image such as a photograph doesn't float in space but instead has a specific location — in a book with a caption, in a family photo album, in a magazine advertisement, on a Web page — that tells us a great deal about why the photograph was taken and what purpose it is intended to serve. But even without the external context, there are often clues within a photograph that suggest its origins.

We could guess the approximate date of the photograph on page 85 by the content of the billboard. By the end of the 1950s, long-distance travel by passenger train was being replaced by airline travel, so the picture must have been taken before then. The name of the railroad, Southern Pacific, along with the barren landscape, indicates that the photograph was taken in the southwestern United States. In fact, this photograph was taken in 1937 by Dorothea Lange (1895–1955), who gave it the title "Toward Los Angeles, California."

One approach to critical viewing is to examine a photograph in terms of its **composition**. In Lange's photograph the lines of the shoulder

of the road, the highway, and the telephone poles slope toward a vanishing point on the horizon, giving the image a sense of great distance. At the same time, the image divides into ground and sky with the horizon line in the center. The two figures in dark clothing walking away contrast to a rectangular billboard with a white background and white frame.

Another approach to critical viewing is to **analyze the content**. In 1937 the United States was in the midst of the Great Depression and a severe drought, which forced many small farmers in middle America to abandon their homes and go to California in search of work. The luxury portrayed on the billboard contrasts with the two walking figures, who presumably do not have bus fare, much less enough money for a luxury train. By placing the figures and the billboard beside each other (a visual relationship called **juxtaposition**), Lange is able to make an ironic commentary on the lives of well-off and poor Americans during the depression.

No one set of questions can cover the great variety of images, but a few general questions can assist you in developing a critical response.

- What kind of an image or visual is it?
- Who created this image (movie, advertisement, television program, and so on)?
- What is it about? What is portrayed in the image?
- Where did it first appear? Where do you usually find images like this one?
- When did it appear?

The following questions are primarily for still images. For animations, movies, and television, you also have to ask questions about how the story is being told.

- What attracts your eye first? If there is an attention-grabbing element, how does it connect with the rest of the image?
- What impression of the subject does the image create?
- How does the image appeal to the values of the audience? (For example, politicians love to be photographed with children.)
- How does the image relate to what surrounds it?
- Was it intended to serve purposes other than art and entertainment?

Exercise 5.2   Find an interesting photo in your textbook, a magazine, a newspaper, or online. Write a brief (one- or two-page) analysis of this photo following the process outlined in Section 5d. Pay particular attention to the last question: After you have thought about this picture, how has your first impression changed?

Exercise 5.3   Altered photos can have a huge impact, especially when they rewrite history or are used to "prove" the essence of some other-worldly beast. Faced with such grand hoaxes, though, we often overlook the prevalence of altered images in our daily lives. Find an image that has clearly been altered in an advertisement, on TV (shows such as *Saturday*

Night Live and *The Daily Show with Jon Stewart* alter images for comedic effect), on the Internet, in the newspaper (newspapers like the *National Enquirer* and *Sun* routinely alter images), or even in a textbook (some publishers routinely remove logos, tattoos, firearms, alcoholic drinks, and tobacco products from images). Write a few paragraphs about this image. What has been altered? Is the producer of the image up front about the alteration? What, do you think, was the purpose behind the alteration of this photo? What are the possible implications?

Exercise 5.4 Advertising has become so much a part of our lives that we are very nearly blind to its more subtle manifestations. Look around your room; how many corporate logos and brand names do you see? Make a list of all that you find and compare your list with your classmates' lists. Are you surprised by the results?

5e Recognize Visual Fallacies

Misleading images

The era of digital imaging has made it possible to create images of lifelike dinosaurs chasing humans, interactions between people now living and those long dead, and human feats that defy human limits and the laws of physics. However, the manipulation of images is not new to the digital era. One of the best-known images from the Civil War is an image of a dead Confederate sharpshooter behind a rock barricade on the Gettysburg battlefield. The photograph reproduced here was made by Alexander Gardner (1821–1882) in July 1863. Gardner titled the photograph "The Home of a Rebel Sharpshooter, Gettysburg," and for over a century historians accepted that description. Gardner claimed that he saw the body again in November 1863 in the same place with the rusted rifle still beside him.

A modern historian, William Frassanito, studied other photographs Gardner took at Gettysburg and discovered pictures of the dead soldier in another, much less dramatic location. He also noted that the rifle in the

photograph was not the type of weapon used by sharpshooters. Frassanito surmised that Gardner had moved the body and added a rifle as a photographic prop. Furthermore, he doubted that Gardner had seen the body again four months later since all the bodies had been buried by that time and the battlefield had been thoroughly scavenged for souvenirs.

Pictures are not always what they claim to be. Critical viewers ask questions about images similar to those they ask about texts.

Misleading charts

A special category of visual fallacies is misleading charts. For example, the fictitious company Glitzycorp might use the chart in Figure 5.1 to attract investors. The chart shows what looks like remarkable growth from 2005 to 2007 and projects additional sales for 2008. But is the picture quite as rosy as it is painted?

Figure 5.1 Misleading. The starting point on the y-axis is $20 million, not 0.

Figure 5.2 Accurate. The actual increase from 2005 to 2006 was less than 5%.

Notice that the bars in Figure 5.1 start at 20 rather than at 0. The effect is to make the $22 million sales in 2006 appear to double the $21 million sales of 2005, even though the increase was less than 5%. Three years is also a short span to use to project a company's future profits. Figure 5.2 shows the sales of Glitzycorp over seven years, and it tells quite a different story. The big growth years were in the early 2000s, followed by a collapse in 2004 and slow growth ever since.

Glitzycorp's sales charts illustrate how facts can be manipulated in visual presentations.

Write to Analyze

Apply your critical reading and viewing skills to particular subjects.

6a Understand the Goal of a Rhetorical Analysis

The goal of a **rhetorical analysis** is to understand how a particular act of writing or speaking influenced particular people at a particular time. Rhetorical analysis is not limited to speaking and writing. The tools of rhetorical analysis have been applied to understanding how meaning is made by other human creations, such as art, buildings, photographs, dance, memorials, Web sites, music, advertisements—any kind of symbolic communication.

Writing a rhetorical analysis (also called "critical analysis" or "textual analysis") is frequently an assignment in college. A rhetorical analysis requires you to step back from a text and consider it from multiple perspectives. Writing a rhetorical analysis can give you a heightened awareness of a text and a better appreciation of what the author accomplished.

Understanding how communication works or fails to work is a worthy goal by itself, but rhetorical analysis has other benefits. It enables you to think about a text in more depth, to better understand the arguments it makes, and to appreciate how it is put together. In turn, this knowledge helps you in writing your own text. You will have a much better sense of what has been said and written about your subject and where you have opportunities to contribute your own ideas.

6b Analyze the Context and the Text

A rhetorical analysis begins with a text to analyze. If your instructor does not assign a text, select a text that has significance for you, either because it was important when it was written or it is about a subject that is important to you.

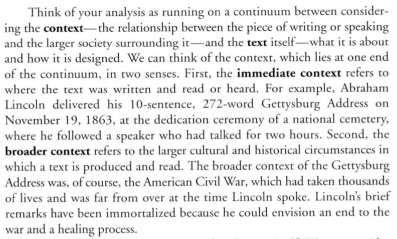

Think of your analysis as running on a continuum between considering the **context**—the relationship between the piece of writing or speaking and the larger society surrounding it—and the **text** itself—what it is about and how it is designed. We can think of the context, which lies at one end of the continuum, in two senses. First, the **immediate context** refers to where the text was written and read or heard. For example, Abraham Lincoln delivered his 10-sentence, 272-word Gettysburg Address on November 19, 1863, at the dedication ceremony of a national cemetery, where he followed a speaker who had talked for two hours. Second, the **broader context** refers to the larger cultural and historical circumstances in which a text is produced and read. The broader context of the Gettysburg Address was, of course, the American Civil War, which had taken thousands of lives and was far from over at the time Lincoln spoke. Lincoln's brief remarks have been immortalized because he could envision an end to the war and a healing process.

At the other end of the continuum lies the text itself. We can consider a text as if it were a piece in a museum, where we closely scrutinize it. For example, if you look carefully at the language of the Gettysburg Address, you'll begin to appreciate Lincoln's tactics and skill. He says of his purpose: "We have come to dedicate a portion of that field, as a final resting place for those who here gave their lives that that nation might live."

But then he immediately turns this purpose on its head: "But in a larger sense, we can not dedicate—we can not consecrate—we can not hallow—this ground. The brave men, living and dead, who struggled here, have consecrated it, far above our poor power to add or detract." Lincoln's words become powerful because they defy expectation: we cannot consecrate the field because the field is already consecrated. Lincoln does not once refer to "the enemy" in the Gettysburg Address. Instead he says, "The brave men, living and dead, who struggled here." Even though the cemetery was a burying ground for Union soldiers, Lincoln's language invokes the heroism and sacrifice of both sides.

Often in the back and forth movement between text and context, you gain surprising insights about how a text achieves certain effects. These questions will help you get started in composing a rhetorical analysis.

The Gettysburg Address

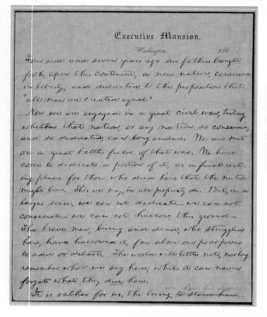

■ Text

■ Broader context

■ Immediate context

Analyze the immediate context

Examine the author

- What is the author's purpose: to change beliefs? to inspire action? to teach about a subject? to praise or blame? to amuse?
- How did the author come to this subject?
- What else did the author write?

Examine the audience

- Who was the intended audience?
- What were their attitudes and beliefs about the subject?
- What were their attitudes and beliefs about the author?
- What does the author assume about the audience?

Analyze the broader context

Examine the larger conversation

- Why did this text appear at this particular time?
- What else has been said or written about this subject?
- What was going on at the time that influenced this text?

Examine the larger society

- What social, political, and economic influences can you find in the text?

Analyze the text

Examine the kind of text

- What kind of text is it: speech? essay? letter? editorial? advertisement?
- What is the medium: print? Web site? voice recording?

Summarize the content

- What is the author's main claim or main idea?
- How is the main claim or main idea supported?
- How is the text organized?

Examine the appeals

- *Ethos:* How does the author represent him or herself? How does the author build or fail to build trust?
- *Logos:* What kinds of facts and evidence does the author use?
- *Pathos:* How does the author appeal to values shared with the audience?

Examine the language and style

- Is the style formal? informal? academic?
- Does the author use humor or satire?
- What metaphors are used?

6c Organize and Write a Rhetorical Analysis

When you have completed your initial analysis, you are ready to begin writing. Expect to discover additional ideas you can use in the analysis while you are writing and to go back and forth with your analysis.

❶ Before you write

Take stock of your initial analysis

- If your selected text isn't working for the assignment, find one that works better.

- Look at your notes on the author, the audience, the circumstances of original publication or delivery, what other texts the author was responding to, and what else was going on at the time.

- Spend some time thinking about how to organize your analysis.

Think about your readers

- How much do readers know about your text? the author? the events surrounding the text? other texts like it?

- What will readers gain from reading your analysis?

➋ Write an introduction

Begin your analysis by giving the necessary background

- Inform your readers about the author and why the author selected this particular topic.

- Tell readers about the original audience and the conversation about the topic that was going on at the time the text was written.

Make a claim

- Make a claim about how the text you are analyzing uses rhetoric for particular purposes.

➌ Organize and write the body of your paper

Support your claim with your detailed analysis of the text and context

- Give examples from the text to show how the author builds credibility with the audience, appeals to their values and beliefs, and convinces them with facts and evidence.

- Analyze the author's style, tone, and language, including metaphors.

- Analyze how the author responded to the immediate context and to the broader context.

➍ Write a conclusion

End with more than a summary

- Draw larger implications from your analysis.

- End with a vivid example from the text.

(continued)

⑤ Revise, revise, revise

Evaluate your draft

- Make sure your analysis meets the requirements of the assignment.
- Consider where you might provide more information about the context.
- Consider where you might provide more evidence supporting your claim about the text.
- When you have finished revising, edit and proofread carefully.

Exercise 6.1   Public speeches are usually intended to persuade. You can find many examples of public speeches on the Web. Many politically oriented Web sites contain transcripts of speeches and often the audio and video. (For example, go to www.whitehouse.gov for speeches by the president, or to a history site, such as the History Channel, for other famous speeches). Select a speech to analyze and answer the following questions:

1. What is the **rhetorical purpose**? What did the speech intend to achieve?
2. Where was the speech given? How does the speaker connect with the beliefs and attitudes of the **audience**?
3. What **appeals** does the speech rely upon: the rational appeal (logos), the emotional appeal (pathos), or the ethical appeal (ethos)?
4. How is the speech **organized**?
5. How formal or informal is the **style**? Is humor used?
6. Does the speaker use any **metaphors** and for what purpose?

When you have completed your analysis, formulate a thesis about the speech.

6d Sample Rhetorical Analysis

Jackson 1

Samantha Jackson

Professor Janis

English 100

4 May 2007

Rhetorical Strategies in Sojourner Truth's

"Ain't I a Woman?"

Sojourner Truth was born into slavery in 1797 and given the name Isabella Baumfree. Between 1797 and her escape from slavery in 1827, Isabella was "owned" by five different masters. Her last owner, John Dumont, sometimes bragged that she could "do a good family's washing in the night and be ready to go into the field the next morning, where she would do as much raking and binding as his best hands" (Washington 15). However, in 1817, the New York Legislature had passed a law that slavery in New York would end ten years later, on July 4, 1827. With this date fast approaching, Dumont decided to strike a deal with Isabella: he would release her one year early if she worked hard throughout 1826. Isabella agreed,

Jackson's opening provides background to help readers understand why Truth's personal history is relevant.

Jackson 2

but at the end of the year Dumont refused to release

her. Enraged, Isabella escaped. After experiencing

mystical visions from God on June 1, 1843, at the age

of forty-six, Isabella changed her name to Sojourner

Truth and pledged to "'sojourn' the land and speak the

'truth' of God's word" (Washington 15).

This paragraph uses examples to show how slavery and the Women's Suffrage movement shaped the rhetorical situation.

As debates over slavery raged, Sojourner was

sometimes harassed. Once she was told that a

building she was scheduled to speak in would be

burned down if she lectured there. She replied, "Then

I will speak to the ashes" (Washington 11). As the

Women's Suffrage movement became more popular in

the late 1840s, Truth took notice. In 1851 she

traveled to Akron, Ohio, to attend a women's rights

convention aimed at getting Ohio to add more rights

for women in its state constitution. Many Ohioans

were against this goal. Many local men, including

several ministers, attended the convention just to

In these two sentences, Jackson makes a claim about the persuasive power of Truth's speech.

heckle speakers. Sojourner Truth delivered her famous

"Ain't I a Woman?" speech in this intense atmosphere.

In her spontaneous lecture, Truth used her own

physical and intellectual credibility to make powerful

Jackson 3

emotional appeals and convincing logical claims. Her
arguments redefined the word "womanhood" and
made direct connections between women's rights and
the abolition of slavery for an all-white audience. Her
powerful speech was so successful that her words are
the main reason this convention is remembered today.

When Truth began to speak, her words displayed her
experience and wisdom. Rather than addressing her
audience as "Ladies and gentlemen," or, "Members of
the convention," Truth begins this way: "Well children,
when there is so much racket there must be something
out of kilter" (268). By using the word "children" to
address her adult, white audience, Truth draws
attention to her age and wisdom, and at the same time
proves that she is equal to, not subservient to, these
white adults. She also refers to the heated arguments
between the women and men attending the convention
as "so much racket," a statement that takes her out of
the arguments she is witnessing and therefore makes her
seem like a voice of reason in a chaotic environment.

Another reason Truth was such an effective
speaker at this convention was how she used humor

Jackson demonstrates how Truth established her relationship to her audience in the opening of her speech.

Jackson discusses the humor employed by Truth to defuse tension and put her audience at ease.

to break down arguments against women's rights. Just after she notes that the convention has become a "racket," she offers a tongue-in-cheek observation: "I think that 'twixt the negroes of the South and the women at the North, all talking about rights, the white men will be in a fix pretty soon" (268). Although Truth is making the serious point that when white women and African Americans get equal rights, white men will be less powerful, she uses humor to break up some of the tension of the moment.

> This paragraph demonstrates how Truth built her argument by drawing on personal experience and by using emotional appeals to her audience's sense of shame.

Once Truth has her audience listening through this light tone, she begins to use her status as a former slave woman to bring out feelings of guilt and shame in her audience. She builds her argument slowly. First, she shows the fallacy in the argument that women do not need rights because male chivalry protects them from harm and guarantees them protection. Truth restates this argument: "That man over there says that women need to be helped into carriages, and lifted over ditches, and to have the best place everywhere." She points out that as a poor, black woman, she is excluded from this definition of womanhood: "Nobody ever helps me into carriages, or

Jackson 5

over mud puddles, or gives me any best place! And ain't I a woman?" (268).

She next shows the connection between women's rights and abolition by referring to the unique horrors of womanhood under slavery: "I could work as much and eat as much as a man—when I could get it—and bear the lash as well! And ain't I a woman? I have borne thirteen children, and seen them most all sold off to slavery, and when I cried out with a mother's grief none but Jesus heard me" (268-69). By using emotional appeals to produce shame in her audience, Truth connects women's rights and abolition. She argues that people who believe women should be protected and treated to "the best" are obliged to treat all women, black and white, with "chivalry."

Although Truth is appealing to her audience's shame here, and asking them to reconsider their positions on women's rights and abolition, her main way of arguing is through logic. Truth tries to expose the flaws in arguments against women's rights, and also in arguments against equal rights for African Americans. First, Truth points out that claiming that chivalry makes rights unnecessary for women is illogical because her

Jackson analyzes Truth's use of logic to expose fallacies in common arguments against women's rights.

Jackson 6

audience's definition of "woman" is flawed. Women, she

argues, are not only people who need assistance getting

into fancy carriages, or those who wear expensive

clothes that must be protected from mud puddles.

Women are also people like her, who "have ploughed

and planted, and gathered into barns" (268).

Jackson describes the process Truth used to counter arguments that the Bible authorized male supremacy.

Truth's most powerful logical argument for this

audience of mostly religious men is her argument

about God, Eve, and women's rights. She first restates

their argument: that "women can't have as much

rights as men, 'cause Christ wasn't a woman." Then

she exposes the flaws in that argument: she asks

"Where did your Christ come from?" and answers,

"From God and a woman. Man had nothing to do with

Him." Then, turning to her audience's argument that

women should not have rights because of Eve's sins, she

asks, "If the first woman God ever made was strong

enough to turn the world upside down all alone, these

women together ought to be able to turn it back, and get

it right side up again!" She is arguing here that if these

men credit the first woman, Eve, with such a huge

amount of power, then they should see that other women

are equally powerful and should be given equal rights. If

Jackson 7

Eve turned the world upside down, these women can turn
it right-side up again, Truth argues: "And now they is
asking to do it, the men better let them."

Finally, Truth addresses the topic of intelligence:
"Then they talk about this thing in the head; what's
this they call it?" (269). An audience member reminds
her that the word is "intellect," and she replies, "That's
it, honey." She then asks, "What's that got to do with
women's rights or negro's rights?" (269). This question
is deceptive. Although at first it seems like Truth is
agreeing with sexist notions when she characterizes
women's minds as capable of "hold[ing] but a pint"
while male minds can "hold a quart," it becomes clear
that she is using flattery as a manipulative tool: "if my
cup won't hold but a pint, and yours holds a quart,
wouldn't you be mean not to let me have my little half
measure full?" Clearly, a speaker who can develop such
convincing logical arguments is just as intelligent as
the audience members whose arguments she exposed as
flawed. It is for this reason that Sojourner Truth's "Ain't
I a Woman?" speech made such an impression then,
and continues to do so today.

Jackson concludes
with a powerful
example of Truth's
wit.

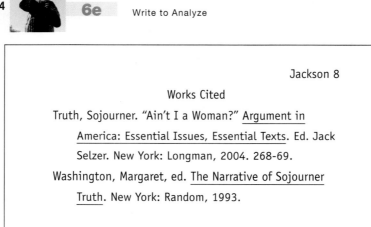

Jackson 8

Works Cited

Truth, Sojourner. "Ain't I a Woman?" Argument in
    America: Essential Issues, Essential Texts. Ed. Jack
    Selzer. New York: Longman, 2004. 268-69.

Washington, Margaret, ed. The Narrative of Sojourner
    Truth. New York: Random, 1993.

*To hear audio commentary on this piece of writing, visit this page
of the E-book at* www.mycomplab.com.

6e Analyze Images and Other Kinds of Visual Texts

The word *text* typically brings to mind words on a printed page. But in the sense that anything that can be "read" can be a text, then nearly everything is a text. We see hundreds of visual texts every day distributed on television, the Web, films, newspapers, advertisements, product labels, clothing, signs, buildings—indeed, on nearly everything. We can analyze how these images create meaning by the same means we use to analyze verbal texts—by examining the relationship between the text and its contexts.

Some culturally significant images, significant at least at the time they were created, are public art and public sculpture. On one of the bridge houses of the Michigan Avenue Bridge crossing the Chicago River in downtown Chicago is a large relief sculpture depicting the massacre of settlers fleeing Fort Dearborn in 1812. The size of the sculpture and its

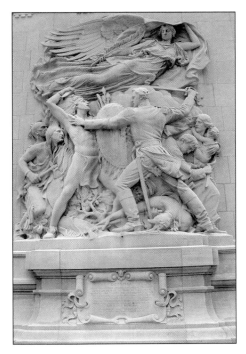

■ Relief sculpture of the Fort Dearborn
Massacre, on the Michigan Avenue Bridge,
Chicago

placement on the busiest and most famous street in Chicago attests to its
significance at the time it was commissioned.

Two central figures—an American soldier and a Potawatomi Indian—
battle as an angel hovers above. On the left another Indian is stealthily approaching, crouched with a tomahawk in hand. On the right a man shields
a woman and a child from the threat. The sculpture uses a familiar stereotype of American Indians to make a visual argument: The Indians are
attacking because they are bloodthirsty and sneaky; the innocent settlers

bravely resist. The sculpture does not speak to the circumstances of the massacre: The Potawatomis allied with the British during the War of 1812 to resist settlers who were taking their land, and the settlers waited too long to evacuate Fort Dearborn in the face of growing numbers of Indians surrounding the fort.

It's not surprising that the sculpture represents the settlers as heroic. The bridge and monument were part of a grand plan, begun in 1909, to enhance Chicago's waterfront. Thus, the monument plays its part in obscuring the actual history of the area. Viewers who are unaware of the facts may feel a sense of patriotic pride in the actions of the soldier and the woman. Viewers who are familiar with the whole story may take a different view.

Exercise 6.2 The leaders of classical Rome were keenly aware of the persuasive power of public buildings and monuments. In addition to statues and columns, Romans built arches to commemorate emperors and military victories. Visitors and citizens of Rome alike were reminded of the power of Imperial Rome when they walked under an arch. The massive size of the arch suggested the might and majesty of Rome while the intricate decorative details commemorated specific military conquests and the triumphs celebrated afterward.

Find an example of public architecture in your city or town or on the Internet. What messages does it convey? What do you think the designers and city leaders had in mind when they built it?

Write to Reflect

By sharing our significant experiences, we learn about ourselves.

7a Find a Reflective Topic

Reflecting on experience

Reflections, whether they appear in print, video, or any other medium, often deal with personal and private experiences, but they do not have to be based on explicitly personal topics. In some cases, being too personal or confessional can limit a writer's ability to connect to his or her audience. The goal of reflection should not be simply to vent pent-up feelings or to expose secrets. Instead, the goal should be to allow the audience to share with the writer his or her discovery of the significance of an experience.

Discovering a reflective topic

Listing is a good way to identify possibilities for reflective essays based on memories.

- List five people who have been significant in your life.
- List five events that have been important in your life. Think about one-time events, such as getting a scholarship, and recurring events, such as a yearly family get-together.
- List five places that have been important in your life.
- Now look through your lists and check the items that are especially vivid.

Another set of possibilities can be drawn from looking at family photographs (see Melissa Dodd's reflection on a family photograph in

Section 7d). In addition to constructing the context for the photograph, you can point to details in the picture that have significance. You can also write about objects that have special significance for your family or just for you, such as a scrapbook that you kept in elementary school.

Once you have selected a topic, try freewriting to stimulate your memories and explore your present perspective (see Section 2b). Take five to ten minutes to write about the event, person, or place as you remember it. Then write for five to ten minutes about how you think about the event, person, or place today. What has changed from your first experience? Why do you feel differently now?

Not all reflective topics are about the past. You can visit a place or go to an event and focus on your interaction with the place or event instead of on the place or event itself.

Exercise 7.1   Look at your immediate work space. Are you at home, at the library, at a coffeehouse, or elsewhere? If you are someplace that is familiar to you, list the first five people that this place makes you think about, the first five things that this place makes you think about, and the first five events in your past that you associate with this place. Can you connect any of these into a brief narrative? Write a one-paragraph narrative of a memory this place inspires using the items from your lists.

If the place isn't familiar to you, choose an object, person, or aspect of the atmosphere that reminds you of something else. Does the smell of the coffee bring back a memory? Does the person napping across the table from you at the library remind you of anyone? Use your moment now to frame a memory you could associate with this particular place.

7b Identify a Focus

Reflections do not often have a formal thesis, but they typically have a **focus** that makes the reflection coherent by communicating a central idea to readers. Why is this experience important? Why is it memorable? In short, why is it worth writing about?

Often the focus comes not in the big idea but in the small details that call for reflection. In one of the most powerful essays ever written about capital punishment, George Orwell, while serving as a minor British colonial official in Burma (now Myanmar), describes the routine execution of a nameless prisoner convicted of a nameless crime. All of those present quietly do their jobs—the prison guards, the hangman, the superintendent, and even the prisoner, who offers no resistance when he is bound and led to the gallows. All is routine until a very small incident changes Orwell's awareness of what is happening: The prisoner, gripped tightly by the guards, steps lightly around a puddle on his way to the gallows. Orwell writes, "It is curious; but till that moment I had never realized what it means to destroy a healthy, conscious man."

Exercise 7.2 Find a short reflective piece of writing in a newspaper, a magazine, a book, or on the Internet. The *New York Times Magazine,* for example, has a regular feature in which people tell brief stories about a key moment in their lives—many other magazines have similar features. Talk shows and interviews are also good places to look for brief personal narratives. Write a paragraph in which you analyze the format of the message. Does the intended purpose actually line up with the way in which the message is presented? Is the message conveyed to the intended audience? Why or why not?

7c Organize and Write a Reflection

When you have a topic and a focus that communicates the importance of the experience or event to your readers, then it's time to write your reflection. You might not follow this order, as writing is often a back-and-forth process.

① Before you write

Think about your readers

- What attitudes are your readers likely to have about your subject?
- How can you make readers care about your subject?
- What will readers gain from reading your reflection?

② Write an introduction

Engage your readers quickly

- Choose a title that will interest readers.
- Start with the incident, place, or person that is the focus.

③ Organize and write the body of your paper

Should you use a chronological organization?

- Use chronological order to let readers re-live events with you.

Should you use a conceptual organization?

- Use conceptual order to show connections and links between ideas.

Communicate experiences with details

- Give specifics such as dates and names to provide background information.
- Augment visual details with other sensory details (smells, sounds, tastes, tactile feelings).
- Choose specific words to convey details.
- Identify people by more than how they look. Think about typical mannerisms, gestures, and habits.
- If people interact, use dialogue to convey the interaction.

Consider your voice and tone

- Your writing should sound like you. Be yourself.

- If your writing sounds like the voice that makes announcements in the airport, try rewriting as you would talk.

- Let yourself go in the first draft. If you become excessive, you can adjust the language when you revise.

④ Write a conclusion

End by inviting further reflection

- Share any discoveries you made in the process of reflecting.

- Avoid a simple moral lesson, but your conclusion should help your readers to make sense of your reflection.

⑤ Revise, revise, revise

Evaluate your draft

- Make sure your reflection meets the requirements of the assignment.

- Consider how you might sharpen the focus and significance of your reflection.

- Consider where you might provide more details, dialogue, or background information.

- When you have finished revising, edit and proofread carefully.

7d Sample Reflective Essay

In her film studies class, Melissa Dodd was asked to read excerpts from Michelle Citron's *Home Movies and Other Necessary Fictions,* in which Citron asks why home movies of her childhood do not correspond with her memories of her family. For a course assignment, Melissa Dodd decided to write her own reflection on a family snapshot. The focus of Dodd's reflection is that the objects in a photograph give clues not only to the dynamics of the moment the photo claims to capture, but also to what is missing.

Dodd 1

Melissa Dodd

Professor Mendoza

Introduction to Film

25 April 2007

My Sister and Me on Grandma's Lap

Dodd begins with a descriptive paragraph, bringing the reader into the photo.

This picture was taken at my paternal grandmother's house in Enid, Oklahoma. I'm on Grandma's lap, and my sister Rhonda is on the floor.

Dodd 2

I believe this picture was taken around 1989 or 1990 because I look about two or three years old. It is after supper, and Grandma is reading to me.

This photograph is interesting to me because it reflects two points that Michelle Citron makes in her book, Home Movies and Other Necessary Fictions. First, the person taking the picture is asserting control over the interpretation of the memory. Second, there are clues within the frame that signify what has actually been left out of the frame. The item missing from this picture is my mother.

My father took the picture in order to show me wearing the moccasins my maternal grandfather had just bought for me when we visited him in Holdenville, Oklahoma. My mother had remained there, while we went on to Enid. She rarely came with us to visit Grandma because they did not get along. Like her own mother, my mother could be moody, distant, and bad-tempered. Grandma, on the other hand, was somewhat meddlesome, but affectionate, and over-indulgent with us kids. Consequently, they argued over how we should be treated.

The summary of Citron's *Home Movies* is used to pose a question about why Dodd's mother was missing from the photo.

A detail in the photo, the moccasins, leads to a description of conflict between mother and grandmother.

Dodd steps back to reflect on the photograph in the context of what was happening in the family.

Grandma is pointing to the moccasins, which signify my mother's absence. In some ways, the photo is a conciliatory gesture; my father is acknowledging his in-laws' contribution to my happiness and well being. In another, less obvious way, it is an act of spite. Since my mother refused to be there, my father replaced her with his own mother in this happy family scene he has created.

Dodd examines how her sister was affected by family conflicts by contrasting her appearance in this photo with her appearance in others.

Her absence is also highlighted by the presence of my sister, Rhonda, who was about nine or ten. When I was a baby, Rhonda and I were always in pictures together. Usually she's playing "mommy" and holding me on her lap. She was very protective of me and would not let me out of her sight. Taking the role of my guardian often got her in trouble, especially when my mother's temper flared. Here, she looks silly and relaxed, more childlike than she does in other family pictures.

Dodd moves one step further to explore how good memories are manufactured in family photographs by banishing what is disruptive.

Citron argues that since they are selective and often taken by men, home movies and family photographs assert a balance of power within the family and strive to promote the "good" memory of

Dodd 4

family: "parents in control, men in charge, families together" (15). What she does not overtly mention, however, is that these created memories are also punitive. It is the people, things, or events that disrupt the image of the ideal family that are banished from the frame. Importantly, my mother's temper and her refusal to make peace with my grandmother led to her omission from my father's carefully constructed scene of domestic tranquillity.

In the end, what is most significant is the fact that this manufactured memory works. Until I began to look at this picture through Citron's eyes, I simply had a memory of my Grandma's house—its warmth, and that it always smelled like bacon and Dr Pepper. Unfortunately, this is not the whole picture. But this pleasant memory does not have to go away just because I now see things in more detail. By recognizing what is missing, I hope I can work to reconcile the fiction to the reality and come to a more complete understanding of my family's dynamics.

Dodd 5

Work Cited

Citron, Michelle. <u>Home Movies and Other Necessary</u>
<u>Fictions</u>. Minneapolis: U of Minnesota P, 1999.

 To hear audio commentary on this piece of writing, visit this page of the E-book at www.mycomplab.com.

Exercise 7.3   Return to the paragraph you wrote for Exercise 7.1. Develop this paragraph into a full response using the advice provided in Section 7c. Find a focus for your response, and add details to make the reflection come alive for the reader. Remember to give your response an attention-getting introduction and thoughtful conclusion.

Chapter 8

Write to Inform

Learn to write clear, informative reports.

8a Find an Informative Topic

Many of the writing tasks assigned in college are informative—from lab reports and essay exams to analyses of literature, research papers, and case studies. At the beginning of any such assignment, it is critical to understand what kind of information your instructor expects. Look at your assignment for key words such as *study, analyze, explain,* and *explore,* which indicate what kind of writing you are expected to produce (see Section 2a). Informative writing has four primary functions: to report new or unfamiliar information; to analyze for meaning, patterns, and connections; to explain how to do something or how something works; and to explore questions and problems.

Reporting information

Reporting information takes many forms, ranging from reports of experimental research and reports of library research to simple lists of information. In one sense, writing to reflect (discussed in Chapter 7) and writing to persuade (Chapter 9) also report information. The main difference is that the focus of a report and other informative kinds of writing is on the subject, not on the writer's reflections or on changing readers' minds or on getting them to take action. Writers of reports usually stay in the background and keep their language as neutral as possible, giving the impression of an objective, impartial observer.

Analyzing meaning, patterns, and connections

Writers not only report what they read and observe. They often construct meaning through selecting what and what not to include and in organizing that information. Sometimes this construction of meaning is made explicit as **analysis**. The complexity of the world we live in requires making connections. For example, scientists now agree that the earth has become warmer over the last few decades, but to what extent this warming has been caused by the burning of fossil fuels remains controversial. Advertisers know that certain kinds of ads (for example, ads that associate drinking beer with social life) sell the product, but often they do not know exactly how these ads work or why some ads are more effective than others. Historians debate the importance of certain historical events (for example, the Treaty of Versailles following World War I) and how those events led to subsequent events (World War II).

Explaining how

Often what you know well is difficult to explain to others. You may know how to solve certain kinds of difficult problems, such as how to fix a problem in your car's electrical system, but if you have to tell someone else how to do it over the phone, you may quickly become very frustrated. Often you have to break down a process into steps that you can describe in order to explain it. Explaining a process sometimes requires you to think about something familiar in a new way.

Exploring questions and problems

Not all informative writing is about topics with which you are familiar or ones that you can bring to closure. Often college writing involves issues or problems that perplex us and for which we cannot come to a definitive conclusion. The goal in such writing is not the ending but the journey. Tracing the turns of thought in a difficult intellectual problem can result in writing far beyond the ordinary. Difficult issues often leave us conflicted; readers appreciate it when we deal honestly with those conflicts.

Finding a topic

When your general subject is specified in your assignment, you can make your work more enjoyable by choosing a specific topic that is either more familiar to you or that you find particularly interesting. Your level of engagement in a topic can have a real impact on your readers' level of interest. Here are guidelines you can use when choosing a topic.

- Choose a topic you will enjoy writing about.
- Choose a topic that readers will enjoy reading about.
- Choose a topic that you know something about or can readily find information about.
- Choose a topic for which you can make a contribution of your own, perhaps by viewing something familiar in a new way.
- If you choose an unfamiliar topic, you must be strongly committed to learning more about it.

Exercise 8.1 Informative writing in college often involves explaining a concept. Pick a particular academic discipline that interests you and that you already know something about (such as psychology, biology, engineering, art, and so on) or another broad subject area (such as online gaming, college athletics, fashion, and so on). List at least five central concepts for that discipline or area of interest. When you finish, review your list and select one concept as a possible topic.

Take five minutes to write what you know about that concept. Why does it interest you? What else would you like to know about it?

Next, make a quick survey of information about the concept. If your library has online resources such as specialized encyclopedias, look up the concept. Otherwise, go to the library. Do a Web search using a search engine. After an hour or two, you should know whether you can find enough information to write about this concept.

8b Narrow Your Topic and Write a Thesis

A central difficulty with writing to inform is determining where to stop. For any large subject, even a lifetime may be insufficient. The key to success is to limit the topic. Find a topic you can cover thoroughly in the space you have. Broad, general topics are nearly impossible to cover in an essay of five pages. Look for ways of dividing large topics such as *the use of steroids among college students* into smaller categories and select one that is promising. *Why college athletes ignore the risks of steroids* is a topic that you are more likely to be able to cover in a short paper.

Often your readers will lack initial interest in your topic. If you ignore their lack of interest, they in turn will likely ignore you. Instead, you can take your readers' knowledge and interest into account when you draft your thesis. For example, someone who knows a lot about birds in the parks of your city might write this informative thesis:

> Watching birds in urban areas is interesting because unusual birds often show up in city parks.

It doesn't sound like a topic that most college students would find as interesting as the writer does. But if the writer puts the audience's attitude in the foreground, challenging them to consider a subject they have likely not thought much about, a college audience might read beyond the title:

> Although most college students think of bird watching as an activity for retired people, watching birds gives you a daily experience with nature, even in urban areas.

This thesis also gives the writing a stance from which to approach the topic.

Exercise 8.2 Look back at the topic you explored in Exercise 8.1. If you did not complete Exercise 8.1, look back at a paper you have written for this or another class, or think of a topic you would like to write a paper about for this or another class. Your task now is to develop this topic into a thesis.

An informative thesis statement should contain the topic and indicate your focus. To sharpen that focus, ask the following questions.

1. Who are your readers? What are they likely to know about your topic?
2. What particular features of this topic have led to your interest in it?
3. What are the main subtopics your topic can be broken down into? Which ones would you focus on?
4. What key terms are important to your topic?

Write a clear, focused thesis based on your answers to these questions.

8c Organize and Write an Informative Essay

Successful reporting of information requires a clear understanding of the subject and clear presentation. How much information you need to include depends on your readers' knowledge of and potential interest in your topic. You might not follow this order as writing is often a back-and-forth process.

1 Before you write

Think about your readers

- What do your readers already know about the subject?

- What questions or concerns might they have about your subject?

- What is their attitude toward the subject? If it is different from yours, how can you address the difference?

Review your thesis and scope

- When you learn more about your topic, you should be able to identify one aspect or concept that you can cover thoroughly.

(continued)

Write an introduction

Engage your readers quickly

- Write a title and an introduction that will make readers take an interest in your topic.

Organize and write the body of your paper

Think about your main points

- Use an idea map to organize your main points (see Section 2b).

- Make a working outline to identify your main points and the relationships among them.

Decide how your points are best ordered

- Chronological organization often works best for a topic that occurs over time.

- Conceptual organization focuses on how important concepts are related.

- Compare and contrast organization helps to show how two things are similar or different.

Write a conclusion

End with more than a summary

- Make a point that readers can take away.

- Raise an interesting question.

- End with a vivid example.

Revise, revise, revise

Evaluate your draft

- Make sure your informative essay meets the requirements of the assignment.

- Examine the order of your ideas and reorganize them if necessary.

- Add detail or further explanation where needed.

- When you have finished revising, edit and proofread carefully.

WRITING SMART

Use visuals to report information

Complex statistical data can often be presented effectively in a table or a chart. Other visuals such as maps and photos can help readers to understand your subject. Be sure to provide the sources of your data and the source of any visual that you do not create.

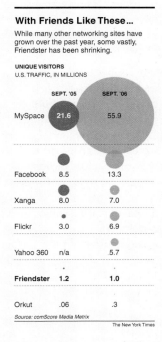

With Friends Like These...

While many other networking sites have grown over the past year, some vastly, Friendster has been shrinking.

UNIQUE VISITORS
U.S. TRAFFIC, IN MILLIONS

	SEPT. '05	SEPT. '06
MySpace	21.6	55.9
Facebook	8.5	13.3
Xanga	8.0	7.0
Flickr	3.0	6.9
Yahoo 360	n/a	5.7
Friendster	**1.2**	**1.0**
Orkut	.06	.3

Source: comScore Media Metrix

The New York Times

■ The proliferation of MySpace over twelve months from September 2005 to September 2006 in comparison to other social networking sites, especially its predecessor Friendster, is evident at a glance.

Source: McPherson, Bruce. "With Friends Like These. . . ." Drawing. *New York Times*. 15 Oct. 2006, final ed. sec. 3: 9.

Exercise 8.3   The way you should organize your information in an informative essay depends on the subject you have chosen. If you are writing about a topic that occurs over time, a **chronological organization** works best. If your subject requires you to identify the major aspects of a subject and discuss each in turn a **conceptual organization** may work best. (Outlines and idea maps are useful tools for this.) If you are writing about two things that are similar or different, a **compare and contrast organization** is appropriate. In this case, you might describe one thing and then the other, closing with a summary of similarities or differences.

Which of the methods of organization described above would work best for each of the following topics?

1. How to interview for a job
2. The unseen stresses felt by teenaged girls
3. An analysis of the causes of the Spanish-American War
4. A description of Egyptian burial practices
5. How to install software on a computer
6. A comparison of two different proposals to solve the same problem
7. A description of the Battle of Little Bighorn
8. An analysis of the rhetorical styles of Malcolm X and Martin Luther King, Jr.
9. An analysis of a proposal to make a course in English grammar mandatory for all entering freshmen
10. A continent-by-continent survey of the various styles of Stone Age cave painting

8d Sample Informative Essay

Schumaker 1

Jon Schumaker

Professor Kim

English 1102

9 April 2007

Search Engine Optimization: How Google Is Making

Sure Link Bombs Fail Miserably

Many people view the Internet as a democratic

enterprise, one that is based on the ideal of equal

access for all users. However, most people are unaware

of the extent to which Web searching can be

manipulated by advertisers and others who wish to

control their presence online. In fact, there are a

number of practices, collectively referred to as search

engine optimization (SEO), which allow people to

manipulate the order in which search results appear on

sites like Google. This kind of manipulation can be

profitable for businesses because there is a huge

difference between having your site appear at the top

of the first search results page instead of buried

several pages later. Because Google's success is

founded in part on its users' belief in the objectivity of

The introduction places the audience's attitudes in the foreground.

Schumaker 4

The thesis is placed early in the paper.

its results—the belief that all Web sites are created equal—it has been necessary for them, and other search engines like them, to fight back against these practices.

One common SEO technique is known as "link bombing" or "Google bombing," a process of manipulating the order Web pages appear in search

Google's search process is broken down into steps for easier explanation.

results or associating a particular page with particular keywords. Google claims its search engine works by counting links on Web pages, "interpret[ing] a link from page A to page B as a vote" for page B. These "votes" are tabulated and ranked by the popularity of the site where they are found (how many sites link to page A) and the keywords associated with them. When a user then searches for those keywords, the pages with the most links from the most popular sites are placed at the top of the results. Google bombing works by "creat[ing] dozens of Weblogs . . . filled with positive stories and keywords" in order to associate a person's or company's name with those keywords or to drive a particular page higher up on a list of search results (Glaser).

Schumaker 4

Fig. 1. Results of a Google search for "miserable failure" before Google changed the algorithm in January 2007.

The most famous example of a Google bomb was the association of the words "miserable failure" with George W. Bush's official biography (see Fig. 1). While this example was a prank, marketers can use Google bombs to manipulate Google's "voting" results, thus damaging the objectivity of those results.

In damaging Google's objectivity, link bombing harms the search engine's credibility; Google employee

Schumaker analyzes the effects of link bombing by making connections between this practice and Google's reputation.

Schumaker 5

Matt Cutts and his colleagues note that many people
might react to the "miserable failure" bomb by thinking
that Google itself is biased against President Bush.
More critically, Google bombs that are used for
marketing purposes make it more difficult for searchers
to find the information they need. As one user tells
Mark Glaser, companies that use link bombs and other
SEO practices know that they are "deceitful" because
SEO is "not about providing value for people" or
"providing a great information resource." Instead, "it's
about flooding the Web with crap." Since this "crap" is
presented to the user as coming from Google's search
results, it makes the company seem less like a
multinational information manager and more like a
door-to-door fertilizer salesman.

To combat the damage that this tampering may
cause its reputation, Google has introduced the "no
follow" tag. If a blog's author places the "no follow"
tag at the end of her or his post, the tag "will signal to
Google as it indexes the Web that [those comments]
are to be overlooked" (Olsen). This tag is especially
helpful for the authors of blogs, since blog comments

Margin notes:

Information reporting is combined with analysis to provide a fuller description of the problem.

A conceptual organization has been used to explain the process of Google bombing, the effects of this practice, and the ways in which Google is responding to it.

Schumaker 5

are one of the primary means of executing Google bombs. Additionally, Cutts, Moulton, and Carattini note that Google has updated its algorithm so that SEO practices are less effective. By constantly updating its software and tailoring specific responses to the problem, such as the "no follow" tag, they claim that Google has been able to "minimiz[e] the impact" of Google bombs. This response has already had some success; the "miserable failure" bomb no longer works. By continually monitoring SEO practices, search engines like Google are working to prevent search "vote" tampering, thereby maintaining the integrity of their results.

The conclusion outlines Google's response and indicates the ongoing nature of the issue.

Schumaker 6

Works Cited

Cutts, Matt, Ryan Moulton, and Kendra Carattini.
"A Quick Word about Googlebombs."
Official Google Webmaster Central Blog.
Blog. 25 Jan. 2007. 31 Mar. 2007 <http://
googlewebmastercentral.blogspot.com/2007/01/
quick-word-about-googlebombs.html>.

Glaser, Mark. "Companies Subvert Search Results To
Squelch Criticism." Online Journalism Review
1 Jun. 2005. 31 Mar. 2007 <http://www.ojr.org/
ojr/stories/050601glaser/>.

Google. "Our Search: Google Technology." 2 Apr. 2007
<http://www.google.com/technology/>.

Olsen, Stefanie. "Google Aims To Outsmart Search
Tricksters." CNET News.com 18 Jan. 2005. 31 Mar.
2007 <http://www.news.com/
Google+aims+to+outsmart+search+tricksters/
2100-1024_3-5540740.html>.

WRITING IN THE WORLD

Informative podcasts

Podcasts are digital media files that are distributed on the Internet for playback. Podcasts differ from similar digital media in that they can be downloaded automatically onto personal computers or media players.

The initial use of podcasts was to allow individuals the capability of producing and distributing their own "radio" shows. Quickly other uses were discovered, including the distribution of music, scholarly and popular journal articles, newspaper articles, television shows, theater performances, museum tours, interviews, lectures, language lessons, and public service programs. User-friendly software such as Apple's GarageBand makes it easy to create a podcast, and there are now several free hosting sites available.

■ Students from Marymount College listen to an informative podcast about an exhibit at the Museum of Modern Art in New York.

Chapter 9

Write Arguments

Clear, carefully reasoned arguments are highly valued.

9a Position Arguments and Proposal Arguments

When you imagine an argument, you might think of two people, or two groups of people, with different views, engaged in a heated debate— maybe even shouting slogans. In college courses, in public life, and in professional careers, written arguments are meant to persuade readers who refuse to accept a **claim** when it is expressed as a slogan. Extended written arguments attempt to change people's minds by convincing them that a new idea or point of view is valid, or that a particular course of action is the best one to take. Written arguments not only offer evidence and reasons but also often examine the assumptions on which they are based, explore opposing arguments, and anticipate objections. How you develop a written argument depends on your goals. You may want to convince your readers to change their way of thinking about an issue or perhaps get them to consider the issue from your perspective. Or you may want your readers to take some course of action based on your argument. These two kinds of arguments can be characterized as **position** and **proposal arguments**.

Position arguments

In a position argument, you make a claim about a controversial issue. You

- define the issue,
- take a clear position,
- make a convincing argument, and
- acknowledge opposing views.

Proposal arguments

In a proposal argument, you present a course of action in response to a recognizable problem. The proposal says what can be done to improve the situation or change it altogether. You

- define the problem,
- propose a solution or solutions, and
- explain why the solution will work and is feasible.

9b Find an Arguable Topic

You probably know people who will argue about almost anything. If you think long enough, you too can find ways to argue about almost anything. Some topics, however, are much better suited than others for writing an extended argument. One way to get started is to make a list of topics you care about. Below are examples of other starting points.

Make a list of possible campus issues

Think about issues that are debated on your campus.

Should smoking be banned on campus?
Should varsity athletes get paid for playing sports that bring in revenue?
Should admissions decisions be based exclusively on academic achievement?
Should fraternities be banned from campuses if they are caught encouraging alcohol abuse?

Make a list of possible community issues

Think about issues that are debated in your community.

Should people who ride bicycles and motorcycles be required to wear helmets?
Should the public schools be privatized?

WRITING SMART

Find arguments on the Web

Because the Web is a grass-roots medium with millions of people putting up Web sites, it's no surprise that the Web has turned out to be a vast forum for arguments. Many organizations and individuals have taken advantage of the low cost of the Web to publicize their stands on issues. To get a sense of the range of interest groups that use the Web to publicize their views, go to Yahoo's directory of issues and causes (dir.yahoo.com/Society_and_Culture/Issues_and_Causes/). As you will see from the list, the issues extend from abortion, affirmative action, and animal rights to welfare reform, xenotransplantation, and zoos.

Yahoo! My Yahoo! Mail Welcome, **Guest** [Sign In]

YAHOO! SEARCH
Directory

Search: ⦿ the Web | ○ the Directory | ○ this category

[   ] (Search)

Issues and Causes

Directory > Society and Culture > **Issues and Causes**

CATEGORIES (What's This?)

- Abortion@
- Activism Resources@
- Affirmative Action (20)
- Afrocentrism@
- Age Discrimination (14)
- Animal Rights@
- Anti-Semitism (37)
- Breastfeeding in Public@
- Campaign Finance Reform@
- Child Advocacy@
- Child Modeling@
- Child Soldiers@
- Church-State@
- Civil Rights (200)
- Climate Change@
- Cloning@
- Computers@
- Conflict Diamonds (7)
- Conservation@
- Consumer Advocacy and Information (631)

- Incest@
- Internet@
- K-12 Education@
- Language Policy@
- Lesbian, Gay, and Bisexual@
- Literacy@
- Media Ethics and Accountability@
- Men's Movement@
- Militia Movement (24)
- Minimum Wage@
- Mining@
- Multiculturalism (22)
- Native American@
- Oil and Gas@
- Ozone Depletion@
- Patriotism@
- Peace and Nonviolence (186)
- Peak Oil@
- Philanthropy (1800)
- Political Issues@

■ Yahoo's Issues and Causes index (dir.yahoo.com/Society_and_Culture/ Issues_and_Causes/)

Proposal arguments

In a proposal argument, you present a course of action in response to a recognizable problem. The proposal says what can be done to improve the situation or change it altogether. You

- define the problem,
- propose a solution or solutions, and
- explain why the solution will work and is feasible.

9b Find an Arguable Topic

You probably know people who will argue about almost anything. If you think long enough, you too can find ways to argue about almost anything. Some topics, however, are much better suited than others for writing an extended argument. One way to get started is to make a list of topics you care about. Below are examples of other starting points.

Make a list of possible campus issues

Think about issues that are debated on your campus.

Should smoking be banned on campus?
Should varsity athletes get paid for playing sports that bring in revenue?
Should admissions decisions be based exclusively on academic achievement?
Should fraternities be banned from campuses if they are caught encouraging alcohol abuse?

Make a list of possible community issues

Think about issues that are debated in your community.

Should people who ride bicycles and motorcycles be required to wear helmets?
Should the public schools be privatized?

WRITING SMART

Find arguments on the Web

Because the Web is a grass-roots medium with millions of people putting up Web sites, it's no surprise that the Web has turned out to be a vast forum for arguments. Many organizations and individuals have taken advantage of the low cost of the Web to publicize their stands on issues. To get a sense of the range of interest groups that use the Web to publicize their views, go to Yahoo's directory of issues and causes (dir.yahoo.com/Society_and_Culture/Issues_and_Causes/). As you will see from the list, the issues extend from abortion, affirmative action, and animal rights to welfare reform, xenotransplantation, and zoos.

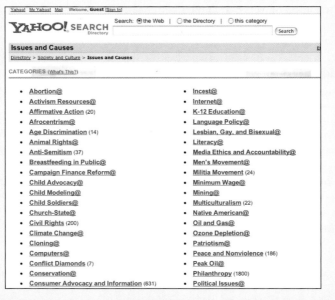

■ Yahoo's Issues and Causes index (dir.yahoo.com/Society_and_Culture/ Issues_and_Causes/)

Should bike lanes be built throughout your community to encourage more people to ride bicycles?

Should more tax dollars be shifted from building highways to public transportation?

Make a list of possible national and international issues

Think about national and international issues.

Should advertising be banned on television shows aimed at preschool children?

Should capital punishment be abolished?

Should the government be allowed to monitor all phone calls and all email to combat terrorism?

Should handguns be outlawed?

Should the United States punish nations with poor human rights records?

Read about your issue

What are the major points of view on your issue?

Who are the experts on this issue? What do they have to say?

What major claims are being offered?

What reasons are given to support the claims?

What kinds of evidence are used to support the reasons?

How can you add to what has been said about your subject?

Exercise 9.1 Which of the following statements are arguable claims? Which are statements of fact, personal taste, or claims of belief? If a statement seems borderline, how could it be made into an arguable claim?

1. The United States has by far the highest rate of deaths by handguns in the world.
2. Allowing teachers to carry handguns would eliminate school shootings.
3. *The Lord of the Rings* trilogy is the best series of fantasy films ever made.

4. Buddhism is superior to other religions because it considers that the root of evil lies in craving—both sensual pleasures and material possessions.
5. Buddhism began in India in the sixth century BCE.
6. Graffiti should be considered art and not vandalism.
7. Any sport performed to music is not really a sport and should not be included in the Olympics.

9c   Make an Arguable Claim

Slogans versus arguable claims

The difference between a slogan, such as *Vote for candidate X*, and an arguable claim, such as *Vote for candidate X because she will lower taxes and improve schools*, is the presence of a reason linked to the claim. A reason is typically offered in a **because clause**, a statement that begins with the word *because* and provides a supporting reason for the claim. The word *because* signals a **link** between the reason and the claim.

Regardless of their sloganizing, many bumper stickers can still be considered as starting points for written arguments. For example, the bumper sticker *Buy American* (Figure 9.1) offers the beginnings of an arguable claim.

Figure 9.1

We have to do some work to unpack this bumper sticker. First, we may want to know exactly what the writer means by *Buy American*, since the components for many products are made overseas and assembled here. Second, we need to know exactly what the writer means by *It's our future*. Presumably the phrase means that if people in the United States buy products made in the United States, more jobs will be created, which in turn will lead to greater prosperity. When we start fleshing out what the bumper sticker might mean, we find a proposal argument.

Supporting claims with reasons

To move beyond simple assertion—or a shouting match—a claim must have one or more supporting reasons, and the reasons must be linked to the claim in order to be accepted by readers. An argument in college writing, therefore, consists of a claim and a series of appropriately linked supporting reasons:

> Buy American   because   it's our future.
> CLAIM ◄———— LINK (**because**) ◄———— REASON

The problem lies in convincing a reader to accept that the reasons provided are linked to the claim. A reader might challenge the bumper sticker's claim by asking *How? So what?* or *Why?*

> Buy American   because   it's our future.
> CLAIM ◄———— LINK (**because**) ◄———— REASON
> ↑
> CHALLENGES (**How? So what? Why?**)

The argument should not end simply because it is challenged. Instead, you must often generate a **series of claims**, each of which is supported by evidence that your readers will accept:

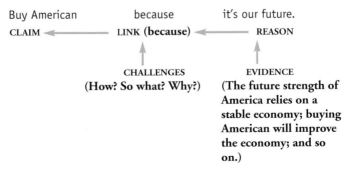

> Buy American   because   it's our future.
> CLAIM ◄———— LINK (**because**) ◄———— REASON
> ↑   ↑
> CHALLENGES   EVIDENCE
> (**How? So what? Why?**)   (**The future strength of America relies on a stable economy; buying American will improve the economy; and so on.**)

Recognize what is not arguable

Certain topics can be argued only in limited ways.

- **Statements of fact.** Statements of fact are usually not considered arguable since they can usually be verified by research. You can easily verify that George W. Bush is the forty-third president of the United States. Claims of fact are arguable only if you can challenge the basis of the fact. For example, since Grover Cleveland served two nonconsecutive terms, he is considered both the twenty-second and twenty-fourth presidents. If you argue for counting Cleveland only once, George W. Bush becomes the forty-second president.
- **Personal taste.** Another category of claims that are not arguable is claims of personal taste. If you hate peas, no argument can convince you that you like them. But just as some statements of fact turn out to be arguable, so too do many claims of personal taste turn out to be value judgments based on arguable criteria.
- **Claims of belief.** Many claims rest on **belief** or **faith**. If a person accepts a claim as a matter of faith or religious belief, that claim is true for that person and cannot be refuted. Of course, people still argue about the existence of God, and which (if any) religion reflects the will of God. But those who hold to irrefutable beliefs will not be convinced by those arguments.

Claims must be specific and contestable

In addition to being supported by reasons that are appropriately linked to it, your claim must also be *specific*. Broad general claims such as *The United States has become too crowded* are nearly impossible to argue effectively. Often general claims contain more restricted claims that can be argued, such as *The United States should increase its efforts to reduce illegal immigration* or *The amount of land in national parks should be doubled to ensure adequate wild spaces for future generations.*

Your claim must also be contestable. Your claim that you like sour cream on a baked potato is specific, but it is not contestable. No matter how many times you are told that a baked potato is less fattening without sour cream, the fact that you like sour cream won't change. You may stop eating the sour cream, but you won't stop wanting to eat it.

Exercise 9.2   Collect five slogans from advertisements, posters, the news, T-shirts, the Internet, or even bumper stickers and evaluate whether or not each presents an arguable claim by answering the questions below.

1. Is there a reason linked to the claim? If not, is it assumed that the audience knows the reason?
2. Is there evidence to stand up to the challenges *So what? Why?* and *How?* If so, what is this evidence? If not, what evidence is needed to support the argument against the challenges?
3. Is the claim specific or is it too broad? How could it be made more specific?
4. Is the claim contestable? Why or why not?

9d Organize and Write a Position Argument

Thinking of reasons to support a claim is not hard. What *is* hard is convincing your audience that your reasons are good ones. Imagine you will have critical readers—people who are going to listen carefully to what you have to say but who are not going to agree with you automatically. Whenever you put forward a reason, they will ask *So what?* You will have to have evidence, and you will have to link that evidence to your claim in ways they will accept if they are to agree that your reason is a good reason. Be open to new ideas while you are writing. Often you will go back and forth in developing a position argument.

① Before you write

Think about your readers

- What do your readers already know about the subject?

- What is their attitude toward the subject? If it is different from your position, how can you address the difference?

- What are the chances of changing the opinions and beliefs of your readers? If your readers are unlikely to be moved, can you get them to acknowledge that your position is reasonable?

- Are there any sensitive issues you should be aware of?

② Write an introduction

Engage your readers quickly

- Get your readers' attention with an example of what is at stake.

- Define the subject or issue.

- State your thesis to announce your position.

③ Organize and write the body of your paper

Develop reasons

- Can you argue from a definition? Is _____ a _____?

  EXAMPLES

  > Are cheerleaders athletes?
  >
  > Are zoos guilty of cruelty to animals?

- Can you compare and contrast? Is _____ like or unlike _____?

- Can you argue that something is good (better, bad, worse)?

- Can you argue that something caused (or may cause) something else?

- Can you refute objections to your position?

Support reasons with evidence

- Can you support your reasons by going to a site and making observations?

- Can you find facts, statistics, or statements from authorities to support your reasons?

Consider opposing views

- Acknowledge other stakeholders for the issue, and consider their positions.

- Explain why your position is preferable.

- Make counterarguments if necessary.

4 Write a conclusion

End with more than a summary

- Think of a strong way to end by offering more evidence in support of your thesis, reinforcing what is at stake, or giving an example that gets at the heart of the issue.

5 Revise, revise, revise

Evaluate your draft

- Make sure your position argument meets the requirements of the assignment.

- Can you sharpen your thesis to make your position clearer?

- Can you add additional reasons to strengthen your argument?

- Can you supply additional evidence?

- Examine your language for bias and emotionally loaded words and reword if needed.

- When you have finished revising, edit and proofread carefully.

Exercise 9.3 Return to the slogans that you found for Exercise 9.2. Choose one that is particularly interesting or that presents a wealth of possible arguments. Try to come up with a thesis based on the slogan for each line of argument (definition, value, comparison/contrast, consequence).

9e Sample Position Argument

Martinez 1

Mariela Martinez

Professor Barnes

English 102

13 April 2007

Should Students Have the Right

of Freedom of Speech?

In January 2002, students at Juneau-Douglas

High School in Juneau, Alaska, were dismissed from

classes for a parade sponsored by a local business for

the Winter Olympic Torch Relay, which passed in front of

the school. Across the street and off of school grounds,

high school senior Joseph Frederick, who had not

attended school that day, and his friends waited until

the torch and cameras approached. They then unfurled a

banner that read "Bong Hits 4 Jesus." The outraged

school principal, Deborah Morse, ran across the street

and seized the banner. She then suspended Frederick

for five days and later increased the penalty to ten

days when Frederick quoted Thomas Jefferson on the

right of freedom of speech (Sherman).

The first and
second paragraphs
give the
background of an
issue that likely is
unfamiliar to most
readers.

Martinez 2

Frederick appealed to the Superintendent and the
Juneau School Board, which denied his appeal. He then
filed suit against Morse and the school board, claiming
they had violated his First Amendment right to freedom
of speech. The federal district court ruled in favor of
Morse and the school board. The United States Court of
Appeals for the Ninth Circuit, however, reversed the district court in a unanimous decision, ruling that Frederick's right to freedom of speech had been violated (Hussain). The Juneau School Board then took the case to
the United States Supreme Court, which heard oral
arguments on March 19, 2007. Kenneth Starr, the
Whitewater prosecutor during the Clinton
administration, presented the case for the school board.

At first glance the incident seems blown
enormously out of proportion, certainly unworthy of
consuming many hours of a federal judge's time.
Frederick's banner was a stupid prank done in poor
taste by an adolescent. He is far from the ideal
poster child for free speech. But the underlying issue
is huge. I maintain that there is no reason to restrict
the First Amendment rights of students when they are

In the third
paragraph,
Martinez gives her
interpretation that
the event was not
worthy of the
attention it
received. Then she
states her thesis
that students' right
to freedom of
speech should be
protected.

Martinez 3

not disrupting the school. To give school authorities
the right to control anything a student says anywhere
far exceeds any reasonable interpretation of our
Constitution.

Martinez examines
the opposing
position. She
concludes that the
evidence cited by
the opposition
does not apply to
the Juneau case.

Attorney Kenneth Starr argued before the
Supreme Court that Morse's censorship of Frederick
was justified because of the precedent set in Bethel
School District v. Fraser. In that 1986 case, the Supreme
Court ruled that public schools could limit student
speech at a school assembly. Vulgar or obscene speech
could be censored. The court decided that "[T]he
undoubted freedom to advocate unpopular and
controversial views in schools and classrooms must be
balanced against the society's countervailing interest in
teaching students the boundaries of socially appropriate
behavior." But that case involved a school assembly on
school property. Starr argued that Frederick v. Morse is
comparable because students had been collectively
released from school to watch the Olympic torch pass by
and were accompanied by their teachers.

The case Morse v. Frederick is not, as Starr
maintained, about protecting young people from "the

Martinez 4

scourge of drugs." The drug reference is a red herring. Frederick described the words as nonsense meant to get the attention of the television cameras (Biskupic). The banner was not pornographic or obscene. The banner did not incite violence. The only violent act was the principal's seizing the banner. Neither could it be interpreted as attacking Christianity. Organizations that litigate on behalf of the religious right including the Christian Legal Society and the American Center for Law and Justice, founded by the Rev. Pat Robertson, have sided with Frederick (Greenhouse).

> Martinez argues that Frederick's banner neither broke any laws nor did it insult Christian organizations because the religious right sided with Frederick.

Instead the case is an effort by school administrators supported by their professional organizations to get the Supreme Court to allow them to censor anything they disagree with. This effort is chilling because they currently have the power to censor obscene, violent, and libelous speech. It is an attempt to use the public's fear about illegal drugs to justify heavy-handed authoritarian control of student expression, whether on or off campus. Morse and Starr may not like to admit it, but the First Amendment does apply in our nation's public schools. The U.S.

> Martinez supplies evidence that students do have the right of political expression when they are not disruptive.

Martinez 5

Supreme Court decided in 1969, in the case of Tinker et
al. v. Des Moines Independent Community School
District, that students do have the right of political
expression. The court ruled that as long as the
student's expression does not disrupt the educational
environment, officials cannot suppress it (Haynes). The
Supreme Court has long maintained that speech that is
unpleasant or uncomfortable is nonetheless protected.

In her conclusion, Martinez reiterates that she does not think Frederick's prank was a good idea, but the principal was wrong to deny his right to freedom of speech off of school property. She gives additional evidence that the Supreme Court has ruled in the past that students do have freedom of speech.

Frederick's prank was stupid and boorish, but
imagine that Frederick held up a banner protesting racial
segregation in the South in 1961. We would now see his
act as courageous. Indeed, students were at the
forefront of the Civil Rights movement, and many school
administrators opposed their actions. Principal Morse
was not wrong to disagree with Frederick's message, but
she was wrong to censor it. The Supreme Court declared
in its Tinker ruling in 1969 that students do not "shed
their constitutional rights to freedom of speech or
expression at the 'schoolhouse gate.'" The First
Amendment is fundamental to our sense of what the
United States is about, and we should always be vigilant
when those in power seek to limit freedom of speech.

Martinez 6

Works Cited

Bethel School Dist. v. Fraser. No. 478-674. Supreme
Ct. of the US. 7 Jul. 1986.

Biskupic, Joan. "Justices Debate Student's Suspension
for Banner." USA Today 20 Mar. 2007: 3A.

Greenhouse, Linda. "Free Speech Case Divides Bush and
Religious Right." New York Times 18 Mar. 2007,
late ed.: A22.

Haynes, Charles C. "T-shirt Rebellion in the Land of the
Free." First Amendment Center 14 Mar. 2004. 4
Apr. 2007 <http://www.firstamendmentcenter.org/
commentary.aspx?id=12854>.

Hussain, Murad. "The 'Bong' Show: Viewing Frederick's
Publicity Stunt Through Kulmeier's Lens." Yale Law
Journal Pocket Parts 9 Mar. 2007.
2 Apr. 2007 <http://thepocketpart.org/
2007/3/9/hussain.html>.

Sherman, Mark. "'Bong Hits 4 Jesus' Banner Case Reaches
Supreme Court." Lansing State Journal 16 Mar. 2007.
2 Apr. 2007 <http://www.lansingstatejournal.com:
apps:pbcs.dll:article%3FAID=:20070316:NEWS01:
703160379:1001:RSS>.

Martinez 7

Tinker et al. v. Des Moines Independent Community
School Dist. No. 393-503. Supreme Ct.
of the US. 24 Feb. 1969.

*To hear audio commentary on this piece of writing, visit this page
of the E-book at* www.mycomplab.com.

9f Organize and Write a Proposal Argument

Every day we hear people say that something should be fixed or changed
for the better. But it's rarer when people try to convince others that they
should take action. Even though doing nothing is an easy choice, many
people aren't satisfied with doing nothing about a problem they find
important. They want things to improve. Every large-scale project, every
major scientific endeavor, even every form of constitutional government
starts with an argument for change. These kinds of arguments are called
proposal arguments and they take the classic form: *We should (or should
not) do something.*

Writing an effective proposal argument takes time. Often you start out
with something that bothers you but no one seems to be doing much
about. Writing about the problem can inspire you to learn more about
what causes it and how the solution you are proposing might actually be
put into practice.

① Before you write

Think about your readers

- How much are your readers affected by the problem you are addressing?

- Do your readers agree that the problem you are addressing is important?

- If your readers are unaware of the problem, how can you make them think that solving the problem at least partially is important?

② Write an introduction

Identify the problem

- Do background research on what has been written about the problem and what solutions have been attempted.

- Summarize the problem for your readers and identify whose interests are at stake.

- Describe what is likely to happen if the problem isn't addressed.

③ Organize and write the body of your paper

Describe other solutions that have been attempted or proposed

- Explain why other solutions don't solve the problem or are unrealistic.

Present your solution

- Make clear the goals of your solution. Some solutions do not completely solve the problem.

- Describe the steps of your proposal in detail.

- Describe the positive consequences (or how negative consequences might be avoided) as a result of your proposal.

Argue that your solution can be done

- Your proposal is a good idea only if it can be put into practice, so explain how it is feasible.

(continued)

- If your proposal requires money, explain where the money will come from.

- If your proposal requires people to change their present behavior, explain how they can be convinced to change.

④ Write a conclusion

End with a call to action

- Think about shared community values—such as fairness, justice, or clean air and water—that you might raise with your readers.

- Put your readers in a position that if they agree with you, they will take action.

- Explain exactly what they need to do.

⑤ Revise, revise, revise

Evaluate your draft

- Make sure your proposal argument meets the requirements of the assignment.

- Can you better explain the problem or provide more evidence about it?

- Can you add additional evidence that your proposal will solve the problem?

- Can you supply additional evidence that your proposal can be implemented?

- Do you explain why your solution is better than other possible solutions?

- When you have finished revising, edit and proofread carefully.

9g Sample Proposal Arguments

You can find a sample proposal argument that uses MLA-style documentation in Section 23l and a sample proposal argument that uses APA-style documentation in Section 24f.

WRITING SMART

Use visuals to support an argument

Pictures alone don't make arguments, but they often provide vivid evidence in support of arguments. Charts, graphs, and maps can also bring supporting evidence. All visuals should have captions, and their relevance to the argument should be made clear in the main text.

■ Richard Scruggs sits on the foundation of his home in March 2007 after it was destroyed by Hurricane Katrina in August 2005. Scruggs has used images of the catastrophic destruction caused by Katrina in his battle to get insurance companies to pay for more of the damage.

Source: Cheryl Gerber, "Katrina Insure." Photograph. *New York Times*. 1 Mar. 2007, late ed.: C1.

Writing in the Disciplines

Learn to Write in Academic Disciplines

Each academic discipline has its own writing requirements.

10a Become an Academic Writer

In any discipline, good writing is likely to exhibit similar qualities: it will be clear, concise, and logical, supplying appropriate evidence in sufficient amounts to persuade the audience. But because disciplines have different purposes, they use different vocabularies, formats, and evidence to make and support claims. What kinds of questions does a botanist ask? How does a sociologist solve problems? What kinds of evidence will be most convincing to a banker or stockbroker? Learning to communicate with professionals in your field helps you think like a professional in that field.

In college, the many fields and majors are organized into disciplines. These groupings can vary from one institution to another, but the chart on pages 156–157 shows the most common divisions. Note, however, that there is significant overlap and sharing of knowledge among various fields. For example, archaeology is often housed in humanities programs, yet the study of ancient civilizations combines many of the scientific methods used in natural sciences like paleontology. Engineers rely heavily on natural sciences like mathematics and physics; advertising majors will need to know quite a bit about psychology and human behavior to be successful; and so on.

It is also becoming more and more common for researchers to collaborate with experts in other fields to solve problems. Thus a sociologist might work with a professional in business administration to study the group dynamics of a large organization or a historian might collaborate with colleagues in natural sciences to understand the effects of an epidemic in years past.

DISCIPLINES, PURPOSES, AND GENRES

Discipline	Common fields or majors	Purposes	Genres	Preferred documentation style
Fine Arts	Theater, dance, studio art, art history, music	Creation of artwork; history and reception of art	Essay, critique, review, visual analysis, iconography, research paper, grant proposal, creative writing	MLA and CMS (see Ch. 23 and 25)
Humanities	Literature, history, classics, government, languages, philosophy, law	Interpreting, appreciating, and imagining the human experience	Essay, research paper, abstract, case study, grant proposal, oral history, ethnography	Primarily MLA, but also APA and CMS (see Ch. 23, 24, and 25)
Education	Curriculum and instruction, education administration	Training teachers and developing effective teaching methods	Lesson plan, literature review, abstract, case study, grant proposal	APA (see Ch. 24)
Social Sciences	Psychology, sociology, anthropology, geography, social work, human ecology	Exploring human behavior in individuals and groups—both in the past and the present—with a strong desire to learn to predict human behavior in the future	Literature review, abstract, case study, oral history, grant proposal, poster presentation	Primarily APA (see Ch. 24)

DISCIPLINES, PURPOSES, AND GENRES				
Discipline	**Common fields or majors**	**Purposes**	**Genres**	**Preferred documenta-tion style**
Natural Sciences	Physics, math, astronomy, bi-ology (botany, zoology, marine science), geol-ogy, ecology, chemistry. Also health science fields like nurs-ing, pharmacy, kinesiology	The study of living things, inanimate mat-ter, systems, and processes	Literature re-view, lab re-port, abstract, grant proposal, poster presen-tation	APA and CSE (see Ch. 24 and 26); some sciences, like chemistry and physics, have their own style guides
Business	Finance, business administration, management, accounting, marketing, public relations	Building and maintaining healthy busi-nesses and markets	Summary, letter, email, memo, busi-ness plan, speech/presen-tation, market-ing plan, case study, market analysis	CMS and APA (see Ch. 25 and 24)
Media/ communi-cations	Journalism, radio/televi-sion/film stud-ies, advertising, information management	Informing and entertaining the public, promot-ing commerce, and effecting the exchange of information	Article, analy-sis, advertising, scripts, screen-plays	APA and CMS (see Ch. 24 and 25)
Engineering	Civil, industrial, chemical, petroleum, aerospace, biomedical, mechanical, electrical (in-cluding com-puter science)	Practical application of science and technology to improve human civilization	Case study, de-sign report, progress re-port, lab report, proposal	Primarily CSE and APA (see Ch. 26 and 24)

Ask your instructor for advice and for examples of the writing genres common in your field. Some genres, like lab reports and case studies, vary considerably from discipline to discipline, so locate an example from your field.

> **Exercise 10.1** Look at some journals or textbooks that are used frequently in your field of study. Do you notice any common elements of format, style, or language? Do some journals follow a style that differs from others in the field? Why do you think this is? Write out a list of the elements that define writing in your field.

10b What Counts as Evidence in the Disciplines?

Experts in most fields prefer certain types of evidence. Although any kind of logical evidence can be, and is, used in almost any field, the types noted on page 161 are those that carry the most weight. If you have any doubts about the kind of evidence to use, you should always check with your instructor.

Experts in the various disciplines look for different kinds of evidence because they are trying to solve different problems. For example, here are questions the experts in sixteen fields might ask in beginning to explore the topic of global climate change:

Field	Possible questions
Geography	What constitutes a "normal" range of global climate conditions?
Geology	What do worldwide coal deposits tell us about the global Paleolithic climate?

Field	Possible questions
Astronomy	What can humans' impact on Earth's atmosphere and climate teach us about making other planets habitable?
Biology	Is recent deforestation responsible for an increase in CO_2 in the earth's atmosphere?
Chemistry	To what extent has the reduced production of chlorofluorocarbons "solved" the problem of ozone depletion?
Psychology	How has the "clean energy" movement changed individuals' norms regarding fossil fuels?
Sociology	How does a community's assumptions about socioeconomic value affect its response to the threat of global climate change?
Economics	What burdens do carbon dioxide emissions controls impose on large versus small businesses?
Business	Which "clean" energy sources are most likely to become profitable in the next twenty years?
Engineering	How can engineers protect coastal urban areas from the stronger hurricanes associated with global warming?
Government	How might rising sea levels affect the stability of governments in coastal third-world nations?
History	What percentage of recorded famines might be attributable in part to global climate change?
Archaeology	What effect did global climate change have on ancient human population and migration patterns?

Field	Possible questions
Classics	What ancient texts describe possible effects of global climate change, and what can these texts tell us about humans' response to such change?
Literature	How do literary descriptions of climate-related catastrophes (floods, drought, hurricanes) change over time?
Fine Arts	How might a performance piece utilizing dance and music demonstrate the impact of global climate change on human beings?

10c Where Do You Find Sources for a Discipline?

The best place to begin to find sources for a discipline is on your library's Web site. Your library has online resources for researching particular disciplines. Look for "Research by Subject" on your library's research page.

Research by Subject

You might also like to consult . . .

> ► How Do I Find a Subject Librarian?
> ► How Do I Get Started with My Research?
> ► How Do I Find Articles on a Topic?
> ► How Do I Evaluate a Web Site?

Subjects Listed Alphabetically

A | B | C | D | E | F | G | H | I | J | K | L | M | N | O | P | Q | R | S | T | U | V | W | X | Y | Z

A

Accounting and Tax
Advertising
African and African American Studies
Agriculture
American Studies
Anthropology

Your library has a subject directory on its Web site.

FIELDS OF STUDY AND TYPES OF EVIDENCE

Field	Controlled experimental data	Non-participatory observation	Participatory observation	Material data (fossil record, human artifacts, material properties)	Historical records (letters, maps)	Literary texts	Man-made artifacts: buildings, paintings	Pre-existing, gathered statistics	Interviews, surveys	Articles by other experts
Literature					✓	✓				✓
Classics					✓	✓	✓			✓
Archaeology				✓	✓	✓	✓			✓
History	✓				✓	✓	✓	✓	✓	✓
Government	✓				✓			✓	✓	✓
Geography	✓		✓	✓	✓			✓		✓
Astronomy	✓	✓		✓	✓			✓		✓
Chemistry	✓			✓				✓		✓
Biology	✓	✓		✓				✓		✓
Psychology	✓	✓	✓	✓	✓			✓	✓	✓
Sociology	✓	✓			✓			✓	✓	✓
Economics	✓				✓			✓	✓	✓
Business	✓	✓						✓	✓	✓
Engineering	✓	✓	✓	✓			✓	✓		✓
Fine Arts	✓	✓				✓	✓	✓		✓

Chapter 11

Write in Specific Genres

Learn to write in the many academic formats.

11a Write an Essay Exam

Instructors use essay exams to test your understanding of course concepts and to assess your ability to analyze ideas independently. To demonstrate these skills, you must write an essay that responds directly and fully to the question being asked.

Elements of an exam essay

Introduction	Briefly restate the question, summarizing the answer you will provide.
Body paragraphs	Each paragraph should address a major element of the question. Order them so the reader can tell how you are responding to the question.
Conclusion	*Briefly* restate your answer to the question, not the question itself.

What you need to do

- Make sure you understand the question. Respond with the kinds of information and analysis the question asks you to provide.
- Plan your response before you begin writing, with an outline, list, or diagram. Note how much time you have to write your response.
- Address each element of the question, providing supporting evidence.
- Save a few minutes to proofread and add information where needed.

162

Sample exam essay

HIS 312: Early American History Describe the economic, cultural, and political variables that led to the establishment of slavery in the American South.

Amy Zhao began her response to the essay question by jotting down ideas for each of the three categories mentioned. Her outline also served as a map for the structure of her essay.

economic	cultural	political
plantation economy	racist ideologies	elite leadership of southern colonies
trade with Europe	divide with indentured servants	legislature limited to large landowners
need for cheap labor		

Multiple variables in economics, culture, and politics combined to help institutionalize slavery in the American South. Most important among these variables were the plantation economy, racist ideologies, conflict among the lowest social classes, and the stranglehold of elite landowners on the legislative process. Economic variables arose primarily from the Southern colonies' unique geographical situation. Physically isolated from the large markets of Europe but blessed with huge quantities of arable land, the region required cheap labor in order to exploit its full economic potential. Relatively wealthy white colonists secured large tracts of land and strongly resisted any forces that pushed for the breakup of these plantations into smaller, individually-owned farm holdings. The concentrated wealth and power of the plantation owners allowed them to arrange conditions to protect their land. Slavery came to be seen as the best way to maintain their power.

Amy uses the key terms from the question to indicate where she is addressing that element of the question.

11b Write an Observation

Observations are common in the natural sciences and in social science disciplines such as psychology, sociology, and education. They begin as notes taken firsthand by the writer as he or she observes an event, phenomenon, or place. Observations should include as many relevant and specific details as possible.

Elements of an observation

Title	Include a precise title. **EXAMPLE** Doppler Profile of the Structure of Tornadoes Near Attica, Kansas, on 12 May 2004
Description and context	Be specific about what or whom you are observing. How did you limit your site or subject? What background information do readers need? How will a deeper understanding of your subject help people? **EXAMPLE** Eleven mixed-breed puppies six weeks old were observed during feeding and play periods over a five-week period. Each puppy's tendency to exhibit alpha- or omega-dog behaviors changed relatively little over this period.
Record of observations	Report what you observed in some logical order: chronologically, from most obvious features to least obvious, or some other pattern.
Conclusion or summary	Give your readers a framework in which to understand your observations. What conclusions can you draw from them? What questions are left unanswered?

What you need to do

- Carry a notebook and make extensive field notes. Provide as much information as possible about the activities you observe.
- Record in your notebook exactly when you arrived and left, where you were, and exactly what you saw and heard.
- Analyze your observations before you write about them. Identify patterns, and organize your report according to those patterns.

Sample observation

Animal Activity in Barton Springs Pool

from 15 April to 22 April 2007

Barton Springs Pool is a 225-meter-long, natural spring-fed pool in a limestone creek bed in Austin, Texas. It is both a wildlife habitat and a busy hub of human activity. Because of the constant flow from the springs, the water temperature is constant at 68°F (20°C), allowing swimmers to use the pool year around.

My first observation was on 15 April from 1:45–4:00 p.m. on a warm sunny day with the air temperature at 74°F (23°C). I used a mask and snorkel to observe below the water. It was remarkable how oblivious people and wildlife were of each other. While from forty to fifty-five Austinites splashed on the surface, many fish (mostly smallmouth bass with two large channel catfish on the bottom) swam below them, and large numbers of crayfish crept along the rocky portion of the pool's bottom. Eight small turtles (red-eared sliders) alternately swam at the surface or dove below near the dam at the deep end. Twelve endangered Barton Springs salamanders (Eurycea sosorum), ranging in color from bright orange to paler yellow, were active by the larger spring at the center of the pool.

At the times when humans are not present or nearly absent, animal activity noticeably increases. From the side of the pool on 16 April (clear, 72°) from 7:25 p.m. until closing at 8 p.m., I observed smallmouth bass schooling near the dam and feeding on mosquitoes and mayflies. Nine ducks (seven lesser scaup and two mallards) landed on the pool at 7:40 p.m. and remained when I left. (Lesser scaup migrate to the area in large numbers in the winter; the mallards are likely domesticated ducks.) A pair of wood ducks (male and female) were also on the cliff above the shallow end.

> Specific times, weather conditions, numbers of individual species, and behaviors are recorded.

11c Write a Case Study

Case studies are used in a wide range of fields such as nursing, psychology, business, and anthropology. Case studies are narrow in focus, providing a rich, detailed portrait of a specific event or subject.

Elements of a case study

Introduction	Explain the purpose of your study and how or why you selected your subject. Use language appropriate to your discipline, and specify the boundaries of your study.
Methodology	Explain the theories or formal process that guided your observations and analysis during the study.
Observations	Describe the "case" of the subject under study by writing a narrative, utilizing interviews, research, and other data to provide as much detail and specificity as possible.
Discussion	Explain how the variables in your case might interact. Don't generalize from your case to a larger context; stay within the limits of what you have observed.
Conclusion	What does all this information add up to? What is implied, suggested, or proven by your observations? What new questions arise?
References	Using the appropriate format, cite all the outside sources you have used. (See Chapter 24 for APA documentation and Chapter 26 for CSE documentation.)

What you need to do

- Understand the specific elements of your assignment. Ask your instructor about what your case study should include.
- Use careful observation and precise, detailed description to provide a complex picture with a narrow focus.
- Write your observations in the form of a narrative, placing yourself in the background (avoid using *I* or *me*).
- Analyze your findings and interpret their possible meanings, but draw your conclusions from the observed facts.

Sample case study

Underage Drinking Prevention Programs

in the Radisson School District

INTRODUCTION

This study examines the effect of Smith and Bingham's drinking-prevention curriculum on drinking rates in the Radisson School District, 2000-2006. Prior to 2002, the Radisson School District offered no formal drinking-prevention education. In 2000, as part of a state initiative, the district proposed several underage drinking education curricula for possible adoption. After substantial debate and input from parents, Smith and Bingham's curriculum was chosen for implementation in ninth through twelfth grades. This study tracks student drinking rates from 2000 to 2006, and compares the results after introduction of the curriculum to district rates prior to implementation.

DISCUSSION

The data from this study showed no correlation between the curriculum and student drinking rates. Drinking rates remained unchanged before, during, and after the implementation of the curriculum. Additionally, survey data indicate that levels of student drinking remained constant as well. Therefore, Smith and Bingham's curriculum had minimal effect on changing students' drinking behavior.

CONCLUSION

In terms of reducing student drinking, Smith and Bingham's curriculum does not appear to be any more effective than no drinking-prevention education at all. Since no measurable results were obtained, the strong administrative support for the curriculum in the school district cannot be attributed to its success. . . .

Some disciplines require title pages. See page 448 for an example of an APA title page.

The introduction identifies both the problem and the particular subject of the case study.

The conclusion sums up what has been observed. Many case studies do not give definitive answers but rather raise further questions to explore.

11d Write a Lab Report

Lab reports follow a strict structure, enabling specialists in a given field to assess quickly the experimental methods and findings in any report. Check with your instructor for the specific elements required for your lab report.

Elements of a lab report

Title	The title of a lab report should state exactly what was tested using language specific to the field.
Abstract	The abstract briefly states the questions and the findings in the report.
Introduction	The introduction gives the full context of the problem, defining the hypothesis being tested.
Methods	Describe the materials used as well as the method of investigation. Your methods and procedure sections should be specific enough to allow another researcher to replicate your experiment.
Procedure	Step by step, narrate exactly what you did and what happened. In most fields, you will use the passive voice.
Results	State the outcomes you obtained, providing well-labeled charts and graphics as needed.
Discussion	State why you think you got the results you did, using your results to explain. If there were anomalies in your data, note them as well.
Conclusion	Briefly, what was learned from this experiment? What still needs to be investigated?
References	Using the appropriate format, cite all the outside sources you have used. (See Chapter 24 for pyschology lab reports and Chapter 26 for science lab reports.)

What you need to do

- Understand the question you are researching and the process you will use before you begin. Ask your instructor if you need clarification.
- Take thorough notes at each step of your process. You may be asked to keep a lab notebook with a specific format for recording data. Review your notes before you begin drafting your report.
- Don't get ahead of yourself. Keep methods, procedure, discussion, and conclusion sections separate. Remember that other scientists will look at specific sections of your report expecting to find certain kinds of information. If that information isn't where they expect it to be, your report will not make sense.
- Write your abstract last. Writing all the other sections of the report first will give you a much clearer picture of your findings.

Sample lab report

Wave interference in visible light using
the double-slit method

Abstract

Filtered light was projected through one slit in a piece of cardboard, producing a single bar of light, brightest in the center and shaded darker toward the edges, on the wall behind the cardboard. When a second slit was added to the cardboard, the projected image changed to alternating bands of bright light and darkness. The conclusion reached is that wavelength patterns in the light cancelled or reinforced one another as they reached the wall, increasing or decreasing the observed light. These results are consistent with the wave theory of light.

11e Write a Letter of Application

Successful letters of application place the reader's needs first and show why you are the best candidate. Great jobs attract many applicants. Convince your readers that you are worthy of an interview. A well-written letter of application is the way you get your foot in the door.

Elements of a letter of application

Inside address and salutation	Use the name and title of the person doing the hiring whenever possible. If you don't know them, call the organization for the person's name and official title.
First paragraph	Name the position for which you are applying.
Body	Explain why your education, experience, and skills make you a good candidate for the position.
Conclusion	Mention that you've enclosed your résumé and your contact information.

What you need to do

- Limit yourself to one page.
- Find out as much as you can about the organization or company.
- Don't fall into the trap of emphasizing why the job would be good for you; instead, show why you are well suited for the employer's needs.
- List in your résumé the qualifications and work experience that make you well suited for the position, then describe them in your letter and remember to bring them up if you get an interview.

Sample letter of application

609 McCaslin Lane
Manitou Springs, CO 80829

November 2, 2007

Ann Darwell
100 Pine Street
Colorado Springs, CO 80831

Dear Ms. Darwell:

Please consider my application for Fox 45's *Kids' Hour* production assistant position.

During my senior year at Boston College, I interned for the Emmy-winning children's program *Zoom*. Through the internship I learned not only the technical skills necessary to produce a weekly, hour-long show, but the finesse required to manage an all-child cast.

My experience as the producer of *All the News* also gave me intensive training in the skills of a successful producer. Under my direction, a staff of fifteen crew members and reporters regularly broadcast creative campus news pieces. Because I produced this weekly show for three years, I would need little initial supervision before being able to make significant contributions to *Kids' Hour*.

After one year at *Zoom*, I want to continue production work in a position that offers more responsibility in the field of children's television. My work at *Zoom*, particularly my authoring and producing a series of spots to teach children Spanish, has given me hands-on experience in creating the kind of innovative television for which *Kids' Hour* is known.

Thank you for considering my application. Enclosed is my résumé. I would be happy to send my references if you wish to see them. You can reach me at (719) 555-0405 or c.popolo@hotmail.com. I look forward to speaking with you about the production assistant position.

Sincerely,

Christian Popolo

Christian Popolo

11f Write a Résumé

Finding the right job depends on writing a successful résumé, one of the most important pieces of writing that you will ever compose. The secret of a successful résumé is understanding its purpose—to place you in the small group of candidates to be interviewed.

Elements of a résumé

Objective section	Target the objective section to the position you are applying for. Be as specific as possible. **EXAMPLE** Special education teacher in the greater Atlanta area specializing in brain-injured patients and requiring familiarity with coordinating ARDS and completing IED documentation.
Overview section	List your education in reverse chronological order, beginning with certificates or degrees earned. List work experience in reverse chronological order, focusing on your more recent jobs and including details of your duties.

What you need to do

- Focus on the employer's needs. Imagine you are the person hiring. List the qualifications and work experience an ideal candidate would have.
- Make a list of your qualifications and work experience.
- Compare the two lists. What qualifications and work experience do you have that make you well suited for the position? Put checks beside the items on your list that you find are most important.
- Create two printed résumés—a scannable résumé and a traditional résumé. Many companies now scan résumés and store the information in a database. Make your scannable résumé simple, and avoid any graphics such as bulleted points and lines.

Sample résumé

Christian Popolo
609 McCaslin Lane
Manitou Springs, CO 80829
(719) 555-0405
c.popolo@hotmail.com

OBJECTIVE
Production assistant position for an innovative Colorado television program requiring prior experience in children's television and a strong technical background.

SUMMARY OF SKILLS
On-location production, studio-based production, news production, children's television, management, fundraising, animation, AVID Media Composer, AVID Xpress DV, MS Word, MS Office, fluent Spanish, detail-oriented, articulate, excellent writer

EDUCATION
Bachelor of Arts in Communications, Boston College, May 2007, GPA: 3.65/4.0

WORK EXPERIENCE
Producer, *All the News,* BCTV Campus Television, Chestnut Hill, MA, August 2004–May 2007. Produced a weekly, half-hour campus news program. Supervised seven studio staffers and eight reporters. Spearheaded successful initiative to increase Student Services funding of the program by fifteen percent.
Intern, *Zoom,* Boston, MA, May 2006–May 2007. Interned in the production department of award-winning national children's television program. Wrote and produced three 2-minute "Hablamos" segments, designed to teach Spanish phrases.
Technician, Communications Media Lab, Chestnut Hill, MA, August 2003–April 2006. Maintained over $300,000 worth of the latest filming and editing technology.

HONORS
Presidential Scholar, August 2004–May 2007
BCTV Excellence Award, May 2005 and May 2006

REFERENCES
Available upon request from the Career Center, Boston College, Southwell Hall, Chestnut Hill, MA 02467 at (617) 555-3430.

To hear audio commentary on each example in this chapter, visit Chapter 11 of the E-book at www.mycomplab.com.

Chapter 12

Write About Literature

Concentrate on developing a reading of your own.

12a Become a Critical Reader of Literature

Reading literature requires a set of practices different from those you might use while reading the Sunday paper or a magazine article. Think of yourself as an active critical observer. Carry on a dialogue with the text using marginal notes. Although writing in the margins as you read may seem like extra work at first, you will soon discover that it saves time and, before long, sharpens your reading skills. Keeping a record of your reading will force you to engage with a text; being an active reader is practice toward being a thoughtful reader. And marginal comments will be your best source from which to generate a paper topic.

As you read make notes using the following list as a guide.

- Study the plot of the story. Determine how the events in the story relate to each other. What is the conflict and how is it resolved?
- Examine the principal characters in the story. What are their most defining characteristics? Are there minor characters? What purpose do they serve?
- Describe the setting of the story. What role does it play?
- Identify the point of view—that is, the perspective from which the story is told. Does a major character relay the events? A minor character? Or a fly on the wall?
- Look for shifts in the tone, style, and language of the story.
- Look for symbols, imagery, and interesting metaphors. Are sounds, images, or motifs repeated? What roles do they play?

- Identify the story's central theme or main idea. Consider the title of the story and how the main characters fit the theme.

When reading poetry also pay attention to the following.

- Identify the rhyme scheme. For example, when the first and third lines rhyme and the second and fourth, the rhyme scheme is *abab*.
- Listen to the meter. The most common meter in English is *iambic*, where an unstressed syllable is followed by a stressed syllable (for example, "To swell the gourd, and plump the hazel shells," from John Keats' "To Autumn").
- Listen for alliteration, the repetition of initial consonant sounds (for example, *b*aby *b*oomer, *M*arch *m*adness, *r*oad *r*age, *W*orld *W*ide *W*eb).
- Note the stanza, the unit of poetry. The shortest stanza is the two-line couplet.

12b Develop an Interpretation

Assignments for English classes tend to be more open-ended than writing assignments in other disciplines so you can focus on an aspect of the text that interests you. Develop an original idea. Ideally your audience will see the text differently after reading your interpretation.

Opinion versus interpretation

Papers about literature are often called *critical analyses*. Don't let the term trip you up. *Critical* in this sense doesn't mean judgmental. The fact is, your understanding of the text is much more interesting to a reader than whether you like it or not. Avoid making an argument about your opinion of a text unless the assignment specifically asks for one. Instead, develop an interpretation that illuminates some aspect of the text.

WRITING SMART

Electronic resources for writing about literature

While libraries are still the best places for literary research, you can find a number of handy resources online.

- **Bartleby.com** (www.bartleby.com) features free e-texts of well-known poetry, prose, and reference works, including the *Cambridge History of English and American Literature.*
- **MLA Bibliography** is a searchable bibliography of literary criticism available on your library's Web site.
- **Oxford English Dictionary,** available on your library's Web site, records the history of a word's meaning, tracking where it first appeared and how its definition has changed through the years.
- **Project Gutenberg** (www.gutenberg.net) offers free e-texts of hundreds of works of literature.

Exercise 12.1 Review the descriptions of electronic resources for writing about literature and try out a few online. Which resource or resources would be the best place to look for . . .

1. a searchable version of the King James Bible?
2. recent works of literary criticism about E. M. Forester's *Howard's End?*
3. the origins of the word *carnival?*
4. full text versions of different translations of *Beowulf?*
5. a searchable encyclopedia of world history?

Develop your thesis

Ask *what, how,* and *why* questions. These questions will lead you from observation, to exploration, to an interpretation.

Observation: What's going on in the text?

What did you observe in the text that was unexpected, odd, powerful, or central? What questions did you ask? Wonderful interpretations frequently evolve from a question or confusion about the text.

> Why does the concluding scene of *Pride and Prejudice* feature the Gardiners, two secondary characters?

Although you won't have an interpretation yet, answering *why* questions will help you narrow your focus to a potentially fruitful topic for interpretation.

Exploration: How does the text do what it's doing?

The answer to this question may consider technical, stylistic, or thematic aspects of the text. At this point you'll begin to develop the first stages of your interpretation.

> How does Austen feature the Gardiners in the last scene of *Pride and Prejudice*? Throughout the novel Austen shows us strained or broken marriages, but the Gardiners are an exception. She presents them as a well-matched, well-adjusted couple.

Analysis and interpretation: Why does the text do what it's doing?

Consider to what end or for what purpose the text functions as it does. What are the ultimate implications of this feature of the text? Frequently answers will fall into one of the following lines of inquiry:

- It advances or complicates a major theme of the text.
- It engages in commentary about larger political, social, philosophical, or literary issues of the author's day.
- It reflects the influence of another writer or text.
- It advances the plot or adds depth to a character.
- It's attempting to be technically innovative. It highlights a capability or limitation in the author's choice of theme, genre, structure, stylistic elements, or narrative technique.

Why does the end of *Pride and Prejudice* feature secondary characters, the Gardiners? The Gardiners exemplify successful marriage. By ending the novel with them, Austen lends a note of hope for Elizabeth and Darcy's union. The novel, then, is not a condemnation of marriage as an institution but of the social forces that promote bad matches. We can analyze Austen's characterization of the Gardiners to better understand the kind of marriage making she wants to advocate.

12c Write a Literary Analysis

Keep your audience in mind when writing a literary analysis. Those who have already read the work will be bored by plot summary. Quote or paraphrase passages that advance your interpretation. Never use the text as evidence without analyzing it. Your analysis should be a close reading of the text that explains how the text you've chosen illustrates your interpretation.

1 Before you write

Read and analyze closely

- You should have a text. If the first text you select isn't working for the assignment, find another one.

- Go through your text line by line, annotating your responses.

- Develop a thesis for your interpretation that might start with a question and turn into a claim.

- When you have a thesis, reread the text to look for evidence.

2 Write an introduction

Engage your reader

- Raise what is at stake in your literary text. Many literary texts speak to large issues, whether about art or about life. What issues does your text raise?

Organize and write the body of your paper

Use literary concepts to examine your text

- Take into account literary concepts such as character, setting, theme, motif, symbol, point of view, and imagery to express your ideas.

- Your analysis will likely answer such questions as who are the characters, what is the setting and what role does it play, what are themes or motifs in the text, from what point of view is the work told, what language choices are made, and what is the significance of the title?

Support your interpretation

- Cite the precise passages in the text that support your interpretation.

- Attribute every direct quotation and explain its significance.

- If your instructor asks you to use secondary sources, either literary criticism or biographical information about the author, decide where these sources are relevant.

Write a conclusion

End with more than a summary

- Draw larger implications from your analysis.

- End with a vivid example from the text.

Revise, revise, revise

Evaluate your draft

- Make sure your analysis meets the requirements of the assignment.

- Make sure your thesis is specific and significant. If you identify a pattern but say nothing about why it is important, your reader will ask "So what?" What does the pattern contribute to an overall interpretation?

- Make sure your evidence and examples are relevant to your thesis. Explain the significance of the evidence for your thesis.

- When you have finished revising, edit and proofread carefully.

Incorporating critical strategies

Your instructor might ask you to use particular critical strategies, such as to consider a literary work from a feminist approach. Ask your instructor to recommend major critical books and articles that deal with your topic. Then consider ways you can advance or revise the conversation about your topic. Does your interpretation of the text advance or complicate an existing critical perspective? Is there a scene or an aspect of the text that the critics don't consider but should? By developing original responses to these questions, you enter the critical conversation.

STAYING ON TRACK

Use the literary present tense

The disciplinary convention in English is to employ the **literary present tense**. The literary present tense requires the use of present tense when analyzing any literary text such as a poem, a play, a work of fiction, an essay, or a sermon. Also use the present tense when discussing literary criticism.

Incorrect   In *Song of Myself* Walt Whitman **tempered** his exuberant
Past tense   language with undercurrents of doubt about whether
language **could** do all he **asked** of it.

Correct   In *Song of Myself* Walt Whitman tempers his exuberant
Present tense   language with undercurrents of doubt about whether
language can do all he asks of it.

However, you should employ the past tense when discussing literary history. The author's life, the creation of the text, the text's publication, and the critical reception of the text all exist outside the work itself and require the past tense. The following passage uses the past tense to discuss the publication history and critical reception of *Leaves of Grass*.

(Continued on next page)

Correct Past tense	Beyond doubting whether his audience would understand the spirit of his verse, Whitman worried that *Leaves of Grass* would never reach an audience at all. He was so concerned, in fact, that he published reviews of the book under false names to drum up publicity.

12d Sample Literary Analysis

The following student paper responds to the assignment topic "Analyze how W. B. Yeats's poem 'A Prayer for My Daughter' uses poetic language to describe a father's ambitions for his child's future. What does the speaker's 'prayer' tell us about his own conceptions of femininity?"

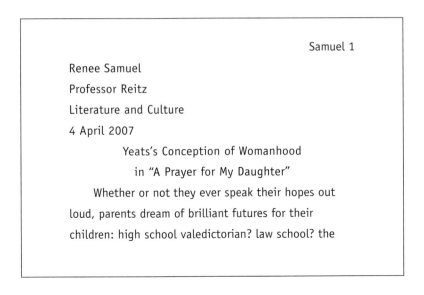

Samuel 1

Renee Samuel

Professor Reitz

Literature and Culture

4 April 2007

Yeats's Conception of Womanhood

in "A Prayer for My Daughter"

Whether or not they ever speak their hopes out

loud, parents dream of brilliant futures for their

children: high school valedictorian? law school? the

ballet? the White House? Although these dreams are usually well-intentioned, often a parent's definition of his or her child's "brilliant future" is filtered through that parent's own desires, fears, and prejudices. The speaker in W. B. Yeats's 1919 poem "A Prayer for My Daughter" is a father who at first seems to have his daughter's best interests at heart. As his child sleeps in her cradle, immune to a raging storm outside, the speaker "walk[s] and pray[s] for this young child" for hours on end (9). But despite such protective behavior, the father's prayers contain old-fashioned and conservative notions about femininity. By describing the kind of woman he hopes his daughter will one day become, Yeats's speaker also gives the reader a definition of his "perfect woman." By analyzing this definition, we learn more about how this father's past has influenced his ideas about women than we do about his concern for his daughter's future.

　　This father's first prayer for his daughter concerns ideal beauty. He prays, "May she be granted beauty and yet not / Beauty to make a stranger's eye

Samuel 3

distraught, / Or hers before a looking glass" (17-19).
The speaker wants his daughter to be beautiful, but
not *too* beautiful, because "being . . . beautiful
overmuch" might allow her to slide by on her beauty
and "consider beauty a sufficient end" (20-21). The
father fears that this vanity will lead to other life
problems: she will "lose natural kindness," miss out
on "heart-revealing intimacy," and worst of all,
"never find a friend" (12-24).

By "a friend" the speaker means a husband, and
Yeats makes this clear in the next stanza when the
speaker declares that he wants his less-than-
beautiful daughter "chiefly learned" in the art of
"courtesy" (33), because "Hearts are not had as a gift
but hearts are earned / By those that are not entirely
beautiful" (34-35). According to the speaker, men
who have been seduced by and "played the fool" for
"beauty's very self" (37) will eventually prefer a
woman with "glad kindness" instead of "charm" (40).
The father also prays that his daughter will not
be too intellectual or opinionated, because such
women are unattractive and "choked with hate" (52).

Samuel 4

He states that "Intellectual hatred is the worst" (57)
and prays that his daughter will grow up to "think
opinions are accursed" (58). In this way she will
avoid becoming like a woman her father once knew,
who:

> Because of her opinionated mind
> Barter[ed] that horn and every good
> By quiet natures understood
> For an old bellows full of an angry wind?
> (61-64)

If his daughter follows this definition of ideal
womanhood (ideal women are courteous rather than
too beautiful, and avoid the bitterness caused by
intellect and opinion), this father believes she will
marry well, live in "a house / where all's accustomed,
ceremonious" (73-74) and "be happy" (72).

This father's prayer for his daughter is not all bad;
surprisingly, this poem's speaker idolizes non-perfect
women and believes that true love should come from
courtesy and kindness rather than just lust. As Elizabeth
Cullingford argues, "It is refreshing to be offered the
'not-entirely-beautiful' woman as an ideal. . . . Pleasing,

too, is the notion of love as a gradual development rather than a thunderbolt" (136). However, behind this open-mindedness is anger over how he was treated by beautiful, opinionated women in his past, and anxiety over the dying out of old traditions. This anger and anxiety leads to some very sexist ideas about femininity.

For most of his early life, Yeats was in love with Maud Gonne, a beautiful, smart, opinionated, and political woman who rejected his affection. However, Yeats felt that she used her beauty to manipulate him into writing beautiful poetry about her. In 1917, Yeats finally married a less beautiful, but also less independent woman: Georglie Hyde-Lees. When the poem's speaker prays that his daughter will be "not entirely beautiful," he is also wishing that she will be more gentle and kind, and less opinionated, than Maud Gonne with her "opinionated mind" and "angry wind" (61, 64). Here we see the father's protective sexism: he would selfishly prefer a submissive daughter over a smart one who would remind him of the "loveliest woman born" (57) for whom he once "played the fool" (36).

Furthermore, this kind of daughter will be less likely to "dance to [the] frenzied drum" (15) of modern womanhood. Instead, she will carry on old traditions, and "live like some green laurel / Rooted in one dear perpetual place" (47-48). Here, the speaker shows his desire to keep his daughter protected against the modern violence of the twentieth century (which Yeats symbolizes through images of "howling," "roof-leveling" storms and "flooded," "murderous" seas) by hiding her away in past traditions. The father prays that his daughter will marry into a family rooted in old aristocratic tradition, and he chooses this "hypothetical son-in-law" not because he is a good match for his daughter, but "because of his aristocratic social status and ownership of landed property" (Cullingford 138). The father is so anxious about the future that he prays his daughter will give up her individual identity and free will to become an "innocent," "beautiful" ambassador of tradition (Cullingford 76).

Even though the speaker in "A Prayer for My Daughter" selfishly projects his own past onto his

Samuel 7

daughter's future, Yeats does not seem to want us to think we are hearing the prayer of an unreliable narrator. Although Yeats believed in gender equality, this poem "marks a regression in Yeats's acceptance of changing gender roles" (Cullingford 136). Perhaps the point, though, is just this: When it comes to their children's futures, even open-minded parents sometimes become conservative and reactionary.

Samuel 8

Works Cited

Cullingford, Elizabeth. <u>Gender and Sexuality in Yeats's Love Poetry</u>. Syracuse: Syracuse UP, 1996.

Yeats, W. B. "A Prayer for My Daughter." <u>The Collected Poems of W. B. Yeats</u>. Ed. Richard J. Finneran. New York: Collier, 1989.

To hear audio commentary on this piece of writing, visit this page of the E-book at www.mycomplab.com.

Designing and Presenting

Color   Swatches   Styles

Chapter 13

Communicate with Words, Images, and Graphics

Good design, like good writing, begins with a focus on your audience.

13a Write in Multimedia

During the past few hundred years in Western culture, people typically communicated using one medium at a time. The more highly they valued the communication, the more likely they would use only one medium. The most valued writing, such as great literature, academic books and articles, and legal contracts, had dense pages of print with no illustrations. Great art was limited to a few materials: oil on canvas or chiseled stone. Great music was performed on orchestral instruments by formally dressed musicians.

Computer technologies now make it possible for individuals to create multimedia texts that formerly required production staffs. Today, word processing programs not only permit you to control type styles and size but also allow you to insert pictures, add tables and other graphics, print in color, and prepare sophisticated visuals for presentations.

The problem today is not whether you can add images and graphics but when to add them and for what effects. Just as for other rhetorical situations, it finally comes down to what you hope to accomplish—your purpose for communicating.

■ Sometimes, images are used in place of words.

■ Sometimes words bring images to mind.

13b Think About Verbal and Visual Relationships

Knowing when to use images and graphics and when to use words requires you to think about them as **media**—as different means of conveying information and ideas. The word *writing* makes us think of words, yet in our daily experience reading newspapers, magazines, advertisements, posters, and signs, we find words combined with images and graphics. On the flip side, television uses words extensively (think of the words you see on commercials when you have the sound off or the text running across the bottom of the screen on news, sports, and financial programs).

Many ideas and concepts can be explained more effectively with a combination of words, graphics, and images. One example is the creation of the Waterpocket Fold, a nearly 100-mile-long wrinkle in the earth's crust, a major landmark in southern Utah. (See below and the next page.)

Verbal explanation

The Waterpocket Fold is a classic monocline: a regional fold with one very steep side in an area of otherwise nearly horizontal layers. A monocline is a "step-up" in the rock layers. The rock layers on the west side of the Waterpocket Fold have been lifted more than 7000 feet higher than the layers on the east. Major folds are almost always associated with underlying faults. The Waterpocket Fold formed between 50 and 70 million years ago when a major mountain building event in western North America, the Laramide Orogeny, reactivated an ancient buried fault. When the fault moved, the overlying rock layers were draped above the fault and formed a monocline.

More recent uplift of the entire Colorado Plateau and the resulting erosion has exposed this fold at the surface only within the last 15 to 20 million years.

—National Park Service

Visual explanation

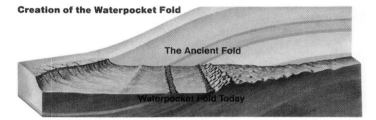

Creation of the Waterpocket Fold

The Ancient Fold

Waterpocket Fold Today

▤ The creation of the Waterpocket Fold

Images

▤ Unless you have seen the Waterpocket Fold, it's hard to imagine what it looks like without a photograph.

Organization in Verbal Texts

Organization is the path the writer creates for readers to follow. Even in a reference book like this one, in which readers consult particular chapters and sections according to their needs, there is still a path from beginning to end. Sentences, paragraphs, sections, and chapters are the writer's materials in constructing the pathway. The various subjects the writer treats are the places along the pathway. If the trail is well marked and the places identified, the reader can follow without getting lost and can revisit particular places.

Mapping of ideas

Some kinds of writing demand particular kinds of organization. A short memo in an office typically begins with an announcement of the subject. But in other kinds of writing, the organization is not so predictable. How you begin and how you take the reader along a pathway depend on what you are trying to achieve. Thinking about your purpose often helps you to map out the organization.

Titles, headings, and paragraphs

Titles and headings combine verbal and visual indicators of levels of importance and major divisions in subject matter. Paragraphs give visual cues to the progression of ideas in verbal texts. Other visual indicators such as boldface and italics provide emphasis at the level of words and phrases. Print, after all, is a visual as well as a verbal medium.

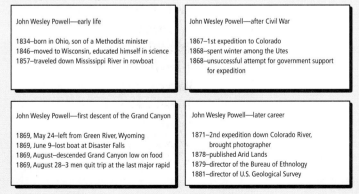

John Wesley Powell—early life

1834–born in Ohio, son of a Methodist minister
1846–moved to Wisconsin, educated himself in science
1857–traveled down Mississippi River in rowboat

John Wesley Powell—after Civil War

1867–1st expedition to Colorado
1868–spent winter among the Utes
1868–unsuccessful attempt for government support
for expedition

John Wesley Powell—first descent of the Grand Canyon

1869, May 24–left from Green River, Wyoming
1869, June 9–lost boat at Disaster Falls
1869, August–descended Grand Canyon low on food
1869, August 28–3 men quit trip at the last major rapid

John Wesley Powell—later career

1871–2nd expedition down Colorado River,
brought photographer
1878–published Arid Lands
1879–director of the Bureau of Ethnology
1881–director of U.S. Geological Survey

■ Notecards are a traditional method for mapping ideas.

Organization in Visual Texts

Organization is often called *composition* by photographers, artists, and designers. The materials for photographers and artists are objects placed in space.

Both of the pictures below are of the same subject. Which do you find more appealing, the image on the left or the one on the right?

Static versus dynamic

The image on the left is a typical snapshot. The person is placed at the exact center, and the horizon is about at the midpoint. Putting the subject in the exact center is what happens when people take snapshots without thinking about how they are composed. The effect is static because the focus is on the object.

The image on the right moves the person away from the center and places him in relation to a large rock illuminated by the setting sun. Instead of focusing on the man, we now see him in relation to objects on the beach and the sea and sky behind.

When the picture is divided into thirds horizontally and vertically, we can see that the prominent rock and the man are placed at the intersections of these imaginary lines. This principle of organization is known as the "rule of thirds." While there is no beginning and ending in a photograph, principles of organization still apply.

Point of View in Verbal Texts

At the most basic level, **point of view** means selecting among first person (*I, we*), second person (*you*), and third person (*he, she, it*) when you write about your subject. Using *I* emphasizes the writer or the teller of the story in fiction. Using *you* puts the relationship between writer and reader in the foreground. Using *he, she,* or *it* keeps the focus more on the subject and diminishes the prominence of the writer.

Point of view is also determined by how you locate yourself in relation to your subject. Whether you write in first or third person, you can write about a subject from close, firsthand experience or you can place yourself at a distance from your subject, giving the sense of being an impartial observer offering an overview.

You can write about the Grand Canyon as if you were looking out from the window of an airplane.

The Grand Canyon is 218 miles long, from 4 to 18 miles wide, and over a mile deep in some places. From the sky the contrast between the north and south rims of the Grand Canyon is striking. The north rim is above 9,000 feet and covered by a thick forest; the south rim is about 1,200 feet lower than the north rim and has much less vegetation. The bottom of the canyon is the northernmost extension of the Sonoran Desert, where several different species of cacti, thistle, and other desert plants are found.

You can write about the Grand Canyon from the bottom.

On a late afternoon in August with the temperature well over 100°, we paddled our kayaks into Elves Chasm after getting pounded most of the day by some of the biggest rapids in the Grand Canyon—Granite, Hermit, Crystal, Serpentine, and Waltenberg—taking our casualties in turbulent swims when rolls failed. The cool trickle from the waterfall brought relief to the scorching canyon. The droplets glistened on the intense green moss and ferns like thousands of gems.

Point of View in Visual Texts

Where we choose to stand when we take a photograph makes all the difference in how the audience sees the subject. The photographer gives the audience a vantage point to take in the subject by allowing the audience to see what the photographer sees, creating an effect comparable to the use of *I* in writing. But photographers can also diminish the immediacy of a photograph by placing subjects at a distance or photographing them in stereotypical ways.

Three views of a bullpen

The bullpen is the area of a baseball park where relief pitchers warm up and wait their turn to pitch. What difference does point of view make in how we see the bullpen?

Photographers also create a *you* relationship with their subjects. Photographing people at close range creates a sense of interaction between subject and photographer.

Focus and Frame in Verbal Texts

When you write, maintain focus on one subject at a time. You achieve focus by what you choose to include and what you choose either to leave out or to postpone until later.

When you write about a complex subject, often you think about many things at once and try to get them all into your prose.

Our era is not unique as a time of uncertainty. In the past the Four Horsemen of the Apocalypse—war, disease, famine, and death—represented uncertainty. Today much of the risk is produced by humans. Science and technology are both the cause of and the solution to our problems. In the past spirits or demons took the blame for catastrophes; today the blame circles back on us. The media tell us that things go wrong because we choose the wrong lifestyle or the wrong partner or the wrong kind of food or the wrong occupation, and it's our responsibility to fix what is wrong.

When you write about a complex subject, sort the issues and present them one at a time.

Our era is not unique as a time of uncertainty. The Four Horsemen of the Apocalypse—war, disease, famine, and death—have been the daily reality for most humans in times before modernity and for many living now. There are two major differences between uncertainty today and in the past.

First is the degree to which risk is produced by humans. Science and technology are both the cause of and the solution to our present risks. Every new technology brings associated risks; trains brought the risk of train wrecks, airplanes brought plane crashes, automobiles brought traffic accidents and smog, nuclear power brought radiation leaks, the Internet brought rapidly spreading computer viruses.

Second is the absence of traditions to account for risks. In the past spirits or demons took the blame for catastrophes. Today the blame circles back on us. We chose the wrong lifestyle or the wrong partner or the wrong kind of food or the wrong occupation. When things go wrong, it is the individual's responsibility to seek counseling, to retrain herself, to pull himself up by his bootstraps.

Focus and Frame in Visual Texts

Just as in writing, make the subject of your images clear to the viewer. Beginning photographers tend to see only what is at the center of the viewfinder. More experienced photographers pay attention to the edges of the frame because they know the frame is critical to how the viewer sees the subject.

What's the subject of this picture? The soccer players? The spectators? The two kids playing behind the spectators?

If the subject is soccer, then change the frame to one that focuses on the action.

Most of the time, you should aim for simplicity in images.

When your subject is complex, you can still achieve simplicity by paying close attention to point of view and frame.

Interest in Verbal Texts

Readers will plow through pages of boring writing if they have a strong purpose for reading, such as a financial report for a company they plan to invest in. Most of the time, however, you have to create and hold readers' interest if you expect them to finish what you write. When you create interest, you also build your credibility as a writer.

Details make writing lively

Lamesa is typical of the hard towns of west Texas, which you quickly learn to associate with the smell of sulfur. Coming into town you pass the lots of the oil field suppliers surrounded by chain-link fences with red dirt blown over the lower third. Inside are rusted oil tanks, mutated steel skeletons of derrick parts, and squat buildings with plank porches lined with orange and blue oil drums—model railroad buildings blown up to full scale. On the small lots in between are shabby motels and windowless liquor stores with names like "Pinkies" on art deco signs above.

Dialogue brings people to life

When we reached the pass, we stood for a moment and looked again at Glacier Peak and, far below us, the curving white line of the Suiattle. Park said, "When you create a mine, there are two things you can't avoid: a hole in the ground and a dump for waste rock. Those are two things you can't avoid."

Brower said, "Except by not doing it at all."

—John McPhee, *Conversations with the Archdruid*

Humor rewards readers and can make points memorable

Large, naked, raw carrots are acceptable as food only to those who live in hutches eagerly awaiting Easter.

Inhabitants of underdeveloped nations and victims of natural disasters are the only people who have ever been happy to see soybeans.

—Fran Lebowitz, *Metropolitan Life*

Interest in Visual Texts

Interest in visual texts is created by composition and subject matter. Some subjects possess inherent interest, but the photographer or artist must build on that interest. Kittens and puppies are cute, but viewers' interest fades quickly if the images are predictable.

Even potentially interesting subjects can be rendered boring if they are photographed in stereotypical ways.

Children often express a spontaneity lacking in adults, which provides visual interest.

Lines

Lines create interest in photographs. Strong diagonal lines can create dynamic photographs. Curved lines can produce graceful images.

13c Know Where Images and Graphics Work Best

"A picture is worth a thousand words" is an old cliché. We could just as easily turn the cliché around to say that certain words such as *justice, truth,* and *faith* are worth a thousand pictures. It's not that images are necessarily more powerful than words but that images and words are different media. Our eyes and brains are able to take in a great deal of visual information and sort that information for relevance. People have little difficulty distinguishing familiar faces in a crowd or recognizing familiar patterns.

For example, we've now become accustomed to deciding whether we'll need to wear a sweater outdoors tomorrow by looking at the colors on a weather map. But even then, we depend on words to tell us whether the forecast is for today or tomorrow and what each color signifies. Visuals are typically used in combination with text. Visuals work well when they

- Deliver spatial information, especially through maps, floor plans, and other graphic representations of space.
- Represent statistical relationships.
- Produce a strong immediate impact, even shock value.
- Emphasize further a main point you've made in words.

13d Know Where Words Work Best

Words can do many things that images cannot. Written words work best when they

- Communicate abstract ideas.
- Report information.
- Persuade using elaborated reasoning.
- Communicate online using minimal bandwidth.
- Adapt to specific users' needs. (Computers can convert words from spoken to written language for those who are hearing impaired or from written to spoken for those who are visually impaired.)

If you've ever visited a Web site that opens with a glitzy Flash screen that takes forever to load and then discovered there was no significant content behind the opening screen, you know the problem of style without substance. While more of our communication in the digital era will take advantage of the multimedia capabilities of new technologies, these technologies will not replace the need for effective writing.

> **Exercise 13.1**   Find an example of words and visuals used effectively to convey a message. This can be an advertisement, a poster announcing a public service, a brochure, an article in a periodical, a page in a textbook or other book, a manual, a work of art, a flyer for a concert or show, a Web site, or anything else that appeals to you to use. Describe the work accomplished by the visuals and by the text, both separately and in combination with one another. Why is the example you've chosen effective?

Chapter 14

Design for Print and the Screen

Successful design should be both functional and handsome.

14a Start with Your Readers

Imagine yourself in the shoes of your reader. What do you, the reader, want from the writer?

Tell your reader what you are writing about

An accurate and informative title is critical for readers to decide if they want to read what you have written. Some genres require **abstracts**, which are short summaries of the overall document. Abstracts are required for scholarly articles in the sciences and social sciences as well as for dissertations. Business reports and other reports often have executive summaries, which are similar to abstracts but often briefer.

Make your organization visible to readers

Most longer texts and many shorter ones include **headings,** which give readers an at-a-glance overview and make the text easier to follow and remember. Some genres have specific formats for organization, such as the APA-style report of research that is divided into four parts: introduction, method, results, and discussion. If you are writing in a genre that requires a specific format, follow it. Readers will be irritated if you don't. (For more information on academic genres, see Chapter 11.)

> A writer's scarcest resource is the reader's attention. Sidebars and pull quotes can be effective for creating interest.

Help your reader to navigate your text

Do the little things that help readers. Remember to include page numbers—something that word processing software can insert for you. Make cross references to other parts of your document when a subject is covered elsewhere.

14b Design Pages

Word processing and other easy-to-use software allow you to achieve what required a team of designers to accomplish just a few years ago.

Format pages

Your word processor can set standard margins of one inch (usually the default setting) and take care of other small issues such as double spacing. But you can do a great deal more, even within standard formats, such as MLA guidelines for formatting.

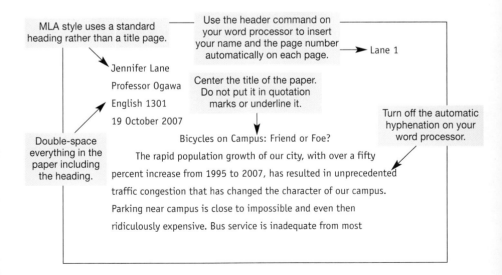

MLA style uses a standard heading rather than a title page.

Use the header command on your word processor to insert your name and the page number automatically on each page.

Lane 1

Jennifer Lane

Professor Ogawa

English 1301

19 October 2007

Center the title of the paper. Do not put it in quotation marks or underline it.

Turn off the automatic hyphenation on your word processor.

Double-space everything in the paper including the heading.

Bicycles on Campus: Friend or Foe?

The rapid population growth of our city, with over a fifty percent increase from 1995 to 2007, has resulted in unprecedented traffic congestion that has changed the character of our campus. Parking near campus is close to impossible and even then ridiculously expensive. Bus service is inadequate from most

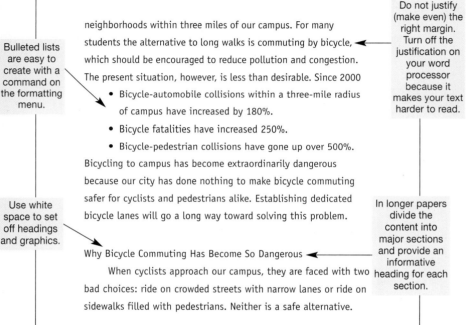

Bulleted lists are easy to create with a command on the formatting menu.

neighborhoods within three miles of our campus. For many students the alternative to long walks is commuting by bicycle, which should be encouraged to reduce pollution and congestion. The present situation, however, is less than desirable. Since 2000

- Bicycle-automobile collisions within a three-mile radius of campus have increased by 180%.
- Bicycle fatalities have increased 250%.
- Bicycle-pedestrian collisions have gone up over 500%.

Bicycling to campus has become extraordinarily dangerous because our city has done nothing to make bicycle commuting safer for cyclists and pedestrians alike. Establishing dedicated bicycle lanes will go a long way toward solving this problem.

Why Bicycle Commuting Has Become So Dangerous

When cyclists approach our campus, they are faced with two bad choices: ride on crowded streets with narrow lanes or ride on sidewalks filled with pedestrians. Neither is a safe alternative.

Do not justify (make even) the right margin. Turn off the justification on your word processor because it makes your text harder to read.

Use white space to set off headings and graphics.

In longer papers divide the content into major sections and provide an informative heading for each section.

Figure 14.1 The first page of a paper in standard MLA format. Your instructor may have specific formatting requirements. Ask your instructor for formatting instructions if they are not specified in the assignment.

Use color effectively

Color can provide contrast to draw attention to headings and emphasized words. Color printing is now affordable, and color is expected on Web sites. We are surrounded by so much color that sometimes the strongest effects are created by using color in minimal ways. Limited use of warm colors—yellow, orange, and especially red—can make an impact.

London

**Spring Break
March 8-16, 2008**

You'll see

Plays
Six outstanding plays including a performance by the Royal Shakespeare Company

Sights of London
Buckingham Palace, the Tower of London, Westminster Abbey, St. Paul's Cathedral, the Houses of Parliament, Big Ben, 10 Downing Street—the residence of the Prime Minister

Museums
National Gallery of Art, the new Tate Modern, the restored Globe Theatre, the British Museum

Sponsored by the Drama Club

**For information contact
Karen Clark, President
Drama Club
405 Memorial Union
482-1564**

Figure 14.2 The red used in the titles and headings both matches and balances the red uniforms in the image.

Design brochures and other documents

With today's word processing and other easy-to-use software, you can produce a professional-looking project. Handsome brochures are one example. Templates take care of the basic layout, allowing you to focus on the content and design. If you are creating a brochure, select the size of paper you want, fold the sheet of paper, and number the panels. Make a sketch of what you want to appear on each panel, including headings, text, images, and graphics.

Determine the main subdivisions of your subject, and divide your text into units with informative headings.

Bulleted points are most effective when they are parallel in structure.

Signal what is different by using a different design or a different color (as in this case).

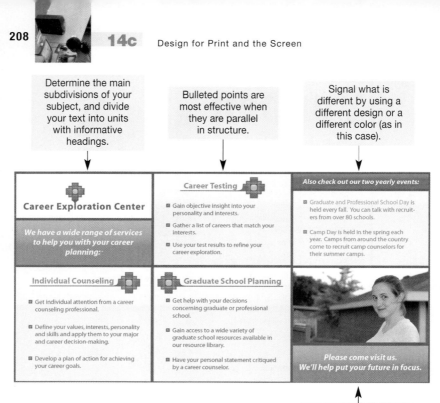

Career Exploration Center

We have a wide range of services to help you with your career planning:

Career Testing

■ Gain objective insight into your personality and interests.

■ Gather a list of careers that match your interests.

■ Use your test results to refine your career exploration.

Also check out our two yearly events:

■ Graduate and Professional School Day is held every fall. You can talk with recruiters from over 80 schools.

■ Camp Day is held in the spring each year. Camps from around the country come to recruit camp counselors for their summer camps.

Individual Counseling

■ Get individual attention from a career counseling professional.

■ Define your values, interests, personality and skills and apply them to your major and career decision-making.

■ Develop a plan of action for achieving your career goals.

Graduate School Planning

■ Get help with your decisions concerning graduate or professional school.

■ Gain access to a wide variety of graduate school resources available in our resource library.

■ Have your personal statement critiqued by a career counselor.

Please come visit us.
We'll help put your future in focus.

Choose images that aid in communicating the content.

Figure 14.3 The inside panels of a three-panel brochure fold out to show the services offered by the Career Exploration Center.

 Choose Type

Writing on a computer enables you to use dozens of different typefaces and fonts. (A particular style of type is called a **typeface**, such as Times New Roman or Arial. A specific kind of typeface, such as Verdana bold, is called a **font**.) At first, typefaces may all appear similar, but when you pay attention to various typefaces, you will notice how they differ.

Use typefaces effectively

Serif type

Serif and **sans serif** are major categories of typefaces. Serif (rhymes with *sheriff*) faces were developed first. Serifs are the little wedge-shaped ends on letter forms, which scribes produced with wedge-tipped pens. Serif typefaces also have thick and thin transitions on the curved strokes. Four of the most common serif typefaces are

Times

Palatino

Bookman

Garamond

Serif typefaces were designed to be easy to read. They don't call attention to themselves. Thus they are well suited for long stretches of text and are used frequently.

Sans serif type

Sans serif (*sans* is French for *without*) typefaces don't have the little wedge-shaped ends on letters, and the thickness of the letters does not vary. Popular sans serif typefaces include

Helvetica

Arial

Verdana

Sans serif typefaces work well for headings and short stretches of text. They give a crisp, modern look. Some sans serif typefaces are easy to read on a computer screen. Verdana, Helvetica, and Arial are sans serif typefaces that most computers now have installed, which is why they are popular on Web sites.

Script and decorative type

There are many script and decorative typefaces. These typefaces tend to draw attention to themselves. They are harder to read, but sometimes they can be used for good effects. Script typefaces imitate handwriting or calligraphy, which is why they often appear on diplomas, formal invitations, and similar documents.

Popular script typefaces include Nuptial Script and Dorchester Script:

When you want only the very best

Snead, Potter, and Jones, Attorneys at Law

Some decorative typefaces, including Lazyvermont and ComicStrip Classic, are informal, almost irreverent:

That's a no brainer.

Totally awesome!

Use a readable type size

It's easy to change the size of type when you compose on a computer. For long stretches of text, use at least 10- or 12-point type. Use larger type for headings and for text that will be read on a screen.

Use other effects as needed

Finally, word processing programs allow you to use type fonts such as **boldface**, *italics*, and underlining. All three are used for emphasis.

14d Compose Images

Think about what an image communicates

- Think about your readers' expectations for the medium you are using. Most essays don't use images. Most Web sites and brochures do use images.
- Think about the purpose for an image. Does it illustrate a concept? highlight an important point? show something that is hard to explain in words alone? If you don't know the purpose, you may not need the image.

- Think about the focus of an image. Will readers see the part that matters? If not, you may need to crop the image.
- Provide informative captions for the images you use and refer to them in your text.

Format images for the medium you are using

Images that you want to print need to be of higher quality than those intended for the Web or the screen. Pay attention to the settings on your camera or scanner.

Digital cameras frequently make images with 72 dpi (dots per inch), which is the maximum you can display on the screen. Most printers use a resolution from 300 to 600 dpi. Use the high-quality setting on your camera for images you intend to print.

Scanners typically offer a range of resolution from 72 to 1600 dpi. The higher the number, the finer the image, but the file size becomes larger. Images on the Web or a screen display at 72 dpi, so higher resolutions do not improve the quality but do make the image slow to load.

Take pictures that aren't boring

No matter how easy it is now to take photographs, the great majority of pictures look alike. Why? It's because most people hold their cameras at eye level and put the subject in the center.

STAYING ON TRACK

Scanning and the law

Images in books and magazines published in the last seventy-five years are almost always owned by someone. If you copy an image for redistribution of any kind, including putting it on a Web site, you must find out who holds the copyright and obtain permission to use the image. Always give credit for any image that you copy, even if it is in the public domain.

Learn what your camera can do

Many digital cameras have special features, such as the macro setting that captures much more detail than the standard setting when photographing at close range. Read the manual that came with your camera, and try the different settings.

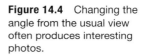

Figure 14.4 Changing the angle from the usual view often produces interesting photos.

Figure 14.5 Look for details. If your camera has a zoom, use it.

Figure 14.6   The macro setting on your camera (usually a flower symbol) allows you to take finely detailed photos from a few inches away.

Figure 14.7   Usually the closer you can get to your subject, the better.

Fill the frame

Most people include too much in their photographs. Decide what is essential and concentrate on getting those elements in the frame.

14e Edit Images

No matter which image editor you use, there are a few manipulations that you will need to use frequently. It's always a good idea to copy an image first and work on the copy.

- **Cropping.** Most images can be trimmed to improve visual focus and file size. To crop an image, select the rectangle tool, draw the rectangle over the area you want to keep, and select the **Crop** or **Trim** command (see Figure 14.8). The part of the image outside the rectangle will be discarded. Every pixel you can squeeze out of an image intended for use on the Web makes the image display faster on a user's screen.

- **Rotating images.** Often you'll find that you held your camera at a slight angle when taking pictures, especially if your subjects were moving. You can make small adjustments by using the **Rotate Image** command. You can also rotate images 90° to give them a vertical orientation.

Figure 14.8 Cropping often improves the image by emphasizing details. Smaller images use less memory and thus are able to load faster on the screen.

WRITING SMART

Save a copy of an image before editing it

Always keep a copy of your original scan or digital photo. Once you change an image and save it, you cannot restore what you changed. Use the **Save As** command to save a copy before you start editing an image.

- **Sizing images.** All photo editing programs will tell you the height and width of an image. You can resize images to fit in a particular area of a Web page or printed page. You can also change the resolution in the dpi window. Remember that if the image is intended for the Web, 72 dpi is the maximum the screen will display. Higher resolution images look no better and are slower to load.

- **Adjusting colors.** Often the colors in photographs that you scan appear "off" when you view the image on a computer monitor. The image may appear too dark or lack contrast. Sometimes the color balance appears off and you want to correct it. The basic controls for brightness, contrast, and color saturation are similar to those on your color TV. Be aware that colors look different on different monitors and what you print may not show the colors you saw on your screen.

14f Create Tables, Charts, and Graphs

Tables, charts, and graphs are easy to create in word processing programs, spreadsheet applications, presentation software, and Web page editors, and they can be imported from one program (e.g., Excel) to another (e.g., Word). While software does much of the formatting of tables, charts, and graphs, you still have to supply the labels for the different parts of the graphic and an accurate title or caption.

Like any graphic, tables, charts, and graphs can be used to mislead readers. Small differences can be exaggerated, for example, or relevant differences concealed (see Section 5e). You have an ethical responsibility to create accurate tables, charts, and graphs.

STAYING ON TRACK

Use and evaluate tables

When to use tables
- To present a summary of several factors
- To present exact numbers
- To give an orderly arrangement so readers can locate and compare information

Evaluating tables
- Does the table have a clear purpose?
- Does the title indicate the purpose?
- What units do the numbers represent (dollars, people, voters, percentages, and so on)?
- What is the source of the data?
- Is the table clearly organized?
- Is the table clearly labeled?

Name of item	Factor 1	Factor 2	Factor 3
AAA	000	00	0
BBB	00	0	000
CCC	0	000	00

Tables

Extensive statistical data can be dull or cumbersome to communicate in sentences and paragraphs. Readers can more quickly and easily grasp data when they are displayed in a table. A table allows readers to view an entire set of data at once or to focus only on relevant aspects (see Table 14.1).

**Table 14.1 Violent Crime in the United States, by Volume
and Rate per 100,000 Inhabitants, 1986–2005**

Year	Population	Violent crime	Violent crime rate
1986	240,132,887	1,489,169	620.1
1987	242,288,918	1,483,999	612.5
1988	244,498,982	1,566,221	640.6
1989	246,819,230	1,646,037	666.9
1990	249,464,396	1,820,127	729.6
1991	252,153,092	1,911,767	758.2
1992	255,029,699	1,932,274	757.7
1993	257,782,608	1,926,017	747.1
1994	260,327,021	1,857,670	713.6
1995	262,803,276	1,798,792	684.5
1996	265,228,572	1,688,540	636.6
1997	267,783,607	1,636,096	611.0
1998	270,248,003	1,533,887	567.6
1999	272,690,813	1,426,044	523.0
2000	281,421,906	1,425,486	506.5
2001	285,317,559	1,439,480	504.5
2002	287,973,924	1,423,677	494.4
2003	290,788,976	1,383,676	475.8
2004	293,656,842	1,360,088	463.2
2005	296,410,404	1,390,695	469.2

Source: United States. Department of Justice. Federal Bureau of Investigation. *Crime in the
United States: 2005.* Sept. 2006. 4 May 2007 <www.fbi.gov/ucr/05cius/
data/table_01.html>.

Bar charts

Bar charts are useful for comparing data. Multiple bars can be combined, as shown in Figure 14.9, which compares the earnings of men and women according to level of education.

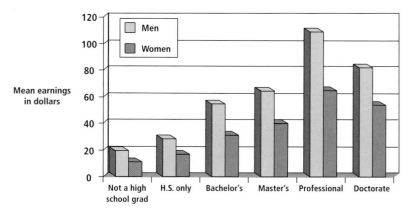

Earnings by highest degree earned: 2001

Figure 14.9 Bar charts are useful for comparing data.
Source: United States. Census Bureau. *Statistical Abstract of the United States: 2003.* Washington: GPO, 2003. 154.

Line graphs

Line graphs are well suited for displaying changes in data across time. Line graphs can have one line, or two or more sets of data can be displayed on different lines, emphasizing the comparative rates of change (see Figure 14.10).

Pie charts

Pie charts are commonly used to represent the relationship of parts to a whole. They provide overviews that are quickly understood. For example,

Percentage of College Freshmen, 1975-2005

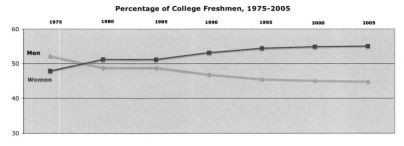

Figure 14.10 Line graphs are useful for displaying data across time.
Source: United States. Census Bureau. *Statistical Abstract of the United States: 2007.*
Washington: GPO, 2007. 177.

Figure 14.11 shows that in 2002 half the people in the United States had at least some college education. You must have data in percentages to use a pie chart, and the slices of the pie must add up to 100%. If the slices are too small, a pie chart becomes confusing. Six or seven slices are about the limit for a pie chart that is easy to interpret.

Educational attainment for persons
in the U.S. aged 25 and over: 2002

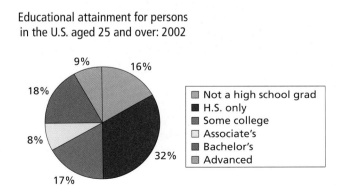

Figure 14.11 Pie charts display the relationship of parts to a whole.

Organizational charts and flowcharts

Presentation software and the drawing module in word processing programs allow you to create organizational charts and flowcharts. You can make organizational and flowcharts by selecting shapes and arrows on the drawing module and inserting them. Select the text tool for typing labels on the shapes (see Figure 14.12).

Stage 1: Planning

Figure 14.12 Flowcharts are useful for representing steps in a process.

STAYING ON TRACK

Use and evaluate charts

When to use charts
- To direct readers to what is important
- To give evidence for claims
- To show factual information visually
- To show statistical relationships more clearly than either words or numbers alone permit

(Continued on next page)

STAYING ON TRACK *(continued)*

Selecting the right chart

	Bar charts	Make comparisons in particular categories
	Line graphs	Show proportional trends over time
	Pie charts	Show the proportion of parts in terms of the whole
	Flowcharts	Show the steps in a process

Evaluating charts

- Does the chart have a clear purpose?
- Does the title indicate the purpose?
- What do the units represent (dollars, people, voters, percentages, and so on)?
- What is the source of the data?
- Is the type of chart appropriate for the information presented?
- Is there any distortion of information (see Section 6e)?

14g Design a Web Site

Web authoring software makes it easy to compose Web pages, but the software doesn't tell you how to design an effective Web site. Visitors to Web sites often don't read pages one after the other as they do in books. Visitors expect to be able to move through your site according to their own interests.

Determine your structure

Think in advance about the structure of your site. Decide on the major topics that should be on separate pages. Draw a map of your site that shows the pages and the links to other pages.

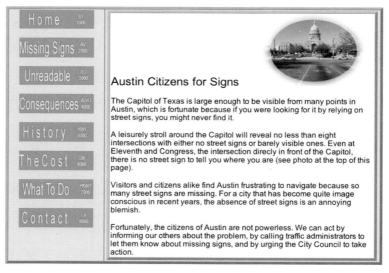

AUSTIN CITIZENS FOR SIGNS

Austin Citizens for Signs

The Capitol of Texas is large enough to be visible from many points in Austin, which is fortunate because if you were looking for it by relying on street signs, you might never find it.

A leisurely stroll around the Capitol will reveal no less than eight intersections with either no street signs or barely visible ones. Even at Eleventh and Congress, the intersection direcly in front of the Capitol, there is no street sign to tell you where you are (see photo at the top of this page).

Visitors and citizens alike find Austin frustrating to navigate because so many street signs are missing. For a city that has become quite image conscious in recent years, the absence of street signs is an annoying blemish.

Fortunately, the citizens of Austin are not powerless. We can act by informing our others about the problem, by calling traffic administrators to let them know about missing signs, and by urging the City Council to take action.

Figure 14.13   Home page on *Austin Citizens for Signs*.

To hear audio commentary on this Web site, visit this page of the E-book at www.mycomplab.com.

Kat Schwegel created the multipage *Austin Citizens for Signs* for a course project. Her subject was something that bothered her: the absence of street signs at many intersections in her city. She wanted fellow students and fellow citizens to contact city council members about the problem. She composed separate pages describing the missing signs, the consequences of their absence, the history of the problem, the cost of installing signs, and what readers could do to address the problem.

Make your site visually effective

A consistent look and feel make a Web site appear unified and support the content. A Web site does not need a loud background or flashy animations to achieve a visual theme. Instead, little things such as selecting a simple set of colors for the text, headings, links, and background do more to create a consistent visual theme than an attention-grabbing image. Similar graphics and images should be the same size, and often their placement can be repeated from page to page.

Make the text readable

Long stretches of text on the Web tend not to get read. You can make your text more readable on the Web if you do the following.

- **Divide your information into chunks.** If your information runs longer than a page, consider placing it on two Web pages.
- **Use shorter paragraphs when possible.** Long paragraphs are harder to read on the screen than in print.
- **Use a sans serif typeface.** You can specify typefaces using the font command on your Web editing software.
- **Control for line width.** Lines of type that run across the entire page are often difficult to read. Divide your page into columns.
- **Use white space to separate elements** and to give visual relief.

Make navigation easy

People typically scan a Web site quickly and move around a lot. They are likely to click on links, following their interests. If you put content on more than one page, provide a navigation bar so readers can navigate easily. A navigation bar can be a simple text bar or icons that are easy to create with image editing software.

Evaluate the design of a Web site

You can learn a great deal about effective Web design by keeping these criteria in mind when you visit Web sites. Some will be more critical than others, depending on the site. For example, good navigational tools become more important on extensive sites.

1. **Audience and purpose:** How does the site identify its intended audience? Why was the site created?
2. **Content:** How informative is the content? Has the site been updated recently? What do you want to know more about? Are there any mechanical, grammatical, or style problems?
3. **Readability:** Is there sufficient contrast between the text and the background to make it legible? Are the margins wide enough? Are there paragraphs that go on too long and need to be divided? Are headings inserted in the right places, and if headings are used for more than one level, are the levels indicated consistently? Is high-contrast text, including text in boldface and all caps, kept short?
4. **Visual design:** Does the site have a consistent visual theme? Where is the focal point on each page? Do the images contribute to the visual appeal or do they detract from it?
5. **Navigation:** Does the first page indicate what else is on the site? How easy or difficult is it to move from one page to another on the site? Is a consistent navigation scheme used throughout the site? Are there any broken links?
6. **Accessibility:** Web accessibility means that people with disabilities and people with slow Internet connections can access the information and interaction available on the Web. W3C, the World Wide Web Consortium, offers guidelines and tools for assessing Web accessibility (see www.w3.org/WAI/eval/Overview.html).

Exercise 14.1 Make two lists. On one list, write out the Web sites you always enjoy visiting and why you like them. Are they updated frequently? easy to navigate? quick to load? Do they act as indexes to other useful sites? What else do you like about them?

On the other list, write out the Web sites that you often have to visit but almost always find annoying or frustrating, and explain why you don't like them. Are they hard to navigate? What else do you find frustrating about these sites?

Compare your two lists. What conclusions can you draw about what makes an effective Web site? Do any of the conclusions also hold true for your own essays?

Chapter 15

Design Presentations

An engaging presentation requires careful planning.

15a Plan a Presentation

The key to success is remembering that your purpose is to communicate effectively. In any medium, your goals, your subject, and your audience should shape your presentation. Look closely at what you are being asked to present and how long you will have. Decide early on what kind of presentation you will give and what visuals you will incorporate. If you want to use visual elements, make sure the presentation room has the equipment you need.

Select your topic

Choosing and researching a topic for an oral presentation is similar to preparing for a written assignment. If you have a broad choice of topics, make a list of subjects that interest you. Then go through your list and answer these questions.

- Will you enjoy speaking on this topic?
- Does the topic fit the situation for your presentation?
- Do you know enough to speak on this topic?
- If you do not know enough, are you willing to do research to learn more about the topic?

If your presentation requires research, you will need to document the sources of your information just as you would for a research paper (see Chapters 16–20 on planning and conducting research). Provide your audience with those sources either in your talk or in a handout.

Consider your audience

Unlike writing for readers you've never seen, speaking allows you to have your audience directly before you. That audience will give you concrete feedback during your presentation by smiling or frowning, by paying attention or losing interest, by asking questions or sitting passively.

Think about the general characteristics of your audience—their ages, their occupations, their educational level, their ethnic and cultural background, and the mix of men and women. Think specifically about your audience in relation to your topic.

- Will your audience be interested in your topic?
- Are there ways you can make them more interested?
- What is your audience likely to know or believe about your topic?
- What does your audience probably not know about your topic?
- What key terms will you have to define or explain?
- What assumptions do you hold in common with your audience?
- How is your audience most likely to disagree with you?
- What questions is your audience likely to ask?

Organize your presentation

After you have done your research and analyzed your audience, it's time to organize your presentation.

- **Make a list of key points.** Think about the best order for your major points. If you use visuals, they should indicate your major points.
- **Plan your introduction.** Your success depends on your introduction. You must gain the attention of your audience, introduce your topic, indicate why it's important, and give a sense of where you are headed. It's a tall order, but if you don't engage your audience in the first two minutes, you will lose them.
- **Plan your conclusion.** You want to end on a strong note. Stopping abruptly or rambling on only to tail off leaves your audience with a bad impression. Give your audience something to take away, a compelling example or an idea that captures the gist of your presentation.

Support your presentation

When you have organized your main points, you need to decide how to support those points. Look at your research notes and think about how best to incorporate the information you found. Consider a strategy based on one or more of these elements.

- **Facts.** Speakers who know their facts build credibility.
- **Statistics.** Effective use of statistics can give the audience the impression that you have done your homework. Statistics can also indicate that a particular example is representative.
- **Statements by authorities.** Quotations from credible experts can support key points.
- **Narratives.** Narratives are brief stories that illustrate key points. Narratives can hold the attention of the audience—but keep them short or they will become a distraction.
- **Humor.** Humor is one of the best ways to convince an audience to share your point of view. You have to know the audience well, however, to predict with confidence what they will think is funny.

Organize a group presentation

Changing speakers is a distraction for the audience in a group presentation. For the group presentation to succeed, each speaker must have a clear role and the transition from one speaker to the next should be smooth.

- **Determine the roles and the goals.** Each member of the group must understand his or her role in the presentation and the goal of that segment. For example, the first speaker may serve as the host and provide transitions from one speaker to the next.
- **Coordinate research.** Each speaker should be well informed on the subtopic he or she is to present. The audience will expect answers to in-depth questions.
- **Coordinate visuals.** An advantage of group presentation is that a person not speaking can handle the visuals, allowing the speaker to focus on the delivery. This advantage is gained by practicing in advance.

- **Rehearse.** Groups that try to make a presentation on the fly rarely succeed. Timing is critical. Pausing to read notes is a sure way to lose the audience.

WRITING IN THE WORLD

Home field advantage

Athletes know that home field advantage involves much more than having the crowd behind them. Each field and court has its own special characteristics. In many cases small bits of knowledge acquired from playing on the field (such as a position from which the sun is blinding at a certain time of day) can mean the difference between winning and losing. Visiting teams practice on the opponent's field or court before the game to learn as much as possible.

In college many or all presentations will be in your classroom, which can give you your own home field advantage. You'll know whether the acoustics are good, whether it is easy to see visuals from everywhere in the room, and so on. In the workplace, you may be required to give presentations in unfamiliar places such as a client's site. You will have to work a little harder to ensure success.

Practice your presentation in the room where you will deliver it. Bring a friend who can tell you whether you can be heard in the back of the room and whether your visuals can be read at that distance. Make sure any equipment you need is working.

Have a back-up plan for visuals. If your presentation depends on a projector that stops working unexpectedly, think about what you will do if you suddenly cannot use the visuals you brought. For example, you can write a few main points on a white board or flip chart if necessary.

Remember that the audience is with you. Most people are patient when something goes wrong. They have been in similar situations themselves. If, for example, a projector bulb burns out and another one is available, ask the audience to give you a minute or two.

15b ▶ Design Visuals for a Presentation

Visuals focus the attention of the audience and can keep your audience oriented throughout your presentation while providing you with memory aids. Charts, pictures, and diagrams can help you emphasize major points and provide information that would be tedious to describe verbally.

Visuals also give your audience something to look at besides you, which helps you to relax. At a minimum, consider putting an outline of your talk on an overhead transparency or a slide. Visuals take time to prepare, so start planning them early.

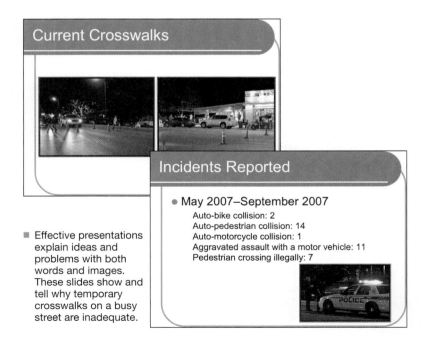

Current Crosswalks

Incidents Reported

● May 2007–September 2007

Auto-bike collision: 2
Auto-pedestrian collision: 14
Auto-motorcycle collision: 1
Aggravated assault with a motor vehicle: 11
Pedestrian crossing illegally: 7

■ Effective presentations explain ideas and problems with both words and images. These slides show and tell why temporary crosswalks on a busy street are inadequate.

Guidelines for creating and using visuals effectively

Visuals can make or break a presentation. Poor-quality visuals destroy your credibility.

- **Keep the text short.** In general, put no more than six words on a line and have no more than six lines on a single slide.
- **Always proofread.** Typos and misspelled words make you appear careless and can distract the audience from your point.
- **Use a readable type size.** You probably have been in the audience for a presentation where the type size was too small to read. And you probably found it annoying.
- **Use dark text on a white or light-colored background.** Light text on a dark background is often hard to read.
- **Focus on one element per slide.** Outlines, charts, photographs, and maps are all easy to create.
- **Keep the design simple.** Use a consistent style and color scheme.
- **Plan your timing when using visuals.** Usually you can leave a slide on the screen for one to two minutes, which allows your audience time to read the slide and connect it to what you are saying.

Exercise 15.1 Think about oral presentations you have recently seen—class lectures, presentations at work, public talks—and choose one that you felt was the most effective and one that you felt was the least effective. Make two lists—one on what makes a presentation effective and another on what makes a presentation ineffective.

15c Deliver an Effective Presentation

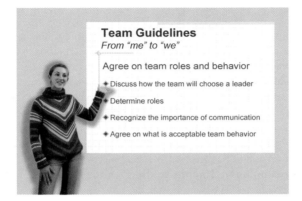

Nervousness

Nervousness is usually invisible. If you make a mistake, remember that your audience will understand. Stage fright is normal, and often you can draw off that energy. Take a deep breath before you begin, and smile.

Practice

There is no substitute for rehearsing your speech several times.

- You will become more confident.
- You will be more comfortable using your visuals.
- You will know how long your presentation will take.

Effective techniques

- Talk, don't read.
- Stand, don't sit.
- Make eye contact.
- Signal main points with gestures.
- Speak loudly and not too quickly.
- Use effective visuals.
- Give an overview in the introduction.
- Give a conclusion that ends with a key idea or example.
- Believe in what you say; enthusiasm is contagious.
- Finish on time.

Researching

Plan Your Research

Understand the different kinds of research and plan your strategy.

16a Analyze the Research Task

Research is a creative process, which is another way of saying it is a messy process. Often there are false starts and dead ends. Sometimes the direction you take starting out leads you to places you didn't expect. That's why research can be fun.

Even though the process is complex, your results will turn out better if you keep the big picture in mind while you are immersed in research. If you have an assignment that requires research, look closely at what you are being asked to do. The assignment may ask you to review, compare, survey, analyze, evaluate, or prove that something is true or untrue. Your purpose and an awareness of your potential audience will help guide your strategies for research.

Determine your purpose

Often the assignment itself will tell you what is expected. Look for key words:

- An *analysis* or *examination* requires you to look at an issue in detail, explaining how it has evolved, whom or what it affects, and what is at stake.
- A *review of scholarship* requires you to summarize what key scholars and researchers have written about the issue.
- A *survey* requires you to gather opinion about a particular issue, either by a questionnaire or by interviews.

- An *evaluation* requires you to make critical judgments.
- An *argument* requires you to assemble evidence in support of a claim you make.

Ask your instructor for guidance if you remain unsure of what is expected.

Identify your potential readers

Think about your readers.

Who exactly are your readers?

- How familiar are your readers likely to be with your subject?
- What are they likely to know and not know about your subject?
- What aspects of your subject might interest them the most?
- What background information will you need to supply?

What exactly do you want to do?

- Do you want to inform readers about a subject?
- Do you want to analyze how something caused something else to happen?
- Do you want to argue for a position on an issue?
- Do you want your readers to take action in solving a problem?

What will your readers expect of you?

- Do they expect you to write in a standard format such as MLA (see Section 23l) or APA (see Section 24f)?
- Will they expect you to include research and expert opinions that run counter to your position?
- Will they expect you to present new knowledge about your subject?
- Will they expect you to help them understand a problem or event?

How will readers respond to your claim?

- If your subject is controversial, what opinions or beliefs are your readers likely to have about it?
- If some readers are likely to disagree with you, how can you convince them?

Assess the project's length and scope

Think about exactly what you are expected to produce.

- What kind of research are you being asked to do? Library research? survey research? field observations?
- How long is the paper you are writing or how extensive is the Web site you are creating?
- How many sources are you expected to include?
- What steps are required by your instructor in advance of the final draft? A topic proposal? a first draft? a working bibliography?

WRITING SMART

Set a schedule

The secret to a successful research project is allowing enough time to do the job well. Fill in the date your final draft is due and work backward to the present. Remember that your schedule is a rough guide that you may need to change as your project evolves. You might accomplish some goals more quickly than you expected, or you may find you need to return to earlier phases and do more work. You can use your schedule to make a research log in which you keep track of your progress.

(Continued on next page)

WRITING SMART *(continued)*

Schedule for research project

Task to complete	Date
Find a topic (16b)	___
Determine what kind of research you need (16c)	___
Draft a working thesis (16d)	___
Start a working bibliography (16e)	___
Find, read, and evaluate your sources (17, 18, 19, 20)	___
Create an annotated bibliography (16e)	___
Summarize and paraphrase your sources (21e)	___
Review your goals and research (22a)	___
Plan your organization (22b)	___
Write the first draft (22c)	___
Decide what material from your sources to include (22d)	___
Review your draft (22e)	___
Revise, edit, and check the formatting of your revised draft (22f)	___
Submit final draft	___

Exercise 16.1 Determine the research strategy required for each of the assignment topics below: analysis/examination, review of scholarship, survey, evaluation, or argument.

1. How does the student body feel about a proposed raise in tuition?
2. What do scientists know about the effectiveness of acupuncture in treating various forms of addiction?

3. Did Sacha Baron Cohen exploit the poverty of the nation of Kazakhstan in his 2006 movie, *Borat: Cultural Learnings of America for Make Benefit Glorious Nation of Kazakhstan?*
4. What has caused hurricanes to increase in intensity in the 21st century?
5. How far should the government go to prevent terrorism?

16b Find a Topic

If you ask meaningful questions, research will be enjoyable. Your courses may give you ideas about questions to ask, or you may simply want to pursue an interest of your own. One good way to begin is by browsing, either in your library or on the Web. Browsing may lead you to topics you hadn't yet considered; it may also show you the breadth of possibilities included in a topic you have already selected.

For example, perhaps you're interested in emerging computer technologies like virtual reality. But as you browse on this topic, you realize that virtual reality is being used not just to create gaming systems, but for many practical applications as well. There are many areas where you might focus your research—for example, on the topic of augmented reality technologies like optical camouflage clothing.

Browse a Web subject directory

Web subject directories, including Yahoo Directory (dir.yahoo.com), are useful when you want to narrow a topic or learn what subcategories a topic might contain. (See Figure 16.1 for the Yahoo directory for augmented reality.) In addition to the Web subject directories, the Library of Congress Virtual Reference Shelf (www.loc.gov/rr/askalib/virtualref.html) may help you identify sites relevant to your topic.

Consult a general encyclopedia

General encyclopedias, which provide basic information about a wide range of topics, are also a good starting point for browsing. Popular edited

Figure 16.1   Yahoo subject directory for augmented reality (dir.yahoo.com/
Computers_and_Internet/Virtual_Reality/Augmented_Reality/)

online encyclopedias include Britannica Online (www.britannica.com) and
Columbia Encyclopedia (www.bartleby.com/65/). Your library's Web site
likely has others.

Consult a specialized encyclopedia

Specialized encyclopedias focus on a single area of knowledge, go into more
depth about a subject, and often include bibliographies. Specialized encyclopedias are available for virtually any area that may interest you, from the
Encyclopedia of Accounting Systems to the *Encyclopedia of Zoroastrianism*. Your
library's Web site will have links to specialized encyclopedias under Research
by Subject or a similar heading.

Look for topics as you read

When you read actively, you ask questions and respond to ideas in the text (see Section 5b). Review what you wrote in the margins or on a computer file about something you read that interested you. You may find a potential topic.

STAYING ON TRACK

Decide if a topic is manageable

It can be tricky to find a balance between what you want to say about a topic and the amount of space you have to say it in. Usually your instructor will suggest a length for your paper, which should help you decide how to limit your topic. If you suspect your topic is becoming unmanageable and your paper may be too long, look for ways to narrow your focus.

Off track   A 5-page paper on European witch hunts

On track   A 5-page paper tracing two or three major causes of the European witch hunts of the fifteenth and sixteenth centuries

Off track   A 10-page paper on accounting fraud

On track   A 10-page paper examining how a new law would help prevent corporate accounting fraud

---

Exercise 16.2   Think of a general topic you might write about for one of your courses (the human genome, the European Union, pragmatism, the National Parks, the Negro Leagues of baseball, or any other). Then, gather lists of subtopics using a Web directory, a general encyclopedia, and a specialized encyclopedia (if applicable). Answer the questions that follow.

1. What subtopics do all of the resources provide for this general topic?
2. Do any of the subtopics lead to other subtopics? Which ones?
3. Which resource produced the most useful list of subtopics for this general topic?
4. Which of the subtopics generated seems the most fruitful to pursue? Why?

16c Determine What Kind of Research You Need

When you first begin your research, you will have to make a few educated guesses about where to look. Ask these questions before you start.

- How much information do you need? The assignment may specify the number of sources you should consult.
- Are particular types of sources required? If so, do you understand why those sources are required?
- How current should the information be? Some assignments require you to use the most up-to-date information you can locate.
- Do you need to consider point of view? Argument assignments sometimes require you to consider opposing viewpoints on an issue.

Secondary research

Most people who do research rely partly or exclusively on the work of others as sources of information. Research based on the work of others is called **secondary research**. In the past this information was contained almost exclusively in collections of print materials housed in libraries, but today enormous amounts of information are available on the Internet and in various recorded media. Chapters 17 through 19 explain in detail how to find and evaluate database, Web, and print sources.

Primary research

Much of the research done at a university creates new information through **primary research**: experiments, data-gathering surveys and interviews, detailed observations, and the examination of historical documents. Although most undergraduates do not do primary research, sometimes you have to gather the needed information yourself. If you are researching a campus issue such as the problem of inadequate parking for students, you may need to conduct interviews, make observations, and take a survey. Or, if you are training in a field where primary research is important, you may be required to conduct research in order to learn research methods. Chapter 20 explains how to plan and conduct three types of field research: interviews (20b), surveys (20c), and observations (20d).

WRITING SMART

Find the right kinds of sources

Type of Source	Type of Information	How to Find Them
Scholarly books (see Chapter 19)	Extensive and in-depth coverage of nearly any subject	Library catalog
Scholarly journals (see Chapter 17)	Reports of new knowledge and research findings by experts	Online library databases

(Continued on next page)

WRITING SMART *(continued)*

Type of Source	Type of Information	How to Find Them
Trade journals (see Chapter 17)	Reports of information pertaining to specific industries, professions, and products	Online library databases
Popular magazines (see Chapter 17)	Reports or summaries of current news, sports, fashion, entertainment subjects	Online library databases
Newspapers (see Chapter 17)	Recent and current information; foreign newspapers are useful for international perspectives	Online library databases
Government publications (see Chapter 18)	Government-collected statistics, studies, and reports; especially good for science and medicine	Library catalog and city, state, and federal government Web sites
Videos, audios, documentaries, maps (see Chapter 18)	Information varies widely	Library catalog, Web, and online library databases

Exercise 16.3 What kind of research (primary, secondary, or both) would each of the following topics require?

1. The programs a local public radio station should add to or remove from its schedule.
2. The history of the color line in American sports.
3. How people applying for unemployment could be better served.
4. The emotional, physical, and social health of children raised by same-sex parents.
5. Japanese *manga* (comic strip narratives) as a working-class art form.

16d Draft a Working Thesis

Often you'll be surprised by the amount of information your initial browsing uncovers. You may be tempted to start finding sources or preparing for your field research, but your research will be more efficient and more productive if you first ask **researchable questions** about your topic and formulate an initial answer. This **working thesis** will be the focus of the remainder of your research and ultimately your research paper.

Ask questions about your topic

When you have a topic that is interesting to you, manageable in scope, and possible to research using sources or doing field research, then your next task is to ask researchable questions.

Explore a definition

- While many (most) people think X is a Y, can X be better thought of as a Z?

  Most people think of deer as harmless animals that are benign to the environment, but their overpopulation devastates young trees in forests, leading to loss of habitat for birds and other species that depend on those trees.

Evaluate a person, activity, or thing

- Can you argue that a person, activity, or thing is either good, better, or best (or bad, worse, or worst) within its class?

  Fender Stratocasters from the 1950s remain the best electric guitars ever made because of their versatility, sound quality, and player-friendly features.

Compare or contrast

- Can you think of items or events or situations that are similar or dissimilar to the one you are writing about?

  Television viewing in Great Britain is not plagued by frequent commercials because television programming is financed through a flat-rate fee rather than through advertising.

Examine why something happened

- Can you argue that while there were obvious causes of Y, Y would not have occurred had it not been for X?

  College students are called irresponsible when they run up high credit card debts that they cannot pay off, but these debts would not have occurred if credit card companies did not aggressively market cards and offer high lines of credit to students with no income.

- Can you argue for an alternative cause rather than the one many people assume?

  The defeat of the Confederate Army at the Battle of Gettysburg in July 1863 is often cited as the turning point in the Civil War, but in fact the South was running out of food, equipment, and soldiers, and it lost its only real chance of winning when Great Britain failed to intervene on its side.

Counter objections to a position

- Can the reverse or opposite of an opposing claim be argued?

  New medications that relieve pain are welcomed by runners and other athletes who put their joints and muscles under extreme stress, but these drugs also mask important signals that our bodies send us, increasing the risk of serious injury.

Argue why something matters

- Can you challenge commonly held attitudes to show why something that many people haven't considered actually matters a great deal?

   Although most people think of wind- and solar-generated electricity as the main alternatives to using coal, oil, and gas, increasing nuclear-generated power and reducing electricity consumption are the only alternatives that have the potential to reduce greenhouse gas emissions.

Turn your answers into a working thesis

1. **Topic**   Reading disorders

   Researchable question   Why do some people learn to read top-to-bottom Chinese characters more easily than left-to-right alphabetic writing?

   Working thesis   The direction of text flow may be an important factor in how an individual learns to read.

2. **Topic**   Historical changes in plant life in the Brazos River valley

   Researchable question   Why does this area of the state feature such dense undergrowth compared to 200 years ago?

   Working thesis   Overgrazing by cattle in the Brazos River valley allowed inedible undergrowth to flourish.

Remember, your research may end up showing you that your working thesis is wrong. That doesn't mean you have to start your project over. Return to your researchable question and think of other possible answers.

Exercise 16.4   Choose one of the subtopics you found for Exercise 16.2. Do some preliminary research on this subject and develop a topic, research question, and working thesis, using the advice given in Section 16d.

16e Start a Working Bibliography

As you begin to collect your sources, make sure you get full bibliographic information for everything you might want to use in your project: articles, books, Web sites, and other materials. Decide which documentation style you will use. If your instructor does not tell you which style is appropriate, ask. (The major documentation styles—MLA, APA, CMS, and CSE—are dealt with in detail in Chapters 23–26.)

Find the necessary bibliographic information

Chapters 17, 18, and 19 give instructions on what information you will need to collect for each kind of source. In general, as you research and develop a working bibliography, the rule of thumb is to write down more information rather than less. A working bibliography is an aid that you may refer to often during your research and writing process, so make it as helpful to you as possible. You can always delete unnecessary information when it comes time to format your citations according to your chosen documentation style (APA, MLA, CMS, or CSE), but it is time-consuming to go back to sources to find missing bibliographic information.

Record bibliographic information

There are many ways to record and organize your sources. You can record each source's bibliographic information on individual notecards; you can print out or photocopy relevant pages from each source; you can email articles to yourself from library databases; and you may be able to use your library's bibliographic software to manage citations (for example, Endnote or RefWorks). Whichever way you choose, always check that you have complete and accurate information for each source.

Sample notecard

A notecard for George Crile's book *Charlie Wilson's War* would look like the one at the top of the next page.

> DS
> 371.2
> C75
> 2003
> Crile, George. *Charlie Wilson's War: The*
>   *Extraordinary Story of the Largest Covert*
>   *Operation in History*. New York, Atlantic
>   Monthly P, 2003.
> Crile uses research and interviews to trace the
>   role of Texas congressman Charlie Wilson in
>   supporting covert U.S. action against the
>   Soviet Union in Afghanistan.

The same information should appear in any computer file you are generating to build your bibliography.

If you make notes in a computer file or on a notecard, be sure to distinguish your summary from material you quote directly. You will also need to identify by page number any quoted material.

> Crile explains how Wilson's support for Nicaraguan
> dictator Anastasio Somoza shaped his future
> approach to foreign policy.
> p. 39 "In retrospect, the Somoza fiasco was a
> turning point for Wilson, and only later would he
> realize its positive impact. He had discovered
> that, even with a wildly unpopular cause, he had
> the power to intimidate the most high-level
> bureaucrats."

Alternatives to copying from a source are cutting and pasting into a file (for online sources) or making photocopies (for a print source). Both methods ensure accuracy in copying sources, but in either case make sure you attach full bibliographic information to the file or photocopy. It's easy to get confused about where the material came from (see Chapter 21 for information on incorporating sources and avoiding plagiarism). In Chapter 23 you'll find detailed instructions on how to find the information you need for MLA documentation. See Chapter 24 for APA, Chapter 25 for CMS, and Chapter 26 for CSE documentation.

WRITING SMART

Determine the relevance of sources

Whether you use print or online sources, a successful search will turn up many more items than you can expect to use in your final product. You have to make a series of decisions as you evaluate your material. Use your research question and working thesis to create guidelines for yourself about importance and relevance.

For example, if your research question asks why the Roman Empire declined rapidly at the end of the fourth and beginning of the fifth centuries AD, you may find older sources as valuable as new ones. Edward Gibbon's three-volume history, *The Decline and Fall of the Roman Empire,* remains an important source even though it was published in 1776 and 1781.

But if you ask a research question about contemporary events—for example, why Chinese businesses are thriving in African nations at a time when the Western presence is dwindling—you will need to find current information. Statistics such as the growth of Chinese trade with Africa to $55 billion in 2006 or the fact that over 750,000 Chinese live and work in Africa describe the trend, but statistics alone do not explain why. An article on the new popularity of Chinese food in some African cities might be interesting, but it is not relevant. Relevant articles will discuss China's willingness to invest in factories and businesses in Africa while Western investment in the continent has decreased.

Use these guidelines to determine the importance and relevance of your sources to your research question.

- Does your research question require you to consult primary or secondary sources?
- Does a source you have found address your question?
- Does a source support or disagree with your working thesis? (You should not throw out work that challenges your views.)
- Does a source add significant information?
- Is the material you have found persuasive?
- What indications of possible bias do you note in the source?

Create an annotated bibliography

A working bibliography is an alphabetized list of sources a writer has used to research a paper on a specific topic. This list includes the author and title of each source, as well as bibliographic information. An **annotated bibliography** builds on this basic citation by adding a brief summary or an evaluation of each source. One type of annotated bibliography adds a comment to the summary of the source's content concerning its relevance to the research topic. For example, a student preparing an annotated bibliography on whether the United States government should offer amnesty to workers who enter the country illegally might comment on how the source could strengthen her argument.

> Massey, Douglas S. *Beyond Smoke and Mirrors: Mexican Immigration in an Era of Economic Integration*. New York: Sage, 2003. Massey provides statistical research on U.S.-Mexico border control efforts and their effects. He provides solid data to back up my claim that stricter border controls have done much harm and not much good.

Annotated bibliographies assist writers in the early stages of research gathering. By taking the time to write a brief summary and evaluation of each source you locate, you create building materials that you can use when it comes time to narrow your focus and start outlining and drafting.

Sample annotated bibliography

Rebecca Ashbury is researching the topic of global hunger. As she locates sources, she is taking careful notes on each source's main points and on how she thinks this information will help her construct her main arguments. Her instructor has asked that she turn in an annotated list of five sources that she thinks will be crucial for her thesis.

Ashbury 1

Rebecca Ashbury

Professor Zapati

English 1302

3 May 2007

Annotated Bibliography

Hawkes, Corinna, and Marie Ruel. "The Linkages

Between Agriculture and Health: An Inter-

sectoral Opportunity to Improve the Health

and Livelihoods of the Poor." Bulletin of the

World Health Organization 84 (2006): 984-90.

This article looks at the links between

agriculture and nutrition, and unlike my

other sources, it talks about the ways local

agriculture can have a negative impact on

health. This source is an important counter-

argument to proposals favoring local farming.

"Hunger Facts: International." Bread.org. 2007.

1 May 2007.

This nonprofit Web site has detailed

information on many aspects of the world

hunger problem, plus it is all referenced and

sometimes even hyperlinked directly

to the sources.

Ashbury 2

Millstone, Erik, and Tim Lang. The Penguin Atlas of
    Food. New York: Penguin, 2003.
        Millstone and Lang map the sources and
        movement of all kinds of food worldwide. This
        book explains the concentration of
        global food sources in the west and the
        causes of famine in underdeveloped
        countries.

Shiva, Vandana. Stolen Harvest: The Hijacking of the
    Global Food Supply. Cambridge: South End
    P, 2000.
        Shiva looks in detail at how local food
        production can be carried out successfully.
        She also talks about how Big Agriculture
        has adverse effects that can be avoided
        with more traditional methods. Her
        argument gives a good picture of what
        one solution to world hunger might
        look like.

United States. Department of Agriculture. Food Security
    Assessment 2005, GFA 17. May 2006.
        1 May 2007 <http://www.ers.usda.gov/
        Publications/GFA17/>.

Ashbury 3

This USDA report gives a detailed snapshot of world hunger in 2005. It also makes predictions about where hunger will worsen in the near future, which will be helpful in arguing for a specific plan to end world hunger.

To see another sample annotated bibliography, visit this page of the E-book at www.mycomplab.com.

Exercise 16.5   Here is a working bibliography on hate crimes. Evaluate these sources as if you would be using them for a research paper dealing with hate crime legislation in Texas. Answer these two questions for each:

How relevant is this source (very, somewhat, slightly, not at all)? Why?

How reliable is this source (very, somewhat, slightly, not at all)?

1. United States. Federal Bureau of Investigation. Hate Crime Statistics, 2005. 2007. 17 Sept. 2007 <http://www.fbi.gov/ucr/hc2005/index.html>. Government site distributing hate crime statistics. The most recent statistics available are for 2005.

2. "Governor of Texas Signs New Hate Crime Bill." Jet 28 May 2001: 16. Short article (262 words) about Governor Perry signing the James Byrd Jr. Hate Crime Act.

3. Spong, John. "The Hate Debate." Texas Monthly April 2001: 64.
   Article dealing specifically with the controversy over
   hate crime legislation in Texas.

4. Levin, Jack, and Jack McDevitt. Hate Crimes: The Rising Tide of
   Bigotry and Bloodshed. Boulder: Westview, 2001.
   Scholarly study of the causes of the recent increase in
   hate crimes in the United States.

5. National Criminal Justice Referral Service. In the Spotlight: Hate
   Crimes. 2001. 17 Sept. 2007 <http://www.ncjrs.org/
   hate_crimes/hate_crimes.html>.
   Site for a nonprofit organization affiliated with the Department of Justice. The site is a clearinghouse for various forms of information about hate crimes (statistics,
   legal information, reports, links to other sites).

Chapter 17

Find and Evaluate Sources in Databases

Library databases combine convenience with the reliability of a library.

17a Know the Strengths of Database Sources

Sources found through library databases have already been filtered for you by trained librarians. They will include some common sources like popular magazines and newspapers, but the greatest value of database sources are the many journals, abstracts, studies, and other writing produced by specialists whose work has been scrutinized and commented upon by other experts. When you read a source from a library database, chances are you are hearing an informed voice in an important debate. Such sources can sometimes be found on the Web, of course, but there they are vastly outnumbered by sources that are not useful for typical academic research purposes.

17b Find Information in Databases

You must first locate databases in order to use them. Usually you can find them on your library's Web site (see Figure 17.1). Sometimes you will find a list of databases. Sometimes you select a subject, and then you are directed to databases. Sometimes you select the name of a database vendor such as EBSCO, FirstSearch, or Ovid. The vendor is the company that provides databases to the library. It can be confusing to determine the name of the database and the name of the vendor, but you will need to understand this distinction in order to document your research. LexisNexis, for example, is both the name of the database and the name of the vendor.

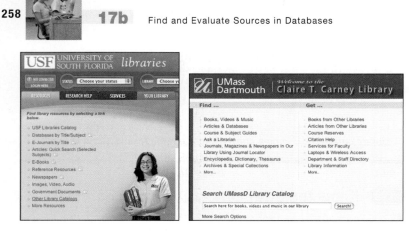

Figure 17.1 You can find a link to your library's database collection on the library's home page.

In contrast, Academic Search Premier and Academic Search Complete are databases offered by EBSCO, and in some libraries you click on EBSCOhost to access either Academic Search Premier or Academic Search Complete.

You can learn how to use databases in your library with the help of a reference librarian. Your library may also have online and printed tutorials on using databases. Once you know how to access the databases you need, you can work from computers in other locations. Many colleges and universities allow you to access databases from your home, apartment, or dormitory room with your student login name and password.

WRITING SMART

Know the advantages of database versus Web sources

	Library database sources	**Web sources**
Speed	✓ Users can find information quickly	✓ Users can find information quickly
Accessibility	✓ Available 24/7	✓ Available 24/7

Organization	✓ Materials are organized for efficient search	User must look in many different places for information
Consistency and quality	✓ Librarians review and select resources	Anyone can claim to be an "expert," regardless of qualifications
Comprehensiveness	✓ Collected sources represent a wide body of knowledge	No guarantee that the full breadth of an issue will be represented
Permanence	✓ Materials remain available for many years	Materials can disappear or change in an instant
Free of overt bias	✓ Sources are required to meet certain standards of documentation and rigor	Sources are often a "soapbox" for organizations or individuals with particular agendas
Free of commercial slant	✓ Sources are largely commercial-free	Sources often try to sell you something

Exercise 17.1 Explore five of the following databases through the Web or your library: Google Scholar (Web), MedlinePlus (Web), Academic OneFile (your library), Academic Search Premier (may be listed as EBSCOhost, your library), FirstSearch, JSTOR, LexisNexis (your library), ProQuest (your library). In which of these would you be able to find

1. full issues of the journal *Art History?*
2. full-text general interest articles about religious trends in Ireland?

3. articles about methods of teaching academic vocabulary to elementary students?
4. a transcript of an ABC News interview with Nancy Pelosi?
5. articles discussing the HPV vaccination controversy?

17c Construct Effective Database Searches

To use databases effectively, make a list of keywords in advance. Keywords might come from your researchable question or your working thesis. You will need keywords to search in a database. For example, a search for voter participation trends among young adults might begin with the terms young adult and voters. You will probably want to focus on the most recent information you can find. It's important to know if voter participation among young adults is increasing or decreasing, for example.

WRITING SMART

Learn the art of effective keyword searches

Keyword searches on databases are similar to using search engines on the Web (see Chapter 18) and in your library's online catalog subject index (see Chapter 19).

As you generate your list of possible keywords, there are two important methods you can use. First, think of keywords that make your search *more specific.* For example, a search for sources related to youth voter participation might focus more specifically on young adults *and*

  voter registration
  party affiliation
  historical participation rates
  voter turnout

You should also think about *more general* ways to describe what you are doing—what synonyms can you think of for your existing terms? Other people may have discussed the topic using those terms instead. Instead of relying on "young adult," you can also try keywords like

> youth
> under 30
> Generation Y
> college students

You can even search using terms that refer to related people, events, or movements that you are familiar with.

> Rock the Vote
> MTV voter registration drive
> Michael Stipe voter registration

Many databases have a thesaurus that can help you find more keywords.

Your next decision is to choose a database to begin your research. To research voter participation among young adults, you'll need to access newspapers, popular journals, and scholarly journals. You'll need to use a general database such as Academic Search Premier or Academic Search Complete, Expanded Academic ASAP, or LexisNexis Academic.

Academic Search Premier and Academic Search Complete

Academic Search Premier and its successor Academic Search Complete are good general databases to research current topics. You can find them either on a list of databases or under EBSCOhost on your library's Web site. If you wish to get only full-text articles, you can check that option (see Figure 17.2). Full-text documents give you the same text you

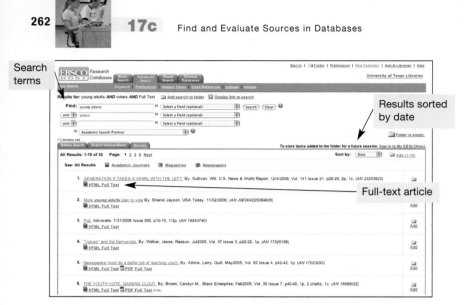

Figure 17.2 Results of a full-text search for *young adult* and *voters* on Academic Search Premier. Articles in PDF format are scans of the printed text with page numbers. Articles in HTML format usually do not contain the page numbers.

would find in print. Sometimes the images are not reproduced in the HTML versions, but the PDF versions show the actual printed copy.

LexisNexis Academic

Another major database for researching current issues is LexisNexis Academic, which offers full-text and summary versions of articles from thousands of newspapers and magazines. It also gives you access to company profiles, financial reports, government documents, and other databases. LexisNexis Academic allows you to limit a search by the kind of publication and by date, or you can sort your results by publication type or date. For example, the results of a search for *young adult voters* are shown in Figure 17.3. Often you can determine by the title of an article if it is relevant to your topic.

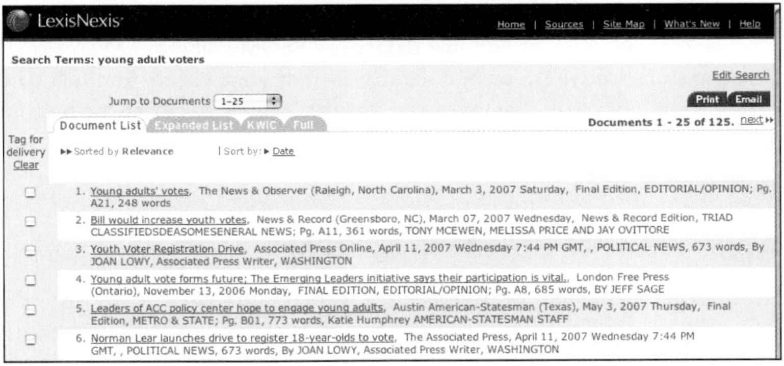

Figure 17.3 Results of a LexisNexis Quick Search for *young adult voters*

WRITING SMART

Adjust searches to improve results

If your search turns up hundreds or thousands of hits,

- Try more specific search terms.
- Combine the words with AND.
- Use a phrase within quotation marks or specify "the exact phrase."
- Specify NOT for terms you are not interested in finding.
- Limit your search by a date range.
- Limit the search by domain name (.edu, .gov).

If your search turns up fewer than twenty-five hits,

- Check your spelling.
- Try broader search terms.
- Use OR instead of AND, or specify "find any of the words."
- Try another index or search engine.

Exercise 17.2 Select two or three keywords related to your topic as search terms. Then find five databases on your library's Web site. If you are unsure where to find databases, visit your library and talk to a reference librarian. Compare the results. Which database turned up more results? Which turned up more scholarly journals (see Section 19c)? Which turned up more popular journals and newspapers?

17d Evaluate Database Sources

Because database sources have been screened and classified by subject, they will be more pertinent to your research than general Web sources. Furthermore, database sources are usually more reliable, but you still have to evaluate them. A very wide range of authors, organizations, and document types are represented among the sources found in databases.

WRITING SMART

Checklist for evaluating database sources

1. **Source.** Who published the article? Scholarly books and articles in scholarly journals are reviewed by experts in the field before they are published.
2. **Author.** Who wrote the article? What are the author's qualifications? What organization does he or she represent?
3. **Timeliness.** How current is the source? If you are researching a fast-developing subject such as changes in breast cancer rates, then currency is very important. Even historical topics are subject to controversy or revision.
4. **Evidence.** Where does the evidence in the article come from—facts, interviews, observations, surveys, or experiments? Is the evidence adequate to support the author's claims?
5. **Biases.** Can you detect particular biases of the author? How do the author's biases affect the interpretation offered?

17e Locate Elements of a Citation in Database Sources

Sometimes you will find exactly what you are looking for by using a database, but then you may become frustrated when you cannot find it again. It's critical to keep track of how you get to a particular article or other material—both to find it again and to cite the item in your list of works cited.

You must document information you get from database sources just as for print sources. The reason you document sources is to allow your readers to view exactly the same sources you looked at. Consequently, when you find a source on a database, you must give the name of the database in addition to what you would include for a print source.

LexisNexis Academic

Figure 17.4 shows an article from the LexisNexis Academic search for *young adult voters*. From the first paragraph you can surmise that this article will be useful to discuss efforts to increase voter turnout among young adults. To cite this article you'll need the information pointed out in Figure 17.4.

MLA style requires you to provide the name of the library where you accessed the database and the URL of the vendor's home page. In this case, you would give the name of the library you used (U of Kentucky Lib.) and the URL of LexisNexis (http://www.lexisnexis.com/). (The vendor's URL can often be found by following links like "home" or "terms and conditions.")

The citation for the article in Figure 17.4 would appear as follows in an MLA-style works-cited list (see Section 23f).

> Shefner, Ruth. "Politics Deserve Teens' Attention." Post-Standard [Syracuse]. 28 Nov. 2006, final ed.: B3. LexisNexis Academic. LexisNexis. U of Kentucky Lib. 28 Apr. 2007 <http://www.lexisnexis.com/>.

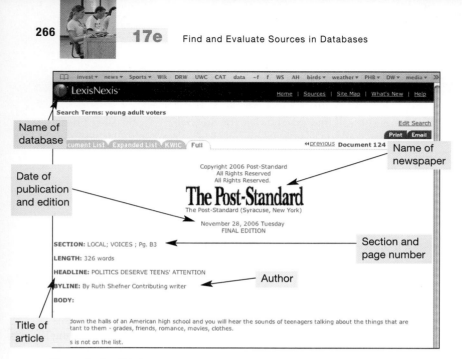

Figure 17.4 Citing a database article from LexisNexis Academic

Author's name	Shefner, Ruth
Title of article	"Politics Deserve Teens' Attention"
Publication information	
Name of periodical	Post-Standard [Syracuse]
Date of publication (and edition for newspapers)	28 Nov. 2006, final ed.
Section and page number	B3
Database information	
Name of database	LexisNexis Academic
Name of vendor	LexisNexis
Name of library	U of Kentucky Lib.
Date you accessed the site	28 Apr. 2007
URL of vendor's home page	http://www.lexisnexis.com/

APA style does not require that you give the name of the library, the date of retrieval, or the URL of the vendor. Here's how the citation for the article in Figure 17.4 would appear in an APA-style references list (see Section 24d).

> Shefner, R. (2006, November 28). Politics deserves teens' attention. *The Post-Standard,* p. B3. Retrieved from LexisNexis Academic database.

Academic Search Complete

Figure 17.5 shows an article from the Academic Search Complete search for *young adult* AND *voters.* The confusing part of citing this example is distinguishing between the database and the vendor. The vendor's name often appears at the top of the screen, making the vendor's name look like the name of the database. In this case, EBSCO is the vendor—the company that sells your library access to Academic Search Complete and many other databases. Often you have to look carefully to find the name of the database.

Here's how the citation for the article in Figure 17.5 would appear in an MLA-style works-cited list.

> Jayson, Sharon. "More Young Adults Plan to Vote." USA Today 2 Nov. 2006, 11D. Academic Search Complete. EBSCO. U of Texas Lib. 29 Apr. 2007 <http://www.epnet.com/>.

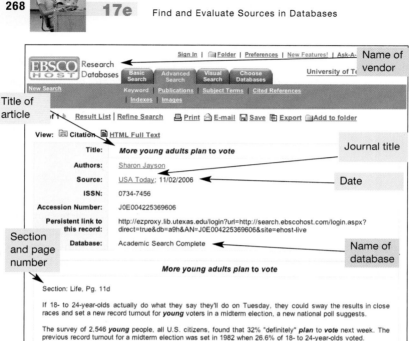

Figure 17.5   Citing a database article from Academic Search Complete

And here's how it would appear in an APA-style references list.

> Jayson, S. (2006, November 2). More young adults plan to vote.
> *USA Today*, p. 11D. Retrieved from Academic Search Complete
> database.

You can find more examples of how to cite database sources in Chapters 23 and 24.

For a tutorial on finding and citing information using databases, visit this page of the E-book at www.mycomplab.com.

Chapter 18

Find and Evaluate Sources on the Web

The Web has many traps for unwary researchers.

18a Know the Strengths and Weaknesses of Web Sources

The World Wide Web puts an astonishing amount and variety of information literally at your fingertips. It may seem like anything a person could ever want to know is available online somewhere.

But the fact is that you often get what you pay for—much of the "free" information on the Web is worthless or incomplete. Much important information (including most books) still isn't available on the Web. Much of what is on the Web is not useful to researchers because Web sites often contain misleading or incorrect information, even deliberately misleading information. Knowing how to find and evaluate Web sources is crucial if you want to get the most out of your online research (see the "Writing Smart" box on database vs. Web sources in section 17a).

18b Find Reliable Web Sources

Because anyone can publish on the Web, there is no overall quality control and there is no system of organization—two strengths we take for granted in libraries. Nevertheless, the Web offers you some resources for current topics that would be difficult or impossible to find in a library. The key to success is knowing where you are most likely to find current and accurate information about the particular question you are researching, and knowing how to access that information.

Search engines

Search engines designed for the Web work in ways similar to library databases and your library's online catalog but with one major difference. Databases typically do some screening of the items they list, but search engines potentially take you to everything on the Web—millions of pages in all. Consequently, you have to work harder to limit searches on the Web or you can be deluged with tens of thousands of items.

Kinds of search engines

A search engine is a set of programs that sort through millions of items at incredible speed. There are four basic kinds of search engines.

1. **Keyword search engines**   (e.g., Ask.com, Google, MSN, Yahoo). Keyword search engines give different results because they assign different weights to the information they find.
2. **Web directories**   (e.g., Britannica.com, Yahoo Directory). Web directories classify Web sites into categories and are the closest equivalent to the cataloging system used by libraries. On most directories professional editors decide how to index a particular Web site. Web directories also allow keyword searches.
3. **Metasearch agents**   (e.g., Dogpile, HotBot, MetaCrawler). Metasearch agents allow you to use several search engines simultaneously. While the concept is sound, metasearch agents are limited by the number of hits they can return and their inability to handle advanced searches.
4. **Specialized search engines**   Specialized search engines include
   - regional search engines (e.g., Baidu for China)
   - medical search engines (e.g., WebMD)
   - legal search engines (e.g., Lexis)
   - job search engines (e.g., Monster.com)
   - property search engines (e.g., Zillow)
   - comparison-shopping search engines (e.g., Froogle)
   - children-oriented search engines (e.g., Yahoo.kids)

No doubt we'll see many more specialized search engines develop.

Online government sources

The federal government has made many of its publications available on the Web. Also, many state governments now publish important documents on the Web. Often the most current and most reliable statistics are government statistics. Among the more important government resources are the following:

- **Bureau of Labor Statistics** (www.bls.gov/). Source for official U.S. government statistics on employment, wages, and consumer prices.
- **Census Bureau** (www.census.gov/). Contains a wealth of links to sites for population, social, economic, and political statistics, including the *Statistical Abstract of the United States* (www.census.gov/compendia/statab/).
- **Centers for Disease Control** (www.cdc.gov/). Authoritative and trustworthy source for health statistics.
- **CIA World Factbook** (www.cia.gov/library/publications/the-world-factbook/). Resource for geographic, economic, demographic and political information on the nations of the world.
- **Library of Congress** (www.loc.gov/). Many of the resources of the largest library in the world are available on the Web.
- **National Institutes of Health** (www.nih.gov/). Extensive health information including MedlinePlus searches.
- **NASA** (www.nasa.gov/). A rich site with much information and images concerning space exploration and scientific discovery.
- **THOMAS** (thomas.loc.gov/). The major source of legislative information, including bills, committee reports, and voting records of individual members of Congress.
- **USA.gov** (www.usa.gov/). The place to start when you are not sure where to look for government information.

Archives

An archive is traditionally a physical place where historical documents, such as manuscripts and letters, are stored. Recently the term has come to mean any collection of documents, typically preserved for educational purposes, and many are now available online.

WRITING SMART

Keep track of Web research

One of the easiest ways to return to Web sites you find useful for your research is to use the **Add to Favorites** or **Add Bookmark** command on your browser. You can arrange the sites you mark in folders and even download them onto a keychain drive or other storage device so you can retrieve the Web sites on other computers.

You can also use the **History** menu on your browser to obtain a list of sites you have visited. Most allow you to go back a few days, so if you remember a site you visited but didn't add to your favorites list, you can probably find it again.

For example, if you want to do a research project on how people living at the time of the American Civil War understood the war, you will need to look at documents written at the time—letters, diaries, newspapers, speeches, and sermons. The Valley of the Shadow project has made available on the Web thousands of documents written at the time of the Civil War from Augusta County, Virginia, and Franklin County, Pennsylvania (http://valley.vcdh.virginia.edu/).

Other extensive archive sites include

- **American Memory** (lcweb2.loc.gov/amhome.html) Library of Congress site offering over 11 million digital items from more than a hundred historical collections.
- **A Chronology of U.S. Historical Documents** (www.law.ou. edu/hist) Sponsored by the University of Oklahoma College of Law, this site contains chronologically ordered primary sources ranging from the *Federalist Papers* to recent presidential addresses.
- **JSTOR: The Scholarly Journal Archive** (www.jstor.org) Electronic archive of the back issues of over a hundred scholarly journals, mainly in the humanities and social sciences fields.

- **University of Michigan Documents Center** (www.lib.umich. edu/govdocs) Huge repository of local, state, federal, foreign, and international government information. Includes an extensive subject directory.

Search Internet forums

The Internet allows you to access other people's opinions on thousands of topics. Millions of people post messages on Web applications called "discussion groups," "message boards," "discussion forums," and various similar names. Messages are displayed either in chronological order or as threaded discussions on the same subject. Much of what you read on these sites is undocumented and highly opinionated, but you can still gather important information about people's attitudes and get tips about other sources, which you can verify later.

Depending on your research topic, it might be useful to check out these forums. For example, if you wanted to examine how the negative reports of SUV safety have affected SUV owners, you might look at the Town Hall discussion forum on www.edmunds.com, a popular car-buying advice site.

These search engines are specialized for Internet forums:

- **Big Boards** (www.big-boards.com). Tracks the most active discussion forums.
- **Google Groups** (groups.google.com). Archives discussion forums dating back to 1981.
- **Yahoo Groups** (groups.yahoo.com). A directory of groups by subject.

Search blogs

Blogs began as online diaries in the 1990s, but they have since moved closer to mainstream media and are now published by politicians, political consultants, news editors, and various experts. At times blogs can be an important source of current news. Following the December 2004 tsunami in Asia and Hurricane Katrina in New Orleans in 2005, bloggers who were

STAYING ON TRACK

Know the limitations of Wikipedia

Wikipedia is a valuable resource for popular culture topics that are not covered in traditional encyclopedias. You can find out SpongeBob SquarePants's original name ("SpongeBoy" but that had already been copyrighted), how many home runs Sammy Sosa hit in 1998 (66; Mark McGwire hit 70 the same year), whether David Lee Roth or Sammy Hagar was the lead singer on Van Halen's "Finish What Ya Started" (Hagar), and in what years the Red Hot Chili Peppers were the headliners at Coachella (2003 and 2007).

Wikipedia, however, is not considered a reliable source of information for a research paper by many instructors and the scholarly community in general. The problem with Wikipedia is that anyone can change an entry, and there are too many anonymous abusers. Wikipedia had to tighten its rules in 2005 after a journalist complained that his biography on Wikipedia claimed for four months that he was suspected in the assassinations of John F. Kennedy and Robert F. Kennedy.

Even with steps to correct some of the worst problems, too much erroneous information remains on Wikipedia. To be on the safe side, treat Wikipedia as you would a blog. It can be a source of ideas, but confirm any facts you want to include in your paper.

James Gandolfini

From Wikipedia, the free encyclopedia

> **This article or section does not adequately cite its references or sources.**
> Please help improve this article by adding citations to reliable sources. (help, get involved!)
> Any material not supported by sources may be challenged and removed at any time. This article has been tagged since **April 2007**.

> 🔒 **Editing of this article by unregistered or newly registered users is currently disabled.** If you are prevented from editing this article, and you wish to make a change, please discuss changes on the talk page, request unprotection, log in, or create an account.

▪ Wikipedia now attaches warning labels to articles that are incomplete, lack sources, or may contain mistakes.

able to maintain power provided eyewitness reports. Specialized search engines allow you to find subjects discussed in blogs.

- **Bloglines** (www.bloglines.com). Searches blogs and Internet forums.
- **Google Blog Search** (blogsearch.google.com). Searches blogs in several languages besides English.
- **IceRocket** (blogs.icerocket.com). Searches blogs and MySpace.
- **Technorati** (www.technorati.com). Searches blogs and other user-generated content.

18c Construct Effective Web Searches

Subject searches require keywords, so it's important to start your search with a good list of keywords. See the Writing Smart box on pages 260–261 for advice on generating keywords.

As you look through your initial search results, keep these facts in mind.

- Results that come up at the top of a list aren't necessarily the best sources when the reasons behind the ranking of results aren't obvious (see Figure 18.1). Search engines rank results in different ways, based on factors like the degree of match with your keywords, the current popularity of a site, and the total traffic at the site hosting the page.
- Commercial search engines often return some results that are actually paid advertisements. These ads will usually be related to your search, but they may not be at all helpful.

You can adjust your search, using the tips in Section 17c to improve your results.

Google   Web   Images   Video^(New!)   News   Maps   more »

ritalin   (Search)   Advanced Search / Preferences

Web   Results 1 - 10 of about **6,070,000** for **ritalin** [definition]. (0.05 seconds)

Ritalin   Sponsored Link
www.DEAdiversion.usdoj.gov   Purchasing Drugs Online May Be A Crime. Learn The Law
Before Buying.

Refine results for **ritalin**:
Drug uses   Interactions   For patients   From medical authorities
Side effects   Warnings/recalls   For health professionals

InfoFacts - Methylphenidate (Ritalin)
Trends in **Ritalin** Use. Monitoring the Future (MTF) Survey * ... MTF 2005 data on annual**
use indicate that 2.4 percent of 8th-graders used **Ritalin**. ...
www.nida.nih.gov/Infofax/ritalin.html - 27k - Cached - Similar pages

Ritalin Information: Side Effects, Cautions, Alternatives, ADD, ADHD
Ritalin Information: Side Effects, Cautions, Adderall, stimulants, ADD, ADHD, Adderall,
stimulants, **Ritalin** class action suit, amphetamines, addiction. ...
www.breggin.com/ritalin.html - 9k - Cached - Similar pages

Methylphenidate - Wikipedia, the free encyclopedia
These generic versions of methylphenidate tend to outsell brand-name "**Ritalin**" four-to-one. In
Belgium the product is sold under the name "Rilatine" for ...
en.wikipedia.org/wiki/Methylphenidate - 89k - Cached - Similar pages

Death from Ritalin: the ADHD Truth
Information for parents about Attention Deficit Hyperactivity Disorder(ADHD)when considering
treatment with **Ritalin**. Includes information on alternative ...
www.ritalindeath.com/ - 83k - Cached - Similar pages

Methylphenidate
Relative bioavailability of the **Ritalin** SR tablet, compared to the **Ritalin** tablet, measured by
the urinary excretion of the methylphenidate major metabolite ...
www.mentalhealth.com/drug/p30-r03.html - 26k - Cached - Similar pages

Ritalin Information from Drugs.com
Ritalin methylphenidate from Drugs.com, includes side effects, interactions, indications.
www.drugs.com/ritalin.html - 53k - Cached - Similar pages

Ritalin
Description Monographs include chemistry, chemical structure, inactive ingredients.
www.rxlist.com/cgi/generic/methphen.htm - 21k - Cached - Similar pages

Ritalin Side Effects?
Managing the side effects of **Ritalin**. Dexedrine and other stimulants.
www.ncpamd.com/Stimulant_Side_Effects.htm - 25k - Cached - Similar pages

Why to Avoid RITALIN®*
RITALIN-SR: methylphenidate hydrochloride USP (stimulant drug) is addictive. Sometimes
called 'speed' or 'uppers.' **Ritalin** produces a short-term mood ...
healthysource.com/ritalin.html - 13k - Cached - Similar pages

Sponsored Links

Kids Need Your Help Now
You need to see to learn
Start the school year off right!
www.2020advocacy.com

ADHD Treatment
Does your child have ADHD? Sign up
& discover how Concerta® can help
www.eversave.com

Ritalin Alternatives
Review safe **ritalin** alternatives.
Learn how natural products help ADD
www.usmedicalresearch.org

Focus in with Focuset
Naturally supports focus and energy
Use code "google10" to save 10% !
www.focuset.com

Drugs For ADHD?
Avoid Dangerous ADHD Drugs!
Proven Alternative 100% Guaranteed.
Synaptol.com

No ADHD Quick Fix Here
Original drug-free program if ready
to work hard to remedy ADHD/ADD.
www.LearningBreakthrough.com

Natural ADD/ADHD Medicine
Dr. Formulated & Clinically-Proven.
No Side-Effects. 1-Year Guarantee!
www.NoMoreADD.com

ADHD Drug Lawyer
ADHD drugs linked to liver damage
and suicide. Learn more here.
www.jimsokolove.com

More Sponsored Links »

Figure 18.1   The first ten hits on Google often give you a dog's stew of results, especially for controversial subjects. A Google search for *Ritalin* retrieves a mix of two factual government sites from the National Institutes of Health, a Wikipedia entry with an attached warning that its information may be unreliable, sites condemning the use of Ritalin, and a commercial site with links to online drug sellers.

WRITING SMART

Know how to use Google and other search engines effectively

Search engines often produce too many hits and are therefore not always useful. If you look only at the first few items, you may miss what is most valuable. The alternative is to refine your search. Most search engines offer you the option of an advanced search, which gives you the opportunity to limit numbers.

The advanced searches on Google and Yahoo! give you the options of using a string of words to search for sites that contain (1) all the words, (2) the exact phrase, (3) any of the words, or (4) that do not contain certain words. They also allow you to specify the language of the site, the date range, the file format, and the domain. For example, if you want to limit a search for multiple sclerosis to government Web sites such as the National Institutes of Health, you can specify the domain as **.gov.**

Google Advanced Search | Advanced Search Tips |

Find results	with **all** of the words	multiple sclerosis		10 results	Google Search
	with the **exact phrase**				
	with **at least one** of the words				
	without the words				
Language	Return pages written in		any language		
File Format	Only return results of the file format		any format		
Date	Return web pages updated in the		anytime		
Numeric Range	Return web pages containing numbers between	and			
Occurrences	Return results where my terms occur		anywhere in the page		
Domain	Only return results from the site or domain		.gov		
			e.g. google.com, .org More info		

■ Limiting a Google search for *multiple sclerosis* to the domain .gov eliminates commercial sites.

18d Find Visual Sources Online

Visual databases and the Web give you access to many visual sources that were difficult to locate just a few years ago. Before you search for visuals, have a clear idea of what you are looking for and why a particular visual would be effective in your research paper.

Visual databases

Several libraries have made large collections of photographs and other visual materials available on their Web sites. The American Memory collection in the Library of Congress offers an important visual record of the history of

the United States (memory.loc.gov). You can do keyword searches for the entire photographic collection or for particular collections to find photographs and popular culture artifacts. For example, if you are researching public attitudes toward women's suffrage at the beginning of the twentieth century, you might want to look at political cartoons. They can be located using the search terms "cartoon women's suffrage" (see Figure 18.2).

Figure 18.2 A 1909 political cartoon comments on women achieving voting rights.

Visual sources on the Web

Millions of images have been published on the Web, and you can find them using search engines that allow you to specify searches for images. For example, if you are writing a research paper on Chinese accounts of the supernova in AD 1054 that created the Crab Nebula, you might want to include a picture of the nebula. In Google, choose **Images** and type *Crab Nebula* in the search box, and you'll find a selection of images of the nebula.

Three major search engines are designed specifically to find images:

- **Google Image Search** (images.google.com/). The most comprehensive image search tool.
- **Picsearch** (www.picsearch.com/). Provides thumbnails of images linked to the source on the Web.
- **Yahoo Search** (images.search.yahoo.com). Has tools to limit results on the Advanced Search similar to Google.

In addition to images, you can find statistical data represented in charts and graphs on government Web sites. Especially useful is the Statistical Abstract of the United States for finding charts and graphs of population statistics (www.census.gov/compendia/statab/). You can also find thousands of maps on the Web. (See www.lib.utexas.edu/maps/map_sites/map_sites.html for a directory of map sites.)

Downloading and inserting images

Images can be downloaded from Web sites by right-clicking on the image and selecting **Save Image As** in Windows (on a Mac, hold the mouse button down and select **Save This Image As**). When you have the image file on your desktop, you can use the **Insert** command on your word processing or Web editing program; in some programs you can simply drag and drop the image into your text. Often you will need to resize the image after you insert it by clicking on the corners and dragging the mouse to make the image bigger or smaller.

Image copyright

Just because images are easy to download from the Web does not mean that every image is available for you to use. Look for the image creator's copyright notice and suggested credit line. This notice will tell you if you can reproduce the image. For example, the Cascades Volcano Observatory makes their images available to all: "The maps, graphics, images, and text found on our website, unless stated otherwise, are within the Public Domain. You may download and use them. Credit back to the USGS/Cascades Volcano Observatory is appreciated." Most images on government Web sites can be reproduced, but check the copyright restrictions. You should acknowledge the source of any image you use.

In many cases you will find a copyright notice that reads, "Any use or retransmission of text or images in this website without written consent of the copyright owner constitutes copyright infringement and is prohibited." You must write to the creator to ask permission to use an image from a site that is not in the public domain, even if you cannot find a copyright notice.

Exercise 18.1   Use all three of the image search engines mentioned in this chapter (Google Images, Picsearch, and Yahoo Search) to research images for either a newsworthy event (Hurricane Katrina), a controversial topic (torture), a controversial person (Britney Spears), or a controversial concept (terrorism, patriotism). Compare the first few rows of images. What differences do you see? What similarities? What might this tell you about the sources for the images? Why do you think the images are presented in this order on each site? How are the sources for the images presented on each site? Can you think of instances when you might choose one image search site over another?

18e Evaluate Web Sources

The Web gives everyone with online access a voice. No one is banned from the Web, no matter what the person's opinions or motives may be. Thus it's no surprise that much of what is on the Web is highly opinionated or false (or both).

Some Web sites are put up as jokes. Other Web sites are deliberately misleading. Many prominent Web sites draw imitators who want to cash in on the commercial visibility. The Web site for the Campaign for Tobacco-Free Kids (www.tobaccofreekids.org), for example, has an imitator (www.smokefreekids.com) that sells software for antismoking education. The .com URL is often a tip-off that a site has a profit motive. Always approach Web sites with an eye toward evaluating content. Seemingly legitimate sites with objective sounding URLs can be anything but objective. For example, you might think that www.martinlutherking.org could be a source for objective information about Martin Luther King, Jr., but in fact it aims to repeal the national holiday that honors King. Only by scrolling to the bottom of the page do you find a link to the sponsor of the site, a white supremacist group.

One method of assessing the objectivity of a Web site is to find out what sites link to it using the **Advanced Search** in Google. One of the options on the Advanced Search allows you to find links to a particular page. Often Web sites that advocate for a cause or particular viewpoint link to similar pages.

WRITING SMART

Checklist for evaluating Web sources

Web sources present special challenges for evaluation. When you find a Web page by using a search engine, you will often go deep into a complex site without having any sense of the context for that page. To evaluate the credibility of the site, you would need to examine the home page, not just the specific page you get to first.

Use these criteria for evaluating Web sites.

1. **Source.** What organization sponsors the Web site? Look for the site's ownership in the Web address. If a Web site doesn't indicate ownership, then you have to make judgments about who put it up and why.

(Continued on next page)

WRITING SMART *(continued)*

2. **Author.** Is the author identified? Often Web sites give no information about their authors other than an email address, if that. In such cases it is difficult or impossible to determine the author's qualifications. Be cautious about information on an anonymous site.

3. **Timeliness.** When was the Web site last updated? Many Web pages do not list when they were last updated; thus you cannot determine their currency.

4. **Evidence.** Are sources of information listed? Any factual information should be supported by indicating where the information came from. Reliable Web sites that offer information will list their sources.

5. **Biases.** Does the Web site offer a balanced point of view? Many Web sites conceal their attitude with a reasonable tone and seemingly factual evidence such as statistics. Citations and bibliographies do not ensure that a site is reliable. Look carefully at the links and sources cited.

6. **Advertising.** Is the Web site trying to sell you something? Many Web sites are infomercials that might contain useful information, but they are no more trustworthy than other forms of advertising.

Exercise 18.2 A recent search on Google with the phrase *hate crimes* resulted in a list of the following URLs. Answer the questions below. Look for clues provided by the URLs before visiting the sites.

(A) www.fbi.gov/ucr/ucr.htm

(B) www.ncjrs.gov/App/Topics/Topic.aspx?Topicid=63

(C) unquietmind.com/hate_crime.html

(D) caag.state.ca.us/civilrights/content/hatecrimes.htm

(E) www.infoplease.com/spot/hatecrimes.html

(F) www.rickross.com/groups/hategroups.html

1. On which of the sites are you most likely to find advertisements?
2. Which site is most likely to feature the opinions of an individual?
3. Which site is most likely to provide you with information on hate crime legislation in California?
4. Which site probably contains out-of-date information?
5. Which site is probably funded by grants from the government or public donations?
6. Which site provides information from the federal government?

18f Locate Elements of a Citation in Web Sources

As you conduct your online research, make sure you collect the necessary bibliographic information for everything you might want to use as a source. Web sources, because of their potential volatility (they can and do disappear overnight), require extra information. Depending on the citation format you use, you'll arrange this information in different ways.

For example, if you are doing research on alternative fuels, you might cite the article shown in Figure 18.3, which discusses current research. Collect the following information about a Web site:

Author's name, if available (if not, use the associated institution or organization)	Pollitt, Michael
Title of article	"Sweet Smell of Success for Biofuel Expert"
Publication information	
Name of site or online journal	Guardian Unlimited
Sponsoring organization if available	N/A
Date of publication (for an article) or of site's last update	26 Apr. 2007
Date you accessed the site	2 May 2007
URL	http://environment.guardian.co.uk/ energy/story/ 0,,2065244,00.html

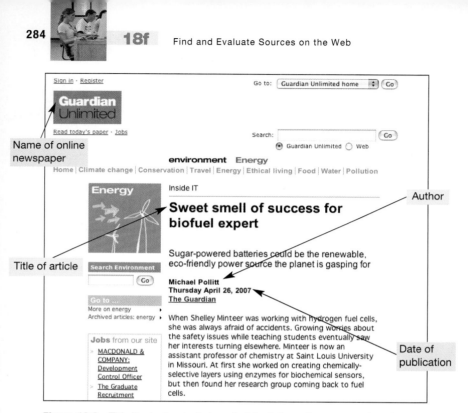

Figure 18.3 This illustration includes all of the information you need to cite a Web source. This information appears in different places on different sites and sometimes is missing.

Source: "Sweet Smell of Success for Biofuel Export" by Michael Pollitt, *The Guardian*, April 26, 2007, from *Guardian Unlimited* website, www.guardian.co.uk. Copyright Guardian News & Media Ltd. 2007. Reprinted with permission.

An MLA works-cited entry for this article would look like this:

Pollitt, Michael. "Sweet Smell of Success for Biofuel Expert." Guardian Unlimited 26 Apr. 2007. 2 May 2007 <http://environment.guardian.co.uk/energy/story/ 0,,2065244,00.html>.

In an APA references list, the citation would look like this:

> Pollitt M. (2007, April 26). Sweet smell of success for biofuel
> expert. *Guardian Unlimited*. Retrieved from
> http://environment.guardian.co.uk/

You can find more examples of how to cite Web sources in MLA style
(Section 23g) and APA style (Section 24d).

Chapter 19

Find and Evaluate Print Sources

Your professional librarian can help you locate sources.

19a Know the Strengths of Print Sources

Print sources may seem "old fashioned" if you grew up with the Internet. You might even feel a little bit intimidated by them. But they are the starting point for much of the research done by experts. In college and beyond, they are indispensable. No matter how current the topic you are researching, you will likely find information in print sources that is simply not available online, but which will help you understand, explain, or question that topic.

The print sources in your library offer a range and depth of expertise you can't find on the Web. They have other advantages as well.

- Books are shelved according to subject, allowing easy browsing.
- Books often have bibliographies, directing you to other research on the subject.
- You can search for books in multiple ways: author, title, subject, or call letter.
- The majority of print sources have been evaluated by scholars, editors, and publishers, who decided whether they merited publication.
- Print sources in your library have also been evaluated by trained librarians, whose job is to get the best materials that will be the most useful research tools.

19b Find Books

Scholarly books offer you in-depth analyses of many subjects. They also contain bibliographies that can help you find other resources on the particular subject. Libraries have well-developed systems for locating books.

Nearly all libraries now shelve books according to the Library of Congress Classification System, which uses a combination of letters and numbers to give you the book's unique location in the library. The Library of Congress call number begins with a letter or letters that represent the broad subject area into which the book is classified.

Locating books in your library

A subject search for "obesity" AND "children" might turn up the following record in your library.

The floors of your library where books are shelved are referred to as the stacks. The call number will enable you to find the item in the stacks. You will need to consult the locations guide for your library, which gives the level and section where an item is shelved.

■ The signs in the stacks guide you to the books you are looking for.

Author, title, and publication information

Brief Record

Author	Ellin, Abby
Title	Teenage waistland: a former fat kid weighs in on living large, losing weight, and how parents can (and can't) help
Published	New York: Public Affairs, 2005.
Description	xli, 257 p.; 25 cm.
Notes	Includes bibliographical references (p. 223-248) and index.
Subjects	Ellin, Abby
	Overweight children--United States--Biography.
	Obesity in children--Treatment.
	Camps for overweight children.
	Child rearing.
ISBN	1586482289
OCLC NUMBER	58422627
Call Number and Library for item location	RJ 399 C6 E387 2005 Main Library Stacks

Subject terms can help you find other books on the same topic

Call number and location

Finding book reviews

You may want to consult book reviews to learn about the content of particular books and whether reviewers find them important. You need to know the author's name, the title of the book, and the date of original publication in order to search for book reviews. Book reviews are included in databases (see Chapter 17). The most comprehensive index dedicated to book reviews is *Book Review Digest* (1905–), which includes excerpts and some full-text reviews.

19c Find Journal Articles

Like books, scholarly journals provide in-depth examinations of subjects. The articles in scholarly journals are written by experts, and they usually contain lists of references that can guide you to other research on a subject.

Examples of scholarly journals include *American Journal of Mathematics; College English; JAMA: Journal of the American Medical Association;* and *Psychological Reports.*

Popular magazines are useful for gaining general information. Articles in popular magazines are usually short with few, if any, source references and are typically written by journalists. Some instructors frown on using popular magazines, but these journals can be valuable for researching current opinion on a particular topic. Examples of popular journals include *Cosmopolitan, GQ, Rolling Stone, Sports Illustrated,* and *Time.*

Searching for articles in scholarly journals and popular magazines works much the same way as searching for books. Indexes for scholarly journals and magazines are available on your library's Web site (see Chapter 17 for in-depth advice on database searching). Databases increasingly contain the full text of articles, allowing you to read and copy the contents onto your computer. Others give you a citation, which you then have to find in your library's resources.

Your library has a list of databases and indexes by subject. If you can't find this list on your library's Web site, ask a reference librarian for help. Follow these steps to find articles:

1. Select an index appropriate to your subject. (For researching multiple sclerosis, you might start with Health Reference Center, MEDLINE, and PsycINFO.)

2. Search the index using relevant subject heading(s). (You could start with multiple sclerosis and then combine MS with other terms to narrow your search.)
3. Print or email to yourself the complete citation to the article(s).
4. Print or email to yourself the full text if it is available.
5. If the full text is not available, check the online library catalog to see if your library has the journal.

Your library will probably have printed handouts or information on the Web that tells you which specialized index to use for a particular subject. Ask a librarian who works at the reference or information desk to help you. Take advantage of your librarian's experience in searching for information.

Exercise 19.1   Decide what kind of periodical (popular or scholarly) you would turn to for information on each of the following topics.

1. Results of a recent study on the long-term physiological effects of Prozac
2. A first-person account of one woman's experiences with depression
3. A review of a self-help book titled *Be Your Own Therapist*
4. An essay arguing that Mary Shelley's *Frankenstein* was heavily influenced by the author's struggles with depression
5. A description of a new reading skills program for students with mild learning disabilities

19d Evaluate Print Sources

Determining the reliability of sources is a problem not only on the Web. Print sources contain their share of biased, inaccurate, and misleading information. But because books are expensive to print and distribute, book publishers generally protect their investment by providing some level of editorial oversight.

WRITING SMART

Checklist for evaluating print sources

Over the years librarians have developed a set of criteria for evaluating print sources.

1. **Source.** Who published the book or article? Scholarly books and articles in scholarly journals are generally more reliable than popular magazines and books, which tend to emphasize what is sensational or entertaining at the expense of accuracy and comprehensiveness.
2. **Author.** Who wrote the book or article? What are the author's qualifications?
3. **Timeliness.** How current is the source? If you are researching a fast-developing subject such as treating ADHD, then currency is very important, but even historical topics are subject to controversy or revision.
4. **Evidence.** Where does the evidence come from—facts, interviews, observations, surveys, or experiments? Is the evidence adequate to support the author's claims?
5. **Biases.** Can you detect particular biases of the author? How do the author's biases affect the interpretation offered?
6. **Advertising.** Is advertising a prominent part of the journal or newspaper? How might the ads affect what gets printed?

Exercise 19.2 Return to the subject you researched and developed a topic and working thesis for in Exercise 16.4. Do some research in the library and find two print sources that seem well suited to your topic. Evaluate their usefulness and credibility using the criteria presented in this section.

19e Locate Elements of a Citation in Print Sources

As you begin to collect your sources, make sure you get full bibliographic information for everything you might want to use in your project. Decide which documentation style you will use. If your instructor does not tell you which style is appropriate, ask. (The major documentation styles—MLA, APA, Chicago, and CSE—are dealt with in detail in Chapters 23–26.)

For books you will need, at minimum, the following information, which can typically be found on the front and back of the title page.

Author's name	Ojito, Mirta
Title of the book	Finding Manaña: A Memoir of a Cuban Exile
Publication information	
Place of publication	New York
Name of publisher	Penguin
Date of publication	2005

Here's how the book would be cited in an MLA-style works-cited list.

> Ojito, Mirta. Finding Manaña: A Memoir of a Cuban Exile. New York: Penguin, 2005.

Here's the APA citation for the same book.

> Ojito, M. (2005). *Finding manaña: A memoir of a Cuban exile.* New York: Penguin.

You will also need the page numbers if you are quoting directly or referring to a specific passage, and the title and author of the individual chapter if your source is an edited book with contributions by several people.

For journals you will need the following.

Author's name	Longaker, Mark Garrett
Title of article	"Idealism and Early-American Rhetoric"
Publication information	
Name of journal	Rhetoric Society Quarterly
Volume number (and issue number if paginated by issue)	36
Date of publication (and edition for newspapers)	2006
Page numbers of the article	281–308

An entry in an MLA-style works-cited list would look like this:

Longaker, Mark Garrett. "Idealism and Early-American Rhetoric." Rhetoric Society Quarterly 36 (2006): 281-308.

And in APA style, like this:

Longaker, M. G. (2006). Idealism and early-American rhetoric. *Rhetoric Society Quarterly, 21,* 281–308.

In general, as you research and develop a working bibliography, the rule of thumb is to write down more information rather than less. You can always delete unnecessary information when it comes time to format your citations according to your chosen documentation style (APA, MLA, CMS, or CSE), but it is time-consuming to go back to sources to find missing bibliographic information.

Plan Field Research

Gather information through interviews, surveys, and observations.

20a Know What You Can Obtain from Field Research

Even though much of the research you do for college courses will be secondary research conducted at a computer or in the library, some topics do call for primary research, requiring you to gather information on your own. Field research of this kind can be especially important for exploring local issues. It is also used extensively in professions that you may be joining after college.

Remember, you're not a huge polling organization with thousands of employees and unlimited resources. The data you collect will necessarily be limited in scope. You won't be able to sample a wide range of people in a survey, and you can't spend years observing wildlife in a distant location. But you can use field research to provide concrete evidence about attitudes, environments, and opinions in your immediate location. If you are making an argument about a local issue, local opinions or conditions are an important part of that argument. Field research that directly measures those opinions or conditions will give your argument much more credibility.

Be aware that the ethics of conducting field research require you to inform people about what you are doing and why you are gathering information. If you are uncertain about the ethics of doing field research, talk to your instructor.

Three types of field research that can usually be conducted in college are **interviews, surveys,** and **observations.**

- **Interviews.** College campuses are a rich source of experts in many areas, including those on the faculty and in the surrounding community. Interviewing experts on your research topic can help build your knowledge base. You can use interviews to discover what the people most affected by a particular issue are thinking and feeling.
- **Surveys.** Extensive surveys that can be projected to large populations, like the ones used in political polls, require the effort of many people. Small surveys, however, often can provide insight on local issues.
- **Observation.** Local observation can be a valuable source of data. For example, if you are researching why a particular office on your campus does not operate efficiently, observe what happens when students enter and how they are handled by the staff.

20b Conduct Interviews

Before you contact anyone to ask for an interview, think carefully about your goals; knowing what you want to find out through your interviews will help you determine whom you need to interview and what questions you need to ask.

- Decide what you want or need to know and who best can provide that for you.
- Schedule each interview in advance, and let the person know why you are conducting the interview.
- Plan your questions in advance. Write down a few questions and have a few more in mind. Listen carefully so you can follow up on key points.
- Come prepared with a notebook and pencil for taking notes and jotting down short quotations. Record the date, time, place, and subject of the interview. A tape recorder sometimes can intimidate the person you are interviewing. If you want to use a tape recorder, ask for permission in advance.

- When you are finished, thank your subject and ask his or her permission to get in touch again if you have additional questions.
- When you are ready to incorporate the interview into a paper or project, think about what you want to highlight from the interview and which direct quotations to include.

Exercise 20.1   Think of a specific person who fits one of the categories below. Then, think of a specific purpose and write 5–10 interview questions to solicit the information you need. For example, you might write questions to ask your U.S. Senator about immigration policy.

- a politically active celebrity
- a potential employer or employee
- the author of a book you read recently
- the director of a film you saw recently
- the CEO of a controversial company
- someone in the service or maintenance industry that you see every day but rarely interact with
- a scientist in a field you know little about

20c Administer Surveys

Use surveys to find out what large groups of people think about a topic (or what they are willing to admit they think). Surveys need to be carefully designed. There are two important components: the survey instrument itself—which is the list of questions you will ask—and the place, time, and way in which the survey will be administered.

- Write a few specific questions. Make sure that they are unambiguous; people will fill out your survey quickly, and if the questions are confusing, the results will be meaningless. To make sure your questions are clear, test them on a few people before you conduct the survey.

- Include one or two open-ended questions, such as "What do you like about X?" "What don't you like about X?" Open-ended questions can be difficult to interpret, but sometimes they turn up information you had not anticipated.
- Decide whom you need to survey and how many people to include. If you want to claim that the results of your survey represent the views of residents of your dormitory, your method of selecting respondents should give all residents an equal chance to be selected. Don't select only your friends.
- Decide how you will contact participants in your survey. If you are going to mail or email your survey, include a statement about what the survey is for and a deadline for returning it. You may need to get permission to conduct a survey in a public place.
- Think about how you will interpret your survey. Multiple-choice formats make data easy to tabulate, but often they miss key information. Open-ended questions will require you to figure out a way to analyze responses.
- When writing about the results, be sure to include information about who participated in the survey, how the participants were selected, and when and how the survey was administered.

An example of a survey on study habits that a student could administer in the student union or library appears on page 299.

STAYING ON TRACK

Keep survey language impartial

Writers of effective surveys must take into account people's subconscious biases, reading, writing, and listening patterns, and other subtle factors. For a small survey, you probably won't be able to control many of the variables important in large polls. Still, you want your survey results to be

(Continued on next page)

STAYING ON TRACK *(continued)*

as accurate and credible as possible. That means you have to let people make up their own minds. So take care that the questions you ask don't actively encourage people to give the answers you may want to hear.

Off track Would you like the library to stop closing at the ridiculous hour of 9 p.m.?

On track Would you like the library to stay open later at night?

Off track Do you want the Student Council spending your student fees on things like chips and soda?

On track Do you think the Student Council should have discretion to use student fees for entertainment costs?

■ Students in a marketing class at MIT conducted a survey at a ski resort in Vermont to test whether simulated trading could predict consumer trends.

Study Habits Survey

Your answers to these questions will help me determine if the library's schedule ought to be altered.

1. How often do you use the library?	• Daily • Three or more times a week • Once a week • Once a month • Once a semester • Never
2. At what time do you most often use the library?	• 8 a.m.-noon • Noon-4:00 p.m. • 4 p.m.-8 p.m. • After 8 p.m.
3. Have you ever had to leave the library because it was closing?	• Yes • No
4. Have you ever had to wait to use the library because it wasn't yet open?	• Yes • No
5. In general, how well do the library's current hours meet your study needs?	• Not at all well • Somewhat well • Quite well • Extremely well
6. What for you would be the ideal hours for the library to be open?	

20d Make Observations

Simply observing what goes on in a place can be a very effective research tool. Your observations can inform a controversy or topic by providing a vivid picture of real-world activity. For example, you might observe a local swimming pool to see what age groups use it the most and at what times of day. Or you might observe a drainage pond to see what forms of wildlife it attracts. Here are some tips on making observations.

- Choose a place where you can observe with the least intrusion. The less people wonder about what you are doing, the better.
- Carry a notebook and write extensive field notes. Get down as much information as you can, and worry about analyzing it later.
- Record the date, exactly where you were, exactly when you arrived and left, and important details like the number of people present.
- Write on one side of your notebook so you can use the facing page to note key observations and analyze your data later.

A sample page of observations of a preschool classroom might look like this.

Observations	Analysis
8 a.m.	
Dimonte and Lilly dropped off. Lilly cries when her mother leaves.	Lilly's teacher says she always cries when her mother drops her off, but not when her father does. Some of the other children also exhibit this pattern.
8:15	
Carissa tries to take the scissors outside onto the playground and is stopped by a teacher.	

Observations	Analysis
8:30	
All the children are playing outside; the noise level has gradually increased.	It's interesting that the morning starts off fairly quietly, then gets louder and louder until snack time. Are the kids getting reacquainted with each other every morning, or just waking up?
8:40	
Carissa has managed to sneak the scissors outside again. The teacher takes them away.	Carissa does this over and over again during the day; does anyone know what she wants to do with the scissors outside?
8:45	
Snack time. Carissa shares her goldfish crackers with Lilly.	The girls are sharing more often now, although they also use "not sharing" as a way to punish others or show their displeasure.

Once you begin taking extensive notes about what you observe, you will collect a great deal of data. At some point you have to interpret the data. When you analyze your observations, think about what constitutes normal and unusual activities for this place. What can you determine about the purposes of these activities?

Chapter 21

Incorporate Sources and Avoid Plagiarism

Build on the research of others by using sources accurately and fairly.

21a Understand the Purposes of Sources

Knowledge building

From a student's point of view, documenting sources can seem like learning Latin—something obscure and complicated that has little use in daily life. You don't see footnotes or lists of works cited in magazines and newspapers, so you may wonder why they are so important in college writing. Careful documentation of sources, however, is essential to developing knowledge and allows scholars and researchers to build on the work of other scholars and researchers. Large bodies of knowledge that have been accumulated over many years allow a scholar to reinterpret the fall of the Roman Empire or a researcher to advance a new hypothesis about how moving plates shape the surface of the earth.

Knowledge is built through ongoing conversations that take place in writing as well as talking. The practice of citing sources provides a disciplinary map, indicating the conversation in which the writer is participating and how that writer responds to what has been said before. Often knowledge building does not move in a straight line but reflects wrong turns and backtracking. Tracing these movements would be extremely difficult if writers did not acknowledge their sources.

Accurate referencing of sources allows you or any reader the opportunity to consult those sources. For example, historians who write about the distant past must rely on different kinds of evidence, including letters, records, public documents, newspaper articles, legal manuscripts and other material from that time; they also take into account the work of contemporary scholars. Other historians working in the same area must be able to find and read these primary sources to assess the accuracy of the interpretation. The system of citing sources requires that summaries and paraphrases be accurate, that words taken from the original be set off in quotation marks, and that full information be provided for locating the source.

Fairness

Another basic issue is fairness. When historians draw on the interpretations of other historians, they should give those historians credit. In this respect citing sources builds community with writers of both the present and the past. When you begin to read the published research in an academic discipline, your awareness of that community takes shape. But the issue of fairness also is part of the much larger issues of intellectual property and scholastic honesty—issues that need to be considered carefully when you use sources.

21b Incorporate Sources

Sources offer evidence for claims

A common saying is that 88% of all statistics (or whatever percentage) are made up on the spot, which of course is an example of the error it describes. Readers expect to see evidence to support claims, and they want to know where the evidence came from. Polls and studies are often funded by those who have an interest in the outcome. In studies of global warming, for example, oil companies, environmental groups, politicians, and government agencies all have a stake in what is reported.

Your obligation is to find the most reliable evidence and to document the sources of that evidence. Let's look at an example of a student writing a research project. George Abukar had a friend who was a victim of identity theft when her driver's license was stolen. The thief then applied for a credit card in his friend's name and made thousands of dollars of fraudulent purchases. None of the people who could have stopped the thief did so: the credit card company did not bother to verify the friend's identity, and the three major credit card reporting agencies did not remove the information about unpaid bills from her file, leaving her with a bad credit rating. Abukar's thesis proposes that the United States Congress pass federal legislation making credit-reporting agencies liable for damages when their actions or negligence leads to loss from identity theft.

Sources can help you build a case for why your claim matters. To argue for his thesis, Abukar had to establish first that the problem affected many more people besides his friend. He cites a report from the General Accounting Office that estimates the cost of identity theft.

Readers expect evidence to support claims and reasons.
> In a report to Congress, the General Accounting Office of the United States estimated that check-related fraud losses in 1999 were $2.2 billion (40). That was double the figure for 1997, so it is reasonable to assume costs are much higher today. Fraud losses from credit card fraud for Mastercard and Visa were over $1 billion in 2000 (43).

Sources provide points of departure

All good research writing responds to sources. Every significant issue has an extensive history of discussion with various points of view. Your task as a researcher is to enter this discussion by "talking" to your sources. Just as you would in a conversation with several people who hold different views, you may disagree with some people, agree with some, and agree with others only up to a point and then disagree.

You can sort your sources into three categories: "No" for those you disagree with, "Yes" for those you agree with, and "Yes, but" for those you agree with up to a point. George Abukar uses all three strategies to position his sources in relation to his argument.

No—Disagreeing with a source

> A common way of thinking about this issue is _____, but this view is mistaken because _____.

George Abukar argues that there are inadequate safeguards against identity theft because credit card companies and reporting agencies have no financial interest in preventing identity theft and in some ways even profit from it. He needed to establish that a common view is that individuals are responsible for identity theft. He found a Federal Trade Commission Web site that puts forth this view and included a quotation from the site in his paper.

Abukar quotes common sense advice from the FTC Web site.

> Mostly, consumers are being told to protect themselves. The Federal Trade Commission has an entire Web site devoted to telling consumers how to minimize their risk of identity theft. Some of their advice is obvious, like "Keep your purse or wallet in a safe place at work." Some tips are more obscure: "Treat your mail and trash carefully." Some assume that people have a lot more time, patience, and knowledge than they really do:
>
> > Ask about information security procedures in your workplace or at businesses, doctor's offices or other institutions that collect your personally identifying information. Find out who has access to your personal information and verify that it is handled securely. Ask about the disposal procedures for those records as well. Find out if your information will be shared with anyone else. If so, ask how your information can be kept confidential. (Minimizing)

Abukar points out how impractical the FTC advice is.

> However, not many people are prepared to spend twenty minutes grilling the checkout person at Old Navy when she asks for their phone number.

Yes—Agreeing with a source with an additional point

> I agree with _____ because my experience confirms that _____.

Sources should not make your argument for you. Indicate exactly how they support your position by making an additional point.

The credit reporting agencies are not content with letting consumers and banks foot the bill for their sloppy handling of our digital identities. They want to make more money off the insecurity they have created. Kevin Drum reports in Washington Monthly:

The source describes how credit card reporting agencies make money off the fear of identity theft, supporting Abukar's claim.

> For their part, the major credit-reporting bureaus—Experian, Equifax, and TransUnion—don't seem to care much about the accuracy of their credit reports. In fact, they actually have a positive incentive to let ID theft flourish. Like mobsters offering "protection" to frightened store owners, credit-reporting agencies have recently begun taking advantage of the identity-theft boom to offer information age protection to frightened consumers. For $9.95 a month, Equifax offers "Credit Watch Gold," a service that alerts you whenever changes are made to your credit report. Experian and TransUnion offer similar services. In effect, customers are being asked to pay credit agencies to protect them from the negligence of those same agencies.

Abukar makes an additional point that builds on his source.

Unlike consumers, who usually at least try to act responsibly to protect their credit rating, credit-reporting agencies avoid responsibility for, and profit from, identity theft. Therefore, the most important step to take in reducing identity theft is to implement legislation that holds credit reporting agencies responsible for the damage their actions or inactions cause consumers.

Yes, but—Agreeing and disagreeing simultaneously with a source

I agree with _____ up to a point, but I disagree with the conclusion _____ because _____.

Incorporating sources is not a matter of simply agreeing or disagreeing with sources. Often you will agree with a source up to a point, but you will object to the conclusions. Or you may agree with the conclusions but not with the reasoning. In other words, you may find someone's views are correct but not for the reasons put forth.

Abukar used a source with which he was in basic agreement, but he found one part of the argument in the source much stronger than the other part.

Abukar summarizes the position of his source.

In his book The Digital Person: Technology and Privacy in the Information Age, Daniel J. Solove proposes that the way to reduce identity theft is to change the structure, or "architecture," of the systems we use to collect and store personal information. He recommends giving individuals more control over their personal information, and requiring the companies that use that information to inform people whenever something unusual happens to their files. While Solove's plan sounds good, he

Abukar goes on to argue that the source misses how the solution proposed might be implemented.

neglects the key for implementing the solution. Solove says that any new system should be "premised on the notion that the collection and use of personal information is an activity that carries duties and responsibilities" (121). This statement is an indirect way of saying, "Companies that handle personal information ought to be held liable for damages caused by identity theft." I would argue that if you make companies responsible to consumers by making them liable (the second half of Solove's plan), then they will automatically give consumers more control over their own information (the first half).

WRITING SMART

Determine the relationship of each source to your thesis

Gather the list of sources you have found in your research. You may have assembled these sources in a working bibliography or an annotated bibliography. Examine each source in relation to your working thesis. Note beside each source how it relates to your argument, using the "no," "yes," and "yes, but" strategy.

(Continued on next page)

> ## WRITING SMART *(continued)*
>
> - Does the source provide evidence for your claim or your reasons?
> - Do you disagree with the source and can you use it as a jumping off point for your argument?
> - Do you agree with the source and find you can expand on it?
> - Do you agree with the source up to a point and can you use it to show how your argument is different and perhaps better?

21c Avoid Plagiarism

What is Plagiarism?

Plagiarism means claiming credit for someone else's intellectual work no matter whether it's to make money or get a better grade. Intentional or not, plagiarism has dire consequences. Reputable authors have gotten into trouble through carelessness by taking notes from published sources without acknowledging those sources. A number of famous people have had their reputations tarnished by accusations of plagiarism, and several prominent journalists have lost their jobs and careers for copying the work of other writers and passing it off as their own.

The use of the Web has increased instances of plagiarism in college. Some students view the Internet as a big free buffet where they can grab anything, paste it in a file, and submit it as their own work. Cut-and-paste plagiarism is easy to do, but instructors quickly recognize when a student's writing style changes in mid-essay. It's also easy for instructors to use the Web to trace sources stolen off the Web.

You know that copying someone else's paper word for word or taking an article off the Web and turning it in as yours is plagiarism. That's plain stealing, and people who take that risk should know that the punishment can be severe. But if plagiarism also means using the ideas, melodies, or images of someone else without acknowledging them, then the concept is much broader and more difficult to define. If you think about it, you might wonder whether it is even possible to avoid plagiarizing in the strictest sense when you write. How many phrases and ideas are truly original? And how can you know where every idea comes from?

WRITING IN THE WORLD

The consequences of plagiarism

Most colleges and universities consider plagiarism a serious form of cheating that deserves severe penalties, including failure of a course for first-time offenders and expulsion for those who are caught cheating more than once. Colleges have to take a strong stance against plagiarism. They attempt to make the playing field level for all students; if some get by without doing the required work, it affects every other student. Professional schools and employers look down on graduates of schools that have a reputation for tolerating scholastic dishonesty. Students who blatantly plagiarize often do not realize how much harm they might do to themselves down the road. Employers do not want to hire students who have been caught cheating.

Businesses also have to take a hard line on plagiarism. In many professions, the product is a written document. If that document turns out to be plagiarized, the reputation of the entire company is tarnished.

What you don't have to document

Fortunately, common sense governs issues of academic plagiarism. The standards of documentation are not so strict that the source of every fact you cite must be acknowledged. Suppose you are writing about the causes of maritime disasters and you want to know how many people drowned when the *Titanic* sank on the early morning of April 15, 1912. You check the Britannica Online Web site and find that the death toll was around 1,500. Since this fact is available in many reference works, you would not need to cite Britannica Online as the source.

Plagiarism in college writing

If you find any of the following problems in your academic writing, you may be guilty of plagiarizing someone else's work. Because plagiarism is usually inadvertent, it is especially important that you understand what constitutes using sources responsibly. Avoid these pitfalls.

• **Missing attribution.** Make sure the author of a quotation has been identified. Include a lead-in or signal phrase that provides attribution to the source, and identify the author in the citation.

• **Missing quotation marks.** You must put quotation marks around material quoted directly from a source.

• **Inadequate citation.** Give a page number to show where in the source the quotation, paraphrase, or summary is drawn from.

• **Paraphrase relies too heavily on the source.** Be careful that the wording or sentence structure of a paraphrase does not follow the source too closely.

• **Distortion of meaning.** Don't allow your paraphrase or summary to distort the meaning of the source, and don't take a quotation out of context, resulting in a change of meaning.

• **Missing works-cited entry.** The Works Cited page must include all the works cited in the paper.

• **Inadequate citation of images.** A figure or photo must appear with a label, number, caption, or citation to indicate the source of the image. If material includes a summary of data from a visual source, an attribution or citation must be given for the graphic being summarized.

But let's say you want to challenge the version of the sinking offered in the 1998 movie *Titanic,* which repeats the usual explanation that the

Titanic sideswiped an iceberg, ripping a long gash along the hull that caused the ship to go down. Suppose that, in your reading, you discover that a September 1985 exploration of the wreck by an unmanned submersible did not find the long gash previously thought to have sunk the ship. The evidence instead suggested that the force of the collision with the iceberg broke the seams in the hull, allowing water to flood the ship's watertight compartments. You would need to cite the source of your information for this alternative version of the *Titanic*'s demise.

What you do have to document

For facts that are not easily found in general reference works, statements of opinion, and arguable claims, you should cite the source. You should also cite the sources of statistics, research findings, examples, graphs, charts, and illustrations. As a reader you should be skeptical about statistics and research findings when the source is not mentioned. When a writer does not cite the sources of statistics and research findings, there is no way of knowing how reliable the sources are or whether the writer is making them up. From the writer's perspective, careful citing of sources lends credibility. If you take your statistics from a generally trusted source, your readers are more likely to trust your conclusions. When in doubt, always document the source.

Be careful when taking notes and copying material online

The best way to avoid unintentional plagiarism is to take care to distinguish source words from your own words. Don't mix words from the source with your own words. If you copy anything from a source when taking notes, you will need to place those words in quotation marks and note the page number(s) where those words appear (see Section 16e). You should also write down all the information you need for a list of works cited or a list of references (see Part 6).

If you copy words from an online source, you need to take special care to note the source. You could easily copy online material and later not be able to find where it came from. Instead of cutting and pasting words straight from an online document, print out the entire source so you can refer to it later. Having photocopies of printed sources also allows you to double-check later that you haven't used words from the source by mistake and that any words you quote are accurate.

Exercise 21.1   Decide which of the following are instances of plagiarism or scholastic dishonesty and which are not.

1. You cut and paste information from a Web site into your notes for an economics paper that is due tomorrow. Unfortunately, you lose track of what information you quoted directly, what you paraphrased, and what you summarized. You do your best to sort out which ideas are yours and which came from the Web site, but you don't have time to check everything before your paper is due.

2. A paper for a required government course is due on the same day that a really important paper for a core class in your major is due. You borrow a paper from your roommate, but you rewrite it in your own words and you hand it in.

3. A passage in your English paper is a paraphrase of a lecture your history instructor gave. Your English instructor did not require you to use any outside sources, so you do not create a works-cited sheet for the paper.

4. You are in a real crunch for time, so your friend, an English major, edits your paper. She rewrites a few awkward sentences and corrects a few of your facts. You type in her changes before turning in the paper.

5. You scan a picture from the cover of a CD to put on your personal Web site. Everyone knows where the picture came from, so you don't cite the source.

Exercise 21.2   Which of the following pieces of information require a citation and which do not?

1. Elvis Presley was born in Tupelo, Mississippi, on January 8, 1935.
2. Peter Guralnick wrote *Last Train to Memphis*, which chronicles Elvis's youth in Tupelo, Mississippi, and Memphis, Tennessee.
3. In this book, Guralnick tries to present as complete a picture as possible of Elvis as a teenager, and not as the superstar he was to become.
4. Frank Sinatra thought that Elvis's music inspired destructive behavior in young people.
5. Critics denounce Elvis for stealing the style, rhythms, and, in some cases, the actual lyrics of black music, but many black artists, like Jackie Wilson, felt that this was not the case.
6. Graceland, Elvis Presley's former home, is in Memphis.
7. On December 31, 1956, the *Wall Street Journal* reported that sales of Elvis Presley memorabilia had grossed over $22 million in the past few months.
8. Elvis's mother, Gladys, died on August 14, 1958.
9. Friends and family say Elvis and his mother shared a special bond that made others, including Elvis's father, Vernon, feel like outsiders.
10. Elvis Presley died at Graceland on August 16, 1977.

21d Quote Sources Without Plagiarizing

Most people who get into plagiarism trouble lift words from a source and use them without quotation marks. Where the line is drawn is easiest to illustrate with an example. In the following passage, Nell Irvin Painter discusses the African Diaspora, the dispersion of African people from their native lands in Africa. She describes the cultural differences that distinguish contemporary African Americans from their ancestors.

■ Nell Irvin Painter

The three centuries separating African Americans from their immigrant ancestors profoundly influenced their identity. A strong case can be made for seeing African Americans as a new, Creole people, that is, as a people born and forged in the Western Hemisphere. Language provides the most obvious indicator: people of African descent in the Diaspora do not speak languages of Africa as their mother tongue. For the most part, they speak Portuguese, Spanish, English, and French as a mother tongue, although millions speak Creole languages (such as Haitian Creole and South Carolinian Gullah) that combine African grammars and English vocabulary.

As the potent engine of culture, language influences thought, psychology, and education. Language boundaries now divide descendants whose African ancestors may have been family and close neighbors speaking the same language. One descendant in Nashville, Tennessee, may not understand the Portuguese of her distant cousin now living in Bahia, Brazil. Today, with immigrants from Africa forming an increasing proportion of people calling themselves African American, the woman in Nashville might herself be an African immigrant and speak an African language that neither her black neighbors in Tennessee nor her distant cousin in Brazil can understand. Religion, another crucial aspect of culture, distinguishes the different peoples of the African Diaspora. Millions of Africans are Muslims, for instance, while most African Americans see themselves as Christian. They would hardly agree to place themselves under the Sharia, the legal system inspired by the Koran, which prevails in Northern Nigeria.

—Nell Irvin Painter. *Creating Black Americans: African-American History and Its Meanings, 1619 to the Present.* New York: Oxford UP, 2006. 5.

If you were writing a paper or creating a Web site that concerned African American cultural heritage, you might want to refer to Painter's arguments about cultural differences resulting from different languages. Your options are to paraphrase the source or to quote it directly.

If you quote directly, you must place quotation marks around all words you take from the original:

> One scholar notes the numerous linguistic differences among Americans of African descent: "[P]eople of African descent in the Diaspora do not speak languages of Africa as their mother tongue. For the most part, they speak Portuguese, Spanish, English, and French as a mother tongue" (Painter 5).

Notice that the quotation is introduced and not just dropped in. This example follows Modern Language Association (MLA) style, where the citation goes outside the quotation marks but before the final period. In MLA style, source references are made according to the author's last name, which refers you to the full citation in the works-cited list at the end. Following the author's name is the page number where the quotation can be located. (Notice also that there is no comma after the name.) If you want to cite a newspaper article without a byline or another anonymous source, you use the first important word or two of the title to make the reference. This system allows you to find the reference easily in the list of works cited, since the list is arranged alphabetically by author and title.

If the author's name appears in the sentence, cite only the page number, in parentheses:

> According to Nell Irvin Painter, "people of African descent in the Diaspora do not speak languages of Africa as their mother tongue" (5).

If you want to quote material that is already quoted in your source, use single quotes for that material:

> Nell Irvin Painter traces a long history of African American interest in Egyptian culture: "Hoping that past greatness portended future glory, black Americans often recited a verse from the Bible that inspired this hope: 'Princes shall come out of Egypt; Ethiopia shall soon stretch forth her hands unto God' (Psalms 63:31)" (7).

Exercise 21.3 Using the following excerpts from two sources and an essay that incorporates quotations from both, rewrite the essay to correct punctuation and citation errors.

Source 1: Chris Brice, "Literary Illusion?" *The Advertiser.* 9 Feb. 2002: M20. [copied directly from the source]

American author Armistead Maupin's latest novel [*The Night Listener*] is tangled up in the divide between truth and fiction, and not even he can be sure which is which. It centers around the bizarre story of Anthony Godby Johnson, the boy author of a best-selling book who was once described as "the bravest teen in America."

. . . Maupin is just one of many thousands of people who have been moved by Tony Johnson's 1993 memoir, *A Rock and a Hard Place*, published when Johnson was just 15 years old, and telling of a life of horrific physical and sexual abuse.

. . . Maupin now says *The Night Listener* was not entirely "a fanciful concoction on the part of a novelist with far too vivid imagination," but was drawn from his own experiences of the "real-life Hitchcockian mystery of Tony Johnson."

Source 2: Tad Friend, "Virtual Love." *The New Yorker.* 26 Nov. 2001. [copied directly from the source]

Tony has become a symbol of modern victimhood, his body torn apart by the most appalling end-of-the millennium traumas—child abuse and AIDS. (88)

. . . When I visited Maupin again recently, I noticed that he had removed Tony's picture from his living room. But he told me, "Tony's still more real to me than many people who demonstrably do exist. I wrote the ending of the book the way I'd like it to be in life, because I'd have great trouble killing that child in my head." (99)

Essay

Tony Johnson, child survivor of abuse and AIDS as well as the author of the best-selling book *A Rock and a Hard Place*, has a problem. Many of his celebrity friends don't believe he exists. One of the most outspoken of these friends is Armistead Maupin, who is one of many thousands of people who have been moved by Tony Johnson's 1993 memoir. But why have so many people been taken in by this boy author? According to Friend, "Tony has become a symbol of modern victimhood, his body torn apart by the most appalling end-of-the millennium traumas—child abuse and AIDS." No one, however, has ever met Tony Johnson.

After a series of events that caused him to doubt Tony's existence, Maupin wrote the novel, *The Night Listener*, in which the lives of characters Donna and Pete bear a striking resemblance to that of Tony and his adopted mother, Vicki Johnson. The novel was published in 2000 and was met with instant controversy. Maupin, however, afraid that Tony still might actually exist, insisted that the story was "a fanciful concoction on the part of a novelist with far too vivid imagination." ("Literary" 20) Later, he admitted that the book was inspired by his own experiences as a character in the real-life Hitchcockian mystery of Tony Johnson (Friend 20). However, the novel and its controversial story line do not signify that Maupin bears Tony, whoever or whatever he may be, any ill will. Quite the contrary:

> When I visited Maupin again recently, I noticed that he had removed Tony's picture from his living room. But he told me, "Tony's still more real to me than many people who demonstrably do exist. I wrote the ending of the book the way I'd like it to be in life, because I'd have great trouble killing that child in my head.

To this day, no one really knows if Tony Johnson ever existed.

21e Summarize and Paraphrase Sources Without Plagiarizing

Summarize

When you summarize, you cite your source but, instead of quoting it directly, you state the major ideas of the entire source, or part of a source, in a paragraph or perhaps even a sentence. The key is to put the summary in your own words.

Plagiarized

> Nell Irvin Painter argues in *Creating Black Americans* that we should consider **African Americans as a new Creole people, born and forged in the Western Hemisphere.**

Most of the words are lifted directly from the original.

Acceptable summary

> Nell Irvin Painter argues in *Creating Black Americans* that African Americans' experiences in the Western Hemisphere made them so culturally different from their ancestors that we can think of them as a separate people.

Paraphrase

When you paraphrase, you represent the idea of the source in your own words at about the same length as the original. You still need to include the reference to the source of the idea. The following example illustrates what is not an acceptable paraphrase.

Plagiarized

> Nell Irvin Painter contends that cultural factors like language and religion divide African Americans from their ancestors. **People of African descent** no longer speak the **languages of Africa** as their first language. Since language is a **potent engine of culture,** the **thought, psychology, and education** of contemporary African Americans is radically different from that of their ancestors. **Religion, another crucial aspect of culture,** also divides African Americans from Africans. **Sharia, the legal system inspired by the Koran,** may **prevail in Northern Nigeria,** but it is foreign to Christian African Americans (5).

Even though the source is listed, this paraphrase is unacceptable. Too many of the words in the original are used directly here, including much or all of entire phrases. When a string of words is lifted from a source and inserted without quotation marks, the passage is plagiarized. Changing a few words in a sentence is not a paraphrase. Compare these two sentences:

Source

People of African descent in the Diaspora do not speak languages of Africa as their mother tongue.

Unacceptable paraphrase

People of African descent no longer **speak the languages of Africa** as their first language.

The paraphrase keeps the structure of the original sentence and substitutes a few words. It is much too similar to the original.

A true paraphrase represents an entire rewriting of the idea from the source.

Acceptable paraphrase

Nell Irvin Painter contends that cultural factors like language and religion divide African Americans from their ancestors. Black Americans speak a wide variety of languages, but usually these are not African. Painter notes how important language is in shaping our cultural identity; it dictates in large part how we think and feel. Linguistic differences create significant boundaries between peoples. Religion, like language, is a fundamental part of how many people identify themselves. Many African Americans identify as Christians, and they would probably see sharp contrasts between their faith and the Muslim faith common in much of Africa (5).

Even though there are a few words from the original in this paraphrase, such as *identity* and *language*, these sentences are original in structure and wording while accurately conveying the meaning of the source.

Exercise 21.4 Two sources dealing with Abraham Lincoln and his association in American pop culture with the log cabin are excerpted here. Decide whether the numbered paraphrases and summaries of the two sources are correct. If not, rewrite to eliminate problems.

Source 1: "Lincoln, Abraham," *Encarta*. 2007. Microsoft. 31 Oct. 2007 <http://encarta.msn.com/>.

In the winter of 1816 the Lincolns took their meager possessions, ferried across the Ohio River, and settled near Pigeon Creek, close to what is now Gentryville, Indiana. Because it was winter, Thomas Lincoln immediately built a crude, three-sided shelter that served as home until he could build a log cabin. A fire at the open end of the shelter kept the family warm. At this time southern Indiana was a heavily forested wilderness. Lincoln described it as a "wild region, with many bears and other wild animals in the woods."

Source 2: James W. Loewen, *Lies My Teacher Told Me: Everything Your American History Textbook Got Wrong*. New York: New P, 1995. 178.

The strange career of the log cabin in which Abraham Lincoln was born symbolizes in a way what textbooks have done to Lincoln. The actual cabin fell into disrepair probably before Lincoln became president. According to research by D. T. Pitcaithley, the new cabin, a hoax built in 1894, was leased to two amusement park owners, went to Coney Island, where it got commingled with the birthplace cabin of Jefferson Davis (another hoax), and was finally shrunk to fit inside a marble pantheon in Kentucky, where, reassembled, it still stands. The cabin also became a children's toy: Lincoln Logs, invented by Frank Lloyd Wright's son John in 1920, came with instructions on how to build both Lincoln's log cabin and Uncle Tom's cabin! The cabin still makes its archetypal appearance in our textbooks, signifying the rags-to-riches legend of Abraham Lincoln's upward mobility. No wonder one college student could only say of him, in a much-repeated blooper, "He was born in a log cabin which he built with his own hands."

1. The description that *Encarta* gives of Lincoln's childhood—the hard work, the honest poverty, and the succession of hand-hewn log cabins—is the story we are taught as schoolchildren.

2. James Loewen, in his book *Lies My Teacher Told Me*, focuses instead on the career of the log cabin Lincoln grew up in. He argues that the cabin's story symbolizes in some way what the textbooks students read have done to Lincoln (178).

3. It is interesting how the depiction of Lincoln's life in *Encarta* is so focused on the domestic details. We can almost see the Lincoln family, huddled in the corner of their three-sided shelter, a small fire burning, as they wait for Father to build yet another log cabin.

4. According to Loewen, however, Lincoln's cabin has led a comparatively unhealthy life. In his research he found that a new "Lincoln" cabin, a hoax built in 1894, was leased to two amusement park owners, went to Coney Island, where it got commingled with the birthplace cabin of Jefferson Davis. The cabin, shrunk down to fit inside a marble pantheon, now stands in Kentucky (178). Has the legend of Lincoln suffered the same fate?

Chapter 22

Write and Revise the Research Project

Thorough research gives you a wealth of ideas to communicate.

22a Revisit Your Research

Before you begin writing your paper, review the assignment and your goals (see Chapter 16). Your review of the assignment will remind you of your purpose (analysis, review, survey, evaluation, argument), your potential readers, your stance on your subject, and the length and scope you should aim for.

Take stock of your research

Gather the source material and any field research you have generated (see Chapters 17, 18, 19, and 20). Often additional questions come up in the course of your research. Group your notes by subject. Ask yourself

- Which sources provide evidence that supports your thesis or main points?
- Which sources turned out not to be relevant?
- Which ideas or points lack adequate sources? You may need to do additional research before starting to write your paper.

Revise your working thesis

Often you will find that one aspect of your topic turned out to be more interesting and produced more information. If you have ample material, narrowing your subject is a benefit. At this stage in the writing process, your working thesis may be rough and may change as you write your draft, but having a working thesis will help keep your paper focused.

Revise or write out your working thesis.

> I plan to (analyze, review, survey, evaluate, argue) that _____.
> This subject matters to my readers because _____.

Exercise 22.1   Go back to the working thesis you developed in Exercise 16.4. After doing research on this topic, you likely changed your thesis, and perhaps even your topic and research questions. Revise your topic, research questions, and thesis to reflect these changes.

22b Plan Your Organization

After you have drafted a thesis, look back over your notes and determine how to group the ideas you researched. Decide what your major points will be, and how those points support your thesis. Group your research findings so that they match up with your major points.

Now it is time to create a working outline. Always include your thesis at the top of your outline as a guiding light. Some writers create formal outlines with roman numerals and the like; others compose the headings for the paragraphs of their paper and use them to guide their draft; still others may start writing and then determine how they will organize their draft when they have a few paragraphs written (see Section 2e). Experiment and decide which method works best for you.

Exercise 22.2   Using the advice given in Section 3d, develop an outline for your research paper (Exercise 22.1). Remember that your outline does not have to be formal; use a system that works best for you.

22c Write a Draft

Write a specific title

A bland, generic title says to readers that you are likely to be boring.

Generic   Good and Bad Fats

Specific titles are like tasty appetizers; if you like the appetizer, you'll probably like the main course.

Specific   The Secret Killer: Hydrogenated Fats

Write an engaging introduction

Get off to a fast start. If, for example, you want to alert readers to the dangers of partially hydrogenated oils in the food we eat, you could begin by explaining the difference in molecular structure between natural unsaturated fatty acids and trans fatty acids. And you would probably lose your readers by the end of the first paragraph.

Instead, let readers know what is at stake along with giving some background and context (see Section 3f). State your thesis early on. Then go into the details in the body of your paper.

> Americans today are more heath conscious than ever before, yet most are unaware that they may be ingesting high levels of dangerous fat in the form of partially hydrogenated oils. Hydrogenation is the process of passing hydrogen bubbles through heated oil, which makes the oil taste like butter. Nearly all processed food contains some level of hydrogenated oils. The food tastes good, but the oil it contains will make you fat and can eventually kill you.

Write a strong conclusion

The challenge in writing ending paragraphs is to leave the reader with something provocative, something beyond pure summary of the previous paragraphs. Connect back to your thesis, and use a strong concluding image, example, question, or call to action to leave your readers with something to remember and think about (see Section 3f).

Use transitions to indicate relationships

Transitions are words and phrases that let readers know relationships among your ideas. Research projects are often complex, and readers can easily miss seeing how your ideas fit together.

Give your readers clues. If you are giving readers an example, tell them "For example." If you are comparing or contrasting points, begin with a transition like "Similarly" or "In contrast." If you are signaling an effect, use "As a result" or "Consequently" (see page 52 for a list of transitional terms).

Include visuals where appropriate

Readers judge the quality of research projects by the quality of the evidence. Readers also expect evidence to be presented as clearly as possible. If you have statistical evidence to present, consider using a chart, graph, or table. Images, diagrams, and maps can also be useful to present evidence. See Figure 22.1.

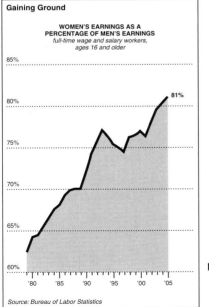

Figure 22.1 Women's earnings have gained steadily in comparison to men's earnings since 1980.

WRITING SMART

Use visuals in a research project

Here are guidelines for incorporating visual sources into your research paper.

- **Use visuals for examples and supporting evidence, not for decoration.** For example, if the subject of your research is Internet crime in San Francisco, including a picture of the Golden Gate Bridge is irrelevant and will detract from your project.
- **Refer to images and other graphics in the body of your research paper.** Explain the significance of any images or graphics in the body of your paper. The relevance of the visual should not be left to the reader to guess.
- **Include captions for images and other graphics.** Describe the content of the image or graphic in the caption.
- **Respect the copyright of visual sources.** You may need to request permission to use a visual from the Web. Use public domain material whenever possible.
- **Download images when you find them.** They may be gone when you return to the site.
- **Get complete citation information.** You are required to cite visual sources in your list of works cited just as you are for other sources.

22d Select and Introduce Quotations

Use sources to support what you say; don't expect them to say it for you. Next to plagiarism, the worst mistake you can make with sources is to string together a series of long quotations. This strategy leaves your readers wondering whether you have anything to say. Relying too much on quotations from others also makes for a bumpy read. Think about how each source relates to your thesis (see Section 21b).

When to quote and when to paraphrase

The general rule in deciding when to include direct quotations and when to paraphrase lies in the importance of the original wording. If you want to refer to an idea or fact and the original wording is not critical, make the point in your own words. Save direct quotations for language that is memorable or conveys the character of the source.

Suppose you are writing about the effects of the Internet on literacy, and you want to acknowledge those who maintain that the effects are largely negative. You find books by Sven Birkerts (*The Gutenberg Elegies: The Fate of Reading in an Electronic Age*), Mark Slouka (*War of the Worlds: Cyberspace and the High-Tech Assault on Reality*), and Clifford Stoll (*Silicon Snake Oil*) that argue the Internet is a disorganized wasteland that discourages people from thinking for themselves. You also find a book by Jay David Bolter (*The Writing Space: The Computer, Hypertext and the History of Writing*), someone more sympathetic to digital technologies who also sees them as a threat to the power of prose. You could paraphrase each argument, but you realize that there are common themes that run through these books, so you decide to summarize these sources by making a list of the themes expressed. You want to use a direct quote from Bolter that articulates the themes. You might write:

> The rapid spread of the Internet has produced many critics, such as Sven Birkerts, Mark Slouka, and Clifford Stoll, who all complain about how the Internet is destroying the foundations of literacy—that critical thinking and reflection, a sense of order, logical relations in texts, depth of analysis, trails of sources, and the reform mission of public discourse are going to be lost. Even those who take a more balanced view fear the multimedia capability of the Web will undermine the power of prose. Jay David Bolter writes,
>
> > The new media . . . threaten to drain contemporary prose of its rhetorical possibilities. Popular prose responds with a desire to emulate computer graphics. Academic and other specialized forms respond by a retreat into jargon or willful anachronism. (270)

> The coming of the Web, however, does not have to be viewed as a loss to literacy. Images and words have long coexisted on the printed page and in manuscripts, but relatively few people possessed the resources to exploit the rhetorical potential of images combined with words.

You would include all four books in your works-cited list.

WRITING SMART

Use quotations effectively

Quotations are a frequent problem area in research papers. Review every quotation to ensure that each is used effectively and correctly.

- **Limit the use of long quotations.** If you have more than one block quotation on a page, look closely to see if one or more can be paraphrased or summarized. Use direct quotations only if the original wording is important.
- **Check that each quotation is supporting your major points rather than making major points for you.** If the ideas rather than the original wording are what's important, paraphrase the quotation and cite the source.
- **Check that each quotation is introduced and attributed.** Each quotation should be introduced and the author or title named. Check for verbs that signal a quotation: Smith *claims*, Jones *argues*, Brown *states*.
- **Check that each quotation is properly formatted and punctuated.** Prose quotations longer than four lines (MLA) or forty words (APA) should be indented ten spaces in MLA style or five spaces in APA style. Shorter quotations should be enclosed within quotation marks.
- **Check that you cite the source for each quotation.** You are required to cite the sources of all direct quotations, paraphrases, and summaries.

- **Check the accuracy of each quotation.** It's easy to leave out words or mistype a quotation. Compare what is in your paper to the original source. If you need to add words to make the quotation grammatical, make sure the added words are in brackets. Use ellipses to indicate omitted words.
- **Read your paper aloud to a classmate or a friend.** Each quotation should flow smoothly when you read your paper aloud. Put a check beside rough spots as you read aloud so you can revise later.

Block quotations

As you see in the example above, when a direct quotation is long, it is indented from the margin instead of being placed in quotation marks. In MLA style, a quotation longer than four lines should be indented ten spaces. A quotation of forty words or longer is indented five spaces in APA style. In both MLA and APA styles, long quotations are double-spaced. When you indent a long quotation this way, it is called a **block quotation**. You still need to integrate a block quotation into the text of your paper by mentioning who wrote or said it. Note three points about form in the block quotation.

- No quotation marks appear around the block quotation.
- Words quoted in the original retain the double quotation marks.
- The page number appears after the period at the end of the block quotation.

It is a good idea to include at least one or two sentences following the quotation to describe its significance to your thesis.

Whether they are long or short, you should double-check all quotations you use to be sure they are accurate and that all words belonging to the original are set off with quotation marks or placed in a block quotation. If you wish to leave out words from a quotation, indicate the omitted words with ellipses (. . .), but make sure you do not alter the meaning of the original quote (see Section 44e). If you need to add words of your own to a quotation to make the meaning clear, place your words in square brackets (see Section 44d).

STAYING ON TRACK

Weave sources into your paper

Sources should be well integrated into your paper. A common mistake is to drop in quotations without introducing them or indicating their significance. We don't know how the following long quotation fits into the writer's argument.

Off track   Cell phones and the Internet have not made the world a more harmonious place just because people have the increased potential to talk with each other.

I see a world where people can't talk to each other in any meaningful way. Global networking will be a tool of business communication, consumerism, propaganda, banal conversations, and mindless entertainment. We will have forgotten how to tell stories or how to hear them. The majority of the world's population will be very young people without extended families or intact cultures, with fanatical allegiances to dead religions or live dictatorships. We have what Jonas Salk called a "wisdom deficit." (Laurel 102)

Introduce each quotation and make clear its significance to your text. Compare the following paragraph with the paragraph above.

On track   Cell phones and the Internet have not made the world a more harmonious place just because people have the increased potential to talk with each other. The tone of public discourse—be it in political campaigns, opinion in print and in pixels, talk radio, and discussion boards—has taken a turn toward the ugly. More information seems to have led to less understanding. Brenda Laurel, one of the more insightful commentators on the effects of digital media, fears we are moving toward "a world where people can't talk to each

(Continued on next page)

STAYING ON TRACK *(continued)*

other in any meaningful way," a world where "we will have forgotten how to tell stories or how to hear them" (102). Laurel uses Jonas Salk's description of our culture as suffering from a "wisdom deficit" to sum up her point (103).

The second example introduces Brenda Laurel in relation to the writer's claim that more information has led to less understanding. The writer weaves Brenda Laurel's words into his own but preserves Laurel's distinctive voice.

Remember: Quotations don't speak for themselves.

WRITING SMART

Use signal verbs to attribute quotations

Signal verbs often indicate your stance toward a quotation. Introducing a quotation with "X says" or "X believes" tells your readers nothing. Find a more lively verb that suggests how you are using the source. For example, if you write "X contends," your reader is alerted that you likely will disagree with the source.

acknowledge	answer	compare	describe
add	argue	complain	disagree
admit	ask	concede	discuss
advise	assert	conclude	dispute
agree	charge	contend	emphasize
allow	claim	criticize	explain
analyze	comment	declare	express

(Continued on next page)

WRITING SMART (continued)

find	maintain	refute	show
grant	note	reject	state
illustrate	object	remark	suggest
imply	observe	reply	think
insist	offer	report	write
interpret	point out	respond	

Integrate quotations

You should also check to see that all sources are well integrated into the fabric of your paper. Introduce quotations by attributing them in your text:

> Even those who fought for the United States in the U.S.-Mexican War of 1846 were skeptical of American motives: "We were sent to provoke a fight, but it was essential that Mexico should commence it" (Grant 68).

This quotation is used correctly, but it loses the impact of the source. Compare it with the following:

> Many soldiers who fought for the United States in the U.S.-Mexican War of 1846 were skeptical of American motives, including Civil War hero and future president Ulysses S. Grant, who wrote: "We were sent to provoke a fight, but it was essential that Mexico should commence it" (68).

Integrate summaries and paraphrases

Summaries and paraphrases likewise need introductions (see Section 21e). The following paragraph is the summary of a book. The source is noted at the end, but the reader cannot tell exactly which ideas come from the source.

> In 2001 it became as fashionable to say the Internet changes nothing as it had been to claim the Internet changes everything just two years before. While the profit-making potential of the Internet was overrated, the social effects were not. The

Internet is demolishing old castles of expertise along with many traditional relationships based on that expertise (Lewis).

In the following summary, signal phrases make it clear which ideas come from the source. The summary also indicates the stance of Lewis and includes a short quotation that gives the flavor of the source.

> In 2001 it became as fashionable to say the Internet changes nothing as it had been to claim the Internet changes everything just two years before. In the midst of the Internet gloom, one prominent contrarian has emerged to defend the Internet. Michael Lewis observes in Next: The Future Just Happened that it's as if "some crusty old baron who had been blasted out of his castle and was finally having a look at his first cannon had said, 'All it does is speed up balls'"(14). Lewis claims that while the profit-making potential of the Internet was overrated, the social effects were not. He sees the Internet demolishing old castles of expertise along with many traditional relationships based on that expertise.

Exercise 22.3 For each of the following rhetorical situations, decide whether you would quote, paraphrase, or summarize the sources mentioned.

1. You are writing an article arguing that a local judge is a racist. You have collected several inappropriate remarks made by this judge as she conducted the business of the court.
2. You are writing an email to your mother comparing two recipes for chicken and dumplings you got from shows on the Food Network.
3. You are trying to get the school computer lab you work at to buy some new multimedia software. Your supervisor hands you a stack of technical manuals and asks you to submit a proposal for the ones you think the school should purchase.
4. You are writing a paper on how Poe uses coded language in the poem "Annabel Lee" to criticize his deceased wife's family.
5. You are writing a response to a letter in the newspaper. You want to emphasize the other author's lack of information about the subject.

22e Review Your Draft

After you've finished your first draft, you'll want to get comments from other writers. A good source of help is fellow students. Your instructor may include a peer review session as part of the assignment. Before going to your peer review session, run one last spell-check, then print a double-spaced version of your paper for each member of your group.

Reading another student's paper

It is usually best to read through a paper twice, looking at different levels (see Chapter 4). The first time you read through a paper, concentrate on comprehension and overall impressions. See if you can summarize the paper after reading it once. Ask yourself whether the writing is convincing or informative.

On your second reading show the writer where you got confused or highlight parts that were especially good by adding comments in the margins. Consider the following questions when reading a research paper:

- Does the title describe the subject of the paper? Does it create interest in the subject?
- Are the introductory paragraphs effective and relevant to the paper that follows?
- Is the thesis clearly stated in the beginning paragraphs of the paper?
- Does the writer offer support for the thesis from a variety of valid and reliable sources?
- Does the paper go into enough detail to support the thesis, and are the details relevant to the thesis?
- Do the arguments presented in the paper flow logically? Is the paper well organized?
- Is the tone of the paper consistent throughout? Is the word choice varied and appropriate throughout?
- Did you have to read some parts more than once to fully understand them?

- Are quotations properly introduced and integrated into the text?
- Are all facts and quotations that are not common knowledge documented?
- Is the documentation in the correct form?
- Is the paper free of errors of grammar and punctuation?

Once you've read through the paper a second time, write concluding suggestions and comments about how the writer could improve the paper, using the questions as your guide. Be specific. Saying "I liked your paper" or "It's a good first draft" does not help the writer. Comments like "You need to cite more sources," "You might consider switching paragraphs 2 and 4," or "Try to use a more formal tone in your introductory and concluding paragraphs" give the writer specific areas to concentrate on in the revision. It is important to be supportive in the peer editing process, so try to offer comments that are positive and encouraging.

Reading your own paper

If others read and comment on your paper, you cannot expect them to tell you everything you need to do in a revision. You need to be able to read your own draft with the same distance that you have when you read the drafts of others. Sometimes you will not have another person available who can comment on your paper.

Reading your paper aloud to yourself will help you find rough places. Parts that are difficult for you to speak aloud are going to be hard for your readers to get through. Try to imagine yourself as a reader who does not know much about your subject or who holds a viewpoint different from yours. What could you add that would benefit that reader?

22f Revise, Revise, Revise

After you've gone through the peer editing process or assessed your own draft, sit down with your paper and consider the changes you need to make. Start from the highest level, reorganizing paragraphs and possibly even cutting large parts of your paper and adding new sections (see Sections 4b and 4c). If you make significant revisions, likely you will want to repeat the overall evaluation of your revised draft when you finish.

When you feel your draft is complete, you should begin the editing phase. Use the guidelines in Section 4d to revise style and grammatical errors. Finally, you should proofread your paper, word by word, checking for mistakes (see Section 4e). After you print out the final paper, check each page for formatting errors (see Section 23l for MLA-style formatting and Section 24f for APA-style formatting). Make sure all the pages were printed and that all are readable.

STAYING ON TRACK

Check for missing documentation

When you reach the proofreading stage, make one pass though your draft to check for missing documentation. Print your draft and your work-cited list, then place them beside each other.

1. Check that every parenthetical citation and every mention of an author's name in your text has an entry in your works-cited list. Put a check beside each when you find they match and note what is missing.

2. Read your text carefully for missing citations. For example, if you find a sentence similar to the following, you'll need to insert a parenthetical citation.

Off track   One critic of the exuberance over Web 2.0 writes, "today's amateur monkeys can use their networked computers to publish everything from uninformed political commentary, to unseemly home videos, to embarrassingly amateurish music, to unreadable poems, reviews, essays and novels."

(Continued on next page)

STAYING ON TRACK *(continued)*

On track   One critic of the exuberance over Web 2.0 writes, "today's amateur monkeys can use their networked computers to publish everything from uninformed political commentary, to unseemly home videos, to embarrassingly amateurish music, to unreadable poems, reviews, essays and novels" (Keen 3).

3. Check for missing page numbers for sources that have pagination.

Off track   Andrew Keen describes Wikipedia as "an online encyclopedia where anyone with opposable thumbs and a fifth-grade education can publish anything on any topic from AC/DC to Zoroastrianism."

On track   Andrew Keen describes Wikipedia as "an online encyclopedia where anyone with opposable thumbs and a fifth-grade education can publish anything on any topic from AC/DC to Zoroastrianism" (3).

Remember: Faulty documentation hurts your credibility as a researcher and can be a cause of plagiarism (see Section 21d).

Documenting

Five Steps for Documenting Sources

In academic writing you are expected to document your sources for three major reasons:

1. The ethics of research require that you give credit to other writers for their words and ideas. If you don't give proper credit, you are plagiarizing from your sources (see Chapter 21).

2. Scholars expect to be able to examine the sources of information. They often share your interests and want to know more about the larger conversation about your subject.

3. Your citations give a record of the intellectual journey you traveled. They support your credibility by illustrating the thoroughness with which you researched your topic and making clear what your original contribution is.

Follow the basic steps by answering these five questions when documenting and citing your sources.

1. **Which documentation style do I use?**
2. **What kind of source am I using?**
3. **When do I cite sources?**
4. **How do I cite a source in my paper?**
5. **How do I cite sources at the end of my paper?**

1 Which documentation style do I use?

Different disciplines use different styles of documentation. If you are unsure about which documentation style to use, ask your instructor.

- **MLA** (Modern Language Association) is the preferred style in the humanities and fine arts (see Chapter 23).
- **APA** (American Psychological Association) is followed in the social sciences and education (see Chapter 24).
- **CMS** (*Chicago Manual of Style*) offers flexibility in documentation style and the option of using footnote documentation (see Chapter 25).
- **CSE** (Council of Science Editors) covers all scientific disciplines (see Chapter 26).

The examples in this guide follow MLA style documentation.

2 What kind of source am I using?

The major types of sources are:

- **Books** are mostly in print but are migrating to online and audio formats. A book source can mean either an entire book or a chapter inside a book.

- **Scholarly journals** have traditionally been printed but now are increasingly available on online library databases.

- **Popular magazines and newspapers** now are distributed both in print and online.

- **Library databases**, accessed through your library's Web site, contain books, scholarly journals, magazines, newspapers, government documents, company reports, illustrations, and sources of other information.

- **Other online sources** include Web sites, discussion forums, blogs, online newspapers, online magazines, online government documents, and email messages.

- **Multimedia sources** include films, CDs, DVDs, television programs, cartoons, maps, advertisements, and performances.

3 When do I cite sources?

Quotations

Readers expect to find the original source of any words that are taken directly from a source. All words quoted from a source must be placed within quotation marks and the source must be cited.

How to cite a quotation

Let's say you read an article by Kermit Campbell and decided to quote in your paper the sentence that is highlighted in the paragraph below.

> This kind of control, this kind of juice among America's purveyors of middle-class virtue suggests to me that as writing teachers we cannot allow whiteness and middle-classness to go unchecked in the classroom. If we abandon the critical perspective here because we see the values of one group as superior to the others', as the principal aim of composition pedagogy, then we really aren't preparing students to become—as many of my fair-skinned colleagues like to say—citizens, active participants in the shaping of our democracy. Being citizens of a democracy, in my view, shouldn't be about class, aspiring to or being middle class; it should be about learning to live peaceably and justly with other citizens, especially with those who differ from the middle-class ideal. If composition is what Bloom perceives it to be, then the democracy we are preparing students for doesn't look so democratic after all.

Campbell, Kermit E. "There Goes the Neighborhood: Hip Hop Creepin' on a Come Up at the U." College Composition and Communication 58 (2007): 325–44.

You can either mention Kermit Campbell in the text of your paper or you can place the author's name inside parentheses following the quotation. In both cases, include the page number where you found the quotation inside parentheses.

A.　　Kermit Campbell argues that literacy education has a broader purpose than economic empowerment: "Being citizens of a democracy, in my view, shouldn't be about class, about aspiring to or being middle class; it should be about learning to live peaceably and justly with other citizens" (339).

B. An influential scholar concludes, "Being citizens of a democracy, in my view, shouldn't be about class, about aspiring to or being middle class; it should be about learning to live peaceably and justly with other citizens" (Campbell 339).

Ideas that you summarize or paraphrase

When you use information or ideas from a source, cite that source even if you do not use the writer's exact words. Any of the writer's words that you do use should be in quotation marks.

How to cite a summary or paraphrase

Note the specific page where the idea appears.

MLA The underlying causes of identity theft lie in the systems we use for storing data (Solove 115).

Facts that are not common knowledge or are unfamiliar to your readers

The source of facts that aren't generally known or are unfamiliar to your readers should be cited. That the Battle of Gettysburg was fought from June 30 to July 3, 1863 is common knowledge, but that some of Robert E. Lee's generals urged that the battle be fought elsewhere is unfamiliar to those who haven't studied Civil War history; thus the source needs to be cited.

How to cite the source of a fact

Note the specific page where the fact appears.

MLA Shakespeare may have drawn the plot of King Lear from a widely discussed lawsuit in 1603, when the elder daughters of feeble Brian Annesley attempted to take over his estate and were opposed by Annesley's youngest daughter, Cordell (Greenblatt 357).

4 How do I cite a source in my paper?

Citing sources is a two-part process. When readers find a reference to a source in the body of your paper, they can turn to the list of sources at the end and find the full publication information. This list is called "Works Cited" in MLA and "References" in APA.

This example quotes a passage from page 196 of the book *Emergence: The Connected Lives of Ants, Brains, Cities, and Software*, by Stephen Johnson.

In-text citation	Describing humans as "innate mind readers," one observer argues that "our skill at imagining other people's mental states ranks up there with our knack for language and our opposable thumbs" (Johnson 196).

Entry in the works-cited list	Works Cited Johnson, Steven. Emergence: The Connected Lives of Ants, Brains, Cities, and Software. New York: Scribner's, 2001.

How to cite an entire work, a Web site, or other electronic source

If you wish to cite an entire work (a book, a film, a performance, and so on), a Web site, or an electronic source that has no page numbers or paragraph numbers, MLA prefers that you mention the name of a person (for example, the author or director) in your paper with a corresponding entry in the works-cited list. You do not need to include the author's name in parentheses. If you cannot identify the author, mention the title in your paper.

Author's name mentioned in your paper	Michelle Tsai observes that while nonalphabetic languages cannot have spelling bees, Chinese children participate in dictionary contests and Japanese children compete in various writing and pronunciation skills.

Works Cited
Tsai, Michelle. "Bees Overseas." Slate 29 May 2007. 7 June 2007 <http://www.slate.com/id/2167194/>.

5 How do I cite sources at the end of my paper?

During your research you will need to collect information about each source to create your works-cited list. Go through your paper and find every reference to a work external to your paper. Each reference should have an entry in your works-cited list.

Organize your works-cited list alphabetically by authors' last names or, if no author is listed, the first word in the title other than *a, an,* or *the.* (See pages 412–415 for a sample works-cited list.) MLA style uses four basic forms for entries in the works-cited list: books, periodicals (scholarly journals, newspapers, magazines), online library database sources, and other online sources (Web sites, discussion forums, blogs, online newspapers, online magazines, online government documents, and email messages).

1. Works-Cited Entries for Books

Entries for books have three main elements. See pages 362–363 for where to find this information.

Sterling, Bruce. Shaping Things. Cambridge: MIT P, 2005.

I. Author's name.
- List the author's name with the last name first, followed by a period.

2. Title of book.
- Find the exact title on the title page, not on the cover.
- Separate the title and subtitle with a colon.
- Underline the title and put a period (not underlined) at the end.

3. Publication information.

Publication information for books includes:
- The place (usually the city) of publication,
- The name of the publisher,
- The date of publication.
  Use a colon after the place of publication; the publisher's name (using accepted abbreviations) is followed by a comma and then the publication date.

2. Works-Cited Entries for Periodicals

Entries for periodicals (scholarly journals, newspapers, magazines) have three main elements. See pages 370–371 and 374–375 for where to find this information.

Swearingen, C. Jan. "Feminisms and Composition." <u>College Composition and Communication</u> 57 (2006): 543-51.

1. Author's name.

- List the author's name with the last name first, followed by a period.

2. "Title of article."

- Place the title of the article inside quotation marks.
- Insert a period before the closing quotation mark.

3. Publication information.

- Underline the title of the journal.
- Follow immediately with the volume number.
- List the date of publication, in parentheses, followed by a colon.
- List the page numbers, followed by a period. Use a hyphen in the page range.

3. Works-Cited Entries for Library Database Sources

Basic entries for library database sources have four main elements. See pages 380–381 for where to find this information.

> Cooke, William. "Hrothulf: A Richard III, or an Alfred the Great?" Studies in Philology 104 (2007): 175-98. Academic Search Premier. EBSCO. U of Texas Lib. 3 Aug. 2007 <http://www.epnet.com/>.

1. Author's name.

- List the author's name with the last name first, followed by a period.

2. "Title of article."

- Place the title of the article inside quotation marks.
- Insert a period before the closing quotation mark.

3. Print publication information.

- Give the print publication information in standard format, in this case for a periodical (see page 370).

4. Database information.

- Underline the name of the database, which you will have to look for.
- Give the name of the vendor, which is usually at the top.
- Give the name of the library or library system you used.
- List the date you looked at the source just before the URL. No period follows.
- Put the URL of the vendor inside angle brackets followed by a period.

GO

4. Works-Cited Entries for Other Online Sources

Basic entries for online sources (Web sites, discussion forums, blogs, online publications, online government documents, and email) have three main elements. Sometimes information such as the author's name or the date of publication is missing from the online source. Include the information you are able to locate. See pages 382–383.

There are many formats for the different kinds of electronic publications. Here is the format of an entry for an online article.

> Smith, Patrick. "Ask the Pilot." Salon 1 June 2007. 24 Aug. 2007
> <http://www.salon.com/tech/col/smith/2007/06/01/
> askthepilot234/>.

1. Author's name.

- List the author's name with the last name first, followed by a period.

2. "Title of article."

- Place the title of the Web page inside quotation marks.
- Insert a period before the closing quotation mark.

3. Publication information.

- Underline the title of the entire site or the online journal.
- Put a period after the title of an entire site. Do not put a period after the name of an online journal.
- Give the date of electronic publication.
- List the date of access just before the URL.
- Place the URL inside angle brackets, followed by a period.

APA style includes the same information in its list of references but uses a different format. For the format of entries in APA's list of references, see pages 461–463.

3. Works-Cited Entries for Library Database Sources

Basic entries for library database sources have four main elements. See pages 380–381 for where to find this information.

> Cooke, William. "Hrothulf: A Richard III, or an Alfred the Great?" Studies in Philology 104 (2007): 175-98. Academic Search Premier. EBSCO. U of Texas Lib. 3 Aug. 2007 <http://www.epnet.com/>.

1. Author's name.
- List the author's name with the last name first, followed by a period.

2. "Title of article."
- Place the title of the article inside quotation marks.
- Insert a period before the closing quotation mark.

3. Print publication information.
- Give the print publication information in standard format, in this case for a periodical (see page 370).

4. Database information.
- Underline the name of the database, which you will have to look for.
- Give the name of the vendor, which is usually at the top.
- Give the name of the library or library system you used.
- List the date you looked at the source just before the URL. No period follows.
- Put the URL of the vendor inside angle brackets followed by a period.

4. Works-Cited Entries for Other Online Sources

Basic entries for online sources (Web sites, discussion forums, blogs, online publications, online government documents, and email) have three main elements. Sometimes information such as the author's name or the date of publication is missing from the online source. Include the information you are able to locate. See pages 382–383.

There are many formats for the different kinds of electronic publications. Here is the format of an entry for an online article.

> Smith, Patrick. "Ask the Pilot." Salon 1 June 2007. 24 Aug. 2007
> <http://www.salon.com/tech/col/smith/2007/06/01/
> askthepilot234/>.

1. Author's name.
- List the author's name with the last name first, followed by a period.

2. "Title of article."
- Place the title of the Web page inside quotation marks.
- Insert a period before the closing quotation mark.

3. Publication information.
- Underline the title of the entire site or the online journal.
- Put a period after the title of an entire site. Do not put a period after the name of an online journal.
- Give the date of electronic publication.
- List the date of access just before the URL.
- Place the URL inside angle brackets, followed by a period.

APA style includes the same information in its list of references but uses a different format. For the format of entries in APA's list of references, see pages 461–463.

Chapter 23

MLA Documentation

MLA is the preferred style in the humanities and fine arts.

In-text Citations

Works-Cited Entries

MLA style is the norm for the humanities and fine arts disciplines. If you have questions that the examples in this chapter do not address, consult the *MLA Handbook for Writers of Research Papers*, sixth edition (2003), and the *MLA Style Manual and Guide to Scholarly Publishing*, second edition (1998).

23a In-text Citations in MLA Style

Paraphrase, summary, or short quotation

A short quotation takes four lines or fewer in your paper.

> The computing power of networked technology is growing at an accelerating rate, prompting some visionaries to argue that the Internet "may actually become self-aware sometime in the next century" (Johnson 114).

Here, the author's name is provided in the parenthetical reference.

> Science writer and cultural critic Steven Johnson poses the question this way: "Is the Web itself becoming a giant brain?" (114).

Note that the period goes *after* the parentheses.

The author of the quotation is named in this sentence, so only a page number is needed in the parenthetical reference.

WHEN DO YOU PROVIDE A PAGE NUMBER?

- If the source is longer than one page, provide the page number for each quotation, paraphrase, and summary.
- If an online source includes paragraph numbers rather than page numbers, use *par.* with the number.

  (Cello, par. 4)

- If the source does not include page numbers, consider citing the work and the author in the text rather than in parentheses.

  In a hypertext version of James Joyce's Ulysses, . . .

Quotations longer than four lines

The sentence introducing the quotation names the author, so only the page number needs to appear in the parenthetical reference.

Technology writer and cultural commentator Steven Johnson relates how he often responded to questions about whether or not networked computers would ever be able to think or develop awareness:

> For there to be a single, global consciousness, the Web itself would have to be getting smarter, and the Web wasn't a single, unified thing—it was just a vast sum of interlinked data. You could debate whether the Web was making us smarter, but that the Web itself might be slouching toward consciousness seemed ludicrous. (114)

Despite his initial scepticism, however, Johnson slowly began to change his mind about the idea of artificial consciousness or intelligence.

Note that the period appears *before* the parentheses in an indented block quote.

Sample in-text citations for sources in general

1. **Author named in your text**

Put the author's name in a signal phrase in your sentence.

Sociologist Daniel Bell called this emerging U.S. economy the "postindustrial society" (3).

2. Author not named in your text

> In 1997, the Gallup poll reported that 55% of adults in the United States think secondhand smoke is "very harmful," compared to only 36% in 1994 (Saad 4).

3. Work by one author

The author's last name comes first, followed by the page number. There is no comma.

> (Bell 3)

4. Work by two or three authors

The authors' last names follow the order of the title page. If there are two authors, join the names with *and*. If there are three, use a comma between the first two names and a comma with *and* before the last name.

> (Francisco, Vaughn, and Lynn 7)

5. Work by four or more authors

You may use the phrase *et al.* (meaning "and others") for all names but the first, or you may write out all the names. Make sure you use the same method for both the in-text citations and the works-cited list.

> (Abrams et al. 1653)

6. Work by no named author

Use a shortened version of the title that includes at least the first important word. Your reader will use the shortened title to find the full title in the works-cited list.

> A review in the New Yorker of Ryan Adams's new album focuses on the artist's age ("Pure" 25).

Notice that "Pure" is in quotation marks because it is the shortened title of an article. If it were a book, the short title would be underlined.

7. Work by a group or organization

Treat the group or organization as the author. Try to identify the group author in the text and place only the page number in parentheses.

> According to the Irish Free State Handbook, published by the Ministry for Industry and Finance, the population of Ireland in 1929 was approximately 4,192,000 (23).

8. Quotations longer than four lines

NOTE: When using indented ("block") quotations of longer than four lines, the period appears *before* the parentheses enclosing the page number.

> In her article "Art for Everybody," Susan Orlean attempts to explain the popularity of painter Thomas Kinkade:
>> People like to own things they think are valuable. . . . The high price of limited editions is part of their appeal: it implies that they are choice and exclusive, and that only a certain class of people will be able to afford them. (128)
> This same statement could also explain the popularity of phenomena like PBS's Antiques Road Show.

If the source is longer than one page, provide the page number for each quotation, paraphrase, and summary.

9. Two or more works by the same author

Use the author's last name and then a shortened version of the title of each source.

> The majority of books written about coauthorship focus on partners of the same sex (Laird, Women 351).

Note that *Women* is underlined because it is the name of a book.

10. Different authors with the same last name

If your list of works cited contains items by two or more different authors with the same last name, include the initial of the first name in the parenthetical reference. Note that a period follows the initial.

> Web surfing requires more mental involvement than channel surfing (S. Johnson 107).

11. Two or more sources within the same sentence

Place each citation directly after the statement it supports.

> Many sweeping pronouncements were made in the 1990s that the Internet is the best opportunity to improve education since the printing press (Ellsworth xxii) or even in the history of the world (Dyrli and Kinnaman 79).

12. Two or more sources within the same citation

If two sources support a single point, separate them with a semicolon.

> (McKibbin 39; Gore 92)

13. Work quoted in another source

When you do not have access to the original source of the material you wish to use and only an indirect source is available, put the abbreviation *qtd. in* (quoted in) before the information about the indirect source.

> National governments have become increasingly what Ulrich Beck, in a 1999 interview, calls "zombie institutions"—institutions which are "dead and still alive" (qtd. in Bauman 6).

Sample in-text citations for particular kinds of sources

14. Web sources including Web pages, blogs, podcasts, wikis, videos, and other multimedia sources

MLA prefers that you mention the author in your text instead of putting the author's name in parentheses.

> Andrew Keen ironically used his own blog to claim that "blogs are boring to write (yawn), boring to read (yawn) and boring to discuss (yawn)."

If you cannot identify the author, mention the title in your text.

> The podcast "Catalina's Cubs" describes the excitement on Catalina Island when the Chicago Cubs came for spring training in the 1940s.

15. Work in an anthology

Cite the name of the author of the work within an anthology, not the name of the editor of the collection. Alphabetize the entry in the list of works cited by the author, not the editor. For example, Melissa Jane Hardie published the chapter "Beard" in *Rhetorical Bodies*, a book edited by Jack Selzer and Sharon Crowley.

> In "Beard," Melissa Jane Hardie explores the role assumed by Elizabeth Taylor as the celebrity companion of gay actors including Rock Hudson and Montgomery Cliff (278-79).

Note that Hardie, not Selzer and Crowley, is named in a parenthetical citation.

> (Hardie 278-79)

16. Work in more than one volume

Give the volume number in the parenthetical reference before the page number, with a colon and a space separating the two.

> Contrary to the legend that Vincent van Gogh succumbed to personal demons before his suicide in 1890, his letters from the last two months describe feelings of calmness and an end to his recurrent nightmares (Walther and Metzger 2: 647).

17. Poems, plays, and classic works

Poems

If you quote all or part of two or three lines of poetry that do not require special emphasis, put the lines in quotation marks and separate the lines using a slash (/) with a space on each side.

> John Donne's "The Legacy" associates the separation of lovers with death: "When I died last, and, Dear, I die / As often as from thee I go" (1-2).

Plays

Give the act, scene, and line numbers when the work has them, the page numbers when it does not. Abbreviate titles of famous works (like *Hamlet*).

> (Ham. 3.2.120-23).

Classic Works

To supply a reference to classic works, you sometimes need more than a page number from a specific edition. Readers should be able to locate a quotation in any edition of the book. Give the page number from the edition that you are using, then a semicolon and other identifying information.

> "Marriage is a house" is one of the most memorable lines in Don Quixote (546; pt. 2, bk. 3, ch. 19).

23b Books in MLA-Style Works Cited

TITLE PAGE

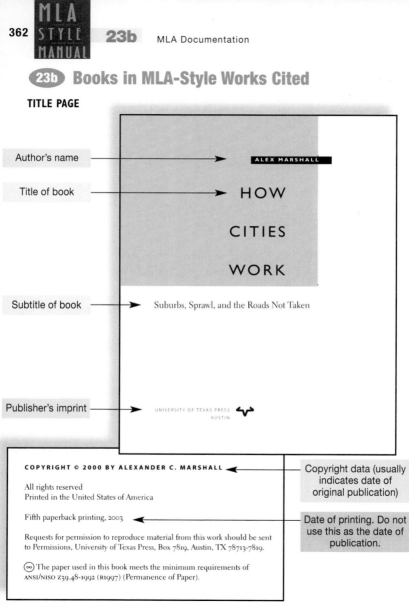

Author's name → ALEX MARSHALL

Title of book → HOW

CITIES

WORK

Subtitle of book → Suburbs, Sprawl, and the Roads Not Taken

Publisher's imprint → UNIVERSITY OF TEXAS PRESS
AUSTIN

COPYRIGHT © 2000 BY ALEXANDER C. MARSHALL ← Copyright data (usually indicates date of original publication)

All rights reserved
Printed in the United States of America

Fifth paperback printing, 2003 ← Date of printing. Do not use this as the date of publication.

Requests for permission to reproduce material from this work should be sent to Permissions, University of Texas Press, Box 7819, Austin, TX 78713-7819.

∞ The paper used in this book meets the minimum requirements of ANSI/NISO Z39.48-1992 (R1997) (Permanence of Paper).

DETAIL OF COPYRIGHT PAGE

Marshall, Alex. How Cities Work: Suburbs, Sprawl, and the

Roads Not Taken. Austin: U of Texas P, 2000.

AUTHOR'S OR EDITOR'S NAME

The author's last name comes first, followed by a comma and the first name.

For edited books, put the abbreviation *ed.* after the name, preceded by a comma:

Kavanagh, Peter, ed.

BOOK TITLE

Use the exact title, as it appears on the title page (not the cover).

Underline the title.

All nouns, verbs, pronouns, adjectives, adverbs, and subordinating conjunctions, and the first word of the title are capitalized. Do not capitalize articles, prepositions, or coordinating conjunctions unless they are the first word of the title.

PUBLICATION INFORMATION

Place of publication

If more than one city is given, use the first.

For cities outside the U.S., add an abbreviation of the country or province if the city is not well known.

Publisher

Use a short form of the name.

Omit words such as *Press, Publisher,* and *Inc.*

For university presses, use *UP*:
New York UP

Shorten the name. For example, shorten *Addison, Wesley, Longman* to *Longman; W. W. Norton & Co.* to *Norton.*

Date of publication

Give the year as it appears on the copyright page.

If no year of publication is given, but can be approximated, put a *c.* ("circa") and the approximate date in brackets: [c. 1999].

Otherwise, put *n.d.* ("no date"):
Boston: Harvard UP, n.d.

Sample works-cited entries for books

ONE AUTHOR

18. **Book by one author**

> Friedman, Alice T. Women and the Making of the Modern House.
> New Haven: Yale UP, 2007.

19. **Two or more books by the same author**

In the entry for the first book, include the author's name. In the second entry, substitute three hyphens and a period for the author's name. List the titles of books by the same author in alphabetical order.

> Grimsley, Jim. Boulevard. Chapel Hill: Algonquin, 2002.
> ---. Dream Boy. New York: Simon, 1995.

MULTIPLE AUTHORS

20. **Book by two or three authors**

The second and subsequent authors' names appear first name first.

> Burger, Edward B., and Michael Starbird. Coincidences, Chaos, and
> All That Math Jazz. New York: Norton, 2006.

21. **Book by four or more authors**

You may use the phrase *et al.* (meaning "and others") for all authors but the first, or you may write out all the names. Use the same method in the in-text citation as you do in the works-cited list.

> North, Stephen M., et al. Refiguring the Ph.D. in English Studies.
> Urbana: NCTE, 2000.

ANONYMOUS AND GROUP AUTHORS

22. Book by an unknown author

Begin the entry with the title.

Encyclopedia of Americana. New York: Somerset, 2001.

23. Book revised by a second author

Place the editor's name after the book title.

Strunk, William. Elements of Style. Ed. E. B. White. 4th ed.
    Boston: Allyn, 2000.

24. Book by a group or organization

Treat the group as the author of the work.

United Nations. The Charter of the United Nations: A Commentary.
    New York: Oxford UP, 2000.

FOREIGN AND EMBEDDED TITLES

25. Title within a title

If the title contains the title of another book or a word normally italicized, do not underline that title or word.

Higgins, Brian, and Hershel Parker. Critical Essays on Herman
    Melville's Moby-Dick. New York: Hall, 1992.

26. Title in a foreign language

If the title is in a foreign language, copy it exactly as it appears on the title page.

Fontaine, Jean. Etudes de Littérature Tunisienne. Tunis: Dar
    Annawras, 1989.

IMPRINTS, REPRINTS, AND UNDATED BOOKS

27. Book published before 1900

You may omit the publisher for books published prior to 1900.

Rodd, Renell. <u>Rose Leaf and Apple Leaf</u>. Philadelphia, 1882.

28. Books that include a special imprint of the publisher

In the example below, Flamingo is a special imprint of Harper.

O'Brien, Flann. <u>The Poor Mouth</u>. London: Flamingo-Harper, 1993.

29. Book with no publication date

If no year of publication is given, but it can be approximated, put a *c.* ("circa") and the approximate date in brackets: [c. 1999]. Otherwise, put *n.d.* ("no date").

O'Sullivan, Colin. <u>Traditions and Novelties of the Irish Country Folk</u>. Dublin [c. 1793].

James, Franklin. <u>In the Valley of the King</u>. Cambridge: Harvard UP, n.d.

30. Reprinted works

For works of fiction that have been printed in many different editions or reprints, give the original publication date after the title.

Wilde, Oscar. <u>The Picture of Dorian Gray</u>. 1890. New York: Norton, 2001.

PARTS OF BOOKS

31. Introduction, foreword, preface, or afterword

Give the author and then the name of the specific part being cited. Next, name the book. Then, if the author for the whole work is different, put that author's name after the word *By*. Place inclusive page numbers at the end.

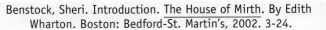

> Benstock, Sheri. Introduction. The House of Mirth. By Edith
> Wharton. Boston: Bedford-St. Martin's, 2002. 3-24.

32. Single chapter written by the same author as the book

> Ardis, Ann. "Mapping the Middlebrow in Edwardian England."
> Modernism and Cultural Conflict: 1880-1922. Cambridge:
> Cambridge UP, 2002. 114-42.

33. Selection from an anthology or edited collection

> Sedaris, David. "Full House." The Best American Nonrequired
> Reading 2004. Ed. Dave Eggers. Boston: Houghton, 2004.
> 350-58.

34. More than one selection from an anthology or edited collection

Multiple selections from a single anthology can be handled by creating a complete entry for the anthology and shortened cross-references for individual works in that anthology.

> Adichie, Chimamanda Ngozi. "Half of a Yellow Sun." Eggers 1-17.

> Eggers, Dave, ed. The Best American Nonrequired Reading 2004.
> Boston: Houghton, 2004.

> Sedaris, David. "Full House." Eggers 350-58.

35. Article in a reference work

You can omit the names of editors and most publishing information for an article from a familiar reference work. Identify the edition by date. There is no need to give the page numbers when a work is arranged alphabetically. Give the author's name, if known.

> "Utilitarianism." The Columbia Encyclopedia. 6th ed. 2001.

A full entry is required for less familiar works.

RELIGIOUS TEXTS

36. Religious texts

Underline The Bible and other titles of sacred texts only when you are citing a specific edition.

> Holy Bible. King James Text: Modern Phrased Version.
>   New York: Oxford UP, 1980.

Use a period to separate the chapter and verse in the in-text note. Books of the Bible are commonly abbreviated (Gen. for Genesis, Exod. for Exodus, and so on).

> (Deut. 34.7)

EDITIONS AND TRANSLATIONS

37. Book with an editor—focus on the editor

When the focus is on the work of an editor, begin with the editor's name followed by a comma and the abbreviation *ed.* List the author's name after the title preceded by the word *By*.

> Lewis, Gifford, ed. The Big House of Inver. By Edith Somerville and
>   Martin Ross. Dublin: Farmar, 2000.

38. Book with an editor—focus on the author

The usual order is to begin with the author's name, then give the title and editor's name preceded by the abbreviation *Ed.*

> Somerville, Edith, and Martin Ross. The Big House of Inver.
>   Ed. Gifford Lewis. Dublin: Farmar, 2000.

39. Book with a translator

For a translation begin with the author's name, then give the title and translator's name preceded by the abbreviation *Trans.*

> Mallarmé, Stéphane. Divagations. Trans. Barbara Johnson.
>   Cambridge: Harvard UP, 2007.

40. Second or subsequent edition of a book

Hawthorn, Jeremy, ed. A Concise Glossary of Contemporary Literary Theory. 3rd ed. London: Arnold, 2001.

MULTIVOLUME WORKS

41. One volume of a multivolume work

If you cite only one volume of a multivolume work, give the publication information for only that volume. List the volume number after the abbreviation *Vol.*

Samuel, Raphael. Theatres of Memory. Vol. 1. London: Verso, 1999.

42. More than one volume of a multivolume work

List the total number of volumes in Works Cited.

Samuel, Raphael. Theatres of Memory. 2 vols. London: Verso, 1999.

Identify the specific volume in your in-text citations.

(Samuel 2: 36-37)

43. Book in a series

Give the series name just before the publishing information.

Watson, James. William Faulkner: Self-Presentation and Performance. Literary Modernism Series. Austin: U of Texas P, 2000.

23c Journals and Magazines in MLA-Style Works Cited

JOURNAL COVER

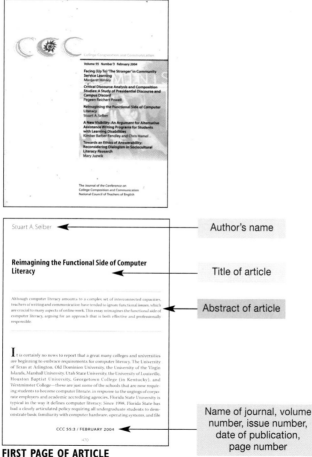

Author's name

Title of article

Abstract of article

Name of journal, volume number, issue number, date of publication, page number

FIRST PAGE OF ARTICLE

Selber, Stuart A. "Reimagining the Functional Side of

Computer Literacy." <u>CCC</u> 55 (2004): 470-503.

AUTHOR'S NAME

The author's last name comes first, followed by a comma and the first name.

For two or more works by the same author, consult the sample works-cited list on page 414.

TITLE OF ARTICLE

Use the exact title, which appears at the top of the article.

Put the title in quotation marks. If a book title is part of the article's title, underline the book title. If a title requiring quotation marks is part of the article's title, use single quotation marks.

All nouns, verbs, pronouns, adjectives, adverbs, and subordinating conjunctions, and the first word of the title are capitalized. Do not capitalize articles, prepositions, or coordinating conjunctions unless they are the first word of the title.

PUBLICATION INFORMATION

Name of journal

Underline the title of the journal.

Abbreviate the title of the journal if it commonly appears that way (as in this example).

Volume, issue, and page numbers

- For journals paginated separately by issue, list the volume number, a period, and then the issue number before the year and page numbers.

- For continuously paginated journals, include the volume number before the year, but do *not* include the issue number (as in this example).

Date of publication

- For magazines and journals identified by the month or season of publication, use the month (or season) and year in place of the volume.

- For weekly or biweekly magazines, give both the day and month of publication, as listed on the issue. Note that the day precedes the month and no comma is used.

Sample works-cited entries for journals and magazines

JOURNAL AND MAGAZINE ARTICLES

44. Article by one author

> Bhabha, Jacqueline. "The Child—What Sort of Human?" PMLA 121 (2006): 1526-35.

45. Article by two or three authors

> Shamoo, Adil E., and Jonathan D. Moreo. "Ethics of Research Involving Mandatory Drug Testing of High School Athletes." American Journal of Bioethics 1 (2004): 25-31.

46. Article by four or more authors

You may use the phrase *et al.* (meaning "and others") for all authors but the first, or you may write out all the names.

> Breece, Katherine E., et al. "Patterns of mtDNA Diversity in Northwestern North America." Human Biology 76 (2004): 33-54.

47. Article by an unknown author

> "Idol Gossip." People 12 April 2004: 34-35.

48. Article with a title in a foreign language

Copy the title exactly as it appears on the title page.

> Frostin, Georges. "Les Colons de Saint Dominique." Revue Historique 237 (1967): 67-78.

MONTHLY, WEEKLY, AND BIWEEKLY MAGAZINES

49. Monthly or seasonal magazines or journals

Use the month (or season) and year in place of the volume. Abbreviate the names of all months except May, June, and July.

> Barlow, John Perry. "Africa Rising: Everything You Know about Africa Is Wrong." Wired Jan. 1998: 142-58.

50. Weekly or biweekly magazines

For weekly or biweekly magazines, give both the day and month of publication, as listed on the issue.

Toobin, Jeffrey. "Crackdown." New Yorker 5 Nov. 2001: 56-61.

DIFFERENT TYPES OF PAGINATION

51. Article in a journal paginated by volume

Include the volume number but do not include the issue number.

Lerer, Seth. "Medieval English Literature and the Idea of the Anthology." PMLA 118 (2003): 1251-67.

52. Article in a journal paginated by issue

List the volume number, a period, and then the issue number before the year and page numbers.

Morris, James. "Off the Road." Wilson Quarterly 31.1 (2007): 14-17.

REVIEWS, EDITORIALS, LETTERS TO THE EDITOR

53. Review

If there is no title, just name the work reviewed.

Mendelsohn, Daniel. "The Two Oscar Wildes." Rev. of The Importance of Being Earnest, dir. Oliver Parker. New York Review of Books 10 Oct. 2002: 23-24.

54. Letter to the editor

Patai, Daphne. Letter. Harper's Magazine Dec. 2001: 4.

55. Editorial

If the editorial is unsigned, put the title first.

"Stop Stonewalling on Reform." Editorial. Business Week 17 June 2002: 108.

56. Published interview

Olson, Gary A., and Lester Faigley. "Language, Politics, and Composition: A Conversation with Noam Chomsky." JAC 11 (1991): 1-35.

57. Article on microfilm

Cite an article on microfilm or microfiche as you would the original.

Bowen, Elizabeth. "The Case for Summer Romance." Glamour 43 (1960): 94-95, 180.

23d Newspapers in MLA-Style Works Cited

MASTHEAD ON THE FRONT PAGE OF THE NEWSPAPER

Name of newspaper

Edition

Date

FIRST PAGE OF ARTICLE (PAGE A1)

Title of article

Author

CONTINUATION OF ARTICLE (PAGE A3)

Title of article

Source: "Once World Cause, South Africa Lowers Voices on Human Rights" by Michael Wines, March 24, 2007. Copyright © 2007 by *The New York Times*. Reprinted with permission.

Wines, Michael. "Once World Cause, South Africa Lowers Voice on Human Rights." New York Times 24 Mar. 2007, late ed.: A1+.

AUTHOR'S NAME

The author's last name comes first, followed by a comma and the first name.

For two or more works by the same author, consult the sample works-cited list on page 414.

TITLE OF ARTICLE

Use the exact title, which appears at the top of the article.

Put the title in quotation marks. If a book title is part of the article's title, underline the book title. If a title requiring quotation marks is part of the article's title, use single quotation marks.

All nouns, verbs, pronouns, adjectives, adverbs, and subordinating conjunctions, and the first word of the title are capitalized. Do not capitalize articles, prepositions, or coordinating conjunctions unless they are the first word of the title.

PUBLICATION INFORMATION

Name of newspaper

Underline the name.

Omit introductory articles. (New York Times *not* The New York Times).

If the city is not mentioned in the name of the paper, add it in square brackets after the name.

Section and page numbers

Provide the section label (usually A, B, C, and so on).

Include the page number. If the article continues to a nonconsecutive page, add a plus sign after the number of the first page.

Date of publication and edition

Give the complete date for a newspaper—day, month, and year.

Abbreviate the names of all months except May, June, and July.

Do *not* give the volume and issue numbers for a newspaper.

Specify the edition if one is given on the masthead: *natl. ed., final ed., suburban ed.*

Place a colon after the edition if an edition name or number is given. If no edition is listed, place the colon after the date.

Sample works-cited entries for newspapers

NEWSPAPER ARTICLES

58. Article by one author

> Boyd, Robert S. "Solar System Has a Double." Montreal Gazette 14
> June 2002, final ed.: A1.

59. Article by two or three authors

The second and subsequent authors' names are printed in regular
order, first name first:

> Davis, Howard, June Allstead, and Jane Mavis. "Rice's Testimony to
> 9/11 Commission Leaves Unanswered Questions." Dallas
> Morning News 9 Apr. 2004, final ed.: C5.

Notice that a comma separates the authors' names.

60. Article by four or more authors

You may use the phrase *et al.* (meaning "and others") for all authors
but the first, or you may write out all the names. Use the same method in
the in-text citation as you do in the works-cited list.

> Watson, Anne, et al. "Childhood Obesity on the Rise." Daily
> Missoulian 7 July 2003: B1.

61. Article by an unknown author

Begin the entry with the title.

> "Democratic Candidates Debate Iraq War." Austin American-
> Statesman 19 Jan. 2004: A6.

62. Article with a title in a foreign language

If the title is in a foreign language, copy it exactly as it appears on the
title page, paying special attention to accent marks and capitalization.

> "Iraq, Liberati gli Ostaggi Sudcoreani." Corriere Della Sera 8 Apr.
> 2004: A1.

63. **Article that continues to a nonconsecutive page**

Add a plus sign after the number of the first page.

Kaplow, Larry, and Tasgola Karla Bruner. "U.S.: Don't Let Taliban Forces Flee." Austin American-Statesman 20 Nov. 2001, final ed.: A11+.

REVIEWS, EDITORIALS, LETTERS TO THE EDITOR

64. **Review**

Fox, Nichols. "What's for Dinner?" Rev. of Eating in the Dark: America's Experiment with Genetically Engineered Food, by Kathleen Hart. Washington Post 16 June 2002: T9.

65. **Letter to the editor**

Leach, Richard E. Letter. Boston Globe 2 Apr. 2007, first ed.: A10.

66. **Editorial**

Add the word *Editorial* after the title.

Pachon, Harry P. "Pricing Out New Citizens." Editorial. Los Angeles Times 2 Apr. 2007, home ed.: A13.

67. **Unsigned editorial**

If the editorial is unsigned, put the title first.

"High Court Ruling Doesn't Mean Vouchers Will Work." Editorial. Atlanta Journal and Constitution 28 June 2002, home ed.: A19.

68. **Article on microfilm**

Cite an article on microfilm or microfiche as you would the original.

Greenhouse, Linda. "Supreme Court Roundup; Court to Review Suits on H.M.O. Policies." New York Times 4 Nov. 2003, final ed.: A9.

23e Government Documents, Pamphlets, Dissertations, and Letters in MLA-Style Works Cited

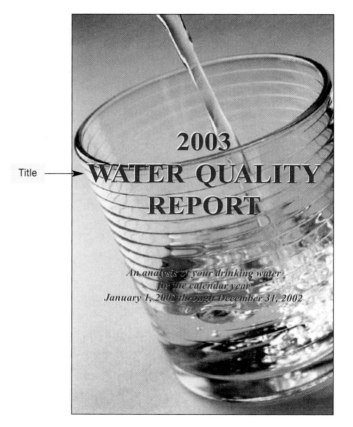

Title ——▶ **WATER QUALITY REPORT**

2003 Water Quality Report. Lafayette, CO: City of Lafayette Water Division, 2003.

69. Government documents other than the *Congressional Record*

Malveaux, Julianne. "Changes in the Labor Market Status of Black Women." A Report on the Study Group on Affirmative Action to the Committee on Education and Labor. 100th Cong., 1st sess. H. Rept. 100-L. Washington: GPO, 1987. 231-55.

70. *Congressional Record*

Cong. Rec. 8 Feb. 2000: 1222-46.

71. Bulletin or pamphlet

The Common Cold. Austin: U of Texas Health Center, 2007.

72. Published letter

Wilde, Oscar. "To Lord Alfred Douglas." 17 Feb. 1895. In The Complete Letters of Oscar Wilde. Ed. Merlin Holland and Rupert Hart-Davis. New York: Holt, 2000. 632-33.

73. Unpublished letter

Welty, Eudora. Letter to Elizabeth Bowen. 1 May 1951. Harry Ransom Humanities Research Center, Austin, TX.

74. Published dissertation or thesis

Mason, Jennifer. Civilized Creatures: Animality, Cultural Power, and American Literature, 1850-1901. Diss. U of Texas at Austin, 2000. Ann Arbor: UMI, 2000. 9992865.

75. Unpublished dissertation or thesis

Schorn, Susan. "The Merciful Construction of Good Women: Actresses in the Marriage-Plot Novel." Diss. U of Texas at Austin, 2000.

76. Published proceedings of a conference

Abadie, Ann, and Robert Hamblin, eds. Faulkner in the Twenty-first Century: Proceedings of the 27th Faulkner and Yoknapatawpha Conference, Aug. 10-16, 2000. Jackson: U of Mississippi P, 2003.

23f Library Database Sources in MLA-Style Works Cited

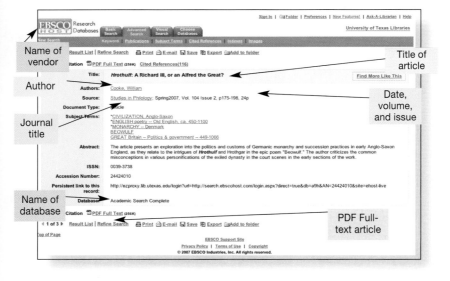

Name of vendor — EBSCO HOST Research Databases

Author — Authors: Cooke, William

Journal title

Name of database — Database: Academic Search Complete

Title of article — Title: *Hrothulf:* A Richard III, or an Alfred the Great?

Date, volume, and issue — Source: Studies in Philology; Spring2007, Vol. 104 Issue 2, p175-198, 24p

PDF Full-text article

77. Journal article from a library database

Snider, Michael. "Wired to Another World." Maclean's 3 Mar. 2003:
  23-24. Academic Search Premier. EBSCO. Harold B. Lee Lib.,
  Brigham Young U. 9 Apr. 2007 <http://www.epnet.com/>.

78. Newspaper article from a library database

Franciane, Valerie. "Quarter Is Ready to Rock." Times-Picayune
  [New Orleans] 3 Apr. 2007: 1. LexisNexis Academic.
  LexisNexis. George A. Smathers Lib., U of Florida. 14 Oct.
  2007 <www.lexisnexis.com/>.

Cooke, William. "Hrothulf: A Richard III, or an Alfred the Great?"

Studies in Philology 104 (2007): 175-98. Academic Search

Premier. EBSCO. U of Texas Lib. 3 Aug. 2007

<http://www.epnet.com/>.

AUTHOR'S NAME

The author's last name comes first, followed by a comma and the first name.

For two or more works by the same author, consult the sample works-cited list on page 414.

TITLE OF ARTICLE

Use the exact title, which appears at the top of the article.

Put the title in quotation marks. If a book title is part of the article's title, underline the book title. If a title requiring quotation marks is part of the article's title, use single quotation marks.

PUBLICATION INFORMATION

Name of journal or newspaper

Underline the title of the journal or newspaper.

Abbreviate the title of the journal or newspaper if it commonly appears that way.

Volume, issue, date, and page numbers

List the same information you would for a print item. See pages 370–377.

DATABASE INFORMATION

Name of database and name of vendor

Underline the name of the database, which you will have to look for.

Give the name of the vendor, which is usually at the top.

Name of library or library system

Give the name of the library or library system you used.

Date of access

List the date you looked at the source just before the URL. No period follows.

URL of vendor

Put the URL of the vendor inside angle brackets followed by a period. The URL of the vendor is not the URL of the page. You may have to enter the name of the vendor in a search engine to find the URL.

23g Online Publications in MLA-Style Works Cited

HOME PAGE

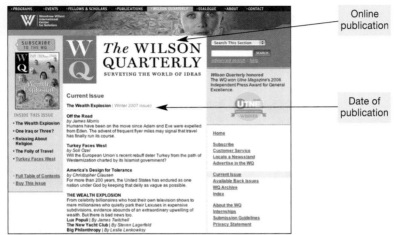

Online publication

Date of publication

FIRST PAGE OF THE ARTICLE

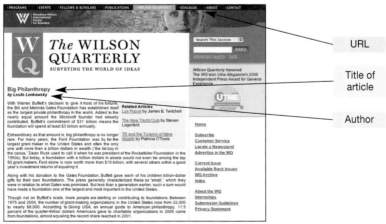

URL

Title of article

Author

Lenkowsky, Leslie. "Big Philanthropy." <u>Wilson Quarterly</u> Winter 2007.

30 May 2007 <http://www.wilsoncenter.org/

index.cfm?fuseaction=wq.essay&essay_id=216352>.

AUTHOR'S NAME

Authorship is sometimes hard to discern for online sources. If you know the author or creator, follow the rules for books and journals.

If the only authority you find is a group or organization, list its name after the date of publication or last revision.

TITLE OF PAGE OR ARTICLE

Use the exact title of the pagr or article. Put the title in quotation marks.

Capitalize all words except articles, prepositions, and coordinating conjuctions unless they are the first word of the title.

PUBLICATION INFORMATION

Name of online publication

Underline the title of the online publication.

Dates

List two dates for each online publication.

1. List the publication date (often at the bottom of the page; might also be a copy-right date). This date might be just a year.

2. List the date you accessed the publication. Place this second date just before the URL. Notice that there is no period after the date of access.

URL

Copy the address exactly as it appears in your browser window. You can even copy and paste the address into your text for greater accuracy. Put it in angle brackets followed by a period.

COMMON QUESTIONS ABOUT CITING ONLINE SOURCES

Where do I find the title?

Web sites are often made up of many separate pages or articles. Each page or article on a Web site may or may not have a title. If you are citing a page that has a title, treat the title like that of an article in a periodical. Otherwise, treat the name of the Web site itself as you would a book.

How do I handle very long URLs?

If the URL is excessively long and complicated, give the URL of the site's search page. If the document is from a subscription service, give the URL of the service's home page or the keyword assigned, preceded by the word *Keyword*. You can also give the sequence of links you followed, preceded by the word *Path*. Place a colon after *Keyword* or *Path*.

Note: Be sure to test your URLs as part of your proofreading process.

Sample works-cited entries for online publications

ONLINE PUBLICATIONS

79. **Publication by a known author**

> Boerner, Steve. "Leopold Mozart." The Mozart Project: Biography. Ed. Steve Boerner. 23 Mar. 1998. The Mozart Project. 3 Dec. 2007 <http://www.mozartproject.org/biography.mozart_1.html>.

80. **Publication by a group or organization**

> "State of the Birds, USA 2004." Audubon. 2004. National Audubon Society. 19 Nov. 2007 <http://www.audubon.org/bird/stateofthebirds/>.

81. Publication where the author's name is a pseudonym

If the author's or creator's name is a pseudonym or is unconventional, list it exactly as it appears on the Web site.

Akma. "Two Points." Blog posting. 26 Mar. 2007. Akma's Random Thoughts. 1 Apr. 2007 <http://akma.disseminary.org>.

ONLINE PERIODICALS

NOTE: Because most online periodicals do not have page numbers, you should identify the site in your paper. That way, you can avoid awkward parenthetical citations.

82. Article in an online scholarly journal

The volume and issue number follow the name of the journal. The date in parentheses is the date of publication.

Caramanica, Laura. "Shared Governance: Hartford Hospital's Experience." Online Journal of Issues in Nursing 9.1 (2004). 12 July 2007 <http://www.nursingworld.org/ojin/topic23/ tpc23_2.htm>.

83. Article in an online newspaper

The first date is the date of publication, the second is the date of access.

Roig-Franzia, Manuel. "Mexican President Criticizes 'Absurd' U.S. Border Policies." Washingtonpost.com 17 Mar. 2007. 23 Sept. 2007 <http://www.washingtonpost.com/wp-dyn/ content/article/2007/03/16/AR2007031602753.html>.

84. **Article in an online magazine**

The first date is the date of publication, the second is the date of access.

Hulbert, Ann. "Inside Autism." Slate 28 Mar. 2007. 23 Nov. 2007
    <http://www.slate.com/id/2162836/>.

85. **Online review**

Stein, Ruthe. "Leave It to Mama to Clean Up the Mess." Rev. of
    Volver, dir. Pedro Almodóvar. SFGate.com 22 Nov. 2006. 23 Jan.
    2007 <http://www.sfgate.com/cgi-bin/article.cgi?f=/
    c/a/2006/11/22/DDGQRMGP7D1.DTL>.

ONLINE BOOKS AND SCHOLARLY PROJECTS

86. **Online book**

Prebish, Charles S., and Kenneth K. Tanaka. The Faces of Buddhism
    in America. Berkeley: U of California P, 2003. 22 May 2007
    <http://ark.cdlib.org/ark:/13030/ft1v19n7k4/>.

87. **Online scholarly project**

If you are citing a page that has a title, treat the title like that of an article in a periodical. Otherwise, treat the name of the Web site itself as you would a book, as in the following example.

The Valley of the Shadow: Two Communities in the American
    Civil War. Ed. Edward L. Ayres, 2001. Virginia Center for Digital
    History, U of Virginia. 1 July 2007
    <http://www.iath.virginia.edu/vshadow2/>.

88. Document within a scholarly project

Give the author and title of the work first, as well as its date and place of publication if it is a book. Then give the name of the project or database, its editor, version or revision date, affiliation, and date of access. The URL is the address of the document itself.

> Calhoun, John C. "The Southern Address." Nineteenth Century
> Documents Project. Ed. Lloyd Bensen. 2000. Furman U.
> 23 Nov. 2007 <http://www.furman.edu/~benson/docs/
> calhoun.htm>.

SUBSCRIPTION SERVICES

89. Work from a personal subscription service

For a personal subscription service that allows you to retrieve material by entering a keyword, write *Keyword* followed by a colon and the word you entered at the end of the entry.

> "Anasazi." Compton's Encyclopedia Online. Vers. 2.0. 1997.
> America Online. 12 Dec. 2007. Keyword: Compton's.

ONLINE GOVERNMENT PUBLICATIONS

90. Online government publication

Begin with the same information you would give for printed government works and conclude with information for the electronic source.

> United States. Dept. of the Treasury. Your Federal Income Tax.
> Publication 17. 2006. 12 Apr. 2007
> <http://www.irs.gov/publications/p17/index. html>.

23h CD-ROM, Software, and Unedited Online Sources in MLA-Style Works Cited

PUBLICATIONS ON CD-ROM

91. CD-ROM by a known author

When page numbers are not available, use the author's name in the text to avoid an awkward parenthetical citation.

> Hagen, Edward, and Phillip Walker. Human Evolution: A Multimedia Guide to the Fossil Record. 2002 ed. CD-ROM. New York: Norton, 2002.

92. Multidisc CD-ROM

Follow the publication medium with either the total number of discs or the number of the specific disc you are using. Mentioning the CD-ROM in the text itself is preferable to a parenthetical citation.

> The Norton Anthology of English Literature Audio Companion. CD-ROM. 2 discs. New York: Norton, 2001.

SOFTWARE

93. Computer software

Provide the author's name (if known), the version number (if any), the manufacturer, and the date. You can also list the operating system, if relevant.

> AOL. Vers. 9.0. America Online, 2004.

UNEDITED ONLINE SOURCES

94. Wiki entry

Wiki content is written collaboratively, thus no author is listed. Provide the title of the article, the name of the Wiki, the date of publication or last revision, the sponsor, the date of access, and the URL.

> Snowboard. Wikipedia. 10 Apr. 2007. Wikipedia Foundation.
> 11 Apr. 2007 <http://en.wikipedia.org/wiki/Snowboard>.

95. Online synchronous communication (MOOs, MUDs)

Provide the speaker and/or site, the title and date of the session, the forum for communication (if specified), the date of access, and the electronic address.

> Sirius, B. Discussion of popularity of Harry Potter. 12 Dec. 2000.
> LinguaMOO. 24 Nov. 2001 <telnet:lingua.utdallas.edu8090>.

96. Email communication

Give the name of the writer, the subject line, a description of the message, and the date.

> Wilson, Samuel. "Digital Authenticity." Email to the author. 18
> Sept. 2007.

97. Online posting to a discussion list

Give the author's name (or alias), the subject line, the descriptor *Online posting,* the date of posting, the name of the discussion list, the date of access, and the URL of the list or the email address of the moderator.

> Green, Angela. "A Doctor on Writing." Online posting. 3 Apr. 2007.
> WPA Discussion List. 23 Nov. 2007 <http://wpacouncil.org>.

98. Course home page

Begin with the instructor's name, the name of the course, the words *Course home page*, the dates of the course, the name of the department, school, date of access, and URL.

> Kirkpatrick, Judith. American Literature Online. Course home
>   page. Jan.-May 2003. Dept. of English. Kapi'olani CC. 23
>   Feb. 2003. <http://www2.hawaii.edu/~kirkpatr/s03/
>   s03250syllabus.html>.

99. Personal home page

If there is no title for the Web site, list it by author or creator. If it is a personal home page, place the words *Home page* after the name of the owner of the page.

> Stallman, Richard. Home page. 2007. 8 Apr. 2007
>   <http://www.stallman.org/>.

100. Blog (Web log) entry

Citing a blog (or Web log) entry is similar to citing other Web sites. In many cases the author's name will be only a first name, pseudonym, or email address. Often there is no sponsoring organization mentioned. MLA does not offer an example entry for a blog, so this entry is based on MLA guidelines for postings to an online discussion list.

> Leitch, Will. "This Was Not Done by Aliens." Blog posting. 3 Apr.
>   2007. Deadspin. 2 May 2007 <http://deadspin.com/sports/
>   baseball/this-was-not-done-by-aliens-249187.php>.

WORKS PUBLISHED IN MULTIPLE FORMATS

101. Work in more than one medium

Specify all of the media that constitute the publication (e.g., book, CD-ROM, diskette) or list only the media you used.

> Scowen, Paul. 21st Century Astronomy. Book, CD-ROM. New York: Norton, 2002.

23i Visual Sources in MLA-Style Works Cited

102. Cartoon

> Chast, Roz. "Are You in Your Goddess Years?" Cartoon. New Yorker 10 Mar. 2004: 113.

103. Advertisement

> Discover Card. Advertisement. Newsweek 29 Oct. 2001: 40-41.

104. Map, graph, or chart

> Baltimore Street Map and Visitor's Guide. Map. Baltimore: MAP, 1999.

105. Table reproduced in your text

This is how a table might appear in your text:

In The Republic, Plato explains how the three parts of the individual soul should be repeated in the structure of the ideal city-state (see Table 1).

Table 1
Plato's Politics

Soul	Reason	Courage	Appetites
State	Elite guardians	Soldiers	Masses

Source: Richard Osborne, Philosophy for Beginners (New York: Writers and Readers, 1992) 15.

This is how a table appears in your list of works cited.

Work Cited

Plato's Politics. Table. New York: Writers and Readers, 1992. 15.

106. Painting, sculpture, or photograph

Provide the artist's name, the title of the work, the date, the name of the institution or individual who owns the work, and the city.

Cloar, Carroll. Odie Maude. 1990. David Lusk Gallery, Memphis.

If you are citing a photograph of a work, give the information for the work, followed by the publication information for the source that you got the photograph from. Include the slide, plate, figure, or page number, as relevant. In the text, mentioning the work and the artist in the text itself is preferable to a parenthetical citation.

107. Online map

> "Xpeditions Atlas." Map. National Geographic.com. 2003.
> National Geographic Society. 24 Nov. 2006
> <http://www.nationalgeographic.com/xpeditions/atlas/>.

108. Online work of art

> Bontecou, Lee. Untitled. 1997. Museum of Modern Art, New York. 10
> Apr. 2007 <http://www.moma.org/exhibitions/2004/
> LeeBontecou.html>.

109. Online cartoon

> Kelley, Steve. "The Swan." Cartoon. Daryl Cagle's Professional
> Cartoonist's Index. 9 Apr. 2004. 12 Apr. 2007 <http://
> cagle.slate.msn.com/politicalcartoons/PCcartoons/kelley.asp>.

23j Multimedia Sources in MLA-Style Works Cited

110. Musical composition

If you have the sheet music or a score, list the publication information. If not, just provide the composer, the title of the composition, and the year.

> Gershwin, George. "Cuban Overture." 1932.

111. Sound recording

> Williams, Lucinda. Essence. Lost Highway Records, 2001.

112. Podcast

MLA does not give an example for documenting a Podcast. Provide all relevant information including the name of the host, the name of the program, the name of the site, the word *Podcast*, the number of the episode, the date of access, and the URL. If the Podcast is a rebroadcast of a program, also provide the information for the original broadcast.

> Sussingham, Robin. "All Things Autumn." HighLifeUtah. Podcast. 20 Nov. 2006. No. 2. 11 Apr. 2007 <http://www.highlifeutah.com/>.

113. Online video clip

> Busterwiand. "Shark Tags Tuna." Video. YouTube. 11 Mar. 2007. 5 May 2007 <http://www.youtube.com/watch?v=B7JtZXUVDYs&NR=1>.

114. Film

> The Departed. Dir. Martin Scorsese. Perf. Leonardo DiCaprio and Matt Damon. Warner Bros., 2006.

115. DVD

> Napoleon Dynamite. Dir. Jared Hess. Perf. Jon Heder, Jon Gries, and Efren Ramirez. DVD. 20th Century Fox, 2004.

116. Television or radio program

Provide the title of the episode or segment, followed by the title of the series (if any). After the titles, list any performers, narrators, directors, or others who might be pertinent. Then give the name of the network and the broadcast date.

> "Philippi." Rome. Dir. Robert Young. HBO. 18 Feb. 2007.

117. Telephone interview

> Minnelli, Liza. Telephone interview. 5 Mar. 2003.

118. Broadcast interview

> Cage, Nicolas. Interview with Terry Gross. <u>Fresh Air</u>. WHYY-FM.
> Philadelphia. 13 June 2002.

119. Musical, dramatic, dance, or artistic performance

> <u>Lipstick Traces</u>. By Griel Marcus. Adapted by Kirk Lynn. Dir. Shawn
> Sides. Perf. Lana Lesley and Jason Liebrecht. Off Center.
> Austin. 31 Aug. 2000.

120. Speech, debate, mediated discussion, or public talk

> Clinton, William Jefferson. Liz Carpenter Distinguished Lecture
> Series, U of Texas at Austin. 12 Feb. 2003.

23k Informational Notes

The MLA style is designed to avoid the need for either footnotes or end-notes. Documentation should be handled using in-text citations and a list of works cited. However, two kinds of notes sometimes appear in MLA style. Notes may be placed at the bottom of the page or at the end of the paper.

Content notes supply additional information that would interrupt the flow of the text, yet may be important to provide the context of a source.

> Much speculation has blamed electronic media, especially television, for an alleged decline in literacy, following Newton N. Minow's famous 1961 description of television as a "vast wasteland."[1]

The note explains who Minow was and why the remark was newsworthy.

> [1]Minow, the newly appointed chairman of the Federal
> Communications Commission, told the assembled executives
> of the National Association of Broadcasters in May 1961
> that "[w]hen television is bad, nothing is worse" (Adams).
> Minow's efforts to upgrade programming were met with cries of
> censorship from the television industry, and Minow resigned two
> years later.

You need to include any sources you use in notes in the list of works cited.

> ### Work Cited
> Adams, Val. "F.C.C. Head Bids TV Men, Reform 'Vast Wasteland.'"
>   New York Times 10 May 1961, late ed.: 11.

Bibliographic notes give either evaluative comments about sources or additional references.

> "Fordism" is a summary term for the system of mass production
> consolidated by Henry Ford in the early decades of this century.[1]

The note gives the origin of the term "Fordism."

> [1]The term Fordism was first used by Italian political theorist
> Antonio Gramsci in his prison notebooks, written while he was
> jailed under Mussolini's fascist dictatorship.

> ### Work Cited
> Gramsci, Antonio. Selections from the Prison Notebooks of Antonio
>   Gramsci. Ed. and trans. Quintin Hoare and Geoffrey Nowell
>   Smith. New York: International, 1971.

 Sample Research Paper with MLA Documentation

Chapters 16 through 22 discuss how to plan and write a research paper. The following research paper, written by Ashley Walker, makes a proposal argument. The paper is annotated to show specific features of MLA style and to show how the works-cited page is organized.

FORMATTING A RESEARCH PAPER IN MLA STYLE

MLA offers these general guidelines for formatting a research paper.

- **Use white, 8½-by-11-inch paper.** Don't use colored or lined paper.
- **Double-space everything—the title, headings, body of the paper, quotations, and works-cited list.** Set the line spacing on your word processor for double spacing and leave it there.

- **Put your last name and the page number at the top of every page, aligned with the right margin, one-half inch from the top of the page.** Your word processor has a header command that will automatically put a header with the page number on every page.
- **Specify one-inch margins.** One-inch margins are the default setting for most word processors.
- **Do not justify (make even) the right margin.** Justifying the right margin throws off the spacing between words and makes your paper harder to read. Use the left-align setting instead.

- **Indent the first line of each paragraph one-half inch (5 spaces).** Set the paragraph indent command or the tab on the ruler of your word processor at one-half inch.
- **Use the same readable typeface throughout your paper.** Use a standard typeface such as Times New Roman, 12 point.
- **Use block format for quotations longer than four lines.** See page 358.
- **MLA does not require a title page.** Unless your instructor asks for a separate title page, put one inch from the top of the page your name, your instructor's name, the course, and the date on separate lines. Center your title on the next line. Do not underline your title or put it inside quotation marks.

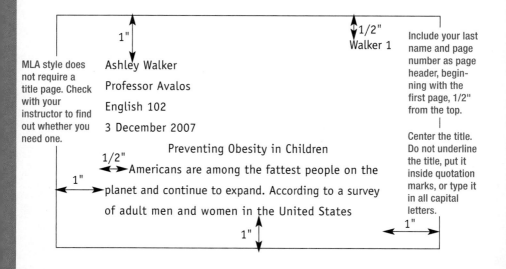

1"

1/2"
Walker 1

MLA style does not require a title page. Check with your instructor to find out whether you need one.

Ashley Walker

Professor Avalos

English 102

3 December 2007

Preventing Obesity in Children

1/2"
◄─►Americans are among the fattest people on the

1"
─►planet and continue to expand. According to a survey

of adult men and women in the United States

1"

Include your last name and page number as page header, beginning with the first page, 1/2" from the top.

Center the title. Do not underline the title, put it inside quotation marks, or type it in all capital letters.

1"

Walker 2

during 2003-2004, published in <u>JAMA: The Journal</u>
<u>of the American Medical Association</u>, 32.5% of
American adults are obese and two-thirds (66.3%)
are overweight (Ogden et al. 1553). Excess weight is
not just a matter of looks. Obesity magnifies the risk
of heart disease, diabetes, high blood pressure, and
other ailments—already overtaking tobacco as the
leading cause of chronic illness (Brownell and
Horgen 4). An especially disturbing aspect of this
trend is that children are increasingly obese. The
Center for Disease Control and Prevention reports
that the percentage of obese children aged 6 to 11
almost quadrupled from 4% in 1974 to 15% in 2000,
and the percentage of obese children aged 12 to 19
increased from 6% in 1974 to 15% in 2000 (United
States; see Fig. 1). Obese children have a 70%
chance of becoming obese adults with a much
higher risk of serious illness than those of normal
weight (Brownell and Horgen 46). Furthermore,
obese children suffer many serious health
problems today. Pediatricians now routinely treat
atherosclerosis and type II diabetes, diseases

Specify 1"
margins all
around. Double-
space every-
thing.

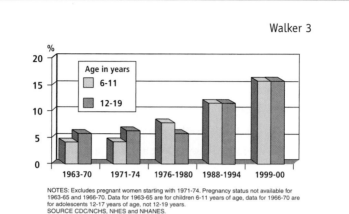

NOTES: Excludes pregnant women starting with 1971-74. Pregnancy status not available for 1963-65 and 1966-70. Data for 1963-65 and 1966-70 are for children 6-11 years of age, data for 1966-70 are for adolescents 12-17 years of age, not 12-19 years.
SOURCE CDC/NCHS, NHES and NHANES.

Fig. 1. Prevalence of overweight among children and adolescents ages 6-19 years, chart from United States, Department of Health and Human Services, Centers for Disease Control and Prevention, Prevalence of Overweight Among Children and Adolescents: United States, 1999-2000 (24 Oct. 2002 <http://www.cdc.gov/nchs/products/pubs/pubd/hestats/overwght99.htm>).

that used to be frequent only among older people (Tyre 38). Today's children are among the first generation in American history who may die at earlier ages than their parents.

Walker 4

For most people in the United States, obesity is a matter of individual choice and old-fashioned willpower (Lee and Oliver). The usual advice for overweight people is to eat less and exercise more, but how applicable is this advice for children unless they have strong guidance from adults? How can children make intelligent choices about eating in an environment where overeating is normal and where few adults know what's in the food they eat? The United States has been successful in addressing teenage health problems: drug use has dropped, teenage pregnancy has been reduced, and teen smoking has declined. We need to take a similar proactive response by taking concrete steps to reverse the trend toward more obese children.

Many have blamed the rise in obesity on a more sedentary life style, including the move to the suburbs, where people drive instead of walk, and increased viewing of television. One study of children watching television found a significant drop in the average metabolic rate during viewing (Klesges, Shelton, and Klesges). Another study reports that

Indent each paragraph five spaces (1/2" on the ruler in your word processing program).

Walker's thesis appears here, at the end of her second paragraph. The preceding questions establish a context for her thesis.

Cite publications within the text by the name of the author (or authors).

Walker 5

reducing children's television viewing also affects their
eating behavior (Robinson and Killen). No doubt that
children who exercise less tend to weigh more, but the
couch potato argument does not explain why the
enormous weight gains have occurred over the past
twenty-five years. The move to the suburbs and the
widespread viewing of television began in the 1950s.
Furthermore, the couch potato argument neglects the
extraordinary rise of female participation in athletics.
The number of young women playing a sport in high
school has risen from 294,015 in 1971-72 to 2,953,355
in 2005-06, a tenfold increase ("Participation"). Yet
girls, like boys, have gained weight.

The simple answer to why Americans of all ages
have steadily gained weight over the past three
decades is that we're consuming more calories—
about 500 more per person per day in 2000 than in
1984. Marion Nestle, the chair of the Department of
Nutrition and Food Studies at New York University,
observes that "food is so overproduced in the U.S.
that there are 3,800 calories per person per day, and
we only need about half of that" (qtd. in Spake and

Sources not identified with an author are referenced in text by title.

Marcus 43). We're eating more food high in calories and high in fat than ever before.

Patterns of eating in America have changed over the past three decades. With more people working longer hours and fewer staying at home, annual spending in adjusted dollars at restaurants increased nearly by a factor of ten between 1970 and 2003, from $42.8 billion to $426.1 billion ("Industry"). The growth was most rapid among fast-food chains,

Do not include a page number for items without pagination, such as Web sites.

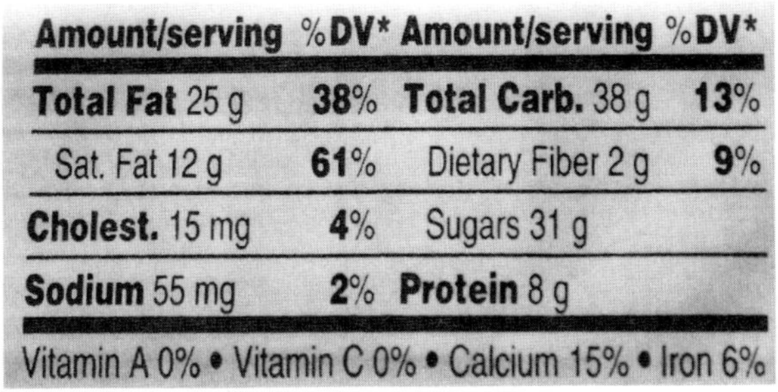

Amount/serving	%DV*	Amount/serving	%DV*
Total Fat 25 g	**38%**	**Total Carb.** 38 g	**13%**
Sat. Fat 12 g	**61%**	Dietary Fiber 2 g	**9%**
Cholest. 15 mg	**4%**	Sugars 31 g	
Sodium 55 mg	**2%**	**Protein** 8 g	
Vitamin A 0% • Vitamin C 0% • Calcium 15% • Iron 6%			

Fig. 2. Nutritional information label for a typical snack food. This chocolate bar with almonds contains 38% of the recommended daily total fat intake and a remarkable 61% of an entire day's recommended intake of saturated fat.

If more than one publication is by the same author, include an abbreviated title in the reference.

which by 1999 were opening a new restaurant every two hours (Schlosser, "Bitter"). According to Eric Schlosser,

Quotations of more than four lines should be indented 1" or ten spaces. Do not use quotation marks. Introduce block quotations rather than just dropping them into the text.

> In 1970, Americans spent about $6 billion on fast food; in 2001, they spent more than $110 billion. Americans now spend more money on fast food than on higher education, personal computers, computer software, or new cars. They spend more money on fast food than on movies, books, magazines, newspapers, videos, and recorded music—combined. (Fast 3)

As the restaurant business became more competitive, fast-food chains realized that the cost of the food they served was small in comparison to the costs of buildings, labor, packaging, and advertising, so they began increasing the size of portions. Amanda Spake and Mary Brophy Marcus note: "When McDonald's opened, its original burger, fries, and 12-ounce Coke provided 590 calories. Today, a supersize Extra Value Meal with a Quarter Pounder With Cheese, supersize fries, and a supersize drink is 1,550 calories" (44).

Walker 8

Large portions may represent good value for the dollar, but they are not good value for overall health.

Another significant change in the American diet beginning in the 1970s has been the introduction of high-fructose corn syrup into many foods. Listed at the top of food labels today are fructose, dextrose, maltrose, or a similar name—all corn syrup products—in foods like peanut butter, crackers, and ketchup not associated with high levels of sugar. Food producers found that sweetness is an important component of taste, and they have been dumping in sweet corn syrup ever since. High-fructose corn syrup is cheap to produce and enjoys government subsidies, enabling soft drink manufacturers to increase size without increasing cost. The 8-ounce soft drink bottle of the 1950s has been replaced with the 12-ounce can, 20-ounce bottle, and 32-ounce fountain drink. Harvard researcher David Ludwig has found that food high in sugar makes people hungrier in a short time because it creates a spike in blood sugar followed by a crash, triggering overeating (Uhlenhuth). In other words, one cookie does lead to another.

Walker 9

Also contributing to the rise of obesity is the widespread availability of food. Stores that formerly did not sell food, such as drug stores, now have aisles of food. Gas stations have been replaced by mini-marts. Vending machines are found nearly everywhere, particularly in cash-strapped schools. And food companies have produced an endless line of good-tasting snack foods for consumption at home and at work. When we eat food high in sugar and feel hungry two hours later, usually food is close by.

These factors have contributed to a general rise in obesity, but they do not explain why the rate of obesity among children has skyrocketed. One prominent cause is the huge increase in marketing food to children, which has not only doubled since 1992 but also become increasingly sophisticated. An average child in the United States who watches television now sees a food ad on Saturday morning every 5 minutes and a total of over 10,000 a year, overwhelmingly ads for high-sugar and high-fat food (Brownell and Horgen 101-02). Restaurant and food companies spend fifteen billion dollars in marketing

Give page numbers for paraphrases as well as direct quotations.

Walker 10

to children each year with sophisticated advertising campaigns that include product tie-ins (Barboza C1). Even children of parents who limit or ban television watching are exposed to a massive amount of food advertising in movies and video games, on the Internet, and even in schools. Walter Willett, a Harvard professor of nutrition, observes, "The vast majority of what [food companies] sell is junk. . . . How often do you see fruits and vegetables marketed?" (qtd. in Barboza C1).

Obesity in children is a health crisis comparable to the illnesses caused by smoking. Defenders of the food industry argue that smoking is voluntary, but everyone has to eat. The crisis for children is more analogous to secondhand smoke, which has been proven to be harmful to children. To blame children for choosing to be fat is like blaming a baby for being born to parents who smoke. Most children lack the knowledge to make intelligent food choices, and they often have no access to healthy food. Parents of course can make a difference, but parents do not control much of the environment where children eat, including school lunch programs and vending machines in schools. Furthermore, the majority of adults have inadequate skills for controlling their weight.

Some changes have begun to occur. West Virginia has eliminated junk food in vending machines in schools (Tyre 40). McDonald's and other fast-food companies have begun to offer healthier alternatives to their fat-laden foods. Kraft Foods, the largest food company in the United States, has begun an antiobesity initiative by reducing portions of popular snacks and providing more nutritional information (Walker). But these are small steps in addressing the biggest health crisis of the twenty-first century.

The first major step in reducing obesity in children is to restrict marketing of junk food to children. When the American public realized how effective Joe Camel ads were in reaching children, their outrage led to a ban on many forms of cigarette advertising. The food industry has no such restrictions and uses popular cartoon characters and actors to pitch their products. According to advertising professor Vijay Netaji, children under age eight cannot distinguish programs from advertising,

Walker 12

particularly when the same characters are participating in both. Other countries including Belgium, Greece, Norway, and Sweden now limit advertising directed toward children (Brownell and Horgen 123). The United States should join these nations.

The second major step is to develop a campaign to educate children and parents about healthy and unhealthy food. Children and their parents need to know more about the health risks of obesity and how to follow healthier eating habits. Parents play an important role in selecting what children eat, but children also need to be able to make good choices about eating on their own.

The third major step is to promote a healthy lifestyle through more exercise. Exercise, like eating, is not simply a matter of personal choice. Many schools cannot afford to provide physical education programs and activities that encourage exercise, and many communities lack public space and facilities where people can exercise. More exercise for children needs to be made a priority in schools and communities.

Walker 13

Step one can be accomplished either by voluntary restriction of marketing to children or by legislation, but steps two and three will require major funding sources. Margo Wootan of the consumer advocacy group Center for Science in the Public Interest proposes that food companies support a public service campaign to promote healthier eating and more exercise ("Generation"). Wootan's proposal may be too idealistic for the highly competitive food industry where profits mean survival. Advocates for children's health have proposed instead taxes on unhealthy food and soft drinks similar to taxes on tobacco products that fund the campaign to reduce teenage smoking (Brownell). Food tax proposals have been extremely controversial. The Center for Consumer Freedom, a group supported by the restaurant and food industry, has launched ads against "fat taxes" and legal actions against junk food, arguing that healthy food is a choice ("CCF"). The choice argument, however, is more difficult to make for children.

If a source consists of a single page, do not give the page number in the citation.

Walker 14

If food taxes are the best way to promote healthier eating and more exercise among children, would Americans support such a tax? A 2003 opinion poll sponsored by the Harvard Forums on Health found that Americans are overwhelmingly in favor of measures to fight obesity in children including banning vending machines that sell unhealthy foods in schools and providing healthier school lunches ("Obesity"). Over three quarters of the people sampled in the poll support a government-sponsored advertising campaign for healthier eating and the creation of more public spaces for exercise. The poll indicates that Americans are willing to pay higher taxes for these programs, although the majority opposed specific taxes on junk food. Just as Americans eventually woke up to the risks of smoking among young people and took decisive action, they are gradually becoming aware of the threat of obesity to their children's future and, more important, starting to do something about it.

Works Cited

Barboza, David. "If You Pitch It, They Will Eat."

New York Times 3 Aug. 2003, late ed.: C1+.

Brownell, Kelly D. "Get Slim with Higher Taxes."

New York Times 15 Dec. 1994, late ed.: A29+.

Brownell, Kelly D., and Katherine Battle Horgen.

Food Fight: The Inside Story of the Food Industry,

America's Obesity Crisis, and What We Can Do

about It. Chicago: Contemporary, 2004.

"CCF Ad Campaigns." ConsumerFreedom.com. 2003.

Center for Consumer Freedom. 18 Nov. 2007 <http://

www.consumerfreedom.com/ad_campaign.cfm>.

"Generation XL: Middle Ground on Obesity." Editorial.

Boston Globe 11 Oct. 2003, 3rd ed.: A18.

"Industry at a Glance." Restaurant.org. 2003. National

Restaurant Association. 18 Nov. 2007

<http://www.restaurant.org/research/

ind_glance.cfm>.

Klesges, Robert C., Mary L. Shelton, and Lisa M.

Klesges. "Effects of Television on Metabolic

Rate: Potential Implications for Childhood

Obesity." Pediatrics 91 (1993): 281-86. Academic

Side annotations:

Center "Works Cited" on a new page.

Double-space all entries. Indent all but the first line in each entry five spaces.

Alphabetize entries by the last names of the authors or by the first important word in the title if no author is listed.

Underline the titles of books and periodicals.

Walker 16

OneFile. Thomson Gale. U of Texas Lib. 20 Nov.
    2007 <http://www.gale.com/>.

Lee, Taeku, and J. Eric Oliver. "Public Opinion and the
    Politics of America's Obesity Epidemic." May 2002.
    John F. Kennedy School of Government, Harvard
    U. 12 Nov. 2007 <ksgnotes1.harvard.edu/
    Research/wpaper.nsf/rwp/RWP02-017/$File/
    rwp02_017_lee.pdf>.

Netaji, Vijay. Telephone interview. 20 Nov. 2007.

"Obesity as a Public Health Issue: A Look at Solutions."
    Harvard University Program for Health Systems
    Improvement. 2003. Harvard Forums on Health. 18
    Nov. 2007 <http://www.phsi.harvard.edu/
    health_reform/focus_on_obesity.php>.

Ogden, Cynthia L., et al. "Prevalence of Overweight and
    Obesity in the United States, 1999-2004."
    JAMA 295 (2006): 1549-55.

"Participation in High School Sports Increases Again;
    Confirms NFHS Commitment to Stronger Leadership."
    16 Sept. 2006. National Federation of State
    High School Associations. 14 Nov. 2007

Walker 17

<http://www.nfhs.org/web/2006/09/
participation_in_high_school_sports_increases_
again_confirms_nf.aspx>.

Robinson, Thomas N., and Joel D. Killen. "Obesity
Prevention for Children and Adolescents."
Body Image, Eating Disorders, and Obesity in
Youth: Assessment, Prevention, and Treatment. Ed.
J. Kevin Thompson and Linda Smolak. Washington,
DC: APA, 2001. 261-92.

Schlosser, Eric. "The Bitter Truth about Fast Food."
Guardian 7 Apr. 2001, weekend sec.: 13.

---. Fast Food Nation: The Dark Side of the All-American
Meal. New York: Perennial, 2002.

Spake, Amanda, and Mary Brophy Marcus. "A Fat Nation."
U.S. News & World Report 19 Aug. 2002: 40-47.

Tyre, Peg. "Fighting 'Big Fat.'" Newsweek 5 Aug. 2002:
38-40.

Uhlenhuth, Karen. "Spoonful of Sugar Makes Appetites
Go Up." Advertiser 19 Jan. 2003: 39. LexisNexis
Academic. LexisNexis. U of Texas Lib. 20 Nov. 2007
<http://www.lexis-nexis.com/>.

If an author has more than one entry, list the entries in alphabetical order by title. Use three hyphens in place of the author's name for the second and subsequent entries.

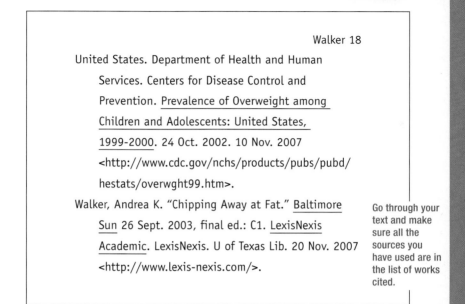

Walker 18

United States. Department of Health and Human
 Services. Centers for Disease Control and
 Prevention. Prevalence of Overweight among
 Children and Adolescents: United States,
 1999-2000. 24 Oct. 2002. 10 Nov. 2007
 <http://www.cdc.gov/nchs/products/pubs/pubd/
 hestats/overwght99.htm>.

Walker, Andrea K. "Chipping Away at Fat." Baltimore
 Sun 26 Sept. 2003, final ed.: C1. LexisNexis
 Academic. LexisNexis. U of Texas Lib. 20 Nov. 2007
 <http://www.lexis-nexis.com/>.

Go through your text and make sure all the sources you have used are in the list of works cited.

To hear audio commentary on this piece of writing, visit this page of the E-book at www.mycomplab.com.

FORMATTING THE WORKS CITED IN MLA STYLE

- **Begin the works-cited list on a new page.** Insert a page break with your word processor before you start the works-cited page.
- **Center "Works Cited" on the first line at the top of the page.**
- **Double-space all entries.**
- **Alphabetize each entry by the last name of the author or, if no author is listed, by the first content word in the title (ignore *a, an, the*).**
- **Indent all but the first line in each entry one-half inch (five spaces).**
- **Underline the titles of books and periodicals.**
- **If an author has more than one entry, list the entries in alphabetical order by title. Use three hyphens in place of the author's name for the second and subsequent entries.**

> Murphy, Dervla. <u>Cameroon with Egbert</u>. Woodstock, NY: Overlook, 1990.

> ---. <u>Full Tilt: Ireland to India with a Bicycle</u>. London: Murray, 1965.

- **Go through your paper to check that each source you have used is in the works-cited list.**

Chapter 24

APA Documentation

APA style is followed in the social sciences and education.

In-text Citations

References

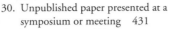

Social sciences disciplines—including government, linguistics, psychology, sociology, and education—frequently use the American Psychological Association (APA) documentation style. The APA style is similar to the MLA style in many ways. Both styles use parenthetical citations in the body of the text, with complete bibliographical citations in the list of references at the end. Both styles avoid using footnotes for references. For a detailed treatment of APA style, consult the *Publication Manual of the American Psychological Association*, fifth edition (2001) and the *APA Style Guide to Electronic References* (2007), available online.

APA style emphasizes the date of publication. When you cite an author's name in the body of your paper, always include the date of publication. Notice too that APA style includes the abbreviation for page (p.) in front of the page number. A comma separates each element of the citation.

> Zukin (2004) observes that teens today begin to shop for themselves at age 13 or 14, "the same age when lower-class children, in the past, became apprentices or went to work in factories" (p. 50).

If the author's name is not mentioned in the sentence, the reference looks like this:

> One sociologist notes that teens today begin to shop for themselves at age 13 or 14, "the same age when lower-class children, in the past, became apprentices or went to work in factories" (Zukin, 2004, p. 50).

The corresponding entry in the references list would be

> Zukin, S. (2004). *Point of purchase: How shopping changed American culture.* New York: Routledge.

24a In-text Citations in APA Style

Paraphrase, summary, or short quotation

In APA style a short quotation has fewer than 40 words.

> "The appeal of a shopping spree," one sociologist comments, "is not that you'll buy a lot of stuff; the appeal is that, among all the stuff you buy, you'll find what you truly desire" (Zukin, 2004, p. 112).

The author's name is provided in the parenthetical reference.

In this example, the author's name is provided inside the parentheses at the end of the sentence. Put the author's name in a signal phrase in your sentence, particularly when you want to add an affiliation or title to indicate the authority of your source.

> "The appeal of a shopping spree," noted sociologist Sharon Zukin (2004) comments, "is not that you'll buy a lot of stuff; the appeal is that, among all the stuff you buy, you'll find what you truly desire" (p. 112).

Put the page number in parentheses after the quotation. Note that the period comes *after* the parentheses.

When the author of the quotation is clearly named in the sentence, add the date in parentheses after the author's name.

WHERE DO YOU PUT THE DATE?

You have two choices. You can put the date (1) in your text in parentheses:

> Zhang, Liu, and Cao (2001) specify . . .

or (2) between the author's name and the page number in the citation note:

> . . . visual languages (Zhang, Liu, & Cao, 2001, p. 192).

For translations, reprints, and later editions, either put *trans.* or *revised* before the date of the source you have, or give the original date, if known.

> (O'Brien, trans. 1973) or (O'Brien 1941/1973).

Quotations 40 words or longer

> Orlean (2001) has attempted to explain the popularity of the painter Thomas Kinkade:
>> People like to own things they think are valuable. . . . The high price of limited editions is part of their appeal; it implies that they are choice and exclusive, and that only a certain class of people will be able to afford them. (p. 128)

The sentence introducing the quotation names the author.

Note that the period appears before the parentheses in an indented "block" quote.

The date appears in parentheses immediately following the author's name.

WHEN DO YOU NEED TO GIVE A PAGE NUMBER?

- Give the page number for all quotations.
- APA encourages including page numbers for paraphrases, but they are not required.
- For electronic sources that do not provide page numbers, give the paragraph number when available. Use the abbreviation *para.* or the symbol ¶.
- If the source does not include page numbers, it is preferable to reference the work and the author in the text.

   In Martin Scorsese's 2006 film *The Departed*, . . .

Sample in-text citations

1. Author named in your text

The influential sociologist Daniel Bell (1973) noted a shift in the United States to the "postindustrial society" (p. 3).

2. Author not named in your text

In 1997, the Gallup poll reported that 55% of adults in the United States think secondhand smoke is "very harmful," compared to only 36% in 1994 (Saad, 1997, p. 4).

3. Work by a single author

(Bell, 1973, p. 3)

4. Work by two authors

List both authors' last names, joined with an ampersand.

(Suzuki & Irabu, 2002, p. 404)

When you cite the authors' names in a sentence, use *and* in place of the ampersand.

Suzuki and Irabu (2002) report . . .

5. Work by three to five authors

The authors' last names follow the order of the title page.

(Francisco, Vaughn, & Romano, 2006, p. 7)

Subsequent references can use the first name and *et al.*

(Francisco et al., 2006, p. 17)

6. Work by six or more authors

Use the first author's last name and *et al.* for all in-text references.

(Swallit et al., 2007, p. 49)

7. Work by a group or organization

Identify the group in the text and place the page number in parentheses.

The National Organization for Women (2001) observed that this "generational shift in attitudes towards marriage and childrearing" will have profound consequences (p. 325).

If you use the name of the group in an in-text citation, the first time you cite the source put its acronym (if there is one) in brackets.

> (National Organization for Women [NOW], 2001)

Use the acronym in subsequent in-text citations.

> (NOW, 2001)

8. Work by an unknown author

Use a shortened version of the title (or the full title if it is short) in place of the author's name. Capitalize all key words in the title. If it is an article title, place it inside quotation marks.

> ("Derailing the Peace Process," 2003, p. 44)

9. Two works by one author with the same copyright date

Assign the dates letters (*a*, *b*, etc.) according to their alphabetical arrangement in the references list.

> The majority of books written about coauthorship focus on partners of the same sex (Laird, 2007a, p. 351).

10. Parts of an electronic source

If an online or other electronic source does not provide page numbers, use the paragraph number preceded by either the paragraph symbol ¶ or the abbreviation *para.*

> (Robinson, 2007, ¶7)

11. Two or more sources within the same sentence

Place each citation directly after the statement it supports.

> Some surveys report an increase in homelessness rates (Alford, 2004) while others chart a slight decrease (Rice, 2006a) . . .

If you need to cite two or more works within the same parentheses, list them in the order they appear in the references list.

> (Alford, 2004; Rice, 2006a)

12. Work quoted in another source

Give the full citation for the secondary source (in this case Rice, 2006a) in the list of references.

> Saunders and Kellman's study (as cited in Rice, 2006a)

24b Book and Nonperiodical Sources in the APA-Style References List

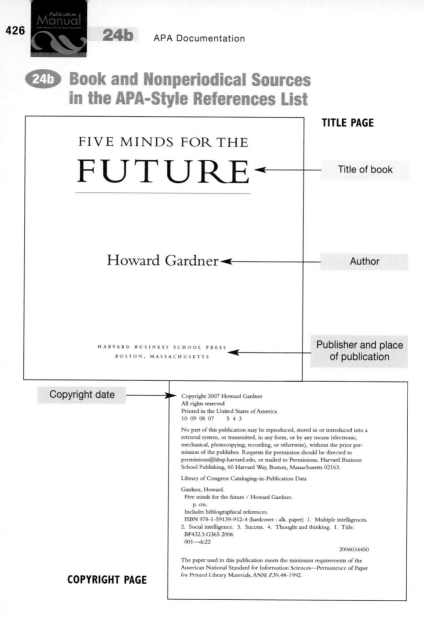

TITLE PAGE

FIVE MINDS FOR THE

FUTURE ←

Title of book

Howard Gardner ←

Author

HARVARD BUSINESS SCHOOL PRESS
BOSTON, MASSACHUSETTS

Publisher and place of publication

Copyright date

Copyright 2007 Howard Gardner
All rights reserved
Printed in the United States of America
10 09 08 07   5 4 3

No part of this publication may be reproduced, stored in or introduced into a
retrieval system, or transmitted, in any form, or by any means (electronic,
mechanical, photocopying, recording, or otherwise), without the prior permission of the publisher. Requests for permission should be directed to
permissions@hbsp.harvard.edu, or mailed to Permissions, Harvard Business
School Publishing, 60 Harvard Way, Boston, Massachusetts 02163.

Library of Congress Cataloging-in-Publication Data

Gardner, Howard.
     Five minds for the future / Howard Gardner.
          p. cm.
     Includes bibliographical references.
     ISBN 978-1-59139-912-4 (hardcover : alk. paper) 1. Multiple intelligences.
2. Social intelligence. 3. Success. 4. Thought and thinking. I. Title.
     BF432.3.G365 2006
     001—dc22

                                                        2006034450

The paper used in this publication meets the minimum requirements of the
American National Standard for Information Sciences—Permanence of Paper
for Printed Library Materials, ANSI Z39.48-1992.

COPYRIGHT PAGE

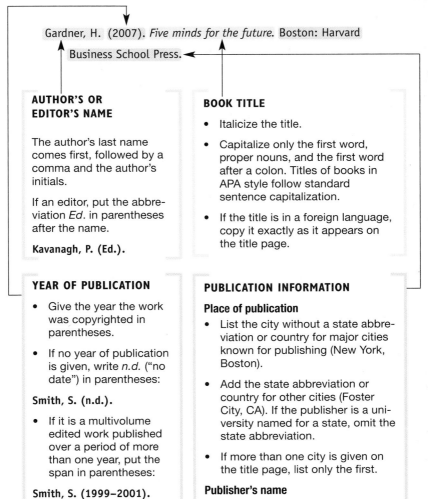

Gardner, H. (2007). *Five minds for the future*. Boston: Harvard Business School Press.

AUTHOR'S OR EDITOR'S NAME

The author's last name comes first, followed by a comma and the author's initials.

If an editor, put the abbreviation *Ed*. in parentheses after the name.

Kavanagh, P. (Ed.).

YEAR OF PUBLICATION

- Give the year the work was copyrighted in parentheses.

- If no year of publication is given, write *n.d.* ("no date") in parentheses:

Smith, S. (n.d.).

- If it is a multivolume edited work published over a period of more than one year, put the span in parentheses:

Smith, S. (1999–2001).

BOOK TITLE

- Italicize the title.

- Capitalize only the first word, proper nouns, and the first word after a colon. Titles of books in APA style follow standard sentence capitalization.

- If the title is in a foreign language, copy it exactly as it appears on the title page.

PUBLICATION INFORMATION

Place of publication

- List the city without a state abbreviation or country for major cities known for publishing (New York, Boston).

- Add the state abbreviation or country for other cities (Foster City, CA). If the publisher is a university named for a state, omit the state abbreviation.

- If more than one city is given on the title page, list only the first.

Publisher's name

Do not shorten or abbreviate words like *University* or *Press*. Omit words such as *Co.*, *Inc.*, and *Publishers*.

Sample references for books

ONE AUTHOR

13. Book by one author

The author's last name comes first, followed by a comma and the first initial of the author's first name and middle initial, if any.

> Ball, E. (2000). *Slaves in the family*. New York: Ballantine Books.

If an editor, put the abbreviation *Ed.* in parentheses after the name.

> Rasgon, N. L. (Ed.). (2006). *The effects of estrogen on brain function*. Baltimore: Johns Hopkins University Press.

14. Two or more books by the same author

Arrange according to the date, with the earliest publication first, or alphabetically according to the names of additional authors.

> Jules, R. (2003). *Internal memos and other classified documents*. London: Hutchinson.
> Jules, R. (2004). *Derelict cabinet*. London: Corgi-Transworld.

MULTIPLE AUTHORS

15. Book by two authors

> Hardt, M., & Negri, A. (2000). *Empire*. Cambridge, MA: Harvard University Press.

If editors, use *(Eds.)* after the names.

> McClelland, D., & Eismann, K. (Eds.).

16. Book by three or more authors

Write out all of the authors' names up to six. The seventh and subsequent authors can be abbreviated to *et al.*

> Anders, K., Child, H., Davis, K., Logan, O., Petersen, J., Tymes, J., et al.

17. Authors listed with the word *with*

> Bettinger, M. (with Winthorp, E.).

UNKNOWN AND GROUP AUTHORS

18. **Book by an unknown author**

Survey of developing nations. (2003). New York: Justice for All Press.

19. **Book by a group or organization**

Centers for Disease Control and Prevention. (2003). *Men and heart disease: An atlas of racial and ethnic disparities in mortality*. Atlanta, GA: Author.

TRANSLATIONS, EDITIONS, AND MULTIVOLUME BOOKS

20. **Translated book**

Voltaire. (1959). *Candide* (R. Aldington, Trans.). Garden City, NY: Hanover. (Original work published 1759)

21. **Revised or later edition of a book**

Weintraub, A. (2004). *Yoga for depression: A compassionate guide to relieve suffering through Yoga* (2nd ed.). New York: Broadway Books.

22. **Multivolume book**

Theweleit, K. (1993). *Male fantasies* (Vol. 1). Minneapolis: University of Minnesota Press.

PARTS OF BOOKS

23. **Chapter written by the same author as the book**

Add the word *In* after the chapter title and before the book title. Include inclusive full page numbers for the chapter inside parentheses.

Savage, T. (2004). Challenging mirror modeling in group therapy. In *Collaborative practice in psychology and therapy* (pp. 130–157). New York: Haworth Clinical Practice Press.

24. **Chapter in an edited collection**

McCracken, J. L. (1995). Northern Ireland, 1921–66. In T. W.
Moody & F. X. Martin (Eds.), *The course of Irish history*
(pp. 313–324). Niwot, CO: Roberts Rinehart.

25. **Chapter in a volume in a series**

Jackson, E. (1998). Politics and gender. In F. Garrity (Series Ed.) &
M. Halls (Vol. Ed.), *Political library: Vol. 4. Race, gender, and
class* (2nd ed., pp. 101–151). New York: Muse.

26. **Article in a reference work**

Viscosity. (2001). In *The Columbia encyclopedia* (6th ed.).
New York: Columbia University Press.

27. **Selection reprinted from another source**

Thompson, H. S. (1997). The scum also rises. In K. Kerrane &
B. Yagoda (Eds.), *The art of fact* (pp. 302–315). New York:
Touchstone. (Reprinted from *The great shark hunt*,
pp. 299–399, by H. S. Thompson, 1979, New York:
Simon & Schuster)

RESEARCH REPORTS, CONFERENCE PROCEEDINGS, AND DISSERTATIONS

28. **Technical and research reports**

Austin, A., & Baldwin, R. (1991). *Faculty collaboration: Enhancing the
quality of scholarship and teaching* (ASCHE-ERIC Higher Education
Report 7). Washington, DC: George Washington University.

29. **Published conference proceedings**

Abarkan, A. (1999). Educative physical planning: Housing and the
emergence of suburbia in Sweden. In T. Mann (Ed.), *Power of
imagination. Proceedings of the 30th annual conference of the*

> *Environmental Design Research Association* (pp. 24–32).
> Edmond, OK: Environmental Design Research Association.

30. Unpublished paper presented at a symposium or meeting

> Kelly, M. (2004, November). *Communication in virtual terms.* Paper presented at the annual meeting of the National Communication Association, Chicago.

31. Poster session

Poster sessions are common at social sciences conferences. Give the year and month of the meeting following the author's name, and give the name of the meeting.

> Wilson, W. (2005, September). *Voting patterns among college students, 1992–2004.* Poster session presented at the annual meeting of the American Political Science Association, Washington, DC.

32. Unpublished dissertation or thesis

> Davis, J. (2004). *A quantitive analysis of student activism and the effects of online communication, 1994–2002.* Unpublished doctoral dissertation, New York University.

33. Published dissertation or thesis

If the dissertation you are citing is published by University Microfilms International (UMI), provide the order number as the last item in the entry.

> Price, J. J. (1998). Flight maps: Encounters with nature in modern American culture. *Dissertation Abstracts International, 59* (5), 1635. (UMI No. 9835247)

GOVERNMENT AND LEGAL DOCUMENTS

34. Government document

When the author and publisher are identical, use the word *Author* as the name of the publisher.

U.S. Environmental Protection Agency. (2002). *Respiratory health effects of passive smoking: Lung cancer and other disorders.* (EPA Publication No. 600/6–90/006 F). Washington, DC: Author.

In-text

(U.S. Environmental Protection Agency [EPA], 2002)

35. *Congressional Record* (Senate resolution)

S. Res. 103, 107th Cong., 147 Cong. Rec. 5844 (2001) (enacted).

In-text

(S. Res. 103, 2001)

36. Online government publication

U.S. Public Health Service. Office of the Surgeon General. (2001, March 11). *Women and smoking.* Retrieved April 25, 2004, from http://www.surgeongeneral.gov/library/womenandtobacco/

In-text

(U.S. Public Health Service [USPHS], 2001)

RELIGIOUS TEXTS, PAMPHLETS, INTERVIEWS, AND LETTERS

37. Religious or classical texts

Reference entries are not required for major classical works or the Bible, but in the first in-text citation, identify the edition used.

John 3.16 (Modern Phrased Version)

38. Bulletins or pamphlets

> University Health Center. (2001). *The common cold* [Brochure].
> Austin, TX: Author.

39. Published interview

List a published interview under the name of the interviewer. Then list the date of the interview and the subject's name in brackets. Follow with the publication information.

> Bush, L. (2001, April). [Interview with P. Burka]. *Texas Monthly*,
> pp. 80–85, 122–124.

40. Unpublished letter

Personal communications are not listed on the references list; they are cited in text only.

> (B. O'Nolan, personal communication, May 1, 2004)

24c Periodical Sources in the APA-Style References List

COMMUNICATION EDUCATION

(ISSN 0363-4523) VOLUME 52 • NUMBER 1 • JANUARY 2003

ARTICLES

Name of journal, volume,
issue number, date

ix   Note from the Editor   Don Rubin

1   Practicing Engineers Talk about the   Ann L. Darling and
     Importance of Talk: A Report on the   Deanna P. Dannels
     Role of Oral Communication in the
     Workplace

     In the last decade engineering education and industry have requested
     assistance from communication educators. Responding to increased atten-
     tion on the changing expectations for practicing engineers and an attendant
     need for better communication skills, these teams of engineering and
     communication educators have been working to incorporate speaking and
     writing in engineering education. Despite a great deal of anecdotal evidence
     that communication is important to working engineers, relatively little data
     based information is available to help us understand better the specifics of
     how and why communication is important for these particular professionals.
     This paper reports the results of practicing engineers' descriptions of the
     importance of oral communication. These data suggest that engineering
     practice takes place in an intensely oral culture and while formal presenta-
     tions are important to practicing engineers, daily work is characterized more
     by interpersonal and small group experiences. Communication skills such
     as translation, clarity, negotiation, and listening are vital.

17   An Examination of Academic Mentoring   Paul Schrodt,
     Behaviors and New Faculty Members'   Carol Stringer Cawyer,
     Satisfaction with Socialization and   and Renee Sanders
     Tenure and Promotion Processes

     This study explored the relationship between academic mentoring behav-
     iors and the organizational socialization of new faculty members within the
     communication discipline. Participants included 259 faculty members from
     the National Communication Association. Results indicated that mentors'
     tendencies to provide support and encouragement, a sense of collegiality,
     and research assistance are related to an organizational newcomer's feelings
     of connectedness and ownership with the work environment. Overall, the
     results suggested that the benefits of mentoring are reciprocal and benefit the
     institution as well as the protégé.

30   Loss of the Creature: The Obscuring of   Lesley A. Rex
     Inclusivity in Classroom Discourse

     Amidst few empirical studies of the effects of high stakes testing on class-
     room talk, this study concretely illustrates erosion of inclusive teacher-
     student interaction. Using discourse analysis, it compares K-12 classroom
     instructional practices before and after the imposition of standardized testing
     and illuminates the negative transformation of five inclusionary discursive
     practices. Before testing mandates: 1) diversity was regarded as a resource
     for opportunities to learn something valuable; 2) standards for academic
     achievement provided a wide range of possible performances; 3) teachers
     and students were flexible in their stances toward what constituted academic
     performance; 4) students' constructed student "selves" were part of a
     dialogue about academic expectations; and 5) students' personal texts were
     a legitimate part of the curriculum. In test impacted classrooms, in contrast,

CONTENTS PAGE

Title of article

Authors' names

Abstract

Practicing Engineers Talk about the
Importance of Talk:
A Report on the Role of Oral
Communication in the Workplace

Ann L. Darling and Deanna P. Dannels

*In the last decade engineering education and industry have requested assistance from
communication educators. Responding to increased attention on the changing expectations for
practicing engineers and an attendant need for better communication skills, these teams of
engineering and communication educators have been working to incorporate speaking and
writing in engineering education. Despite a great deal of anecdotal evidence that communication is important to working engineers, relatively little data based information is available to
help us understand better the specifics of how and why communication is important for these
particular professionals. This paper reports the results of practicing engineers' descriptions of the
importance of oral communication. These data suggest that engineering practice takes place in
an intensely oral culture and while formal presentations are important to practicing engineers,
daily work is characterized more by interpersonal and small group experiences. Communication
skills such as translation, clarity, negotiation, and listening are vital.* **Keywords:** communication in the professions, workplace teams, engineering education, oral presentations

Increasingly, oral communication is recognized as an essential element of the
curriculum in technical disciplines (Beaufait, 1991; Bjorklund & Colbeck, 2001;
Deston, 1998; Yu & Liaw, 1998). Disciplines such as biology, chemistry, engineering, and mathematics, with a long curricular tradition focused on technical knowledge, have begun to explore the role of oral performance as both a learning tool
(e.g., use of cooperative learning groups) and outcome (i.e., students in these
disciplines are expected to be proficient both technically and communicatively).
    Engineering is one such discipline experiencing a shift toward incorporating oral
communication instruction within a highly technical curriculum (Beaufait, 1991).
The 1995 report from the National Board of Engineering Education includes
recommendations for a redesign of the engineering curriculum toward a more
professional focus with specific attention on instruction in communication. Additionally, the Accreditation Board for Engineering and Technology (ABET) has developed new standards for accreditation to evaluate departments and colleges of
engineering around the country. Specifically, ABET assessment procedures are
driven by 11 student outcome measures, one of which states that students should

Publication information

FIRST PAGE OF ARTICLE

*Ann L. Darling (PhD, University of Washington) is Associate Professor and Chair of the Department
of Communication at the University of Utah. Deanna P. Dannels (PhD, University of Utah) is
Assistant Professor of Communication and Assistant Director of the Campus Writing and Speaking
Program at North Carolina State University. The authors wish to thank the gracious and abundant
contributions of the College of Engineering at the University of Utah, especially on the part of
Professor Robert Roemer.*

Communication Education, Vol. 52, No. 1, January 2003, pp. 1–16
Copyright 2003, National Communication Association

Darling, A. L., & Dannels, D. P. (2003). Practicing engineers talk
about the importance of talk: A report on the role of oral
communication in the workplace. *Communication Education,*
52, 1–16.

AUTHOR'S NAME

The author's last name comes first, followed by the author's initials.

Join two authors' names with a comma and an ampersand.

DATE OF PUBLICATION

Give the year the work was published in parentheses.

Most popular magazines are paginated per issue. These periodicals might have a volume number, but are more often referenced by the season or date of publication.

TITLE OF ARTICLE

- Do not use quotation marks. If there is a book title in the article title, italicize it.

- The first word of the title, the first word of the subtitle, and any proper nouns in the title are capitalized. Titles of articles in APA style follow standard sentence capitalization.

PUBLICATION INFORMATION
Name of journal

- Italicize the journal name.

- All nouns, verbs, and pronouns, and the first word of the title are capitalized. Do not capitalize any article, preposition, or coordinating conjunction unless it is the first word of the title or subtitle.

- Put a comma after the journal name.

- Italicize the volume number followed by a comma.

Volume, issue, and page numbers

See sample references 47 and 48 for more on different types of pagination.

JOURNAL AND MAGAZINE ARTICLES

41. Article by one author

Kellogg, R. T. (2001). Competition for working memory among writing processes. *American Journal of Psychology, 114*, 175–192.

42. Article by two authors

Note that APA uses an ampersand, not *and,* for two authors.

Fecica, A. M., & Stoltz, J. A. (2008). Facial affect and temporal order judgments: Emotions turn back the clock. *Experimental Psychology, 55*, 3–8.

43. Article by three or more authors

The seventh and subsequent authors can be abbreviated to *et al.*

Andis, S., Franks, D., Girardeau, J., Kellog, K., Oppenheimer, G., Zales, D., et al.

44. Authors listed with the word *with*

Bettinger, M. (with Winthorp, E.).

45. Article by an unknown author

Insert works with no author in the references list in alphabetical order by the first significant word in the title (in this case, *green*).

The green gene revolution. (2004, February). [Editorial]. *Scientific American, 291*, 8.

46. Article by a group or organization

See example 7 on page 423–424 for how to create in-text citations for groups and organizations.

National Organization for Women. (1980). Where to find feminists in Austin. *The NOW guide for Austin women*. Austin, TX: Chapter Press.

47. Article in a journal with continuous pagination

Include only the volume number and the year, not the issue number. Note that the title and the volume number are italicized.

> Engen, R., & Steen, S. (2000). The power to punish: Discretion and sentencing reform in the war on drugs. *American Journal of Sociology, 105*, 1357–1395.

48. Article in a journal paginated by issue

List the issue number in parentheses (not italicized) after the volume number.

> Davis, J. (1999). Rethinking globalisation. *Race and Class, 40*(2/3), 37–48.

MONTHLY, WEEKLY, AND BIWEEKLY PERIODICALS

49. Weekly or biweekly periodicals

If available, list the volume number in italics. If a volume number is not available, list by the date that appears on the issue.

> Hurtley, Stella. (2004, July 16). Limits from leaf litter. *Science, 305*, 311–313.
>
> Toobin, J. (2001, November 5). Crackdown. *The New Yorker*, 56–61.

50. Monthly publications

> Barlow, J. P. (1998, January). Africa rising: Everything you know about Africa is wrong. *Wired*, 142–158.

ABSTRACTS

51. Abstract from an original source

> de Watteville, C. (1904). On flame spectra [Abstract]. *Proceedings of the Royal Society of London, 74*, 84.

52. Abstract from a printed secondary source

APA prefers that you cite the original article, not the abstract.

Van Schaik, P. (1999). Involving users in the specification of functionality using scenarios and model-based evaluation. *Behaviour and Information Technology, 18*, 455–466. Abstract obtained from *Communication Abstracts*, 2000, *24*, 416.

53. Electronic copy of an abstract retrieved from a database

APA no longer requires a date of retrieval for items from a widely used database.

Putsis, W. P., & Bayus, B. L. (2001). An empirical analysis of firms' product line decisions. *Journal of Marketing Research, 37*(8), 110–118. Abstract retrieved from PsychINFO database.

NEWSPAPERS

54. Newspaper article

If a newspaper article appears on more than one page, list all the pages.

McFadden, R. D. (2005, January 1). Relief delivery lags as deaths pass 140,000. *New York Times*, pp. A1, A9.

If an article has no author, list and alphabetize by the first significant word in the title of the article.

Incorrect cancer tests can be costly. (2004, December 16). *USA Today*, p. 8D.

REVIEWS AND LETTERS TO THE EDITOR

55. Review

Inside brackets identify the type of medium being reviewed (book, television program, theater) and the title of the work. If the review is untitled (as in this case), use the material in brackets as the title.

> Berger, S. E. (1999). [Review of the book *The evolution of the book*]. *Library Quarterly, 69,* 402.

56. Letter to the editor or editorial

> Wilkenson, S. E. (2001, December 21). When teaching doesn't count [Letter to the editor]. *The Chronicle of Higher Education,* p. B21.

24d Online Sources in the APA-Style References List

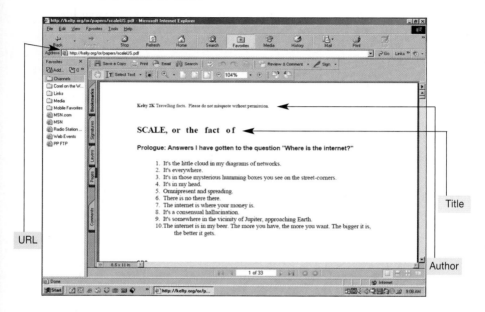

URL

Title

Author

TITLES AND URLS IN APA-STYLE REFERENCES

Web sites are made up of many separate pages or articles. Each page on a Web site may or may not have a title. If you are citing a page or article that has a title, treat the title like an article in a periodical. No retrieval date is necessary if the content is not likely to be changed or updated.

Heiney, A. (2004). A gathering of space heroes. Retrieved from the National Aeronautics and Space Administration Website: http://www.nasa.gov/missions/shuttle/f_ahofpreview.html

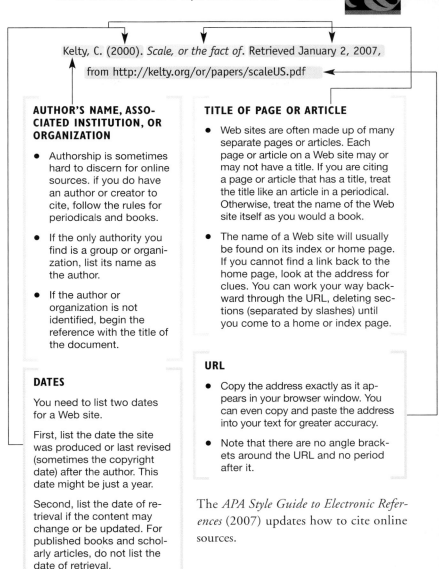

Kelty, C. (2000). *Scale, or the fact of.* Retrieved January 2, 2007, from http://kelty.org/or/papers/scaleUS.pdf

AUTHOR'S NAME, ASSOCIATED INSTITUTION, OR ORGANIZATION

- Authorship is sometimes hard to discern for online sources. if you do have an author or creator to cite, follow the rules for periodicals and books.

- If the only authority you find is a group or organization, list its name as the author.

- If the author or organization is not identified, begin the reference with the title of the document.

DATES

You need to list two dates for a Web site.

First, list the date the site was produced or last revised (sometimes the copyright date) after the author. This date might be just a year.

Second, list the date of retrieval if the content may change or be updated. For published books and scholarly articles, do not list the date of retrieval.

TITLE OF PAGE OR ARTICLE

- Web sites are often made up of many separate pages or articles. Each page or article on a Web site may or may not have a title. If you are citing a page or article that has a title, treat the title like an article in a periodical. Otherwise, treat the name of the Web site itself as you would a book.

- The name of a Web site will usually be found on its index or home page. If you cannot find a link back to the home page, look at the address for clues. You can work your way backward through the URL, deleting sections (separated by slashes) until you come to a home or index page.

URL

- Copy the address exactly as it appears in your browser window. You can even copy and paste the address into your text for greater accuracy.

- Note that there are no angle brackets around the URL and no period after it.

The *APA Style Guide to Electronic References* (2007) updates how to cite online sources.

ONLINE PUBLICATIONS

57. Online publication by a known author

Carr, A. (2003, May 22). AAUW applauds Senate support of title IX
    resolution. Retrieved from http://www.aauw.org/about
    /newsroom/press_releases/030522.cfm

58. Online publication by a group or organization

Girls Incorporated. (2003). Girls' bill of rights. Retrieved from
    http://www.girlsinc.org/gc/page.php?id=9

59. Online publication with an author and a group affiliation

Identify the host before giving the URL for the document itself. Precede the URL with a colon.

Bjork, O. (2004, May 5). MOO bots. Retrieved from CWRL White
    Papers Web site: http://www.cwrl.utexas.edu/professional
    /whitepapers/2004/040512-1.pdf

60. Online publication with no known author or group affiliation

Begin the reference with the title of the document.

Halloween costumes from my warped mind. (n.d.). Retrieved from
    http://home.att.net/~jgola/hallow01.htm

61. Online publication with no copyright or revision date

If no copyright or revision date is given, use *(n.d.)*, as shown in entry 60.

ONLINE PERIODICALS

Because URLs frequently change, many scholarly publishers have begun to use a Digital Object Identifier (DOI), a unique alphanumeric string that is permanent. If a DOI is available, use the DOI instead of the URL.

62. Online article with DOI assigned

The article was retrieved from the PsychARTICLES database, but there is no need to list the database, the retrieval date, or the URL if the DOI is listed.

Erdfelder, E. (2008). Experimental psychology: Good news. *Experimental Psychology, 55*(1), 1-2. doi: 0.1027 /1618-3169.55.1.1

63. Online article with no DOI assigned

Brown, B. (2004). The order of service: the practical management of customer interaction. *Sociological Research Online, 9*(4). Retrieved from http://www.socresonline.org.uk /9/4/brown.html

64. Article in an online newspaper

Erard, M. (2001, November 16). A colossal wreck. *Austin Chronicle*. Retrieved from http://www.austinchronicle.com/

65. Article in an online magazine

McClure, L. (2003, February 18). The Salon interview: Molly Ivins. *Salon*. Retrieved from http://www.salon.com

ONLINE DATABASES AND ENCYCLOPEDIAS

66. Document from a database

APA no longer requries listing the names of well-known databases. Include the name of the database only for hard-to-find books and other items.

Holloway, J. D. (2004). Protecting practitioners' autonomy. *Monitor on Psychology, 35*(1), 30.

67. **Online encyclopedia**

> Swing. (2002). In *Britannica Online*. Retrieved April 29, 2007,
>   from http://www.britannica.com/

UNEDITED ONLINE SOURCES

68. **Blog entry**

> Albritton, C. (2004, May 19). Greetings from Baghdad. *Back to Iraq*.
>   Retrieved from http://www.back-to-iraq.com/

69. **Message posted to a newsgroup, online forum, or discussion group**

Only use messages that are archived and accessible by readers.

> Truett, S. (2007, September 17). Where are the historians in
>   popular political discourse? Message posted to http://
>   www.h-net.org/~border/, archived at http://h-net.mus.edu/

70. **Wiki**

Because Wikis change frequently, the date of retrieval is important.

> Mount Everest. (n.d.). Retrieved November 12, 2007, from
>   Wikipedia: http://en.wikipedia.org/wiki/Mt._Everest

71. **Email**

Email sent from one individual to another should be cited as a personal communication. Personal communication is cited in text but not included in the reference list.

> (S. Wilson, personal communication, August 18, 2007)

24e Visual, Computer, and Multimedia Sources in the APA-Style References List

MULTIMEDIA

72. Television program

> Frolov, D., Schneider, A., Chase, D., & Weiner, M. (Writers), & Van Patten, T. (Director). (2007). Soprano home movies [Television series episode]. In D. Chase (Producer), *The sopranos*. New York: HBO.

73. Film, Video, or DVD

> Miller, G. (Director). (2006). *Happy feet* [Motion picture]. United States: Warner Brothers.

74. Musical recording

> Waits, T. (1980). Ruby's arms. On *Heartattack and vine* [CD]. New York: Elektra Entertainment.

75. Audio recording

> King, M. L., Jr. (Speaker). (1968). *In search of freedom* (Cassette Recording No. SR61170). Los Angeles: Mercury Records.

76. Graphic, audio, or video files

> Aretha Franklin: A life of soul. (2004, January 24). *NPR Online*. Retrieved April 30, 2004, from http://www.npr.org/features /feature.php?wfId=1472614

Sample Research Paper with APA Documentation

Major kinds of papers written in APA style include the following.

Reports of research

Reports of experimental research follow a specific organization in APA style:

- **The abstract** gives a brief summary of the report.
- **The introduction** identifies the problem, reviews previous research, and states the hypothesis that was tested.
- **The methods section** describes how the experiment was conducted and how the participants were selected.
- **The results section** reports the findings of the study. This section often includes tables and figures that provide statistical results and tests of statistical significance.
- **The discussion section** interprets the findings and often refers to previous research.

Case studies

Case studies report material about an individual or a group that illustrates some problem or issue of interest to the field. See Section 11c.

Reviews of literature

Reviews of literature summarize what has been published on a particular subject and often evaluates that material to suggest directions for future research.

Thesis-driven argument

Thesis-driven arguments are similar to reviews of research, but they take a particular position on a theoretical or a real-life issue. The APA paper that follows by John M. Jones is a thesis-driven proposal argument that advocates a particular course of action.

FORMATTING A RESEARCH PAPER IN APA STYLE

APA offers these general guidelines for formatting a research paper.

- **Use white, 8¹/₂-by-11-inch paper.** Don't use colored or lined paper.
- **Double-space everything—the title page, abstract, body of the paper, quotations, and list of references.** Set the line spacing on your word processor for double spacing and leave it there.
- **Put a shortened title (50 characters or under) and the page number at the top of every page, with 5 spaces between the title and page number, aligned with the right margin, one-half inch from the top of the page.** Your word processor has a header command that will automatically put a header with the page number on every page.
- **Specify one-inch margins.** One-inch margins are the default setting for most word processors.
- **Do not justify (make even) the right margin.** Justifying the right margin throws off the spacing between words and makes your paper harder to read. Use the left-align setting instead.
- **Indent the first line of each paragraph one-half inch (5 spaces).** Set the paragraph indent command or the tab on the ruler of your word processor at one-half inch.
- **Use the same readable typeface throughout your paper.** Use a standard typeface such as 12-pt Times Roman or 12-pt Courier.
- **Use block format for quotations longer than 40 words.** See page 421.
- **Create an abstract.** The abstract appears on a separate page after the title page. Insert and center "Abstract" at the top. Do not indent the first line of the abstract. The abstract should be a brief (120 words or under) summary of the paper.
- **Create a title page.** Follow the format below for your title page. It should have
  1. a shortened title and page number one-half inch from the top,
  2. a descriptive title that is centered at the top of the page with all words capitalized except *a, an, the*, prepositions, and conjunctions under 4 letters,
  3. your name centered on a separate line,
  4. your school centered on a separate line.

Surveillanomics   1

Include a running head, consisting of a short version of your title and the page number, separated by 5 spaces. This header should be about 1/2 inch from the top of the page. Set the margins of your paper to 1".

Center your title in the top half of the page, below the running head. The title should clearly describe the content of the paper and should be around 10 words long. If the title runs to 2 lines, double-space it.

Surveillanomics: The Need for Governmental

Regulation of Video Surveillance

John M. Jones

The University of Texas at Austin

On the line below the title, include your name, also centered. On the next line below, include the name of your school. Double-space between these lines.

Abstract

Because recent technological advances have made
it possible to use surveillance video to gather
information about private citizens, and because
unregulated data-mining has made this information
economically valuable, the collection and use of
video surveillance data should be regulated by the
government. This regulation, based on the model
introduced by Taylor (2002), should mandate that all
video surveillance must be in accordance with the
law, have a legitimate objective, and be necessary for
the maintenance of a free society. These guidelines
would ensure that surveillance data could not be
used for purposes other than those for which it was
collected, and would make the primary concerns in
debates over the use of surveillance democratic, not
economic as they are now.

The abstract
appears on a
separate page
with the title
Abstract cen-
tered at the top.

Do not indent
the first line of
the abstract.

The abstract
should be a brief
(120 words or
fewer) summary
of your paper's
argument.

Center your title at the beginning of the body of your paper. If it runs to 2 lines, double-space it.

Surveillanomics: The Need for Governmental Regulation of Video Surveillance

On September 5, 2005, the operators of the social networking site Facebook gave the service a facelift. One of the innovations they introduced was the "news feed" feature, which "automatically alerted users when their friends made changes to their online profiles," like changing personal details or adding new "friends" (Meredith, 2006). This service, which was automatically installed for all accounts, outraged users, 700,000 of whom formed the group "Students Against Facebook News Feeds." Before Facebook altered its implementation of this feature, the members of this group were preparing to protest the changes at the company's headquarters.

At first, this negative reaction by users took the company completely by surprise. As Schneier (2006) puts it, in their eyes, all they had done "was take available data and aggregate it in a novel way for what [they] perceived was [their] customers' benefit"; however, users realized that this change "made an enormous difference" in the way that their information could be aggregated, accessed, and distributed. In other words, although

Surveillanomics   4

Facebook news feeds did nothing more than take information that was already publicly available and repackage it in a new form, this new information source was seen by users as a massive invasion of their privacy.

In light of this reaction, it is interesting to note that right now companies referred to as "data brokers" are creating their own "news feeds" of private citizens' lives, collating individuals' public information, like credit reports and vehicle registration histories, and then selling that information to practically anyone who can pay for it. Whereas Facebook was semiprivate—in September 2005 its membership was restricted to those with .edu email addresses and news feeds were distributed only to a member's online friends—data brokers like USAData, Acxiom, and ChoicePoint collect information about anyone, then package and sell that information to third parties in what has become "a multibillion-dollar, unregulated business that's growing larger by the day" (Whiting, 2006). This "unregulated" activity, known as data-mining, has recently come under increased scrutiny, the need for which was highlighted when ChoicePoint sold sensitive

All quotations should be cited by author, date, and page number. A page number does not appear in this example because the source is a Web page without paragraph numbers.

Surveillanomics   5

information to thieves who posed as the
representatives of legitimate businesses.

The rapid growth of data-mining has provoked
worries that continually improving technology has made
it possible to mine other kinds of data as well. Like the
consumer information already gathered by data brokers,
the video collected by surveillance cameras and webcams
is quickly becoming an economically valuable data
source. Department stores can now analyze movement in
video data to prevent shoplifting or to increase sales, and
face recognition software can be used to find particular
individuals on security tapes (O'Harrow, 2005, p. 296).
Similarly, Sweeney and Gross (2005) have developed
software that can monitor public webcams for suspicious
activity. Currently, video data is largely in the hands of
private companies, for, as Koskela (2003) has noted,
"cameras run by private market forces outnumber those
used by the authorities" such that governments "have
very little control on how and where surveillance is used"
(p. 302). In short, surveillance has become an economic
activity managed by "private market forces" and data
miners, and this surveillanomics represents a significant
new challenge to personal privacy.

If you include the author's name in the text, include the publication year in parentheses immediately after it. If necessary, include the page number in parentheses with the abbreviation *p.* following the citation.

Surveillanomics   6

In light of these facts, it is clear that we are in dire need of governmental regulation of video surveillance. Following the model for surveillance regulation in the European Convention on Human Rights as outlined by Taylor (2002), I argue that the government should mandate that all video surveillance must be in accordance with the law, have a legitimate objective, and be necessary for the maintenance of a free society (pp. 67–69). Further, any organization, public or private, that uses video surveillance should be required to register with the government in order to ensure that the use of surveillance data does not violate these three guidelines (p. 78). While the first guideline, that video surveillance practices be in accordance with the law, would reinforce the applicability of current statutes to surveillance activity—for example, the documented tendency of surveillance camera operators to voyeuristically stalk women in public spaces (Koskela, 2000, pp. 255–256; O'Harrow, 2005, p. 179)—for the purposes of this paper I will focus more on the necessity of the latter two guidelines and their beneficial effects.

In the first place, demanding that video surveillance operations have a legitimate objective would place

If you cite the works of multiple authors in a sentence, format as normal, but separate the individual sources with a semicolon.

Surveillanomics 7

surveillance video out of the reach of data miners.
Under these guidelines, in order to obtain permission
to install surveillance equipment, it would be necessary
for potential operators to establish a clear objective for
their surveillance. The resulting data could then be
used only for purposes relevant to that objective. A
similar restriction has been successfully implemented
in a program to limit weigh-station stops by trucks.
While truckers were initially skeptical of the program
because they feared that the system of transponders
used to track weight information "would be used to
catch them for speeding or check their routines"
(O'Harrow, 2005, p. 217), the data collected was used
only for a single, clear purpose—automating the
weighing process. After that task was accomplished,
the data was destroyed, making it impossible for it to
be used for other purposes, like tracking speeders, as
some tollbooth cameras are used now (Nieto,
Johnston-Dodds, & Simmons, 2002, p. 24). Following
this example, if the government were to use video
surveillance in airports to look for terrorist activity,

In a parenthetical citation, use & instead of *and* when listing more than one author.

that video would not be allowed to be used for other
applications, like using facial recognition to find
private citizens with outstanding arrest warrants.
Having clear objectives for the collection of video
surveillance, and regulating the use of the data
collected through surveillance operations so as to
prevent it from being used for other purposes, would
eliminate surveillance video as a source for data-
mining, thus protecting individual privacy.

Second, since video surveillance would be subject
to government regulation, defining what "needs"
necessitate the use of video surveillance would be the
subject of open debate. The last guideline, that video
surveillance be conducted only for the purpose of
maintaining a free society, would help define the terms
of that debate in such a way as to make the needs of
private citizens of primary concern. Currently, the use
of video surveillance and the storage of surveillance
data is primarily motivated by economic concerns. In
the past ten years, video surveillance has become a
billion-dollar industry (see Table 1). As pointed out
earlier, most video surveillance is conducted by private

Title tables by number (Table 1, Table 2, . . .).

Table 1

Sales Revenues Generated by CCTV Surveillance
Cameras

Provide your table with a descriptive title that is italicized and flush with the left margin.

Year	Sales (in billions)
1996	0.29
1997	0.31
1998	0.49
1999	0.7
2000	1
2001	1.6

Note. From the Security Industry Association, 2001, qtd.
in Nieto et al. (2002).

companies (Koskela, 2003). Although arguments for
surveillance systems are generally described in terms
of public safety, when used in public places like
shopping malls, video surveillance has become a key
element of what Koskela (2000) calls "policing for
profit," for it excludes "groups that are marginal in
relation to the mall's purpose": consumption (p. 246).
In malls

the guards' routine work is to use surveillance
cameras to look for 'undesirables' (Sibley, 1995: xi).

Surveillanomics   10

The reason for excluding someone is that person's appearance. A person's appearance is considered as reflecting that person's ability to consume (Crawford, 1992: 27): one must always look as if one has bought something or is about to buy (Shields, 1989: 160) [. . .] Thus, ostensibly public spaces are not public for everyone—public space can be seen as if it 'refers to places under public scrutiny' (Domosh, 1998: 209). (p. 246)

The transformation of public spaces into "places under public scrutiny" is contrary to the democratic principle of freedom of movement. Unfortunately, the shopping mall, where any activity that is considered "undesirable"—defined by a person's "ability to consume"—is excluded, has become the template for public space (Koskela, 2000, p. 246).

Although some might argue that giving market forces a free hand would lead the best solution to the surveillance problem, this is not necessarily true, for economists have shown that market solutions are not always the best ones (Waldrop, 1992, pp. 40–41). In either case, as a society do we really want economic

Quotations of more than 40 words should be indented 5 spaces or $1/2$" from the margin. Include citations from the original text, but do not list those works in your references unless you cite them again elsewhere in the paper.

For blocked quotations, parenthetical citations go outside of closing punctuation.

24f APA Documentation

concerns to determine how video surveillance is used? Based on current trends, if surveillance standards are left entirely in private hands, or if individual government agencies are allowed to determine standards for surveillance use independently, this will certainly be the result. However, if the government were to regulate surveillance and to base its regulation on the principle of a free and open society, this economic motive could be subverted through the use of openly debatable standards based on individual rights, rights that are unlikely to be protected in a situation dominated by economic concerns.

I believe that this solution—government regulation of video surveillance—is the best one because it responds to both of the problems I have outlined: the ability of private companies to mine video sources for information about private citizens, and the use of economic concerns to define surveillance standards. Before this solution is likely to be accepted, however, it will be necessary to deal with a possible objection to government regulation: the fear that giving the government control of video

Surveillanomics   12

surveillance would turn it into a de facto Big Brother. As
Mieszkowski (2003) reports, some argue that the fact
that the government conducts video surveillance is
already a sign that we are entering an Orwellian future.
If the government were to regulate video surveillance,
the argument might go, this situation would only get
worse, for it would have access to all public and
private surveillance data, thereby realizing Orwell's dark
vision of the future. However, Lee (2005) points out
that in current practice the government *already* has
access to this data, for private surveillance video is
regularly provided to government agencies when they
request it. What, then, would be the danger in allowing
the government to regulate information it already has
access to? The government already regulates many
important aspects of our personal lives without
widespread panic over the potential for abuse: the FDA
regulates our food and medicine, the SEC regulates our
finances, and the FCC regulates telecommunications.
While no one would argue that the government is
perfect, it does occasionally get things right. At the
very least, if it gets policies wrong, it can be held

Surveillanomics   13

accountable for its mistakes and faulty policies can be changed. If the guidelines I have presented here were to be adopted, neither the government nor any other entity would be allowed to access video data for purposes other than those for which that data was collected, a fact which would reduce the chances of Big-Brother-type outcomes. Further, there would be the added benefits of open, debatable standards for government surveillance and a marked increase in accountability for private sector surveillance activities.

Allowing the government to regulate video surveillance would eliminate the access of data-miners and government agencies to surveillance data. More important, in the face of the rampant use of surveillance technology, decisions over how that technology is implemented, how the data it produces is stored, and who gets to have access to it should be decided in an open, democratic manner, not a private, economic one. Governmental regulation is our best chance for achieving this end.

References

Koskela, H. (2000). 'The gaze without eyes': Video-
surveillance and the changing nature of urban space.
Progress in Human Geography, 24(2), 243–265.

Koskela, H. (2003). 'Cam era'—the contemporary urban
panopticon. *Surveillance & Society, 1*(3), 292–313.
Retrieved February 23, 2007, from http://
www.surveillance-and-society.org

Lee, J. (2005, May 22). Caught on tape, then just caught;
private cameras transform police work. *The New York
Times*. Retrieved from http://www.nytimes.com

Meredith, P. (2006, September 22). Facebook and the
politics of privacy. *Mother Jones*. Retrieved from
http://www.motherjones.com

Mieszkowski, K. (2003, September 25). We are all
paparazzi now. *Salon.com*. Retrieved from
http://archive.salon.com

Nieto, M., Johnston-Dodds, K., & Simmons, C. W.
(2002). *Public and private applications of video
surveillance and biometric technologies*.
Sacramento, CA: California Research Bureau,
California State Library. Retrieved from
http://www. library.ca.gov/CRB/02/06/02-006.pdf

Center
References at
the top.

Alphabetize
entries by last
name of the first
author.

Indent all but the
first line of each
entry 5 spaces
or $^1/_2$".

Double-space all
entries.

Surveillanomics   15

O'Harrow, R. (2005). *No place to hide*. New York: Free Press.

Schneier, B. (2006, September 21). Lessons from the
Facebook riots. *Wired News*. Retrieved from
http://www.wired.com/

Sweeney, L., & Gross, R. (2005). *Mining images in
publicly-available cameras for homeland security*.
Paper presented at the AAAI Spring Symposium on
AI Technologies for Homeland Security, Palo Alto,
CA. Retrieved from http://privacy.cs.cmu.edu
/dataprivacy/projects/videocount/index.html

Taylor, N. (2002). State surveillance and the right to
privacy. *Surveillance & Society, 1*(1), 66–85. Retrieved
from http://www.surveillance-and-society.org

Waldrop, M. M. (1992). *Complexity: The emerging
science at the edge of order and chaos*. New York:
Simon & Schuster.

Whiting, R. (2006, July 10). Data brokers draw
increased scrutiny. *InformationWeek*. Retrieved
from http://www.informationweek.com

Go through your text and make sure that everything you have cited, except for personal communication, is in the list of references.

FORMATTING THE REFERENCES IN APA STYLE

- **Begin the references on a new page.** Insert a page break with your word processor before you start the references page.

- **Center "References" on the first line at the top of the page.**

- **Double-space all entries.**

- **Alphabetize each entry by the last name of the author or, if no author is listed, by the first content word in the title (ignore *a, an, the*).**

- **Indent all but the first line in each entry one-half inch (5 spaces).**

- **Italicize the titles of books and periodicals.**

- **Go through your paper to check that each source you have used (except personal communication) is in the list of references.**

To hear audio commentary on this piece of writing, visit this page of the E-book at www.mycomplab.com.

Chapter 25

CMS Documentation

CMS style offers flexibility and the option of using footnotes.

25a Books and Nonperiodical Sources 467

25b Periodical Sources 474

Writers who publish in business, social sciences, fine arts, and humanities outside the discipline of English often use *The Chicago Manual of Style* (CMS) method of documentation. CMS guidelines allow writers a clear way of using footnotes and endnotes (rather than MLA and APA in-text citations) for citing the sources of quotations, summaries, and paraphrases. If you have questions after consulting this chapter, you can consult the full CMS style manual, *The Chicago Manual of Style*, fifteenth edition (Chicago: University of Chicago Press, 2003), or visit the Web site (www.chicagomanualofstyle.org).

In-text citations

CMS describes two systems of documentation, one similar to APA and the other a style that uses footnotes or endnotes, which is the focus of this chapter. In the footnote style CMS uses a superscript number directly after any quotation, paraphrase, or summary. Notes are numbered consecutively throughout the essay, article, or chapter. This superscript number corresponds to either a footnote, which appears at the bottom of the page, or an endnote, which appears at the end of the text.

> In *Southern Honor: Ethics and Behavior in the Old South*, Wyatt-Brown argues that "paradox, irony, and guilt have been three current words used by historians to describe white Southern life before the Civil War."[1]

Note

> 1. Bertram Wyatt-Brown, *Southern Honor: Ethics and Behavior in the Old South* (Oxford: Oxford University Press, 1983), 3.

Bibliography

> Wyatt-Brown, Bertram. *Southern Honor: Ethics and Behavior in the Old South*. Oxford: Oxford University Press, 1983.

Footnotes and endnotes

Footnotes appear at the bottom of the page on which each citation appears. Begin your footnote four lines from the last line of text on the page. Footnotes are single-spaced, but you should double-space between multiple notes on a single page.

Endnotes are compiled at the end of the text on a separate page entitled *Notes*. Center the title at the top of the page and list your endnotes in the order they appear within the text. The entire endnote section should be double-spaced—both within and between each entry. Even with endnotes it's still possible to include explanatory footnotes, which are indicated by asterisks or other punctuation marks.

CMS Bibliography

Because footnotes and endnotes in CMS format contain complete citation information, a separate list of references is often optional. This list of references can be called the *Bibliography*, or if it has only works referenced directly in your text, *Works Cited, Literature Cited,* or *References*. Generally, CMS bibliographies follow the MLA works-cited format.

Books and Nonperiodical Sources in CMS Style

Note

> 1. Nell Irvin Painter, *Creating Black Americans: African-American History and Its Meanings, 1619 to the Present* (New York: Oxford University Press, 2006), 5.

Bibliography

> Painter, Nell Irvin. *Creating Black Americans: African-American History and Its Meanings, 1619 to the Present.* New York: Oxford University Press, 2006.

AUTHOR'S OR EDITOR'S NAME

Note: the author's name is given in normal order.

Bibliography: give the author's name last name first. If an editor, put *ed.* after the name.

BOOK TITLE

Use the exact title, as it appears on the title page (not the cover).

Italicize the title.

Capitalize all nouns, verbs, adjectives, adverbs, and pronouns, and the first word of the title and subtitle.

PUBLICATION INFORMATION

In a note, the place of publication, publisher, and year of publication are in parentheses.

Place of publication

- Add the state's postal abbreviation or country when the city is not well known (Foster City, CA) or ambiguous (Cambridge, MA, or Cambridge, UK).
- If more than one city is given on the title page, use the first.

Publisher's name

- You may use acceptable abbreviations (e.g., Co. for Company).
- For works published prior to 1900, the place and date are sufficient.

Year of publication

- If no year of publication is given, write *n.d.* ("no date") in place of the date.
- If it is a multivolume edited work published over a period of more than one year, put the span of time as the year.

Sample citations for books and nonperiodical sources

BOOKS

1. Book by one author

In a note the author's name is given in normal order.

> 1. Elizabeth Bowen, *The Mulberry Tree: Selected Writings* (London: Vintage, 1999), 33–41.

In subsequent references, cite the author's last name only:

> 2. Bowen, 231.

If the reference is to the same work as the preceding note, you can use the abbreviation *Ibid.*:

> 3. Ibid., 231.

In the bibliography, give the author's name in reverse order.

> Bowen, Elizabeth. *The Mulberry Tree: Selected Writings*. London: Vintage, 1999.

For edited books, put *ed.* after the name.

> Kavanagh, Patrick, ed. *Lapped Furrows*. New York: Hand Press, 1969.

2. Book by two or three authors

In a note, put all authors' names in normal order. For subsequent references, give only the authors' last names:

> 4. McClelland and Eismann, 32.

In the bibliography, give second and third names in normal order.

> Hauser, Taylor, and June Kashpaw. *January Blues*. Foster City, CA: IDG Books, 2003.

3. Book by four or more authors

In a note, give the name of the first author listed, followed by *and others*.

> 5. Jacqueline Jones and others, *Created Equal: A Social and Political History of the United States* (New York: Longman, 2003), 243.

List all the authors in the bibliography.

Jones, Jacqueline, Peter H. Wood, Elaine Taylor May, Thomas Borstelmann, and Vicki L. Ruiz. *Created Equal: A Social and Political History of the United States*. New York: Longman, 2003.

4. Book by an unknown author

Begin both the note and the bibliography entries with the title.

Note

> 6. *Remarks upon the Religion, Trade, Government, Police, Customs, Manners, and Maladys of the City of Corke* (Cork, 1737), 4.

Bibliography

> *Remarks upon the Religion, Trade, Government, Police, Customs, Manners, and Maladys of the City of Corke*. Cork, 1737.

5. Book by a group or organization

Treat the group or organization as the author of the work.

Note

> 7. World Health Organization. *Advancing Safe Motherhood through Human Rights* (Geneva, Switzerland: World Health Organization, 2001), 18.

Bibliography

> World Health Organization. *Advancing Safe Motherhood through Human Rights*. Geneva, Switzerland: World Health Organization, 2001.

PARTS OF BOOKS

6. A single chapter by the same author as the book

Note

> 1. Ann Ardis, *"The Lost Girl, Tarr, and the Moment of Modernism,"* In *Modernism and Cultural Conflict, 1880–1922* (New York: Cambridge University Press, 2002), 78–113.

Bibliography

Savage, Gail. "The Ministry of Labour: Accentuating the Negative." Chap. 5 in *The Social Construction of Expertise*. New York: Routledge, 1996.

7. **A selection in an anthology or a chapter in an edited collection**

Note

2. J. L. McCracken, "Northern Ireland, 1921–66," in *The Course of Irish History*, eds. T. W. Moody and F. X. Martin (Niwot, CO: Roberts Rinehart, 1995), 313–23.

Bibliography

Cook, Martha E. "Background in Tennessee: Recovering a Southern Identity." In *Evelyn Scott: Recovering a Lost Modernist*, edited by Paul Jones and Dorothy Scura, 123–29. Knoxville: University of Tennessee Press, 2001.

8. **Article in a reference work**

Publication information is usually omitted from citations of well-known reference volumes. The edition is listed instead. The abbreviation *s.v.* (*sub verbo* or "under the word") replaces an entry's page number.

4. *Benet's Reader's Encyclopedia*, 1987 ed., s.v. "Lampoon."

9. **Introduction, foreword, preface, or afterword**

When citing an introduction, foreword, preface, or afterword written by someone other than the book's main author, the other writer's name comes first, and the main author's name follows the title of the book.

Note

5. Edward Larkin, introduction to *Common Sense*, by Thomas Paine (New York: Broadview, 2004).

Bibliography

Larkin, Edward. Introduction to *Common Sense*, by Thomas Paine. New York: Broadview, 2004.

REVISED EDITIONS, VOLUMES, AND SERIES

10. A revised or later edition of a book

Note

> 1. Jeremy Hawthorn, ed., *A Concise Glossary of Contemporary Literary Theory*, 2nd ed. (London: Arnold, 1994), 30.

Bibliography

> Hawthorn, Jeremy, ed. *A Concise Glossary of Contemporary Literary Theory*. 2nd ed. London: Arnold, 1994.

11. Work in more than one volume

Note

> 1. Oscar Wilde, *The Complete Works of Oscar Wilde*, vol. 3 (New York: Dragon Press, 1998), 1024.

Bibliography

> Wilde, Oscar. *The Complete Works of Oscar Wilde*. Vol. 3. New York: Dragon Press, 1998.

EDITIONS AND TRANSLATIONS

12. Book with an editor

Note

> 1. Thomas Hardy, *Jude the Obscure*, ed. Norman Page (New York: Norton, 1999), 35.

Bibliography

> Hardy, Thomas. *Jude the Obscure*. Edited by Norman Page. New York: Norton, 1999.

13. Book with a translator

Follow the style shown in entry 12, but substitute "trans." for "ed." in the note and "Translated" for "Edited" in the bibliographic entry.

GOVERNMENT DOCUMENTS

14. Government document

Note

> 5. U.S. Department of Health and Public Safety, *Grade School Hygiene and Epidemics* (Washington, DC: GPO, 1998), 21.

Bibliography

> U.S. Department of Health and Public Safety. *Grade School Hygiene and Epidemics*. Washington, DC: GPO, 1998.

15. *Congressional Record*

Note

> 6. *Congressional Record,* 100th Cong., 1st sess., 1987, 70, pt. 2:750–51.

Bibliography

> U.S. Congress. *Congressional Record*. 100th Cong., 1st sess., 1987. Vol. 70, pt. 2.

RELIGIOUS TEXTS

16. Religious texts

Citations from religious texts appear in the notes but not in the bibliography. Give the version in parentheses in the first citation only.

Note

> 4. John 3:16 (King James Version).

LETTERS

17. Published letter

Note

> 5. Oscar Wilde to Robert Ross, 25 November 1897, in *The Complete Letters of Oscar Wilde*, ed. Merlin Holland and Rupert Hart-Davis (New York: Holt, 2000), 992.

Bibliography

Wilde, Oscar. Letter to Robert Ross. 25 November 1897. In *The Complete Letters of Oscar Wilde*. Edited by Merlin Holland and Rupert Hart-Davis, 992. New York: Holt, 2000.

18. **Personal letter to author**

Personal communications are not usually listed in the bibliography because they are not accessible to the public.

Note

7. Ann Williams, letter to author, May 8, 2007.

DISSERTATIONS AND CONFERENCE PROCEEDINGS

19. **Unpublished dissertation**

Note

7. James Elsworth Kidd, "The Vision of Uncertainty: Elizabethan Windows and the Problem of Sight" (PhD diss., Southern Illinois University, 1998), 236.

Bibliography

Kidd, James Elsworth. "The Vision of Uncertainty: Elizabethan Windows and the Problem of Sight." PhD diss., Southern Illinois University, 1998.

20. **Published proceedings of a conference**

Note

8. Joyce Marie Jackson, "Barrelhouse Singers and Sanctified Preachers," in *Saints and Sinners: Religion, Blues, and (D)evil in African-American Music and Literature: Proceedings of the Conference held at the Université de Liège*, 14–28 (Liège: Société Liègeoise de Musicologie, 1996).

25b Periodical Sources in CMS Style

Note

1. Michael Hutt, "A Nepalese Triangle: Monarchists, Maoists, and Political Parties," *Asian Affairs* 38 (2007): 11–22.

Bibliography

Hutt, Michael. "A Nepalese Triangle: Monarchists, Maoists, and Political Parties." *Asian Affairs* 38 (2007): 11–22.

AUTHOR'S OR EDITOR'S NAME

Note: the author's name is given in normal order.

Bibliography: give the author's last name first.

TITLE OF ARTICLE

- Put the title in quotation marks. If there is a title of a book within the title, italicize it.
- Capitalize nouns, verbs, adjectives, adverbs, and pronouns, and the first word of the title and subtitle.

PUBLICATION INFORMATION

Name of journal

- Italicize the name of the journal.
- Journal titles are normally not abbreviated in the arts and humanities unless the title of the journal is an abbreviation (*PMLA, ELH*).

Volume, issue, and page numbers

- Place the volume number after the journal title without intervening punctuation.
- For journals that are paginated from issue to issue within a volume, do not list the issue number.
- When citing an entire article, with no page numbers, place the abbreviation *vol.* before the volume number.

Date

- The date or year of publication is given in parentheses after the volume number, or issue number, if provided.

Sample citations for periodical sources

JOURNAL ARTICLES

21. Article by one author

Note

> 1. Nick Cullather, "The Foreign Policy of the Calorie," *American Historical Review* 112 (2007): 336–64.

In subsequent references, cite the author's last name only:

> 2. Cullather, 346.

If the reference is to the same work as the reference before it, you can use the abbreviation *Ibid.*:

> 3. Ibid., 348.

Bibliography

Cullather, Nick. "The Foreign Policy of the Calorie." *American Historical Review* 112 (2007): 336–64.

22. Article by two or three authors

Note

> 3. Pamela R. Matthews and Mary Ann O'Farrell, "Introduction: Whose Body?" *South Central Review* 18, no. 3–4 (Fall–Winter 2001): 1–5.

All authors' names are printed in normal order. For subsequent references, give both authors' last names.

> 4. Matthews and O'Farrell, 4.

Bibliography

Matthews, Pamela R., and Mary Ann O'Farrell. "Introduction: Whose Body?" *South Central Review* 18, no. 3–4 (Fall–Winter 2001): 1–5.

23. **Article by more than three authors**

Note

Give the name of the first listed author, followed by *and others*.

> 5. Thompson and others, 602.

Bibliography

List all the authors (inverting only the first author's name).

Thompson, Michael J., Jorgen Christensen-Dalsgaard, Mark S.
     Miesch, and Juri Toomre. "The Internal Rotation of the Sun."
     Annual Review of Astronomy and Astrophysics 41 (2003):
     599–643.

24. **Article by an unknown author**

Note

> 6. "Japan's Global Claim to Asia," *American Historical Review*
> 109 (2004): 1196–98.

Bibliography

> "Japan's Global Claim to Asia." *American Historical Review* 109
>   (2004): 1196–98.

DIFFERENT TYPES OF PAGINATION

25. **Journals paginated by volume**

Note

> 4. Susan Welsh, "Resistance Theory and Illegitimate
> Reproduction," *College Composition and Communication* 52
> (2001): 553–73.

Bibliography

> Welsh, Susan. "Resistance Theory and Illegitimate Reproduction."
>   *College Composition and Communication* 52 (2001): 553–73.

26. Journals paginated by issue

For journals paginated separately by issue, list the issue number after the volume number.

Note

> 5. Tzvetan Todorov, "The New World Disorder," *South Central Review* 19, no. 2 (2002): 28–32.

Bibliography

> Todorov, Tzvetan. "The New World Disorder." *South Central Review* 19, no. 2 (2002): 28–32.

POPULAR MAGAZINES

27. Weekly and biweekly magazines

For a weekly or biweekly popular magazine, give both the day and month of publication as listed on the issue.

Note

> 5. Roddy Doyle, "The Dinner," *New Yorker*, February 5, 2001, 73.

Bibliography

> Doyle, Roddy. "The Dinner." *New Yorker*, February 5, 2001, 73.

28. Regular features and departments

Do not put titles of regular features or departments of a magazine in quotation marks.

> 3. Conventional Wisdom, *Newsweek*, May 14, 2007, 8.

REVIEWS AND EDITORIALS

29. A review

Provide the title, if given, and name the work reviewed. If there is no title, just name the work reviewed.

Note

> 1. Jeff Severs, review of *Vanishing Point,* by David Markson, *Texas Observer*, February 2, 2004.

Bibliography

> Severs, Jeff. Review of *Vanishing Point,* by David Markson. *Texas Observer*, February 2, 2004.

30. A letter to the editor or an editorial

Add *letter* or *editorial* after the name of the author (if there is one). If there is no author, start with the descriptor.

Note

> 2. Mary Castillo, letter to the editor, *New York Magazine*, May 14, 2007, 34.

Bibliography

> Castillo, Mary. Letter to the editor. *New York Magazine*, May 14, 2007, 34.

NEWSPAPERS

31. Newspaper article

> 1. Melena, "Off the Beaten Beat," *New York Times*, May 11, 2007, late edition, sec. E.

- The month, day, and year are essential in citations of materials from daily newspapers. Cite them in this order: Month—Day—Year (November 3, 2007).
- For an item in a large city newspaper that has several editions a day, give the edition after the date.
- If the newspaper is published in sections, include the name, number, or letter of the section after the date or the edition (sec. C).
- Page numbers are usually omitted. If you put them in, use *p.* and *col.* (column) to avoid ambiguity.

25c Online and Computer Sources in CMS Style

ONLINE PUBLICATIONS

32. Document or page from a Web site

To cite original content from within a Web site, include as many descriptive elements as you can: author of the page, title of the page, title and owner of the Web site, and the URL. Include the date accessed only if the site is time-sensitive or is frequently updated. If you cannot locate an individual author, the owner of the site can stand in for the author.

Note

> 11. National Organization for Women, "NOW History," http://www.now.org/history/history.html.

Bibliography

> National Organization for Women. "NOW History." http://www.now.org.history/history.html.

CITING ONLINE SOURCES IN CMS STYLE

CMS advocates a style for citing online and electronic sources that is adapted from its style used for citing print sources. Titles of complete works are italicized. Quotation marks and other punctuation in citations for online sources should be used in the same manner as for print sources.

Access dates: CMS does not generally recommend the use of access dates, except in time-sensitive fields such as law or medicine.

Revision dates: Due to the inconsistency in the practice of Internet sites stating the date of last revision, CMS also recommends against using revision dates in citations.

URLs: If a URL has to be broken at the end of a line, the line break should be made after a slash (/) or double slash (//). CMS does not advocate the use of angle brackets (<>) to enclose URLs.

For details not covered in this section, consult *The Chicago Manual of Style*, fifteenth edition, sections 17.4–17.15, "The Advent of Electronic Sources."

33. Online book

Note

> 12. Angelina Grimké, *Appeal to the Christian Women of the South* (New York: New York Anti-Slavery Society, 1836), http://history.furman.edu/~benson/docs/grimke2.htm.

Bibliography

> Grimké, Angelina. *Appeal to the Christian Women of the South*. New York: New York Anti-Slavery Society, 1836. http://history.furman.edu/~benson/docs/grimke2.htm.

34. Online article

Note

> 13. Emily Bazelon, "Little Geniuses," *Slate* (May 11, 2007): http://www.slate.com/id/2165995/.

Bibliography

> Bazelon, Emily. "Little Geniuses." *Slate* (May 11, 2007): http://www.slate.com/id/2165995/.

OTHER ELECTRONIC SOURCES

35. Posting to a discussion list or group

To cite material from archived Internet forums, discussion groups, MOOs, or blogs, include the name of the post author, the name of the list or site, the date of the posting, and the URL. Limit your citation to notes or in-text citations.

> 16. Jason Marcel, post to U.S. Politics Online Today in Politics Forum, April 4, 2004, http://www.uspoliticsonline.com/forums/forumdisplay.php?f=24.

36. Email

Since personal emails are not available to the public, they are not usually listed in the bibliography.

Note

> 11. Erik Lynn Williams, "Social Anxiety Disorder," email to author, August 12, 2007.

25d Multimedia Sources in CMS Style

37. **Musical recording**

Note

    8. Judy Garland, "Come Rain or Come Shine," *Judy at Carnegie Hall: Fortieth Anniversary Edition*, compact disc, Capitol B000059QY9.

Bibliography

Garland, Judy. "Come Rain or Come Shine." *Judy at Carnegie Hall: Fortieth Anniversary Edition*. Capitol B000059QY9 (compact disc).

38. **Film or video**

Note

    9. *Flags of Our Fathers*, DVD, directed by Clint Eastwood (2006; Hollywood, CA: Paramount Pictures, 2007).

Bibliography

Flags of Our Fathers. DVD. Directed by Clint Eastwood. Hollywood, CA: Paramount Pictures, 2007.

39. **Speech, debate, mediated discussion, or public talk**

Note

    16. Ellen Arthur, "The Octoroon, or Irish Life in Louisiana" (paper presented at the 2001 Annual Convention of the American Conference for Irish Studies, New York, June 2001).

Bibliography

Arthur, Ellen. "The Octoroon, or Irish Life in Louisiana." Paper presented at the 2001 Annual Convention of the American Conference for Irish Studies, New York, June 2001.

40. **Interview**

Note

15. Ira Glass, interview by Terry Gross, *Fresh Air*, National Public Radio, November 17, 2000.

Bibliography

Glass, Ira. Interview by Terry Gross. *Fresh Air*. National Public Radio, November 17, 2000.

41. **Illustrations, figures, and tables**

When citing figures from sources, use the abbreviation *fig.*. However, spell out the word when citing tables, graphs, maps, or plates. The page number on which the figure appears precedes any figure number.

16. Christian Unger, *America's Inner-City Crisis* (New York: Childress, 2003), 134, fig. 3.4.

25e Sample Pages with CMS Documentation

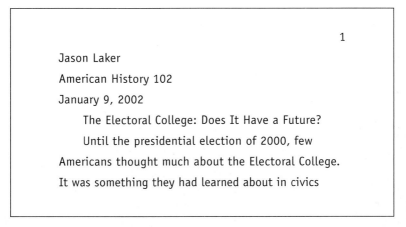

1

Jason Laker

American History 102

January 9, 2002

The Electoral College: Does It Have a Future?

Until the presidential election of 2000, few Americans thought much about the Electoral College. It was something they had learned about in civics

2

class and had then forgotten about as other, more pressing bits of information required their attention. In November 2000, however, the Electoral College took center stage and sparked an argument that continues today: Should the Electoral College be abolished?

The founding fathers established the Electoral College as a compromise between elections by Congress and those by popular vote.[1] The College consists of a group of electors who meet to vote for the president and vice president of the United States. The electors are nominated by political parties within each state and the number each state gets relates to the state's congressional delegation. The process and the ideas behind it sound simple, but the actual workings of the Electoral College remain a mystery to many Americans.

The complicated nature of the Electoral College is one of the reasons why some people want to see it abolished. One voter writes in a letter to the editor of the *New York Times* that the elimination of the Electoral College is necessary "to demystify our voting system in the eyes of foreigners and our own citizenry."[2] Other detractors claim that it just does not work, and they cite the presidential elections of 1824, 1876, 1888, and, of

3

course, 2000 as representative of the failures of the College. Those who defend the Electoral College, however, claim that the failures of these elections had little to do with the Electoral College itself.[3]

According to Gary Gregg, director of the McConnell Center for Political Leadership, a new study shows that much of what Americans think we know about the Electoral College is wrong. Consequently, we should actively question the wisdom of those who want to see it abolished.[4] . . .

4

Notes

1. Lawrence D. Longley and Neal R. Peirce, *The Electoral College Primer 2000* (New Haven: Yale University Press, 1999).

2. William C. McIntyre, "Revisiting the Electoral College," *New York Times*, November 17, 2001, late edition, sec. A.

3. Avagara, *EC: The Electoral College Webzine*, http://www.avagara.com/e_c/.

5

4. Gary Gregg, "Keep the College," *National Review Online*, November 7, 2001, http://www.lexisnexis.com/universe/.

Bibliography

Avagara. *EC: The Electoral College Webzine*. http://www.avagara.com/e_c/.

Gregg, Gary. "Keep the College." *National Review Online*, November 7, 2001. http://www.lexisnexis.com/ universe/.

Longley, Lawrence D., and Neal R. Peirce. *The Electoral College Primer 2000*. New Haven: Yale University Press, 1999.

McIntyre, William C. "Revisiting the Electoral College." *New York Times*. November 17, 2001. Late edition, sec. A.

Chapter 26

CSE Documentation

CSE style applies for all scientific disciplines.

Within the disciplines of the natural and applied sciences, citation styles are highly specialized. Many disciplines follow the guidelines of particular journals or style manuals within their individual fields. Widely followed by writers in the sciences is the comprehensive guide published by the Council of Science Editors: *Scientific Style and Format: The CSE Manual for Authors, Editors, and Publishers*, seventh edition (2006).

The preferred documentation system in CSE places references in the body of the text marked by a superscript number placed inside punctuation. For example:

> Cold fingers and toes are common circulatory problems found in most heavy cigarette smokers[1].

This number corresponds to a numbered entry on the CSE source list, titled *References.*

The CSE References page lists all sources cited in the paper. To create a CSE References page, follow these guidelines:

1. Title your page "References," and center this title at the top of the page.
2. Double-space the entire References page, both within and between citations.
3. List citations in the order they appear in the body of the paper. Begin each citation with its citation number, followed by a period, flush left.
4. Authors are listed by last name, followed by initials. Capitalize only first words and proper nouns in cited titles. Titles are not underlined, and articles are not placed in quotations. Names of journals should be abbreviated where possible.
5. Cite publication year, and volume or page numbers if applicable.

26a In-text References in CSE Style

CSE documentation of sources does not require the names of authors in the text but only a number that refers to the References list at the end.

> In 1997, the Gallup poll reported that 55% of adults in the United States think secondhand smoke is "very harmful," compared to only 36% in 1994[1].

The superscript[1] refers to the first entry on the References list, where readers will find a complete citation for this source.

What if you need more than one citation in a passage?

If the numbers are consecutive, separate with a dash. If nonconsecutive, use a comma.

The previous work[1, 3, 5–8, 11]

26b Books and Nonperiodical Sources in CSE-Style References

1. Nance JJ. What goes up: the global assault on our atmosphere. New York: W Morrow; 1991. 324 p.

AUTHOR'S OR EDITOR'S NAME

The author's last name comes first, followed by the initials of the author's first name and middle name (if provided). If an editor, put the word *editor* after the name.

BOOK TITLE

- Do not italicize or under-line titles.

- Capitalize only the first word and proper nouns.

PUBLICATION INFORMATION

Year of publication

- The year comes after the other publication information. It follows a semicolon.

- If it is a multivolume edited work, published over a period of more than one year, give the span of years.

Page numbers

- When citing an entire book, give the total number of pages: *324 p*.

- When citing part of a book, give the page range for the selection: *p. 60–90*.

Sample references

BOOKS

1. Book by a single author/editor

2. Minger TJ, editor. Greenhouse glasnost: the crisis of global warming. New York: Ecco; 1990. 292 p.

2. Book by two or more authors/editors

3. O'Day DH, Horgen PA, editors. Sexual interactions in eukaryotic microbes. New York: Academic Press; 1981. 407 p.

3. Book by a group or organization

4. IAEA. Manual on radiation haematology. Vienna: IAEA; 1971. 430 p.

4. Two or more books by the same author

Number the references according to the order in which they appear in the text.

5. Gould SJ. The structure of evolutionary theory. Cambridge: Harvard University Press; 2002. 1433 p.

8. Gould SJ. Wonderful life: the Burgess Shale and the nature of history. New York: Norton; 1989. 347 p.

PARTS OF BOOKS

5. A single chapter written by the same author as the book

6. Ogle M. All the modern conveniences: American household plumbing, 1840–1890. Baltimore: Johns Hopkins University Press; 2000. Convenience embodied; p. 60–92.

6. **A selection in an anthology or a chapter in an edited collection**

> 7. Kraft K, Baines DM. Computer classrooms and third grade development. In: Green MD, editor. Computers and early development. New York: Academic; 1997. p. 168–79.

REPORTS

7. **Technical and research reports**

> 9. Austin A, Baldwin R, editors. Faculty collaboration: enhancing the quality of scholarship and teaching. ASCHE-ERIC Higher Education Report 7. Washington, DC: George Washington University; 1991.

26c Periodical Sources in CSE-Style References

> 1. Bohannon J. Climate change: IPCC report lays out options for taming greenhouse gases. Science. 2007;316(5826): 812–814.

AUTHOR'S NAME

The author's last name comes first, followed by the initials of the author's first name and middle name (if provided).

TITLE OF ARTICLE

- Do not italicize or underline titles.

- Capitalize only the first word and proper nouns.

PUBLICATION INFORMATION

Name of journal

- Do not abbreviate single-word titles. Abbreviate multiple-word titles according to the National Information Standards Organization (NISO) list of serials.

- Capitalize the journal title, even if abbreviated.

Date of publication, volume, and issue numbers

- Include the issue number inside parentheses if it is present in the document. Leave no spaces between these items.

JOURNAL ARTICLES

8. **Article by one author**

> 1. Board J. Reduced lodging for soybeans in low plant population is related to light quality. Crop Science. 2001;41:379–387.

9. **Article by two or more authors/editors**

> 2. Simms K, Denison D. Observed interactions between wild and domesticated mixed-breed canines. J Mamm. 1997; 70:341–342.

10. **Article by a group or organization**

> 4. Center for Science in the Public Interest. Meat labeling: Help! Nutrition Action Health Letter: 2. 2001 Apr 1.

11. **Article with no identifiable author**

Use [Anonymous].

12. **Journals paginated by issue**

Use the month or season of publication (and day, if given) for journals paginated by issue. Include the issue number in parentheses after the volume number.

> 8. Barlow JP. Africa rising: everything you know about Africa is wrong. Wired. 1998 Jan:142–158.

26d Online Sources in CSE-Style References

13. Online journal articles

> 2. Schunck CH, Shin Y, Schirotzek A, Zwierlein MW, Ketterle A. Pairing without superfluidity: the ground state of an imbalanced fermi mixture. Science [Internet]. 2007 [cited 2007 June 15]; 316(5826):867–870. Available from: http://www.sciencemag.org/cgi/content/full/3165826/867/DC1

14. Scientific databases on the Internet

> 3. Comprehensive Large Array-data Stewardship System [Internet]. 2007. Release 4.2. Silver Spring (MD): National Environmental Satellite, Data, and Information Service (US). [updated 2007 May 2; cited 2007 May 14]. Available from: http://www.class.noaa.gov/saa/products/welcome

26e Sample Pages with CSE Documentation

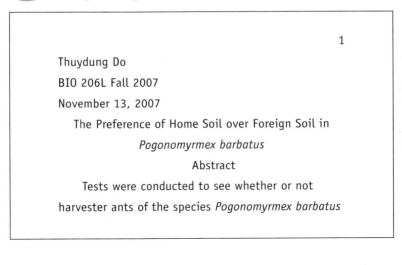

1

Thuydung Do

BIO 206L Fall 2007

November 13, 2007

The Preference of Home Soil over Foreign Soil in

Pogonomyrmex barbatus

Abstract

Tests were conducted to see whether or not

harvester ants of the species *Pogonomyrmex barbatus*

2

can actually distinguish home soil from foreign soil.
These ants were exposed to different types of soils
and the time they spent on each soil was recorded.
The Wilcoxan Signed Rank test was performed to
analyze the collected data. It was observed that
Pogonomyrmex barbatus does show preference for
home soil over foreign soil.

Introduction

Pieces of food are sometimes seen surrounded by
hundreds of ants a while after they were dropped on
the table or on the ground. There are also trails of
ants that line up in an orderly fashion leading from
the food to the nests. How do these ants know to
follow each other in a line instead of scattering all
over? The main method is through releasing
pheromones[1]. The pheromones allow the ants to trail
after one another, but where will they go? What
makes these different ant mounds unique from one
another? Based on research done by Wagner and her
group, soil biota and soil chemistry of each nest can
set themselves apart[2]. Can the harvester ants detect
these differences in the soils at all or are all soils the

3

same to them? In this experiment, the null
hypothesis that harvester ants *Pogonomyrmex
barbatus* cannot distinguish home soil from foreign
soil and neutral soil was tested in attempt to find
the answer to this question.

. . .

4

References

1. Holldobler B, Morgan ED, Oldham NJ, Liebig J.
   Recruitment pheromone in the harvester ant genus
   Pogonomyrmex. J Insect Phys. 2001;47:369–374.
2. Wagner D, Brown M, Gordon D. 1997. Harvester ant
   nests, soil biota and chemistry. Oceologia. 1997;
   112:232–236.

Effective Style and Language

Chapter 27

Write with Power

Learn how to write an efficient sentence.

Keeping a few principles in mind can make your writing a pleasure to read instead of a boring slog.

In visuals
You imagine actions when subjects are captured in motion.

In writing
Your readers expect actions to be expressed in verbs: *gallop, canter, trot, run, sprint, dash, bound, thunder, tear away.*

In visuals
Viewers interpret the most prominent person or thing as the subject—what the visual is about.

In writing
Readers interpret the first person or thing they meet in a sentence as what the sentence is about (the jockey, the horse). They expect that person or thing to perform the action expressed in the verb.

27a Pay Attention to Verbs

A teacher may once have told you that verbs are "action words." Where are the action words in the following paragraph?

> In August 1996, Tiger Woods became a professional golfer with the announcement, "Hello world," and endorsement deals worth $60 million from Nike and Titleist. He was the winner of two events in the next three months and was a qualifier for the PGA Tour Championship. The following April, Woods was the winner of The Masters by a record margin of twelve strokes. After an off year in 1998, Woods was the winner seventeen times in the next two years and in 2001 was the first golfer to hold all four major professional championships at the same time.

No action words here! The paragraph describes a series of actions, yet most of the verbs are *was*. These sentences typify writing that uses *be* verbs (*is, are, was, were*) when better alternatives are available. Think about what the actions are and choose powerful verbs that express those actions.

STAYING ON TRACK

Express actions as verbs

Many sentences contain words that express action, but those words are nouns instead of verbs. Often the nouns can be changed into verbs. For example:

> The arson unit ~~conducted an investigation of~~ investigated the mysterious fire.

> The committee ~~had a debate over~~ debated how best to spend the surplus funds.

Notice that changing nouns into verbs also eliminates unnecessary words.

In August 1996, Tiger Woods announced "Hello world," launching his career as a professional golfer by signing endorsement deals worth $60 million from Nike and Titleist. He won two events in the next three months and qualified for the PGA Tour Championship. The following April, Woods obliterated the field to win his first major tournament, The Masters, by a record margin of twelve strokes. After slumping in 1998, Woods roared back with seventeen victories in the next two years, becoming in 2001 the first golfer to hold all four major professional championships at the same time.

27b Stay Active

When you were a very young child, you learned an important lesson about language. Perhaps you can remember the day you broke the cookie jar. Did you tell Mom, "I knocked over the jar"? Probably not. Instead, you might have said, "The jar got broken." This short sentence accomplishes an amazing sleight of hand. Who broke the jar and how the jar was broken remain mysterious. Apparently, it just broke.

"Got" is often used for "was" in informal speech. In written language, the sentence would read, "The jar was broken," which is an example of the passive voice. Passives can be as useful for adults as for children to conceal who is responsible for an action:

> The laptop containing our customers' personal information was misplaced.

Who misplaced the laptop? Who knows?

Sentences with transitive verbs (labeled "TV" below; verbs that need an object; see Section 35c) can be written in the active or passive voice. In the active voice the subject of the sentence is the actor. In the passive voice the subject is being acted upon.

STAYING ON TRACK

Prefer the active voice

To write with power, consider different ways of saying the same thing. The extra effort will bring noticeable results.

Passive   A request on your part for special consideration based on your experience working in the profession **will be reviewed** by the admissions committee.

Active   If you ask for special consideration because you have worked in the profession, the graduate admissions committee will review your request.

           ┌————— SUBJ —————┐ ┌—TV—┐

Active   **Leonardo da Vinci** painted *Mona Lisa* between 1503 and 1506.

           ┌—— SUBJ ——┐ ┌——TV——┐

Passive   *Mona Lisa* was painted by Leonardo da Vinci between 1503 and 1506.

The passive is created with a form of *be* and the past participle of the main verb. In a passive voice sentence, you can either name the actor in a *by* phrase following the verb or omit the actor altogether.

Passive   *Mona Lisa* was painted between 1503 and 1506.

Exercise 27.1 Underline the active or passive verbs in the following paragraph. If a sentence contains a passive, rewrite the sentence to make it active.

Example   Many kinds of human behavior <u>are</u> now <u>being understood</u> as the products of brain structures by researchers in neuroscience.

Rewrite   Researchers in neuroscience now understand many kinds of human behavior as the products of brain structures.

It has been reported by researchers in neuroscience that food advertising often succeeds because of the structure of our brains. Some people are surprised by this finding. That people buy things they don't need because of advertising has long been rejected by economists. Studies using brain imaging have proven otherwise. When people see and smell their favorite food, a brain structure called the dorsal striatum is stimulated. This brain structure was found to be different from the neural circuits that are stimulated when we are truly hungry. When the dorsal striatum is activated, food is desired to be consumed, even if we are not hungry. Probably the dorsal striatum was important for human survival in past times when food wasn't plentiful. Food needed to be eaten and stored in our bodies for times when food wouldn't be available. But today with food everywhere, an epidemic of obesity is caused by the drive to eat when we aren't hungry.

27c Find Agents

The **agent** is the person or thing that does the action. The most powerful writing usually highlights the agent in a sentence.

Focus on people

Read the following sentence aloud.

Mayoral approval of the recommended zoning change for a strip mall on Walnut Street will negatively impact the traffic and noise levels of the Walnut Street residential environment.

It sounds dead, doesn't it? Think about the meaning of the sentence for a minute. It involves people—the mayor and the people who live on Walnut Street. Putting those people in the sentence makes it come alive.

With people

> If the mayor approves the recommended zoning change to allow a strip mall on Walnut Street, people who live on the street will have to endure much more noise and traffic.

Identify characters

If people are not your subject, then keep the focus on other types of characters.

Without characters

> The celebration of Martin Luther King Day had to be postponed because of inclement weather.

With characters

> A severe ice storm forced the city to postpone the Martin Luther King Day celebration.

STAYING ON TRACK

Include people

Including people makes your writing more emphatic. Most readers relate better to people than to abstractions. Putting people in your writing also introduces active verbs because people do things.

Without people

> The use of a MIDI keyboard for playing the song will facilitate capturing it in digital form on our laptop for the subsequent purpose of uploading it to our Web site.

With people

> By playing the song on a MIDI keyboard, we can record the digitized sound on our laptop and then upload it to our Web site.

Exercise 27.2   The following paragraph includes nouns used to express action. Underline all nouns that show action and the *be* verbs they follow. Then rewrite the entire paragraph, changing the underlined nouns to verbs and deleting be verbs. More than one set of correct answers is possible.

> **Example**   An amputee <u>is</u> likely to have the <u>experience</u> of "phantom limb sensations," as the brain can misinterpret activity from the nervous system.
>
> **Rewrite**   An amputee may feel "phantom limb sensations," as the brain can misinterpret activity from the nervous system.

Though few people celebrate the experience of pain, the human body is dependent on unpleasant impulses for survival. Without pain, an individual is at a disadvantage in terms of self-preservation. When a diseased brain is a failure at communication, the entire body is in jeopardy. Pain is a signal to the body of injured or strained joints, bones, or muscles and is integral in forcing an individual to alter his or her behavior to aid the healing process. Those who are without the ability to sense pain often die by early adulthood, as unchecked infections and injuries overwhelm the body.

Exercise 27.3   In the following paragraph, underline the subject of each sentence. Then rewrite the entire paragraph so that living agents are performing the actions expressed by the verbs.

> **Example**   <u>Halloween customs and traditions</u> have been traced back in time to the ancient Druids.
>
> **Rewrite**   Historians have traced Halloween customs back to the times of the ancient Druids.

The observation of these old customs in parts of Europe where the inhabitants are Celtic proves their Druid origin. To mark the beginning of winter, the burning of fires on November 1 was customary. These Halloween fires are lit even today in Scotland and Wales. Also, it was the belief of Druid custom that on the night of November 1, the earth was roamed by such groups as

witches, demons, and evil spirits. To greet the beginning of "their season," Halloween was the night when these demons celebrated the long nights and early sunsets of the coming winter. It was important to have fun at the expense of mortals on this night, and to offer treats as appeasement was the only way mortals could stop the evil, demonic tricks. To give these treats became a tradition, which has continued into modern Halloween celebrations.

27d Vary Your Sentences

Read the following passage.

> On the first day Garth, Jim, and I paddled fourteen miles down Johnstone Strait. The strait is off the northeast coast of Vancouver Island. The morning was moist and deceptively calm. We stopped to watch a few commercial fishing boats net salmon on the way. Then we set up camp on a rocky beach. We headed down the strait about five more miles to Robson Bight. It is a famous scratching place for orcas. The Bight is a small bay. We paddled out into the strait so we could see the entire Bight. There were no orcas inside. By this time we were getting tired. We were hungry. The clouds assumed a wintry dark thickness. The wind was kicking up against us. Our heads were down going into the cold spray.

The subject matter is interesting, but the writing isn't. The paragraph is a series of short sentences, one after the other, that have a thumpety-thump, thumpety-thump rhythm. When you have too many short sentences one after the other, try combining a few of them. For example, the second and third sentences can be merged into the first sentence (see the paragraphs marked "Revised" on pages 507–508).

The choppiness of the last five sentences destroys the effect of impending danger. These sentences can easily be combined (see the revised paragraphs).

This next passage suffers from a different problem. The sentences are not short, but too many are linked by *and*.

Ahead of us we heard what sounded like a series of distant shotgun blasts, and when it happened again, we could see the fins of a pod of orcas, and we stopped paddling. The orcas were feeding on the salmon, and they were surfacing at six- to eight-second intervals, and they were coming straight at us. They swam in twos and threes, and there were at least twelve of them. There was a mix of the long fins of the bulls and the shorter, more rounded fins of the cows, and the noise of their exhaling was becoming louder and louder.

The paragraph builds to a climax but, as in the previous passage, the effect is lost. The use of too many *and*s becomes monotonous. The passage becomes more intense when the paddlers first see the orcas swimming toward them. The sentence should reflect this intensity, speeding up the pace as the paddlers' hearts start racing. Several of the *and*s can be eliminated and short sentences joined (see the revision below). The result of combining some (but not all) short sentences and revising other statements joined by *and* is a paragraph with sentences that raise interest and control the pace.

Revised

On the first day Garth, Jim, and I paddled fourteen miles down Johnstone Strait off the northeast coast of Vancouver Island on a moist and deceptively calm morning. We stopped to watch a few commercial fishing boats net salmon before we set up camp on a rocky beach and headed down the strait about five more miles to Robson Bight, a small bay known as a famous scratching place for orcas. We paddled out into the strait so we could see the entire Bight, but there were no orcas inside. By this time we were tired and hungry, the clouds had assumed a wintry dark thickness, and the wind was kicking up against us—our heads dropped going into the cold spray.

Ahead of us we heard what sounded like a series of distant shotgun blasts, and when it happened again, we could see the fins of a pod of orcas. We stopped paddling. The orcas were feeding on the salmon, surfacing at six- to eight-second

> intervals, coming straight at us, swimming in twos and
> threes, at least twelve of them, a mix of the long fins of
> the bulls and the shorter, more rounded fins of the cows,
> the noise of their exhaling becoming louder and louder.

Another kind of sentence monotony sets in when sentences are consistently long and complex. The solution to this problem is to simplify some of them and eliminate excess words (see Chapter 28).

27e Give Your Writing Personality

Nobody likes listening to the voice of a robot. Good writing—no matter what the genre—has two unfailing qualities: a human personality that bursts through the page or screen and a warmth that suggests the writer genuinely wishes to engage the readers.

> From age eleven to age sixteen I lived a spartan life without the usual adolescent uncertainty. I wanted to be the best swimmer in the world, and there was nothing else.
>
> —Diana Nyad

> You don't choose your family. They are God's gift to you, as you are to them.
>
> —Desmond Tutu

> If you worried about falling off the bike, you'd never get on.
>
> —Lance Armstrong

Sentences like these convince your readers that you are genuinely interested in reaching out to them.

Write Concisely

Make your writing lean and mean.

Clutter creeps into our lives every day.

Clutter also creeps into our writing in the form of unnecessary words, inflated constructions, and excessive jargon.

> **In regards to** the Web site, the content is **pretty** successful **in consideration of** the topic. The site is **fairly** good **writing-wise** and is **very** unique in telling you how to adjust the rear derailleur one step at a time.

The words in **red** are clutter. Get rid of the clutter. You can say the same thing with half the words and gain more impact as a result.

> The well-written Web site on bicycle repair provides step-by-step instructions on adjusting your rear derailleur.

28a Eliminate Unnecessary Words

Empty words resemble the foods that add calories without nutrition. Put your writing on a diet.

COMMON ERRORS

Empty intensifiers

Intensifiers modify verbs, adjectives, and other adverbs, and they often are overused. One of the most overused intensifiers is *very*.

> The new copper roof was **very bright** on a sunny day.

A new copper roof reflects almost all light. *Very bright* isn't an accurate description. Another adjective would be more accurate:

> The new copper roof was blinding on a sunny day.

Very and *totally* are but two of a list of empty intensifiers that usually can be eliminated with no loss of meaning. Other empty intensifiers include *absolutely, awfully, definitely, incredibly, particularly,* and *really.*

Remember: When you use *very, totally,* or another intensifier before an adjective or adverb, always ask yourself whether there is a more accurate adjective or adverb you could use instead to better express the same thought.

For step-by-step discussion, examples, and practice exercises, visit this page of the E-book at www.mycomplab.com.

Redundancy

Some words act as modifiers, but when you look closely at them, they repeat the meaning of the word they pretend to modify. Have you heard expressions such as *red in color, small in size, round in shape, several in number, past history, attractive in appearance, visible to the eye,* or *honest truth*? Imagine *red* not referring to color or *round* not referring to shape.

Legalese

Legal language often attempts to remove ambiguity through repetition and redundancy. For example, think about what a flight attendant says when your plane arrives.

> Please remain seated, with your seatbelt fastened, until the airplane has come to a full and complete stop; when you deplane from the airplane, be sure to take with you all your personal belongings.

Is there a difference between a *full* stop and a *complete* stop? Can you *deplane* from anything but an airplane? Would you have any *nonpersonal* belongings?

Some speech situations like the flight attendant's instructions may require redundancy to ensure that listeners understand, but in writing, say it once.

Exercise 28.1 The following paragraph is littered with redundant words and phrases. Rewrite wordy sentences to make them concise.

Example ~~Threatening in concept, a~~ black hole is often incorrectly
thought of as an*ₐ*astronomical force that possesses a pull
so strong ~~in force~~ it can engulf anything in its path.

Because we cannot visibly see a black hole up close
distance-wise, we must use our own imaginations to consider its

characteristic properties. For example, imagine taking a jumping leap feet first into a black hole. As you fall, you would descend downward at a slow speed; however, from your personal perception you would seem to be falling faster in speed as time elapsed. In fact, a personal friend observing your downward descent would see that you were in fact moving more and more slowly. In addition, that self-same friend would see that your body was being elongated lengthwise as the center of the black hole pulled more strongly in force on the part of your body which was closest in distance to its center. Simultaneously, your body would begin to start collapsing toward its center, as the forceful force pulled both sides of your body toward the middle of the black hole's center. Unlike in science fiction make-believe, black holes do not serve as either a menacing threat to human life or as a possible means of space or time travel.

Exercise 28.2   In the following paragraph, underline empty intensifiers and the modifiers they intensify. Replace them with more specific and effective modifiers.

Example   The American CIA conducted a <u>very long</u> search for a drug that could serve as a truth serum.

Rewrite   The American CIA conducted an extensive search for a drug that could serve as a truth serum.

In 1942, the American Office of Strategic Services (OSS) Chief William Donovan gathered six incredibly respected scientists to develop a truth serum. The American Psychiatric Association and the Federal Bureau of Narcotics, both very respectable organizations, also participated in this rather secretive search for the truth drug. After definitely varying results and very interesting visions occurred with drugs such as peyote and scopolamine, the group turned to marijuana as a really serious possibility. Creating very different forms of the drug, both strong and diluted, the group tested knowing and unknowing subjects. They tried incredibly unique methods of administering the drug, such as placing a laced gel in foods or injecting a serum into cigars or cigarettes, but they found it very hard to settle on an exact dosage or suitable method. Also, they discovered that individuals did not react very regularly, and the drug could cause a subject to become either absolutely too talkative or particularly quiet. Despite the initial setbacks with marijuana, the American government would really pursue its quest to find a really good substance to serve as a truth serum.

28b Reduce Wordy Phrases

We acquire bad writing and speaking habits because we read and hear so much wordy language. Many inexperienced writers use phrases like "It is my opinion that" or "I think that" to begin sentences. These phrases are deadly to read. If you find them in your prose, cut them. Unless a writer is citing a source, we assume that the ideas are the writer's. (See "When to use *I*" on pages 532–533.)

Coaches are among the worst in using many words for what could be said in a few:

> After much deliberation about Brown's future in football with regard to possible permanent injuries, I came to the conclusion that it would be in his best interest not to continue his pursuit of playing football again.

The coach might have said simply:

> Because Brown risks permanent injury if he plays football again, I decided to release him from the team.

Perhaps the coach wanted to sound impressive, authoritative, or thoughtful. But the result is the opposite. Speakers and writers who impress us are those who use words efficiently.

STAYING ON TRACK

Replace wordy phrases

Certain stock phrases plague writing in the workplace, in the media, and in academia. Many wordy phrases can be replaced by one or two words with no loss in meaning.

Wordy   **Within the time period of no more than** the past decade, email has replaced handwritten and printed personal letters.

Concise   **In** the past decade email has replaced handwritten and printed personal letters.

Wordy	Concise
at this point in time	now
at that point in time	then
due to the fact that	because
for the purpose of	for
have the ability to	can
in spite of the fact that	although
in the event that	if
in the modern world of today	today
in the neighborhood of	about
it is possible that there might be	possibly
make an attempt	try
met with her approval	she approved
The great writer by the name of Henry David Thoreau	Henry David Thoreau

Exercise 28.3 The following paragraph includes many wordy phrases. Rewrite each sentence to eliminate wordiness. Make sure you retain the original meaning of each sentence.

Example ~~Due to the fact that at this point in time~~ *Because* historians
~~dispute~~ *now* the origin of the necktie, I will not ~~make an~~ *try*

~~attempt~~ to provide one conclusive answer.

In the modern world today, it seems the necktie is considered one of the oldest fashion creations and one of the earliest items created for the sole purpose of decorating the human form. One of the main theories locates the predecessor of the modern necktie in the neighborhood of the mid-sixteen hundreds when Croatian soldiers arrived in France adorned with tasseled scarves of linen and muslin. It was at this point in time when the French dubbed these types of garments "croates," which soon became "cravats." In a very real sense, this garment with regard to social practice developed a significance for the purpose of determining levels of proper masculinity; as a matter of fact, at one point in time, the ability to properly tie a necktie served as an initiation ritual for marriage or military service. In spite of the fact that the emphasis placed on tie tying has waned, some historians use this association of proper masculinity with the practice of tie tying in order to explain the short life of the clip-on tie.

28c Simplify Tangled Sentences

Long sentences can be graceful and forceful. Such sentences, however, often require several revisions before they achieve elegance. Too often long sentences reflect wandering thoughts that the writer did not bother to go back and sort out. Two of the most important strategies for untangling long sentences are described in Chapter 27: using active verbs (Section 27a) and naming your agents (Section 27c). Here are some other strategies.

Revise expletives

Expletives are empty words that can occupy the subject position in a sentence. The most frequently used expletives are *there is*, *there are*, and *it is*.

Wordy   There is another banking option that gives you free checking.

To simplify the sentence, find the agent and make it the subject.

Revised   Another banking option gives you free checking.

Wordy   There were several important differences between their respective positions raised by the candidates in the debate.

STAYING ON TRACK

Focus on the main clause

The main clause should express the main idea of the sentence. When you find a tangled, hard-to-read sentence, try revising it by finding the main clause and putting it at the front, letting the details follow.

Tangled

When you approach the ice cream parlor area of the building, you see that the back and side walls of the ice cream parlor area are covered with Bertram High School memorabilia, such as clothing like varsity jackets, cheerleader uniforms, and football jerseys, and other stuff like newspaper clippings and photographs.

Untangled

The back and side walls of the ice cream parlor are covered with Bertram High School memorabilia: varsity jackets, cheerleader uniforms, football jerseys, newspaper clippings and photographs.

Revised The candidates raised several important differences between their respective positions in the debate.

A few kinds of sentences—for example, *It is raining*—do require you to use an expletive. In most cases, however, expletives add unnecessary words, and sentences usually read better without them.

Use positive constructions

Sentences become wordy and hard to read when they include two or more negatives such as the words *no, not* and *nor* and the prefixes *un-* and *mis-*. For example:

Difficult A **not un**common complaint among employers of new college graduates is that they **cannot** communicate effectively in writing.

Revised Employers frequently complain that new college graduates cannot write effectively.

Even simpler Employers value the rare college graduate who can write well.

Phrasing sentences positively usually makes them more economical. Moreover, it makes your style more forceful and direct.

Simplify sentence structure

Long sentences can be hard to read, not because they are long but because they are convoluted and hide the relationships among ideas. Consider the following sentence.

When the cessation of eight years of hostility in the Iran-Iraq war occurred in 1988, it was not the result of one side defeating the other but the exhaustion of both after losing thousands of people and much of their military capability.

This sentence is hard to read. To rewrite sentences like this one, find the main ideas, then determine the relationships among them.

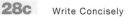

After examining the sentence, you decide there are two key ideas:

1. Iran and Iraq stopped fighting in 1988 after eight years.
2. Both sides were exhausted from losing people and equipment.

Next ask what the relationship is between the two ideas. When you identify the key ideas, the relationship is often obvious; in this case (2) is the cause of (1). Thus the word you want to connect the two ideas is *because*.

> Iran and Iraq stopped fighting after eight years of an indecisive war **because** both sides had lost thousands of people and most of their equipment.

The revised sentence is both clearer and more concise, reducing the number of words from forty-three to twenty-five.

Exercise 28.4 The following paragraph includes negative constructions and expletives (*there is, it is*). Rewrite the sentences for clarity and concision. Some expletives may remain.

Example ~~Not unlike~~ *Similar to* anthropology and sociology, *the discipline of* paleontology ~~is an attempt~~ *attempts* to uncover information ~~that is yet unknown~~ about both living things and civilizations.

There are a number of ways fossils can help paleontologists gain additional information about ancient eras. Though not without problems and informational gaps, fossils aid in locating data that are missing regarding location, time, and traits of both past and future organisms. For example, data have been determined by the not uncontested notion of "uniformitarianism," a theory that assumes certain interactions of matter have not been inconsistent throughout time. Because there is this assumption regarding the constancy of certain processes, it is not illogical to believe there is a way by which fossil age and other characteristics may be determined by considering the effects of constant processes on the aged relic. There is controversy in the scientific community, however, regarding the constancy of such scientific processes and interactions.

Chapter 29

Write with Emphasis

Make your key ideas stand out and not get lost.

29a Manage Emphasis in Sentences

Put your main ideas in main clauses

Emphasize your most important information by placing it in main clauses and your less important information in subordinate clauses (for a description of main and subordinate clauses, see Section 32c).

In the following paragraph all the sentences are main clauses.

> Lotteries were common in the United States before and after the American Revolution. They eventually ran into trouble. They were run by private companies. Sometimes the companies took off with the money. They didn't pay the winners.

This paragraph is grammatically correct, but it does not help the reader understand which pieces of information the author wants to emphasize. Combining the simple sentences into main and subordinate clauses and phrases can significantly improve the paragraph.

First, identify the main ideas.

> Lotteries were common in the United States before and after the American Revolution. They eventually ran into trouble.

These ideas can be combined into one sentence.

> Lotteries were common in the United States before and after the American Revolution, but they eventually ran into trouble.

Now think about the relationship of the three remaining sentences to the main ideas. Those sentences explain why lotteries ran into trouble; thus the relationship is *because*.

> Lotteries were common in the United States before and after the American Revolution, but they eventually ran into trouble because they were run by private companies that sometimes took off with the money instead of paying the winners.

Put key ideas at the beginning and end of sentences

Read these sentences aloud.

1 *Courage Under Fire* and *Good Will Hunting*, films marking the actor's transition from teen idol to adult actor, starred Matt Damon.

2 Films such as *Courage Under Fire* and *Good Will Hunting*, both starring Matt Damon, helped the actor make the difficult transition from teen idol to adult actor.

3 Matt Damon made the difficult transition from teen idol to adult actor, starring in films such as *Courage Under Fire* and *Good Will Hunting*.

Most readers put the primary emphasis on the words at the beginning and end of sentences. Usually at the front of a sentence is what is known: the topic. At the end is the new information about the topic. Subordinate information is in the middle. If a paragraph is about Matt Damon, we would not expect the writer to choose sentence 2 over 1 or 3. In sentence 2 Damon is buried in the middle.

Photographs and writing gain energy when they emphasize key ideas

In visuals

Photographers create emphasis by composing the image to direct the attention of the viewer. Putting people and objects in the foreground and making them stand out against the background gives them emphasis.

In writing

You have many tools for creating emphasis. Writers can design a page to gain emphasis by using headings, white space, type size, color, and boldfacing. Just as important, learning the craft of structuring sentences will empower you to give your writing emphasis.

Exercise 29.1   The following paragraph includes many short sentences. Locate the main and subordinate ideas, and combine groups of sentences into longer, more concise, and clearer sentences. In the revised sentences, underline the main information twice and the subordinate information once.

Example   ~~Muscular Christianity was~~ *P*opular in the late nineteenth and early twentieth centuries. *. Muscular Christianity sought to regain* ~~It focused on regaining~~ the church for men, *by changing* ~~It sought to change~~ the image of Jesus Christ.

Rewrite   Popular in the late nineteenth and early twentieth centuries, <u>Muscular Christianity sought to regain the church for men</u> by changing the image of Jesus Christ.

American religion was thought of as very feminine in the nineteenth century. It catered to moralism. Some thought it deterred market capitalism. There were more women than men in congregations. Pictures of Jesus Christ portrayed a sickly, effeminate man. Men wanted to reclaim religion. They did not want to aspire to an effeminate God. They wanted to change the image of Jesus. They refocused on Jesus' carpentry. Carpentry was associated with America's self-made man. Billy Sunday was a major spokesman for Muscular Christianity. He was an ex-professional baseball player. He had left baseball. He disapproved of the fact that one did not need morality for success in baseball. He demanded men be manly like Jesus. He was popular. American Magazine voted him the eighth greatest man in the United States. This vote was in 1914. This helped to rejuvenate religion. Men were allowed to be religious. They were also allowed to be strong.

29b Forge Links Across Sentences

When your writing maintains a focus of attention across sentences, the reader can distinguish the important ideas and how they relate to each other. To achieve this coherence, control which ideas occupy the positions of greatest emphasis. The words and ideas you repeat from sentence to sentence act as links.

Link sentences from front to front

In front-to-front linkage, the subject of the sentence remains the focus from one sentence to the next. In the following sequence, sentences 1 through 5 are all about Matt Damon. The subject of each sentence refers to the first sentence by using the pronouns *he* and *his*.

1 Matt Damon was born in 1970 and grew up in Boston.

2 His first movie role was a one-line part in *Mystic Pizza* with Julia Roberts in 1988.

3 He dropped out of Harvard twelve credits short of graduating to pursue his acting career full time.

4 His first major role was a Gulf War vet-turned-heroin-addict in *Courage Under Fire* in 1996.

5 Since then he has frequently starred with his real-life best friend, Ben Affleck.

Each sentence adds more information about the repeated topic, Matt Damon.

Link sentences from back to front

In back-to-front linkage, the new information at the end of the sentence is used as the topic of the next sentence. Back-to-front linkage allows new material to be introduced and commented on.

1 Matt Damon's one-line part in *Mystic Pizza* was his first film role.

2 Hollywood film brokers recognized in *Chasing Amy* the potential of pairing Damon with his childhood friend Ben Affleck.

3 Affleck and Damon next wrote the screenplay for *Good Will Hunting*, in which they co-star.

Back-to-front linkage is useful when ideas need to be advanced quickly, as when you are telling stories. Rarely, however, will you use either front-to-front linkage or back-to-front linkage for long. You will mix them, using front-to-front linkage to add more information and back-to-front linkage to move the topic along.

STAYING ON TRACK

Check links across sentences

Where in the following paragraph is your attention disrupted?

> In February 1888, Vincent van Gogh left cloudy Paris for Arles in the sunny south of France. Later that year he persuaded fellow painter Paul Gauguin to join him. Gauguin, who had traveled in the tropics, did not find Arles colorful and exotic. Critics hail this period as the most productive in van Gogh's brilliant but short career.

The last sentence connects distantly with what has come before by mentioning art and van Gogh, but it jars you when you read it because new information, "critics," comes where we expect to find known information. Adding a clause provides a bridge between the old and new information.

> In February 1888, Vincent van Gogh left cloudy Paris for Arles in the sunny south of France. Later that year he persuaded fellow painter Paul Gauguin to join him. Gauguin, who had traveled in the tropics, did not find Arles colorful and exotic. **Although van Gogh and Gauguin argued and soon parted company,** critics hail this period as the most productive in van Gogh's brilliant but short career.

29c Use Parallel Structure with Parallel Ideas

What if Patrick Henry had written "Give me liberty or I prefer not to live"? Would we remember those words today? We do remember the words he did write: "Give me liberty or give me death." Writers who use parallel structure often create memorable sentences:

> Uncommon valor was a common virtue.
>
> —Chester Nimitz describing the Marines at Iwo Jima

> Bread that must be sliced with an ax is bread that is too nourishing.
>
> —Fran Lebowitz

> If a free society cannot help the many who are poor, it cannot save the few who are rich.
>
> —John F. Kennedy

Use parallelism with *and, or, nor, but*

When you join elements at the same level with coordinating conjunctions, including *and, or, nor, yet, so, but*, and *for*, use parallel grammatical structure.

Awkward

In today's global economy, **the method of production and where factories are located** has become relatively unimportant in comparison with **the creation of new concepts and marketing those concepts.**

Parallel

In today's global economy, how goods are made and where they are produced has become relatively unimportant in comparison with creating new concepts and marketing those concepts.

COMMON ERRORS

Faulty parallel structure

When writers neglect to use parallel structure, the result can be jarring. Reading your writing aloud will help you catch problems in parallelism. Read this sentence aloud.

> At our club meeting we identified problems in **finding** new members, **publicizing** our activities, and **maintenance** of our Web site.

The end of the sentence does not sound right because the parallel structure is broken. We expect to find another verb + *ing* following *finding* and *publicizing*. Instead, we run into *maintenance*, a noun. The problem is easy to fix: Change the noun to the *-ing* verb form.

> At our club meeting we identified problems in finding new members, publicizing our activities, and **maintaining** our Web site.

Remember: Use parallel structure for parallel ideas.

For step-by-step discussion, examples, and practice exercises, visit this page of the E-book at www.mycomplab.com.

Use parallelism with *either/or, not only/but*

Make identical in structure the parts of sentences linked by correlative conjunctions: *either ... or, neither ... nor, not only ... but also, whether ... or.*

Awkward

> Purchasing the undeveloped land **not only** gives us a new park **but also** is something that our children will benefit from in the future.

Parallel

Purchasing the undeveloped land **not only** will give our city a new park **but also** will leave our children a lasting inheritance.

The more structural elements you match, the stronger the effect the parallelism will achieve.

Correct

Either we find a way to recruit new members or we settle for the current number of sailboats.

Improved

Either we find a way to recruit new members or we drop the plan to increase our fleet.

The first sentence is correct but still clunky. The parallelism is limited to *we find/we settle*. The second sentence delivers more punch by extending the parallelism: *we find a way to recruit new members/we drop the plan to increase our fleet*. Matching structural elements exactly—verb for verb, article for article, adjective for adjective, object for object—provides the strongest parallelism.

Exercise 29.2   The following paragraph contains many examples of nonparallel sentence structure. Find the faulty constructions and either delete them or replace them with parallel constructions, as necessary.

Example   Sesame Street introduced America to educational children's television and ~~providing~~ *provided* children with informational furry friends.

Sesame Street entered the American consciousness in 1969, playing, singing, and to teach. Joan Ganz Cooney, a major mastermind of Sesame Street, proposed to join child-friendly techniques with commercial television standards, and accelerating the speed

of teaching. These standards and techniques would aid teachers' goals of teaching symbolic representation, cognitive processes, and teaching social and physical environments. These goals were accomplished with the help of live actors, using puppeteers, and animation. In its more than thirty-year run, Sesame Street has managed to educate three generations of school children, finding a home in over 140 countries, and garner more Emmys than any other show in history.

29d Use Parallel Structure with Lists

Lists are frequently used in visual aids for oral presentations and in announcements, brochures, instructions, and other kinds of writing. The effectiveness of a bulleted list is lost, however, when the items are not in parallel form. In a list of action items, such as a list of goals, beginning each item with a verb emphasizes the action. See the example on the next page.

Exercise 29.3   You're invited to Howard's party on Saturday. The following directions to Howard's house contain several examples of faulty parallelism. Revise the directions, making the structure of each parallel to the first entry.

Directions to Howard's

1. Turn left onto Route 22 N at the end of Maple Street.
2. You'll come to the Dewdrop Inn after following Route 22 N 3 miles.
3. There's a sharp right turn onto Geoffrey Drive at the fourth traffic signal after the Dewdrop.
4. The red mailbox you're looking for is halfway down the block.
5. Directly across from the mailbox there's a driveway—turn in there.
6. You can reverse the directions and follow them to come home.

Sailing Club goals

- Increase the membership by 50% this year
- Compete in all local regattas
- Offer beginning and advanced classes
- Purchase eight new Flying Juniors
- Organize a spring banquet
- Publicize all major events

29e Use Parallel Structure in Paragraphs

Use parallelism to create rhythm

Parallel structure does not have to be used in rigid, mechanical ways. Repeating elements of structure can build a rhythm that gives your prose a distinctive voice.

> If you don't like my book, write your own. If you don't think you can write a novel, that ought to tell you something. If you think you can, do.
>
> —Rita Mae Brown, from *A Note*

Use parallel structure to pair ideas

Parallel structure is also useful to pair ideas. The closer the similarity in structure, the more emphasis you will achieve.

> Being a grown-up means assuming responsibility for yourself, for your children, and—here's the big curve—for your parents. In other words, you do get to stay up later, but you want to go to sleep sooner.
>
> —Wendy Wasserstein, from *Bachelor Girls*

■ Parallel structure in images also creates emphasis. Notice how the horse and the groom have a parallel stance—both tense, both with knees bent, both looking away—connected only by the hand on the rein.

Chapter 30

Find the Right Words

Use precise language to express your ideas effectively.

Styles in dress and in writing have become more casual in recent years; just as you might see someone wearing flip-flops in a fancy restaurant, you can see terms like *spam* and *flame* from informal email turning up in newspapers, magazines, and even in academic writing. Nevertheless, most applicants for good jobs don't show up for interviews in flip-flops. Instead, they carefully select their clothing to give the right impression. Selecting the right words in your writing can be just as important for conveying your ideas.

30a Be Aware of Levels of Formality

Colloquialisms

Colloquialisms are words or expressions that are used informally, often in conversation but less often in writing.

> I'm not happy with my grades, but that's the way the cookie crumbles.

> I've had it up to here with all of Tom's complaining.

> Liz is always running off at the mouth about something.

Aside from carrying meanings that aren't always obvious to your reader, colloquialisms usually indicate a lack of seriousness that runs counter to what you'll be trying to accomplish in most academic and professional writing. Colloquialisms can suggest a flippant attitude, carelessness, or even thoughtlessness.

College writing does not mean, however, that you should try to use big words when small ones will do as well, or that you should use ten words instead of two.

Slang

The most conspicuous kind of language to be avoided in most college writing is slang. The next time a friend talks to you, listen closely to the words he or she uses. Chances are you will notice several words that you probably would not use in a college writing assignment. Slang words are created by and for a particular group—even if that group is just you and your friend.

> Joey's new ride is totally pimped out.

> The party was bumpin' with all my peeps.

Aside from being a fun way to play with language, slang asserts a sense of belonging to a group. But because slang excludes those who are not members of the group, it is best avoided in college writing.

STAYING ON TRACK

When to use *I*

You may have been taught to avoid the first person *(I, we)* in academic and professional writing. Some instructors feel that first-person references reflect a self-indulgence that is inappropriate outside of autobiography. Sentences beginning with *I* refer to the author and make him or her the subject. In a sentence such as *I think Florida's west coast beaches are better in every way than those on the east coast,* the reader's attention is divided between the beaches and the person evaluating the beaches.

(Continued on next page)

> **STAYING ON TRACK** (continued)
>
> Another reason some instructors prohibit use of the first person is the tendency of writers to overuse it. Some writers feel that nothing can be invalidated as long as each potentially arguable assertion starts with *I think* or *I feel*. *I* becomes a shield, which the writer uses to escape the work of building an argument.
>
> Occasionally, the use of *I* is redundant. In the following sentence, the nature of the assertion clearly indicates that it's the writer's opinion:
>
> **Redundant *I***   I think the Panama Canal is the greatest engineering achievement of the United States.
>
> Here you can safely drop *I think* without changing the sentence's meaning. Sometimes, however, you will want to indicate plainly that an assertion is tentative. *I* is critical to the meaning of this sentence:
>
> **Tentative *I***   I thought that the dim, distant light was a planet.
>
> If you're unsure whether or not first-person references are permissible, ask your instructor.

Exercise 30.1   Sue Mills wrote the following note to thank her friend Hannah Le Chat for lunch. How would the language of the note change if Sue Mills were writing a letter to a potential employer, thanking her for a luncheon interview? Rewrite the note, making the potential employer the audience. Note how eliminating colloquialisms changes a letter's level of formality.

Dear Hannah,

I'm so glad that we were finally able to catch up on things at lunch on Friday. I thought the eggplant was totally off the hook, the beans were to die for, and the cheesecake melted in my mouth. All in all, you totally raised the roof with that one. Even if my back were against the wall, I would still be a fish out of water in the kitchen. As a matter of fact, ever since my junior high cooking teacher bawled me out in front of the class, I've really had a chip on my shoulder about my culinary skills. Anyway, I just wanted to give you props for the lunch and let you know I hope we can strap on the old feedbag again sometime soon.

Well, I should split.

Sue

Exercise 30.2   The following paragraph was taken from a rough draft of a research paper for an environmental ecology class. The instructor asked the writer to eliminate any use of first person, colloquial language, unnecessarily big words, and wordiness. Use the advice from this section to revise the paragraph according to the instructor's comments.

Example   Many geologists and conservationists in the United States have views that are diametrically opposed on whether to support or fight mining and commercialization in sacrosanct public acreage.

Rewrite   Many U.S. geologists and conservationists disagree on whether to mine or commercialize public lands.

David Brower, who died in 2000, was a person who was the president of the American wilderness preservation club called the Sierra Club. As this organization's preeminent leader he was the human personification of preservation. Brower took a no-holds-barred approach to fighting the infidels of mining and tourism in America's wilderness areas. I think his most perspicacious campaign against these factors that threaten the wilderness must have been when he published an ad to fight the commercialization of the Grand Canyon. His placement of newspaper advertisements telling people about plans to open businesses at the base of the canyon deterred this development. I think that most who believe in conservation would agree that these achievements make David Brower a hero for the American environment.

30b Be Aware of Denotation and Connotation

When you see a Jeep covered with mud, you know the driver has probably been off the pavement. Car manufacturers regularly take advantage of associations like this one. While some advertisements show shiny new cars, ads for Jeeps and similar vehicles show them caked with mud, emphasizing their ruggedness.

Words likewise carry associations from the places they have been. Words have both literal meanings, called **denotations**, and associated meanings, called **connotations**. The contrast is evident in words that mean roughly the same thing but have different connotations. For example, some people are set in their opinions, a quality that can be described positively as *persistent, firm,* and *steadfast* or negatively as *stubborn, bull-headed,* and *close-minded.*

In college and professional writing, writers are expected not to rely on the connotations of words to make important points. For example, the statement *It's only common sense to have good schools* carries high positive connotations but is not precise enough for college writing. Most people believe in common sense, and most people want good schools. What is common sense for one person, however, is not common sense for another; how a good school is defined varies greatly. You have the obligation in college writing to support any judgment with evidence.

Exercise 30.3 The following sets of words have negative connotations. Replace each set with (a) two words that each have a similar denotative meaning but a positive connotation, and (b) one word that has a similar denotative meaning but a neutral connotation. If you are unsure of the meaning of a word, use a dictionary.

1. skinny, gaunt, emaciated, bony, skeletal
2. cacophony, discord, racket, clamor
3. drudge, workaholic, plodder, drone
4. flakey, indecisive, wishy-washy, dithering
5. stubborn, pig-headed, inflexible, obstinate

30c Use Specific Language

Be precise

Effective writing conveys information clearly and precisely. Words such as *situation, sort, thing, aspect,* and *kind* often signal undeveloped or even lazy thinking.

Vague   The violence aspect determines how video games are rated.

Better   The level of violence determines how video games are rated.

When citing numbers or quantities, be as exact as possible. A precise number, if known, is always better than slippery words like *several* or *many,* which some writers use to cloak the fact that they don't know

---

STAYING ON TRACK

Find the exact word

When you use words like *things,* always ask if there is a more specific word.

Vague   Members of the kayaking club also enjoy things like mountain biking, caving, and climbing.

Specific   Members of the kayaking club also enjoy outdoor activities like mountain biking, caving, and climbing.

Animals, birds, insects, fish, trees, flowers, clouds, and rocks all have names. If you don't know the names of what you are writing about, look them up.

Vague   A big flock of black birds came to roost on the big tree beside our apartment.

Specific   Over three hundred boat-tailed grackles descended on the four-story live oak beside our apartment to roost for the night.

the quantity in question. If you know an approximate quantity, indicate the quantity but qualify it: *about twenty-five* tells readers much more than *many*.

Use a dictionary

There is no greater tool for writers than the dictionary. When you write always have a dictionary handy—either a book or an online version—and get into the habit of using it. In addition to checking spelling, you can find additional meanings of a word that perhaps you had not considered, and you can find the etymology—the origins of a word. In many cases knowing the etymology of a word can help you use it to better effect. For example, if you want to argue that universities as institutions have succeeded because they bring people together in contexts that prepare them for their lives after college, you might point out the etymology of *university*. *University* can be traced back to the late Latin word *universitas*, which means "society or guild," thus emphasizing the idea of a community of learning.

COMMON ERRORS

Words often confused

Words with different meanings that are pronounced in the same way are called **homonyms**. Be particularly careful that you select the correct one. These pairs can cause confusion.

bare—unadorned
bear—(1) an animal; (2) to carry

capital—(1) government seat; (2) material wealth; (3) uppercase letter
capitol—a building housing a government seat

(Continued on next page)

COMMON ERRORS *(continued)*

cite—(1) to make mention of; (2) to quote as an example
sight—something seen
site—place, location

coarse—rough
course—plotted-out site or matter

counsel—(1) advice; (2) lawyer; (3) to advise
council—a deliberative body

complement—to go with, as in *That tie complements that suit.*
compliment—to flatter

fair—(1) just; (2) carnival
fare—(1) ticket price; (2) to get along

hear—to listen to
here—location

passed—went by
past—time before the present

patience—the state of calmly waiting
patients—people receiving medical care

peace—serenity
piece—a part of

plain—(1) simple; (2) level land
plane—(1) short for airplane; (2) level surface; (3) carpenter's tool

principal—(1) head of an organization; (2) a sum of money
principle—a basic law or guideline

wear—(1) to don clothes; (2) to erode
where—location

(Continued on next page)

COMMON ERRORS *(continued)*

weather—climatic condition
whether—if

Other words do not sound exactly alike, only similar. The words in the following pairs are frequently confused:

accept—to receive
except (as preposition)—excluding

advice—a suggestion
advise—to suggest

affect—to act upon or to have an effect on something or somebody
effect—a change caused by an action

allude—to make reference to
elude—to evade

allusion—an indirect reference
illusion—a false impression

conscience—moral compass
conscious—aware

continually—(1) consistently; (2) regularly
continuously—without stopping

desert—(1) geographical feature; (2) to abandon
dessert—sweet snack

elicit—to bring out
illicit—unlawful

loose—not tight
lose—(1) to misplace; (2) to fail to win a game

personal—(1) individual; (2) private
personnel—staff

(Continued on next page)

COMMON ERRORS *(continued)*

presence—opposite of absence
presents—(1) gifts; (2) introduces

respectfully—demonstrating respect
respectively—in the given order

Remember: Use a dictionary to check that you are using the right word.

For step-by-step discussion, examples, and practice exercises, visit this page of the E-book at www.mycomplab.com.

Exercise 30.4 The following paragraph, taken from a research paper, contains slang that may not be appropriate for an academic audience. Revise the paragraph to make all the sentences suitable for college readers.

Example Sally Ride is ~~super~~ famous *most famous* as the first American woman in space and as the youngest astronaut to orbit in the Challenger shuttle.

In her youth, Ride was a radical tennis player. However, instead of becoming a professional athlete, she went to Stanford and received her doctorate in x-ray physics. While at Stanford, Ride was selected out of a group of 8,000 other folks to be part of NASA's astronaut class. On June 18, 1983, Ride took her totally extreme first trip to space. In 1989, Ride split NASA and became a professor of physics at USSD, where she directs the California Space Institute. Ride was so awesome in space that she totally had an impact on women in scientific and technical careers.

Exercise 30.5   This paragraph, from a research paper about space exploration, contains vague and incorrect language. Revise it to eliminate vague language, misused homonyms, and misused sound-alike words. Information needed to eliminate vague language is included in parentheses.

Example   Astronauts have been exploiting space for quite a few years now.

Rewrite   Astronauts have been exploring space since at least the 1960s.

Space missions can adversely affect an astronaut's health. A more than minor culprit is the lack of gravity in space; one of the affects that weightlessness has on astronauts is that it causes bone loss, which might be really bad. A sort-of older (45) astronaut may have such serious bone deterioration that after a mission, her bones resemble those of an old lady (like an 80-year-old). Other continuous effects are the interruption of sleeping patterns and the deterioration of the immune system and mussels. But perhaps the scariest affect sited by experts is radiation exposure, especially during visits to Mars. None knows what the cancer risks from this exposure might be.

Exercise 30.6   Circle the correct word in parentheses in the following paragraph. Look up the words in a dictionary if you are not sure of their meaning.

Butchering a hog requires (patience, patients) and hard work. First, find a (cite, sight, site) outside (wear, where) you will have plenty of space. After killing the pig, dunk it in hot water to loosen the (coarse, course) hair. Scrape the hair with a knife (continually, continuously) until the skin is completely (bare, bear). Thread a gambling stick (threw, through) the hamstrings, and hang the pig head-down from a post. Remove the head, cut down the length of the underbelly, and remove the organs. Then cut down the length of the spine and remove the tenderloin, fatback, ribs, middlin' meat, shoulders, and hams (respectfully, respectively). While some people are squeamish about eating hogs' heads and organs, in (principal, principle) nearly every part of the animal is edible.

30d   Use Effective Figurative Language

Figurative language—figures of speech that help readers get a more vivid sense of an object or idea—is what you use when literal descriptions seem insufficient.

Literal   The prosecutor presented a much stronger legal case than did the defense attorney.

Figurative   The prosecutor took the defense attorney apart like a dollar watch.

The two most common figures of speech are the simile and the metaphor. A **simile** usually begins with *as* or *like*, and makes an explicit comparison.

In the past talking about someone's children was like talking about the weather.

Metaphor is from a Greek term that means "carry over," which describes what happens when you encounter a metaphor: You carry over the meaning from one word to another. Metaphor makes a comparison without using *like* or *as*.

She reached the pinnacle of her profession.

[highest point ————→ best]

Two other forms of figurative language are **synecdoche**, in which the part is used to represent the whole (a hood ornament that represents a car) and **metonymy**, in which something related stands in for the thing itself (*White House* for the executive branch; *brass* for military officers).

If not used imaginatively, figurative language merely dresses up a literal description in fancy clothes without adding to the reader's understanding of the object or idea. The purpose of figurative language is to convey information vividly to help the reader grasp your meaning.

You'll want to avoid **clichés**, which are relics of figurative language, phrases used so often that they have become tired and stripped of meaning. Among countless others, the following expressions have hardened into clichés.

better late than never	out like a light
blind as a bat	playing with fire
easier said than done	pride and joy
hard as a rock	thin as a rail
ladder of success	water under the bridge
nutty as a fruitcake	wise as an owl

STAYING ON TRACK

Think fresh

You might find yourself resorting to clichés when you're low on inspiration or energy. Read your drafts aloud to yourself to identify clichés, listening for the phrases that you've used or heard before. Make a note of them and either change the clichés to literal description or, better still, create fresh new phrases to convey what you were trying to say with the cliché.

Cliché

When we entered the old café with the screen door banging behind us, we knew **we stood out like a sore thumb**.

Specific

When we entered the old café with the screen door banging behind us, we knew we stood out like our hybrid Prius in the parking lot full of pickup trucks.

Exercise 30.7 The following paragraph is filled with clichés. Underline each cliché and replace it with fresh language.

Example Cephalopods are a group of marine mollusks that many Americans would not touch with a ten-foot pole.

Rewrite Cephalopods are a group of marine mollusks that many Americans find distasteful.

However, in Japan and in the Mediterranean, squid, octopus, and cuttlefish are an important food source and sell like hot cakes. Unfortunately, myths about giant squid sinking boats and octopus drowning swimmers persist in the United States, and information that giant squid are weak as kittens and that an octopus has never drowned anyone falls on deaf ears. The Japanese attitude is a step in the right direction; they see the octopus as a cheerful, friendly creature and often use its image as a toy or mascot. Our culinary pleasures could grow by leaps and bounds if more of us opened our minds to the joys of fried calamari dipped in marinara sauce and squid sushi with plenty of wasabi. We need to wake up and smell the coffee in the United States that cephalopods are an underexploited marine resource.

Chapter 31

Write to Be Inclusive

Be sure to reach all of your potential readers.

Except for comedians and angry people, few writers want to insult their readers. Often when readers are offended by a writer's language the writer did not intend this result. Instead, the writer likely expressed assumptions that readers rejected as biased. If you want to reach all your potential readers, you should avoid biased language.

Although the conventions of inclusiveness change continually, three guidelines for inclusive language toward all groups remain constant.

- Do not point out people's differences unless those differences are relevant to your argument.
- Call people whatever they prefer to be called.
- When given a choice of terms, choose the more accurate one.

31a Be Aware of Stereotypes

Reject stereotypes

A **stereotype** makes an assumption about a group of people by applying a characteristic to all of them based on the knowledge of only a few of them. The idea that Asian women are submissive, for instance, is a stereotype; it tries to apply one personality trait to many individuals whose only shared characteristics are their gender and ethnicity. Such a stereotype is just as ridiculous as a belief that all Idahoans are potato farmers.

Of course you want to avoid obviously harmful (not to mention inaccurate) stereotypes such as *People on welfare are lazy, gays are effeminate*, or *NASCAR fans are rednecks*. More subtle stereotypes, however, may be harder to identify and eliminate from your writing. If you want to offer an engineer as an example, will you make the engineer a man? If you want your reader to envision a child living in subsidized housing, will you describe the child as an African American? Instead of using these examples that perpetuate stereotypes, try to choose cases that go against them.

Watch for assumptions about what's "normal"

Assumptions about what's "normal" or "regular" can create bias. Calling one person or group "normal" implies that others are abnormal.

Problematic norm

Gloria Nuñez isn't like the regular sprinters at the Greater Detroit Meet; while other runners gingerly settle their feet into the blocks, Nuñez plants her prosthetic foot in the block and waits for the starting gun.

Better

Gloria Nuñez is one sprinter at the Greater Detroit Meet who might surprise you; while other runners gingerly settle their feet into the blocks, Nuñez plants her prosthetic foot in the block and waits for the starting gun.

Exercise 31.1   Identify your pet peeves in writing. Do you have any words or phrases that you find unnecessary, annoying, or wrong? Write down as many of them as possible. Then, consider where and how you acquired the negative attitudes toward them.

Bring the list of your pet peeves and the sources of your attitudes. Then, discuss with your classmates when those words and phrases may be useful or appropriate.

STAYING ON TRACK

Stereotypical images

Most Americans now realize that overtly racist images are offensive. The notable exception to this awareness is representations of American Indians. American Indian mascots used by college and professional sports teams have long been controversial. Most were adopted in the early decades of the twentieth century when European Americans enjoyed putting on paint and feathers and "playing Indian." Supporters of the mascots claim that they honor American Indians. Critics argue that the mascots perpetuate stereotypes of American Indians as primitive, wild, and bellicose. Furthermore, fans of schools that compete with those that have Indian mascots often create derogatory images of American Indians.

Subtle stereotyping comes through the media. Based on images in the news media, many Americans think that women in Islamic countries cover their faces in public, but this practice is typical only in Saudi Arabia and the most conservative sectors of Islamic society. While some people in Holland still wear wooden shoes, wooden shoes are hardly everyday Dutch footwear.

■ Sign over a service station in New Mexico

31b Be Inclusive about Gender

Gender is a term that refers to the social designations of men, women, and their sexual orientations.

Avoid exclusive nouns and pronouns

Don't use masculine nouns and pronouns to refer to both men and women. *He, his, him, man,* and *mankind* are outmoded and inaccurate terms for both genders.

- Don't say *boy* when you mean *child.*
- Use *men and women* or *people* instead of *man.*
- Use *humanity* or *humankind* in place of *mankind.*

Eliminating *he, his,* and *him* when referring to both men and women is more complicated. Many readers consider *he/she* to be an awkward alternative. Try one of the following approaches instead.

- Make the noun and its corresponding pronoun plural. The pronoun will change from *he, him,* or *his* to *they, them,* or *theirs.*

Biased masculine pronouns

An undercover agent won't reveal **his** identity, even to other agents, if **he** thinks it will jeopardize the case.

Better

Undercover agents won't reveal **their** identities, even to other agents, if **they** think it will jeopardize the case.

- Replace the pronoun with another word.

Biased masculine pronoun

Anyone who wants to rent scuba gear must have **his** certification.

Better

Anyone who wants to rent scuba gear must have **diver** certification.

Use gender-neutral names for professions

Professional titles that indicate gender—*chairman, waitress*—falsely imply that the gender of the person doing the job changes the essence of the job being done. Terms like *woman doctor* and *male nurse* imply that a woman working as a doctor and a man working as a nurse are abnormal. Instead, write simply *doctor* and *nurse*.

Biased, gender-specific	Better, gender-neutral
chairman	chair, chairperson
clergyman	member of the clergy
congressman	representative or senator
fireman	firefighter
foreman	supervisor
hostess	host
mailman	mail carrier
manpower	personnel, staff

Biased, gender-specific	Better, gender-neutral
policeman	police officer
salesman	salesperson
stewardess	flight attendant
waitress	server
weatherman	meteorologist
workmen	workers

Eliminate bias when writing about sexual orientation

Sexual orientation refers to a person's identification as bisexual, heterosexual, homosexual, or transsexual. *Heterosexual* and *homosexual* carry a somewhat clinical connotation. Referring to people who are homosexual as *gays* can lead to confusion: It sometimes connotes men and women, sometimes just men. Instead, use *gay men* and *lesbians*. Again, the principle is to use terms that individuals in specific groups prefer.

31c Be Inclusive about Race and Ethnicity

Use the terms for racial and ethnic groups that the groups use for themselves. Use *black* to write about members of the Black Coaches' Association and *African American* to write about members of the Society for African American Brotherhood.

If you are still in doubt, err on the side of specificity. For instance, while *Latino(a)*, *Hispanic*, and *Chicano(a)* are all frequently accepted terms for many people, a term that identifies a specific country (*Mexican* or *Puerto Rican*) would be more accurate. *Asian* is currently preferred over *Oriental*; however, terms like *Vietnamese* and *Japanese* are even more specific. Also, *English* and *British* are different. The people who live in England are English, but people from elsewhere in Great Britain—Scotland, Wales, Northern Ireland—will be quick to tell you that they are not English. Call people from Wales *Welsh* and those from Scotland *Scots*.

When discussing an American's heritage, often the best term to use is the country of origin plus the word *American*, as in *Swedish American* or *Mexican American*. Currently *black* and *African American* are acceptable. Some people prefer *Native American* over *American Indian*, but both terms are used. In Canada the preferred name for indigenous peoples is *First Peoples* (or Inuit for those who live in the far north). First Peoples is increasingly used by indigenous peoples in the United States in solidarity with their Canadian relatives. If you are writing about specific people, use the name of the specific American or Canadian Indian group (Cree, Hopi, Mi'kmaq, Ute).

31d Be Inclusive about Other Differences

Writing about people with disabilities

The *Publication Manual of the American Psychological Association* (5th ed.) offers some good advice: "Put people first, not their disability" (75). Write *people who are deaf* instead of *the deaf* and *a student who is quadriplegic* instead of *a quadriplegic student*. Discuss *a man who has depression*, not *a depressive*, and *a woman who uses a wheelchair*, not *a wheelchair-bound woman*.

Writing about people of different ages

Avoid bias by choosing accurate terms to describe age. If possible, use the person's age rather than an adjective, like *elderly* or *older*, which might offend. *Eighty-two-year-old Adele Schumacher* is better than *elderly Adele Schumacher* or *Adele Schumacher, an older resident.*

Writing about people of different financial statuses

When writing about financial status, be careful not to make assumptions (*People who live in trailer parks are uneducated*) or value judgments (*Dishwashing is a less respectable job than managing a restaurant*). While *upper class* and *middle class* are acceptable terms, *lower class* implies a bias. Instead use *working class.*

Writing about people of different religions

Avoid making assumptions about someone's beliefs or practices based on religious affiliation. Even though the Vatican opposes capital punishment, many Roman Catholics support it. Likewise, not all Jewish men wear yarmulkes. The tremendous variation within religions and among individual practitioners makes generalizations questionable.

Exercise 31.2 Read the descriptions of situations below and decide if inclusive language is or is not being used in each. If it is not, explain why. Then, explain how the language might be made more inclusive.

- A humor writer jokes about how nervous he is going to his lady doctor.
- A principal speaks to the school board about purchasing new materials to help teach the increasing number of Vietnamese children in her school.
- A writer for a liberal political blog calls Catholic beliefs about birth control "medieval."
- A comedian refers to some audience members as Afro-Americans.

- A reporter asks a runner who uses a specially designed prosthetic leg how it feels to race against normal runners.
- A talk show host jokes about bigoted white men.
- An interviewer asks an artist how her art reflects her Hispanic heritage.
- A caller to a radio show argues that a clergyman shouldn't advise married couples unless he is also married.

31e Recognize International Varieties of English

English today comes in various shapes and forms. Many applied linguists now speak of "World Englishes" in the plural, to highlight the diversity of the English language as it is used worldwide. English has long been established as the dominant language in Australia, Canada, New Zealand, the United Kingdom, and the United States, although many people in those countries also speak other languages at home and in their communities. Englishes used in these countries share many characteristics, but there also are differences in sentence structures, vocabulary, spelling, and punctuation. For example:

| **British English** | Have you got your ticket? |
| **U.S. English** | Do you have your ticket? |

| **British English** | What's the price of petrol (petroleum) these days? |
| **U.S. English** | What's the price of gas (gasoline) these days? |

Newer varieties of English have emerged outside of traditionally English-speaking countries. Many former British and U.S. colonies — Hong Kong, India, Malaysia, Nigeria, Papua New Guinea, the Philippines, Singapore, and others — continue to use a local variety of English for both public and private communication. Englishes used in many of these countries are based primarily on the British variety, but they also include many features that reflect the local context.

| **Indian English** | Open the air conditioner. |
| **U.S. English** | Turn on the air conditioner. |

Indian English	They're late always.
U.S. English	They're always late.
Phillipine English	You don't only know.
U.S. English	You just don't realize.
Phillipine English	I had seen her yesterday.
U.S. English	I saw her yesterday.
Singaporean English	I was arrowed to lead the discussion.
U.S. English	I was selected to lead the discussion.
Singaporean English	I am not sure what is it.
U.S. English	I am not sure what it is.

Remember that what is correct differs from one variation of English to another.

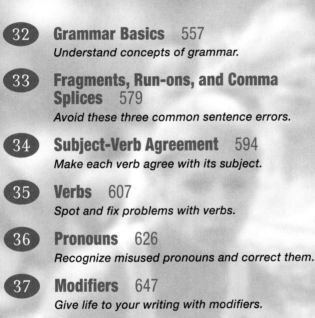

PART

8

Understanding Grammar

32 **Grammar Basics** 557
Understand concepts of grammar.

33 **Fragments, Run-ons, and Comma Splices** 579
Avoid these three common sentence errors.

34 **Subject-Verb Agreement** 594
Make each verb agree with its subject.

35 **Verbs** 607
Spot and fix problems with verbs.

36 **Pronouns** 626
Recognize misused pronouns and correct them.

37 **Modifiers** 647
Give life to your writing with modifiers.

Chapter 32

Grammar Basics

Understand concepts of grammar.

32a Sentence Basics

Sentences are the basic units in writing. Many people think of a sentence as a group of words that begins with a capital letter and ends with a period, but that definition includes grammatically incomplete sentences called **fragments** (see Section 33a).

Subjects and predicates

Regular sentences must have a subject and a predicate that includes a main verb. Typically the subject announces what the sentence is about, and the predicate says something about that subject or conveys the action of the subject.

Subject	Predicate
I	want a new monitor.
Your Web site	loads quickly.
By 1910, 26 million Americans	were going to the movies at nickelodeon theaters every week.

The exception to this rule is a class of sentences called **imperatives,** in which the subject is usually implied. In these sentences, we know that the subject is *you* without stating it.

Quit bothering me.

Help me carry in the groceries.

Sentence patterns

Sentences can be classified into four major patterns according to function.

- **Declaratives.** Declarative sentences make statements.

  The house on the corner was built in 2001.

- **Interrogatives.** Interrogatives are usually referred to as questions.

  Who will be the first to volunteer?

- **Imperatives.** Imperatives request or demand some action.

  Stop complaining.

- **Exclamations.** Exclamations are used to express strong emotion.

  What an incredible performance you gave!

Sentences can be classified as either **positive** or **negative**. A sentence can be made negative by inserting a negative word, usually *not* or a contracted form of *not* (*can't, isn't*).

Positive   Juanita has worked here for a year.

Negative   Juanita has not worked here for a year.

Sentences with transitive verbs (see Section 32c) can be considered as **active** or **passive** (see Section 27b). Sentences can be made passive by changing the word order.

Active   The House of Representatives selected Thomas Jefferson as president in 1800 when the electoral vote ended in a tie.

Passive   Thomas Jefferson was selected president by the House of Representatives in 1800 when the electoral vote ended in a tie.

Exercise 32.1   Classify each of the following sentences according to (a) its pattern (declarative, interrogative, imperative, or exclamatory), (b) whether it is positive or negative, and (c) whether it is passive or active.

Example   America boasts some of the world's strangest museums, from the American Sanitary Plumbing Museum to the Museum of Questionable Medical Devices. (Declarative, positive, active)

1. Don t miss the Spam memorabilia display in Austin, Minnesota s First Century Museum.
2. The Combat Cockroach Hall of Fame in Plano, Texas, displays a roach dressed like Marilyn Monroe!
3. Does the Elvis Is Alive Museum in Wright City, Missouri, really have a Tomb Room?
4. Stand in the mouth of a four-and-a-half-story-high fiberglass muskie at the National Fresh Water Fishing Hall of Fame in Hayward, Wisconsin.
5. The Desert of Maine Museum was not built in a desert at all, but in snowy Freeport, Maine.

32b Word Classes

Like players in a team sport who are assigned to different positions, words are classified into parts of speech. The different positions on a team have different functions. The forwards in soccer and hockey do most of the scoring; goalies are responsible for preventing scoring. The parts of speech also serve different functions in sentences. And just as individuals can play more than one position on a team, so too can individual words belong to more than one part of speech. *Try* is a noun in *The third try was successful,* but a verb in *I would not try it.*

Nouns

A noun is the name of a person, place, thing, concept, or action. Names of particular persons, places, organizations, companies, titles, religions, languages, nationalities, ethnicities, months, and days are called **proper nouns** and are almost always capitalized. More general nouns are called

common nouns and are seldom capitalized unless they begin a sentence (see Section 46a). Most common nouns can be made plural, and most are preceded by articles (*a, an, the*). Nouns have several functions:

- **Subject:** The cat climbed the tree.
- **Object:** Please feed the cat.
- **Subject complement:** This is the cat.
- **Object of a preposition:** This is for the cat.
- **Modifier of other nouns:** She moved on cat feet.
- **Appositive of other nouns:** My best friend, my cat, eats mice.
- **Possessive noun:** The cat's ball is under the sofa.

Nonnative speakers should see Chapter 49 for more on count and non-count nouns.

Exercise 32.2 The underlined words in the following paragraph are nouns. Identify the function of each. Does it serve as the subject, object, subject complement, object of a preposition, or modifier of another noun?

SUBJ   OBJ OF PREP   SUBJECT COMPLEMENT

Example   The original title for *Casablanca* was *Everybody Comes to Rick's*.

The boyish Ronald Reagan was the studio's first choice for the male lead. Instead, the studio chose Humphrey Bogart, the shrapnel-scarred tough guy, to portray the owner of Rick's nightclub. The Swedish actress Ingrid Bergman was eventually cast as the female lead. The unexpected chemistry between Bergman and Bogart made *Casablanca* one of the greatest films of all time.

Pronouns

Pronouns are a subclass of nouns and are generally used as substitutes for nouns. Pronouns themselves are divided into several subclasses.

- **Personal pronouns:** *I, you, he, she, it, we, they, me, him, her, us, them*

  I gave my old racquet to her. She gave me a CD in return.

- **Possessive pronouns:** *my, mine, his, hers, its, our, ours, your, yours, their, theirs*

  My old racquet is now hers.

- **Demonstrative pronouns:** *this, that, these, those*

  Those are the mittens I want.

- **Indefinite pronouns:** *all, any, anyone, anybody, anything, both, each, either, everyone, everything, many, neither, no one, none, nothing, one, some, someone, somebody, something*

  Everyone was relieved that the driver's injuries were minor.

- **Relative pronouns:** *that, which, what, who, whom, whose, whatever, whoever, whomever, whichever*

  The house, which hung off a steep ridge, had a stunning view of the bay.

- **Interrogative pronouns:** *who, which, what, where*

  What would you like with your sandwich?

- **Reflexive pronouns:** *myself, ourselves, yourself, yourselves, himself, herself, itself, themselves*

  The twins behaved themselves around their grandfather.

- **Reciprocal pronouns:** *each other, one another*

  The brothers didn't like each other.

See Chapter 36 for more on pronouns.

Exercise 32.3 The underlined words in the following paragraph are pronouns. Identify the function of each. Does it serve as a personal, possessive, demonstrative, indefinite, relative, interrogative, reflexive, or reciprocal pronoun?

> **Example**   On November 20, 1820, a sperm whale rammed and
> sank the whaleship *Essex*, but all the sailors escaped
> with <u>their</u> lives.
> <small>POSS</small>

> The ramming was no accident; after the whale hit the *Essex* once, <u>it</u> turned around to hit the ship a second time. The sailors found <u>themselves</u> adrift in three whaleboats, 1,200 miles from the nearest islands. However, the crew feared that <u>those</u> were populated by cannibals. After a month starving at sea, the sailors found a small island, <u>which</u> offered little to eat. Crushed by hunger, the crew convinced <u>each other</u> to eat a fellow sailor who had died of starvation. <u>Who</u> could say that <u>anybody</u> would act differently if placed in similar circumstances? <u>Their</u> chances of survival weakened with each passing day. Yet, first mate Owen Chase navigated <u>his</u> whaleship for eighty-eight days until the crew was rescued by a merchant ship.

Verbs

Verbs indicate actions, states of mind, occurrences, and states of being. Verbs are divided into two primary categories: **main verbs** and **auxiliaries**. A main verb must be present in the predicate. The main verb may be the only word in the predicate.

> She slept.

> When he heard the starting gun, Vijay sprinted.

Auxiliaries (often called *helping verbs*) include forms of *be, have,* and *do.* A subset of auxiliaries are **modals**: *can, could, may, might, must, shall, should, will, would.*

You will be satisfied when you see how well they painted your car.

She might have been selected for the lead role in the ballet if her strained muscle had healed.

See Chapters 34 and 35 for more on verbs.

Exercise 32.4 Underline the verbs in the following paragraph. Decide whether each verb is a main verb or an auxiliary verb. If it is an auxiliary verb, note whether or not it is a modal verb.

Example Frank Oz <u>has</u> <u>created</u> some of the best known
        AUX NOT MODAL   MAIN
characters on *Sesame Street,* including Bert, Cookie Monster, and Grover.

Frank Oz was born in Hereford, England, in 1944 and began staging puppet shows when he was 12. You may know him best as the voice of Yoda in the *Star Wars* series. Oz could have remained a puppeteer, but he has decided to embark on a second career as a movie director. You might have seen one of his movies such as *Indian in the Closet* or *In and Out.* The Muppet Fozzie Bear is named after Oz, using his first initial and his last name.

Verbals

Verbals are forms of verbs that function as nouns, adjectives, and adverbs. The three kinds of verbals are infinitives, participles, and gerunds.

- **Infinitives:** An infinitive is the base or *to* form of the verb. Infinitives can be used in place of nouns, adjectives, or adverbs.

  ⌐NOUN⌐
  To fly has been a centuries-old dream of people around the world.

                            ⌐ ADJECTIVE ⌐
  Keeping your goals in mind is a good way to succeed.

- **Participles:** Participles are either present (*flying*) or past (*defeated*). They always function as adjectives.

The *flying* insects are annoying.

Napoleon's *defeated* army faced a long march back to France.

- **Gerunds:** Gerunds have the same form as present participles, but they always function as nouns.

Flying was all that she wanted to do in life.

Exercise 32.5 Underline the verbals in the following paragraph and identify whether they are infinitives, participles, or gerunds. In addition, specify whether the participle is past or present.

Example   gerund Casting the "evil eye" is a superstition past participle recognized in cultures around the world.

The evil eye is a focused gaze, supposedly causing death and destruction. Writings of the Assyrians, Babylonians, Greeks, and Romans all document an abiding belief in this supernatural concept. Old women and those thought to be witches are often accused of having the evil eye. To ward off the effects of the evil eye, people have resorted to praying, hand gestures, and purifying rituals.

Adjectives

Adjectives modify nouns and pronouns. Some adjectives are used frequently: *good, bad, small, tall, handsome, green, short*. Many others are recognizable by their suffixes: *-able* (*dependable*), *-al* (*cultural*), *-ful* (*hopeful*), *-ic* (*frenetic*), *-ive* (*decisive*), *-ish* (*foolish*), *-less* (*hopeless*), *-ous* (*erroneous*).

The *forgetful* manager was always backed up by her *dependable* assistant.

Adjectives often follow linking verbs.

That drumbeat is *relentless*.

Numbers are considered adjectives.

Only **ten** team members showed up for practice.

See Chapter 37 for more about adjectives and adverbs.

Adverbs

Adverbs modify verbs, other adverbs, adjectives, and entire clauses. The usual suffix for adverbs is *-ly*. Many adverbs do not have suffixes (*then, here*) and others have the same form as adjectives (*fast, hard, long, well*).

That drummer plays **well**. [modifies the verb *plays*]

That drummer plays **very** well. [modifies the adverb *well*]

That answer is **partly** correct. [modifies the adjective *correct*]

Frankly, I could care less. [modifies the clause *I could care less*]

Conjunctive adverbs often modify entire clauses and sentences. Like coordinating conjunctions, they indicate the relationship between two clauses or two sentences. Commonly used conjunctive adverbs include *also, consequently, furthermore, hence, however, indeed, instead, likewise, moreover, nevertheless, otherwise, similarly, therefore, thus.*

The Olympics brings together the best athletes in the world; **however**, the judging often represents the worst in sports.

Exercise 32.6 The underlined words in the following paragraph are modifiers. Label each modifier as adjective or adverb, and state which word it modifies.

Example

After initially living the life of an average middle-class
ADV MOD LIVING / ADJ MOD WOMAN / ADJ MOD WOMAN

woman, Dorothy Parker ultimately became one
ADV MOD BECAME

of the most infamous wits of the twentieth century.
ADV MOD INFAMOUS / ADJ MOD WITS / ADJ MOD CENTURY

Parker's father encouraged her to pursue "feminine arts" such as piano and poetry, but just following his death in 1913, she rushed into what turned out to be a profitable foray into the world of literature. Almost immediately, *Vanity Fair* purchased one of her poems, leading her into a full-time writing position with *Vogue*. It was life-changing, as Parker's flair for clever prose swiftly led her into the inner sanctum of New York literary society. Parker was fired from *Vanity Fair*'s editorial board in 1919 after harshly panning an advertiser's film. Despite her early departure from magazines, Parker gained lasting fame as a prolific writer and critic.

Prepositions

Prepositions indicate the relationship of nouns or pronouns to other parts of a sentence. Prepositions come before nouns and pronouns, and in this sense prepositions are "prepositioned." The noun(s) or pronoun(s) that follow are called the objects of prepositions.

　　　　　　　　PREP　　OBJ　　　　　PREP　　　　OBJ

She took the job **of speechwriter for the president.**

Here are some common prepositions.

about	behind	from	than
above	below	in	through
across	beside	inside	to
after	between	of	toward
against	but	off	under
among	by	on	until
around	despite	out	up
as	down	over	upon
at	during	past	with
before	for	since	without

Some prepositions are compounds.

according to	due to	in front of	next to
as well as	except for	in spite of	out of
because of	in addition to	instead of	with regard to

Exercise 32.7 Underline the prepositional phrases in the following paragraph and circle the prepositions.

Example (In) 2006, Apple Inc. launched an advertising campaign (in) the United States, United Kingdom, and Australia called "Get a Mac."

The ads in the campaign are easily recognizable because they were shot against an empty, white background. In addition to looking the same, each ad follows a standard pattern: a man dressed in casual clothes says "Hello, I'm a Mac." Then another man, wearing a rumpled suit and tie, enters and stands beside the Mac. He introduces himself, saying "And I'm a PC." The two then talk about the differences between Macs and PCs, showing that the Mac is better at fun, creative tasks than the PC. Despite the popularity of the ads, they have been criticized by media critics for emphasizing style over substance.

Conjunctions

Conjunctions indicate the relationship between words or groups of words. The two classes of conjunctions are **coordinate**, indicating units of equal status, and **subordinate**, indicating that one unit is more important than the other.

- **Coordinating conjunctions:** The seven coordinating conjunctions are *and, but, or, yet, for, so,* and *nor.*

  Do you want cake or ice cream?

  I graduated a semester early, but I had to go to work immediately to pay off loans.

- **Subordinating conjunctions:** Subordinating conjunctions introduce subordinate clauses. Common subordinating conjunctions are *after, although, as, because, before, if, since, that, unless, until, when, where, while.*

  After the value of the NASDAQ dropped by more than two-thirds between March 2000 and April 2001, some of the new dotcom millionaires found out the party was over.

Exercise 32.8   Fill in the blanks in the following paragraph with an appropriate coordinating or subordinating conjunction. More than one conjunction may fit.

Example   Scientists used to believe that sharks attacked people intentionally, *but* they now assert that sharks attack humans only when mistaking them for natural prey.

Only four of the 400 species of shark attack humans: bull sharks, whitetips, tiger sharks, _____ great whites. _____ sharks committed 74 fatal attacks in the past 100 years, 75% of all shark-attack victims have survived. Peter Benchley, the author of *Jaws*, describes sharks as "fragile" _____ their numbers seem to be declining. _____ the populations of some shark species have declined by 80%, some nations have enacted laws to protect them. People are coming to see sharks as an important part of ocean environments, _____ they are acting accordingly.

Articles

There are two classes of articles:

- **Definite article:** *the*
- **Indefinite article:** *a, an*

Nonnative speakers should see Section 49d for more on articles.

Interjections

Interjections are words like *oops, ouch, ugh,* and *ah.* They are usually punctuated separately, and they do not relate grammatically to other words.

Exercise 32.9 Each underlined word in these paragraphs represents one of the word classes explained in this section. Identify nouns, pronouns, verbs, verbals, adjectives, adverbs, prepositions, conjunctions, articles, and interjections.

Example
<small>PREP</small>
In 1874, Colonel George Armstrong Custer
<small>VERB</small> <small>NOUN</small>
announced the discovery of gold on French Creek
<small>ADJ</small>
near present-day Custer, South Dakota.

Gold! This discovery not only triggered the Black Hills gold rush but also gave rise to the lawless town of Deadwood, which reached a population of around 5,000 within the next two years. Many scheming business people flocked to Deadwood, hoping to strike it rich by offering supplies and entertainments, many of them illegal, to the gold miners. Deadwood also quickly gained a reputation as a place where murders, such as that of Wild Bill Hickok, were frequent and murderers went unpunished.

As the gold vein became the property of mining companies, Deadwood lost its rough and rowdy character and gradually settled down into a prosperous town. However, a fire on September 26, 1879, devastated the town, destroying over 300 buildings. Without the opportunities that characterized the town's early days, many of those who had lost their belongings in the fire left town to try their luck elsewhere.

32c Clauses

Clauses are the grammatical structures that underlie sentences. Each clause has a subject and a predicate, but not all clauses are sentences. The variety of clauses is nearly infinite because phrases and other clauses can be embedded within them in a multitude of ways. Nevertheless, a few basic patterns are central to English clause structure.

Subject-verb-object

On the predicate side of a clause, you always find a main verb and often a direct object that is affected by the action of the verb.

┌ S ┐ ┌ V ┐ ┌ DO ┐
Ahmad kicked the ball.

This basic pattern, called **subject-verb-object** or **S-V-O**, is one of the most common in English. Verbs that take objects (*kick, revise*) are called **transitive verbs**. Some transitive verbs can take two objects: a **direct object** that completes the sentence and an **indirect object**, usually a person, indirectly affected by the action.

┌ S ┐ ┌ V ┐ ┌ IO ┐ ┌ DO ┐
Ahmed gave Sally the ball.

Clauses without objects

Not all clauses have objects.

┌ S ┐ ┌ V ┐
Maria slept.

┌ S ┐ ┌ V ┐
The engine runs rough. [*Rough* is an adverb, not an object.]

┌ S ┐ ┌ V ┐
The staff cannot work on weekends. [*On weekends* is a prepositional phrase.]

This clause pattern is **subject-verb** or **S-V**. Verbs that do not require objects are called **intransitive verbs**. Many verbs can be both transitive and intransitive.

Intransitive   Ginny runs fast.

Transitive   Ginny runs the company.

For more on the verbs *lay/lie, set/sit,* and *raise/rise,* see Section 35c.

Linking-verb clauses

A third major pattern links the subject to a noun or an adjective that follows the verb and restates or describes the subject. The most commonly used verbs for this pattern are forms of *be.*

McKinley was **president** in 1900.

Rosalia Fernandez is **the assistant manager.**

The results of the MRI were **negative.**

What follows the verb is the subject complement, either a noun or noun phrase (*president, assistant manager*) or a predicate adjective describing the subject (*negative*).

Other linking verbs besides *be* are *appear, become, feel, look, remain,* and *seem.* These linking verbs often refer to people's perceptions or senses.

Jennifer felt nervous when she accepted the award.

Main versus subordinate clauses

All the examples of clauses we have looked at up to now can stand by themselves as sentences. These clauses are called **main** or **independent clauses.** Other clauses have the necessary ingredients to count as clauses—a subject and a main verb—yet they are incomplete as sentences.

Where you choose to go to college

Which was the first to be considered

As fast as my legs could pedal

These clauses are examples of **subordinate** or **dependent clauses**. They do not stand by themselves but must be attached to another clause:

I rode my bike as fast as my legs could pedal.

Subordinate clauses serve three main functions.

- **Noun clauses:** Noun clauses serve all the functions that nouns perform, including subjects, objects, complements, and appositives. They are usually formed with either a relative pronoun (*that, which, what, who, whom, whose, whatever, whoever, whichever*) or with *when, where, why,* or *how.*

As subject	That the entry fee included all the food made the price reasonable.
As direct object	I could not **find** where it was located.
As subject complement	**The newest version** is what she wants.
As appositive	**The reason** that I am here today is obvious.
As object of preposition	He listened **to** what she had to say.

- **Adjective clauses:** Adjective clauses modify nouns and pronouns. They are also called **relative clauses** and usually begin with a relative pronoun.

  Steroids that are used to increase muscle density have many harmful side effects.

  The site where the fort once stood was washed away by a hurricane.

- **Adverb clauses:** Adverb clauses function as adverbs, modifying verbs, other adverbs, adjectives, and entire clauses. They begin with a subordinating conjunction such as *after, although, as, because, before, if, since, that, unless, until, when, where, while.*

Modifies verb	She **arrived** after we had carried all of our furniture into our new apartment.
Modifies adverb	Jeff laughed **nervously** whenever the boss came around.
Modifies adjective	The forward was not as **tall** as the media guide stated.
Modifies clause	When you see a person faint, **you should call 911.**

Exercise 32.10 Identify which of the three main clause patterns each of the following sentences exemplifies: subject-verb-object, subject-verb, or subject-linking verb.

Example In 1954, the United States Supreme Court ordered school desegregation. (Subject-verb-object)

1. Arkansas Governor Orval Faubus refused to obey the order.
2. The Arkansas militia seemed impenetrable.
3. Nine African American students retreated from the school.
4. President Dwight Eisenhower ordered National Guard troops to escort the African American students.
5. The guardsmen were successful.

Exercise 32.11 The subordinate clauses in the following sentences are in italics. Identify whether they are noun, adjective, or adverb clauses.

Example   *Although many cultures abhor the practice of* ADVERB CLAUSE
                NOUN CLAUSE
                cannibalism, that it has taken place in many areas

                is indisputable.

1. Tribes in the West Indies *who sought dominance over neighboring peoples* often ate human flesh.
2. Some practitioners in New Guinea and West Africa believed *that consuming the body of an enemy would transfer the special attributes of the conquered to themselves.*
3. It is important to note that not all tribes *who practiced human sacrifice* necessarily condoned consumption of the dead.
4. *Unless there were dire circumstances of famine* most tribes perceived cannibalism solely as a byproduct of military conquest.
5. *That cannibalism is a purely non-Western phenomenon* is a common misconception; *because Mediterranean histories cite instances of cannibalism,* we must concede that it has had a long and diverse cultural existence.

32d Phrases

Phrases add to a sentence groups of words that modify or develop parts of the sentence. Some phrases can be confused with clauses, but phrases lack either a subject or a main verb.

Prepositional phrases

Prepositional phrases consist of a preposition and its object, including modifiers of the object. They can modify nouns, verbs, or adjectives.

┌NOUN┐ ┌ PREP PHRASE ┐
The **carton** of orange juice froze solid.

┌VERB┐   ┌ PREP PHRASE ┐
They will **bring** the pizza on time.

┌ ADJ ┐┌ PREP PHRASE ┐
She was **rich** in spirit.

Verbal phrases

Each of the three kinds of verbals—infinitives, participles, and gerunds—can be used to create phrases.

- **Infinitive phrases:** Infinitive phrases can function as nouns, adverbs, and adjectives. As nouns they can be subjects, objects, or complements.

  <u>To succeed where others had failed</u> was her goal.
      SUBJECT

- **Participial phrases:** Participial phrases are formed with either present participles (*flying*) or past participles (*defeated*); they function as adjectives.

  The freighter, listing noticeably to the port side, left the port without balancing the load.

- **Gerund phrases:** Gerund phrases formed from the present participle (*-ing*) function as nouns.

  <u>Feeding stray cats</u> became my next-door neighbor's obsession.
     SUBJECT

Appositives

Appositive phrases modify nouns and are often set off by a pair of commas. They usually follow the noun they modify. They are quite useful as identifying tags for nouns.

Andy, my old linguistics teacher, became one of my best friends.

Absolutes

Absolute phrases are nearly clauses because they include a noun or pronoun and a verb; however, the verb is a participle ending in *-ing* or *-ed* and not a main verb. Absolute phrases can appear anywhere in a sentence and are set off by commas.

He struggled at the beginning of his speech, his voice trembling.

32e Sentence Types

Simple sentences

A simple sentence consists of one main clause and no subordinate clauses. Simple sentences can be quite short.

> ┌ **SUBJ** ┐ ┌**VERB**┐
> The two toy figures spun together.

Simple sentences can become quite long if phrases are added.

> ┌────────── **MAIN CLAUSE** ──────────┐
> The two toy figures spun together, standing on top of their round metal pedestal, teetering back and forth in a jerky, clockwise motion, slowing gradually.

Compound sentences

Compound sentences have two or more main clauses and no subordinate clauses. The main clauses are connected in one of three ways: (1) by a semicolon, (2) by a comma and a coordinating conjunction (*and, but, or, for, so, nor, yet*), or (3) by punctuation and a conjunctive adverb (*furthermore, however, indeed, nevertheless, therefore*).

> ┌──── **MAIN CLAUSE** ────┐ ┌──── **MAIN CLAUSE** ────┐
> Mike walked to his car, and he opened the trunk.
> ┌────── **MAIN CLAUSE** ──────┐ ┌──**MAIN CLAUSE**──┐
> The theater enjoyed record attendance; however, rising costs took all the profits.

Complex sentences

Complex sentences have one main clause and one or more subordinate clauses.

> ┌──── **MAIN CLAUSE** ────┐┌──── **SUBORDINATE CLAUSE** ──┐
> Mike walked to his car when he got out of class.

Compound-complex sentences

Compound-complex sentences have at least two main clauses and at least one subordinate clause.

┌─ **MAIN CLAUSE** ─┐┌─ **SUBORDINATE CLAUSE** ─┐ ┌─ **MAIN CLAUSE** ─┐
Mike walked to his car when he got out of class, but he had to go back for his briefcase.

Exercise 32.12 In each of the following sentences, underline the main clause. If there are subordinate clauses, underline them twice. Then identify what type each sentence is: simple, compound, complex, or compound-complex.

Example Although many cultures consider death an ending or something to fear, various Meso-American civilizations see it as something to embrace, and it is this belief that gives rise to the celebration known as The Day of the Dead. (Compound-complex)

1. The dead reappear during the month-long celebration.
2. The goddess Mictecaclhuati presides over all the festivities, but each culture celebrates the festival in its own unique way.
3. Some revelers celebrate by eating candy skulls with the names of their deceased relatives written on the foreheads.
4. In some parts of Mexico, family members picnic at the spots where the deceased have been buried.
5. Because Spaniards found the ritual blasphemous, they attempted to replace it with the Christian holiday All Saints Day, but their efforts failed, and the celebration still thrives today.

Exercise 32.13 The following are simple sentences. Rewrite each as compound, complex, and compound-complex sentences.

Simple example Baseball, America's national pastime, has endured decades of poor attendance, scandals, and players' strikes.

Compound Baseball has endured decades of poor attendance, scandals, and players' strikes, yet it is still America's national pastime.

Complex Baseball, which many consider America's national pastime, has endured decades of poor attendance, scandals, and players' strikes.

Compound-complex While it has been called America's national pastime for over a century, baseball has endured many trials, yet the game has survived decades of poor attendance, scandals, and players' strikes.

1. Philip K. Wrigley, chewing gum entrepreneur, founded the All-American Girls Professional Baseball League in 1943, bolstering waning interest in baseball during World War II.
2. The league attracted women from all over the United States and Canada, providing them with a previously absent national venue to showcase their athletic talents.
3. The league peaked in 1948 with ten teams and over 900,000 paying fans.
4. Promoting an image of femininity among female athletes, the league insisted on strict regulations regarding dress and public behavior.
5. Lacking audience interest, the league folded in 1954.

Chapter 33

Fragments, Run-ons, and Comma Splices

Avoid these three common sentence errors.

 Fragments

Fragments in speech and writing

Fragments are incomplete sentences. They are punctuated to look like sentences, but they lack a key element—often a subject or a verb—or else are a subordinate clause or phrase. In spoken language we usually pay little attention to fragments.

Missing subject; Missing verb	**Nothing like a hot shower when you're cold and wet.**
Missing subject	I was completely hooked on the game. **And played it constantly.**
Missing verb	**You too?**
Subordinate clause	**If you think so.**

In writing, however, fragments usually interrupt the reader. Consider another example of a full sentence followed by a fragment:

The university's enrollment rose unexpectedly during the fall semester. **Because the percentage of students who accepted offers of admission was much higher than previous years and fewer students than usual dropped out or transferred.**

Such fragments compel a reader to stop and reread. When a sentence starts with *because*, we expect to find a main clause later. But here, the *because* clause refers back to the previous sentence. The writer no doubt knew that the fragment gave reasons why enrollment rose, but a reader must stop to determine the connection.

In formal writing you should avoid fragments. Readers expect words punctuated as a sentence to be a complete sentence. They expect writers to complete their thoughts rather than force readers to guess the missing element.

COMMON ERRORS

Recognizing fragments

If you can spot fragments, you can fix them. Grammar checkers can find some of them, but they miss many fragments and identify other sentences wrongly as fragments. Ask these questions when you are checking for sentence fragments.

- **Does the sentence have a subject?** Except for commands, sentences need subjects:

  Jane spent every cent of credit she had available. **And then applied for more cards.**

- **Does the sentence have a complete verb?** Sentences require complete verbs. Verbs that end in *-ing* must have an auxiliary verb to be complete.

  Ralph keeps changing majors. **He trying to figure out what he really wants to do after college.**

(Continued on next page)

 **COMMON ERRORS** *(continued)*

- **If the sentence begins with a subordinate clause, is there a main clause in the same sentence?** A good test to determine if a subordinate clause is a fragment is to say "I think that" before a possible fragment.

  Even though Seattle is cloudy much of the year, no American city is more beautiful when the sun shines. **Which is one reason people continue to move there.**

  Remember: 1. **A sentence must have a subject and complete verb.**
  2. **A subordinate clause cannot stand alone as a sentence.**

   For step-by-step discussion, examples, and practice exercises, visit this page of the E-book at www.mycomplab.com.

Basic strategies for turning fragments into sentences

Incorporate the fragment into an adjoining sentence.   In many cases you can incorporate the fragment into an adjoining sentence.

She saw him coming. ̶A̶nd looked away. *a*

I was hooked on the game. P̶laying day and night. *game, playing*

Add the missing element.   If you cannot incorporate a fragment into another sentence, add the missing element.

He studying more this semester. *is*

When aiming for the highest returns, a̶nd also t̶h̶i̶n̶k̶i̶n̶g̶ about the possible losses. *investors should think*

Watch for these fragments

1. Pay close attention to sentences that begin with transitional words, coordinating conjunctions, and subordinating conjunctions. Among the most common fragments are those that begin with a transitional word (*also, therefore, however, consequently*), a coordinating conjunction (*and, but, or*), or a word indicating a subordinate clause (*although, because, if, since*). Prepositional or verbal phrase fragments are also common.

Transitional words and phrases such as *also, however,* and *therefore* mark movement from one idea to another, such as introducing another example, a change in direction, or a conclusion. Writers often produce fragments when trying to separate these shifts with a period.

> Susan found ways to avoid working during her shift. T, therefore making more work for the rest of the employees.

Compound predicates are linked by a coordinating conjunction such as *and, but,* or *or*. Because compound predicates share the same subject, the solution for a coordinating conjunction fragment is to incorporate it into the sentence with the subject.

> Heroin use among urban professionals is on the rise in the United States. A and also in Europe, after several decades during which cocaine was the preferred drug among this group.

2. Look for subordinate clause fragments. Subordinate clauses resemble sentences because they contain subjects and verbs. But subordinate clauses cannot stand alone as sentences because their meaning is dependent on another clause. Subordinate clauses begin with words such as *although, after, before, despite, if, though, unless, whether, while, when, who,* and *that*. Subordinate clause fragments often follow the sentence to which they actually belong. You can fix the subordinate clause fragment by incorporating it into the preceding sentence.

> The recent death of former president Gerald Ford has prompted many commentators to interpret his pardoning of Richard Nixon as the best possible solution to the national crisis brought on by the

Watergate scandal. D, despite the fact that at the time of the pardon the decision was widely considered to be an act of political cronyism that damaged Ford's ability to lead the country effectively.

Or you can fix the subordinate clause fragment by turning it into a sentence.

The recent death of former president Gerald Ford has prompted many commentators to interpret his pardon of Richard Nixon as the best possible solution to the national crisis brought on by the Watergate scandal. The current view directly contradicts the widespread opinion of the time that the pardon was an act of political cronyism that damaged Ford's ability to lead the country effectively.

3. Look for phrase fragments. Phrases also cannot stand alone as sentences because they lack either a subject, a verb, or both. There are many kinds of phrase fragments. Prepositional phrase fragments are easy to spot and fix.

As Helen looked over the notes for her autobiography, she mused about how much her life had changed. I, in ways she could not have predicted.

Andrew accepted the university's award for outstanding dissertation. W, with great dignity and humility.

Appositive phrases, which rename or describe a noun, are often fragments.

For his advanced history course, Professor Levack assigned J. J. Scarisbrick's *Henry VIII*. A, an older text historians still regard as essential when studying sixteenth-century English history and politics.

Verbal phrase fragments are sometimes difficult to spot because verbals look like verbs. But remember: They function as adjectives, nouns, or adverbs.

On their last trip to Chicago, Greta went to the Art Institute, but Roger didn't go. Roger, having visited that museum twice already.

4. Watch for list fragments. Do not isolate a list from the sentence that introduces it. Words or phrases such as *for example, for instance, namely,* and *such as* often introduce lists or examples. Make sure these lists are attached to a sentence with a subject and verb.

> Several Ben and Jerry's ice cream flavors are puns.~~S~~, such as Cherry Garcia, Phish Food, and The Full VerMonty.

WRITING IN THE WORLD

Intentional fragments

Most academic and professional writers avoid fragments. Consequently, fragments are not acceptable in formal college writing. If you read carefully, however, you will find fragments in certain kinds of writing.

Fragments used for emphasis

In informal writing that imitates spoken language, you will find fragments used occasionally for emphasis.

> The door-to-door salesman tried to convince us that frozen vegetables taste better than ones picked off the vine. Nonsense.

Fragments in advertising

Advertising copy often uses fragments.

> New and improved! 100% more cleaning power!

Fragments in literary prose

Fragments are common in fiction and literary nonfiction. For example, they can be effective for adding descriptive details if you want those details to stand out.

> An immature bald eagle stood on the bank only thirty feet away, its speckled white and black breast feathers ruffling in the breeze, its massive talons clutching a dead king salmon.

(Continued on next page)

> Wings spread in the indecision of retreat. Powerful beak locked. Eyes and head moving, missing nothing.

This series of details might have been punctuated with commas. Setting off the final three clauses with periods adds additional pauses, as if the writer is moving in to take close-up shots. This strategy, however, should be reserved for special effects. If the ordinary details are punctuated with periods, the result is choppy writing that appears incorrect, even in fiction.

Exercise 33.1   Revise each of the following to eliminate sentence fragments.

Example   Certain mammals, like flying squirrels and sugar gliders, are varieties that actually ~~glide. Which~~ *glide, which* enables them to survive when they are being hunted by nimble predators.

1. Flying squirrels, like typical squirrels except they have flaps of skin that allow them to glide.
2. Flying squirrels glide gracefully. From tree to tree with surprising ease.
3. To gain speed and momentum, flying squirrels often free-fall for several feet. Then to turn in midair, lower one arm.
4. One of the largest known varieties the Japanese giant flying squirrel. Two feet long from its head to its furry tail.
5. Gliding escapes predators and gathers food quickly.

Exercise 33.2   Find the fragments in the following paragraph and revise the paragraph to eliminate them.

Barton Springs still seems like a place not in Texas for those who come from elsewhere. Surrounding hills covered by live oaks and mountain juniper. And ground around the pool shaded by pecan trees whose trunks are a dozen feet in circumference. Banana trees and other tropical plants grow in the roofless dressing areas of the pool. With grackles whistling jungle-like sounds outside. The pool is in a natural limestone creek bed. Which is an eighth of a mile long. Fed by 27,000,000 gallons of 68° water bubbling out of the Edwards Aquifer each day.

33b Run-on Sentences

Run-on sentences are the opposite of sentence fragments. While fragments are incomplete sentences, run-ons jam together two or more sentences, failing to separate them with appropriate punctuation. And while fragments are sometimes acceptable, especially in informal writing, run-on sentences are never acceptable.

Fixing run-on sentences

Take three steps to fix run-on sentences: (1) identify the problem, (2) determine where the run-on sentence needs to be divided, and (3) choose the punctuation that best indicates the relationship between the main clauses.

1. Identify the problem. When you read your writing aloud, run-on sentences will often trip you up, just as they confuse readers. You can also search for subject and verb pairs to check for run-ons. If you find two main clauses with no punctuation separating them, you have a run-on sentence.

> ┌─────── SUBJ ───────┐ ┌──── VERB ────┐
> **Internet businesses** are not bound to specific locations or old ways
> ┌S┐ ┌V┐
> of running a business **they** are more flexible in allowing employees
> to telecommute and to determine the hours they work.

2. Determine where the run-on sentence needs to be divided.

> Internet businesses are not bound to specific locations or old ways of running a business | they are more flexible in allowing employees to telecommute and to determine the hours they work.

COMMON ERRORS

Recognizing run-on sentences

When you read the following sentence, you realize something is wrong.

> **I do not recall what kind of printer it was all I remember is that it could sort, staple, and print a packet at the same time.**

The problem is that the two main clauses are not separated by punctuation. The reader must look carefully to determine where one main clause stops and the next one begins.

> I do not recall what kind of printer it was | all I remember is that it could sort, staple, and print a packet at the same time.

A period should be placed after *was*, and the next sentence should begin with a capital letter:

> I do not recall what kind of printer it wa**s.** All I remember is that it could sort, staple, and print a packet at the same time.

Run-on sentences are major errors.

Remember: Two main clauses must be separated by correct punctuation.

 For step-by-step discussion, examples, and practice exercises, visit this page of the E-book at www.mycomplab.com.

3. Determine the relationship between the main clauses. You will revise a run-on more effectively if you determine the relationship between the main clauses and understand the effect or point you are trying to make. There are several punctuation strategies for fixing run-ons.

- **Insert a period.** This is the simplest way to fix a run-on sentence.

  Internet businesses are not bound to specific locations or old ways of running a business. They are more flexible in allowing employees to telecommute and to determine the hours they work.

  However, if you want to indicate the relationship between the two main clauses more clearly, you may want to choose one of these strategies:

- **Insert a semicolon (and possibly a transitional word indicating the relationship between the two main clauses):**

  Internet businesses are not bound to specific locations or old ways of running a business; therefore, they are more flexible in allowing employees to telecommute and to determine the hours they work.

- **Insert a comma and a coordinating conjunction (*and, but, or, nor, for, so, yet*):**

  Internet businesses are not bound to specific locations or old ways of running a business, so they are more flexible in allowing employees to telecommute and to determine the hours they work.

- **Make one of the clauses subordinate.**

  Because Internet businesses are not bound to specific locations or old ways of running a business, they are more flexible in allowing employees to telecommute and to determine the hours they work.

Exercise 33.3   Correct the following run-on sentences.

Example   Japanese Kabuki theater surfaced in the early ~~1600s its~~ *1600s. Its* origins are often linked to the public, improvised performances of Izumo Grand.

1. The original Kabuki troupes were mostly comprised of female dancers however male performers replaced them after the art became associated with prostitution.

2. Performances included several thematically linked elements such as dance, history, and domestic drama they lasted up to twelve hours.
3. In the 1700s, choreographers and special schools became common-place Kabuki dance became more complex.
4. Kabuki costumes are often quite elaborate actors sometimes need assistance preparing for performances.
5. Since World War II, Western influences have altered the social position of Kabuki ticket prices have risen, making performances more accessible to tourists, but not the average Japanese citizen.

33c Comma Splices

Comma splices are a kind of run-on sentence. They do include a punctuation mark—a comma—but it is not a strong enough punctuation mark to separate two main clauses. Comma splices often do not cause the same problems for readers as run-ons. The following sentence can be read aloud with no problem.

> Most of us were taking the same classes, if someone had a question, we would all help out.

On the page such sentences may cause confusion because commas are used to distinguish between elements within sentences, not to mark the boundary between sentences. Most readers see comma splices as errors, which is why you should avoid them.

Fixing comma splices

You have several options for fixing comma splices. Select the one that best fits where the sentence is located and the effect you are trying to achieve.

1. Change the comma to a period.   Most comma splices can be fixed by changing the comma to a period.

It didn't matter that I worked in a windowless room for 40 hours a ~~week, on~~ week. On the Web I was exploring and learning more about distant people and places than I ever had before.

2. Change the comma to a semicolon. A semicolon indicates a close connection between the two main clauses.

It didn't matter that I worked in a windowless room for 40 hours a ~~week,~~ week; on the Web I was exploring and learning more about distant people and places than I ever had before.

COMMON ERRORS

Recognizing comma splices

When you edit your writing, look carefully at sentences that contain commas. Does the sentence contain two main clauses? If so, are the main clauses joined by a comma and a coordinating conjunction *(and, but, for, or, not, so, yet)*?

Incorrect The **concept** of "nature" **depends** on the concept of human "culture," the **problem is** that "culture" is itself shaped by "nature."
[Two main clauses joined by only a comma]

Correct Even though the concept of "nature" depends on the concept of human "culture," "culture" is itself shaped by "nature."
[Subordinate clause plus a main clause]

Correct The concept of "nature" depends on the concept of human "culture," but "culture" is itself shaped by "nature."
[Two main clauses joined by a comma and coordinating conjunction]

(Continued on next page)

COMMON ERRORS *(continued)*

Treating the word *however* as a coordinating conjunction produces some of the most common comma splice errors. *However* does not function grammatically like the coordinating conjunctions *and, but, or, nor, yet, so,* and *for* (see Section 32b).

Incorrect   The White House press secretary repeatedly avowed the Administration was not choosing a side between the two countries embroiled in conflict, however the developing foreign policy suggested otherwise.

Correct   The White House press secretary repeatedly avowed the Administration was not choosing a side between the two countries embroiled in conflict; however, the developing foreign policy suggested otherwise.
[Two main clauses joined by a semicolon]

Remember: Do not use a comma as a period.

 For step-by-step discussion, examples, and practice exercises, visit this page of the E-book at www.mycomplab.com.

---

3. Insert a coordinating conjunction.   Other comma splices can be repaired by inserting a coordinating conjunction (*and, but, or, nor, so, yet, for*) to indicate the relationship of the two main clauses. The coordinating conjunction must be preceded by a comma.

Digital technologies have intensified a global culture that affects us daily in large and small ways, yet their impact remains poorly understood.

4. Make one of the main clauses a subordinate clause.   If a comma splice includes one main clause that is subordinate to the other, rewrite the sentence using a subordinating conjunction.

Because community
~~Community~~ is the vision of a great society trimmed down to the size of a small town, it is a powerful metaphor for real estate developers who sell a mini-utopia along with a house or condo.

5. Make one of the main clauses a phrase. You can also rewrite one of the main clauses as a phrase.

Community—the vision of a great society trimmed down to the size of a small town—is a powerful metaphor for real estate developers who sell a mini-utopia along with a house or condo.

Exercise 33.4   The following sentences all contain comma splices. Eliminate the splices using the methods indicated in parentheses.

Example   Accused Nazi propagandist Leni Riefenstahl was born
in Germany in ~~1902, her~~ films *Triumph of the Will* and
1902. Her
The Olympiad are said to have captured the essence
of the Nazi era. (Change comma to a period.)

1. Riefenstahl spent her early days performing in Germany as a dancer, a 1924 knee injury derailed her dance career, this accident led her to a successful, scandal-ridden life in film. (Insert a coordinating conjunction; change comma to a period.)
2. Early editing work prepared her to direct her first film, *The Blue Light*, however, national recognition was slow to come. (Change the comma to a semicolon.)
3. The year 1935 saw the release of Riefenstahl s film *Triumph of the Will*, which stunningly captured a Nazi Party rally, to be sure, this film forever cast a shadow over the director s career. (Change comma to a period.)
4. Her pioneering techniques such as the underwater camera in her documentary of the 1936 Berlin Olympics, *The Olympiad*, captured

the spirit of athletics, her place in film history was solidified. (Make one of the main clauses a subordinate clause; insert a coordinating conjunction.)

5. The French imprisoned Riefenstahl because her films were considered Nazi propaganda, she was not an active member of the Nazi Party, her film career was forever damaged by such insinuations. (Make one of the main clauses a phrase; change comma to a period.)

Chapter 34

Subject-Verb Agreement

Make each verb agree with its subject.

34a Agreement in the Present Tense

When your verb is in the present tense, agreement in number is straightforward: The subject takes the base form of the verb in all but the third person singular. For example, the verb *walk* in the present tense agrees in number with most subjects in its base form:

First person singular	I walk
Second person singular	You walk
First person plural	We walk
Second person plural	You walk
Third person plural	They walk

Third person singular subjects are the exception to this rule. When your subject is in the third person singular (*he, it, Fido, Lucy, Mr. Jones*) you need to add an *s* or *es* to the base form of the verb.

Third person singular (add *s*)	He walks. It walks. Fido walks.
Third person singular (add *es*)	Lucy goes. Mr. Jones goes.

34b Singular and Plural Subjects

Sometimes it will be difficult to determine whether your subject is singular or plural, especially when subjects joined by *and* refer to the same thing or idea (*toast and jam, peace and quiet*) or when subjects are linked by *either* . . .

or or *neither . . . nor.* Follow these rules when you have trouble determining whether to use a singular or plural verb form.

Subjects joined by *and*

When two subjects are joined by *and,* treat them as a compound (plural) subject.

> **Mary and Jane** are leaving for New York in the morning.

> **The teacher and the lawyer** are headed west to start a commune.

Some compound subjects are treated as singular. These kinds of compounds generally work together as a single noun. Although they appear to be compound and therefore plural, these subjects take the singular form of the verb:

> **Gin and tonic** is a ritual before dinner in Bermuda.

> **Rock and roll** remains the devil's music, even in the twenty-first century.

Also, when two nouns linked by *and* are modified by *every* or *each,* these two nouns are likewise treated as one singular subject:

> **Every hill and valley** is aglow with light.

> **Each night and day** brings no new news of you.

An exception to this rule arises when the word *each* follows a compound subject. In these cases, usage varies depending on the number of the direct object.

> **The army and the navy each** have their own air forces.

> **The owl and the pussycat each** has a personal claim to fame.

Subjects joined by *or, either . . . or,* or *neither . . . nor*

When a subject is joined by *or, either . . . or,* or *neither . . . nor,* make sure the verb agrees with the subject closest to the verb.

Is it **the sky** ┌─SING─┐ or **the mountains** ┌─────PLURAL─────┐ that are ┌─PL─┐ blue?

Is it **the mountains** ┌─────PLURAL─────┐ or **the sky** ┌──SING──┐ that surrounds ┌──SING──┐ us?

Neither the animals ┌──── PLURAL ──┐ **nor the zookeeper** ┌──── SING ──┐ knows ┌─ SING ─┐ how to relock the gate.

Either a coyote ┌─SING─┐ or **several dogs** ┌── PLURAL ──┐ were ┌─PL─┐ howling last night.

Subjects along with another noun

Verbs agree with the subject of a sentence, even when a subject is linked to another noun with a phrase like *as well as, along with,* or *alongside.* These modifying phrases are usually set off from the main subject with commas.

Chicken, ┌──────── IGNORE THIS PHRASE ────────┐ alongside various steamed vegetables, is my favorite meal.

┌─ IGNORE THIS PHRASE ─┐
Besides David Bowie, **the Beatles** are my favorite band of all time.

COMMON ERRORS

Subjects separated from verbs

The most common agreement errors occur when words come between the subject and verb. These intervening words do not affect subject-verb agreement. To ensure that you use the correct verb form, identify the subject and the verb. Ignore any phrases that come between them.

Incorrect   **Students** at inner-city Washington High **reads** more than suburban students.
┌──────── IGNORE THIS PHRASE ────────┐

Correct   **Students** at inner-city Washington High read more than suburban students.

Students is plural and *read* is plural; subject and verb agree.

Incorrect   **The Whale Shark,** the largest of all sharks, **feed** on plankton.

(Continued on next page)

COMMON ERRORS *(continued)*

Correct   **The Whale Shark,** the largest of all sharks, feeds on plankton.

The plural noun *sharks* that appears between the subject *the whale shark* and the verb *feeds* does not change the number of the subject. The subject is singular and the verb is singular. Subject and verb agree.

Remember: When you check for subject-verb agreement, identify the subject and verb. Ignore any words that come between them.

 For step-by-step discussion, examples, and practice exercises, visit this page of the E-book at www.mycomplab.com.

Ignore the subject complement when determining agreement

With sentences that follow the subject–linking verb–subject complement pattern, ignore the subject complement when deciding to make the verb (v) singular or plural (see Section 32c). A subject complement further identifies the subject but should not be confused with the subject itself.

                                          VERB
      ┌─────── SUBJECT ───────┐ ┌─┴─┐ ┌─────SUBJECT COMPLEMENT─────┐
Tantrums and runny noses are the reality of living with toddlers.

                                       SING V
               ┌──── PLURAL SUBJECT ────┐ ┌─┴─┐
Incorrect   **Tantrums and runny noses** is the reality of living with toddlers.

                                       PL V
               ┌──── PLURAL SUBJECT ────┐ ┌─┴─┐
Correct   **Tantrums and runny noses** are the reality of living with toddlers.

                                 V
   ┌─────── SUBJECT ───────┐ ┌─┴─┐ ┌─────SUBJECT COMPLEMENT─────┐
The beauty of my plan is its simplicity and economy.

Incorrect
┌── SINGULAR SUBJECT ──┐ ┌PL┐
The beauty of my plan are its simplicity and economy.

Correct
┌── SINGULAR SUBJECT ──┐ SING V
The beauty of my plan is its simplicity and economy.

Make the verbs agree with the antecedents of relative pronouns: *who, whom, whose, which,* and *that*

The relative pronouns *who, whom, whose, which,* and *that* begin clauses that modify nouns. For instance, in the following sentence a clause beginning with *who* modifies *engineer.*

CLAUSE MODIFYING ENGINEER
The engineer who works in this lab has twenty-two patents.

To determine whether a verb should be singular or plural, use the antecedent to the relative pronoun. In other words, find the noun that the relative pronoun refers to.

SING ANTECEDENT RELATIVE PRON   SING VERB
The **engineer who** works in this lab **has** twenty-two patents.

PL ANTECEDENT RELATIVE PRON   PL VERB
The **greyhounds that** play in North Park **are** all **retired** from dog racing.

SING ANTECEDENT RELATIVE PRON   SING VERB
The **mechanic whose** tools are all over the garage always **loses** his wrench.

PL ANTECEDENT RELATIVE PRON
My **daughters, to whom** I give a fifteen-dollar allowance weekly,

PL VERB
claim they are always broke.

SINGULAR ANTECEDENT RELATIVE PRON   SING VERB
Baklava, which most Greek restaurants serve, **is** difficult to make.

Titles, institutional and business names, words used as words, and gerunds take singular verbs

Titles of works, institutional and business names, words used as words, and gerunds are all singular subjects, even if they end in *-s*. Thus, they all take singular verbs.

	SINGULAR SUBJECT	SING VERB

Title of a work

The Decline and Fall of the Roman Empire is Edward Gibbon's most popular book.

Title of a work

Kids shocks moviegoers with its sex and drug-laden portrayal of teenagers.
(SING SUBJECT SING VERB)

Institutional name

Big Brothers and Big Sisters hosts a bowling tournament fundraiser each May.
(SINGULAR SUBJECT — SING VERB)

Business name

Armstrong Bikes does the best repairs in town.
(SINGULAR SUBJECT — SING VERB)

Words used as words

Old and Leaky is a better name for our boat than *Hale and Hearty*.
(SINGULAR SUBJECT — SING VERB)

Words used as words

Hamburgers is no longer visible on the Sandwich Paradise sign.
(SING SUBJECT — SING VERB)

Gerunds are *-ing* verbs that act as nouns. They are always singular. Thus, when a gerund or gerund phrase is the subject of a sentence, the verb should be singular as well, in order to agree.

Incorrect

Loitering outside of schools are illegal.
(SING SUBJECT — PL VERB)

Correct

Loitering outside of schools is illegal.
(SING SUBJECT — SING VERB)

Incorrect	SING SUBJECT **Riding** buses PL VERB **reduce** pollution.
Correct	SING SUBJECT **Riding** buses SING VERB **reduces** pollution.

Exercise 34.1   Underline the subject in the following sentences and decide whether it should be treated as singular or plural. Next, circle the verb. If the verb doesn t agree in number with the subject, revise so that it agrees.

Example   Various regions in Italy—including Tuscany,
possess
Lazio, and Umbria—(possesses) rich cultures that
revolve around food preparation and meals.

["Regions" is plural, so the verb needs to be changed to "possess."]

1. Some cite Rome's Marcus Gavius Apicius as the author of the first cookbook, written in the first century.
2. Each Italian city and town in Italy possess a historical rationale for the gastronomical traditions of today.
3. People in central Italy enjoy eating many types of meat, but neither beef nor liver outshine the popularity of the region s top meat, pork.
4. Cheese, as well as foods such as balsamic vinegar and olive oil, is sometimes named for the region where it is produced.
5. Almost every man and woman in America know spaghetti hails from Italy, but many fail to learn about the rich and varied Italian tradition of food.

34c **Indefinite Pronouns as Subjects**

The choice of a singular or plural pronoun is determined by the **antecedent**—the noun that a pronoun refers to. For instance, the sentence *My friend likes soup* might be followed by another sentence, *She makes a new kind daily.* The pronoun must be singular because *she* refers to the singular noun *friend.*

Indefinite pronouns, such as *some, few, all, someone, everyone,* and *each,* often do not refer to identifiable subjects; hence they have no antecedents. Most indefinite pronouns are singular and agree with the singular forms of verbs. Some, like *both* and *many,* are always plural and agree with the plural forms of verbs. Other indefinite pronouns are variable and can agree with either singular or plural verb forms, depending on the context of the sentence.

AGREEMENT WITH INDEFINITE PRONOUNS

Indefinite pronouns that are always singular

anybody	everyone	one
anyone	everything	somebody
anything	neither*	someone
each	nobody	something
either*	no one	
everybody	nothing	

*__Note:__ Although *either* and *neither* are treated as singular when written, they may be treated as singular or plural in spoken English.

Indefinite pronouns that are always plural

both	few
many	several

Indefinite pronouns that are sometimes singular and sometimes plural

all	more	some
any	most	
half	none	

COMMON ERRORS

Agreement errors using *each*

The indefinite pronoun *each* is a frequent source of subject-verb agreement errors. If a pronoun is singular, its verb must be singular. This rule holds true even when the subject is modified by a phrase that includes a plural noun.

A common stumbling block to this rule is the pronoun *each*. *Each* is always treated as a singular pronoun in college writing. When *each* stands alone, the choice is easy to make:

Incorrect   Each are an outstanding student.
Correct   Each is an outstanding student.

But when *each* is modified by a phrase that includes a plural noun, the choice of a singular verb form becomes less obvious:

Incorrect   Each of the girls are fit.
Correct   Each of the girls is fit.

Incorrect   Each of our dogs get a present.
Correct   Each of our dogs gets a present.

Remember: *Each* is always singular.

For step-by-step discussion, examples, and practice exercises, visit this page of the E-book at www.mycomplab.com.

Exercise 34.2   Identify the underlined indefinite pronoun in each sentence as singular or plural. Then circle the verb and correct it if it does not agree in number with the pronoun.

Example   While stand-up comedy has often been considered a

male-dominated industry, *plural* many successful female

comics ~~has~~ *have* carved out places for themselves in the

annals of comic history.

1. Of those who overcame the gender barrier, few ~~has~~ *plural have* had more culturally explosive careers than Ellen Degeneres.
2. When Degeneres was named Funniest Person in America by the
Showtime network in 1982, no one *sing.* was expecting her to gain fame
as a controversial television star.
3. Not everybody *sing.* ~~were~~ *was* thrilled in 1997 when she decided her sitcom
alter ego *plural were* would come out as a lesbian.
4. Many *plural* ~~was~~ *were* forced to cast political feelings aside when she endeared
America as the forgetful fish Dory in the 2003 animated hit *Finding
Nemo.*
5. Everybody *sing.* was surprised when *The Ellen Degeneres Show* became
one of the hottest daytime talk shows of the new millennium.

34d Collective Nouns as Subjects

Collective nouns refer to groups (*administration, audience, class, committee,
crew, crowd, faculty, family, fleet, gang, government, group, herd, jury, mob,
public, team*). When members of a group are considered as a unit, use
singular verbs and singular pronouns.

> The **audience** was patient with the novice performer.

> The **crowd** is unusually quiet at the moment, but it will get noisy soon.

> The **fleet** leaves port on June 29, and it will not return until next year.

When members of a group are considered as individuals, use plural verbs
and plural pronouns.

The **brigade** are in their positions on both flanks.

The **faculty** have their differing opinions on how to address the problems caused by reduced state support.

Sometimes collective nouns can be singular in one context and plural in another. Writers must decide which verb form to use based on sentence context.

The **number** of people who live downtown is increasing.

A **number** of people are moving downtown from the suburbs.

Sports is one of the four main buttons on the newspaper's Web site.

Sports are dangerous for children under five.

Exercise 34.3   The following paragraph contains collective nouns that can be considered either singular or plural depending on the context. Select the form of the verb that agrees with the subject in the context given.

> **Example**   The jury (is/are) ready to deliberate.
>
> [*Jury* is considered singular.]
>
> The jury (believe/believes) that they will resolve their differences in judgment.
>
> [*Jury* is considered plural.]

The administration usually (try/tries) to avoid responsibility for issues concerning students living off campus but also (listen/listens) when the city government (complain/complains) about student behavior. The public (is/are) upset about large parties that last into the morning. The university formed a committee of students, faculty, and neighborhood residents to investigate the problem. Unfortunately, the committee (disagree/disagrees) about the causes of excessive noise.

34e Inverted Word Order

In English a sentence's subject usually comes before the verb: *The nights are tender.* Sometimes, however, you will come across a sentence with inverted word order: *Tender are the nights.* Here the subject of the sentence, *nights*, comes after the verb, *are.* Writers use inverted word order most often in forming questions. The statement *Cats are friendly* becomes a question when you invert the subject and the verb: *Are cats friendly?* Writers also use inverted word order for added emphasis or for style considerations.

Do not be confused by inverted word order. Locate the subject of your sentence, then make sure your verb agrees with that subject.

34f Amounts, Numbers, and Pairs

Subjects that describe amounts of money, time, distance, or measurement are singular and require singular verbs.

Three days is never long enough to unwind.

Two hundred dollars stands as the asking price.

Some subjects, such as courses of study, academic specializations, illnesses, and even some nations, are treated as singular subjects even though their names end in *-s* or *-es.* For example, *economics, news, ethics, measles*, and *the United States* all end in *-s* but are all singular subjects.

Economics is a rich field of study.

News keeps getting more and more commercial.

The United States is a global power.

Other subjects require a plural verb form even though they refer to single items such as *jeans, slacks, glasses, scissors*, and *tweezers.* These items are all pairs.

Your **jeans** look terrific.

My **glasses** are scratched.

Exercise 34.4   Identify whether the underlined subject is singular or plural. Circle the verb and correct the verb if it does not agree in number with the subject.

Example   Despite the racist overtones of nineteenth-century
minstrel shows, the <u>United States</u> have a rich
singular   *has*
tradition of African American theater dating back
to the 1820s.

[The subject is singular so the verb needs to be changed
to "has."]

1. African American <u>theatrics</u> dates back to 1821, the year John Brown organized the first troupe of African American actors.
2. Despite the controversy connected to Brown s involvement in the Harper s Ferry riots, <u>thanks</u> is due to him for creating a space where African Americans could publicly perform works such as *Richard III* and *Othello*.
3. Because American <u>politics</u> was incongruous with supporting serious African American art, the troupe s lead actor, Ira Aldridge, moved to London.
4. <u>Politics</u>, not talent or ambition, was a driving force in determining the success of non-Anglo performers for decades.
5. Despite the success of twentieth-century actors such as Sidney Poitier, James Earl Jones, and Alfre Woodard, nearly <u>one hundred thirty years</u> are a long time for African American actors to wait for popular acceptance.

Chapter 35

Verbs

Spot and fix problems with verbs.

35a Basic Verb Forms

Almost all verbs in English have five possible forms. The exception is the verb *be*. Regular verbs follow this basic pattern:

Base form	Third-person singular	Past tense	Past participle	Present participle
jump	jumps	jumped	jumped	jumping
like	likes	liked	liked	liking
talk	talks	talked	talked	talking
wish	wishes	wished	wished	wishing

Irregular verbs do not follow this basic pattern. See Section 35b for the forms of irregular verbs.

Base form

The base form of a verb is the one you find listed in the dictionary. This form indicates an action or condition in the present.

> I like New York in June.

> We talk often on weekends.

Third-person singular

The base form of the verb changes when used with third-person singular subjects. Third-person singular subjects include *he, she, it,* and the nouns they replace, as well as other pronouns, including *someone, anybody,* and *everything.* (See Section 34c.) Present tense verbs in the third-person singular end with an *s* or an *es.*

> Ms. Nessan speaks in riddles.

> He watches too much television.

Past tense

The past tense describes an action or condition that occurred in the past. For most verbs, the past tense is formed by adding *d* or *ed* to the base form of the verb.

> I called at nine, but no one answered.

> She inhaled the night air.

Many verbs, however, have irregular past tense forms. (See Section 35b.)

Past participle

The past participle is used with *have* to form verbs in the perfect tense, with *be* to form verbs in the passive voice (see Section 27b), and to form adjectives derived from verbs.

Past perfect	They **had** gone to the grocery store prematurely.
Passive	The book **was** written thirty years before it **was** published.
Adjective	In the eighties, teased hair was all the rage.

Present participle

The present participle functions in one of three ways. Used with an auxiliary verb, it can describe a continuing action. The present participle can also function as a noun, known as a **gerund**, or as an adjective. The present participle is formed by adding *ing* to the base form of a verb.

Present participle Wild elks **are** competing for limited food resources.

Gerund Sailing around the Cape of Good Hope is rumored to bring good luck.

Adjective We looked for shells in the ebbing tide.

COMMON ERRORS

Missing verb endings

Verb endings are not always pronounced in speech, especially in some dialects of English. It's also easy to omit these endings when you are writing quickly. Spelling checkers will not mark these errors, so you have to find them while proofreading.

Incorrect Jeremy **feel** as if he's catching a cold.
Correct Jeremy **feels** as if he's catching a cold.

Incorrect Sheila **hope** she would get the day off.
Correct Sheila **hoped** she would get the day off.

Remember: Check verbs carefully for missing *s* or *es* endings in the present tense and missing *d* or *ed* endings in the past tense.

 For step-by-step discussion, examples, and practice exercises, visit this page of the E-book at www.mycomplab.com.

Exercise 35.1   Write the correct form of each underlined verb using the clues given in parentheses.

Example   Although it sound$\overset{s}{\wedge}$(third person singular) simple, noodl$\overset{ing}{e}$$_\wedge$ (present participle-gerund), or catch$\overset{ing}{\wedge}$(present participle-gerund) fish by using only your bare hands, is complicate$\overset{d}{\wedge}$(past participle-adjective).

Flathead catfish are the choose (past participle-adjective) prey for noodle (gerund) because they lives (base form) sedentary lifestyles in holes or under brush. A noodler begin (third person singular) by go (gerund) underwater to depths ranging from only a few feet to a daunt (present participle-adjective) twenty feet. Placing his or her hand inside a discover (past participle-adjective) catfish hole, a noodler use (third person singular) his or her arm as bait to luring (base form) the fish. If all go (third person singular) as plan (past participle-adjective), the catfish will swim forward and fastened (base form) itself onto the noodler's hand and arm. Because catfish often weigh up to 50 to 60 pounds, many a noodler has need (past participle) help lift (gerund) their catch out of the water.

35b Irregular Verbs

A verb is **regular** when its past and past participle forms are created by adding *ed* or *d* to the base form. If this rule does not apply, the verb is considered an **irregular** verb. Here are common irregular verbs and their basic conjugations.

Common irregular verbs

Base form	Past tense	Past participle
arise	arose	arisen
be (is, am, are)	was, were	been
bear	bore	borne or born
beat	beat	beaten
become	became	become
begin	began	begun
bend	bent	bent
break	broke	broken
bring	brought	brought
buy	bought	bought
choose	chose	chosen
cling	clung	clung
come	came	come
cost	cost	cost
creep	crept	crept
deal	dealt	dealt
dig	dug	dug
dive	dived or dove	dived
do	did	done
draw	drew	drawn
drink	drank	drunk
drive	drove	driven
eat	ate	eaten
fall	fell	fallen
feed	fed	fed
feel	felt	felt
fight	fought	fought
fling	flung	flung
fly	flew	flown

(Continued on next page)

Common irregular verbs (Continued)

forbid	forbade or forbad	forbidden
forget	forgot	forgotten or forgot
forgive	forgave	forgiven
freeze	froze	frozen
get	got	got or gotten
give	gave	given
go	went	gone
grow	grew	grown
hang	hung	hung
have	had	had
know	knew	known
lay	laid	laid
lend	lent	lent
lie	lay	lain
make	made	made
read	read	read
run	ran	run
say	said	said
see	saw	seen
send	sent	sent
shine	shone	shone
show	showed	shown or showed
sit	sat	sat
sleep	slept	slept
speak	spoke	spoken
spring	sprang or sprung	sprung
swim	swam	swum
take	took	taken
teach	taught	taught
tell	told	told

(Continued on next page)

Common irregular verbs (Continued)

think	thought	thought
understand	understood	understood
wear	wore	worn
write	wrote	written

Use to be correctly in the past and present

To be is irregular in the present and past tenses.

	Present tense		Past tense	
	singular	**plural**	**singular**	**plural**
First person:	I am	we are	I was	we were
Second person:	you are	you are	you were	you were
Third person:	he/she/it is	they are	he/she/it was	they were

Not all dialects of English use these forms, however. Some use *be* in place of the other present tense forms of the verb, *is* in place of *are*, or *was* in place of *were*. Also, some speakers use *ain't* in place of *am not, isn't,* and *aren't*. In cases where edited American English is called for, be sure to choose the forms of *to be* that correspond to the subject of the sentence.

                        3RD PERSON,
                        SING   INFINITIVE

Dialect   He **be** repainting his house this weekend.

                        3RD PERSON,
                        SING   3RD PERSON, SING

Edited   He **is** repainting his house this weekend.
American English

                        1ST PERSON, PL   3RD PERSON, SING

Dialect   My friends and I **is** tired of reading nothing but bad news in the paper.

                        1ST PERSON, PL   1ST PERSON, PL

Edited   My friends and I **are** tired of reading nothing but
American English   bad news in the paper.

	1ST PERSON, PL	1ST OR 3RD PERSON, SING

Dialect   We was in the right.

	1ST PERSON, PL	1ST PERSON, PL

**Edited
American English**   We were in the right.

	3RD PERSON, SING	NONSTANDARD 3RD PERSON, SING

Dialect   Petula ain't going to take care of any more pets.

	3RD PERSON, SING	3RD PERSON, SING

**Edited
American English**   Petula isn't going to take care of any more pets.

Use *to have* correctly in the past and present

To have is regular in the present tense except for *has* in the third person singular. Some English speakers use *have* in place of *has* and vice versa. When edited American English is appropriate, use *has* in the third person singular present form only and *have* in all the other present tenses.

	3RD PERSON, PL	3RD PERSON, SING

Dialect   My pet rats has more personality than most people think they do.

	3RD PERSON, PL	3RD PERSON, PL

**Edited
American English**   My pet rats have more personality than most people think they do.

	3RD PERSON, SING	3RD PERSON, PL

Dialect   John have chicken pox.

	3RD PERSON, SING	3RD PERSON, SING

**Edited
American English**   John has chicken pox.

Use *to do* correctly in the past and present

To do is regular in the present tense except in the third person singular form, *does*. The negative of the third person singular form is *does not* or *doesn't*. And the negative of all the other present forms is *do not* or *don't*. Speakers of some dialects of English will use *don't* in place of *doesn't*. In cases where you want to use edited American English, however, be sure to use *doesn't* when forming the negative third person singular.

Dialect

3RD PERSON, SING | ALL FORMS EXCEPT 3RD PERSON, SING

My instructor don't accept late papers.

Edited American English

3RD PERSON, SING | 3RD PERSON, SING

My instructor doesn't accept late papers.

COMMON ERRORS

Past tense forms of irregular verbs

The past tense and past participle forms of irregular verbs are often confused. The most frequent error is using a past tense form instead of the past participle with *had*.

Incorrect She had never **rode** a horse before.
PAST TENSE

Correct She had never **ridden** a horse before.
PAST PARTICIPLE

Incorrect He had **saw** many alligators in Louisiana.
PAST TENSE

Correct He had **seen** many alligators in Louisiana.
PAST PARTICIPLE

Remember: Change any past tense verbs preceded by *had* to past participles.

 For step-by-step discussion, examples, and practice exercises, visit this page of the E-book at www.mycomplab.com.

Exercise 35.2   Underline the correct form of the irregular verbs in the following paragraph.

Example   *I Love Lucy*, (thinked/<u>thought</u>) of by many as that funny show with the zany redhead, (<u>drove</u>/drived) many television innovations.

> After marrying in 1940, Lucille Ball and Desi Arnaz (sought/ seeked) to create their own television situation comedy, but the networks (chose/choosed) not to buy the project. Ball and Arnaz decided to fund the show independently, and within a short time the couple (got/gotten) together the money, created Desilu Studios, and (began/begun) shooting their pilot. Soon Americans (eated/ate), (drunk/drank), and (slept/sleeped) *I Love Lucy*. With innovations like the three-camera technique, Desilu Studios (laid/lain/layed) the groundwork for future sitcoms and (rode/ ride/rided) into television history.

35c Transitive and Intransitive Verbs

Lay/lie, set/sit, and *raise/rise*

Do you know whether you raise or rise from bed in the morning? Do your house keys lay or lie on the kitchen table? Does a book set or sit on the shelf? *Raise/rise, lay/lie,* and *set/sit* are transitive and intransitive verbs that writers frequently confuse. Transitive verbs take direct objects, nouns that receive the action of the verb. Intransitive verbs act in sentences that lack direct objects.

The following charts list the trickiest pairs of transitive and intransitive verbs and the correct forms for each verb tense. Pay special attention to *lay* and *lie*, which are irregular.

	lay (put something down)	**lie (recline)**
Present	lay, lays	lie, lies
Present participle	laying	lying
Past	laid	lay
Past participle	laid	lain

Transitive   Once you complete your test, please lay your pencil (direct object, the thing being laid down) on the desk.

Intransitive   The *Titanic* lies upright in two pieces at a depth of 13,000 feet.

	raise (elevate something)	rise (get up)
Present	raise, raises	rise, rises
Present participle	raising	rising
Past	raised	rose
Past participle	raised	risen

Transitive   We raise our glasses (direct object, the things being raised) to toast Uncle Han.

Intransitive   The sun rises over the bay.

	set (place something)	sit (take a seat)
Present	set, sets	sit, sits
Present participle	setting	sitting
Past	set	sat
Past participle	set	sat

Transitive   Every morning Stanley sets two dollars (direct object, the amount being set) on the table to tip the waiter.

Intransitive   I sit in the front seat when it's available.

Exercise 35.3   Decide whether each of the sentences in the following paragraph calls for a transitive or intransitive verb and underline the correct choice.

Example The eastern diamondback rattlesnake (will set/<u>will sit</u>) immobile for hours, sometimes coiled and sometimes stretched to its full length of seven feet.

A rattlesnake will often (lay/lie) in wait for its favorite meal: a rat. When you encounter one of these poisonous snakes, (set/sit) aside your assumptions about aggressive snakes; many are timid. You can tell a rattlesnake feels threatened if its tail (rises/raises) and you hear a sharp rattling sound. If you are hiking in the desert in the southwestern United States, do not (sit/set) down without carefully surveying the ground. To (rise/raise) your chances of avoiding a rattlesnake bite, make noise when you are hiking in wilderness areas.

35d Shifts in Tense

Appropriate shifts in verb tense

Changes in verb tense are sometimes necessary to indicate a shift in time.

	PRESENT TENSE	PAST TENSE
Present to past	I never shop online anymore because I heard that

PRESENT PERFECT TENSE
hackers have stolen thousands of credit card

numbers used in Internet transactions.

	PAST TENSE	FUTURE TENSE
Past to Future	Because Oda won the lottery, she will quit her job

PRESENT TENSE
at the hospital as soon as her supervisor finds a

qualified replacement.

WRITING IN THE WORLD

Verb tenses in academic writing and in reviews

Texts and ideas

Use the present tense to discuss another author's work or ideas. Texts and ideas are enduring; they never become part of the past.

> Garcia and Brink's review of the control groups in fifty-two
> PRESENT TENSE   PRESENT TENSE
> medical studies concludes that doctors grossly overestimate the
> placebo effect.

Be careful to shift tenses when necessary. The sentence that follows cites one pundit's analysis (analysis calls for present tense) about a past event (past events call for past tense).

> ANOTHER'S ENDURING IDEA;   A COMPLETED EVENT;
> USE PRESENT TENSE   USE PAST TENSE
> Gerreau argues that the Monica Lewinsky scandal was the defining
> event of the Clinton presidency.

However, if you are writing in the sciences and using APA style, use past tense when referring to completed studies and events in the past. Stick to the present tense when dealing with your current research, ongoing issues or problems, and accepted ideas.

Completed study	PAST TENSE Bahl (1999) showed that children in day care are no more likely to have depression than children cared for at home.
Event in the past	PAST TENSE The 1986 meteor shower was the biggest ever recorded.
Current research	PRESENT TENSE My study suggests bunions play a role in shin injuries.
Ongoing problem	PRESENT TENSE Melting rates of the polar icecaps indicate the intensification of global climate change.
Accepted idea	PRESENT TENSE The earth revolves around the sun.

(Continued on next page)

Works of art

Use the present tense when discussing works of art, which, like ideas, endure. (See Section 22b for a discussion of the literary present tense.)

> **PRESENT TENSE**
> Rilke's "Archaic Torso of Apollo" captures the potential
> **PRESENT TENSE**
> energy of a frozen block of stone. The poem's imagery refuses
> to portray the headless, limbless sculpture of a Greek god as
> anything less than a powerful, twisting, glowing whole.

Remember to shift verb tenses when your argument shifts from an analysis of an art object, requiring present tense, to a discussion of historical events, requiring past tense.

> **PAST TENSE**
> **HISTORICAL EVENT**   **PAST TENSE**
> Rilke met the sculptor Auguste Rodin in 1902, worked as his
> **PAST TENSE**
> secretary for a time, and later wrote a book about him. His
> **PRES TENSE, ANALYSIS OF ARTWORK**
> experience with Rodin accounts for Rilke's keen eye for the
> plastic arts in his poetry. The "Archaic Torso of Apollo" in
> **PRESENT TENSE**   **PRESENT TENSE**
> particular illustrates how the fluidity of words instills an
> ancient, cold block of stone with new vitality.

Inappropriate shifts in verb tense

Be careful to avoid confusing your reader with unnecessary shifts in verb tense. Once you reach the proofreading stage of your writing, dedicate one careful reading of your text to finding inappropriate tense changes.

> **PRESENT TENSE**
> **Incorrect**   While Brazil looks to ecotourism to fund rainforest
> **PAST TENSE**
> preservation, other South American nations relied on
> foreign aid and conservation efforts.

The shift from present tense (*looks*) to past tense (*relied*) is confusing. The sentence attempts to compare Brazil with other South American countries, but the shift in tenses muddles the comparison. Correct the mistake by putting both verbs in the present tense.

> **PRESENT TENSE**
>
> **Correct**   While Brazil looks to ecotourism to fund rainforest
>
> **PRESENT TENSE**
>
> preservation, other South American nations rely on
>
> foreign aid and conservation efforts.

COMMON ERRORS

Unnecessary tense shift

Notice the tense shift in the following example.

> **PAST TENSE**
>
> **Incorrect**   In May of 2000 the "I Love You" virus crippled the
>
> computer systems of major American companies and
>
> **PAST TENSE**
>
> irritated millions of private computer users. As the
>
> **PRESENT TENSE**   **PRESENT TENSE**
>
> virus generates millions of emails and erases millions
>
> of computer files, companies such as Ford and Time Warner
>
> **PRESENT TENSE**
>
> are forced to shut down their clogged email systems.

The second sentence shifts unnecessarily to the present tense, confusing the reader. Did the "I Love You" virus have its heyday several years ago, or is it still wreaking havoc now? Changing the verbs in the second sentence to the past tense eliminates the confusion.

> **PAST TENSE**
>
> **Correct**   In May of 2000 the "I Love You" virus crippled the com-
>
> **PAST TENSE**
>
> puter systems of major American companies and irritated
>
> **PAST TENSE**
>
> millions of private computer users. As the virus generated
>
> **PAST TENSE**
>
> millions of emails and erased millions of computer files,

(Continued on next page)

COMMON ERRORS *(continued)*

PAST TENSE
companies such as Ford and Time Warner were forced to shut down their clogged email systems.

Remember: Shift verb tense only when you are referring to different time periods.

For step-by-step discussion, examples, and practice exercises, visit this page of the E-book at www.mycomplab.com.

Exercise 35.4   Read the entire paragraph and underline the correct verb tenses.

Example   The American Indian Movement (AIM) (originated/ originates) in Minneapolis in 1968.

Native American activists, including Dennis Banks and Russell Means, (created/create) AIM, a militant organization that fights for civil rights for American Indians. AIM members (participate/ participated) in a number of famous protests, including the occupation of Alcatraz Island (1969–1971) and the takeover of Wounded Knee (1973). The group (has helped/helps) Indians displaced by government programs, (will work/has worked) for economic independence for Native Americans, and (agitates/has agitated) for the return of lands (seize/seized) by the U.S. government. In his book *Agents of Repression: The FBI's Secret War against the Black Panther Party and the American Indian Movement*, Ward Churchill (documented/documents) how the FBI (infiltrated/ infiltrates) AIM in an attempt to destroy it. While most local chapters of AIM (have disbanded/disband), Native American activists today still (fight/fought) for their autonomy and for compensation for centuries of oppression and economic injustice.

35e Shifts in Mood

Indicative, imperative, and subjunctive verbs

Verbs can be categorized into three moods—indicative, imperative, and subjunctive—defined by the functions they serve.

Indicative verbs state facts, opinions, and questions.

Fact	The human genome project seeks to map out human DNA.
Opinion	The scientific advances spurred by the human genome project, including cloning and designer genes, will allow normal people to play God.
Question	How long does it take to map out the entire human genome?

Imperative verbs make commands, give advice, and make requests.

Command	Research the technology being used to carry out the human genome project.
Advice	Try to join a high-profile research project like the human genome project if you want to make a name for yourself in the scientific community.
Request	Could you please explain the role you played in the human genome project?

Subjunctive verbs express wishes, unlikely or untrue situations, hypothetical situations, requests with *that* clauses, and suggestions.

Wish	We wish that unlocking the secrets of our DNA were a surefire way to cure genetic diseases.
Unlikely or untrue situation	If the genome project were as simple as the news media made it out to be, scientists could complete it over a long weekend.
Hypothetical situation	If the genome project were to lose government funding, the scientists working on it would not be able to afford the equipment they need to complete it.

The subjunctive in past and present tenses

Subjunctive verbs are usually the trickiest to handle. In the present tense subjunctive clauses call for the base form of the verb (*be, have, see, jump*).

It is essential that children **be** immunized before they enter kindergarten.

In the past tense they call for the standard past tense of the verb (*had, saw, jumped*), with one exception. In counterfactual sentences the *to be* verb always becomes *were*, even for subjects that take *was* under normal circumstances.

Indicative   I **was** surprised at some of the choices she made.

Subjunctive   If I **were** in her position, I'd do things differently.

Indicative   The young athletes found that gaining muscle **was** not easy.

Subjunctive   If being muscular **were** easy, everyone would look like Arnold Schwarzenegger.

Exercise 35.5   Replace the underlined verb with a verb in the correct mood using the clues in the brackets.

Example   Nitrogen Narcosis resultˢ[indicative] when nitrogen
                 become
                 levels in the bloodstream became [indicative] elevated
                 because of pressure.

    This phenomenon is called "rapture of the deep" because the increase in nitrogen makes a diver feel as if she is [subjunctive] invincible. Being [imperative] very careful, however; this situation is dangerous. Often the combination of nitrogen and excessive oxygen overwhelm [indicative] the diver, causing her to wish that she could got [subjunctive] free of the breathing apparatus. A diver above the surface of the water experience [indicative] one atmosphere of pressure. How much do the pressure increase [indicative] if the diver is 100 feet below the surface? Imagining [imperative] having a 300 pound weight on your chest. That's right—the pressure triple [indicative]. It is crucial that a diver prepares [subjunctive] for the possibility of rapture occurring during a dive. Often divers would inhale [indicative] nitrous oxide to see how they would handle themselves if they was [subjunctive] in the throes of rapture of the deep.

Chapter 36

Pronouns

Recognize misused pronouns and correct them.

36a Pronoun Case

Pronoun case refers to the forms pronouns take to indicate their function in a sentence. Pronouns that function as the subjects of sentences are in the **subjective case**. Pronouns that function as direct or indirect objects are in the **objective case**. Pronouns that indicate ownership are in the **possessive case**.

Subjective pronouns	Objective pronouns	Possessive pronouns
I	me	my, mine
we	us	our, ours
you	you	your, yours
he	him	his
she	her	her, hers
it	it	its
they	them	their, theirs
who	whom	whose

People who use English regularly usually make these distinctions among pronouns without thinking about them.

   S   O   P   S   O   O   S   O
I let him use my laptop, but he lent it to her, and I haven't seen it since.

Nonetheless, choosing the correct pronoun case sometimes can be difficult.

Pronouns in compound phrases

Picking the right pronoun sometimes can be confusing when the pronoun appears in a compound phrase.

> If we work together, you and **me** can get the job done quickly.

> If we work together, you and **I** can get the job done quickly.

Which is correct—*me* or *I*? Removing the other pronoun usually makes the choice clear.

> **Incorrect**   Me can get the job done quickly.

> **Correct**   I can get the job done quickly.

Similarly, when compound pronouns appear as objects of prepositions, sometimes the correct choice isn't obvious until you remove the other pronoun.

> When you finish your comments, give them to Isidora or **I**.

> When you finish your comments, give them to Isidora or **me**.

Again, the choice is easy when the pronoun stands alone:

> **Incorrect**   Give them to I.

> **Correct**   Give them to me.

We and *us* before nouns

Another pair of pronouns that can cause difficulty is *we* and *us* before nouns.

> **Us** friends must stick together.

> **We** friends must stick together.

Which is correct—*us* or *we*? Removing the noun indicates the correct choice.

> **Incorrect**   Us must stick together.

> **Correct**   We must stick together.

Exercise 36.1   Underline the pronoun in each sentence of the following paragraph and replace the pronoun if it is incorrect.

Example   <u>You</u> and ~~me~~ should pay more attention to what we eat.

     If you and a friend go on a road trip, the ADA suggests that you and her limit your stops at fast-food restaurants. The association suggests us snack in the afternoon, provided we choose foods that are healthy for you and I. If your friend wants a cheeseburger for lunch, you should respond that you and her could split the meal. For your sake and me, it is not a good idea to snack after dark.

Who versus *whom*

Choosing between *who* and *whom* is often difficult, even for experienced writers. When you answer the phone, which do you say?

1. To **whom** do you wish to speak?

2. **Who** do you want to talk to?

You probably chose 2. *To whom do you wish to speak?* may sound stuffy, but technically it is correct. The reason it sounds stuffy is that the distinction between *who* and *whom* is disappearing from spoken language. *Who* is more often used in spoken language, even when *whom* is correct.

Pronouns in subordinate clauses

With complex sentences that have one or more subordinate clauses, it can be especially tricky figuring out whether to use *who* or *whom*. Substituting subjective and objective pronouns will help, but first you must (1) isolate the subordinate clause, (2) rearrange the clause so that it leads with the subject, (3) substitute the subjective and objective pronouns to see which sounds right, and (4) choose *who* if the subjective prounoun sounds right and *whom* if the objective pronoun sounds right.

Example   The technology company gave stock options to all employees [who, whom] the Board of Trustees recommended.

1. Isolate the subordinate clause: [who, whom] the Board of Trustees recommended.
2. Rearrange: The Board of Trustees recommended _____.
3. Substitute: The Board of Trustees recommended they. The Board of Trustees recommended them.
4. Choose subjective or objective case: The Board of Trustees recommended whom.

Correct The technology company gave stock options to all employees whom the Board of Trustees recommended.

Pronouns in phrases and clauses that function as objects of prepositions

When a phrase or clause functions as the object of a preposition, the objective pronoun is not automatically the correct choice. Decide whether the pronoun (*who, whom, whoever,* or *whomever*) functions as the subject or object of the verb in the clause.

Correct Phil was excited to meet the film director about whom so much had been written.

Correct Struggling with a bad phone connection, Sylvia tried to speak to whoever was on the other end of the phone.

Pronouns that function as subject complements

When the pronoun functions as a subject complement, always use *who.*

I am who I am.

My mother is the kind of person who likes to cook elaborate meals.

Pronouns that function as subjects or objects of infinitives

When the pronoun functions as the subject or object of an infinitive, always use *whom.*

As Hyun began her job search, she thought about whom to ask for advice.

COMMON ERRORS

Who or *whom*

In writing, the distinction between *who* and *whom* is still often observed. *Who* and *whom* follow the same rules as other pronouns: *Who* is the subject pronoun; *whom* is the object pronoun. If you are dealing with an object, *whom* is the correct choice.

Incorrect   Who did you send the letter to?
                 Who did you give the present to?
Correct   To whom did you send the letter?
                 Whom did you give the present to?

Who is always the right choice for a subject pronoun.

Correct   Who gave you the present?
                 Who brought the cookies?

If you are uncertain of which one to use, try substituting *she* and *her* or *he* and *him*.

Incorrect   You sent the letter to she [who]?
Correct   You sent the letter to her [whom]?

Incorrect   Him [Whom] gave you the present?
Correct   He [Who] gave you the present?

Remember: *Who* = subject
             Whom = object

For step-by-step discussion, examples, and practice exercises, visit this page of the E-book at www.mycomplab.com.

Whoever versus *whomever*

With the same rule in mind, you can distinguish between *whoever* and *whomever*. Which is correct?

> Her warmth touched **whoever** she met.
>
> Her warmth touched **whomever** she met.

In this sentence the pronoun functions as a direct object: Her warmth touched everyone she met, not someone touched her. Thus *whomever* is the correct choice.

> **Exercise 36.2**   In the following sentences, fill in the blank with the correct pronoun: *who, whom, whoever,* or *whomever*.
>
> > **Example**   Soon the Japanese people will select new members of Parliament, some of *whom* are prominent celebrities.
>
> 1. Seats in the Japanese Parliament have lately gone to candidates _____ have high ambitions, fame, and no political experience.
> 2. Atsushi Onita is a professional wrestler _____ cries Fire! when he enters the ring and _____ believes in strict parental disciplining of children.
> 3. One of the candidates for _____ many will vote is Emi Watanabe, a former Olympic figure skater _____ deplores the mounting costs of health care.
> 4. _____ the Japanese vote for, one thing is certain.
> 5. _____ wins will have done so after an unprecedented wave of sports star campaigning.

Pronouns in comparisons

When you write a sentence using a comparison that includes *than* or *as* followed by a pronoun, usually you will have to think about which pronoun is correct. Which of the following is correct?

> Vimala is a faster swimmer than **him**.
>
> Vimala is a faster swimmer than **he**.

The test that will give you the correct answer is to add the verb that finishes the sentence—in this case, *is*.

Incorrect Vimala is a faster swimmer than **him is.**

Correct Vimala is a faster swimmer than **he is.**

Adding the verb makes the correct choice evident.

In some cases the choice of pronoun changes the meaning. Consider these examples:

She likes ice cream more than **me.** [A bowl of ice cream is better than hanging out with me.]

She likes ice cream more than **I.** [I would rather have frozen yogurt.]

In such cases it is better to complete the comparison:

She likes ice cream more than **I do.**

Possessive pronouns

Possessive pronouns are confusing at times because possessive nouns are formed with apostrophes, but possessive pronouns do not require apostrophes. Pronouns that use apostrophes are always **contractions**.

It's   = It is
Who's   = Who is
They're   = They are

The test for whether to use an apostrophe is to determine whether the pronoun is possessive or a contraction. The most confusing pair is *its* and *it's*.

Incorrect **Its** a sure thing she will be elected. [Contraction]
Correct **It's** a sure thing she will be elected. [**It is** a sure thing.]

Incorrect The dog lost **it's** collar. [Possessive]
Correct The dog lost **its** collar.

Whose versus *who's* follows the same pattern.

Incorrect	Who's bicycle has the flat tire? [Possessive]
Correct	Whose bicycle has the flat tire?

Incorrect	Whose on first? [Contraction]
Correct	Who's on first? [**Who is** on first?]

Possessive pronouns before -*ing* verbs

Pronouns that modify an -*ing* verb (called a *gerund*) or an -*ing* verb phrase (*gerund phrase*) should appear in the possessive.

Incorrect	The odds of you making the team are excellent.
Correct	The odds of your making the team are excellent.

Subject complements

Pronouns that function as subject complements are in the subjective case in formal writing. A subject complement is a word that follows a linking verb such as a form of *to be*. Objective pronouns are common in informal contexts, especially *It's me* instead of the more formal *It is I*.

Informal	Driving home, Thomas thought he saw his wife exit the grocery store and later confirmed it was her.
Formal	Driving home, Thomas thought he saw his wife exit the grocery store and later confirmed it was she.

Appositives

When a pronoun functions as an appositive, put it in the same case as the noun to which it refers.

Subjective case	The three company **principals**, Gary, Michelle, and I, decided to hire a financial analyst.
Objective case	My English teacher asked two **students**, Jennifer and me, to stay after class.

Subjects and objects of infinitives

Many people mistakenly put the pronoun subject of an infinitive in the subjective case. But when a pronoun is either the subject or object of an infinitive, it must be in the objective case.

Incorrect subject of infinitive	Our landlord wanted my roommate and **I to replace** the stained carpet.
Correct subject of infinitive	Our landlord wanted my roommate and **me to replace** the stained carpet.
Incorrect object of infinitive	My father asked my sister and me **to visit** our mother and **he** next summer.
Correct object of infinitive	My father asked my sister and me **to visit** our mother and **him** next summer.

Exercise 36.3   The following sentences include all the pronoun uses explained in this section. Underline the correct pronoun in each sentence.

Example   (<u>We</u>/Us) scholars generally look at subjects from a critical distance, but we must never forget to impose that critical distance on our own lives too.

1. The Gurkhas are a division in the British armed forces (who/whom) originate from Nepal.
2. Between 1814 and 1816 several Nepalese hill tribes successfully contained the advancing British army, even though the British were far more technically advanced than (they/them).
3. Thinking that (us/we) warriors should stick together, the British enlisted the Nepalese tribesmen to fight in the specially formed Gurkha division.
4. (Whomever/Whoever) wished to join the Gurkhas had to know someone already serving in the British army; it was an extremely prestigious battalion to be a part of.
5. (Its/It s) amazing to think that nearly 200 years later, money earned from Gurkha pensions and salaries constitutes the largest single source of foreign exchange for the Nepalese economy.

36b Pronoun Agreement

Because pronouns usually replace or refer to other nouns, they must match those nouns in number and gender. The noun that the pronoun replaces is called its **antecedent**. If pronoun and antecedent match, they are in **agreement**. When a pronoun is close to the antecedent, usually there is no problem.

Maria forgot **her** coat.

The band members collected **their** uniforms.

When pronouns and the nouns they replace are separated by several words, sometimes the agreement in number is lost.

When the World Wrestling Federation (WWF) used wrestlers **[PLURAL]** to represent nations, there was no problem identifying the villains. He **[SING]** was the enemy if he **[SING]** came from Russia. But after the Cold War, wrestlers **[PLURAL]** can switch from good guys to bad guys. We don't immediately know how he **[SING]** has been scripted—good or bad.

Careful writers make sure that pronouns match their antecedents.

Collective nouns

Collective nouns (such as *audience, class, committee, crowd, family, herd, jury, team*) can be singular or plural depending on whether the emphasis is on the group or on the particular individuals.

Correct   The **committee** was unanimous in its decision.

Correct   The **committee** put their opinions ahead of the goals of the unit.

Often a plural antecedent is added if the sense of the collective noun is plural.

Correct   The individual committee **members** put their opinions ahead of the goals of the unit.

COMMON ERRORS

Indefinite pronouns

Indefinite pronouns (such as *anybody, anything, each, either, everybody, everything, neither, none, somebody, something*) refer to unspecified people or things. Most take singular pronouns.

Incorrect   **Everybody** can choose **their** roommates.

Correct   **Everybody** can choose **his or her** roommate.

Correct alternative   **All students** can choose **their** roomates.

A few indefinite pronouns (*all, any, either, more, most, neither, none, some*) can take either singular or plural pronouns.

Correct   **Some** of the shipment was damaged when **it** became overheated.

Correct   **All** thought **they** should have a good seat at the concert.

A few are always plural (*few, many, several*).

Correct   **Several** want refunds.

Remember: Words that begin with *any, some,* and *every* are usually singular.

 For step-by-step discussion, examples, and practice exercises, visit this page of the E-book at www.mycomplab.com.

Generic nouns

Related to collective nouns are categorical nouns that identify a person, place, or thing as a member of a particular class or type. With a categorical noun we tend to think immediately of the plural concept and often slip into plural pronoun usage. But you should always look at how the noun functions grammatically in the sentence.

| **Incorrect** | Each French professor at the local college had **their** own office. |
| **Correct** | Each French professor at the local college had *his or her* own office. |

Pronoun agreement with compound antecedents

Antecedents joined by *and* take plural pronouns.

| **Correct** | **Moncef and Driss** practiced *their* music. |

Exception: When compound antecedents are preceded by *each* or *every,* use a singular pronoun.

| **Correct** | **Every male cardinal and warbler** arrives before the female to define *its* territory. |

When compound antecedents are connected by *or* or *nor,* the pronoun agrees with the antecedent closest to it.

Incorrect	**Either the Ross twins or Angela** should bring **their** CDs.
Correct	**Either the Ross twins or Angela** should bring *her* CDs.
Better	**Either Angela or the Ross twins** should bring *their* CDs.

(Continued on next page)

COMMON ERRORS *(continued)*

When you put the plural *twins* last, the correct choice becomes the plural pronoun *their*.

Remember:
1. **Use plural pronouns for antecedents joined by *and*.**
2. **Use singular pronouns for antecedents preceded by *each* or *every*.**
3. **Use a pronoun that agrees with the nearest antecedent when compound antecedents are joined by *or* or *nor*.**

 For step-by-step discussion, examples, and practice exercises, visit this page of the E-book at www.mycomplab.com.

Exercise 36.4 In the following sentences, pronouns are separated from the nouns they replace. Underline the antecedent and fill in the pronoun that agrees with it in the blank provided.

Example Ironically, greyhounds are rarely gray; *their* fur can be all shades of red, brown, gray, and brindle.

1. Canine experts disagree on the origin of the name greyhound, but many believe _____ derives from Greek hound.

2. For over 5,000 years, greyhounds have been prized for _____ regal bearing and grace.

3. Greyhounds were introduced into England by the Cretans around 500 BC, but _____ are best known as the mascot for America s number-one bus line.

4. King Cob was the first notable greyhound sire recorded after England began documenting canine pedigrees in 1858, and _____ fathered 111 greyhounds in three years.

5. Each greyhound King Cob fathered was of the purest pedigree, even though _____ great-grandfather was a bulldog.

Exercise 36.5   Underline the indefinite pronouns, collective nouns, and compound antecedents in the paragraph that follows. Circle the related pronouns, and, if necessary, revise them to agree with their antecedents. In some cases, you may have to decide whether the emphasis is on the group or individuals within the group.

Example   Many stories attempt to explain why the number 13 is
considered unlucky, but they provide no evidence that
Friday is a particularly unlucky day. In fact, if everyone
he or she
were to follow stories from Greek history, they might
be avoiding ladders and sidewalk cracks on Tuesday
the 13th.

Although few would admit it, he or she often take(s) extra precautions on Friday the 13th. Some are so paralyzed by fear that they are simply unable to get out of his or her bed when Friday the 13th comes around. The Stress Management Center and Phobia Institute estimate(s) that more than 17 million people admit to being extra careful as they drive and go about their business on this day. Perhaps they are right to be concerned! A team writing for a British medical journal has shown that there is a significant increase in traffic accidents on Friday the 13th. However, this fear seems to be directed toward cars. According to representatives from both airlines, neither Delta nor Continental Airlines suffer from any noticeable drop in travel on Friday the 13th.

36c Problems with Pronouns and Gender

English does not have a neutral singular pronoun for a group of mixed genders or a person of unknown gender. Referring to a group of mixed genders using male pronouns is unacceptable to many people. Unless the school in the following example is all male, many readers would object to the use of *his*.

Sexist   **Each student** must select **his** courses using the online registration system.

Some writers attempt to avoid sexist usage by substituting a plural pronoun. This strategy, however, produces a grammatically incorrect sentence that also risks putting off some readers.

Incorrect   **Each student** must select **their** courses using the online registration system.

One strategy is to use *his or her* instead of *his.*

Correct   **Each student** must select **his or her** courses using the online registration system.

Often you can avoid using *his or her* by changing the noun to the plural form.

Better   **All students** must select **their** courses using the online registration system.

In some cases, using *his or her* may be necessary. Use this construction sparingly.

COMMON ERRORS

Problems created by the pronoun *one* used as a subject

Some writers use *one* as a subject in an attempt to sound more formal. At best this strategy produces writing that sounds stilted, and at worst it produces annoying errors.

Sexist   **One** can use **his** brains instead of a calculator to do simple addition.

Incorrect   **One** can use **their** brains instead of a calculator to do simple addition. [Agreement error: *Their* does not agree with *one*.]

(Continued on next page)

COMMON ERRORS *(continued)*

Incorrect When **one** runs a 10K race for the first time, **you** often start out too fast. [Pronoun shift error: *One* changes to *you*.]

Correct **One** can use *his or her* brains instead of a calculator to do simple addition.

Correct **One** can use *one's* brains instead of a calculator to do simple addition.

You're better off avoiding using *one* as the subject of sentences.

Better *Use your brain* instead of a calculator for simple addition.

Remember: **Avoid using the pronoun *one* as a subject.**

For step-by-step discussion, examples, and practice exercises, visit this page of the E-book at www.mycomplab.com.

Exercise 36.6 The following sentences contain examples of gender bias. Rewrite the sentences using subject and pronoun formations that are unbiased. Try to avoid using his or her constructions.

Example When an American turns 18, he is bombarded with advertisements that market easy credit.

Revise When *Americans* turn 18, *they* are bombarded with advertisements that market easy credit.

1. When someone is financially overextended, he often considers credit cards as a way of making ends meet.
2. One might begin to convince himself that credit is the only way out.
3. But each adult must weigh the advantages and disadvantages of her own credit card use.

4. Eventually, one may find himself deep in debt because of high credit rates and overspending.
5. Then, one option might be for the individual to find a debt consolidator to assist him.

36d Vague Reference

Pronouns can sometimes refer to more than one noun, thus confusing readers.

> The **coach** rushed past the injured **player** to yell at the **referee**. **She** was hit in the face by a stray elbow.

You have to guess which person *she* refers to — the coach, the player, or the referee. Sometimes you cannot even guess the antecedent of a pronoun.

> The new subdivision destroyed the last remaining habitat for wildlife within the city limits. **They** have ruined our city with their unchecked greed.

Whom does *they* refer to? the mayor and city council? the developers? the people who live in the subdivision? or all of the above?

Pronouns should never leave the reader guessing about antecedents. If different nouns can be confused as the antecedent, then the ambiguity should be clarified.

> **Vague**   Mafalda's pet boa constrictor crawled across Tonya's foot. **She** was mortified.

> **Better**   When Mafalda's pet boa constrictor crawled across Tonya's foot, Mafalda was mortified.

If the antecedent is missing, then it should be supplied.

> **Vague**   Mafalda wasn't thinking when she brought her boa constrictor into the crowded writing center. **They** got up and left the room in the middle of consultations.

> **Better**   Mafalda wasn't thinking when she brought her boa constrictor into the crowded writing center. A few students got up and left the room in the middle of consultations.

Remote pronouns

Pronouns are also vague if they are too far removed from their antecedents. It is confusing and annoying for a reader to have to search back through several sentences to find the noun to which the pronoun refers.

Incorrect Last summer, Joel worked as an intern at the *City Star*, his hometown's local newspaper. His immediate supervisor was Cathy Simon, the features editor. Joel had hoped he would be able to write some feature stories on local environmental issues but soon discovered his job mainly entailed making copies and answering phone calls. After the internship was over, Joel wrote **her** a letter, making suggestions about how the internship program might be improved for future interns.

Better Last summer, Joel worked as an intern at the *City Star*, his hometown's local newspaper. His immediate supervisor was Cathy Simon, the features editor. Joel had hoped he would be able to write some feature stories on local environmental issues but soon discovered his job mainly entailed making copies and answering phone calls. After the internship was over, Joel wrote a letter to **Simon**, making suggestions about how the internship program might be improved for future interns.

Vague use of *which* and *it*

Writers often use *which* or *it* vaguely or too broadly when they assume the reader will know what the pronoun refers to, or when they are uncertain about a point or idea.

Vague This semester, three students were caught copying their papers from the Internet and were only reprimanded, **which** shows how much the school has changed over the past twenty years.

Which fact shows how much the school has changed—the fact that students are cheating or the school's response to the cheating? To avoid vague usage, supply a clear antecedent for the pronoun.

> **Better** This semester, three students were caught copying their papers from the Internet and were only reprimanded, a policy which shows how much the school has changed over the past twenty years.

Implied antecedents

Pronouns should refer to specifically named antecedents. Pronouns cannot refer to an implied noun.

> **Incorrect** Because Susan had enjoyed reading Don DeLillo's novel *White Noise*, she went to **his** book signing at the local bookstore.

> **Correct** Because Susan had enjoyed reading Don DeLillo's novel *White Noise*, she went to **the author's** book signing at the local bookstore.

People commonly mistake a modifier for an antecedent, especially in the case of possessives, as illustrated in the incorrect example. The pronoun *his* requires the antecedent *DeLillo*—not *DeLillo's*, a word that functions as an adjective modifying *novel* in this sentence.

Indefinite use of *it*

Avoid using *they* and *it* as indefinite pronouns. Indefinite pronouns refer to unspecified people or things (see Section 36b), but *they* and *it* should refer to clear antecedents.

> **Incorrect** In the novel *Middlemarch*, **it** details Dorothea Brooke's struggle to escape the constraints of her oppressive marriage to Edward Causabon.

> **Correct** The novel *Middlemarch* details Dorothea Brooke's struggle to escape the constraints of her oppressive marriage to Edward Causabon.

COMMON ERRORS

Vague use of *this*

Always use a noun immediately after *this, that, these, those,* and *some.*

Vague   Enrique asked Meg to remove the viruses on his computer. **This** was a bad idea.

Was it a bad idea for Enrique to ask Meg because she was insulted? Because she didn't know how? Because removing viruses would destroy some of Enrique's files?

Better   Enrique asked Meg to remove the viruses on his computer. This imposition on Meg's time made her resentful.

Remember: Ask yourself "*this* what?" and add the noun that *this* refers to.

For step-by-step discussion, examples, and practice exercises, visit this page of the E-book at www.mycomplab.com.

People versus animals and things

Use *who, whom,* or *whose* to refer to persons. Use *which* or *that* to refer to objects. With named animals (pets) it is common to use *who, whom,* or *whose,* but *which* or *that* for unnamed animals.

Correct   My springer spaniel, Lily, is the kind of dog who loves to sleep all day.

Correct   The deer that live near suburban homes eat as much garbage as foliage.

WRITING IN THE WORLD

Pronouns in legal writing

Legal writing is often difficult to read, in part because lawyers often don't use many pronouns. The following paragraph is typical.

Legalese

Cancellations by participants received within thirty days of departure are subject to loss of the deposit paid in advance by participant plus cancellation costs for services rendered by the travel agency unless a substitute participant is found by the participant or the letter of cancellation from the participant is accompanied by a letter from a physician stating that the participant is not able to travel due to medical reasons, in which case the participant will not pay cancellation costs.

Legal writing does not have to be this difficult to understand. Some attorneys and others who write legal language wrongly believe that they can avoid any possible misunderstanding by not using pronouns. In fact, many states now require consumer contracts to be written in plain English. Using pronouns makes the contract readable.

Plain English

If you cancel within thirty days of departure, you will lose your deposit and you must pay for any services we have provided unless (1) you find a substitute, or (2) you send a letter from a physician stating that you cannot travel for medical reasons, in which case you lose only the deposit.

Chapter 37

Modifiers

Give life to your writing with modifiers.

37a Choose the Correct Modifier

Modifiers come in two varieties: adjectives and adverbs. The same words can function as adjectives or adverbs, depending on what they modify.

Adjectives modify

nouns—*iced* tea, *power* forward
pronouns—He is *brash*.

Adverbs modify

verbs—*barely* reach, drive *carefully*
adjectives—*truly* brave activist, *shockingly* red lipstick
other adverbs—*not* soon forget, *very* well
clauses—*Honestly*, I find ballet boring.

Adjectives answer the questions *Which one? How many?* and *What kind?* Adverbs answer the questions *How often? To what extent? When? Where? How?* and *Why?*

Use the correct forms of comparatives and superlatives

As kids, we used comparative and superlative modifiers to argue that Superman was *stronger* than Batman and recess was the *coolest* part of the day. Comparatives and superlatives are formed differently; all you need to know to determine which to use is the number of items you are comparing.

Comparative modifiers weigh one thing against another. They either end in *er* or are preceded by *more*.

Road bikes are faster on pavement than mountain bikes.

The more courageous juggler tossed flaming torches.

Superlative modifiers compare three or more items. They either end in *est* or are preceded by *most*.

April is the hottest month in New Delhi.

Wounded animals are the most ferocious.

When should you add a suffix instead of *more* or *most*? The following guidelines work in most cases:

Adjectives

- For adjectives of one or two syllables, add *er* or *est*.

  redder, heaviest

- For adjectives of three or more syllables, use *more* or *most*.

  more viable, most powerful

Adverbs

- For adverbs of one syllable, use *er* or *est*.

  nearer, slowest

- For adverbs with two or more syllables, use *more* or *most*.

  more convincingly, most humbly

Some frequently used comparatives and superlatives are irregular. The following list can help you become familiar with them.

Adjective	Comparative	Superlative
good	better	best
bad	worse	worst
little (amount)	less	least
many, much	more	most

Adverb	Comparative	Superlative
well	better	best
badly	worse	worst

Do not use both a suffix (*er* or *est*) and *more* or *most*.

Incorrect The service at Jane's Restaurant is **more slower** than the service at Alphonso's.

Correct The service at Jane's Restaurant is **slower** than the service at Alphonso's.

Be sure to name the elements being compared if they are not clear from the context.

Unclear comparative Mice are **cuter**.
Clear Mice are **cuter than rats**.

Unclear superlative Nutria are the **creepiest**.
Clear Nutria are the **creepiest rodents**.

Absolute modifiers cannot be comparative or superlative

Absolute modifiers are words that represent an unvarying condition and thus aren't subject to the degrees that comparative and superlative constructions convey. How many times have you heard something called *very unique* or *totally unique*? *Unique* means "one of a kind." There's nothing else like it. Thus something cannot be *very unique* or *totally unique*. It is either unique or it isn't. The United States Constitution makes a classic absolute modifier blunder when it begins, "We the People of the United States, in Order to form a more perfect Union. . . ." What is a *more perfect Union*? What's more perfect than perfect itself? The construction is nonsensical.

Absolute modifiers should not be modified by comparatives (*more* + modifier or modifier + *er*) or superlatives (*most* + modifier or modifier + *est*). Note the following list of common absolute modifiers.

absolute	impossible	unanimous
adequate	infinite	unavoidable
complete	main	uniform
entire	minor	unique
false	perfect	universal
fatal	principal	whole
final	stationary	
ideal	sufficient	

Exercise 37.1 Decide whether each word in parentheses should be comparative or superlative. Rewrite the word, adding either the correct suffix (*-er* or *-est*) or *good, best, bad, worst, more, most, less,* or *least*. If you find an absolute modifier (a word that should not be modified), underline it.

Example Volkswagen's Beetle is the (good) *best* selling car in history even though it had the same body for 60 years and had undergone only <u>minor</u> mechanical changes.

1. The Model T is ranked second in sales, but it is perhaps (important) historically than the Beetle because it was the first car to be mass produced, paving the way for cars to be built (cheaply) and (quickly) than ever before.

2. Selling for about $300, the Model T wasn t the (expensive) car on the market in the 1920s, however; that unique honor belongs to the 1922 Briggs & Stratton Flyer, which sold for $125 to $150.

3. With a top speed of over 250 mph and a price well over $1,000,000, the Bugatti Veyron 16.4 is currently the (fast), (powerful), and (expensive) car in the world.
4. However, muscle cars, such as the Camaro, the Corvette, the Firebird, and the Mustang, are considered (dangerous) because they are both (fast) and (expensive) than a Bugatti the ideal car for a young and reckless crowd.
5. The (safe) car in history, the 1957 Aurora, is also the (rare); the one Aurora that was ever built was considered a complete failure.

Double negatives

In English, as in mathematics, two negatives equal a positive. Avoid using two negative words in one sentence, or you'll end up saying the opposite of what you mean. The following are negative words that you should avoid doubling up:

barely	nobody	nothing
hardly	none	scarcely
neither	no one	

Incorrect, double negative	**Barely no one** noticed that the pop star lip-synched during the whole performance.
Correct, single negative	**Barely anyone** noticed that the pop star lip-synched during the whole performance.
Incorrect, double negative	When the pastor asked if anyone had objections to the marriage, **nobody** said **nothing**.
Correct, single negative	When the pastor asked if anyone had objections to the marriage, **nobody** said **anything**.

COMMON ERRORS

Irregular adjectives and adverbs

Switch on a baseball interview and you will likely hear numerous modifier mistakes.

> Manager: We didn't play **bad** tonight. Martinez hit the ball **real good,** and I was glad to see Adamski pitch **farther** into the game than he did in his last start. His fastball was on, and he walked **less** hitters.

While this manager has his sports clichés down pat, he makes errors with five of the trickiest modifier pairs. In three cases he uses an adjective where an adverb would be correct.

Adjectives	Adverbs
bad	badly
good	well
real	really

[*Bad,* an adjective modifying the noun *call.*] The umpire made a **bad** call at the plate.

[*Badly,* an adverb modifying the verb *play.*] We didn't play **badly.**

[*Good,* an adjective modifying the noun *catch.*] Starke made a **good** catch.

[*Well,* an adverb modifying the verb *hit.*] Martinez hit the ball **well.**

Exception: *Well* acts as an adjective when it describes someone's health: Injured players must stay on the disabled list until they feel **well** enough to play every day.

[*Real,* an adjective modifying the noun *wood.*] While college players hit with aluminum bats, the professionals still use **real** wood.

(Continued on next page)

COMMON ERRORS *(continued)*

[*Really*, an adverb modifying the adverb *well*.] Martinez hit the ball really **well**.

The coach also confused the comparative adjectives *less* and *fewer,* and the comparative adverbs *farther* and *further.*

Adjectives
less—a smaller, uncountable amount
fewer—a smaller number of things

Less   Baseball stadiums with pricey luxury suites cater less to families and more to business people with expense accounts.

Fewer   He walked fewer hitters.

Adverbs
farther—a greater distance
further—to a greater extent, a longer time, or a greater number

Farther   Some players argue that today's baseballs go farther than baseballs made just a few years ago.

Further   The commissioner of baseball curtly denied that today's baseballs are juiced, refusing to discuss the matter further.

Remember: *Bad, good, real, less* (for uncountables), and *fewer* (for countables) are adjectives. *Badly, well, really, farther* (for distance), and *further* (for extent, time, or number) are adverbs. *Well* is an adjective when it describes health.

For step-by-step discussion, examples, and practice exercises, visit this page of the E-book at www.mycomplab.com.

Exercise 37.2 Revise the following paragraph to eliminate double negatives. More than one answer may be correct in each case.

Example   One ~~can't~~ *can* hardly survey the history of the American film industry without encountering the story of the Hollywood Ten, a group of artists targeted as communists.

After the creation of the House Un-American Activities Committee (HUAC), Cold War paranoia could not barely hide itself in post–World War II America. HUAC followed on the coattails of the 1938 Special Committee on Un-American Activities. This earlier committee did not focus not solely on communists; extremists from both the far left and the far right were targeted. By the 1940s, however, HUAC focused not on neither white supremacist nor pro-Nazi groups, but instead on the supposed communist infiltration of Hollywood. Scarcely no one could escape the grasp of HUAC; actors, producers, and directors all came under scrutiny. By the end of the proceedings, not hardly nobody remained unscathed. Hundreds in the entertainment industry were either fired or appeared on the infamous HUAC blacklist.

Exercise 37.3 The following words in parentheses are tricky adjective-adverb pairs. Underline the word(s) being modified in the sentence, and circle the correct adjective or adverb from the pair.

Example   To ensure the success of their missions, NASA has tackled the <u>challenge</u> of enabling <u>astronauts</u> to eat (healthy/(healthily)) in space so that <u>they</u> can stay (good/(well)).

In the early days of manned space missions, NASA had (fewer/less) problems feeding astronauts. But the (further/farther) astronauts traveled, the (further/farther) NASA had to go to ensure healthy eating in space. For example, the Mercury missions of the early 1960s took (fewer/less) time than an actual meal, so NASA's (real/really) challenge didn't come until crews were in space for longer periods of time. However, these shorter trips worked (good/well) as tests for experimental astronaut foods. By the mid-1960s, the astronauts on the Gemini missions were offered better ways to prepare and enjoy food in space. Engineers eventually discovered that packaging food in an edible liquid or gelatin container would prevent it from crumbling and damaging the equipment (bad/badly). By the Space Shuttle expeditions of the 1980s and 1990s, (real/really) headway had been made in terms of (good/well) dining technology, and crew members could devise their own menus.

37b Place Adjectives Carefully

As a general rule, the closer you place a modifier to the word it modifies, the less the chance you will confuse your reader. This section and the next elaborate on this maxim, giving you the details you need to put it into practice. Most native speakers have an ear for many of the guidelines presented here, with the notable exception of the placement of limiting modifiers, which is explained in Section 37c.

Place adjective phrases and clauses carefully

Adjective clauses frequently begin with *when, where,* or a relative pronoun like *that, which, who, whom,* or *whose.* An adjective clause usually follows the noun or pronoun it modifies.

> **Adjective clause modifying *salon*:** The **salon** where I get my hair styled is raising its prices.

> **Adjective clause modifying *stylist*:** I need to find a **stylist** who charges less.

Adjective phrases and clauses can also come before the person or thing they modify.

Adjective phrase modifying *girl*: Proud of her accomplishment, the little **girl** showed her trophy to her grandmother.

Adjective phrases or clauses can be confusing if they are separated from the word they modify.

Confusing   Watching from the ground below, the kettle of broadwing hawks circled high above the observers.

Is the kettle of hawks watching from the ground below? You can fix the problem by putting the modified subject immediately after the modifier or placing the modifier next to the modified subject.

Better   The kettle of broadwing hawks circled high above the **observers** who were watching from the ground below.

Better   Watching from the ground below, the **observers** saw a kettle of broadwing hawks circle high above them.

See dangling modifiers in Section 37e.

Exercise 37.4   Underline the adjective phrases and clauses in the following sentences. If any phrase or clause could apply to more than one subject, revise the sentence to eliminate ambiguity.

Example   Arriving June 19, 1865, the Texas slaves were informed of their freedom <u>by Union soldiers</u> two years after the signing of the Emancipation Proclamation.

Rewrite   Arriving June 19, 1865, two years after the signing of the Emancipation Proclamation, Union soldiers informed Texas slaves of their freedom.

1. Now known as Juneteenth, Texas celebrates the day Texan slaves discovered their freedom.
2. A people s event that has become an official holiday, freed slaves celebrated annually their day of emancipation.

3. Celebrated vigorously in the 1950s and 1960s, the Civil Rights movement sparked a renewed interest in the Juneteenth holiday.
4. Still going strong, entertainment, education, and self-improvement are all activities included in the annual celebration.

Place one-word adjectives before the modified word(s)

One-word adjectives almost always precede the word or words they modify.

Pass the hot sauce, please.

When one-word adjectives are not next to the word or words being modified, they can create misunderstandings.

Unclear   Before his owner withdrew him from competition, the **fiercest** rodeo's bull injured three riders.

Readers may think *fiercest* modifies *rodeo's* instead of *bull*. Placing the adjective before *bull* will clarify the meaning.

Better   Before his owner withdrew him from competition, the rodeo's **fiercest** bull injured three riders.

Exception: predicate adjectives follow linking verbs

Predicate adjectives are the most common exception to the norm of single-word adjectives preceding words they modify. Predicate adjectives follow linking verbs such as *is, are, was, were, seem, feel, smell, taste,* and *look.* Don't be fooled into thinking they are adverbs. If the word following a linking verb modifies the subject, use a predicate adjective. If it modifies an action verb, use an adverb. Can you identify the word being modified in the following sentence?

I feel odd.

Odd modifies the subject *I*, not the verb *feel.* Thus, *odd* is a predicate adjective that implies the speaker feels ill. If it were an adverb, the sentence would read *I feel oddly*. The adverb *oddly* modifying *feel* would imply the speaker senses things in unconventional ways. Try the next one:

> The bruise looked bad.

Since *bad* modifies *bruise, bad* is a predicate adjective implying a serious injury. *Looked* is the linking verb that connects the two. If we made the modifier an adverb, the sentence would read *The bruise looked badly*, conjuring the creepy notion that the bruise had eyes but couldn't see well. You can avoid such bizarre constructions if you know when to use predicate adjectives with linking verbs.

Put subjective adjectives before objective adjectives

When you have a series of adjectives expressing both opinion and more objective description, put the subjective adjectives before the objective ones. For example, in

> the sultry cabaret singer

sultry is subjective and *cabaret* is objective.

Put determiners before other adjectives

Determiners are a group of adjectives that include possessive nouns (such as *woman's* prerogative and *Pedro's* violin), possessive pronouns (such as *my, your,* and *his*), demonstrative pronouns (*this, that, these, those*), and indefinite pronouns (such as *all, both, each, either, few,* and *many*). When you are using a series of adjectives, put the determiners first.

> our finest hour
>
> Tara's favorite old blue jeans
>
> those crazy kids

When you are using a numerical determiner with another determiner, put the numerical determiner first.

> both **those** tattoos
>
> all **these** people

Exercise 37.5   Underline the adjectives in the following paragraph. If any are placed ambiguously or incorrectly, revise them.

Example   Johnny Cash was an American *influential American* country singer and songwriter.

Cash was known for his deep voice as well as his dark clothing and demeanor. These traits all earned him the nickname "The Man in Black." Keeping with his dark demeanor, much of Cash's music, especially that of his later career, echoed themes of sorrow, struggle moral, and redemption. One of his popular most songs, "Ring of Fire," was actually penned by his future wife, June Carter. The song may sound happy, but it is dark. It describes inner Carter's turmoil as she wrestled with her forbidden love for the wild, unpredictable Cash. Rocky Johnny Cash and June Carter's relationship was award-winning depicted in the 2005 film, *Walk the Line.*

37c Place Adverbs Carefully

For the most part, the guidelines for adverb placement are not as complex as the guidelines for adjective placement.

Place adverbs before or after the words they modify

Single-word adverbs and adverbial clauses and phrases can usually sit comfortably either before or after the words they modify.

Dimitri quietly **walked** down the hall.

Dimitri **walked** quietly down the hall.

Conjunctive adverbs—*also, however, instead, likewise, then, therefore, thus,* and others—are adverbs that show how ideas relate to one another. They prepare a reader for contrasts, exceptions, additions, conclusions, and other shifts in an argument. Conjunctive adverbs can usually fit well into more than one place in the sentence. In the following example, *however* could fit in three different places.

Between two main clauses

Professional football players earn exorbitant salaries; however, they pay for their wealth with lifetimes of chronic pain and debilitating injuries.

Within second main clause

Professional football players earn exorbitant salaries; they pay for their wealth, however, with lifetimes of chronic pain and debilitating injuries.

At end of second main clause

Professional football players earn exorbitant salaries; they pay for their wealth with lifetimes of chronic pain and debilitating injuries however.

Subordinating conjunctions—words such as *after, although, because, if, since, than, that, though, when,* and *where*—often begin **adverb clauses**. Notice that we can place adverb clauses with subordinating conjunctions either before or after the word(s) being modified:

After someone in the audience yelled, he **forgot** the lyrics.

He **forgot** the lyrics after someone in the audience yelled.

While you have some leeway with adverb placement, follow the advice in Section 37d: Avoid distracting interruptions between the subject and verb, the verb and the object, or within the verb phrase. A long adverbial clause is usually best placed at the beginning or end of a sentence.

Avoid squinting modifiers

In some situations placing a modifier next to the word or phrase it modifies is still unclear; the modifier needs to be on one side or the other. Be especially careful to avoid a **squinting modifier**, an adverb between two verb phrases. The reader won't know which verb phrase it modifies.

Confusing   Tim grabbed the plate hungrily carried by the waiter.

Who's hungry, Tim or the waiter? Placing the adverb before the verb it modifies will clarify.

Better Tim hungrily grabbed the plate carried by the waiter.

Confusing The Chens left the kittens sadly playing in a cage at the pound.

Who's sad, the kittens or the Chens? Again, the sentence will be clearer if we place the adverb efore the verb it modifies.

Better The Chens sadly left the kittens playing in a cage at the pound.

COMMON ERRORS

Placement of limiting modifiers

Words such as *almost, even, hardly, just, merely, nearly, not, only,* and *simply* are called limiting modifiers. Although people often play fast and loose with their placement in everyday speech, limiting modifiers should always go immediately before the word or words they modify in your writing. Many writers have difficulty with the placement of *only*. Like other limiting modifiers, *only* should be placed immediately before the word it modifies.

Incorrect The Gross Domestic Product **only** gives one indicator of economic growth.

Correct The Gross Domestic Product gives **only** one indicator of economic growth.

Remember: Place limiting modifiers immediately before the word(s) they modify.

For step-by-step discussion, examples, and practice exercises, visit this page of the E-book at www.mycomplab.com.

Exercise 37.6 Rewrite each of the following sentences, moving the adverb to eliminate possible confusion. Place adverbs where they make the most logical sense within the context of the sentence. Underline the adverbs in your revised sentences.

> **Example** In the mid-1800s, Father Gregor Mendel developed experiments ingeniously examining the area of heredity.
>
> **Revise** In the mid-1800s, Father Gregor Mendel <u>ingeniously</u> developed experiments examining the area of heredity.

1. Mendel s work focused on initially hybridizing the Lathyrus, or sweet pea.
2. The Lathyrus possessed variations conveniently composed of differing sizes and colors.
3. Hybridizing the plants easily allowed Mendel to view the mathematical effects of dominant and recessive trait mixing.
4. By crossing white-flowered pea pods with red-flowered pea pods, Mendel proved successfully existing pairs of hereditary factors determined the color characteristics of offspring.
5. Though published in 1866, Mendel s theory of heredity remained unnoticed mostly by the biological community until the early 1900s.

37d Revise Disruptive Modifiers

The fundamental way readers make sense of sentences is to identify the subject, verb, and object. Modifiers can sink a sentence if they interfere with the reader's ability to connect the three. Usually, single-word modifiers do not significantly disrupt a sentence. However, avoid placing modifying clauses and phrases between a subject and a verb, between a verb and an object, and within a verb phrase.

Disruptive The forest fire, **no longer held in check by the exhausted firefighters**, jumped the firebreak. [Separates the subject from the verb]

Better No longer held in check by the exhausted firefighters, the forest fire jumped the firebreak. [Puts the modifier before the subject]

Disruptive The fire's heat seemed to melt, **at a temperature hot enough to liquefy metal**, the saplings in its path. [Separates the verb from the object]

Better At a temperature hot enough to liquefy metal, the fire's heat seemed to melt the saplings in its path. [Puts the modifier before the subject]

WRITING IN THE WORLD

Split infinitives

An infinitive is *to* plus the base form of a verb. A split infinitive occurs when an adverb separates *to* from the base verb form.

Infinitive = *To* + Base verb form

Examples: **to feel, to speak, to borrow**

Split infinitive = *To* + Modifier + Base verb form

Examples: **to strongly feel, to barely speak, to liberally borrow**

The most famous split infinitive in recent history occurs in the opening credits of *Star Trek* episodes: "to boldly go where no one has gone before." The alternative without the split infinitive is "to go boldly where no one has gone before." The writers in *Star Trek* no doubt were aware they were splitting an infinitive, but they chose *to boldly go* because they wanted the emphasis on *boldly*, not *go*.

(Continued on next page)

Nevertheless, many split infinitives are considered awkward for good reason.

Awkward	You have to get away from the city lights **to better appreciate** the stars in the night sky.
Better	You have to get away from the city lights to appreciate the stars in the night sky better.
Awkward	**To, as planned, stay** in Venice, we need to reserve a hotel room now.
Better	To stay in Venice as planned, we need to reserve a hotel room now.

When a sentence would sound strange without the adverb's splitting the infinitive, you can either retain the split or, better yet, revise the sentence to avoid the problem altogether.

Acceptable	When found by the search party, the survivors were able to barely whisper their names.
Alternative	When found by the search party, the survivors could barely whisper their names.

Exercise 37.7   Underline the disruptive modifiers in the following paragraph. You may find a modifying clause or phrase that separates major components of a sentence, or you may find a split infinitive. Rewrite the paragraph to eliminate the disruptions. More than one way of revising may be correct.

Example	The Catholic papacy, <u>because of conflict in the Papal States</u>, resided in France for more than seventy years.
Revise	Because of conflict in the Papal States, the Catholic papacy resided in France for more than seventy years.

In the thirteenth and fourteenth centuries, the Italian Papal States, because of militantly rivaling families, were consumed in chaos. In 1305 the cardinals elected, unable to agree on an Italian, a Frenchman as the new pope. He decided to temporarily remain in France. The papacy would, because of various religious and political reasons, remain in France until 1378. Rome, during the papacy's seventy-year absence, would lose both prestige and income.

37e Revise Dangling Modifiers

Some modifiers are ambiguous because they could apply to more than one word or clause. Dangling modifiers are ambiguous for the opposite reason; they don't have a word to modify. In such cases the modifier is usually an introductory clause or phrase. What is being modified should immediately follow the phrase, but in the following sentence it is absent.

After bowling a perfect game, Surfside Lanes hung Marco's photo on the wall.

Neither the subject of the sentence, *Surfside Lanes,* nor the direct object, *Marco's photo,* is capable of bowling a perfect game. Since a missing noun or pronoun causes a dangling modifier, simply rearranging the sentence will not resolve the problem. You can eliminate a dangling modifier in two ways:

1. Insert the noun or pronoun being modified immediately after the introductory modifying phrase.

   After bowling a perfect game, Marco was honored by having his photo hung on the wall at Surfside Lanes.

2. Rewrite the introductory phrase as an introductory clause to include the noun or pronoun.

   After Marco bowled a perfect game, Surfside Lanes hung his photo on the wall.

Exercise 37.8 Each of the following sentences contains a dangling modifier. Revise the sentences to eliminate dangling modifiers according to the methods described in Section 37e. More than one way of revising may be correct.

Example Though it preceded Woodstock, popular music history often obscures the Monterey Pop Festival.

Revise Though the Monterey Pop Festival preceded Woodstock, it is often obscured by popular music history.

1. Lasting for three days in June of 1967, over thirty artists performed.
2. The largest American music festival of its time, attendance totaled over 200,000.
3. With artists such as Ravi Shankar, Otis Redding, and The Who, the fans encountered various musical genres.
4. Performing live for the first time in America, fans howled as Jimi Hendrix set his guitar on fire.
5. Establishing a standard for future festivals, Woodstock and Live Aid would eventually follow suit.

Understanding Punctuation and Mechanics

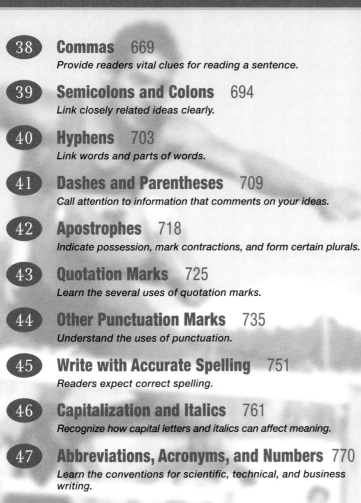

Chapter 38

Commas

Provide readers vital clues for reading a sentence.

38a Commas with Introductory Elements

Introductory elements usually need to be set off by commas. Introductory words or phrases signal a shift in ideas or a particular arrangement of ideas; they help direct the reader's attention to the writer's most important points. Commas force the reader to pause and take notice of these pivotal elements.

Common introductory elements

Conjunctive adverbs	Introductory phrases
however	of course
therefore	above all
nonetheless	for example
also	in other words
otherwise	as a result
finally	on the other hand
instead	in conclusion
thus	in addition

When a conjunctive adverb or introductory phrase begins a sentence, the comma follows.

Therefore, the suspect could not have been at the scene of the crime.

Above all, remember to let water drip from the faucets if the temperature drops below freezing.

When a conjunctive adverb comes in the middle of a sentence, set it off with commas preceding and following.

If you really want to prevent your pipes from freezing, however, you should insulate them before the winter comes.

Conjunctive adverbs and phrases that do not require commas

Occasionally the conjunctive adverb or phrase blends into a sentence so smoothly that a pause would sound awkward.

Awkward Of course, we'll come.

Better Of course we'll come.

Awkward Even if you take every precaution, the pipes in your home may freeze, nevertheless.

Better Even if you take every precaution, the pipes in your home may freeze nevertheless.

Sometimes the presence or absence of a comma can affect the meaning. For example:

Of course, we'll come. [Be reassured that we will come.]

Of course we'll come. [There is no doubt we will come.]

COMMON ERRORS

Commas with long introductory modifiers

Long subordinate clauses or phrases that begin sentences should be followed by a comma. The following sentence lacks the needed comma.

Incorrect Because cell phones now have organizers and email stand-alone personal digital assistants have become another technology of the past.

(Continued on next page)

COMMON ERRORS *(continued)*

When you read this sentence, you likely had to go back to sort it out. The words *organizers and email stand-alone personal digital assistants* tend to run together. When the comma is added, the sentence is easier to understand because the reader knows where the subordinate clause ends and where the main clause begins:

Correct   Because cell phones now have organizers and email, stand-alone personal digital assistants have become another technology of the past.

How long is a long introductory modifier? Short introductory adverbial phrases and clauses of five words or fewer can get by without the comma if the omission does not mislead the reader. Using the comma is still correct after short introductory adverbial phrases and clauses:

Correct   In the long run stocks have always done better than bonds.

Correct   In the long run, stocks have always done better than bonds.

Remember: Put commas after long introductory modifiers.

 For step-by-step discussion, examples, and practice exercises, visit this page of the E-book at www.mycomplab.com.

Exercise 38.1   Underline conjunctive adverbs, introductory phrases, and long introductory modifiers in the following sentences. Then set off those elements with commas when necessary.

Example   <u>Although king cobras have small fangs</u>, one bite is poisonous enough to kill an elephant.

1. King cobras in fact have a poisonous bite from the moment they are born.

2. Even though king cobras carry lethal venom women in Thailand's King Cobra Club dance with the snakes' heads in their mouths.
3. Also many Southeast Asian countries worship the king cobra.
4. Above all avoid provoking king cobras; they are not aggressive animals if left undisturbed.
5. An antidote is available however if you are bitten by a cobra.

38b Commas with Compound Clauses

Two main clauses joined by a coordinating conjunction (*and, or, so, yet, but, nor, for*) form a compound sentence (see Section 32e). Writers sometimes get confused about when to insert a comma before a coordinating conjunction.

Use a comma to separate main clauses

Main clauses carry enough grammatical weight to be punctuated as sentences. When two main clauses are joined by a coordinating conjunction, place a comma before the coordinating conjunction in order to distinguish them.

> Sandy borrowed two boxes full of CDs on Tuesday, and she returned them on Friday.

Very short main clauses joined by a coordinating conjunction do not need commas.

> She called and she called, but no one answered.

Do not use a comma to separate two verbs with the same subject

> **Incorrect**   Sandy borrowed two boxes full of CDs on Tuesday, and returned them on Friday.

Sandy is the subject of both *borrowed* and *returned*. This sentence has only one main clause; it should not be punctuated as a compound sentence.

Correct   Sandy borrowed two boxes full of CDs on Tuesday and returned them on Friday.

Exceptions to this rule occur when there is a lapse of time or after *said.*

He did not study, and failed.

"That's fine," he said, and went on reading.

COMMON ERRORS

Commas in compound sentences

The easiest way to distinguish between compound sentences and sentences with phrases that follow the main clause is to isolate the part that comes after the conjunction. If the part that follows the conjunction can stand on its own as a complete sentence, insert a comma. If it cannot, omit the comma.

Main clause plus phrases

Mario thinks he lost his passport while riding the bus or by absentmindedly leaving it on the counter when he checked into the hostel.

Look at what comes after the coordinating conjunction *or:*

by absentmindedly leaving it on the counter when he checked into the hostel

This group of words is not a main clause and cannot stand on its own as a complete sentence. Do not set it off with a comma.

(Continued on next page)

Main clauses joined with a conjunction

On Saturday Mario went to the American consulate to get a new passport, but the officer told him that replacement passports could not be issued on weekends.

Read the clause after the coordinating conjunction *but*:

the officer told him that replacement passports could not be issued on weekends

This group of words can stand on its own as a complete sentence. Thus, it is a main clause; place a comma before *but*.

Remember:

1. Place a comma before the coordinating conjunction (*and, but, for, or, nor, so, yet*) if there are two main clauses.

2. Do not use a comma before the coordinating conjunction if there is only one main clause.

For step-by-step discussion, examples, and practice exercises, visit this page of the E-book at www.mycomplab.com.

Do not use a comma to separate a main clause from a restrictive clause or phrase

When clauses and phrases that follow the main clause are essential to the meaning of a sentence, they should not be set off with a comma.

Incorrect   Sandy plans to borrow Felicia's record collection, while Felicia is on vacation.

Correct   Sandy plans to borrow Felicia's record collection while Felicia is on vacation.

Incorrect	Sandy plans to borrow Felicia's records while Felicia is on vacation, in order to convert them to CDs.
Correct	Sandy plans to borrow Felicia's records while Felicia is on vacation in order to convert them to CDs.

COMMON ERRORS

Do not use a comma to set off a *because* clause that follows a main clause

Writers frequently place unnecessary commas before *because* and similar subordinate conjunctions that follow a main clause. *Because* is not a co-ordinating conjunction; thus it should not be set off by a comma unless the comma improves readability.

Incorrect	I struggled to complete my term papers last year, because I didn't know how to type.
Correct	I struggled to complete my term papers last year because I didn't know how to type.

But do use a comma after an introductory *because* clause.

Incorrect	Because Danny left his red jersey at home Coach Russell benched him.
Correct	Because Danny left his red jersey at home, Coach Russell benched him.

Remember: Use a comma after a *because* clause that begins a sentence. Do not use a comma to set off a *because* clause that follows a main clause.

 For step-by-step discussion, examples, and practice exercises, visit this page of the E-book at www.mycomplab.com.

Exercise 38.2   Decide which of the coordinating conjunctions in the following sentences should be preceded by commas and add them.

Example   In their heyday, ABBA topped the charts in the United States and Britain‸ and only Volvo was a bigger export in Sweden.

1. The band ABBA was together only from 1974 to 1982 yet their hit "Dancing Queen" is still popular today.

2. ABBA is best known for its music but the group also made a movie titled *ABBA—The Movie*.

3. The quartet's two married couples had success as musicians but not as husbands and wives.

4. After their divorces, group members parted ways and began solo careers.

5. ABBA's songs no longer top the charts but in 2001 their music was featured in a Broadway musical called *Mamma Mia*.

38c Commas with Nonrestrictive Modifiers

Imagine that you are sending a friend a group photo that includes your aunt. Which sentence is correct?

In the back row the woman wearing the pink hat is my aunt.

In the back row the woman, wearing the pink hat, is my aunt.

Both sentences can be correct depending on what is in the photo. If there are three women standing in the back row and only one is wearing a pink hat, this piece of information is necessary for identifying your aunt. In this case the sentence without commas is correct because it identifies your aunt as the woman wearing the pink hat. Such necessary modifiers are **restrictive** and do not require commas.

If only one woman is standing in the back row, *wearing the pink hat* is extra information and not necessary to identify your aunt. The modifier in this case is **nonrestrictive** and is set off by commas.

Distinguish restrictive and nonrestrictive modifiers

You can distinguish restrictive and nonrestrictive modifiers by deleting the modifier and then deciding whether the remaining sentence is changed. For example, delete the modifier *still stained by its bloody Tianamen Square crackdown* from the following sentence:

> Some members of the Olympic Site Selection Committee wanted to prevent China, still stained by its bloody Tianamen Square crackdown, from hosting the 2008 games.

The result leaves the meaning of the main clause unchanged.

> Some members of the Olympic Site Selection Committee wanted to prevent China from hosting the 2008 games.

The modifier is nonrestrictive and should be set off by commas.

In contrast, deleting *who left work early* does change the meaning of this sentence:

> The employees who left work early avoided driving home in the blizzard.

Without the modifier the sentence reads:

> The employees avoided driving home in the blizzard.

Now it sounds as if all the employees avoided driving home in the blizzard instead of just the ones who left early. The modifier is clearly restrictive and does not require commas.

Recognize types and placement of nonrestrictive modifiers

Nonrestrictive modifiers are used frequently to add details. You can add several kinds of nonrestrictive modifiers to a short, simple sentence (see Sections 32c and 32d).

> The student ran across campus,
>
> which left him panting when he got to class. [adjective clause]
> his backpack swaying back and forth. [absolute phrase]
> weaving his way down the crowded sidewalks. [participial phrase]

Nonrestrictive modifiers can be placed at the beginning of sentences.

When he realized his watch had stopped, [adverb clause]
With his thoughts on the intramural championship later that
afternoon, [prepositional phrase]
Rushing to get to class, [participial phrase]

the student ran across campus.

They also can be placed in the middle of sentences.

The student,

who had woken up only fifteen minutes before class, [adjective clause]
my old roommate, [appositive]
wearing a ripped black trenchcoat, [participial phrase]
with one arm in a cast and the other clutching a stack of books,
[prepositional phrase]

ran across campus.

Pay special attention to appositives

Clauses and phrases can be restrictive or nonrestrictive, depending on the context. Often the difference is obvious, but some modifiers require close consideration, especially appositives. An **appositive** is a noun or noun phrase that identifies or adds information to the noun preceding it.

Consider the following pair.

1 The world's most popular music players iPods changed the way people purchase and listen to music.

2 The world's most popular music players, iPods, changed the way people purchase and listen to music.

Which is correct? The appositive *iPods* is not essential to the meaning of the sentence and offers additional information. Sentence 2 is correct.

Here's another pair.

1 The civil rights activist Jesse Jackson runs an organization called the Rainbow Coalition.

2   The civil rights activist, Jesse Jackson, runs an organization called the Rainbow Coalition.

The name *Jesse Jackson* is essential to identifying which of the many civil rights activists is under discussion. Thus, it is a restrictive appositive and should not be set off with commas. Sentence 1 is correct.

Use commas around nonrestrictive clauses within a *that* clause

Restrictive clauses beginning with *that* sometimes have a nonrestrictive clause embedded within them.

Incorrect   I want you to know that despite all the arguments we have had over the past few months I still value your advice.

Correct   I want you to know that, despite all the arguments we have had over the past few months, I still value your advice.

Use commas to mark off parenthetical expressions

A **parenthetical expression** provides information or commentary that is usually not essential to the sentence's meaning.

Incorrect   My mother much to my surprise didn't say anything when she saw my pierced nose.

Correct   My mother, much to my surprise, didn't say anything when she saw my pierced nose.

Some parenthetical expressions are essential to the point of the sentence, especially ones that make contrasts, but they too are set off by commas.

Incorrect   The candidate's conversational skills not her résumé landed her the job.

Correct	The candidate's conversational skills, not her résumé, landed her the job.

However, do not use a comma when the parenthetical expression is one word and its function is not obviously parenthetical.

Incorrect	The Freshmen Studies course is, fundamentally, an introduction to writing arguments.
Correct	The Freshmen Studies course is fundamentally an introduction to writing arguments.

COMMON ERRORS

Commas with *that* and *which* clauses

Writers often confuse when to use commas to set off modifying phrases beginning with *that* and *which*. *That* clauses follow a hard and fast rule: They are used only as restrictive modifiers.

A *that* clause is a restrictive modifier: Omit commas

Two other women were wearing the same dress that Sherice bought specifically to wear to the awards banquet.

Which clauses are usually used as nonrestrictive modifiers. While *which* clauses can also function as restrictive modifiers, careful writers observe the difference and change *which* to *that* if the clause is restrictive.

A *which* clause is a nonrestrictive modifier: Use commas

A student government committee is recommending the allocation of an additional $10,000 for Black History Month festivities, which take place in February, in order to bring a nationally known speaker to campus.

(Continued on next page)

COMMON ERRORS *(continued)*

When a *which* clause acts as a restrictive modifier, change *which* to that

Incorrect   The uncertainty **which** surrounded the selection of the new coach was created by the sudden and unexpected resignation of her predecessor.

Correct   The uncertainty **that** surrounded the selection of the new coach was created by the sudden and unexpected resignation of her predecessor.

Remember:

1. *That* clauses are restrictive modifiers and do not take commas.

2. *Which* clauses can be either restrictive or nonrestrictive, but careful writers use them as nonrestrictive modifiers and set them off with commas.

For step-by-step discussion, examples, and practice exercises, visit this page of the E-book at www.mycomplab.com.

Use commas to mark off absolute phrases

An **absolute phrase** contains at least one noun or pronoun and at least one participle (see Section 32d). Absolutes can modify a noun or a whole sentence.

Incorrect   Her project completed Marianne decided to splurge on a beach vacation.

Correct   Her project completed, Marianne decided to splurge on a beach vacation.

Incorrect	Their recess privileges taken away the boys sat slumped in the classroom's uncomfortable chairs.
Correct	Their recess privileges taken away, the boys sat slumped in the classroom's uncomfortable chairs.

Exercise 38.3 The underlined portions of the following paragraph are modifiers. Identify each modifier as either restrictive or nonrestrictive. Then set off the nonrestrictive modifiers with commas.

Example Marcus Ulpius Traianus, a successful governor and soldier, became the Roman emperor in the year AD 98.
(Nonrestrictive modifier)

Trajan decided to use the Empire's coffers which were brimming with war booty to begin a massive building program. He commissioned the market Mercati Traianei and a lush new forum. In AD 113 he also built a column still on display in Rome today adorned with reliefs depicting his military victories. But the conditions that many Romans faced from day to day stood in stark contrast to the splendor Trajan created. Living in cramped apartment buildings people coped with dark, dirty, and sometimes cold homes.

38d Commas with Items in a Series

In a series of three or more items, place a comma after each item but the last one. The comma between the last two items goes before the coordinating conjunction (*and, or, nor, but, so, for, yet*).

Health officials in Trenton, Manhattan, and the Bronx have all reported new cases of the West Nile virus.

WRITING IN THE WORLD

Commas between the last two items in a series

Whether you should insert a comma between the last two items in a series depends on what kind of writing you're doing. In newspapers and magazines, the comma is typically omitted; however, academic, business, and professional writing includes a comma before the last series item. Omitting the comma sometimes causes confusion.

Journalistic convention	I thank my parents, Robert Pirsig and Harley-Davidson for my outlook on life.
Academic convention	I thank my parents, Robert Pirsig, and Harley-Davidson for my outlook on life.

Exercise 38.4   Insert commas to separate items in a series, following the academic convention. Some sentences may not require commas.

Example   Suburban residents unknowingly spread diseases among deer by feeding them salt, corn, and pellets.

1. White-tailed deer ground squirrels gray squirrels foxes raccoons coyotes opossums and armadillos often wander across my back yard.
2. White-tailed deer and coyotes are among the animals that have adapted best to urban habitats.
3. Deer find cover in urban green belts and thrive on young trees shrubs and flowers that homeowners plant.
4. White-tailed deer reproduce quickly because they have always been prey animals for wolves coyotes mountain lions bobcats and bears.
5. Elimination of predators curtailment of hunting and a high birth rate have led to deer overpopulation in many urban areas.

38e Commas with Coordinate Adjectives

Coordinate adjectives are two or more adjectives that independently modify the same noun. Coordinate adjectives that are not linked by *and* must be separated by a comma.

> After the NASDAQ bubble burst in 2000 and 2001, the Internet technology companies that remain are no longer the fresh-faced, giddy kids of Wall Street.

Distinguish coordinate adjectives

You can recognize coordinate adjectives by reversing their order; if their meaning remains the same, the adjectives are coordinate and must be linked by *and* or separated by a comma. In the following example when the order of the adjectives changes, the description of *lifestyles* retains the same meaning:

> Because border collies are bred to herd sheep, their energetic temperaments may not suit city dwellers' more sedentary, staid lifestyles.

> Because border collies are bred to herd sheep, their energetic temperaments may not suit city dwellers' more staid, sedentary lifestyles.

Do not use commas to link cumulative adjectives

Commas are not used between cumulative adjectives. Cumulative adjectives are two or more adjectives that work together to modify a noun: *deep blue sea, inexpensive mountain bike*. If reversing their order changes the description of the noun (or violates the order of English, such as *mountain inexpensive bike*), the adjectives are cumulative and should not be separated by a comma.

The following example doesn't require a comma in the cumulative adjective series *massive Corinthian*.

> Visitors to Rome's Pantheon pass between the massive Corinthian columns flanking the front door.

We know they are cumulative because reversing their order to read *Corinthian massive* would alter the way they modify *columns*—in this case, so much so that they no longer make sense.

Exercise 38.5   Identify each underlined adjective series as either coordinate or cumulative. Then insert commas to separate coordinate adjectives.

Example   In 2007, Apple announced that over 100 million <u>portable media</u> players, or iPods, have been sold worldwide.
(Cumulative)

This makes the iPod the <u>best-selling music</u> player in history and one of the most <u>successful electronic</u> devices of all time. The idea for the iPod emerged when the company began creating <u>new innovative</u> software for the growing market of <u>consumer digital</u> devices such as digital cameras, personal organizers, and camcorders. All of these items were more successful than not only <u>big clunky digital music</u> players but also <u>small useless digital music</u> players with <u>unbelievably awkward</u> interfaces, both of which were already on the market. Consequently, Apple decided to develop their <u>own Mac-compatible</u> product that would put, according to <u>savvy well-known</u> CEO Steve Jobs, "1000 songs in your pocket."

38f Commas with Quotations

Properly punctuating quotations with commas can be tricky unless you know a few rules about when and where to use commas.

When to use commas with quotations

Commas set off phrases that attribute quotations to a speaker or writer, such as *he argues, they said,* and *she writes.*

"When you come to a fork in the road," said Yogi Berra, "take it!"

If the attribution follows a quotation that is a complete sentence, replace the period that normally would come at the end of the quotation with a comma.

Incorrect "Simplicity of language is not only reputable but perhaps even sacred." writes Kurt Vonnegut.

Correct "Simplicity of language is not only reputable but perhaps even sacred," writes Kurt Vonnegut.

When an attribution is placed in the middle of a quotation, put the comma preceding the attribution within the quotation mark just before the phrase.

Incorrect "Nothing is at last sacred", wrote Emerson in his 1841 essay, "but the integrity of your own mind."

Correct "Nothing is at last sacred," wrote Emerson in his 1841 essay, "but the integrity of your own mind."

When not to use commas with quotations

Do not replace a question mark or exclamation point with a comma.

Incorrect "Who's on first," Costello asked Abbott.

Correct "Who's on first?" Costello asked Abbott.

Not all phrases that mention the author's name are attributions. When quoting a term or using a quotation within a subordinate clause, do not set off the quotation with commas.

"Stonewall" Jackson gained his nickname at the First Battle of Bull Run when General Barnard Bee shouted to his men that "Jackson is standing like a stone wall."

Even a quotation that is a complete sentence can be used in a subordinate clause. Such quotations should not be set off with commas. Pay special attention to quotations preceded by *that, which*, and *because*; these words are the most common indicators of a subordinate clause.

It was Benjamin Franklin's conviction that "Those who would give up essential liberty to purchase a little temporary safety deserve neither liberty nor safety."

Exercise 38.6   Read the following paragraph for errors in comma usage with quotations. Some are used correctly. Cross out unnecessary commas, move misplaced commas, and add omitted commas.

Example   When inspecting a painting for authenticity, try looking for an angle that catches the glare of lights. "You will not be able to see what the paintings show," asserts author James Elkins, "but you'll get a good look at the *craquelure*."

Craquelure is, "the fine network of cracks that scores the surface of . . . paintings" (Elkins 20). Elkins explains that "few museum visitors realize how many paintings have been seriously damaged" and goes on to list possible hazards, such as damage by, "fire, water, vandalism, or just the wear and tear of the centuries" (20). Not all cracks are signs of legitimate age; indeed "Counterfeiters have faked cracks by putting paintings in ovens, and they have even rubbed ink in the cracks to make them look old" (Elkins 22). Though cracks often happen with mishandling, Elkins explains that, "most cracks in paintings that are not caused by accidents are due to the flexing of the canvas or the slow warping of the wood" (22). If you are serious about art history, you may want to learn how to read the cracks in art work. "*Craquelure* is not a hard-and-fast method of classifying paintings," admits Elkins "but it comes close" (24).

38g Commas with Dates, Numbers, Titles, and Addresses

Some of the easiest comma rules to remember are the ones we use every day in dates, numbers, personal titles, place names, direct address, and brief interjections.

Commas with dates

Use commas to separate the day of the week from the month and to set off a year from the rest of the sentence.

> March 25, 1942
>
> Monday, November 18, 2002
>
> On July 27, 2010, the opening ceremony of the World Scout Jamboree will be televised.

Do not use a comma when the month immediately precedes the year.

> 12 June 1988
>
> April 2008

Commas with numbers

Commas mark off thousands, millions, billions, and so on.

> 16,500,000

However, do not use commas in street addresses or page numbers.

> page 1542
>
> 7602 Elm Street

Commas with personal titles

When a title follows a person's name, set the title off with commas.

> Marcus Welby, MD
>
> Jackie Hart, Vice President for Operations, reported that her company's earnings were far ahead of projections.

Commas with place names

Place a comma between street addresses, city names, state names, and countries.

Poughkeepsie, New York

Lima, Peru

Write to the president at 1600 Pennsylvania Avenue, Washington, DC 20500.

Commas in direct address

When addressing someone directly, set off that person's name in commas.

I was happy to get your letter yesterday, Jamie.

Yes, Virginia, there is a Santa Claus.

Commas with brief interjections

Use commas to set off brief interjections like *yes* and *no*, as well as short questions that fall at the ends of sentences.

The director said that, no, the understudy would not have to stand in for the lead tonight.

Have another piece of pie, won't you?

Exercise 38.7 The fictitious business letter that follows is missing commas with dates, numbers, personal titles, place names, direct addresses, and brief interjections. Insert commas where they are needed.

Mazaces' Headquarters
Cairo Egypt
December 13 332 BC

Parmenio
Commander of Syria
Damascus Syria

Dear Parmenio:

Thank you for your latest correspondence dated December 9 332 BC. I am pleased to hear the streets of Damascus remain quiet since our arrival in October 333 and that mighty Syria has adjusted herself to our presence.

To other matters. I write to request 4,000 of your most rested troops be sent to Egypt to arrive no later than January 1 331 BC. The fighting in Gaza was bitter and our enemy merciless; my soldiers are tired and need to recuperate before marching westward.

I busy myself with the construction of the city of Alexandria. Address future correspondence to 12 Conquest Avenue Alexandria where I will soon move in order to oversee the construction directly. Deinocrates head architect has seen to every detail, but of course detail requires time. I remain here until the spring when I intend for our armies to reunite and travel west to Thapsacus Mesopotamia where we will meet Darius King of Persia and secure his defeat for our mutual triumph and to the glory of Greece.

Sincerely,
Alexander the Great (Alex)

38h Commas to Avoid Confusion

Certain sentences can confuse readers if you do not indicate where they should pause within the sentence. Use a comma to guide a reader through these usually compact constructions.

Unclear   With supplies low prices of gasoline and fuel oil will increase.

This sentence could be read as meaning *With supplies, low prices will increase.*

Clear   With supplies low, prices of gasoline and fuel oil will increase.

Exercise 38.8 Some of the sentences in the following paragraph are confusing because they lack clarifying commas. Add commas where readers need more clues about how to read the sentences.

Example Using new ways of dating, scientists can now apply multiple techniques to determine an object's age.

Because geologists used both radiometric and fossil dating we now know that the Colorado River started carving the Grand Canyon only five or six million years ago. Scientists were able to accurately date the Shroud of Turin believed by many Catholics to be Christ's burial covering to between AD 1260 and 1390. This particular example of carbon dating challenged some believers to weigh faith against science. The mysterious Sphinx stands before the pyramid of Khafre dated using the "star method." Scientists determined that the Sphinx and its host pyramid are approximately seventy years younger than was originally believed.

38i Unnecessary Commas

Do not place a comma between a subject and a predicate

Incorrect American children of immigrant parents, often do not speak their parents' native language.

Correct American children of immigrant parents often do not speak their parents' native language.

However, you do use commas to set off modifying phrases that separate subjects from verbs.

Incorrect Steven Pinker author of *The Language Instinct* argues that the ability to speak and understand language is an evolutionary adaptive trait.

Correct Steven Pinker, author of *The Language Instinct*, argues that the ability to speak and understand language is an evolutionary adaptive trait.

Do not use a comma with a coordinating conjunction unless it joins two main clauses

Incorrect   Susana thought finishing her first novel was hard, but soon learned that getting a publisher to buy it was much harder.

Correct   Susana thought finishing her first novel was hard but soon learned that getting a publisher to buy it was much harder.

Correct   Susana thought finishing her first novel was hard, but she soon learned that getting a publisher to buy it was much harder.

Do not use a comma after a subordinating conjunction such as *although, despite,* or *while*

Incorrect   Although, soccer is gaining popularity in the States, it will never be as popular as football or baseball.

Correct   Although soccer is gaining popularity in the States, it will never be as popular as football or baseball.

Do not use a comma before *than*

Some writers mistakenly use a comma with *than* to try to heighten the contrast in a comparison.

Incorrect   Any teacher will tell you that acquiring critical thinking skills is more important, than simply memorizing information.

Correct   Any teacher will tell you that acquiring critical thinking skills is more important than simply memorizing information.

Do not use a comma before a list

A common mistake is to place a comma after *such as* or *like* before introducing a list.

Incorrect Many hourly workers, such as, waiters, dishwashers, and cashiers, do not receive health benefits from their employers.

Correct Many hourly workers, such as waiters, dishwashers, and cashiers, do not receive health benefits from their employers.

Chapter 39

Semicolons and Colons

Link closely related ideas clearly.

39a Semicolons with Closely Related Main Clauses

Why use semicolons? Sometimes we want to join two main clauses to form a complete sentence in order to indicate their close relationship. We can connect them with a comma and a coordinating conjunction like *or, but,* or *and.* However, using those constructions too often can make your writing cumbersome. Instead you can omit the comma and coordinating conjunction, and insert a semicolon between the two clauses.

Semicolons can join only clauses that are grammatically equal. In other words, they join main clauses only to other main clauses, not to phrases or subordinate clauses. Look at the following examples:

Incorrect   ⌐————————————MAIN CLAUSE————————————⌐
Gloria's new weightlifting program will help her recover
⌐——————————⌐ ⌐————————PARTICIPIAL PHRASE————————
from knee surgery; doing a series of squats and presses
⌐——————————⌐
with a physical therapist.

Incorrect   ⌐————————————MAIN CLAUSE————————————⌐
Gloria's new weightlifting program will help her regain
⌐——————————⌐ ⌐————SUBORDINATE CLAUSE————
strength in her knee; which required surgery after she
⌐——————————⌐
injured it skiing.

Correct   ⌐————————————MAIN CLAUSE————————————⌐
Gloria's new weightlifting program will help her recover
⌐——————————⌐ ⌐————————MAIN CLAUSE————————
from knee surgery; a physical therapist leads her through
⌐——————————⌐
a series of squats and presses.

COMMON ERRORS

Main clauses connected with transitional words and phrases

Closely related main clauses sometimes use a conjunctive adverb (such as *however, therefore, moreover, furthermore, thus, meanwhile, nonetheless, otherwise;* see the list in Section 38a) or a transition (*in fact, for example, that is, for instance, in addition, in other words, on the other hand, even so*) to indicate the relationship between them. When the second clause begins with a conjunctive adverb or a transition, a semicolon is needed to join the two clauses. This sentence pattern is frequently used; therefore, it pays to learn how to punctuate it correctly.

Incorrect (comma splice)	The police and city officials want to crack down on drug use at raves, however, their efforts have been unsuccessful so far.
Correct	The police and city officials want to crack down on drug use at raves; however, their efforts have been unsuccessful so far.

The semicolon separates the second main clause from the first. Note that a comma is also needed to separate *however* from the rest of the second clause.

Incorrect (comma splice)	The poster design left much to be desired, for example, the title was printed in garish red, orange, and green.
Correct	The poster design left much to be desired; for example, the title was printed in garish red, orange, and green.

(Continued on next page)

COMMON ERRORS *(continued)*

Note that in addition to the semicolon, a comma separates *for example* from the rest of the second clause.

Remember: Main clauses that use a conjunctive adverb or a transitional phrase require a semicolon to join the clauses.

For step-by-step discussion, examples, and practice exercises, visit this page of the E-book at www.mycomplab.com.

Do not use a semicolon to introduce quotations

Use a comma or a colon instead.

Incorrect	Robert Frost's poem "Mending Wall" contains this line; "Good fences make good neighbors."
Correct	Robert Frost's poem "Mending Well" contains this line: "Good fences make good neighbors."

Do not use a semicolon to introduce lists

Incorrect	William Shakespeare wrote four romance plays at the end of his career; *The Tempest, The Winter's Tale, Cymbeline,* and *Pericles.*
Correct	William Shakespeare wrote four romance plays at the end of his career: *The Tempest, The Winter's Tale, Cymbeline,* and *Pericles.*

39b Semicolons Together with Commas

When an item in a series already includes a comma, adding more commas to separate it from the other items will only confuse the reader. Use semicolons instead of commas between items in a series that have internal punctuation.

Confusing   The church's design competition drew entries from as far away as Gothenberg, Sweden, Caracas, Venezuela, and Athens, Greece.

Clearer   The church's design competition drew entries from as far away as Gothenberg, Sweden; Caracas, Venezuela; and Athens, Greece.

Exercise 39.1   Decide where semicolons should go in the following paragraph. Add any semicolons that would repair run-on sentences, fix comma splices, or clarify a list. Also eliminate any incorrectly used semicolons and insert the correct punctuation.

Example   In the summer of 1947 a flying object crashed in eastern New Mexico⍈ the incident feeds speculation that the government hides evidence of UFOs.

    The media reported that the wreckage of a flying saucer had been discovered on a ranch near Roswell, military spokespeople came up with another explanation. They asserted that the flying saucer was actually a balloon, people stationed at the base, however, reported seeing unidentifiable bodies removed from the wreckage. Initially even UFO enthusiasts believed the government's reports; which seemed plausible at the time. The Air Force has declared the case closed they stated that the bodies at the crash sites were test dummies. Roswell, New Mexico, joins the list of rumored UFO hot spots that includes Delphos, Kansas, Marshall County, Minnesota, Westchester, New York, and Gulf Breeze, Florida.

39c Colons in Sentences

Like semicolons, colons can join two closely related main clauses (complete sentences). Colons indicate that what follows will explain or expand on what comes before the colon. Use a colon in cases where the second main clause interprets or sums up the first.

> Because most victims of bird flu catch the virus from animals, it is not likely to cause a pandemic in its present form: the influenza virus would have to mutate so that it could be easily transmitted from person to person for a pandemic to be possible.

You may choose to capitalize the first word of the main clause following the colon or leave it lowercase. Either is correct as long as you are consistent throughout your text.

Colons linking main clauses with appositives

A colon calls attention to an appositive, a noun, or a noun phrase that renames the noun preceding it. If you're not certain whether a colon would be appropriate, put *namely* in its place. If *namely* makes sense when you read the main clause followed by the appositive, you probably need to insert a colon instead of a comma. Remember, the clause that precedes the colon must be a complete sentence.

> I know the perfect person for the job, namely me.

The sentence makes sense with *namely* placed before the appositive. Thus, a colon is appropriate.

> I know the perfect person for the job: me.

Never capitalize a word following a colon unless the word starts a complete sentence or is normally capitalized (see Chapter 46).

Colons joining main clauses with quotations

Use a colon to link a main clause and a quotation that interprets or sums up the clause. Be careful not to use a colon to link a phrase with a quotation.

Incorrect: noun phrase–colon–quotation

> President Roosevelt's strategy to change the nation's panicky attitude during the Great Depression: "We have nothing to fear," he said, "but fear itself."

Correct: main clause–colon–quotation

President Roosevelt's strategy to end the Great Depression was to change the nation's panicky attitude: "We have nothing to fear," he said, "but fear itself."

Also, a colon is often used after a main clause to introduce an indented block quotation (see Section 22d).

WRITING SMART

Punctuation following quotations

Writing often requires quoting someone else's words. Use the correct sequence of punctuation marks when sharing a quotation with readers.

Place semicolons and colons outside quotation marks

Commas and periods that come after a quotation sit inside the quotation marks. The rule is different, however, for semicolons and colons: They sit outside the quotation marks. Because commas and periods always appear inside the quotation marks, semicolons and colons may seem incorrectly placed if you don't know that they follow a different rule.

Put commas and periods inside the quotation marks
"The length of a film," said Alfred Hitchcock, "should be directly related to the endurance of the human bladder."

Put semicolons outside quotation marks
Chicago mayor Richard Daley said, "The police are not here to create disorder. They're here to preserve disorder"; his misstatement hit at the truth underlying the violent treatment of protestors at the 1968 Democratic Convention.

(Continued on next page)

WRITING SMART *(continued)*

Put colons outside quotation marks

"I believe, absolutely, that if you do not break out in that sweat of fear when you write, then you have not gone far enough"**:** Dorothy Allison reassures would-be writers that they can begin on guts alone.

Remember: Little dogs (commas, periods) sleep in the house. Big dogs (semicolons, colons) sleep outside.

For more on using quotation marks correctly, see Chapter 43.

39d Colons with Lists

Use a colon to join a main clause to a list. The main clauses in these cases sometimes include the phrases *the following* or *as follows*. Remember that a colon cannot join a phrase or an incomplete clause to a list.

Incorrect: noun phrase–colon–list

Three posters decorating Juan's apartment**:** an old Los Lobos concert poster, a view of Mount Rainier, and a Diego Rivera mural.

Correct: main clause–colon–list

Juan bought three posters to decorate his apartment**:** an old Los Lobos concert poster, a view of Mount Rainier, and a Diego Rivera mural.

Incorrect: incomplete clause–colon–list

Volunteers aid biologists in**:** erosion control, trail maintenance, tree planting, and cleanup.

Correct: main clause without a colon

Volunteers aid biologists in erosion control, trail maintenance, tree planting, and cleanup.

COMMON ERRORS

Colons misused with lists

Some writers think that anytime they introduce a list, they should insert a colon. Colons are used correctly only when a complete sentence precedes the colon.

Incorrect   Jessica's entire wardrobe for her trip to Cancun included**:** two swimsuits, one pair of shorts, two T-shirts, a party dress, and a pair of sandals.

Correct   Jessica's entire wardrobe for her trip to Cancun included two swimsuits, one pair of shorts, two T-shirts, a party dress, and a pair of sandals.

Correct   Jessica jotted down what she would need for her trip**:** two swimsuits, one pair of shorts, two T-shirts, a party dress, and a pair of sandals.

Remember: A colon should be placed only after a clause that can stand by itself as a sentence.

 For step-by-step discussion, examples, and practice exercises, visit this page of the E-book at www.mycomplab.com.

Exercise 39.2   Decide where colons should go in the following sentences; add any that are necessary. Eliminate any incorrectly used colons and insert correct punctuation.

Example   Sandra Cisneros has written a number of books, including: *My Wicked, Wicked Ways; Woman Hollering Creek;* and the acclaimed novel *The House on Mango Street.*

1. *The House on Mango Street* tells the story of a Mexican-American girl who has a telling name, Esperanza (Hope).
2. Because *The House on Mango Street* consists of forty-four short vignettes, critics disagree on the book's genre, autobiography, short story, novel, or poetry.
3. Whatever its genre, *The House on Mango Street* has attracted the attention of feminist and Chicano literary critics both groups appreciate the complex portrayal of racism and sexism from a young girl's perspective.
4. Cisneros dedicates the novel to women of the barrio whose stories she wants to tell "For the ones I left behind, for the ones who cannot get out."

Chapter 40

Hyphens

Link words and parts of words.

Hyphens (-) are frequently confused with dashes (—), which are similar but longer. Dashes are used to separate phrases. Hyphens are used to join words.

40a Hyphens with Compound Modifiers

When to hyphenate

Hyphenate a compound modifier that precedes a noun.
When a compound modifier precedes a noun, you should usually hyphenate the modifier. A compound modifier consists of words that join together as a unit to modify a noun. Since the first word modifies the second, compound modifiers will not make sense if the word order is reversed.

middle-class values	self-fulfilling prophecy
best-selling novel	soft-hearted friend
well-known musician	ill-mannered child

Hyphenate a phrase when it is used as a modifier that precedes a noun.

out-of-body experience	step-by-step instructions
all-you-can-eat buffet	all-or-nothing payoff
devil-may-care attitude	over-the-counter drug

Hyphenate the prefixes *pro-*, *anti-*, *post-*, *pre-*, *neo-*, and *mid-* before proper nouns.

pro-Catholic sentiment	mid-Atlantic states
neo-Nazi racism	anti-NAFTA protests
pre-Columbian art	post-Freudian theory

Hyphenate a compound modifier with a number when it precedes a noun.

eighteenth-century drama	one-way street
tenth-grade class	47-minute swim

When not to hyphenate

Do not hyphenate a compound modifier that follows a noun.

Avoid using hyphens in compound modifiers when they come after the noun.

The instructor's approach is student centered.

Among country music fans George Strait is well known.

Do not hyphenate compound modifiers when the first word is *very* or ends in *ly*.

newly recorded data	very cold day
freshly painted bench	very jolly baby

Do not hyphenate chemical terms.

calcium chloride base	hydrochloric acid solution

Do not hyphenate foreign terms used as adjectives.

a priori decision	*post hoc* fallacy

Exercise 40.1   In the following sentences, decide where hyphens should be placed. Some sentences may require more than one hyphen and some sentences may need hyphens deleted.

> **Example**   Since there are few clear enemies of the state in the post‸Soviet era, political parties lack a galvanizing issue.

1. Some people consider the Electoral College to be un-democratic.
2. Independent candidates are often viewed as fly by night long shots with little or no hope of winning positions of power.
3. The tension surrounding the five week wait for the 2000 presidential election results was palpable.
4. Mostly-negative political ads are becoming more common.
5. Local candidates' political debates are rarely considered important enough to interrupt regularly-scheduled programming.
6. Candidates with free market economic policies are often popular with large corporations, which in turn make substantial donations to the candidates with favorable platforms.

40b Hyphens with Compound Nouns

A compound noun is made up of two or more words that work together to form one noun. You cannot change the order of words in a compound noun or remove a word without altering the noun's meaning. No universal rule guides the use of hyphens with compound nouns; the best way to determine whether a compound noun is hyphenated is to check the dictionary.

Some hyphenated compound nouns

T-shirt	one-bagger	time-out
sister-in-law	heart-to-heart	great-grandfather
play-by-play	speed-reading	run-through

Some compound nouns that are not hyphenated

picture window	oneself	time zone
hedgehog	heartland	baby boom
open house	speed of light	playbook

While there's no set rule for all cases of compound nouns, some pre-fixes and suffixes that commonly require hyphens are *ex-*, *all-*, *self-*, and *-elect*.

All-American	president-elect
self-conscious	ex-employee

COMMON ERRORS

Hyphens with numbers

Whole numbers between twenty-one and ninety-nine are hyphenated when they are written as words.

Incorrect   twentysix

Correct   twenty-six

Incorrect   sixteen-hundred

Correct   sixteen hundred

Incorrect   fiftytwo

Correct   fifty-two

(Continued on next page)

COMMON ERRORS *(continued)*

Also, hyphens connect the numerators and denominators in most fractions.

> The glass is one-half full.

A few fractions used as nouns, especially fractions of time, distance, and area, do not take hyphens.

> A half century passed before the mistake was uncovered.

Remember: Numbers between twenty-one and ninety-nine and most fractions are hyphenated when written as words.

For step-by-step discussion, examples, and practice exercises, visit this page of the E-book at www.mycomplab.com.

40c Hyphens That Divide Words at the Ends of Lines

A hyphen can show that a word is completed on the next line. Hyphens divide words only between syllables.

> The Jackson family waited out the tor-
> nado in their storm cellar.

Unless you have a special reason for dividing words at the ends of lines, you should avoid doing it. One special situation might be the need to fit as much text as possible on each line of the narrow columns in a newsletter format. Another might be the need to fit text inside the cells of a table.

WRITING SMART

Automatic hyphenation

Word processing programs, including Microsoft Word, allow automatic hyphenation of your document. Hyphenations that break words at the ends of lines are common in newspaper and magazine articles that are printed in narrow columns. However, this use of hyphens is rarely necessary in academic papers. Unless you are creating a brochure or other document with narrow columns, leave the automatic hyphenation turned off.

40d Hyphens for Clarity

Certain words, often ones with the prefixes *anti-*, *re-*, and *pre-*, can be confusing without hyphens. Adding hyphens to such words will show the reader where to pause to pronounce them correctly.

The courts are in much need of repair.

The doubles final will re-pair the sister team of Venus and Serena Williams.

Reform in court procedure is necessary to bring cases quickly to trial.

The thunderclouds re-formed after the hard rain, threatening another deluge.

Chapter 41

Dashes and Parentheses

Call attention to information that comments on your ideas.

41a Dashes and Parentheses Versus Commas

Like commas, parentheses and dashes enclose material that adds, explains, or digresses. However, the three punctuation marks are not interchangeable. The mark you choose depends on how much emphasis you want to place on the material. Dashes indicate the most emphasis. Parentheses offer somewhat less, and commas offer less still.

Commas indicate a moderate level of emphasis

Bill covered the new tattoo on his bicep, a pouncing tiger, because he thought it might upset our mother.

Parentheses lend a greater level of emphasis

I'm afraid to go bungee jumping (though my brother tells me it's less frightening than a roller coaster).

Dashes indicate the highest level of emphasis and, sometimes, surprise and drama

Christina felt as though she had been punched in the gut; she could hardly believe the stranger at her door was really who he claimed to be—the brother she hadn't seen in twenty years.

Exercise 41.1   Look at the modifying phrases that are underlined in the following paragraph. Use commas, parentheses, or dashes to set them off, based on the level of emphasis you want to create.

Example   Coffee₍ one of the most significant crops of all

time₍ has its origins in Africa₍like so many other

cornerstones of civilization₍.

Coffea arabica the official name for the bean was made
popular in Yemen. The Shadhili Sufi used coffee to inspire visions
and to stimulate ecstatic trances making coffee drinking a
spiritual experience. The use of the beverage spread largely
through other Muslims the Sufi had contact with, and by 1500 it
was well known throughout the Arab world. Cafes originated in
the Middle East. These early cafes one of the few secular public
spaces Muslims could congregate were seen as subversive.

41b Dashes and Parentheses to Set Off Information

Dashes and parentheses call attention to groups of words. In effect, they tell
the reader that a group of words is not part of the main clause and should
be given extra attention. Compare the following sentences.

When Shanele's old college roommate, Traci, picked her up at the
airport in a new car, a Porsche Boxster S convertible, she knew
that Traci's finances had changed for the better.

When Shanele's old college roommate, Traci, picked her up at the
airport in a new car (a Porsche Boxster S convertible), she knew
that Traci's finances had changed for the better.

When Shanele's old college roommate, Traci, picked her up at the
airport in a new car—a Porsche Boxster S convertible—she knew
that Traci's finances had changed for the better.

The Porsche Boxster S convertible is weighted differently in these three sentences because of punctuation. In the first, it is the name of the car. But in the third, it's as if an exclamation point were added—a Porsche Boxster S convertible!

The lesson here is simple enough. If you want to make an element stand out, especially in the middle of a sentence, use parentheses or dashes instead of commas.

Dashes with final elements

A dash is often used to set off an element at the end of a sentence that offers significant comments about the main clause. This construction is a favorite of newscasters, who typically pause for a long moment where the dash would be inserted in writing.

> The *Titanic* sank just before midnight on April 14, 1912, at a cost of over 1,500 lives—a tragedy that could have been prevented easily by reducing speed in dangerous waters, providing adequate lifeboat space, and maintaining a full-time radio watch.

Dashes can also anticipate a shift in tone at the end of a sentence.

> A full-sized SUV can take you wherever you want to go in style—if your idea of style is a gas-guzzling tank.

Parentheses with additional information

Parentheses are more often used for identifying information, afterthoughts or asides, examples, and clarifications. You can place full sentences, fragments, or brief terms within parentheses.

> Some argue that ethanol (the pet solution of politicians for achieving energy independence) costs more energy to produce and ship than it produces.

COMMON ERRORS

Do not use dashes as periods

Do not use dashes to separate two main clauses (clauses that can stand as complete sentences). Use dashes to separate main clauses from subordinate clauses and phrases when you want to emphasize the subordinate clause or phrase.

Incorrect: main clause–dash–main clause

I was one of the few women in my computer science classes— most of the students majoring in computer science at that time were men.

Correct: main clause–dash–phrase

I was one of the few women in computer science—a field then dominated by men.

Remember: Dashes are not periods and should not be used as periods.

For step-by-step discussion, examples, and practice exercises, visit this page of the E-book at www.mycomplab.com.

Exercise 41.2   Insert dashes and parentheses in the following sentences to set off information.

Example   Naples⌃founded by the Greeks, enlarged by the Romans, and ruled later by the Normans, Hohenstaufen, French, and Spanish⌃is one of the few European cities where the links to the ancient world remain evident.

1. Naples is a dirty and noisy metropolis in a spectacular setting a city that sprawls around the Bay of Naples with Mount Vesuvius at its back facing out to the islands of Procida, Ischia, and Capri.

2. The most famous eruption of Mt. Vesuvius the eruption that destroyed Pompeii and Herculaneum occurred in AD 79.

3. Some of the inhabitants of Pompeii decided to flee as the eruptions began, but they ran into several obstacles, such as darkness, un-breathable ash-filled air, and a continuous rain of pumice and *lapilli* small round droplets of molten lava.

4. The minor details in Pompeii graffiti scrawled on the walls give the city a living presence.

5. Herculaneum also known as Ercolano to the west of Pompeii was buried by a mudslide in the same eruption.

41c Other Punctuation with Parentheses

Parentheses with numbers or letters that order items in a series

Parentheses around letters or numbers that order a series within a sentence make the list easier to read.

> Angela Creider's recipe for becoming a great novelist is to (1) set aside an hour during the morning to write, (2) read what you've written out loud, (3) revise your prose, and (4) repeat every morning for the next thirty years.

Parentheses with abbreviations

Abbreviations made from the first letters of words are often used in place of the unwieldy names of institutions, departments, organizations, or terms. In order to show the reader what the abbreviation stands for, the first time it

appears in a text the writer must state the complete name, followed by the abbreviation in parentheses.

> The University of California, Santa Cruz (UCSC) supports its mascot, the banana slug, with pride and a sense of humor. And although it sounds strange to outsiders, UCSC students are even referred to as "the banana slugs."

Parentheses with in-text citations

The various documentation styles require that information quoted, paraphrased, or summarized from an outside source be indicated with a research citation. In several of the styles, including MLA (see Chapter 23) and APA (see Chapter 24), the citation is enclosed in parentheses.

> E. B. White's advice on writing style is to use your natural voice (Strunk and White 70).

COMMON ERRORS

Using periods, commas, colons, and semicolons with parentheses

When an entire sentence is enclosed in parentheses, place the period before the closing parenthesis.

Incorrect   Our fear of sharks, heightened by movies like *Jaws,* is vastly out of proportion with the minor threat sharks actually pose. (Dying from a dog attack, in fact, is much more likely than dying from a shark attack).

Correct   Our fear of sharks, heightened by movies like *Jaws,* is vastly out of proportion with the minor threat sharks actually pose. (Dying from a dog attack, in fact, is much more likely than dying from a shark attack.)

(Continued on next page)

| | **COMMON ERRORS** (continued) |

When the material in parentheses is part of the sentence and the parentheses fall at the end of the sentence, place the period outside the closing parenthesis.

Incorrect Reports of sharks attacking people are rare (much rarer than dog attacks.)

Correct Reports of sharks attacking people are rare (much rarer than dog attacks).

Place commas, colons, and semicolons after the closing parenthesis.

Incorrect Although newspaper editors generally prize concise letters to the editor, (the shorter the better) they will occasionally print longer letters that are unusually eloquent.

Correct Although newspaper editors generally prize concise letters to the editor (the shorter the better), they will occasionally print longer letters that are unusually eloquent.

Remember: When an entire sentence is enclosed in parentheses, place the period inside the closing parenthesis; otherwise, put the punctuation outside the closing parenthesis.

For step-by-step discussion, examples, and practice exercises, visit this page of the E-book at www.mycomplab.com.

Exercise 41.3   Decide where to add parentheses in the following sentences. Be careful to place them correctly in relation to other punctuation marks.

Example   *Saturday Night Live (SNL) is a weekly late-night comedy-variety show based in New York City.*

1. *SNL* has been broadcast live by the National Broadcasting Company NBC on Saturday nights since October 11, 1975.

2. The show was called *NBC's Saturday Night* until 1976 a short-lived variety show hosted by Howard Cosell was also called *Saturday Night Live*.

3. On Saturdays that the show is broadcast live, the cast and crew have to 1 run through the show with props 2 do a full dress rehearsal 3 reorder the script if any sketches are cut and 4 get ready to go live at 11:30 p.m. EST.

4. The premature deaths of a a few well-known cast members John Belushi, Gilda Radner, Phil Hartman, Chris Farley, and Danitra Vance have given rise to a superstition known as the "*Saturday Night Live* Curse."

5. Critics claim that talk of the show's being under a curse is ridiculous, especially because a few untimely deaths are inevitable when a show has had a cast of over 100 people "*SNL* is *Saturday Night Live* on NBC" par. 14.

41d Other Punctuation with Dashes

Dashes with a series of items

Dashes can set off a series. They are especially appropriate when the series comes in the middle of a sentence or when the series simply elaborates on what comes before it without changing the essential meaning of the sentence. Normally commas enclose nonessential clauses; however, placing commas around items separated by commas would confuse readers about where the list begins and ends.

> Rookie Luke Scott became the first player in Major League Baseball history to hit for the reverse cycle—a home run, a triple, a double, and a single in that order—in last night's game against the Diamondbacks.

Dashes with interrupted speech

Dashes also indicate that a speaker has broken off in the middle of a statement.

"Why did everybody get so quiet all of a—"; Silvia stopped in her tracks when she noticed that the customer had a pistol pointed at the clerk.

COMMON ERRORS

The art of typing a dash

Although dashes and hyphens look similar, they are actually different marks. The distinction is small but important because dashes and hyphens serve different purposes. A dash is a line twice as long as a hyphen. Most word processors will create a dash automatically when you type two hyphens together. Or you can type a special character to make a dash. Your manual will tell you which keys to press to make a dash.

Do not leave a space between a dash or a hyphen and the words that come before and after them. Likewise, if you are using two hyphens to indicate a dash, do not leave a space between the hyphens.

Incorrect A well - timed effort at conserving water may prevent long - term damage to drought - stricken farms -- if it's not already too late.

Correct A well-timed effort at conserving water may prevent long-term damage to drought-stricken farms—if it's not already too late.

Remember: Do not put spaces before or after hyphens and dashes.

For step-by-step discussion, examples, and practice exercises, visit this page of the E-book at www.mycomplab.com.

Chapter 42

Apostrophes

Indicate possession, mark contractions, and form certain plurals.

 **Possessives**

Nouns and indefinite pronouns (e.g., *everyone, anyone*) that indicate possession or ownership are in the **possessive case**. The possessive case is marked by attaching an apostrophe and an *-s* or an apostrophe only to the end of a word.

Singular nouns and indefinite pronouns

For singular nouns and indefinite pronouns, add an apostrophe plus *-s: -'s*. Even singular nouns that end in *-s* usually follow this principle.

Iris**'s** coat

everyone**'s** favorite

a woman**'s** choice

today**'s** news

the team**'s** equipment

There are a few exceptions to adding *-'s* for singular nouns:

- **Awkward pronunciations:** *Herodotus' travels, Jesus' sermons*
- **Official names of certain places, institutions, companies:** *Governors Island, Teachers College of Columbia University, Mothers Café, Saks Fifth Avenue, Walgreens Pharmacy.* Note, however, that many companies do include the apostrophe: *Denny's Restaurant, Macy's, McDonald's, Wendy's Old Fashioned Hamburgers.*

Plural nouns

For plural nouns that do not end in -*s*, add an apostrophe plus -*s*: -*'s*.

women**'s** rights

media**'s** responsibility

children**'s** section

For plural nouns that end in -*s*, add only an apostrophe at the end.

dancers**'** costumes

attorneys**'** briefs

the Kennedys**'** legacy

Compound nouns

For compound nouns, add an apostrophe plus -*s* to the last word: -*'s*.

my mother-in-law**'s** house

mayor of Cleveland**'s** speech

Two or more nouns

For joint possession, add an apostrophe plus -*s* to the final noun: -*'s*.

mother and dad**'s** yard

Ben & Jerry**'s** Ice Cream

When people possess or own things separately, add an apostrophe plus -*s* to each noun: -*'s*.

Roberto**'s** and Edward**'s** views are totally opposed.

Dominique**'s**, Sally**'s**, and Vinatha**'s** cars all need new tires.

COMMON ERRORS

Possessive forms of personal pronouns never take the apostrophe

her's, it's, our's, your's, their's

Incorrect The bird sang in **it's** cage.

hers, its, ours, yours, theirs

Correct The bird sang in **its** cage.

Remember: It's = It is

For step-by-step discussion, examples, and practice exercises, visit this page of the E-book at www.mycomplab.com.

Exercise 42.1 The apostrophes have been omitted from the following paragraph. Insert apostrophes in the appropriate places to indicate possession.

Example Pompeii's ruins were excavated during the past two centuries.

Its destruction was caused by an eruption of Mount Vesuvius in AD 79. Survivors stories contain accounts of tunneling through up to sixteen feet of debris after the disaster. The Naples Museums collection contains painted stuccos and other art objects from Pompeii that illustrate the delicate nature of the artisans techniques. More than five

hundred residents bronze seals were found, and these helped identify the occupants of many destroyed homes. Pompeiis ruins provide the worlds most accurate snapshot of Hellenistic and Roman times.

42b Contractions and Omitted Letters

In speech we often leave out sounds and syllables of familiar words. In writing these omissions are noted with apostrophes.

Contractions

Contractions combine two words into one, using the apostrophe to mark what is left out.

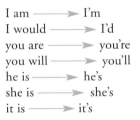
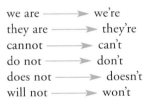

I am ⟶ I'm

I would ⟶ I'd

you are ⟶ you're

you will ⟶ you'll

he is ⟶ he's

she is ⟶ she's

it is ⟶ it's

we are ⟶ we're

they are ⟶ they're

cannot ⟶ can't

do not ⟶ don't

does not ⟶ doesn't

will not ⟶ won't

Omissions

Using apostrophes to signal omitted letters is a way of approximating speech in writing. They can make your writing look informal and slangy, but overuse can become annoying in a hurry.

rock and roll ⟶ rock'n'roll

the 1960s ⟶ the '60s

neighborhood ⟶ 'hood

42c Plurals of Letters, Symbols, and Words Referred to as Words

When to use apostrophes to make plurals

The trend is away from using apostrophes to form plurals of letters, symbols, and words referred to as words. In a few cases adding the apostrophe and *s* is still used, as in this old saying.

> Mind your p's and q's.

Words used as words are italicized and their plural is formed by adding an *s* not in italics, not an apostrophe and *s*.

> Take a few of the **and**s out of your writing.

Words in quotation marks, however, typically use apostrophe and *s*.

> She had too many "probably's" in her letter for me to be confident that the remodeling will be finished on schedule.

WRITING IN THE WORLD

Apostrophes are not used with the plurals of numbers and acronyms

The style manuals of the Modern Language Association (MLA) and the American Psychological Association (APA) do not use apostrophes for indicating plurals of numbers and acronyms. They add only -*s*.

1890**s**	four CEO**s**	several DVD**s**
eight**s**	these URL**s**	the images are all JPEG**s**

When not to use apostrophes to make plurals

Do not use an apostrophe to make family names plural.

> **Incorrect** You've heard of keeping up with the Jones's's.
>
> **Correct** You've heard of keeping up with the Joneses.

COMMON ERRORS

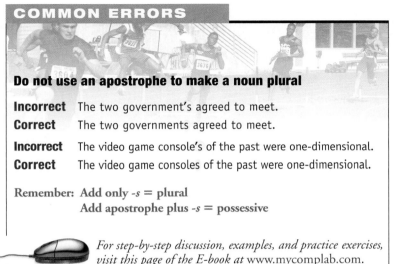

Do not use an apostrophe to make a noun plural

Incorrect The two government's agreed to meet.
Correct The two governments agreed to meet.

Incorrect The video game console's of the past were one-dimensional.
Correct The video game consoles of the past were one-dimensional.

Remember: Add only *-s* = plural
Add apostrophe plus *-s* = possessive

For step-by-step discussion, examples, and practice exercises, visit this page of the E-book at www.mycomplab.com.

Exercise 42.2 In the following sentences some apostrophes were placed correctly, some were placed incorrectly, and others were omitted altogether. Cross out incorrectly used apostrophes and add apostrophes where necessary.

Example Americans have often loved their presidents' nicknames
more than they loved the ~~president's~~ themselves.
presidents

1. Texas VIP's and international diplomats alike affectionately referred to Lyndon B. Johnson as "Big Daddy."
2. There were no *ifs*, *ands*, or *buts* when the "Rough Rider," Theodore Roosevelt, rode into town.

3. Similarly, when old "Give 'Em Hell," also known as Harry Truman, was on the Hill, congressmen could never catch up on their *Z*'s.
4. Jimmy Carters staff learned quickly of his attention to small details, down to the dotting of is and crossing of ts.
5. The last twenty years has seen two George Bush's in the White House.
6. In the 1990's, George H. W. Bush was known as "No New Taxes."

Chapter 43

Quotation Marks

Learn the several uses of quotation marks.

43a Direct Quotations

Use quotation marks to enclose direct quotations

Enclose direct quotations—someone else's words repeated verbatim—in quotation marks.

> Dan Glickman, CEO of the MPAA, the organization that rates U.S. films, argues that smoking is enough of a concern to parents that it should be considered when assigning movie ratings: "There is broad awareness of smoking as a unique public health concern due to nicotine's highly addictive nature, and no parent wants their child to take up the habit. The appropriate response of the rating system is to give more information to parents on this issue."

Even brief direct quotations, such as the repetition of someone else's original term or turn of phrase, require quotation marks.

> Because of the health risk that smoking represents, MPAA CEO Dan Glickman believes that informing parents about on-screen smoking is the "appropriate" thing to do.

Do not use quotation marks with indirect quotations

Do not enclose an indirect quotation—a paraphrase of someone else's words—in quotation marks. However, do remember that you need to cite

your source not only when you quote directly but also when you paraphrase or borrow ideas.

> Dan Glickman of the MPAA thinks that because parents don't want their children to start smoking, they should be warned when movies contain scenes where characters smoke.

Do not use quotation marks with block quotations

When a quotation is long enough to be set off as a block quotation, do not use quotation marks. MLA style defines long quotations as more than four lines of prose or poetry. APA style defines a long quotation as one of more than forty words. In the following example, notice that the long quotation is indented and quotation marks are omitted. Also notice that the parenthetical citation for a long quotation comes after the period.

> Complaints about maintenance in the dorms have been on the rise ever since the physical plant reorganized its crews into teams in August. One student's experience is typical:
>> When our ceiling started dripping, my roommate and I went to our resident director right away to file an emergency maintenance request. Apparently the physical plant felt that "emergency" meant they could get around to it in a week or two. By the fourth day without any word from a maintenance person, the ceiling tiles began to fall and puddles began to pool on our carpet. (Trillo)
> The physical plant could have avoided expensive ceiling tile and carpet repairs if it had responded to the student's request promptly.

Set off quotations in dialogue

Dialogue is traditionally enclosed within quotation marks. Begin a new paragraph with each change of speaker.

> Before Jim and Lester walk fifty yards on a faint animal trail, they hear the brush rattle in front of them and the unmistakable

snorting of a rhino. Jim crouches and looks through the brush. Lester watches Jim, wondering why he isn't retreating, then scrambles up a nearby tree. "Come on back," he yells to Jim, who is now out of sight.

After a few minutes Jim reappears. "I got right next to it but I never did get a good look. I was so close I could even smell it."

"The other one is still out there in the grass. And I heard a third one behind us toward the river."

"We better get out of here before it gets dark. Are you going to spend the night in the tree?"

"I'm thinking about it."

Exercise 43.1 The following sentences contain direct quotations (underlined) and paraphrases from Tony Horowitz's *Confederates in the Attic: Dispatches from the Unfinished Civil War* (New York: Pantheon, 1998). Add, delete, or move quotation marks as needed and correct the placement of citations and the setting of quotes if set incorrectly.

Example After completing his wild and often contradictory ride through two full years, fifteen states, and the contemporary landscape of what he terms the "South's Unfinished Civil War," award-winning journalist and cultural historian Tony Horowitz concluded: "the pleasure the Civil War gave me was hard to put into words" (387).

1. Horowitz's difficulty was finding words that might make sense, as he puts it, to anyone other than a fellow addict (387).

2. There are, Horowitz allows, clear and often-cited reasons why one might develop a passion for the Civil War, however. Everywhere, people spoke of family and fortunes lost in the war (384), Horowitz writes.

3. Horowitz notes that many Southerners, nostalgic for old-time war heroism, still revere men like Stonewall Jackson, Robert E. Lee, and Nathan Bedford Forrest—"figures that he refers to as the marble men of Southern myth (385)."

4. Civil War heroes were, after all, human. And these men, who for some command the status of gods, were also, in Horowitz's words, petty figures who often hurt their own cause by bickering, <u>even challenging each other to duels.</u> (385)

5. The Civil War was also unique because it marked the first war in which the rural landscape of the nineteenth-century United States met a new kind of war technology. Horowitz states: "<u>It was new technology that made the War's romance and rusticity so palpable. Without photographs, rebs and Yanks would seem as remote to modern Americans as Minutemen and Hessians. Surviving daguerreotypes from the 1840s and 1850s were mostly stiff studio portraits. So the Civil War was as far back as we could delve in our own history and bring back naturalistic images attuned to our modern way of seeing</u> (386)."

43b Titles of Short Works

While the titles of longer works such as books, magazines, and newspapers are italicized or underlined, titles of shorter works should be set off with quotation marks. Use quotation marks with the following kinds of titles:

Short stories	"Light Is Like Water," by Gabriel García Márquez
Magazine articles	"Race against Death," by Erin West
Newspaper articles	"Cincinnati Mayor Declares Emergency," by Liz Sidoti
Short poems	"We Real Cool," by Gwendolyn Brooks
Essays	"Self-Reliance," by Ralph Waldo Emerson
Songs	"Purple Haze," by Jimi Hendrix

Speeches, lectures, and sermons	"Zero to Web Page in Sixty Minutes," by Jean Lavre
Chapters	"Last, Best Hope of Earth," Chapter 8 of *The Civil War*, by Shelby Foote
Short films	"Bed Head," by Robert Rodriguez
Episodes of television shows	"Treehouse of Horror," an episode of *The Simpsons*
Episodes of radio shows	"Fiasco," an episode of *This American Life*

The exception. Don't put the title of your own paper in quotation marks. If the title of another short work appears within the title of your paper, retain the quotation marks around the short work. The title of a paper about Jimi Hendrix, for instance, might read:

The History of Hendrix: Riffs on "Purple Haze"

43d Other Uses of Quotation Marks

Quotation marks to indicate the novel use of a word

Quotation marks around a term can indicate that the writer is using the term in a novel way, often with skepticism, irony, or sarcasm. The quotation marks indicate that the writer is questioning the term's conventional definition. Notice the way quotation marks indicate skepticism about the conventional definition of *savages* in the following passage.

In the early days of England's empire building, it wasn't unusual to hear English anthropologists say that conquered native people were savages. Yet if we measure civilization by peacefulness and compassion for fellow humans, those "savages" were really much more civilized than the British.

Quotation marks to indicate that a word is being used as a word

Italics are usually used to indicate that a word is being used as a word, rather than standing for its conventional meaning. However, quotation marks are correct in these cases as well.

> Beginning writers sometimes confuse "their," "they're," and "there."

43d Misuses of Quotation Marks

Do not use quotation marks for emphasis

It's becoming more and more common to see quotation marks used to emphasize a word or phrase. Resist the temptation in your own writing; it's an incorrect usage. In fact, because quotation marks indicate that a writer is using a term with skepticism or irony, adding quotation marks for emphasis will highlight unintended connotations of the term.

> **Incorrect**   "fresh" seafood

By using quotation marks here, the writer seems to call into question whether the seafood is really fresh.

> **Correct**   fresh seafood

> **Incorrect**   Enjoy our "live" music every Saturday night.

Again, the quotation marks unintentionally indicate that the writer is skeptical that the music is live.

> **Correct**   Enjoy our live music every Saturday night.

You have better ways of creating emphasis using your word processing program: **boldfacing**, underlining, *italicizing*, and using color.

Do not use quotation marks around indirect quotations or paraphrases

Incorrect   The airport security guard announced that "all bags will be searched and then apologized for the inconvenience to the passengers."

Correct   The airport security guard announced, "All bags will be searched. I apologize for the inconvenience." [direct quotation]

Correct   The airport security guard announced that all bags would be searched and then apologized for the inconvenience to the passengers. [indirect quotation]

Avoid using quotation marks to acknowledge the use of a cliché

You may have seen other writers enclose clichés in quotation marks. Avoid doing this; in fact, avoid using clichés at all. Clichés are worn-out phrases; fresh words engage readers more.

Incorrect   To avoid "letting the cat out of the bag" about forthcoming products, most large companies employ security experts trained in preventing commercial espionage.

Correct but stale   To avoid letting the cat out of the bag about forthcoming products, most large companies employ security experts trained in preventing commercial espionage.

Correct and Effective   To prevent their savvy competitors from peeking at forthcoming products, most large companies employ security experts trained in preventing commercial espionage.

43e Other Punctuation with Quotation Marks

The rules for placing punctuation with quotation marks fall into three general categories.

Periods and commas with quotation marks

Place periods and commas inside closing quotation marks.

Incorrect   "The smartest people", Dr. Geisler pointed out, "tell themselves the most convincing rationalizations".

Correct   "The smartest people," Dr. Geisler pointed out, "tell themselves the most convincing rationalizations."

Exceptions occur when a parenthetical citation follows a short quotation. In MLA and APA documentation styles, the period follows the closing parenthesis.

Incorrect   "The smartest people," Dr. Geisler pointed out, "tell themselves the most convincing rationalizations." (52)

Correct   "The smartest people," Dr. Geisler pointed out, "tell themselves the most convincing rationalizations" (52).

Colons and semicolons with quotation marks

Place colons and semicolons outside closing quotation marks.

Incorrect   "From Stettin in the Baltic to Trieste in the Adriatic, an iron curtain has descended across the Continent;" Churchill's statement rang through Cold War politics for the next fifty years.

Correct   "From Stettin in the Baltic to Trieste in the Adriatic, an iron curtain has descended across the Continent"; Churchill's statement rang through Cold War politics for the next fifty years.

Exclamation points, question marks, and dashes with quotation marks

When an exclamation point, question mark, or dash belongs to the original quotation, place it inside the closing quotation mark. When it applies to the entire sentence, place it outside the closing quotation mark.

In the original quotation

"Are we there yet?" came the whine from the back seat.

Applied to the entire sentence

Did the driver in the front seat respond, "Not even close"?

COMMON ERRORS

Quotations within quotations

Single quotation marks are used to indicate a quotation within a quotation. In the following example single quotation marks clarify who is speaking. The rules for placing punctuation with single quotation marks are the same as the rules for placing punctuation with double quotation marks.

Incorrect When he showed the report to Paul Probius, Michener reported that Probius "took vigorous exception to the sentence "He wanted to close down the university," insisting that we add the clarifying phrase "as it then existed"" (Michener 145).

Correct When he showed the report to Paul Probius, Michener reported that Probius "took vigorous exception to the sentence 'He wanted to close down the university,' insisting that we add the clarifying phrase 'as it then existed'" (Michener 145).

Remember: Single quotation marks are used for quotations within quotations.

For step-by-step discussion, examples, and practice exercises, visit this page of the E-book at www.mycomplab.com.

Exercise 43.2   The following sentences use a variety of punctuation marks with quotations. Some are used correctly and some are not. Move the punctuation marks that are incorrectly placed in relation to the quotation marks.

> **Example**   In her essay "Survival Is the Least of My Desires," the novelist Dorothy Allison describes herself as being "born poor, queer, and despised."

1. What does Allison mean when she tells gay and lesbian writers, "We must aim much higher than just staying alive if we are to begin to approach our true potential?"

2. She elaborates, "I want to write in such a way as to literally remake the world, to change people's thinking as they look out of the eyes of the characters I create" (212.)

3. "I believe in the truth"; this declaration forms the cornerstone of the philosophy Allison wants to pass on to gay and lesbian writers.

4. According to Allison, "I write what I think are "moral tales." That's what I intend, though I grow more and more to believe that telling the emotional truth of people's lives, not necessarily the historical truth, is the only moral use of fiction." (217)

5. "I believe the secret in writing is that fiction never exceeds the reach of the writer's courage", says Allison.

Chapter 44

Other Punctuation Marks

Understand the uses of punctuation.

44a Periods

Periods at the ends of sentences

Place a period at the end of a complete sentence if it is not a direct question or an exclamatory statement. As the term suggests, a direct question asks a question outright. Indirect questions, on the other hand, report the asking of a question.

Direct question	Mississippi opponents of the Confederate-themed state flag wonder, "Where does the state's pride in its heritage end and its respect for those offended begin?"
Indirect question	Mississippi opponents of the Confederate-themed state flag wonder where the state's pride in its heritage ends and its respect for those offended begins.

Periods with quotation marks and parentheses

When a quotation falls at the end of a sentence, place the period inside the closing quotation marks.

> Although he devoted decades to a wide range of artistic and political projects, Allen Ginsberg is best known as the author of the poem "Howl."

When a parenthetical phrase falls at the end of a sentence, place the period outside the closing parenthesis.

> Mrs. Chen, a grandmother in Seneca Falls, is training for her first 10K race (6.2 miles).

When parentheses enclose a whole sentence, place the period inside the closing parenthesis.

> True to their quirky success, ABBA found a receptive audience in Australia before Americans embraced them. (Australia, in fact, carries the distinction of being the first country to place ABBA at the top of its music charts.)

Periods with abbreviations

Many abbreviations require periods; however, there are few set rules. Use the dictionary to check how to punctuate abbreviations on a case-by-case basis.

John F. Kennedy	Mr.	misc.	Wed.
a.m.	p.m.	a.s.a.p.	etc.

The rules for punctuating two types of abbreviations do remain consistent: Postal abbreviations for states and most abbreviations for organizations do not require periods.

OH for Ohio   ACLU for the American Civil Liberties Union
CA for California   NRA for the National Rifle Association

When an abbreviation with a period falls at the end of a sentence, do not add a second period to conclude the sentence.

Incorrect   Her flight arrives at 6:22 p.m..

Correct   Her flight arrives at 6:22 p.m.

Periods in citations of poetry and plays

Use a period to separate the components of the following kinds of literary citations.

A poem divided into sections such as books or cantos
book.lines   *The Inferno* 27.79-84

A prose play
act.scene   *Beyond Therapy* 1.4

A verse play
act.scene.lines   *Twelfth Night* 3.4.194-98

Periods as decimal points

Decimal points are periods that separate integers from tenths, hundredths, and so on.

99.98% pure silver	98.6° Fahrenheit
on sale for $399.97	2.6 liter engine

Since large numbers with long strings of zeros can be difficult to read accurately, writers sometimes shorten them using decimal points. Notice how the decimal points make the second sentence easier to read than the first.

> With the national debt approaching 6,400,000,000,000 dollars, some senators are salivating at the idea of using a portion of the projected 2,170,000,000,000-dollar budget surplus to pay it down.

> With the national debt approaching $6.4 trillion, some senators are salivating at the idea of using a portion of the projected $2.17 trillion budget surplus to pay it down.

Exercise 44.1   Periods have been omitted from the paragraph that follows. You can see how confusing writing becomes without proper period placement. Add periods and capitalize the first words of sentences correctly to clear up the confusion.

Example   The origins of second wave American feminism are often traced to Ms⊚Betty Friedan of Peoria, Illinois.

Ms Friedan was born February 4, 1921 history will record her as one of the major contributors to modern US feminism in 1963, Friedan penned the monumental *Feminine Mystique* the

book investigated the contemporary malaise of the postwar
US housewife, which she dubbed "the problem that has no
name" Friedan spoke for the millions of housewives who were
wondering why they were discontented as mothers and wives
in 1966, she cofounded the National Organization for
Women (NOW was coconceptualized by African-American
feminist/minister Pauli Murray at the 1966 National Conference
of the Commission on the Status of Women in Washington DC)
Friedan went on to serve as president of NOW (wwwnoworg)
until 1970, and she has since published works such as *It
Changed My Life*, *The Second Stage,* and *Life So Far*

44b Question Marks

Question marks with direct questions

Place a question mark at the end of a direct question. A direct question is
one that the questioner puts to someone outright. In contrast, an indirect
question merely reports the asking of a question. Question marks give
readers a cue to read the end of the sentence with rising inflection. Read
the following sentences aloud. Hear how your inflection rises in the second
sentence to convey the direct question.

Indirect question
Desirée asked whether Dan rode his motorcycle without a helmet.

Direct question
Desirée asked, "Does Dan ride his motorcycle without a helmet?"

Question marks with quotations

When a quotation falls at the end of a direct question, place the question
mark outside the closing quotation mark.

Did Abraham Lincoln really call Harriet Beecher Stowe "the little lady
who started this big war"?

Place the question mark inside the closing quotation mark when only the quoted material is a direct question.

> Slowly scientists are beginning to answer the question, "Is cancer a genetic disease?"

When quoting a direct question in the middle of a sentence, place a question mark inside the closing quotation mark and place a period at the end of the sentence.

> Market researchers estimate that asking Burger World's customers "Do you want fries with that?" was responsible for a 15% boost in their french fries sales.

Question marks to indicate uncertainty about dates or numbers

Place a question mark in parentheses after a date or number whose accuracy is in question.

> After his escape from slavery, Frederick Douglass (1817?-95) went on to become a great orator and statesman.

Exercise 44.2   Periods and question marks have been omitted from the paragraph that follows. Add periods and question marks where needed and capitalize the beginnings of sentences.

> **Example**   What was so Earth-shattering about Friedan's naming of the "problem with no name"?
>
> Betty Friedan's *The Feminine Mystique* addressed the question, "Is this all" She examined why millions of women were sensing a gnawing feeling of discontent Friedan asked, "Can the problem that has no name somehow be related to the domestic routine of the housewife" and examined women's shifting place in postwar America What were women missing

In asking these questions, Friedan legitimized the panic and uneasiness of many women who found the roles of mother and wife not wholly satisfying However, did this naming solve the "problem with no name"

44c Exclamation Points

Exclamation points to convey strong emotion

Exclamation points conclude sentences and, like question marks, tell the reader how a sentence should sound. They indicate strong emotion. As with any display of strong emotion, occasional doses can be invigorating, but too many exclamation points quickly become grating. Instead of relying on exclamation points to convey heightened emotion, use strong words and careful phrasing. Use exclamation points sparingly in formal writing; they are rarely appropriate in academic and professional prose.

Exclamation points with emphatic interjections

Exclamation points can convey a sense of urgency with brief interjections. Interjections can be incorporated into sentences or stand on their own.

Run! They're about to close the doors to the jetway.

Use commas to set off interjections that are not emphatic.

One study has found that, yes, humans can contract a strain of mad cow disease.

Exclamation points with quotation marks

In quotations, exclamation points follow the same rules as question marks. If a quotation falls at the end of an exclamatory statement, place the exclamation point outside the closing quotation mark.

The singer forgot the words of "America the Beautiful"!

When quoting an exclamatory statement at the end of a sentence that is not itself exclamatory, place the exclamation point inside the closing quotation mark.

> Jerry thought his car would be washed away in the flood, but Anna jumped into action, declaring, "Not if I can help it!"

When the quotation of an exclamatory statement does not fall at the end of a sentence, place the exclamation point inside the closing quotation mark and place a period at the end of the sentence.

> Someone yelled "Loser!" when the candidate walked on stage.

44d Brackets

While brackets (sometimes called *square brackets*) look quite similar to parentheses, the two perform different functions. Brackets have a narrow set of uses.

Brackets to provide clarification within quotation marks

Quoted material sometimes requires clarification because it is removed from its context. Adding clarifying material in brackets can allow you to make the quotation clear while still accurately repeating the exact words of your source. In the following example the writer quotes a sentence with the pronoun *they,* which refers to a noun in a previous, unquoted sentence. The material in brackets clarifies to whom the pronoun refers.

> The Harris study found that "In the last three years, they [Gonzales Junior High students] averaged 15% higher on their mathematics assessment tests than their peers in Northridge County."

Brackets within parentheses

Since parentheses within parentheses might confuse readers, use brackets to enclose parenthetical information within a parenthetical phrase.

> Representative Patel's most controversial legislation (including a version of the hate crimes bill [HR 99-108] the house rejected two years ago) has a slim chance of being enacted this session.

WRITING IN THE WORLD

Using quotations that contain errors

In scholarly writing you should copy quotations exactly as they appear in your source, but you must also produce a paper free of grammatical and mechanical errors. So how should you handle a source that contains an error? One way is to rephrase the quotation in your own words, crediting your source for the idea. However, if the quotation is so eloquent or effective that you decide to include it despite the error, use *[sic]* (an abbreviation of the Latin "sicut," meaning *thus*) to indicate that the original source is responsible for the mistake.

Spelling error in original source (*to* instead of *too*)

> "One taste tester reported that the Carb Charge energy bar was to dry; she said it had the consistency of sawdust" (Cisco 22).

Rephrased

> One of the participants in the taste test likened the Carb Charge energy bar to sawdust because it had so little moisture (Cisco 22).

Quote using [sic]

> "One taste tester reported that the Carb Charge energy bar was to [sic] dry; she said it had the consistency of sawdust" (Cisco 22).

44e Ellipses

Ellipses let a reader know that a portion of a passage is missing. You can use ellipses to keep quotations concise and direct readers' attention to what is important to the point you are making. An ellipsis is a string of three periods with spaces separating the periods. MLA style formerly required square brackets around the three periods. Your instructor may prefer that you use brackets surrounding ellipses when you delete words from quotations.

Ellipses to indicate an omission from a prose quotation

When you quote only a phrase or short clause from a sentence, you usually do not need to use ellipses.

> Mao Tse-tung first used "let a hundred flowers blossom" in a Beijing speech in 1957.

Except at the beginning of a quotation, indicate omitted words with an ellipsis. Type a space between each ellipsis dot and between the ellipses and the words preceding and following them.

The original source

> "The female praying mantis, so named for the way it holds its front legs together as if in prayer, tears off her male partner's head during mating. Remarkably, the headless male will continue the act of mating. This brutal dance is a stark example of the innate evolutionary drive to pass genes onto offspring; the male praying mantis seems to live and die only for this moment."

An ellipsis indicates omitted words

> "The female praying mantis . . . tears off her male partner's head during mating."

Note: Retain any punctuation mark falling before the omitted passage if it clarifies the sentence. In this case the comma before the omitted passage would not make the sentence any clearer, so it was not retained.

Ellipses to indicate the omission of a whole line or lines of poetry

Using more than three periods is appropriate in just one instance: to signal the omission of a full line or lines of poetry in the middle of a poetry quotation. In such instances, use an entire line of spaced periods.

Original

My Shakespeare, rise; I will not lodge thee by
Chaucer or Spenser, or bid Beaumont lie
A little further, to make thee a room;
Thou art a monument, without a tomb,
And art alive still, while thy book doth live,
And we have wits to read, and praise to give.

—Ben Jonson, "To the Memory of My Beloved,
the Author, Mr. William Shakespeare" (1623)

Omitted lines of poetry

My Shakespeare, rise;

. . . .
Thou art a monument, without a tomb,
And art alive still, while thy book doth live,
And we have wits to read, and praise to give.

Ellipses to indicate a pause or an interrupted sentence

Ellipses can provide a visual cue that a speaker is taking a long pause or that a speaker has been interrupted.

"And the winner is . . . David Goldstein."

"That ball is going, going, . . . gone!"

"Be careful that you don't spill . . ."

Exercise 44.3   In the following quotations and A. E. Housman's poem "To an Athlete Dying Young," delete the underlined passages and punctuate the quotations with ellipses where necessary. Be sure to leave in clarifying punctuation.

Example   Robert Ward states, "The American culture positions its heroes such that they are destined to end in turmoil, <u>problematizing the desire for eminent success.</u> By elevating them to the position of gods, society gives heroes nowhere to go but down."

Rewrite   Robert Ward states, "The American culture positions its heroes such that they are destined to end in turmoil. . . . By elevating them to the position of gods, society gives heroes nowhere to go but down."

Ward notes, "The phenomenon of the waning star is heavily represented in the last century of English and American culture, <u>ranging from poetry to popular rock music.</u>" In 1896, chronicling the advantage of dying before the glory fades, A. E. Housman published the poem "To an Athlete Dying Young." The following is a passage from that poem:

Now you will not swell the rout
Of lads that wore their honors out,
Runners whom renown outran
And the name died before the man.

<u>So set, before the echoes fade,</u>
<u>The fleet foot on the sill of shade,</u>

And hold to the low lintel up
The still-defended challenge-cup.

And round that early-laurelled head
Will flock to gaze the strengthless dead,
And find unwithered on its curls
The garland briefer than a girl's.

Housman's verses extol the eternal glory of those who pass in their prime. Scholars such as Ona Click have noted the recent proliferation of Housman's theme, citing that "artists such as Neil Young have contemporized this notion with songs such as 'Hey Hey My My.' The song contrasts the fates of two rock stars who ultimately took two very different paths, Elvis Presley and Johnny Rotten of the Sex Pistols; while Presley died in a blaze of glory, Rotten's fleeting stardom waned and dulled the cultural memory of his initial rise to fame." In a related article, she notes this theme traveled into the 1980s as Bruce Springsteen's "Glory Days" recalled the tale of "those who outlive their primes and are forced to reduce their glory to nostalgic reminiscences and fleeting grasps at the past." Though we venerate our heroes, culture notes how their position is tenuous at best.

44f Slashes

Slashes to indicate alternative words

Slashes between two words indicate that a choice between them is to be made. When using slashes for this purpose, do not put a space between the slash and words.

Incorrect	Maya was such an energetic baby that her exhausted parents wished she had come with an on / off switch.
Correct	Maya was such an energetic baby that her exhausted parents wished she had come with an on/off switch.

The following are common instances of the slash used to indicate alternative words:

either/or   actor/director   player/coach
and/or   win/lose   pass/fail
on/off

Slashes to indicate line breaks in short quotations of verse

Line breaks—where the lines of a poem end—are artistic choices that affect how we understand a poem. Thus it is important to reproduce them accurately when quoting poetry. The task is not difficult in MLA style when the quotation is four or more lines long: Simply indent the quoted lines ten spaces and mimic the line breaks of the original verse. When you quote three or fewer lines of poetry, however, and must integrate the quotation into the paragraph rather than setting it off in a block, use slashes to indicate line breaks. Type a space on either side of the slash.

> The concluding lines of T. S. Eliot's "Animula" offer a surprising revision of a common prayer. He writes, "Pray for Floret, by the boarhound slain between the yew trees / Pray for us now and at the hour of our birth." Replacing "death," the final word in the prayer, with "birth" at the end of this dark poem connotes an uneasy sense that we find ourselves adrift in a new and unfamiliar world.

Slashes with fractions

Place a slash between the numerator and the denominator in a fraction. Do not put spaces around the slash.

Incorrect   3 / 4

Correct   3/4

Slashes with dates

In informal writing, slashes divide the month, day, and year in a date. A longer format is appropriate for formal academic and professional writing. Omit the slashes, spell out the month, and place a comma after the day.

Informal Javy, save 1/14/09 on your calendar; I reserved two tickets for the talent show.

Formal It was a pleasure to meet you during my December 14 interview for Universal Oil's marketing internship. As we discussed, I will not be available for full-time employment until my graduation on May 12, 2009. However, I am hopeful that we can work out the part-time arrangement you suggested until that date.

WRITING IN THE WORLD

Should you use *he/she* or *s/he*?

Using *he* as an indefinite pronoun (a pronoun that refers to a person in general rather than to a specific individual) can seem sexist because it omits women. Some writers use *he/she* or the even shorter *s/he* instead. These solutions are unacceptable to many readers, who consider them ugly. Likewise, many readers consider *he or she* annoying. The best solution is to avoid the *he/she* and *he or she* constructions altogether.

Sexist Despite popular lore, a hiker bitten by a snake should never suck out the poison. Instead, **he** should tie a tourniquet above the wound to prevent the poison from circulating to vital organs.

Inclusive but cumbersome Despite popular lore, a hiker bitten by a snake should never suck out the poison. Instead, s/he should tie a tourniquet above the wound to prevent the poison from circulating to vital organs.

(Continued on next page)

Inclusive but cumbersome	Despite popular lore, a hiker bitten by a snake should never suck out the poison. Instead, he or she should tie a tourniquet above the wound to prevent the poison from circulating to vital organs.
Better	Despite popular lore, a hiker bitten by a snake should never suck out the poison. Instead, tying a tourniquet above the wound will prevent the poison from circulating to vital organs.

Chapter 31 offers more tips for avoiding sexist language and awkward indefinite pronouns.

Exercise 44.4   Take a look at the way the following paragraph uses all the punctuation marks discussed in this chapter: periods, question marks, exclamation points, brackets, ellipses, and slashes. Some are used correctly, and others are used incorrectly or omitted altogether. Correct any punctuation mistakes that you find, and add any necessary marks that have been omitted.

Example   Many ask, "Why have snakes become a symbol of religious devotion"(?)

In 1996 alone, over sixty deaths occurred due to religious snake handling. Mark 16-21 in the King James' version of the Bible states, "They shall take up serpents and if they drink any deadly thing it shall not hurt them . . ."! This passage instigated the formation of a religion which thrives among the Irish and English descendants living in Appalachia. (In the 1990s, over 2000 snake handlers lived in Appalachia alone.)

Snake handling has been investigated by both practitioners of the fine arts (Romulus Linney's *Holy Ghosts* (1971) examines snake handling in the South) and news media. One controversial case examined Rev Glenn Summerford who attempted to kill his wife by forcing her to handle rattlesnakes. The general public often sees snake handling as a frightening act of fundamentalism practiced by congregations (often assumed to be undereducated)

Chapter 45

Write with Accurate Spelling

Readers expect correct spelling.

45a Know the Limitations of Spelling Checkers

Spelling checkers do help you to become a better speller. But spelling checkers are quite limited and miss many errors. If you type *ferry tail* for *fairy tale*, your spelling checker will not catch the errors.

WRITING SMART

Electronic dictionaries

A number of reputable dictionaries now maintain searchable electronic versions on CD or on the Internet. If you don't own a dictionary, these Web sites offer a convenient, inexpensive alternative.

General dictionaries

American Heritage Dictionary	bartleby.com/61/
Merriam-Webster Dictionary	www.m-w.com/
Oxford English Dictionary	Most research libraries offer access to an online version free to people with borrowing privileges.

Specialized dictionaries

The Web site *yourDictionary.com* at www.yourdictionary.com/diction4.html lists specialized electronic dictionaries from a variety of disciplines.

Exercise 45.1   The author of the following paragraph ran it through a spelling checker and took all of the checker's advice. The checker missed some errors and created a few new errors. Correct all the spelling mistakes in the paragraph.

Example   ~~Its~~ *It's* indicative of ~~Despond~~ *Desmond* Tutu's feelings of solidarity with his parishioners that he opted to live in ~~Sowed,~~ *Soweto* a poor black neighborhood, rather than in Houghton, a rich suburb.

   Archbishop Despond Tutu's message to the peoples of South Africa is that all are "of infinite worth created in the image of god," and "to be treated . . . with reverence" (Wepman 13). Tutu maintains that this is true fore whites as well as blacks, a position that isn't popular wit some South African. It can be scene from the many awards tutu has received, not least among them the Nobel Peace Prize in 1984, that his commitment to morality and human freedom have had an effect the world over. Archbishop Despond Tutu is a ban who does not waist the potential of hiss powerful role as religious leader. On the contrary, the Archbishop seas many political problems as moral ones and speaks out frequently on human rights issues.

45b Distinguish Homonyms

Homonyms are pairs (*your, you're*) and trios (*their, there, they're*) of words that sound alike but have different spellings and meanings. They are tricky words to spell because we don't learn to distinguish them in spoken language, and spelling checkers don't flag them as errors because they correctly spell other words in their databases. It's easy to type *there* for *their* or *Web sight* for *Web site* and not catch the error when you proofread.

Exercise 45.2   Circle the correct homonyms in the paragraph that follows.

Example   (Except/Accept) for the ethnic cleansings in Rwanda in 1995, one of the worst incidents of genocide in history occurred in the Southeast Asian country of Cambodia.

Modern Cambodia, or Kampuchea, gained its independence from France in 1953, but (by/buy) the early 1970s the country was embroiled in bloody civil war. In 1975, Khmer Rouge guerrillas secured the Cambodian (capital/capitol), Phnom Penh, (where/wear) they ruled the country until 1979. Once in power, the Khmer Rouge killed over 25% of their fellow Cambodians; (all together/altogether) they murdered over 2 million people. Most of those killed met their deaths at a (sight/site) (write/ right) outside of Phnom Penh, known today as the "Killing Fields." The (affects/effects) of the Khmer Rouge's brief, yet defining rule remain all (to/too) apparent in contemporary Cambodia.

COMMON ERRORS

Commonly misspelled words

Is *accommodate* spelled with one *m* or two? Is *harass* spelled with one *r* or two? You'll find a list of words commonly misspelled at the URL below.

Remember: Always check a dictionary when you are unsure of how a word is spelled.

For step-by-step discussion, examples, and practice exercises, visit this page of the E-book at www.mycomplab.com.

45c Learn Spelling Rules

This section addresses four major categories of spelling rules: *i* before *e*; prefixes; suffixes; and plurals. While you'll see that each rule carries a number of exceptions, learning the rules is an important first step toward becoming a better speller.

I before *e*, except after *c* or when pronounced as *ay*

I before *e* is the classic spelling rule you probably learned in grade school. An *i* goes before an *e* except in two cases. The *i* follows the *e* when these letters follow *c* or when they are pronounced *ay*. Other exceptions follow on the next page.

> *i* before *e: brief, hierarchy, obedient*
> except after *c: receipt, perceive, ceiling*
> or when pronounced as *ay: eight, neighbor, heir*

Exceptions to the *i* before *e* rules

ancient	feisty	science
being	foreign	seismic
caffeine	forfeit	seize
conscience	height	species
counterfeit	heist	weird
efficient	leisure	
either	neither	

Prefixes

When adding a prefix to a word, retain the spelling of the root word. (See Section 40a for help determining when a prefix–root word combination should be hyphenated.)

> mis + spelling = misspelling
> hemi + sphere = hemisphere
> un + believable = unbelievable
> un + nerve = unnerve

Suffixes

Double the root word's final consonant if

1. The root word ends in a consonant, and
2. A single vowel comes before the consonant, and
3. The root word is one syllable or the last syllable of the root is stressed.
   rappel + ed = rappelled
   control + ing = controlling
   recur + ence = recurrence
   hit + able = hittable

Do not double the root word's final consonant if

1. The root wood ends in two consonants.
   lift + ing = lifting
   remind + ed = reminded
2. Two vowels come before the consonant.
   head + ing = heading
   repeat + ed = repeated
3. The last syllable of the root is not stressed.
   fó-cus + ed = focused
   trá-vel + ed = traveled
   lá-bel + ing = labeling

Drop the final *e* from a root word if the suffix begins with a vowel.

When adding a suffix that begins with a vowel to a root word that ends with an unpronounced *e*, drop the *e*.

fate + al = fatal
opportune + ity = opportunity
Greece + ian = Grecian

Exceptions.   Keep the *e* if it is preceded by a *c* (*enforceable, noticeable*) or a soft *g* (*advantageous, courageous*).

Keep the final *e* in a root word if the suffix begins with a consonant.

Keep the root word's final unpronounced *e* when the suffix begins with a consonant.

> subtle + ty = subtlety
> fortunate + ly = fortunately
> appease + ment = appeasement

Exceptions

> acknowledge + ment = acknowledgment
> argue + ment = argument
> awe + ful = awful
> judge + ment = judgment
> true + ly = truly
> whole + ly = wholly

When adding a suffix to a root word ending with a consonant and *y*, change the *y* to an *i*.

> beauty + ful = beautiful
> crazy + ness = craziness
> glory + fy = glorify
> hungry + est = hungriest

Exceptions.   When the suffix begins with an *i*, keep the *y* (as in *study, studying* and *dandy, dandyism*) in order to avoid a double *i*. Also keep the *y* when adding 's (*July's* heat, the *spy's* house). Other individual exceptions: *dryness, wryly, spryly.*

When adding a suffix to a root word ending with a vowel and *y*, retain the *y*.

> pay + ment = payment
> stay + ing = staying

boy + hood = boyhood
annoy + ance = annoyance

Exceptions

day + ly = daily   lay + ity = laity
gay + ty = gaiety   pay + ed = paid
lay + ed = laid   say + ed = said

Exercise 45.3   Each of the following root words ends in a consonant-vowel-consonant combination. Write the correct spelling of each word.

occur + ed = occurred
stop + ing = stopping

1. slap + ed   6. run + ing
2. refer + ing   7. refer + ence
3. drop + ed   8. benefit + ed
4. ship + ment   9. commit + ment
5. dim + er   10. forget + able

Exercise 45.4   Each of the following root words ends in a silent e. Write the correct spelling of each word. Pay attention to whether the first letter of the suffix is a consonant or a vowel.

continue + ous = continuous
state + ly = stately

1. definite + ly   6. hate + ful
2. pure + ist   7. judge + ment
3. spine + less   8. debate + able
4. exercise + ing   9. like + able
5. imagine + ation   10. nine + th

Plurals

You can make most words plural simply by adding *s*. Exceptions abound, however. The following rules will help you determine which words do not take just an *s* in the plural.

Compound nouns: Make the most important word plural.

To indicate more than one of a compound noun (several words combining to make a noun) make the most important word plural. Note that the last word isn't always the most important.

sisters-in-law	brigadier generals
attorneys general	passersby
courts-martial	power plays

Add *es* to words ending with *ch*, *s*, *sh*, *x*, *z*, or a consonant and an *o*.

Add *es* to words that end in *ch*, *s*, *sh*, *x*, or *z*, as well as to words that end with a consonant followed by an *o*.

ending with *ch*:	church, churches	catch, catches
ending with *s*:	dress, dresses	trellis, trellises
ending with *sh*:	wash, washes	radish, radishes
ending with *x*:	ax, axes	box, boxes
ending with *z*:	buzz, buzzes	quiz, quizzes
ending with consonant and an *o*:	hero, heroes	tomato, tomatoes

Exceptions

memo, memos	photo, photos
piano, pianos	solo, solos

With words ending in a consonant and *y*, change the *y* to an *i* and add *es*.

Words ending in a consonant followed by a *y* become plural by replacing the *y* with an *i* and adding *es*.

spy, spies
derby, derbies
philosophy, philosophies

With words ending in a vowel and *y*, add *s*.

If a vowel precedes the *y*, simply add an *s* to make the word plural.

day, days
buoy, buoys
lackey, lackeys

Irregular plurals

Some words are irregular in the plural; they don't follow any set rules in English. Some are Latin words that retain their Latin plural endings. The following is a partial list of irregular plurals.

Singular	Plural	Singular	Plural
alumnus	alumni	child	children
analysis	analyses	crisis	crises
axis	axes	criterion	criteria
bacterium	bacteria	curriculum	curricula
basis	bases	datum	data
cactus	cacti	deer	deer
dice	die	parenthesis	parentheses
fish	fish	phenomenon	phenomena
focus	foci	radius	radii
half	halves	self	selves
hypothesis	hypotheses	species	species
life	lives	stimulus	stimuli
locus	loci	stratum	strata
man	men	syllabus	syllabi
medium	media	thesis	theses
memorandum	memoranda	thief	thieves

Singular	Plural	Singular	Plural
mouse	mice	vertebra	vertebrae
octopus	octopi	woman	women
ox	oxen		

Exercise 45.5 In the following paragraph, singular words that should be plural are underlined. Make all the underlined words plural. Where necessary, change verbs so that they agree with the plural words.

Example Why Oscar Wilde, in 1885, brought Lord Queensbury to trial on charges of libel remains one of the great
mysteries
mystery of literary history.

Wilde, a successful author with two child and multiple follower in literary London, made a mistake when he pressed charge against the famous lord. By all account, Wilde was in jovial spirit when he arrived at the Old Bailey courthouse on April 3, 1895. Passerby may have seen the famous writer make one of his characteristically fantastic entrance: Wilde's carriage was outfitted with two horse, several servant, and all the pomp and circumstance his public character demanded. But the series of event that followed led up to one of the great crash of the Victorian era. Wilde lost the libel suit and was then himself tried, twice, based on the body of evidence amassed against him in the first trial. The medium were not sympathetic to Wilde, who had come to embody the multiple threat of moral indecency for conservative Victorian. In the day following his two trial and ultimate conviction for the newly illegal crime of gross indecency, both print article and caricature presenting story from the trial served as knife in the artist's back. Wilde was sentenced to two year of "hard labor," and upon his release from prison fled to France in exile. He died two year later. Wilde lived two life in his brief 47 years; he lived the first under the spotlight of fame, and the second under the glare of infamy. But his philosophy of art and beauty survive, as Wilde predicted they would.

Chapter 46

Capitalization and Italics

Recognize how capital letters and italics can affect meaning.

46a Capital Letters

Capitalize the initial letters of proper nouns and proper adjectives

Capitalize the initial letters of proper nouns (nouns that name particular people, places, and things), including the following:

Names	Sandra Day O'Connor	Bill Gates
Titles preceding names	Dr. Martin Luther King, Jr.	Mrs. Fields
Place names	Grand Canyon	Northwest Territories
Institution names	Department of Labor	Amherst College
Organization names	World Trade Organization	American Cancer Society
Company names	Motorola	JoJo's Café and Bakery
Religions	Protestantism	Islam
Languages	Chinese	Swahili
Months	November	March
Days of the week	Monday	Friday
Nationalities	Italian	Indonesian

Holidays	Passover	Thanksgiving
Departments	Chemistry Department	Department of the Interior
Historical eras	Enlightenment	Middle Ages
Regions	the South	the Midwest
Course names	Eastern Religions	Microbiology
Job title when used with a proper noun		President Benjamin Ladner

Capitalize the initial letters of proper adjectives (adjectives based on the names of people, places, and things).

African American bookstore	Avogadro's number	Irish music

Avoid unnecessary capitalization

Do not capitalize the names of seasons, academic disciplines (unless they are languages), or job titles used without a proper noun.

Seasons	fall, winter, spring, summer
Academic disciplines (except languages)	chemistry, computer science, psychology, English, French, Japanese
Job titles used without a proper noun	The vice president is on maternity leave.

Capitalize titles of publications

In MLA and CMS styles, when capitalizing titles, capitalize the initial letters of all first and last words and all other words except articles, prepositions, and coordinating conjunctions. Capitalize the initial letter of the first word in the subtitle following a colon.

James and the Giant Peach

The Grapes of Wrath

The Writing on the Wall: An Anthology of Graffiti Art

WRITING SMART

Capitalization in email

some people never press the shift key when typing email. while there are no rules for informal email, long stretches of text with no capitalization are tiresome to read, even in email sent between close friends.

SIMILARLY, SOME PEOPLE TYPE EMAIL IN ALL CAPS, WHICH LIKEWISE IS ANNOYING TO READ OVER LONG STRETCHES. ALSO, SOME PEOPLE FEEL READING ALL CAPS IS LIKE BEING SHOUTED AT.

Capitalization conventions are familiar to readers and thus help make messages easy to read. Using both uppercase and lowercase letters, even in the most informal writing, is a friendly act.

COMMON ERRORS

Capitalizing with colons, parentheses, and quotations

Capitalizing with colons

Except when a colon follows a heading, do not capitalize the first letter after a colon unless the colon links two main clauses (which can stand as complete sentences). If the material following the colon is a quotation, a formal statement, or consists of more than one sentence, capitalize the first letter. In other cases capitalization is optional.

Incorrect   We are all being integrated into a global economy that never sleeps: An economy determining our personal lives and our relationships with others.

(Continued on next page)

COMMON ERRORS *(continued)*

Correct   We are all being integrated into a global economy that never sleeps: We can work, shop, bank, and be entertained twenty-four hours a day.

Capitalizing with parentheses

Capitalize the first word of material enclosed in parentheses if the words stand on their own as a complete sentence.

> Beginning with Rachel Carson's *Silent Spring* in 1962, we stopped worrying so much about what nature was doing to us and began to worry about what we were doing to nature. (Science and technology that had been viewed as the solution to problems suddenly became viewed as their cause.)

If the material enclosed in parentheses is part of a larger sentence, do not capitalize the first letter enclosed in the parentheses.

> Beginning with Rachel Carson's *Silent Spring* (first published in 1962), we stopped worrying so much about what nature was doing to us and began to worry about what we were doing to nature.

Capitalizing with quotations

If the quotation of part of a sentence is smoothly integrated into a sentence, do not capitalize the first word. Smoothly integrated quotations do not require a comma to separate the sentence from the rest of the quotation.

> It's no wonder the *Monitor* wrote that Armand's chili was "the best in Georgia, bar none"; he spends whole days in his kitchen experimenting over bubbling pots.

(Continued on next page)

 COMMON ERRORS *(continued)*

But if the sentence contains an attribution and the quotation can stand as a complete sentence, capitalize the first word. In such sentences a comma should separate the attribution from the quotation.

> According to Janet Morris of the *Monitor,* "The chili Armand fusses over for hours in his kitchen is the best in Georgia, bar none."

Remember: For elements following colons or within parentheses or quotation marks, capitalize the first letter only if the group of words can stand as a complete sentence.

For step-by-step discussion, examples, and practice exercises, visit this page of the E-book at www.mycomplab.com.

Exercise 46.1   Nothing in the paragraph that follows has been capitalized. Revise it as necessary.

Example   ͨcourses in ᴬamerican history often disregard the founding
of the ᶠᴮᴵfbi.

The federal bureau of investigation (fbi) has long been considered an american institution that was fathered by president theodore roosevelt. during the early 1900s, the united states was going through what some referred to as the progressive era. (during this period, the american people believed government intervention was synonymous with a just society.) roosevelt, the president during part of this era, aided in the creation of an organization devoted to federal investigations. prior to 1907, federal investigations were carried out by agents-for-hire employed by the department of justice. on wednesday, may 27, 1908, the u.s. congress passed a law prohibiting the employment of agents-for-hire and enabling the establishment of an official secret service directly affiliated with the department. that spring, attorney general charles bonaparte appointed ten agents who would report to a chief examiner. this action is often considered to be the birth of the fbi.

46b Italics

The titles of entire works (books, magazines, newspapers, films) are italicized in print. The titles of parts of entire works are placed within quotation marks. When italicizing is difficult because you are using a typewriter or writing by hand, underline the titles of entire works instead; in papers in MLA style, always underline them.

Books	*Native Son*
Magazines	*Rolling Stone*
Journals	*Journal of Fish Biology*
Newspapers	*The Plain Dealer*
Feature-length films	*Star Wars*
Long poems	*The Divine Comedy*
Plays, operas, and ballets	*Our Town*
Television shows	*The Brady Bunch*
Radio shows and audio recordings	*Prairie Home Companion*
Paintings, sculptures, and other visual works of art	*Starry Night*
Pamphlets and bulletins	*Common Sense*

Also italicize or underline the names of ships and aircraft.

Spirit of St. Louis   *Challenger*
Titanic   *Pequod*

The exceptions. Do not italicize or underline the names of sacred texts.

The text for our Comparative Religions course, *Sacred Texts from around the World,* contains excerpts from the New English Bible, the Qur'an, the Talmud, the Upanishads, and the Bhagavad Gita.

Italicize unfamiliar foreign words

Italicize foreign words that are not part of common English usage. Do not italicize words that have become a common word or phrase in the English vocabulary. How do you decide which words are common? If a word appears in a standard English dictionary, it can be considered as adopted into English.

Incorrect   My favorite Italian restaurant serves six kinds of *risotto, including risotto al radicchio, risotto nero, and risotto ai frutti di mare.*

Correct   My favorite Italian restaurant serves six kinds of risotto, including risotto *al radicchio, risotto nero, and risotto ai frutti di mare.*

In this example, risotto, a dish made with Italian rice and other ingredients, has become familiar enough to appear in standard English dictionaries. The Italian names of specific kinds of risotto are not common and are not included in standard English dictionaries. They should be italicized.

Use italics to clarify your use of a word, letter, or number

In everyday speech, we often use cues—a pause, a louder or different tone—to communicate how we are using a word. In writing, italics help clarify when you use words in a referential manner, or letters and numbers as letters and numbers.

Incorrect   Shannon promised to contact Joel by early next week, but it soon became clear that her **early next week** actually meant Thursday or Friday.

Correct Shannon promised to contact Joel by early next week, but it soon became clear that her *early next week* actually meant Thursday or Friday.

Incorrect Although Giovanni was only two years old, he already knew how to draw **A** and **G**.

Corrrect Although Giovanni was only two years old, he already knew how to draw *A* and *G*.

Incorrect Stephen, who was five years old, did not know how to draw **1** or **2**.

Correct Stephen, who was five years old, did not know how to draw *1* or *2*.

Exercise 46.2 Underline any words in the following paragraph that should be italicized.

Example Both controversial in their own right, the famed clothing designer Coco Chanel and the painter of Guernica, Pablo Picasso, are listed by Time magazine as two of the "Most Interesting People of the Twentieth Century."

Many think Coco Chanel is to fashion what the Bible is to religion. Consequently, various types of media have been used to try to capture the essence of this innovative designer. Films such as Tonight or Never preserve Chanel's designs for future generations, while the failed Broadway musical Coco attempts to embody her life's work. More recently, print and small screen have attempted to encapsulate the impact of the designer in specials like A&E Top 10: Fashion Designers and books such as Chanel: Her Style and Her Life. Chanel was as monumental and self-destructive as the Titanic. She almost single-handedly redefined women's clothing through the popularization of sportswear and the jersey suit. But she also sympathized with Hitler after the release of his book Mein Kampf and the relocation of the Jews, and her image was further tarnished by her wartime romance with a Nazi officer. However, after her initial success waned during World War II, magazines such as Vogue and Life welcomed her back. She reinvented herself and her clothing line in the 1950s, and today she stands as one of the most influential fashion designers in history.

WRITING IN THE WORLD

Italicizing for emphasis

Italicizing a word can show the reader where to place the emphasis, but not all readers find italics appropriate. Use them sparingly. If you often find yourself italicizing words to indicate stresses, try to find stronger words that will do the same work.

Not effective

"You don't *have* to let me win at chess *just because I'm younger,* Lynne."

"I'm not trying to let you win. *I'm just a bad chess player.*"

Effective

"You don't have to let me win at chess just because I'm younger, Lynne."

"I'm *not* trying to let you win. I'm just a bad chess player."

Chapter 47

Abbreviations, Acronyms, and Numbers

Learn the conventions for scientific, technical, and business writing.

47a Abbreviations

Abbreviations are shortened forms of words. Because abbreviations vary widely, you will need to look in the dictionary to determine how to abbreviate words on a case-by-case basis. Nonetheless, there are a few patterns that abbreviations follow.

Abbreviate titles before and degrees after full names

Ms. Ella Fitzgerald	Dr. Suzanne Smith	Driss Ouaouicha, PhD
Prof. Vijay Aggarwal	San-qi Li, MD	Marissa Limon, LLD

Write out the professional title when it is used with only a last name.

Professor Chin	Doctor Rodriguez	Reverend Ames

Write out the professional title when it is used with only a last name.

Professor Chin
Doctor Rodriguez
Reverend Ames

Conventions for using abbreviations with years and times

BCE (before the common era) and CE (common era) are now preferred for indicating years, replacing BC (before Christ) and AD (*anno*

Domini ["the year of our Lord"]). Note that all are now used without periods.

> 479 BCE (or BC)
>
> 1610 CE (or AD, but AD is placed before the number)

The preferred written conventions for times are a.m. (*ante meridiem*) and p.m. (*post meridiem*).

> 9:03 a.m.
>
> 3:30 p.m.

An alternative is military time:

> The morning meal is served from 0600 to 0815; the evening meal is served from 1730 to 1945.

COMMON ERRORS

Making abbreviations and acronyms plural

Plurals of abbreviations and acronyms are formed by adding *s*, not *'s*.

> Technology is changing so rapidly these days that PCs become obsolete husks of circuits and plastic in only a few years.

Use an *'s* only to show possession.

> The NRA's position on trigger locks is that the government should advocate, not legislate, their use.

Remember: When making abbreviations and acronyms plural, add *s*, not *'s*.

 For step-by-step discussion, examples, and practice exercises, visit this page of the E-book at www.mycomplab.com.

Conventions for using abbreviations in college writing

Most abbreviations are inappropriate in formal writing except when the reader would be more familiar with the abbreviation than with the words it represents. When your reader is unlikely to be familiar with an abbreviation, spell out the term, followed by the abbreviation in parentheses, the first time you use it in a paper. The reader will then understand what the abbreviation refers to, and you may use the abbreviation in subsequent sentences.

> The Office of Civil Rights (OCR) is the agency that enforces Title IX regulations. In 1979, OCR set out three options for schools to comply with Title IX.

WRITING IN THE WORLD

Latin abbreviations

Some writers sprinkle Latin abbreviations throughout their writing, apparently thinking that they are a mark of learning. Frequently these abbreviations are used inappropriately. If you use Latin abbreviations, make sure you know what they stand for.

cf.	(*confer*) compare
e.g.	(*exempli gratia*) for example
et al.	(*et alia*) and others
etc.	(*et cetera*) and so forth
i.e.	(*id est*) that is
N.B.	(*nota bene*) note well
viz.	(*videlicet*) namely

In particular, avoid using *etc.* to fill out a list of items. Use of *etc.* announces that you haven't taken the time to finish a thought.

(Continued on next page)

Lazy   The contents of his grocery cart described his eating habits: a big bag of chips, hot sauce, frozen pizza, **etc.**

Better   The contents of his grocery cart described his eating habits: a big bag of chips, a large jar of hot sauce, two frozen pizzas, a twelve-pack of cola, three Mars bars, and a package of Twinkies.

Exercise 47.1   The following is a paragraph from a research paper in which every word is spelled out. Decide which words would be more appropriate as abbreviations and write them correctly. Remember, this is formal academic writing; be sure to follow the conventions for using abbreviations in papers. When you have more than one abbreviation style to choose from, select the one recommended in this section. Note: The term "dense rock equivalent" is abbreviated DRE.

Example   Peter Francis, ~~Doctor of Philosophy~~ PhD, is among the scholars who have written introductory texts on volcanoes.

The unpredictable, destructive nature of volcanoes has attracted the interest of both scholarly and lay circles. Though it erupted in anno Domini 79, Mount Vesuvius is still famous because of its violent decimation of the city of Pompeii. Second to Vesuvius in destructive power is Mount Pelée, which in 1902 killed nearly thirty thousand people (id est, all but four of the citizens of Saint Pierre). Scholars like Professor George Walker have attempted to quantify and predict the effects of volcanoes. Professor Walker developed a system whereby volcanic eruptions are judged by magnitude, intensity, dispersive power, violence, and destructive potential. Walker began using a measurement called dense rock equivalent to measure unwitnessed eruptions. The actual volume of a volcano is converted into dense rock equivalent, which accounts for spaces in the rocks. Walker et alia have continued to perform research which will aid in the study of volcanoes.

47b Acronyms

Acronyms are abbreviations formed by capitalizing the first letter in each word. Unlike other abbreviations, acronyms are pronounced as words.

AIDS for Acquired Immunodeficiency Syndrome
NASA for National Air and Space Administration
NATO for North Atlantic Treaty Organization
WAC for writing across the curriculum

A subset of acronyms is initial-letter abbreviations that have become so common that we know the organization or thing by its initials.

ACLU for American Civil Liberties Union
HIV for human immunodeficiency virus
MLA for Modern Language Association
rpm for revolutions per minute
WNBA for Women's National Basketball Association
YMCA for Young Men's Christian Association

Familiar acronyms and initial-letter abbreviations such as CBS, CIA, FBI, IQ, and UN are rarely spelled out. In a few cases, such as *radar* (*ra*dio *d*etecting *a*nd *r*anging) and *laser* (*l*ight *a*mplification by *s*timulated *e*mission of *r*adiation), the terms used to create the acronym have been forgotten by almost all who use them.

Unfamiliar acronyms and abbreviations should always be spelled out. Acronyms and abbreviations frequent in particular fields should be spelled out on first use. For example, MMPI (Minnesota Multiphasic Personality Inventory) is a familiar abbreviation in psychology but is unfamiliar to those outside that discipline. Even when acronyms are generally familiar, few readers will object to your giving the terms from which an acronym derives on the first use.

The National Association for the Advancement of Colored People (NAACP) is the nation's largest and strongest civil rights organization. The NAACP was founded in 1909 by a group of prominent black and white citizens who were outraged by the numerous lynchings of African Americans.

COMMON ERRORS

Punctuation of abbreviations and acronyms

The trend now is away from using periods with many abbreviations. In formal writing you can still use periods, with certain exceptions.

Do not use periods with

1. **Acronyms and initial-letter abbreviations:** AFL-CIO, AMA, HMO, NAFTA, NFL, OPEC
2. **Two-letter mailing abbreviations:** AZ (Arizona), FL (Florida), ME (Maine), UT (Utah)
3. **Compass points:** NE (northeast), SW (southwest)
4. **Technical abbreviations:** kph (kilometers per hour), SS (sum of squares), SD (standard deviation)

Remember: Do not use periods with postal abbreviations for states, compass points, technical abbreviations, and established organizations.

 For step-by-step discussion, examples, and practice exercises, visit this page of the E-book at www.mycomplab.com.

Exercise 47.2 The following paragraphs from a research paper use some abbreviations correctly and some incorrectly. Revise the paragraphs, adding abbreviations where needed and spelling out the words where needed. You may also need to add or subtract punctuation marks such as parentheses and periods. Remember to make decisions based on whether or not the general population is familiar with the abbreviation.

Example   Burning Man is an eight-day-long festival organized by

Black Rock City, ~~Limited Liability Company~~.
LLC

The festival, which culminates in the burning of a giant
man-shaped effigy, takes place on a playa in the Black Rock
Desert in Nevada, 90 miles (150 kilometers) N-NE of Reno. Black
Rock City, a temporary city which has its own DPW Department of
Public Works, is an experiment in community and self-expression.

As the event has grown, one of the challenges faced by the
organizers has been balancing the freedom of participants with
the requirements of various land management groups, such as
the Bureau of Land Management (BLM), and law enforcement
groups, such as the DEA and the Reno PD. BMO (Burning Man
Organization) is aware of the concerns about the festival's impact
on the environment, so it encourages participants to Leave No
Trace (L.N.T) of their visit to BRC. For example, participants are
told to be very careful not to contaminate the playa with litter
(commonly known as MOOP, or "matter out of place"). However,
scientists are also concerned about how Burning Man contributes
to global warming. Using several scales, including global warming
potential (GWP), they are measuring how much greenhouse gases
(chlorofluorocarbons, HFC's, PFCs) Burning Man participants will
create. The scientists' CoolingMan website suggests ways to offset
the damage caused by the festival, such as planting trees or
investing in alternative energy solutions.

47c Numbers

In formal writing, spell out any number that can be expressed in one or two
words, as well as any number, regardless of length, at the beginning of a sentence. Also, hyphenate two-word numbers from twenty-one to ninety-nine.

My office is **twenty-three** blocks from my apartment—too far to
walk but a perfect bike riding distance.

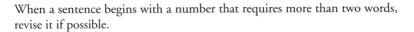

When a sentence begins with a number that requires more than two words, revise it if possible.

Correct but awkward

Fifteen thousand six hundred runners left the Hopkinton starting line at noon in the Boston Marathon.

Better

At the start of the Boston Marathon, 15,600 runners left Hopkinton at noon.

The exceptions.   In scientific reports and some business writing that requires the frequent use of numbers, using numerals more often is appropriate. Most styles do not write out in words a year, a date, an address, a page number, the time of day, decimals, sums of money, phone numbers, rates of speed, or the scene and act of a play. Use numerals instead.

In 2001 only 33% of respondents said they were satisfied with the City Council's proposals to help the homeless.

The 17 trials were conducted at temperatures 12–14°C with results ranging from 2.43 to 2.89 mg/dl.

When one number modifies another number, write one out and express the other in numeral form.

In the last year all four 8th Street restaurants have begun to donate their leftovers to the soup kitchen.

Only after Meryl had run in 12 fifty-mile ultramarathons did she finally win first place in her age group.

Exercise 47.3   All of the numbers in the following paragraph are spelled out. Decide where it would be more appropriate to use the numerals instead and revise. Remember to add hyphens where necessary.

Example   Caused by the dysfunction of two tiny joints near the
ears, a form of temporomandibular joint dysfunction
(TMJ) was identified in ~~nineteen hundred thirty-four~~ *1934*
by Doctor Costen.

Five hundred sixty is the number of times you heard a
popping sound resonating from the jaw of the woman sitting next
to you on the plane. She may be one of over nine point five
million people suffering from TMJ, a condition that often causes
symptoms such as popping, swelling, and aching in the jaw. At
least one study has shown that women on hormone treatments
are seventy seven percent more likely to develop TMJ symptoms.
The disorder goes by at least six names, most of which include
the initials TM, for temporomandibular: Costen's Syndrome, TMJ,
TMD, TMJDD, CMD, and TMPD. Doctors currently prescribe at least
forty nine different treatments for the disorder, ranging from one-
dollar-and-fifty-cent mouth guards to prevent tooth grinding to a
myriad of treatments which could cost thousands of dollars.

If English Is Not Your First Language

Chapter 48

Writing in a Second Language

You can overcome the challenges of writing in a second language.

48a Understand the Demands of Writing in a Second Language

Many multilingual writers find that the main challenges of writing in a second language are more than just grammar and vocabulary. While grammar and vocabulary are important, sometimes too much focus on the details of writing can take your attention away from other issues that affect your ability to communicate effectively. If English is not your first language, you may have noticed some differences between writing in English and in your native language. Some of the differences are relatively easy to identify, such as the direction of writing (left to right instead of right to left or top to bottom), the uses of punctuation (a2,500.00 instead of a2.500,00), and conventions of capitalization and spelling. Other differences are more subtle and complex, such as the citation of sources, the uses of persuasive appeals, and the level of directness expected in a given situation.

Talk with other writers

When you write in an unfamiliar situation, it may be helpful to find a few examples of the type of writing you are trying to produce. If you are writing a letter of application to accompany a résumé, for example, ask your friends to share similar letters of application with you and look for the various ways they present themselves in writing in that situation. Ask them to read their letters out loud and to explain the decisions they made as they wrote and revised their letters. In talking with them about how and why they wrote their letters of application, you will develop a better understanding of the ways writers in English respond to a given writing situation.

Know what is expected in college writing

Understanding what is expected in college writing is as important as understanding English language conventions. College writers are expected to meet the expectations listed on the next page. You will find detailed information on these expectations in other parts of this book.

WRITING SMART

A guide to expectations for writing in college

Address the specific demands of the assignment.	See Sections 2a and 2b for general assignment analysis. See Section 16a for analyzing research assignments.
Use the appropriate format and sources for particular disciplines.	See Chapters 10 and 11.
Pay close attention to document design.	See Chapter 14 for print and onscreen design. See Chapter 15 for presentation design.
Follow specific formatting rules.	See Sections 14b and 23l for MLA style. See Section 24f for APA style.
Document the sources of all ideas not originally yours.	See Chapter 21.

(Continued on next page)

Choose words carefully, and connect ideas clearly.	See Part 7.
Use accepted grammatical forms.	See Part 8. See Chapters 49, 50, and 51 for specific explanations of English grammar and mechanics for second-language speakers.
Spell and punctuate correctly.	See Part 9.
Use your instructor's and peers' comments to revise and improve your writing.	See Chapter 4.

48b Use Your Native Language as a Resource

As you continue to develop your ability to write in English, you will find that many of the strategies you developed in your native language are useful in English as well. The ability to think critically, for example, is important in any language, although what it means to be "critical" may differ from one context to another. Imagery, metaphors, and expressions adapted from your native language may make your writing culturally richer and more interesting to read.

You can also use your native language to develop your texts. Many people, when they cannot find an appropriate word in English, write down a word, a phrase, or even a sentence in their native language and consult a dictionary or a handbook later; it helps to avoid interrupting the flow of thought in the process of writing. Incorporating key terms from your native language is also a possible strategy. Here, for example, a term from Japanese adds flavor and perspective to a sentence: "Some political leaders need to have *wakimae*—a realistic idea of one's own place in the world."

Exercise 48.1   Write a few paragraphs describing the similarities and differences you see between writing in your first language and writing in English. What were the greatest challenges for you in learning to write in English? What strategies have you developed to help you face these challenges? What aspects of writing in your first language have you adapted to help you write in English? What aspects of writing in your first langauge might you use for style or as a rhetorical tool?

48c Use Dictionaries

You can use regular English dictionaries for definitions, but most English dictionaries designed for native English speakers do not include all of the information that many nonnative English speakers find useful. For example, you may know the word *audience* but not whether and when *audience* can function as a count noun. Learner's dictionaries, such as the *Longman Dictionary of American English*, include information about count/noncount nouns and transitive/intransitive verbs (see Chapters 49 and 50). Many of them also provide sample sentences to help you understand how a word is used.

Some nonnative English speakers also find a bilingual dictionary useful. Bilingual dictionaries are especially useful when you want to check your understanding of an English word or when you want to find equivalent words for culture-specific concepts and technical terms. Some bilingual dictionaries also provide sample sentences. When sample sentences are not provided, check the usage in another dictionary or by searching for the word or phrase on the Web.

48d Understand English Idioms

Some English **idioms** function like proverbs, familiar expressions that offer wisdom. In the United States, for example, if someone has to "eat crow," he or she has been forced to admit being wrong about something. When people "walk a fine line," they are being careful not to irritate or anger people on different sides of an argument. Simpler examples of idiomatic usage—word order, word choice, and combinations that follow no obvious or set rules—are common even in the plainest English.

The way certain prepositions are paired with certain words is often idiomatic. It might be possible to use a preposition other than the one usually used, but the preferred combination is accepted as correct because it sounds "right" to longtime English speakers. Any other preposition sounds "wrong," even if it makes sense.

"Incorrect" idiom   Here is the answer *of* your question.

Accepted idiom   Here is the answer *to* your question.

Note that the second sentence is no more logical than the first. But to first-language English speakers, that first sentence sounds imprecise and strange. In a paper written for college, an instructor would likely mark such a sentence as having "poor word choice." See Section 49e for more information on English preposition usage.

Placement order for modifiers is often idiomatic in English—or at least the rules are arbitrary enough that it may make more sense to memorize certain patterns than to try to place modifiers entirely by logic. Say you want to modify the noun "dogs" with three adjectives:

brown
three
small

In English, all these adjectives will be placed before the noun they are modifying. But in what order should they go? The possibilities are

Small three brown dogs
Three brown small dogs
Small brown three dogs
Three small brown dogs
Brown small three dogs
Brown three small dogs

Only two of these options may sound at all correct to first-language English speakers: "Three brown small dogs" and "Three small brown dogs." To put the adjective for number anywhere but first sounds unnatural to native speakers. The other two adjectives, describing size and color, also have a natural "order" to the ears of native speakers. Thus "three small brown dogs" sounds more natural than "three brown small dogs."

Placing the modifier for color ahead of that for size seems peculiar—in fact, doing so might make a native English speaker wonder if there is some special reason to emphasize the out-of-place modifier. Perhaps you are trying to distinguish between several groups of three small dogs, and need to stress that the brown ones (not the gray or black or spotted ones), were the ones you meant. There is no real "reason" to place size before color, but if you don't, readers will assume you *did* have a reason for not following the customary order. Placing modifiers in the order that native speakers expect to hear is important to avoid miscommunication.

Verb phrases in English are also governed by complex rules that most native speakers learn "by ear" rather than from books. These **phrasal verbs** can be particularly tricky for second-language speakers because languages other than English handle such forms quite differently. Yet verb phrases must be used correctly if you wish to avoid confusing readers. English phrasal verbs allow writers to give very specific information about the action taking place, and English speakers expect to receive that information in a consistent way. See Section 50h for information on using phrasal verbs in English.

Though idioms may be frustrating, you can take comfort in the fact that many first-language English speakers struggle with them, especially when using prepositions. Because idioms are not governed by a single set of rules, you can only learn idioms one example at a time. Thus, the more you speak, read, and hear English, the better your grasp of idioms, especially preposition usage, will become. As you are writing, you should check your use of prepositions and other idioms. Dictionaries will often list the prepositions most commonly taken by certain words. Pay particular attention to comments about "word choice" or notations like "awkward phrasing" in your paper drafts. Ask your instructor for more specific instructions, and visit your writing center for more explanation when you need it.

WRITING SMART

Use the Web to check English idioms

Many combinations of English words don't follow hard and fast rules but simply sound right to native speakers of English. If you are unsure whether you should write "disgusted with" or "disgusted for," use Google or another search engine to find out how they are used.

Put the words inside quotation marks in the search box. You'll get many hits for both "disgusted with" and "disgusted for," but you'll see about ten times more for "disgusted with." You'll also notice that many of the hits for "disgusted for" will be examples of "disgusted. For" with "disgusted" at the end of one sentence and "For" at the beginning of the next sentence. You can use this method to determine that "disgusted with" is the better choice.

Exercise 48.2   Choose the idiom commonly used in English. If you are unsure, use Google or another search engine to test the idiom.

1. My girlfriend is the (peach of my eye/apple of my eye).
2. If you (back out/quit out) now, your (name will be mud/name will be muck).
3. That line of research goes (into a closed outlet/up a blind alley).
4. Sunny sang well considering she is still (new as the dew/wet behind the ears).
5. The president of the company is (well heeled/piled with money).
6. He was a (bat on the ceiling/fly on the wall) at the meeting and told us everything that happened.
7. Jianping and Zhao have been dating for years, but they will finally (chain together/tie the knot) this June.

8. (To make a long story short/to make a long distance near), we got lost coming home.
9. Trying to find the address without a map is (an arrow into the sky/a shot in the dark).
10. After losing at tennis, Ahmed had (sour grapes/spoiled milk).
11. Digging up the candidate s 20-year-old statements is a (pickled fish/red herring).
12. When the product didn t sell for the third year in a row, the company decided it was time to (chop the head/pull the plug).

Chapter 49

Nouns, Articles, and Prepositions

Master the conventions for using the common articles the, a, *and* an.

49a Kinds of Nouns

There are two basic kinds of nouns. A **proper noun** begins with a capital letter and names a unique person, place, or thing: *Theodore Roosevelt, Russia, Eiffel Tower.* In the following list, note that each word refers to someone or something so specific that it bears a name.

Proper nouns

Beethoven	Yao Ming	South Korea
Concorde	New York Yankees	Africa
Empire State Building	Picasso	Stockholm
Honda	Queen Elizabeth	Lake Michigan
Thanksgiving	Virginia Woolf	New Hampshire

The other basic kind of noun is called a **common noun**. Common nouns do not name a unique person, place, or thing: *man, country, tower.* Note that the words in the following list are not names and so are not capitalized.

Common nouns

composer	athlete	country
airplane	baseball team	continent
building	painter	city
company	queen	lake
holiday	writer	state

Common nouns can also refer to abstractions, such as *grace, love,* and *power.* In English, proper nouns are names and are always capitalized while common nouns are not names and are not capitalized.

Exercise 49.1   Underline the common nouns in the following paragraph once and underline the proper nouns twice. Correct any errors in capitalization.

Example   In 1903, a fire in ̲c̲hicago led to the new safety ̲Laws.

In 1903, Chicago opened the new iroquois theater on West Randolph street. Around christmas, the Theater held a performance of "Mr. blue beard" starring eddie Foy. Shortly after the play started, a light sparked causing a curtain to catch on fire. Elvira Pinedo said the crowd panicked after a giant Fireball appeared. This panic led to the deaths of more than six hundred people, many of whom died because bodies were pressed against doors that opened inward. Shortly after the Tragedy, mayor Carter h. Harrison was indicted and new laws demanded Theaters have doors that open outward, toward the lobby.

49b   Count and Noncount Nouns

Common nouns can be classified as either *count* or *noncount.* **Count nouns** can be made plural, usually by adding *-s* (*finger, fingers*) or by using their plural forms (*person, people; datum, data*). **Noncount nouns** cannot be counted directly and cannot take the plural form (*information,* but not *informations*; *garbage*, but not *garbages*). Some nouns can be either count or noncount, depending on how they are used. *Hair* can refer to either a strand of hair, when it serves as a count noun, or a mass of hair, when it becomes a noncount noun.

Correct usage of *hair* as count noun

I carefully combed my few hairs across my mostly bald scalp.

Correct usage of *hair* as noncount noun

My roommate spent an hour this morning combing his hair.

In the same way, *space* can refer to a particular, quantifiable area (as in *two parking spaces*) or to unspecified open area (as in *there is some space left*).

If you are not sure whether a particular noun is count or noncount, consult a learner's dictionary. Count nouns are usually indicated as [C] (for "countable") and noncount nouns as [U] (for "uncountable").

Exercise 49.2 The following sentences include various types of plural nouns: count, noncount, and those that can be either, depending on how they are used. Underline the correct plural form from the choices provided.

> **Example** Berry Gordy's Motown Records made much (money/ monies) and introduced America to many (entertainer/ entertainers) who would otherwise not have been heard because of their race.

1. In the late 1950s, Detroit was one of America's many (city/cities) famous for the production of (numbers of automobile/automobiles).

2. Detroit's sound soon changed from the auto industry's assembly line of heavy (pieces of equipment/equipments) to Motown's assembly line of superstar musical (groups of act/acts).

3. Gordy was famous for his (kinds of method/methods) of production; he tailored images down to the styles of performers' (hair/hairs), dances, and musical numbers.

4. The (positions of employment/employments) were clear: (all of the employee/employees) were allowed to perform only the tasks for which they were specifically hired.
5. Though Gordy s techniques led Motown to (much wealth/wealths), the same techniques sent entertainers packing for labels that would provide them with more (personal satisfaction/personal satisfactions).
6. The apartment is unfurnished; you may need to buy (a few pieces of furniture/some furnitures).

49c Singular and Plural Forms

Count nouns usually take both singular and plural forms, while noncount nouns usually do not take plural forms and are not counted directly. A count noun can have a number before it (as in *two books, three oranges*) and can be qualified with adjectives such as *many* (*many books*), *some* (*some schools*), *a lot of* (*a lot of people*), *a few* (meaning several, as in *I ate a few apples*), and *few* (meaning almost none, as in *few people volunteered*).

WRITING IN THE WORLD

Noncount nouns in English

In some languages, all nouns can take singular and plural forms. In English, noncount nouns refer to a collective mass that, taken as a whole, does not have a particular or regular shape. Think of the noncount noun as a mass that can be subdivided into smaller parts without losing its identity. Noncount nouns like *information, garbage, bread,* and *sand* can be broken down into smaller units and remain unchanged in essence: *bits* of information, *piles* of garbage, *slices* of bread, *grains* of sand. Count nouns like *train, finger,* and *ocean* cannot be subdivided without becoming something else: a wheel on a train, a knuckle on a finger, but no longer simply a train or a finger.

Noncount nouns can be counted or quantified in only two ways: either by general adjectives that treat the noun as a mass (*much* information, *little* garbage, *some* news) or by placing another noun between the quantifying word and the noncount noun (two *kinds* of information, three *piles* of garbage, a *piece* of news).

COMMON ERRORS

Singular and plural forms of count nouns

Count nouns are simpler to quantify than noncount nouns. But remember that English requires you to state both singular and plural forms of nouns consistently and explicitly. Look at the following sentences.

Incorrect   The three bicyclist shaved their leg before the big race.

Correct   The three bicyclists shaved their legs before the big race.

In the first sentence, readers would understand that the plural form of *bicyclist* is implied by the quantifier *three* and that the plural form of *leg* is implied by the fact that bicyclists have two legs. (If they didn't, you would hope that the writer would have made that clear already!) Nevertheless, correct form in English is to indicate the singular or plural nature of a count noun explicitly, in every instance.

Remember: English requires you to use plural forms of count nouns even when a plural number is clearly stated.

For more help using count and noncount nouns, try the exercises found on this page of the E-book at www.mycomplab.com.

Exercise 49.3 The following paragraph includes many examples of singular/plural inconsistency. Correct any incorrect versions of nouns.

Example In the history of fashion, many ~~word~~ *words* have lost their original ~~meaning~~ *meanings*.

Every year, thousands of bride and groom don traditional attire while attending their wedding. One garment associated with many of these traditional wedding is the groom's cummerbund or decorative waistband. This garment dates back many century to Persia where they were known as a "kamarband" or "loinband." The cummerbunds was first adopted by a few British military officer in colonial India and later by civilians. These cummerbund were traditionally worn with the pleats facing up to hold ticket stubs and other item. These day, however, cummerbunds are usually worn just for decoration.

 **Articles**

Articles indicate that a noun is about to appear, and they clarify what the noun refers to. There are only two kinds of articles in English, definite and indefinite.

1. **the:** *The* is a **definite article**, meaning that it refers to (1) a specific object already known to the reader, (2) one about to be made known to the reader, or (3) a unique object.

2. **a, an:** The **indefinite articles** *a* and *an* refer to an object whose specific identity is not known to the reader. The only difference between *a* and *an* is that *a* is used before a consonant sound (*man, friend, yellow*), while *an* is used before a vowel sound (*animal, enemy, orange*).

Look at these sentences, identical except for their articles, and imagine that each is taken from a different newspaper story:

Rescue workers lifted the man to safety.

Rescue workers lifted a man to safety.

By use of the definite article *the*, the first sentence indicates that the reader already knows something about the identity of this man and his needing to be rescued. The news story has already referred to him. The sentence also suggests that this was the only man rescued, at least in this particular part of the story.

The indefinite article *a* in the second sentence indicates that the reader does not know anything about this man. Either this is the first time the news story has referred to him or there are other men in need of rescue. When deciding whether to use the definite or indefinite article, ask yourself whether the noun refers to something specific or unique, or whether it refers to something general. *The* is used for specific or unique nouns; *a* and *an* are used for nonspecific or general nouns.

A small number of conditions determine when and how count and noncount nouns are preceded by articles.

1. *A* or *an* is not used with noncount nouns.

Incorrect   The crowd hummed with **an** excitement.

Correct   The crowd hummed with excitement.

2. *A* or *an* is used with singular count nouns whose particular identity is unknown to the reader or writer.

Detective Johnson was reading a book.

3. *The* is used with most count and noncount nouns whose particular identity is known to the reader.

The noun may be known for one of several reasons:

- The noun has already been mentioned.

  I bought a book yesterday. The book is about Iraq.

- The noun is accompanied by a superlative such as *highest, lowest, best, worst, least interesting*, or *most beautiful* that makes its specific identity clear.

  This is the most interesting book about Iraq.

- The noun's identity is made clear by its context in the sentence.

  The book I bought yesterday is about Iraq.

- The noun has a unique identity, such as *the moon*.

  This book has as many pages as the Bible.

4. *The* is not used with noncount nouns meaning "in general."

Incorrect	The war is hell.
Correct	War is hell.

COMMON ERRORS

Articles with count and noncount nouns

Knowing how to distinguish between count and noncount nouns can help you decide which article to use. Noncount nouns are never used with the indefinite articles *a* and *an*.

Incorrect	Maria jumped into a water.
Correct	Maria jumped into the water.

No articles are used with noncount and plural count nouns when you wish to state something that has a general application.

Incorrect	The water is a precious natural resource.
Correct	Water is a precious natural resource.

Incorrect	The soccer players tend to be quick and agile.
Correct	Soccer players tend to be quick and agile.

(Continued on next page)

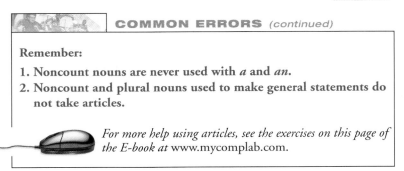

COMMON ERRORS *(continued)*

Remember:

1. Noncount nouns are never used with *a* and *an*.
2. Noncount and plural nouns used to make general statements do not take articles.

For more help using articles, see the exercises on this page of the E-book at www.mycomplab.com.

Exercise 49.4   Underline the correct definite or indefinite articles for the nouns in the following paragraph.

Example   Both (a/an/the) novel and (a/an/the) screenplay have been written about the career of (a/an/the) African American boxer Jack Johnson.

In (a/an/the) early 1900s, boxing films were (a/an/the) extremely popular form of entertainment; (a/an/the) fight would be filmed and shown in movie houses across (a/an/the) country. This practice changed after (a/an) race riot occurred following (a/an) match between (a/an/the) white man, ex-champion Jim Jeffries, and (a/an/the) black man, Jack Johnson. Jeffries had previously refused to fight (a/an) African American boxer, but after Johnson defeated (a/an/the) current white champion, Jeffries agreed to meet (a/an/the) challenger. After Johnson defeated (a/an/the) ex-champion, a nationwide race riot erupted in large portions of (a/an/the) South, as well as (a/an/the) number of other locales. These riots caused alarm in (a/an/the) United States Congress, and within three weeks, (a/an) bill was passed prohibiting (a/an/the) public screening of such films.

Exercise 49.5 The following paragraph includes properly and improperly used articles. Underline the articles, identify the types of nouns they modify (plural or singular, count or noncount), and correct any improperly chosen articles.

Example
Singular count
Troy James Hurtubise is an inventor and conservationist from North Bay, Ontario, who is best known for attempting to develop the suit made for *Singular count* what he calls a "close-quarter bear research." *Noncount*

Rewritten
Troy James Hurtubise is an inventor and conservationist from North Bay, Ontario, who is best known for attempting to develop a suit made for what he calls "close-quarter bear research."

Hurtubise's obsession with the bears began in 1984 when he survived encounter with an adult grizzly bear. Inspired by a movie *Robocop*, Hurtubise decided to build a suit that would withstand the bear attacks. Strangely, he worked to make his suit fireproof as well. Seven years later, he introduced the suit, an *Ursus Mark IV*. Under consultation with a physicists, he tested the suit against the attacks by baseball bat wielding bikers, impact with a swinging 300-pound log, and a flamethrowers. These tests and their results can be seen in documentary *Project Grizzly*.

49e Prepositions

Prepositions are positional or directional words like *to, for, from, at, in, on*, and *with*. They are used before nouns and pronouns, and they also combine with adjectives and adverbs. Each preposition has a wide range of possible meanings depending on how it is used, and each must be learned over time in its many contexts.

Some of the most common prepositional phrases describe time and place, and many are idiomatic.

Incorrect	On midnight
Correct	At midnight

Incorrect	In the counter
Correct	On the counter

Incorrect	In Saturday
Correct	On Saturday

Incorrect	On February
Correct	In February

Over time, you may notice patterns that help you determine the appropriate preposition. For example, *at* precedes a particular time, *on* precedes a day of the week, and *in* precedes a month, year, or other period of time.

COMMON ERRORS

Misused prepositions

The correct use of prepositions often seems unpredictable to nonnative speakers of English. When you are not sure which preposition to use, consult a dictionary.

Of for *about*   The report on flight delays raised criticism ~~of~~ about the scheduling of flights.

On for *into*   The tennis player went ~~on~~ into a slump after failing to qualify for the French Open.

To for *in*   Angry over her low seeding in the tournament, Amy resigned her membership ~~to~~ in the chess club.

(Continued on next page)

COMMON ERRORS *(continued)*

To **for** *of*   The family was ignorant ~~to~~ of the controversial history of the house they purchased.

Remember: When you are uncertain about a preposition, consult a learner's dictionary intended for nonnative speakers of English. See Chapter 48 on the use of learner's dictionaries.

For a list of common verbs with prepositions that follow them, plus additional exercises, visit this page of the E-book at www.mycomplab.com.

Exercise 49.6   Underline the proper preposition in parentheses in the following paragraph.

> **Example**   (<u>In</u>/On/At) the 1940s, several dozen pilots died trying to break Mach one, the speed of sound.

(In, On, At) that time, pilots were familiar (with/in/on) the "wall of air" that existed (in/on/at) the speed of sound. Many airplanes shattered (into/onto/from) a million pieces because of this "wall of air." Pilots were especially afraid (for/on/of) a condition called "compressibility," which would make them lose control (in/of/on) the plane. Air Force pilot Chuck Yeager tried to break the sound barrier (from/with/on) *Glamorous Glennis*, a plane named (from/for/to) his wife. (In/On/At) October 14, 1947, Yeager made an attempt to reach Mach one. The ground crew heard a boom (from/at/in) the distance and feared that *Glamorous Glennis* had crashed. They cheered (with/from/in) joy when they heard Yeager say (with/in/on) the radio a few moments later that he had broken the sound barrier.

Exercise 49.7   The following paragraph contains adjective + preposition phrases. Choose the correct preposition.

Example   The Statue of Liberty was (full for/<u>full of</u>) significance for the millions of immigrants.

The United States remains (grateful to/grateful with) the people of France for the gift of the Statue of Liberty. France supported the colonists during the American Revolution and continues to be (proud for/proud of) its role in creating the United States. Although many Americans today are not (aware of/aware with) the importance of French support in the founding of their country, they are nonetheless (interested in/interested with) French culture and (fond of/fond with) its cuisine.

Chapter 50

Verbs

Learn the special difficulties of English verbs for nonnative speakers.

50a Types of Verbs

The verb system in English can be divided between simple verbs like *run, speak,* and *look* and verb phrases like *may have run, have spoken,* and *will be looking.* In the verb phrases, the words that appear before the main verbs—*may, have, will,* and *be*—are called **auxiliary verbs** (also called **helping verbs**). Helping verbs, as their name suggests, exist to help express something about the action of main verbs: for example, when the action occurs (tense), whether the subject acted or was acted upon (voice), or whether or not an action occurred.

50b *Be* Verbs

Indicating tense and voice with *be* verbs

Like the other auxiliary verbs *have* and *do, be* changes form to signal tense. In addition to *be* itself, the **be verbs** are *is, am, are, was, were,* and *been.* To show ongoing action, *be* verbs are followed by the present participle, which is a verb with an *-ing* ending:

Incorrect   I am **think** of all the things I'd rather **be do.**

Correct   I am thinking of all the things I'd rather be doing.

Incorrect   He **was run** as fast as he could.

Correct   He was running as fast as he could.

To show that an action is being done to, rather than by, the subject, follow *be* verbs with the past participle (a verb usually ending in *-ed, -en,* or *-t*):

Incorrect   The movie **was direct** by John Woo.

Correct   The movie **was directed** by John Woo.

Incorrect   The complaint **will be file** by the victim.

Correct   The complaint **will be filed** by the victim.

WRITING IN THE WORLD

Verbs that express cognitive activity

English, unlike Chinese, Arabic, and several other languages, requires a form of *be* before the present or past participle. As you have probably discovered, however, English has many exceptions to its rules. Verbs that express some form of cognitive activity rather than a direct action are not used as present participles with *be* verbs. Examples of such words include *know, like, see,* and *believe.*

Incorrect   You **were knowing** that I would be late.
Correct   You **knew** that I would be late.

But here's an exception to an exception: A small number of these verbs, such as *considering, thinking,* and *pondering,* can be used as present participles with *be* verbs.

I **am considering** whether to finish my homework first.

Exercise 50.1   The following paragraph is filled with *be* verbs. In each case, underline the correct verb form from the choices provided in parentheses.

Example   Rosh Hashanah, one of the religious High Holy Days, (is celebrated/is celebrating) beginning on the second day of the seventh month of the Jewish calendar, Tishri.

Though many think it marks only the Jewish New Year, those who celebrate Rosh Hashanah (understand/are understanding) that it has many other meanings as well. Rosh Hashanah (is also called/are also called) the day of the blowing of the Shofar, the day of remembrance, and the day of judgment. It long (has been consider/has been considered) the only High Holy Day that warrants a two-day celebration; those who (observe/are observing) the holiday consider the two-day period one extended forty-eight-hour day. Families (feast/are feasting) on foods that (are sweetened/are sweetening) with honey, apples, and carrots, symbolizing the sweet year to come. Challah, the bread that (is eating/is eaten) on the Sabbath, is reshaped into a ring, symbolizing the hope that the upcoming year will roll smoothly.

50c Modal Auxiliary Verbs

Modal auxiliary verbs—*will, would, can, could, may, might, shall, must,* and *should*—are helping verbs that express conditions like possibility, permission, speculation, expectation, obligation, and necessity. Unlike the helping verbs *be, have,* and *do,* modal verbs do not change form based on the grammatical subject of the sentence (*I, you, she, he, it, we, they*).

Two basic rules apply to all uses of modal verbs. First, modal verbs are always followed by the simple form of the verb. The simple form is the verb by itself, in the present tense, such as *have,* but not *had, having,* or *to have.*

Incorrect　She should **studies** harder to pass the exam.

Correct　She should study harder to pass the exam.

The second rule is that you should not use modals consecutively.

Incorrect　If you work harder at writing, you **might could** improve.

Correct　If you work harder at writing, you might improve.

Ten conditions that modals express

- **Speculation:** If you had flown, you would have arrived yesterday.
- **Ability:** She can run faster than Jennifer.
- **Necessity:** You must know what you want to do.
- **Intention:** He will wash his own clothes.
- **Permission:** You may leave now.
- **Advice:** You should wash behind your ears.
- **Possibility:** It might be possible to go home early.
- **Assumption:** You must have stayed up late last night.
- **Expectation:** You should enjoy the movie.
- **Order:** You must leave the building.

Exercise 50.2   The following sentences contain modal auxiliary verbs. Some are used properly and some improperly. Identify the conditions they express (speculation, ability, necessity, and so on) and correct any incorrect modal usage.

> **Example**   The cause of Karen Silkwood's death might could being one of the great conspiracies of recent American history.
>
> **Revise**   The cause of Karen Silkwood's death might be one of the great conspiracies of recent American history. (possibility)

1. In the 1970s, the Kerr-McGee plutonium plant was accused of violations that may shall have endangered workers lives.
2. After becoming contaminated with airborne plutonium, Karen Silkwood decided she would working harder to effect change.
3. Silkwood believed she had information that should have gone public and would having incriminated the company.
4. On the day she would have shared her information, she died in an automobile accident.
5. Some think her death might have been part of a conspiracy carried out by the company.

50d Verbs and Infinitives

Several verbs are followed by particular verb forms. An **infinitive** is *to* plus the simple form of the verb. Here are common verbs that are followed by an infinitive:

afford	expect	promise
agree	fail	refuse
ask	hope	seem
attempt	intend	struggle
claim	learn	tend
consent	need	wait
decide	plan	want
demand	prepare	wish

Incorrect You **learn playing** the guitar by practicing.

Correct You **learn to play** the guitar by practicing.

Some verbs require that a noun or pronoun come after the verb and before the infinitive:

advise	instruct	require
cause	order	tell
command	persuade	warn

Incorrect I would **advise to watch** where you step.

Correct I would **advise you to watch** where you step.

A few verbs, when followed by a noun or pronoun, take an *unmarked infinitive*, which is an infinitive without *to*.

have	let	make

Incorrect I will **let** her **to plan** the vacation.

Correct I will **let** her **plan** the vacation.

Exercise 50.3   Complete the following sentences by choosing the proper verb, pronoun, and infinitive combinations from those provided in parentheses. Underline the correct answer.

Example   Because reality television producers (to struggle/struggle to) attract and keep a wide audience, they have developed many different formulas for their shows.

1. Shows in which a camera (follows/to follow) a person or a group of people around during their everyday life (refer to you/are referred to) as "documentary style."

2. The best known type of documentary style show (forces strangers living/forces strangers to live) together, (causing them to face/causing to face) a variety of conflicts.

3. Other documentary shows follow a professional or group of professionals as they (try completing/try to complete) a project, such as (opening/to open) a restaurant.

4. The extreme competition on some reality shows (causes to cheat participants/causes participants to cheat) against each other so that they will not be (chosen to leave/chosen leaving) the show.

5. A more positive type of show is the improvement or make-over show in which experts (advise to improve someone/advise someone to improve) his or her clothes, home, or overall life.

50e Verbs and *–ing* Verbals

Other verbs are followed by **gerunds**, which are verbs ending in *-ing* that are used as nouns. Here are common verbs that are followed by a gerund.

admit	discuss	quit
advise	enjoy	recommend
appreciate	finish	regret
avoid	imagine	risk
consider	practice	suggest

Incorrect	She will **finish to grade** papers by noon.
Correct	She will **finish grading** papers by noon.

A smaller number of verbs can be followed by either gerunds or infinitives (see Section 50d).

begin	hate	love
continue	like	start

With Gerund   She likes working in the music store.

With Infinitive   She likes to work in the music store.

> *For more help using gerunds and infinitives, see the exercises on this page of the E-book at* www.mycomplab.com.

Exercise 50.4   The following sentences include verbs that should be followed by either gerunds or infinitives. Underline the correct gerund or infinitive from the options provided in parentheses. If both options are correct, underline both.

Example   Children enjoyed (to watch/<u>watching</u>) Pecos Bill in Disney's 1948 animated feature *Melody Time*.

1. Historians risk (misidentifying/to misidentify) actual origins when stories have been passed down simply by word of mouth.
2. Though some like (to believe/believing) that Edward O Reilly found the story of Pecos Bill circulating among American cowboys, it is hard to prove.
3. The story of little Bill, who was raised by coyotes, fails (to go/going) away despite its ambiguous origins.
4. Despite the confusion, stories about Bill s bride Slue-Foot Sue and his horse Widow Maker continue (to spread/spreading) as part of Americana.
5. Because of the debate over authenticity, however, some consider (to call/calling) the story popular culture rather than folklore.

50f Conditional Sentences

Conditional sentences express *if-then* relationships: They consist of a **subordinate clause** beginning with *if,* *unless,* or *when* that expresses a condition, and a **main clause** that expresses a result. The tense and mood of the verb in the main clause and the type of conditional sentence determine the tense and mood of the verb in the subordinate clause.

┌─SUBORDINATE CLAUSE─┐ ┌──────MAIN CLAUSE──────┐
When the wind stops, the sea becomes calm.

Conditional sentences fall into three categories: **factual, predictive**, and **hypothetical**.

Factual conditionals

Factual conditional sentences express factual relationships: If this happens, that will follow. The tense of the verb in the conditional clause is the same as the tense of the verb in the result clause:

Incorrect	When it rains, the ground **would become** wet.
Correct	When it rains, the ground becomes wet.

Predictive conditionals

Predictive conditional sentences express predicted consequences from possible conditions. The verb in the conditional clause is present tense, and the verb in the result clause is formed with a modal (*will, would, can, could, may, might, shall, must,* and *should*) plus the base form of the verb.

Incorrect	If you **take** the long way home, you **enjoy** the ride more.
Correct	If you **take** the long way home, you will enjoy the ride more.

Hypothetical conditionals

Hypothetical conditional sentences express events that are either not factual or unlikely to happen. For hypothetical events in the past, the conditional

clause verb takes the past perfect tense. The main clause verb is formed from *could have, would have*, or *might have* plus the past participle.

Incorrect If we **had fed** the dog last night, he **would not run** away.

Correct If we **had fed** the dog last night, he would not have run away.

For hypothetical events in the present or future, the conditional clause verb takes the past tense and the main clause verb is formed from *could, would,* or *might* and the base form.

Incorrect If we **paid** off our credit cards, we **can** buy a house.

Correct If we **paid** off our credit cards, we could buy a house.

For more help using conditionals, see the exercises on this page of the E-book at www.mycomplab.com.

Exercise 50.5 Rewrite the following sentences to reflect the conditional category represented in the parentheses following the sentence.

Example If you **were to show** irrational fear toward a common object or situation, you **would be diagnosed** with a phobia. (predictive)

Rewrite If you show irrational fear toward a common object or situation, you will be diagnosed with a phobia.

1. If a child was terrified whenever he or she saw a clown, that child had coulrophobia. (factual)
2. If you were ever attacked by birds, you developed ornithophobia. (hypothetical)
3. If someone had claustrophobia, he would not be comfortable in a small cave. (factual)
4. If you develop heliophobia, you do not enjoy sunbathing. (predictive)
5. If a dentist has dentophobia, she has to find a new job. (hypothetical)

50g Participial Adjectives

The present participle always ends in *-ing* (*boring, exciting*), while most past participles end in *-ed* (*bored, excited*). Both participle forms can be used as adjectives.

When participles are used as adjectives, they can either precede the nouns they modify or they can come after a connecting verb.

> It was a thrilling book. [*Thrilling* modifies *book*.]
>
> Stephanie was thrilled. [*Thrilled* modifies *Stephanie*.]

Present participles like *thrilling* describe a thing or person causing an experience, while past participles like *thrilled* describe a thing or person receiving the experience.

Incorrect	Students were **exciting** by the lecture.
Correct	Students were **excited** by the lecture.

Exercise 50.6 The following paragraph includes participial adjectives. Underline each participial adjective once and the word being modified twice.

Example The whirling tornado is often considered one of the world's most damaging natural disasters.

Many tornadoes are created by a special rotating thunderstorm called a supercell. A rising gust of warm wind combines with the raging storm; the warm air begins spinning as the rainfall causes a rushing downdraft. This interaction creates a harrowing twister that is awful for those in its path. The United States is honored to bear the devastating distinction of hosting the world's most tornadoes per year; homeowners in the regions known as "Tornado Alley" and "Dixie Alley" are terrified when they see the funneling tornado heading for their houses.

50h Phrasal Verbs

The liveliest and most colorful feature of the English language, its numerous idiomatic verbal phrases, gives many nonnative speakers the greatest difficulty.

Phrasal verbs consist of a verb and one or two **particles**: either a preposition, an adverb, or both. The verb and particles combine to form a phrase with a particular meaning that is often quite distinct from the meaning of the verb itself. Consider the following sentence:

> I need to go over the chapter once more before the test.

Here, the meaning of *go over*—a verb and a preposition that, taken together, suggest casual study—is only weakly related to the meaning of either *go* or *over* by itself. English has hundreds of such idiomatic constructions, and the best way to familiarize yourself with them is to listen to and read as much informal English as you can.

Like regular verbs, phrasal verbs can be either transitive (they take a direct object) or intransitive. In the preceding example, *go over* is transitive. *Quiet down*—as in *Please quiet down*—is intransitive. Some phrases, like *wake up*, can be both: *Wake up!* is intransitive, while *Jenny, wake up the children* is transitive.

In some transitive phrasal verbs, the particles can be separated from the verb without affecting the meaning: *I made up a song* is equivalent to *I made a song up*. In others, the particles cannot be separated from the verb.

Incorrect   You shouldn't **play** with love **around**.

Correct   You shouldn't **play around** with love.

Unfortunately, there are no shortcuts for learning which verbal phrases are separable and which are not. As you become increasingly familiar with English, you will grow more confident in your ability to use phrasal verbs.

Chapter 51

English Sentence Structure

Convey information accurately with effective sentence structure.

51a Subjects

With the exception of **imperatives** (commands such as *Be careful!* and *Jump!*) and informal expressions (such as *Got it?*), sentences in English usually contain a subject and a predicate. A **subject** names who or what the sentence is about; the **predicate** contains information about the subject.

⌐SUBJECT¬ ⌐PREDICATE¬
The lion is asleep.

Many languages allow the writer to omit the subject if it's implied, but formal written English requires that each sentence include a subject, even when the meaning of the sentence would be clear without it. In some cases, you must supply an **expletive** (also known as a *dummy subject*), such as *it* or *there*, to stand in for the subject.

Incorrect   Is snowing in Alaska.

Correct   It is snowing in Alaska.

Incorrect   Won't be enough time to climb that mountain.

Correct   There won't be enough time to climb that mountain.

Both main and subordinate clauses within sentences require a subject and a predicate. A main clause can stand alone as a sentence, while subordinate clauses can only be understood in the context of the sentence of which they're a part. Still, even subordinate clauses must contain a subject. Look at the underlined subordinate clauses in the following two correct sentences.

We avoided the main highway <u>because it had two lanes blocked off</u>.

We avoided the main highway, <u>which had two lanes blocked off</u>.

In the first example, the subject of the subordinate clause is *it,* a pronoun representing the highway. In the second sentence, the relative pronoun *which*—also representing the highway—becomes the subject. When you use a relative pronoun, do not repeat the subject within the same clause.

Incorrect We avoided the highway, which it had two lanes blocked off.

In this sentence, *it* repeats the subject *which* unnecessarily.

Exercise 51.1 Underline all of the subjects in the following sentences. Some sentences may have more than one subject; some may appear to have none. If the sentence appears to have no subject, supply the needed expletive.

Example Though <u>you</u> may have heard of Lee Harvey Oswald and John Wilkes Booth, many lesser-known <u>individuals</u> have put presidents in harm's way.

1. Though some assassins are widely known, Charles Guiteau and Leon Czolgolsz are relatively obscure.
2. Guiteau shot President James Garfield in 1881, and there was little doubt he would be hung for the murder.
3. Twenty years later, Czolgolsz stood face to face with his victim, President William McKinley.
4. History books are littered with the names of would-be assassins such as Giuseppe Zangara, Samuel Byck, and Sarah Jane Moore.
5. You should protect your leaders because there is no way to tell what the future will bring.

Exercise 51.2 In the following sentences, underline main clauses once and subordinate clauses twice. Circle the subjects in each.

Example When (scientists) explain phenomena such as volcanoes and earthquakes, (they) often use the theory of plate tectonics.

1. Geologists based the theory on an earlier one that had observed that the continents fit together like pieces of a puzzle.
2. In the 1950s and 1960s, scientists found evidence to support the earlier theory, so they were able to confirm its hypothesis regarding continental drift.
3. Although water and earth appear to be distinctly separate, they share a similar underlayer called the asthenosphere.
4. This layer possesses high temperatures and high pressure, and these conditions allow for fluid rock movement.
5. As plates move around, they can create volcanoes or increase and decrease the size of oceans and mountains.

51b English Word Order

All languages have their own rules for sentence structure. In English, correct word order often determines whether or not you succeed in saying what you mean. The basic sentence pattern in English is subject + predicate. A **predicate** consists of at least one main verb (see Section 32a). Although it is possible to write single-verb sentences such as *Stop!* most English sentences consist of a combination of several words. A simple English sentence can be formed with a noun and a verb.

Birds fly.

In the above sentence, the subject (birds) is taking the action *and* receiving the action. There is no other object after the verb. The type of verb that can form a sentence without being followed by an object is called an **intransitive verb**. If the verb is intransitive, like *exist,* it does not take a direct object.

Some verbs are **transitive**, which means they require a **direct object** to complete their meaning. The direct object receives the action described by the verb.

Incorrect   The bird saw.

Correct   The bird saw a cat.

In this sentence, the subject (the bird) is doing the action (saw) while the direct object (a cat) is receiving the action. A sentence with a transitive verb can be transformed into a passive sentence (*A cat was seen by the bird*). See Chapter 27 for active and passive sentences.

Some verbs (*write, learn, read,* and others) can be both transitive and intransitive, depending on how they are used.

Intransitive   Pilots fly.

Transitive   Pilots fly airplanes.

Most learner's dictionaries and bilingual dictionaries indicate whether a particular verb is transitive or intransitive. See Section 48c on the use of dictionaries.

In another simple pattern, the transitive verb is replaced by a linking verb that joins its subject to a following description.

The tallest player was the goalie.

Linking verbs like *was, become, sound, look,* and *seem* precede a *subject complement* (in this example, *the goalie*) that refers back to the subject.

At the next level of complexity, a sentence combines a subject with a verb, direct object, and indirect object.

INDIRECT   DIRECT
OBJ   OBJ

The goalie passed her the ball.

Passed is a transitive verb, *ball* is the direct object of the verb, and *her* is the indirect object, the person for whom the action was taken. The same idea can be expressed with a prepositional phrase instead of an indirect object:

⌐DIRECT┐ ⌐PREP┐
OBJ   PHRASE

The goalie passed the ball to her.

Other sentence patterns are possible in English. (See Chapter 32.) However, it is important to remember that altering the basic subject + verb + object word order often changes the meaning of a sentence. If the meaning survives, the result may still be awkward. As a general rule, try to keep the verb close to its subject, and the direct or indirect object close to its verb.

Exercise 51.3 Label the parts of speech in the following sentences: subject (S), transitive or intransitive verb (TV or IV), linking verb (LV), direct object (DO), indirect object (IO), subject complement (SC), and prepositional phrase (PP). Not all sentences will contain all of these parts, but all will contain some.

Example   Hinduism includes several gods and heroes in its system of beliefs.

1. Ganesh is the god of good luck.
2. Young Ganesh stood at the doorway to his mother s house.
3. He denied his father entry.
4. His father beheaded him.
5. His mother replaced his head with the head of an elephant.

51c Placement of Modifiers

The proximity of a modifier—an adjective or adverb—to the noun or verb it modifies provides an important clue to their relationship. Modifiers, even more than verbs, will be unclear if your reader can't connect them to their associated words. Both native and nonnative speakers of English often have difficulty with misplaced modifiers.

Clarity should be your first goal when using a modifier. Readers usually link modifiers with the nearest word. In the following examples, the highlighted words are adjective clauses that modify nouns.

Unclear   Many pedestrians are killed each year by motorists **not using sidewalks.**

Clear   Many pedestrians **not using sidewalks** are killed each year by motorists.

Unclear	He gave an apple to his girlfriend **on a silver platter**.
Clear	He gave an apple on a silver platter to his girlfriend.

An **adverb**—a word or group of words that modifies a verb, adjective, or another adverb—should not come between a verb and its direct object.

Awkward	The hurricane destroyed **completely** the city's tallest building.
Better	The hurricane completely destroyed the city's tallest building.

While single-word adverbs can come between a subject and its verb, you should avoid placing adverbial phrases in this position.

Awkward	Galveston, **following the 1900 hurricane that killed thousands**, built a seawall to prevent a future catastrophe.
Better	Following the 1900 hurricane that killed thousands, Galveston built a seawall to prevent a future catastrophe.

As a general rule, try to avoid placing an adverb between *to* and its verb. This is called a **split infinitive**.

Awkward	The water level was predicted **to not rise**.
Better	The water level was predicted not to rise.

Sometimes, though, a split infinitive will read more naturally than the alternative. Note also how the sentence with the split infinitive is more concise:

Without split infinitive	Automobile emissions in the city are expected to increase by more than two times over the next five years.
With split infinitive	Automobile emissions in the city are expected to more than double over the next five years.

Certain kinds of adverbs have special rules for placement. Adverbs that describe how something is done—called **adverbs of manner**—usually follow the verb.

The student listened closely to the lecture.

These adverbs may also be separated from the verb by a direct object:

She threw the ball well.

Adverbs of frequency are usually placed at the head of a sentence, before a single verb, or after an auxiliary verb in a verb phrase.

Often, politicians have underestimated the intelligence of voters.

Politicians have often underestimated the intelligence of voters.

It's common practice in English to combine two or more nouns to form a compound noun. Where two or more adjectives or nouns are strung together, the main noun is always positioned at the end of the string:

12-speed road bike, tall oak tree, computer table

Exercise 51.4   The following sentences include confusing modifiers. Underline the confusing modifiers, identify the broken rule (far away from modified word; adverb between verb and direct object; adverbial phrase between subject and verb; split infinitive), and rewrite the sentence clearly.

Example   Japanese film is known by the work of Akira Kurosawa worldwide. *(Far away from modified word)*

Revise   Japanese film is known worldwide by the work of Akira Kurosawa.

1. Kurosawa chose initially painting as his preferred career.
2. Kurosawa, realizing painting would not bring riches, turned to film in 1936.
3. He was able to by 1943 direct his own films.
4. He is remembered for his Samurai films by many.
5. Many of his films, embraced in the West, retold Shakespearean tales.

Exercise 51.5 Underline all the adjectives and adverbs in the following sentences. Label adverbs of manner or adverbs of frequency, and correct improper word order where you find it.

Example
adverb of frequency
Americans associate <u>often</u> cards and dice with <u>shady</u> gamblers <u>Las Vegas</u>.

Revise Americans often associate cards and dice with shady Las Vegas gamblers.

1. By the fourteenth century, cards playing were used widely for gambling and predicting the future.
2. The invention of the printing press directly connects to the proliferation of card games standardized.
3. Ancient dice directly can be traced to Tutankhamen s tomb.
4. Gamblers hollowed frequently the center of an illegally rigged die.
5. These classic games have withstood well the test of time.

COMMON ERRORS

Dangling modifiers

A dangling modifier does not seem to modify anything in a sentence; it dangles, unconnected to the word or words it presumably is intended to modify. Frequently, it produces funny results:

When still a girl, my father joined the army.

It sounds like *father* was once a girl. The problem is that the subject, I, is missing:

When I was still a girl, my father joined the army.

(Continued on next page)

COMMON ERRORS *(continued)*

Dangling modifiers usually occur at the head of a sentence in the form of clauses, with a subject that is implied but never stated.

Incorrect   After lifting the heavy piano up the stairs, the apartment door was too small to get it through.

Correct   After lifting the heavy piano up the stairs, we discovered the apartment door was too small to get it through.

Whenever you use a modifier, ask yourself whether its relationship to the word it modifies will be clear to your reader. What is clear to you may not be clear to your audience. Writing, like speaking, is an exercise in making your own thoughts explicit. The solution for the dangling modifier is to recast it as a complete clause with its own explicit subject and verb.

Remember: Modifiers should be clearly connected to the words they modify, especially at the beginning of sentences.

 For more practice with modifiers, see the exercises on this page of the E-book at www.mycomplab.com.

Exercise 51.6   The following sentences include dangling modifiers. Rewrite the sentences so that the relationship between subject, verb, and modifier is clear.

Example   In his early thirties, France was dealt a hefty blow by Maximilien Robespierre.

Revise   In his early thirties, Maximilien Robespierre dealt France a hefty blow.

1. His philosophical role model, Robespierre followed the writings of Jean Jacques Rousseau.
2. Elected on the eve of the French Revolution, the people were enthralled by his skillful oratory.

3. Gaining further power in the following years, his influence over domestic affairs was unmistakable.

4. A bloodbath known as the Reign of Terror, Robespierre ordered a rash of executions of members of the aristocracy and his political enemies.

5. After they tired of his aggressive tactics, he was overthrown by his own political party.

For more explanation, examples, and practice exercises, visit the Common ESL Errors Workbook on this page of the E-book at www.mycomplab.com.

Glossary of Grammatical Terms and Usage

The glossary gives the definitions of grammatical terms and items of usage. The grammatical terms are shown in **blue**. Some of the explanations of usage that follow are not rules, but guidelines to keep in mind for academic and professional writing. In these formal contexts, the safest course is to avoid words that are described as *nonstandard, informal,* or *colloquial.*

a/an   Use *a* before words that begin with a consonant sound (*a train, a house*). Use *an* before words that begin with a vowel sound (*an airplane, an hour*).

a lot/alot   *A lot* is generally regarded as informal; *alot* is nonstandard.

absolute   A phrase that has a subject and modifies an entire sentence (see Section 32d).

The soldiers marched in single file, their rifles slung over their shoulders.

accept/except   *Accept* is a verb meaning "receive" or "approve." *Except* is sometimes a verb meaning "leave out," but much more often, it's used as a conjunction or preposition meaning "other than."

She accepted her schedule except for Biology at 8 a.m.

active   A clause with a transitive verb in which the subject is the doer of the action (see Section 27b). See also **passive**.

adjective   A modifier that qualifies or describes the qualities of a noun or pronoun (see Sections 32b, 37a, and 37b).

adjective clause   A subordinate clause that modifies a noun or pronoun and is usually introduced by a relative pronoun (see Section 32c). Sometimes called a *relative clause.*

adverb   A word that modifies a verb, another modifier, or a clause (see Sections 32b, 37a, and 37c).

adverb clause   A subordinate clause that functions as an adverb by modifying a verb, another modifier, or a clause (see Section 32c).

advice/advise   The noun *advice* means a "suggestion"; the verb *advise* means to "recommend" or "give advice."

823

affect/effect   Usually, *affect* is a verb (to "influence") and *effect* is a noun (a "result"):

Too many pork chops affect one's health.

Too many pork chops have an effect on one's health.

Less commonly, *affect* is used as a noun and *effect* as a verb. In the following examples, *affect* means an "emotional state or expression," and *effect* means "to bring about."

The boy's affect changed when he saw his father.

The legislators will attempt to effect new insurance laws next year.

agreement   The number and person of a subject and verb must match—singular subjects with singular verbs, plural subjects with plural verbs (see Chapter 34). Likewise, the number and gender of a pronoun and its antecedent must match (see Section 36b).

all ready/already   The adjective phrase *all ready* means "completely prepared"; the adverb *already* means "previously."

The tour group was all ready to leave, but the train had already departed.

all right/alright   *All right*, meaning "acceptable," is the correct spelling. *Alright* is nonstandard.

allude/elude   *Allude* means "refer to indirectly." *Elude* means "evade."

He alluded to the fact that he'd eluded capture.

allusion/illusion   An *allusion* is an indirect reference; an *illusion* is a false impression.

The painting contains an allusion to the Mona Lisa.

The painting creates the illusion of depth.

among/between   *Between* refers to precisely two people or things; *among* refers to three or more.

The choice is between two good alternatives.

The costs were shared among the three participating companies.

amount/number   Use *amount* with things that cannot be counted; use *number* with things that can be counted.

A large amount of money changed hands.

They gave him a number of quarters.

an   See **a/an**.

antecedent   The noun (or pronoun) that a pronoun refers to (see Section 36b). *Jeff* is the antecedent of *his* in the following sentence.

Jeff stopped running when his knee began hurting.

anybody/any body; anyone/any one   *Anybody* and *anyone* are indefinite pronouns and have the same meaning; *any body* and *any one* are usually followed by a noun that they modify.

Anybody can learn English, just as anyone can learn to bicycle.

Any body of government should be held accountable for its actions.

anymore/any more   *Anymore* means "now," while *any more* means "no more." Both are used in negative constructions.

No one goes downtown anymore.

The area doesn't have any more stores than it did in 1960.

anyway/anyways   *Anyway* is correct. *Anyways* is nonstandard.

appositive   A word or a phrase placed close to a noun that restates or modifies the noun (see Section 32d).

Dr. Lim, my physics professor, is the best.

articles   The words *a, an,* and *the* (see Sections 32b and 47d).

as/as if/as though/like   Use *as* instead of *like* before dependent clauses (which include a subject and verb). Use *like* before a noun or a pronoun.

Her voice sounds as if she had her head in a barrel.

She sings like her father.

assure/ensure/insure   *Assure* means "promise," *ensure* means "make certain," and *insure* means to "make certain in either a legal or financial sense."

Ralph assured the new client that his company would insure the building at full value, but the client wanted higher approval to ensure Ralph was correct.

auxiliary verb   Forms of *be, do,* and *have* combine with verbs to indicate tense and mood (see Section 32b). The modal verbs *can, could, may, might, must, shall, should, will,* and *would* are a subset of auxiliaries.

bad/badly   Use *bad* only as an adjective. *Badly* is the adverb.

He was a bad dancer.

Everyone agreed that he danced badly.

being as/being that   Both constructions are colloquial and awkward substitutes for *because*. Don't use them in formal writing.

beside/besides   *Beside* means "next to." *Besides* means "in addition to" or "except."

Does anyone, besides your mother, want to sit beside you when you're coughing like that?

between   See **among/between**.

bring/take   *Bring* describes movement from a more distant location to a nearer one. *Take* describes movement away.

Bring me the most recent issue. You can take this one.

can/may   In formal writing, *can* indicates ability or capacity, while *may* indicates permission.

If I may speak with you, we can probably solve this problem.

case   The form of a noun or pronoun that indicates its function. Nouns change case only to show possession: the **dog**, the **dog's** bowl (see Section 32b). See **pronoun case** (Section 36a).

censor/censure   To *censor* is to edit or ban on moral or political grounds. To *censure* is to reprimand publicly.

The Senate censored the details of the budget.

The Senate censured one of its members for misconduct.

cite/sight/site   To *cite* is to "mention specifically"; *sight* as a verb means to "observe" and as a noun refers to "vision"; *site* is most commonly used as a noun that means "location," but is also used as a verb to mean "situate."

He cited as evidence the magazine article he'd read yesterday.

Finally, he sighted the bald eagle. It was a remarkable sight.

The developers sited the houses on a heavily forested site.

clause   A group of words with a subject and a predicate. A main or independent clause can stand as a sentence. A subordinate or dependent clause must be attached to a main clause to form a sentence (see Section 32c).

collective noun   A noun that refers to a group or a plurality, such as *team, army,* or *committee* (see Section 34d).

comma splice   Two independent clauses joined incorrectly by a comma (see Section 33c).

common noun   A noun that names a general group, person, place, or thing (see Sections 32b and 47a). Common nouns are not capitalized unless they begin a sentence.

complement   A word or group of words that completes the predicate (see Section 32c). See also **linking verb**.

Juanita is my aunt.

complement/compliment   To *complement* something is to complete it or make it perfect; to *compliment* is to flatter.

The chef complemented their salad with a small bowl of soup.

The grateful diners complimented the chef.

complex sentence   A sentence that contains at least one subordinate clause attached to a main clause (see Section 32e).

compound sentence   A sentence that contains at least two main clauses (see Section 32e).

compound-complex sentence   A sentence that contains at least two main clauses and one subordinate clause (see Section 32e).

conjunction   See **coordinating conjunction**; **subordinating conjunction**.

conjunctive adverb   An adverb that often modifies entire clauses and sentences, such as *also, consequently, however, indeed, instead, moreover, nevertheless, otherwise, similarly,* and *therefore* (see Sections 32b and 37c).

continual/continuous   *Continual* refers to a repeated activity; *continuous* refers to an ongoing, unceasing activity.

Tennis elbow is usually caused by continual stress on the joint.

Archaeologists have debated whether Chaco Canyon was inhabited intermittently or continuously.

coordinate   A relationship of equal importance, in terms of either grammar or meaning (see Section 29c).

coordinating conjunction   A word that links two equivalent grammatical elements, such as *and, but, or, yet, nor, for,* and *so* (see Section 32b).

could of   Nonstandard. See **have/of**.

count noun   A noun that names things that can be counted, such as *block, cat,* and *toy* (see Section 47b).

dangling modifier   A modifier that is not clearly attached to what it modifies (see Section 37e).

data   The plural form of *datum*; it takes plural verb forms.

The data are overwhelming.

declarative   A sentence that makes a statement (see Section 32a).

Dover is the capital of Delaware.

dependent clause   See **subordinate clause**.

determiners   Words that initiate noun phrases, including possessive nouns (*Pedro's violin*); possessive pronouns (*my, your*); demonstrative pronouns (*this, that*); and indefinite pronouns (*all, both, many*).

differ from/differ with   To *differ from* means to "be unlike"; to *differ with* means to "disagree."

Rock music differs from jazz primarily in rhythm.

Miles Davis differed with critics who disliked his rock rhythms.

different from/different than   Use *different from* where possible.

Dark French roast is different from ordinary coffee.

direct object   A noun, pronoun, or noun clause that names who or what receives the action of a transitive verb (see Section 32c).

Antonio kicked the ball.

discreet/discrete   Both are adjectives. *Discreet* means "prudent" or "tactful"; *discrete* means "separate."

What's a discreet way of saying "Shut up"?

Over the noise, he could pick up several discrete conversations.

disinterested/uninterested   *Disinterested* is often misused to mean *uninterested*. Disinterested means "impartial." A judge can be interested in a case but disinterested in the outcome.

double negative   The incorrect use of two negatives to signal the same negative meaning.

We don't have no money.

due to the fact that   Avoid this wordy substitute for *because*.

each other/one another   Use *each other* for two; use *one another* for more than two.

effect   See **affect/effect**.

elicit/illicit   The verb *elicit* means to "draw out." The adjective *illicit* means "unlawful."

The teacher tried to elicit a discussion about illicit drugs.

emigrate from/immigrate to   *Emigrate* means to "leave one's country"; *immigrate* means to "settle in another country."

ensure   See **assure/ensure/insure**.

enthused   Nonstandard in academic and professional writing. Use *enthusiastic* instead.

etc.   Avoid this abbreviation for the Latin *et cetera* in formal writing. Either list all the items or use an English phrase such as *and so forth*.

every body/everybody; every one/everyone   *Everybody* and *everyone* are indefinite pronouns referring to all people under discussion. *Every one* and *every body* are adjective-noun combinations referring to all members of a group.

Everyone loves a genuine smile.

Every one of the files contained a virus.

except   See **accept/except**.

except for the fact that   Avoid this wordy substitute for *except that*.

expletive   The dummy subjects *it* and *there* used to fill a grammatical slot in a sentence.

It is raining outside.

There should be a law against it.

explicit/implicit   Both are adjectives; *explicit* means "stated outright," while *implicit* means just the opposite, "unstated."

Even though we lacked an explicit contract, I thought we had an implicit understanding.

farther/further   *Farther* refers to physical distance; *further* refers to time or other abstract concepts.

How much farther is your home?

I don't want to talk about this any further.

fewer/less   Use *fewer* with what can be counted and *less* with what cannot be counted.

There are fewer canoeists in the summer because there is less water in the river.

flunk   In formal writing, avoid this colloquial substitute for *fail*.

fragment   A group of words beginning with a capital letter and ending with a period that looks like a sentence but lacks a subject or a predicate or both (see Section 33a).

further   See **farther/further**.

gerund   An *-ing* form of a verb used as a noun, such as *running, skiing,* or *laughing* (see Section 32b).

good/well   *Good* is an adjective and is not interchangeable with the adverb *well.* The one exception is health. Both she feels *good* and she feels *well* are correct.

The Yankees are a good baseball team. They play the game well.

hanged/hung   Use *hanged* to refer only to executions; *hung* is used for all other instances.

have/of   *Have,* not *of,* follows *should, could, would, may, must,* and *might.*

I should have [not *of*] picked you up earlier.

he/she; s/he   Try to avoid language that appears to exclude either gender (unless this is intended, of course) and awkward compromises such as *he/she* or *s/he.* The best solution is to make pronouns plural (the gender-neutral *they*) wherever possible (see Section 36c).

helping verb   See **auxiliary verb**.

hopefully   This adverb is commonly used as a sentence modifier, but many readers object to it.

I am hopeful [not *Hopefully*] we'll have a winning season.

illusion   See **allusion/illusion**.

immigrate   See **emigrate from/immigrate to**.

imperative   A sentence that expresses a command (see Section 32a). Usually the subject is implied rather than stated.

Go away now.

implicit   See **explicit/implicit**.

imply/infer   *Imply* means to "suggest"; *infer* means to "draw a conclusion."

The ad implied that the candidate was dishonest; I inferred that the campaign would be one of name calling.

in regards to   Avoid this wordy substitute for *regarding*.

incredible/incredulous   *Incredible* means "unbelievable"; *incredulous* means "not believing."

Their story about finding a stack of money in a discarded suitcase seemed incredible; I was incredulous.

independent clause   See **main clause.**

indirect object   A noun, pronoun, or noun clause that names who or what is affected by the action of a transitive verb (see Section 32c).

Antonio kicked the ball to Mario.

infinitive   The word *to* plus the base verb form: *to believe, to feel, to act.* See also **split infinitive.**

infinitive phrase   A phrase that uses the infinitive form of a verb (see Section 32d).

To get some sleep is my goal for the weekend.

interjection   A word expressing feeling that is grammatically unconnected to a sentence, such as *cool, wow, ouch,* or *yikes.*

interrogative   A sentence that asks a question (see Section 32a).

Where do you want to go?

intransitive verb   A verb that does not take an object, such as *sleep, appear,* or *laugh* (see Sections 32c and 35c).

irregardless   Nonstandard for *regardless.*

irregular verb   A verb that does not use either *-d* or *-ed* to form the past tense and past participle (see Section 35b).

it is my opinion that   Avoid this wordy substitute for *I believe that.*

its/it's   *Its* is the possessive of *it* and does not take an apostrophe; *it's* is the contraction for *it is.*

Its tail is missing. It's an unusual animal.

-ize/-wise   The suffix *-ize* changes a noun or adjective into a verb (*harmony, harmonize*). The suffix *-wise* changes a noun or adjective into an adverb (*clock, clockwise*). Some writers are tempted to use these suffixes to convert almost any word into an adverb or verb form. Unless the word appears in a dictionary, don't use it.

kind of/sort of/type of   Avoid using these colloquial expressions if you mean *somewhat* or *rather. It's kind of hot* is nonstandard. Each is permissible, however, when it refers to a classification of an object. Be sure that it agrees in number with the object it is modifying.

This type of engine is very fuel-efficient.

These kinds of recordings are rare.

lay/lie   *Lay* means "place" or "put" and generally takes a direct object (see Section 35c). Its main forms are *lay, laid, laid. Lie* means "recline" or "be positioned" and does not take an object. Its main forms are *lie, lay, lain.*

He lays the papers down. He laid the papers down.

He lies down on the sofa. He lay down on the sofa.

less   See **fewer/less**.

lie   See **lay/lie**.

linking verb   A verb that connects the subject to the complement, such as *appear, be, feel, look, seem,* or *taste* (see Section 32c).

lots/lots of   Nonstandard in formal writing; use *many* or *much* instead.

main clause   A group of words with a subject and a predicate that can stand alone as a sentence (see Section 32c). Also called an *independent clause.*

mankind   This term offends some readers and is outdated. Use *humans, humanity,* or *people* instead.

may/can   See **can/may**.

may be/maybe   *May be* is a verb phrase; *maybe* is an adverb.

It may be time to go.

Maybe it's time to go.

media   This is the plural form of the noun *medium* and requires a plural verb.

The media in this city are biased.

might of   See **have/of**.

modal   A kind of auxiliary verb that indicates ability, permission, intention, obligation, or probability, such as *can, could, may, might, must, shall, should, will,* or *would* (see Section 32b).

modifier   A general term for adjectives, adverbs, phrases, and clauses that describe other words (see Chapter 37).

must of   See **have/of**.

noncount noun   A noun that names things that cannot be counted, such as *air, energy,* or *water* (see Section 47b).

nonrestrictive modifier   A modifier that is not essential to the meaning of the word, phrase, or clause it modifies and should be set off by commas or other punctuation (see Section 38c).

noun   The name of a person, place, thing, concept, or action (see Section 32a). See also **common noun** and **proper noun** (see Section 47a).

noun clause   A subordinate clause that functions as a noun (see Section 32c).

That the city fails to pick up the garbage is ridiculous.

number   See **amount/number**.

object   Receiver of the action within the clause or phrase (see Sections 32c and 32d).

OK, O.K., okay   Informal; avoid using in academic and professional writing. Each spelling is accepted in informal usage.

owing to the fact that   Avoid this wordy, colloquial substitute for *because.*

parallelism   The principle of putting similar elements or ideas in similar grammatical form (see Sections 29c, 29d, and 29e).

participle   A form of a verb that uses *-ing* in the present (*laughing, playing*) and usually *-ed* or *-en* in the past (*laughed, played*). See Section 35a. Participles are either part of the verb phrase (*She had played the game before*) or used as adverbs and adjectives (*the laughing girl*).

participial phrase   A phrase formed either by a present participle (for example, *racing*) or by a past participle (for example, *taken*). (See Section 32d.)

parts of speech   The eight classes of words according to their grammatical function: nouns, pronouns, verbs, adjectives, adverbs, prepositions, conjunctions, and interjections (see Section 32b).

passive   A clause with a transitive verb in which the subject is being acted upon (see Section 27b). See also **active**.

people/persons   *People* refers to a general group; *persons* refers to a collection of individuals. Use *people* over *persons* except when you're emphasizing the idea of separate persons within the group.

"People have the power" was the theme of the rally.

Occupancy by more than 135 persons is illegal.

per   Try to use the English equivalent of this Latin word except in technical writing or familiar usages like *miles per gallon.*

The job paid $20 an hour.

As you requested [not *per your request*], I'll drive up immediately.

phenomena   This is the plural form of *phenomenon* ("observable fact" or "unusual event") and takes plural verbs.

The astronomical phenomena were breathtaking.

phrase   A group of words that does not contain both a subject and a predicate.

plenty   In academic and professional writing, avoid this colloquial substitute for *very.*

plus   Do not use *plus* to join clauses or sentences. Use *and, also, moreover, furthermore,* or another conjunctive adverb instead.

It rained heavily, and it was also [not *plus it was*] bitterly cold.

precede/proceed   Both are verbs but they have different meanings: *precede* means "come before," and *proceed* means "go ahead" or "continue."

In the United States, the national anthem precedes every major league baseball game.

We proceeded to the train station.

predicate   The part of the clause that expresses the action or tells something about the subject. The predicate includes the verb and all its complements, objects, and modifiers (see Section 32a).

prejudice/prejudiced   *Prejudice* is a noun; *prejudiced* is an adjective.

The jury was prejudiced against the defendant.

She knew about the town's history of racial prejudice.

preposition   A class of words that indicate relationships and qualities (see Sections 32b and 35a).

prepositional phrase   A phrase formed by a preposition and its object, including the modifiers of its object (see Section 32d).

pronoun   A word that stands for other nouns or pronouns. Pronouns have several subclasses, including personal pronouns, possessive pronouns, demonstrative pronouns, indefinite pronouns, relative pronouns, interrogative pronouns, reflexive pronouns, and reciprocal pronouns (see Section 32b and Chapter 36).

pronoun case   Pronouns that function as the subjects of sentences are in the **subjective** case (*I, you, he, she, it, we, they*). Pronouns that function as direct or indirect objects are in the **objective** case (*me, you, him, her, it, us, them*). Pronouns that indicate ownership are in the **possessive** case (*my, your, his, her, its, our, their*) (see Section 36a).

proper noun   A noun that names a particular person, place, thing, or group (see Sections 32b and 49a). Proper nouns are capitalized.

question as to whether/question of whether   Avoid these wordy substitutes for *whether*.

raise/rise   The verb *raise* means "lift up" and takes a direct object. Its main forms are *raise, raised, raised*. The verb *rise* means "get up" and does not take a direct object. Its main forms are *rise, rose, risen*.

The workers carefully raised the piano onto the truck.

The piano slowly rose off the ground.

real/really   Avoid using *real* as if it were an adverb. *Really* is an adverb; *real* is an adjective.

The singer was really good.

What we thought was an illusion turned out to be real.

reason is because   Omit either *reason is* or *because* when explaining causality.

The reason he ran is that he thought he was late.

He ran because he thought he was late.

reason why   Avoid using this redundant combination.

The reason he's so often late is that he never wears a watch.

relative pronoun   A pronoun that initiates clauses, such as *that, which, what, who, whom,* or *whose* (see Section 32b).

restrictive modifier   A modifier that is essential to the meaning of the word, phrase, or clause it modifies (see Section 38c). Restrictive modifiers are usually not set off by punctuation.

rise/raise   See **raise/rise**.

run-on sentence   Two main clauses fused together without punctuation or a conjunction, appearing as one sentence (see Section 33b).

sentence   A grammatically independent group of words that contains at least one main clause (see Section 32a).

sentence fragment   See **fragment**.

set/sit   *Set* means "put" and takes a direct object (see Section 35c); its main forms are *set, set, set*. *Sit* means "be seated" and does not take a direct object; its main forms are *sit, sat, sat*. *Sit* should not be used as a synonym for *set*.

Set the bowl on the table.

Please sit down.

shall / will   *Shall* is used most often in first person questions, while *will* is a future tense helping verb for all persons. British English consistently uses *shall* with first person: *I shall, we shall.*

Shall I bring you some water?

Will they want drinks, too?

should of   See **have / of**.

sit / set   See **set / sit**.

some time / sometime / sometimes   *Some time* means "a span of time," *sometime* means "at some unspecified time," and *sometimes* means "occasionally."

Give me some time to get ready.

Let's meet again sometime soon.

Sometimes, the best-laid plans go wrong.

somebody / some body; someone / some one   *Somebody* and *someone* are indefinite pronouns and have the same meaning. In *some body, body* is a noun modified by *some*, and in *some one, one* is a pronoun or adjective modified by *some*.

Somebody should close that window.

"Some body was found on the beach today," the homicide detective said.

Someone should answer the phone.

It would be best if some one person could represent the group.

sort of   See **kind of / sort of / type of**.

split infinitive   An infinitive with a word or words between *to* and the base verb form, such as *to boldly go, to better appreciate* (see Section 37d).

stationary / stationery   *Stationary* means "motionless"; *stationery* means "writing paper."

subject   A noun, pronoun, or noun phrase that identifies what the clause is about and connects with the predicate (see Sections 32a and 32c).

subject-verb agreement   See **agreement**.

subordinate   A relationship of unequal importance, in terms of either grammar or meaning (see Section 29a).

subordinate clause   A clause that cannot stand alone but must be attached to a main clause (see Section 32c). Also called a *dependent clause.*

subordinating conjunction   A word that introduces a subordinate clause. Common subordinating conjunctions are *after, although, as, because, before, if, since, that, unless, until, when, where,* and *while* (see Section 32b).

such   Avoid using *such* as a synonym for *very.* It should always be followed by *that* and a clause that contains a result.

It was a very [not *such a*] hot August.

sure   A colloquial term used as an adverb to mean "certainly." Avoid using it this way in formal writing.

You were certainly [not *sure were*] correct when you said August would be hot.

sure and/sure to; try and/try to   *Sure to* and *try to* are correct; do not use *and* after *sure* or *try.*

Be sure to [not *sure and*] take out the trash this morning.

Try to [not *try and*] finish first.

take   See **bring/take**.

that/which   *That* introduces a restrictive or essential clause. Restrictive clauses describe an object that must be that particular object and no other. Though some writers occasionally use *which* with restrictive clauses, it is most often used to introduce nonrestrictive clauses. These are clauses that contain additional nonessential information about the object.

Let's listen to the CD that Clarence bought.

Clarence's favorite music, which usually puts me to sleep, is too mellow for me.

transition   A word or phrase that notes movement from one unit of writing to another.

transitive verb   A verb that takes a direct object (see Sections 32c and 35c).

verb   A word that expresses action or characterizes the subject in some way. Verbs can show tense and mood (see Section 32b and Chapter 35).

verbal   A form of a verb used as an adjective, adverb, or noun (see Section 32b). See also **gerund, infinitive, participle**.

well/good   See **good/well**.

which/that   See **that/which**.

who/whom   *Who* and *whom* follow the same rules as other pronouns: *Who* is the subject pronoun; *whom* is the object pronoun (see Section 36a).

Sharon's father, who served in the Korean War, died last year.

Sharon's father, whom several of my father's friends knew, died last year.

will/shall   See **shall/will**.

-wise/-ize   See **-ize/-wise**.

would of   See **have/of**.

you   Avoid indefinite uses of *you*. It should only be used to mean "you, the reader."

The [not *your*] average life span in the United States has increased consistently over the past 100 years.

your/you're   The two are not interchangeable. *Your* is the possessive form of "you"; *you're* is the contraction of "you are."

Your car can be picked up after 5 p.m.

You're going to need money to live in Manhattan.

Answers to Selected Exercises

These pages provide answers to selected exercises from Parts 7–10 in *The Penguin Handbook*. Many of the answers below are abbreviated versions of what the full answer would be. These are annotated as "shortened answers."

Chapter 27   Write with Power

EXERCISE 27.1 (p. 502)
Active and passive verbs are underlined. Possible revisions are in parenthesis (shortened answer):

But today with food everywhere, the drive to eat when we aren't hungry has caused an epidemic of obesity. It has been reported by researchers in neuroscience (Researchers in neuroscience have reported) that food advertising often succeeds because of the structure of our brains. Some people are surprised by this finding. (This finding surprises some people.)

EXERCISE 27.2 (p. 505)
The "be" verbs are in bold and the nouns are underlined in the sentences below. Possible revisions are in parenthesis (shortened answer):

Though few people celebrate the experience of pain, the human body **is** dependent (depends) on unpleasant impulses for survival. Without pain, an individual **is** at a disadvantage (The absence of pain disadvantages an individual.) in terms of self-preservation.

EXERCISE 27.3 (p. 505)
The subject of each sentence is underlined below. Possible revisions are in parenthesis (shortened answer):

The observation of these old customs in parts of Europe where the inhabitants are Celtic proves their Druid origin. (Inhabitants of Celtic parts of Europe observed these old customs, proving their Druid origin.) To mark the beginning of winter, the burning of fires on November 1 was customary. (Druids burned fires on November 1 to mark the beginning of winter.)

Chapter 28   Write Concisely

EXERCISE 28.1 (p. 511)
Possible rewrite (shortened answer):

Because we cannot see a black hole up close, we must use our imaginations to consider its properties. For example, imagine jumping feet first into a black hole.

EXERCISE 28.2 (p. 512)
Possible replacements are in brackets (shortened answer).

In 1942, the Chief of the American Office of Strategic Services (OSS), Chief William Donovan, gathered six <u>incredibly respected</u> [prestigious] scientists to develop a truth serum. The American Psychiatric Association and the Federal Bureau of Narcotics, both <u>very respectable</u> [reputable] organizations, also participated in this <u>rather secretive</u> [covert] search for the truth drug.

EXERCISE 28.3 (p. 515)
Possible rewrite (shortened answer):

The necktie is considered one of the oldest fashion creations and one of the earliest items created solely for decorating the human form. One of the main theories locates the predecessor of the modern necktie in the mid-1600s when Croatian soldiers arrived in France adorned with tasseled scarves of linen and muslin.

EXERCISE 28.4 (p. 518)
Possible rewrite (shortened answer):

Fossils can help paleontologists gain additional information about ancient eras in several ways. They aid in locating certain missing data regarding location, time, and traits of both past and future organisms.

Chapter 29 Write with Emphasis

EXERCISE 29.1 (p. 522)
Possible rewrite; main ideas are underlined twice and subordinate ideas are underlined once (shortened answer).

<u>Since popular representations of Jesus portrayed a thin, almost sickly man,</u> <u>men did not identify with Christianity as readily as women did.</u> <u>Those who wanted to change Jesus' image focused on his carpentry</u> because carpentry was associated with America's self-made man.

EXERCISE 29.2 (p. 527)
Replacement constructions are in brackets (shortened answer).

Sesame Street entered the American consciousness in 1969, playing, singing, and <u>to teach</u> [teaching]. Joan Ganz Cooney, a major mastermind of *Sesame Street*, proposed to join child-friendly techniques with commercial television standards, and <u>accelerating</u> [accelerate] the speed of teaching.

EXERCISE 29.3 (p. 528)
1. Correct
2. Follow Route 22 N for 3 miles until you come to the Dewdrop Inn.

Chapter 30   Find the Right Words

EXERCISE 30.1 (p. 533)

Possible rewrite:

Dear Ms. Le Chat,

I am writing to thank you again for arranging our delicious luncheon yesterday. Your choice of restaurant was perfect; the atmosphere, service, and food combined to make the interview a rewarding experience. It was a pleasure meeting and talking with you, and I look forward to our next meeting.

Sincerely,

Susan Aldridge

EXERCISE 30.2 (p. 534)

Possible rewrite (shortened answer):

The late David Brower was president of the Sierra Club, a group devoted to American wilderness preservation. As this organization's leader, Brower personified preservation.

EXERCISE 30.3 (p. 535)

Answers likely will vary. Possible responses below are marked (+) for positive connotation and (=) for neutral denotation.

1. thin (+), slender (+), lean (=), trim (=)
2. music (+), song (+), composition (=), tune (=)

EXERCISE 30.4 (p. 540)

Possible revision (shortened answer):

In her youth, Ride was a <u>superb</u> tennis player. However, instead of becoming a professional athlete, she <u>went</u> to Stanford and received her doctorate in x-ray physics. While at Stanford, Ride was selected out of a group of eight thousand other <u>applicants</u> to be part of NASA's astronaut class.

EXERCISE 30.5 (p. 541)

Possible revision (shortened answer):

Space missions can adversely affect an astronaut's health. A major culprit is the lack of gravity in space; one of the effects that weightlessness has on astronauts is bone loss, which can be severe.

EXERCISE 30.6 (p. 541)

Correct word choices are underlined (shortened answer).

Butchering a hog requires <u>patience</u> and hard work. First, find a <u>site</u> outdoors <u>where</u> you will have plenty of space. After killing the pig, dunk <u>it</u> in hot water to loosen the <u>coarse</u> hair.

EXERCISE 30.7 (p. 544)

Clichés are underlined. Replacements will vary (shortened answer).

However, in Japan and in the Mediterranean, squid, octopus, and cuttlefish are an important food source and <u>sell like hot cakes</u>. Unfortunately, myths about giant squid sinking boats and octopus drowning swimmers persist in the United States, and information that giant squid are <u>weak as kittens</u> and that an octopus has never drowned anyone <u>falls on deaf ears</u>.

Chapter 31   Write to be Inclusive

EXERCISE 31.1 (p. 546)

Answers will vary.

EXERCISE 31.2 (p. 551)

1. No; the writer could refer to his doctor without any gender specification, or make the doctor's gender secondary information.
2. Yes.

Chapter 32   Grammar Basics

EXERCISE 32.1 (p. 558)

1. imperative, negative, active
2. exclamatory, positive, active

EXERCISE 32.2 (p. 560)

Shortened answer:

The boyish <u>Ronald Reagan</u> [subject] was the studio's first <u>choice</u> [subject complement] for the male <u>lead</u> [object of preposition]. Instead, the <u>studio</u> [subject] chose <u>Humphrey Bogart</u> [object], the shrapnel-scarred tough <u>guy</u> [modifier], to portray the <u>owner</u> [object] of <u>Rick's</u> [possessive] <u>nightclub</u> [object of preposition].

EXERCISE 32.3 (p. 562)

Shortened answer:

The ramming was no accident; after the whale hit the *Essex* once, <u>it</u> [personal pronoun] turned around to hit the ship a second time. The sailors found <u>themselves</u> [reflexive pronoun] adrift in three whaleboats, 1,200 miles from the nearest islands.

EXERCISE 32.4 (p. 563)

Shortened answer:

Frank Oz <u>was</u> [aux modal] <u>born</u> [main] in Hereford, England, in 1944 and <u>began</u> [aux modal] <u>staging</u> [main] puppet shows when he was 12. You <u>may</u> [aux modal] <u>know</u> [main] him best as the voice of Yoda in the *Star Wars* series.

Exercise 32.5 (p. 564)

Shortened answer:

The evil eye is a <u>focused</u> [past participle] gaze, supposedly <u>causing</u> [present participle] death and <u>destruction</u>. The Assyrians, Babylonians, Greeks, and Romans all had an <u>abiding</u> [present participle] belief in this supernatural concept.

Exercise 32.6 (p. 565)

Shortened answer:

Parker's father encouraged her to pursue "<u>feminine</u> [adj mod. *arts*] arts" such as piano and poetry, but <u>just</u> [adv mod. *following*] following his death in 1913, she rushed into what turned out to be a <u>profitable</u> [adj mod. *foray*] foray into the world of literature. <u>Almost</u> [adv mod. *immediately*] immediately [adv mod. purchased], *Vanity Fair* purchased one of her poems, <u>leading her</u> into a <u>full-time</u> [adj mod. *position*] <u>writing</u> [adj mod. *position*] position with *Vogue*.

Exercise 32.7 (p. 567)

Prepositions are in bold (shortened answer):

The ads **in** <u>the campaign</u> are easily recognizeable because they were shot **against** <u>an empty, white background</u>. **In addition to** <u>looking the same</u>, each ad follows a standard pattern: a man dressed **in** <u>casual clothes</u> says "Hello, I'm a Mac."

Exercise 32.8 (p. 568)

Shortened answer:

Only four of the 400 species of shark attack humans: bull sharks, whitetips, tiger sharks, <u>and</u> great whites. <u>While</u> *or* <u>Although</u> sharks committed 74 fatal attacks in the past 100 years, 75% of all shark attack victims have survived.

Exercise 32.9 (p. 569)

The word classes are in brackets (shortened answer).

Gold! [interjection] <u>This</u> [pronoun] discovery not only triggered <u>the</u> [article] <u>Black</u> Hills [adjective] <u>gold rush</u> [noun] but [conjunction] also gave rise to the <u>lawless</u> [adjective] town of Deadwood, <u>which</u> [pronoun] reached <u>a</u> [article] population of around 5,000 <u>within</u> [preposition] the next two years.

Exercise 32.10 (p. 573)

1. subject-verb-object
2. subject-linking verb

Exercise 32.11 (p. 573)

1. adjective clause
2. noun clause

EXERCISE 32.12 (p. 577)
1. simple
2. compound

EXERCISE 32.13 (p. 577)
Possible solutions:
1. **Compound:** Philip K. Wrigley was a chewing gum entrepreneur, and he also began the All-American Girls Professional Baseball League in 1943.
Complex: In 1943, when the onset of World War II threatened American interest in the sport of baseball, Philip K. Wrigley, chewing gum entrepreneur, began the All-American Girls Professional Baseball League.
Compound-Complex: Philip K. Wrigley was primarily known as a chewing gum entrepreneur, but in 1943, when American involvement in World War II threatened interest in baseball, he pioneered the All-American Girls Professional Baseball League.

Chapter 33   Fragments, Run-ons, and Comma Splices

EXERCISE 33.1 (p. 585)
1. Flying squirrels are like typical squirrels except they have flaps of skin that allow them to glide.
2. Flying squirrels glide gracefully from tree to tree with surprising ease.

EXERCISE 33.2 (p. 585)
Possible rewrite (shortened answer):

Barton Springs still seems like a place not in Texas for those who come from elsewhere, with its surrounding hills covered by live oaks and mountain juniper, and the ground around the pool shaded by pecan trees whose trunks are a dozen feet in circumference.

EXERCISE 33.3 (p. 588)
Possible rewrites:

1. The original Kabuki troupes were mostly comprised of female dancers; however, male performers replaced them after the art became associated with prostitution.
2. Performances that included several thematically linked elements such as dance, history, and domestic drama lasted up to twelve hours.

EXERCISE 33.4 (p. 592)
Possible rewrites:

1. Riefenstahl spent her early days performing in Germany as a dancer. However, a 1924 knee injury derailed her dance career, detouring her into a successful, scandal-ridden life in film.
2. Early editing work prepared her to direct her first film, *The Blue Light*; however, national recognition was slow to come.

Chapter 34   Subject-Verb Agreement

EXERCISE 34.1 (p. 600)
Items to be circled are in bold; corrected verbs are in brackets.

1. Some, **cite**
2. Each, **possess** [possesses]

EXERCISE 34.2 (p. 602)
Items to be circled are in bold; corrected verbs are in brackets.

1. few, **has** [have] **had**
2. no one, was expecting

EXERCISE 34.3 (p. 604)
The correct verb form is underlined (shortened answer).

The administration usually tries to avoid responsibility for issues concerning students living off campus, but also listens when the city government complains about student behavior.

EXERCISE 34.4 (p. 606)
Items to be circled are in bold; corrected verbs are in brackets.

1. theatrics, **dates**
2. thanks, **is** [are]

Chapter 35   Verbs

EXERCISE 35.1 (p. 610)
The correct form of the verb is underlined (shortened answer).

Flathead catfish are the chosen prey for noodling because they live sedentary lifestyles in holes or under brush. A noodler begins by going underwater to depths ranging from only a few feet to a daunting twenty feet.

EXERCISE 35.2 (p. 616)
The correct form of the verb is underlined (shortened answer).

After marrying in 1940, Lucille Ball and Desi Arnaz sought to create their own television situation comedy, but the networks chose not to buy the project.

EXERCISE 35.3 (p. 617)
The correct form of the verb is underlined (shortened answer).

A rattlesnake will often lie in wait for its favorite meal: a rat. When encountering one of these poisonous snakes, set aside your assumptions about aggressive snakes; many are timid.

EXERCISE 35.4 (p. 622)

The correct form of the verb is underlined (shortened answer).

Native American activists, including Dennis Banks and Russell Means, cre-ated AIM, a militant organization to fight for civil rights for American Indians. AIM members participated in a number of famous protests, including the occu-pation of Alcatraz Island (1969-1971) and the takeover of Wounded Knee (1973).

EXERCISE 35.5 (p. 624)

The correct verb form is underlined (shortened answer).

This phenomenon is called "rapture of the deep" because the increase in ni-trogen makes a diver feel as if she were invincible. Be very careful, however; this situation is dangerous.

Chapter 36 Pronouns

EXERCISE 36.1 (p. 628)

Corrections are in brackets (shortened answer).

If you and a friend go on a road trip, the ADA suggests that you and her [she] limit your stops at fast-food restaurants. The association suggests us [we] snack in the afternoon provided we choose foods that are healthy for you and I [me].

EXERCISE 36.2 (p. 631)

1. who
2. who, who

EXERCISE 36.3 (p. 634)

1. who
2. they

EXERCISE 36.4 (p. 638)

Antecedents are underlined. Pronouns are in bold.

1. name, **it**
2. greyhounds, **their**

EXERCISE 36.5 (p. 639)

Items to be circled are in bold; replacement pronouns are in brackets (shortened answer).

Although few would admit it, **he or she** [they] often take extra precautions on Friday the 13th. Some are so paralyzed by fear that **they** are simply unable to get out of **his or her** [their] bed(s) when Friday the 13th comes around.

EXERCISE 36.6 (p. 641)

Possible rewrites:

1. When some people become financially overextended, they often consider credit cards as a way of making ends meet.
2. Some might begin to convince themselves that credit is the only way out.

Chapter 37   Modifiers

EXERCISE 37.1 (p. 650)

1. The Model T is ranked second in sales, but it is perhaps **more important** historically than the Beetle because it was the first car to be mass produced, paving the way for cars to be built **more cheaply** and **more quickly** than ever before.
2. Selling for about $300, the Model T wasn't the **least expensive** car on the market in the 1920s, however; that unique honor belongs to the 1922 Briggs & Stratton Flyer, which sold for $125 to $150.

EXERCISE 37.2 (p. 654)

Shortened answer:

After the creation of the House Un-American Activities Committee (HUAC), Cold War paranoia could barely hide itself in post-World War II America. HUAC followed on the coattails of the 1938 Special Committee on Un-American Activities.

EXERCISE 37.3 (p. 654)

Items to be circled are in bold (shortened answer).

In the early days of manned space missions, NASA had **fewer** problems feeding astronauts. But the **farther** astronauts traveled, the **further** NASA had to go to ensure healthy eating in space.

EXERCISE 37.4 (p. 656)

All sentences need revision. Possible rewrites:

1. Now known as Juneteenth, the day Texan slaves discovered their freedom, is celebrated in Texas.
2. Freed slaves celebrated annually their day of emancipation, a people's event that has become an official holiday.

EXERCISE 37.5 (p. 659)

Corrected modifier placement is in brackets (shortened answer).

Cash was known for his deep voice as well as his dark clothing and demeanor. These traits all earned him the nickname "The Man in Black." Keeping with his dark demeanor, much of Cash's music, especially that of his later career, echoed themes of sorrow, struggle moral [moral struggle], and redemption.

EXERCISE 37.6 (p. 662)

1. Mendel's work <u>initially</u> focused on hybridizing the Lathyrus, or sweet pea.
2. The Lathyrus <u>conveniently</u> possessed variations composed of differing sizes and colors.

EXERCISE 37.7 (p. 664)

Possible rewrite with formerly disruptive modifiers underlined (shortened answer):

    In the thirteenth and fourteenth centuries, the Italian Papal states were consumed in chaos <u>because of militantly rivaling families</u>. In 1305, <u>unable to agree on an Italian</u>, the cardinals selected a Frenchman as the new Pope.

EXERCISE 37.8 (p. 666)

Possible revisions:

1. Lasting for three days in June of 1967, the festival presented over thirty artists.
2. The largest American music festival of its time, Monterey totaled over 200,000 in attendance.

Chapter 38   Commas

EXERCISE 38.1 (p. 671)

1. King cobras, <u>in fact,</u> have a poisonous bite from the moment they are born.
2. <u>Even though king cobras carry lethal venom</u>, women in Thailand's King Cobra Club dance with the snakes' heads in their mouths.

EXERCISE 38.2 (p. 676)

1. The band Abba was only together from 1974 to 1982[,] yet their hit "Dancing Queen" is still popular today.
2. Abba is best know for their music[,] but they also made a movie entitled *Abba— The Movie*.

EXERCISE 38.3 (p. 682)

Modifiers are identified in parentheses (shortened answer).

    Trajan decided to use the Empire's coffers, <u>which were brimming with war booty</u>, to begin a massive building program. (nonrestrictive modifier). He commissioned the market <u>Mercati Traianei</u> and a lush new forum (restrictive modifier).

EXERCISE 38.4 (p. 683)

1. White-tailed deer[,] ground squirrels[,] gray squirrels[,] foxes[,] raccoons[,] coyotes[,] opossums[,] and armadillos are often in my back yard.
2. no commas necessary

EXERCISE 38.5 (p. 685)

The kinds of adjective series are in parentheses (shortened answer).

This makes the iPod the best-selling music player in history (cumulative) and one of the most successful electronic devices (cumulative) of all time. The idea for the iPod emerged when the company began creating new(,) innovative software (coordinating) for the growing market of consumer digital devices (cumulative) such as digital cameras, personal organizers, and camcorders.

EXERCISE 38.6 (p. 687)

Shortened answer:

Craquelure is "the fine network of cracks that scores the surface of . . . paintings" (Elkins 20). Elkins explains that "few museum visitors realize how many paintings have been seriously damaged," and goes on to list possible hazards, such as damage by "fire, water, vandalism, or just the wear and tear of the centuries" (20).

EXERCISE 38.7 (p. 689)

Shortened answer:

Mazaces' Headquarters
Cairo[,] Egypt
13 December 332 BC

Parmenio
Commander of Syria
Damascus[,] Syria

Dear Parmenio:

Thank you for your latest correspondence dated December 9[,] 332 BC. I am pleased to hear the streets of Damascus remain quiet since our arrival in October 333 BC and that mighty Syria has adjusted herself to our presence.

EXERCISE 38.8 (p. 691)

Shortened answer:

Because geologists used both radiometric and fossil dating[,] we now know that the Colorado River started carving the Grand Canyon only five or six million years ago. Scientists were able to accurately date the Shroud of Turin[,] believed by many Catholics to be Christ's burial covering[,] to between AD 1260–1390.

Chapter 39   Semicolons and Colons

EXERCISE 39.1 (p. 697)

Shortened answer:

The media reported that the wreckage of a flying saucer was discovered on a ranch near Roswell. Military spokespeople came up with another explanation; they asserted that the flying saucer was actually a balloon.

EXERCISE 39.2 (p. 701)

1. *The House on Mango Street* tells the story of a Mexican American girl who has a telling name[:] Esperanza (Hope).
2. Because *The House on Mango Street* consists of 44 short vignettes, critics disagree on the book's genre[:] autobiography, short story, novel, or poetry.

Chapter 40   Hyphens

EXERCISE 40.1 (p. 705)

1. Some people consider the Electoral College to be <u>undemocratic</u>.
2. Independent candidates are often viewed as <u>fly-by-night</u> long shots with little or no hope of winning positions of power.

Chapter 41   Dashes and Parentheses

EXERCISE 41.1 (p. 709)

Answers will vary.

EXERCISE 41.2 (p. 712)

1. Naples is a dirty and noisy metropolis in a spectacular setting—a city that sprawls around the Bay of Naples with Mount Vesuvius at its back, facing out to the islands of Procida, Ischia, and Capri.
2. The most famous eruption of Mount Vesuvius—the eruption that destroyed Pompeii and Herculaneum—occurred in 79 A.D.

EXERCISE 41.3 (p. 715)

1. *SNL* has been broadcast live by the National Broadcasting Company (NBC) on Saturday nights since October 11, 1975.
2. The show was called *NBC's Saturday Night* until 1976 (a short-lived variety show hosted by Howard Cosell was also called *Saturday Night Live*).

Chapter 42   Apostrophes

EXERCISE 42.1 (p. 720)

Shortened answer:

    <u>Its</u> destruction was caused by an eruption of Mount Vesuvius in AD 79. <u>Survivors'</u> stories contain accounts of tunneling through up to sixteen feet of debris after the disaster.

EXERCISE 42.2 (p. 723)

1. Texas <u>VIPs</u> and international diplomats alike affectionately referred to Lyndon B. Johnson as Big Daddy.
2. sentence is correct

Chapter 43   Quotation Marks

EXERCISE 43.1 (p. 727)

1. Horowitz's difficulty was finding words that might make sense, as he puts it, "to anyone other than a fellow addict" (387).
2. There are, Horowitz allows, clear and often-cited reasons why one might develop a passion for the Civil War, however. "Everywhere, people spoke of family and fortunes lost in the war," Horowitz writes (384).

EXERCISE 43.2 (p. 734)

1. What does Allison mean when she tells gay and lesbian writers, "We must aim much higher than just staying alive if we are to begin to approach our true potential"?
2. She elaborates, "I want to write in such a way as to literally remake the world, to change people's thinking as they look out of the eyes of the characters I create" (212).

Chapter 44   Other Punctuation Marks

EXERCISE 44.1 (p. 737)

Shortened answer:

Ms. Friedan was born Feb. 4, 1921. History will record her as one of the major contributors to modern U.S. feminism. In 1963, Friedan penned the monumental *Feminine Mystique.*

EXERCISE 44.2 (p. 739)

Shortened answer:

Betty Friedan's *The Feminine Mystique* addressed the question, "Is this all?" She examined why millions of women were sensing a gnawing feeling of discontent.

EXERCISE 44.3 (p. 745)

Shortened answer:

Ward notes, "The phenomenon of the waning star is heavily represented in the last century of English and American culture . . . ." In 1896, chronicling the perks of dying before the glory has time to fade, A.E. Houseman published the poem "To an Athlete Dying Young."

EXERCISE 44.4 (p. 749)

Shortened answer:

In 1996 alone, over sixty deaths occurred due to religious snake handling. Mark 16.21 in the King James version of the Bible states, "They shall take up serpents and if they drink the deadly thing it shall not hurt them . . .!"

Chapter 45   Write with Accurate Spelling

EXERCISE 45.1 (p. 752)
Shortened answer:

Archbishop <u>Desmond</u> Tutu's message to the <u>people</u> of South Africa is that all are "of infinite <u>worth</u>, created in the image of <u>God</u>," and "to be treated . . . with reverence" (Wepman 13). Tutu maintains that <u>this</u> is true <u>for</u> whites as well as blacks, a position that isn't popular <u>with</u> some South <u>Africans</u>.

EXERCISE 45.2 (p. 753)
Shortened answer:

Modern day Cambodia, or Kampuchea, gained its independence from France in 1953, but <u>by</u> the early 1970s the country was embroiled in bloody civil war. In 1975, Khmer Rouge guerrillas secured the Cambodian <u>capitol</u>, Phnom Penh, <u>where</u> they ruled the country until 1979.

EXERCISE 45.3 (p. 757)
1. slapped
2. referring

EXERCISE 45.4 (p. 757)
1. definitely
2. purist

EXERCISE 45.5 (p. 760)
Shortened answer:

Wilde, a successful author with two <u>children</u> and multiple <u>followers</u> in literary London, made a mistake when he pressed <u>charges</u> against the famous lord. By all <u>accounts</u>, Wilde was in jovial <u>spirits</u> when he arrived at the Old Bailey courthouse on April 3, 1895.

Chapter 46   Capitalization and Italics

EXERCISE 46.1 (p. 765)
Shortened answer:

The Federal Bureau of Investigation (FBI) has long been considered an American institution that was fathered by President Theodore Roosevelt. During the early 1900s, the United States was going through what some referred to as the Progressive Era.

EXERCISE 46.2 (p. 768)

Shortened answer:

Many think Coco Chanel is to fashion what the Bible is to religion. Consequently, various types of media have sought to capture the essence of this innovative designer. Films such as *Tonight or Never* preserve Chanel's designs for future generations, while the failed Broadway musical, *Coco*, attempts to embody her life's work.

Chapter 47   Abbreviations, Acronyms, and Numbers

EXERCISE 47.1 (p. 773)

Shortened answer:

The unpredictable, destructive nature of volcanoes has attracted the interest of both scholarly and lay circles. Though it erupted in AD 79, Mt. Vesuvius is still famous because of its violent decimation of the city of Pompeii.

EXERCISE 47.2 (p. 775)

Shortened answer:

The festival, which culminates in the burning of a giant man-shaped effigy, takes place on a playa in the Black Rock Desert in Nevada, 90 miles (150 km) north to northeast of Reno. Black Rock City (BRC), a temporary city which has its own Department of Public Works (DPW), is an experiment in community and self-expression.

EXERCISE 47.3 (p. 777)

Shortened answer:

Five hundred sixty is the number of times you heard a popping sound resonating from the jaw of the woman sitting next to you on the plane. She may be one of over 9.5 million people suffering from TMJ, a condition that often causes symptoms such as popping, swelling, and aching in the jaw.

Chapter 48   Writing in a Second Language

EXERCISE 48.1 (p. 784)

Answers will vary.

EXERCISE 48.2 (p. 787)

1. My girlfriend is the apple of my eye.
2. If you back out now, your name will be mud.

Chapter 49   Nouns and Articles

EXERCISE 49.1 (p. 790)
Shortened answer:

In <u>1903</u>, <u>Chicago</u> opened the new <u>Iroquois Theater</u> on <u>West Randolph Street</u>. Around <u>Christmas</u>, the <u>theater</u> held a <u>performance</u> of <u>Mr. Blue Beard</u>, starring <u>Eddie Foy</u>.

EXERCISE 49.2 (p. 791)
1. cities, automobiles
2. pieces of equipment, acts

EXERCISE 49.3 (p. 794)
Shortened answer:

Every year, thousands of <u>brides</u> and <u>grooms</u> don traditional attire while attending their <u>weddings</u>; one garment associated with many of these traditional <u>weddings</u> is the groom's cummerbund or decorative waistband. This garment dates back many <u>centuries</u> to Persia, where grooms would wrap their <u>loins</u> in a tight cotton cloth called a "kamarband" or "loin band."

EXERCISE 49.4 (p. 797)
Shortened answer:

In <u>the</u> early 1900s, boxing films were <u>an</u> extremely popular form of entertainment; <u>a</u> fight would be filmed and shown <u>in</u> movie houses across <u>the</u> country. This practice changed after <u>an</u> explosive race riot occurred following <u>a</u> match between <u>a</u> white man, ex-champion Jim Jeffries, and <u>a</u> black man, Jack Johnson.

EXERCISE 49.5 (p. 798)
Corrections are in brackets; types of nouns are in parentheses (shortened answer).

Hurtubise's obsession with [~~the~~] bears (plural, count) began in 1984 when he survived [an] encounter (singular, count) with an adult grizzly bear. Inspired by [~~a~~ the] movie (singular, count) Robocop, Hurtubise decided to build <u>a</u> suit (singular, count) that would withstand [~~the~~] bear attacks.

EXERCISE 49.6 (p. 800)
Shortened answer:

At that time, pilots were familiar <u>with</u> the "wall of air" that existed <u>at</u> the speed of sound. Many airplanes shattered <u>into</u> a million pieces because <u>of</u> this "wall of air."

EXERCISE 49.7 (p. 801)
Shortened answer:

The United States remains <u>grateful to</u> the people of France for the gift of the Statue of Liberty.

Chapter 50   Verbs

EXERCISE 50.1 (p. 803)
Shortened answer:

Though many think it marks only the Jewish New Year, those who celebrate Rosh Hashanah <u>understand</u> that it represents the New Year, the day of the blowing of the Shofar, <u>the day of</u> remembrance, and the day of judgment.

EXERCISE 50.2 (p. 805)
1. may have endangered (possibility)
2. would work (intention)

EXERCISE 50.3 (p. 807)
1. follows, are referred to
2. forces strangers to live, causing them to face

EXERCISE 50.4 (p. 808)
1. misidentifying
2. to believe

EXERCISE 50.5 (p. 810)
1. If a child <u>is</u> terrified whenever he or she <u>sees</u> a clown, that child <u>has</u> coulrophobia.
2. If you <u>had ever been</u> attacked by birds, <u>you could have developed</u> ornithophobia.

EXERCISE 50.6 (p. 811)
Shortened answer:

Many <u>tornadoes</u> are <u>created</u> by a special <u>rotating</u> <u>thunderstorm</u> called a supercell. A <u>rising</u> gust of warm <u>wind</u> combines with the <u>raging</u> <u>storm</u>; however, the warm <u>air</u> <u>is</u> <u>converted</u> as the rainfall causes a <u>rushing</u> <u>downdraft</u>.

Chapter 51   English Sentence Structure

EXERCISE 51.1 (p. 814)
1. Though some <u>assassins</u> are widely known, <u>Charles Guiteau</u> and <u>Leon Czolgolsz</u> are relatively obscure.
2. <u>Guiteau</u> shot President Garfield in 1881, and [there] was little doubt <u>he</u> would be hung for the murder.

EXERCISE 51.2 (p. 815)
Items to be circled are in brackets.
1. [Geologists] based the theory on an earlier one <u>[that] had observed that the continents fit together like pieces of a puzzle</u>.
2. In the fifties and sixties, [scientists] found evidence <u>to support the earlier theory,</u> so [they] <u>were able to confirm its hypothesis regarding continental drift</u>.

EXERCISE 51.3 (p. 817)

1. Ganesh (S) is (LV) the god (SC) of good luck (PP).
2. Young Ganesh (S) stood (IV) at his mother's house (PP).

EXERCISE 51.4 (p. 819)

1. Adverb between verb and direct object; Kurosawa <u>initially</u> chose painting as his preferred career.
2. Adverbial phrase between subject and verb; <u>Realizing</u> painting would not bring riches, Kurosawa turned to film in 1936.

EXERCISE 51.5 (p. 820)

1. By the <u>fourteenth</u> century, <u>playing</u> cards were used <u>widely</u> (adv. of frequency) for <u>gambling</u> and predicting the future.
2. The invention of the <u>printing</u> press connects <u>directly</u> (adv. of manner) to the proliferation of <u>standardized card</u> games.

EXERCISE 51.6 (p. 821)

1. Robespierre followed the writings of Jean Jacques Rousseau, his philosophical role model.
2. Elected on the eve of the French Revolution, he enthralled the people with his skillful oratory.

Index

Credits

Text Credits

2003 Water Quality Report, Lafayette, CO.: City of Lafayette Water Division, 2003. Reprinted with permission.

EBSCO citation for "Hrothuf: A Richard III, or an Alfred the Great? by William Cooke." From Ebsco Publishing website, www.epnet.com. © EBSCO Publishing, Inc. All rights reserved. Reprinted with permission.

EBSCO search for "more young adults plan to vote." From Ebsco Publishing website, www.epnet.com. © EBSCO Publishing, Inc. All rights reserved. Reprinted with permission.

EBSCO search for "young adult" and "voters." From Ebsco Publishing website, www.epnet.com. © EBSCO Publishing, Inc. All rights reserved. Reprinted with permission.

Howard Gardner. *Five Minds for the Future.* Watertown: Harvard Business School Publishing, 2007.

Kelty traveling facts. From "Kelty Traveling Fact" on Christopher Kelty website, www.kelty.org. Reprinted with permission of Christopher M. Kelty.

LexisNexis archive search. From the LexisNexis Academic website.

LexisNexis archive search of *Post Standard Newspaper* article citation. From the LexisNexis Academic Library Service database. Copyright © 2007 LexisNexis, a division of Reed Elsevier Inc. All Rights Reserved. LexisNexis and the Knowledge Burst logo are registered trademarks of Reed Elsevier Properties Inc. and are used with the permission of LexisNexis.

LexisNexis search for "young adult voters." From the LexisNexis Academic Library Service database website. Copyright © 2007 LexisNexis, a division of Reed Elsevier Inc. All Rights Reserved. LexisNexis and the Knowledge Burst logo are registered trademarks of Reed Elsevier Properties Inc. and are used with the permission of LexisNexis.

Michael Wines, "Once World Cause, South Africa Lowers Voices on Human Rights" by Michael Wines, *The New York Times,* March 24, 2007.

Sample document and title page. From *How Cities Work: Suburbs, Sprawl, and the Roads Not Taken* by Alex Marshall, Copyright © 2000. Courtesy of the University of Texas Press.

Sample journal table of contents and article page. *Communication Education,* 52.1, January 2003.

Screen capture "James Gandolfini" from Wikipedia, en.wikipedia.org/wiki/Main_Page. Copyright © 2007, Free Software Foundation, Inc., 51 Franklin Street, Fifth Floor, Boston, MA 02110-1301 USA. Everyone is permitted to copy and distribute verbatim copies of this license document, but changing it is not allowed.

Screen capture from The Wilson Quarterly. Reprinted with permission from *The Wilson Quarterly.* Copyright © 2007 by The Woodrow Wilson International Center for Scholars.

Screen capture from The Wilson Quarterly homepage website. Reprinted with permission from *The Wilson Quarterly,* www.wilsoncenter.org. Copyright © 2007 by The Woodrow Wilson International Center for Scholars. All rights reserved.

Screen capture from University of Massachusetts Dartmouth, Claire T. Carney Library website. Reprinted by permission of the Claire T. Carney Library, University of Massachusetts Dartmouth.

Screen capture from University of South Florida Libraries website, www.lib.usf.edu. Used by permission.

Screen capture of "Big Philanthropy" by Leslie Lenkowsky, The Wilson Quarterly website, www.wilsoncenter.org. Reprinted with permission from The Wilson Quarterly. Copyright © 2007 by The Woodrow Wilson International Center for Scholars. All rights reserved.

Screen capture of "Sweet smell of success for biofuel export" by Michael Pollitt, *The Guardian,* April 26, 2007 from Guardian Unlimited website, www.guardian.co.uk.

Sharon Zukin, *Point of Purchase.* From *Point of Purchase: How Shopping Changed American Culture* by Sharon Zukin. Copyright 2004 by Taylor & Francis Group LLC - Books. Reproduced with permission of Taylor & Francis Group LLC - Books in the format Textbook via Copyright Clearance Center.

Yahoo! Issues and Causes Index. Reproduced with permission of Yahoo! Inc. © 2004 by Yahoo! Inc. Yahoo! and Yahoo! logo are trademarks of Yahoo! Inc.

Yahoo! subject directory for "augmented reality." From Yahoo website, www.yahoo.com. Reproduced with permission of Yahoo! Inc. © 2007 by Yahoo! Inc. Yahoo! and the Yahoo! logo are trademarks of Yahoo! Inc.

Photo Credits

p. 5, Lowe Worldwide

p. 6, top: Substance Abuse and Mental Health Services Administration; p. 6, bottom: Courtesy Rechargeable Battery Recycling Corporation (RBRC) (http://call2recycle.org)

p. 85: Library of Congress

p. 88: Library of Congress

p. 92: Library of Congress (3)

p. 123: The New York Times

p. 131: Librado Romero/The New York Times

p. 151: Cheryl Gerber/The New York Times

p. 193, top: National Park Service

p. 266: Library of Congress

p. 298: Paul O. Boisvery/The New York Times

p. 313: Greater Talent Network

p. 378: Lafayette, CO: City of Lafayette Water Division.

Unless otherwise noted, all photos © Lester Faigley Photos.